LANGUAGE IN SOCIETY 25

American English

Language in Society

GENERAL EDITOR
Peter Trudgill, Chair of English Linguistics,
University of Fribourg

ADVISORY EDITORS
J. K. Chambers, Professor of Linguistics,
University of Toronto

Ralph Fasold, Professor of Linguistics,
Georgetown University

William Labov, Professor of Linguistics,
University of Pennsylvania

Lesley Milroy, Professor of Linguistics,
University of Michigan, Ann Arbor

American English

Dialects and Variation

Second Edition

*Walt Wolfram
and
Natalie Schilling-Estes*

Blackwell
Publishing

BLACKWELL PUBLISHING
350 Main Street, Malden, MA 02148-5020, USA
9600 Garsington Road, Oxford OX4 2DQ, UK
550 Swanston Street, Carlton, Victoria 3053, Australia

First edition published 1998
Second edition published 2006 by Blackwell Publishing Ltd

2   2006

Library of Congress Cataloging-in-Publication Data

Wolfram, Walt, 1941–
American English : dialects and variation / Walt Wolfram and Natalie Schilling-
Estes. – 2nd ed
    p.   cm. – (Language in society; 25)
Includes bibliographical references and index.
ISBN-13: 978-1-4051-1265-9 (hardcover : alk. paper)
ISBN 1-4051-1265-4 (hardcover : alk. paper)
ISBN-13: 978-1-4051-1266-6 (pbk : alk. paper)
ISBN 1-4051-1266-2 (pbk. : alk. paper)
1. English language–Dialects–United States.   2. English language–Variation–United
States.   3. Americanisms.   I. Schilling-Estes, Natalie.   II. Title.   III. Series: Language in
society (Oxford, English); 25.

PE2841.W63   2006
427′.973–dc22
2005009840

A catalogue record for this title is available from the British Library.

Set in 10.5 / 12 pt Ehrhardt
by Graphicraft Ltd, Hong Kong
Printed and bound in the United Kingdom
by TJ International, Padstow, Cornwall

The publisher's policy is to use permanent paper from mills that operate a sustainable
forestry policy, and which has been manufactured from pulp processed using acid-free and
elementary chlorine-free practices. Furthermore, the publisher ensures that the text paper
and cover board used have met acceptable environmental accreditation standards.

For further information on
Blackwell Publishing, visit our website:
www.blackwellpublishing.com

Contents

Series Editor's Preface

Perhaps now is the time to confess that the Language in Society series has always had as one of its secret ambitions the signing up of all the major, significant players in the arena of world sociolinguistics. With the addition of Walt Wolfram to our team, this dream has come one step closer to being achieved, since we now have on our side one of the veterans from the original squad of young scholars who contributed to that first large-scale flowering of American sociolinguistics in the early 1970s, to which many aspects of work in modern sociolinguistics owe so much. That Walt Wolfram has been joined in the authoring of this book by one of the most energetic and gifted scholars from the latest generation of American sociolinguists, Natalie Schilling-Estes, is a source of additional excitement and satisfaction.

The book is very much, as is only appropriate when working with dialectology, a data-based work, with a great deal of the data being – as is typical of practicing sociolinguists – the authors' own, but it is also a ground-breaking work full of important new theoretical contributions and insights. The book is obviously aimed primarily at an American audience, but it will also be of very considerable importance and interest indeed outside the United States. Not only will it be essential for any non-American concerned to learn more about American English; it will also be vital reading for scholars with theoretical interests in historical linguistics, new-dialect formation, variation theory, language and gender, African American Vernacular English, creolization, and many other issues, as well as for practitioners involved in issues to do with mother-tongue education, speech therapy, and dialectological research itself. There is nothing quite like the writings on dialectology of linguists who have been out there and done the fieldwork with real live human beings and analyzed the data themselves. And there are very few dialectologists who have done as much of this type of work – and used the results of their work to do their best to improve the lot of the communities from which they have obtained their data – as these authors.

Peter Trudgill

Preface

There is no end to the writing of books. In fact, we consider the second edition of *American English: Dialects and Variation* to be just another phase in the evolution of a text on language variation in American English. It started for the first author more than three decades ago, with Walt Wolfram and Ralph W. Fasold's *The Study of Social Dialects* (1974) and passed through Wolfram's *Dialects and American English* (1991) on the way to our first edition of *American English: Dialects and Variation* (1998). Though the present edition is a thoroughly revised version of our earlier text, we hope that it is more than that. In addition to revising and updating, we have added a chapter, deleted one, and radically restructured a couple of others. In part, this is an attempt to reflect current emphases in the study of American English dialect variation. For example, we now include a separate chapter on African American English and include separate sections on important sociocultural dialects such as Latino English, Cajun English, and Native American English. We have further strived to more directly adapt our style of presentation for an audience that includes the full range of the students who enroll in a course on dialects. This extends from the curious student with no background at all in linguistics, students in allied disciplines who have a need for information about language diversity, and the student who may wish to specialize in sociolinguistics or the study of American English.

Given the diverse backgrounds and interests of students who end up in a "course on dialects," the challenge is to fashion a text that can meet the needs of a varied audience without oversimplifying the full complexity of the subject matter. In our opinion, such a text should combine an informed approach to the nature of dialect variation, descriptive detail about particular dialects, and a discussion of the broader cultural, political, and educational implications of dialect diversity. We also integrate research from our current studies on regional and sociocultural varieties conducted in the South-eastern and Mid-Atlantic regions of the United States, as well as our ongoing investigation of stylistic variation across a range of varieties. In addition, we have attempted to balance discussion of our own research areas with discussions of the many other important regional and sociocultural varieties in the US.

Throughout the book, we have attempted to keep the diverse nature of the audience in mind, so that the text is readable and relevant for students in English, education, speech and language pathology, cultural anthropology, sociology, and psychology, as well as various branches of linguistic studies. A number of texts are marketed with such broad-based claims; we hope that this will be one of those rare cases where the actual text matches its introductory promises – or at least approaches that ideal. We have tried to keep technical linguistic terminology to a minimum, even with respect to phonetics. For convenience, we have included a skeletal phonetics chart for readers (see pp. xiv–xv); it should be used with the understanding that much phonetic detail is eliminated. In particular, many aspects of vowel pronunciation could have been included in precise phonetic detail, but we have worked under the assumption that most readers will not have an extensive background in phonetics. We can only apologize to linguists with expertise in phonetics who would like to see a bit more discussion of the phonetic nuances of dialect patterning.

We have also tried to avoid linguistic formalism. From our perspective, underlying principles of language variation are much more significant than their formal representation. There are, however, times when technical terms are needed to convey important constructs in the field. To help readers in this regard, a glossary of technical terms is included. Students also should be aided by exercises that are incorporated into the text at relevant points in the discussion rather than at the conclusions of chapters.

We have made an honest attempt to write a text for the full range of students likely to take courses on dialects rather than for professional colleagues who wish to scrutinize the current state of highly specialized knowledge in sociolinguistics. The text should be appropriate for both upper level undergraduate and graduate students in a variety of fields.

Conceptually, the text is divided into four major sections. The first three chapters introduce students to basic notions about the nature of dialectal variation. The next chapter, chapter 4, gives an overview of the history and development of American English dialects. Chapters 5 through 9 offer a descriptive account of some of the major social factors that affect, and are affected by, variation in American English, including region, social status, ethnicity, gender, and style. We have tried to balance approaches from traditional dialectology with advances in the quantitative study of language variation while avoiding the technicalities of such analyses. The final section, chapters 10 and 11, considers the applications of dialect study. We focus on dialects and education but also discuss ways in which researchers can work collaboratively with communities from which they gather data for dialect study.

An updated summary of many of the grammatical and phonological structures that serve to distinguish various social and regional dialects from one another is included in an Appendix as a convenient reference for readers. The Appendix shows an admitted bias in favor of socially significant structures over regionally significant ones, although the relationship between social and regional variation is hardly independent.

We are particularly grateful to a small group of critical readers who provided extensive feedback based on their careful reading of the first edition. These include Kirk Hazen, Matthew J. Gordon, Donald Lance, Peter Patrick, Malcah Yaeger-Dror, and a couple of anonymous reviewers. We would also like to thank Carmen Fought, Norma Medoza-Denton, and Phillip Carter for commenting on the new section on Latino English (in chapter 6) and Sylvie Dubois, Megan Melançon, and Janna Oetting for commenting on the new section on Cajun English. In addition, we wish to thank Janet Fuller, Scott Kiesling, and Christine Mallinson for their help with our discussion of gender and language variation (chapter 8). Dennis Preston offered invaluable assistance in the revision of chapter 5, especially for the new section on perceptual dialectology; he also provided us with several original maps for this section. Further, the second author is indebted to Mary Bucholtz for invaluable insight into this subject area received while participating in her course on Language and Gender at the 2003 Linguistic Society of America Linguistic Institute. Reviewers' comments were invaluable during the process of writing this new edition, even when we haven't shown the wisdom to follow their advice. We also are indebted to those who guided us in other ways along our sociolinguistic path, from the first author's initial teacher in linguistics as an undergraduate student, Roger W. Shuy, to our most recent classes of students at North Carolina State University and Georgetown University. The second author is also grateful to all her colleagues in the Linguistics Department at Georgetown University for their support, inspiration, and friendship. We have been fortunate enough to associate with a group of people who have taught us that professional colleagues can also be good friends: Michael Adams, Carolyn Adger, Bridget Anderson, Guy Bailey, John Baugh, Robert Bayley, Allen Bell, Renee Blake, Charles Boberg, Ron Butters, Jack Chambers, Becky Childs, Donna Christian, Colleen Cotter, Clare Dannenberg, Sylvie Dubois, Connie Eble, Penny Eckert, Ralph W. Fasold, Lisa Green, Gregory Guy, Dave Herman, Brian Jose, Brian Joseph, Bill Kretzschmar, Bill Labov, Lesley Milroy, Ceil Lucas, Tom McClive, Miriam Meyerhoff, Michael Montgomery, Naomi Nagy, Joy Peyton, Shana Poplack, Dennis Preston, Jeffrey Reaser, John Rickford, Edgar Schneider, Dani Schreier, Scott Schwenter, Julie Solomon, Sali Tagliamonte, Erik R. Thomas, Ben Torbert, Peter Trudgill, G. Richard

Tucker, and Tracey Weldon, among many others who should have been named as well. Thanks for your support and friendship. This cast of characters has made academic inquiry much more fun than we ever thought it could be. If students reading this text can just catch a little bit of our respect for and intrigue with language diversity, then we will be satisfied.

Our greatest indebtedness is, as always, reserved for our spouses, Marge Wolfram and Chris Estes. They have given the most – in time, patience, and unfailing encouragement and support throughout this ongoing, seemingly endless process. As we said, the writing of a good text is never done – and this book is no exception. We hope, however, that this is a convenient time to pause and reflect once again on the rich diversity of American English.

Walt Wolfram, William C. Friday Professor
North Carolina State University

Natalie Schilling-Estes
Georgetown University

Phonetic Symbols

Phonemes

Consonants

Symbol	Key words	Phonetic description
[p]	*pit, spit, tip*	voiceless bilabial stop
[b]	*bat, rabbit, rib*	voiced bilabial stop
[t]	*tip, stop, put*	voiceless alveolar stop
[d]	*doom, under, bud*	voiced alveolar stop
[D]	*butter, buddy*	voiced alveolar flap
[k]	*cap, skate, bake*	voiceless velar stop
[g]	*go, buggy, bag*	voiced velar stop
[ʔ]	*bottle, button* (in some dialects)	voiceless glottal stop
[f]	*fee, after, laugh*	voiceless labiodental fricative
[v]	*vote, over, love*	voiced labiodental fricative
[θ]	*thought, ether, both*	voiceless interdental fricative
[ð]	*the, mother, smooth*	voiced interdental fricative
[s]	*so, fasten, bus*	voiceless alveolar sibilant
[z]	*zoo, lazy, fuzz*	voiced alveolar sibilant
[š]	*shoe, nation, bush*	voiceless palatal sibilant
[ž]	*measure, closure*	voiced palatal sibilant
[h]	*hat, behind*	voiceless glottal fricative
[č]	*chew, pitcher, church*	voiceless palatal affricate
[ǰ]	*judge, ranger, dodge*	voiced palatal affricate
[m]	*my, mommy, bum*	bilabial nasal
[n]	*no, funny, run*	alveolar nasal
[ŋ]	*singer, long*	velar nasal
[l]	*look, bully, call*	lateral liquid
[r]	*run, bury, car*	retroflex (bunched tongue) liquid
[w]	*way, quack*	labiovelar glide
[y]	*yes, feud*	palatal glide

Vowels

Symbol	Key words	Phonetic description
[i]	*beet, leap*	high front tense
[ɪ]	*bit, rip*	high front lax
[e]	*bait, grade*	mid front tense
[ε]	*bet, step*	mid front lax
[æ]	*cap, bat*	low front tense
[ə]	*about, afford*	mid central tense
[ʌ]	*shut, was*	mid central lax
[ɑ]	*father, stop*	low central
[u]	*boot, through*	high back tense
[ʊ]	*book, put*	high back lax
[o]	*no, toe*	mid back tense
[ɔ]	*oral, taught*	low back tense
[aʊ]	*crowd, bout*	low central back gliding diphthong
[aɪ]	*buy, lie*	low central front gliding diphthong
[ɔɪ]	*boy, coin*	low back front gliding diphthong
[ɚ]	*mother, bird*	mid central retroflex

forest vs farest
hot vs hat
not vs nat

40 in US Engl.

1

Dialects, Standards, and Vernaculars

Most of us have had the experience of sitting in a public place and eaves-dropping on conversations taking place around us. Though we pretend to be preoccupied, we listen intently. And we form impressions of who we're listening to based not only on the topic of conversation, but on how they are discussing it. In fact, there's a good chance that the most critical part of our impression comes from *how* the people are talking rather than *what* they are discussing. We make judgments about regional background, social status, ethnicity, and a host of other social and personal traits based simply on the kind of language people are using. We may have similar kinds of reactions in telephone conversations, as we try to associate a set of characteristics with an unidentified speaker in order to make claims such as, "It sounds like a salesperson of some type" or "It sounds like the auto mechanic." In fact, it is surprising how little conversation it takes to draw conclusions about a speaker's background – a sentence, a phrase, or even a word is often enough to trigger a regional, social, or ethnic classification.

Assessments of a complex set of social characteristics and personality traits based on language differences are as inevitable as the kinds of judgments we make when we find out where people live, what their occupations are, where they went to school, and who their friends are. In fact, there are some who feel that language differences serve as the single most reliable indicator of social position in our society. When we live a certain way, we are expected to match that lifestyle with our talk. And when we don't match people's expectations of how we should talk, the incongruity between words and behavior is itself a topic for conversation.

Language differences are unavoidable in a society composed of a variety of social groups. They are a fact of life. And, like other "facts of life" in our society, they have been passed on to us with a peculiar mixture of fact and fantasy.

1.1 Defining Dialect

Given the widespread awareness of language differences in our society, just about everyone has some understanding of the term "dialect." However, the technical use of the term in linguistics is different from its popular definition in some important but subtle ways. Professional students of language typically use the term DIALECT as a neutral label to refer to any variety of a language that is shared by a group of speakers. Languages are invariably manifested through their dialects, and to speak a language is to speak some dialect of that language. In this technical usage, there are no particular social or evaluative connotations to the term – that is, there are no inherently "good" or "bad" dialects; dialect is simply how we refer to any language variety that typifies a group of speakers within a language. The particular social factors that correlate with dialect diversity may range from geography to the complex notion of cultural identity. Furthermore, it is important to understand that socially favored, or "standard," varieties constitute dialects every bit as much as those varieties spoken by socially disfavored groups whose language differences are socially stigmatized. The technical definition of dialect simply as a variety of a language typical of a given group of speakers is not rigorous and precise, but it is a sufficient starting point in discussing language variation.

1.2 Dialect: The Popular Viewpoint

Although linguists accept a loosely defined technical definition of dialect, happily arguing about what language features belong to a particular dialect or how two dialects may differ, non-specialists tend to use "dialect" in a somewhat different sense. At first glance, the differences between popular and technical uses seem inconsequential, but closer inspection reveals that its popular uses carry connotations that differ from its technical meaning. At the same time, its popular use gives insight into how dialect differences are perceived in our society. Consider, for example, some commonly held beliefs about dialects demonstrated by popular uses of this term in the following quotes:

1 "We went to Boston for a vacation and the people there sure do speak a dialect."
2 "I know we speak a dialect in the mountains, but it's a very colorful way of speaking."

3 "The kids in that neighborhood don't really speak English; they speak a dialect."

4 "The kids in this school all seem to speak the dialect."

In one popular use, the term "dialect" refers simply to those who speak differently from oneself (Quote 1 above). When the authors of this book were children, growing up in Philadelphia, Pennsylvania, and Maryland, respectively, they didn't necessarily realize that they spoke dialects; it was speakers from other areas who spoke dialects. Of course, we came to realize that this perception could be a two-way street when we attended college in different states and classmates pointed out particular features of our dialects. The perception that only other people speak dialects is obviously shaped by personal experience, as one group's customary way of speaking often turns out to be another group's language peculiarity.

In another common use, the term "dialect" refers to those varieties of English whose features have, for one reason or another, become widely recognized throughout American society (Quote 2). Society at large recognizes a "southern drawl" or a "Boston accent." In other words, if the variety contains some features that are generally acknowledged and commented on by the society as a whole, then it may be recognized as a dialect even by the speakers themselves. If someone keeps telling you that you speak a dialect, after a while you start to believe that you do. Thus, native New Yorkers often believe that they speak a dialect, because their dialect has become a topic of widespread public comment in American society. Similarly, speakers of an Appalachian dialect might recognize that they speak a dialect because of the caricatures and comments that so often appear in the media. On the other hand, the same perception does not hold true of middle-class residents of Ohio whose speech does not receive popular attention. For a variety of historical and social reasons, some dialects have become much more marked than others in American society, and speakers of those varieties therefore accept the dialect label more comfortably. However, this is often more a matter of beliefs and attitudes about language differences than the nature of the differences themselves.

In the most extreme case (Quote 3), dialect is used to refer to a kind of deficient or "corrupted" English. In this case, dialect is perceived as an imperfect attempt to speak "correct" or "proper" English. If, for example, members of a socially disfavored group use phrases like *three mile* instead of the standard English *three miles*, or *Her ears be itching* instead of *Her ears itch*, it is assumed that they have attempted to produce the standard English sentence but simply failed. The result is incorrectly perceived as a "deviant" or "deficient" form of English. Based upon the careful examination of such language structures, however, dialectologists take the position that dialects are *not* deviant forms of language, but simply different systems, with distinct subsets of language patterns. When we talk about language patterning, we are referring to the fact that language features are distributed in systematic and orderly ways rather than used randomly. That is, for any given language feature, there are contexts in which the form may be used and contexts in which it is not typically used.

Exercise 1

An Exercise in Dialect Patterning

In rural dialects of the United States, including in Southern Appalachia, some words that end in *-ing* can take an *a-*, pronounced as *uh*, attached to the beginning of the word (Wolfram 1980, 1988). We call this the *a-* prefix because it attaches to the front of the *-ing* word. The language pattern or "rule" for this form allows the *a-* to attach to some words but not to others. In this exercise, you will figure out this fairly complicated rule by looking at the kinds of *-ing* words that *a-* can and cannot attach to. You will do this using your inner feelings, or "gut reactions," about language. These inner feelings, called INTUITIONS, tell us where we *can* and *cannot* use certain features. As linguists trying to describe a dialect, our task is to figure out the reason for these inner feelings and to state the exact patterns that characterize the usage pattern.

Look at the sentence pairs in **List A** and decide which sentence in each pair sounds better with an *a-* prefix. For example, in the first sentence pair, does it sound better to say *A-building is hard work* or *She was a-building a house*? For each sentence pair, just choose one sentence that sounds better with the *a-*.

List A: Sentence pairs for a- prefixing

1	a	_____	Building is hard work.
	b	_____	She was building a house.
2	a	_____	He likes hunting.
	b	_____	He went hunting.
3	a	_____	The child was charming the adults.
	b	_____	The child was very charming.
4	a	_____	He kept shocking the children.
	b	_____	The store was shocking.
5	a	_____	They thought fishing was easy.
	b	_____	They were fishing this morning.

Examine each of the sentence pairs in terms of the choices for the *a-* prefix and answer the following questions.

- Do you think there is some pattern that guided your choice of an answer? You can tell if there is a definite pattern by checking with other people who did the same exercise on their own.
- Do you think that the pattern might be related to parts of speech? To answer this, see if there are any parts of speech where you *cannot* use the *a-* prefix. Look at *-ing* forms that function as verbs and compare those with *-ing* forms that operate as nouns or adjectives. For example, look at the use of *charming* as a verb and as an adjective in sentence 3.

The first step in figuring out the pattern for the *a-* prefix is related to the part of speech of the *-ing* word. Now let's look at another difference related to prepositions such as *from* and *by*. Based on the sentence pairs in **List B**, say whether or not the *a-* form can be used after a preposition. Use the same technique you used for **List A**. Select the sentence that sounds better for each sentence pair and say whether it is the sentence with or without the preposition.

List B: A further detail for a- patterning

1   a   _____   They make money by building houses.
   b   _____   They make money building houses.
2   a   _____   People can't make enough money fishing.
   b   _____   People can't make enough money from fishing.
3   a   _____   People destroy the beauty of the mountains through littering.
   b   _____   People destroy the beauty of the mountains littering.

We now have another detail for figuring out the pattern for *a-* prefix use related to prepositions. But there is still another part to the pattern of *a-* prefix use. This time, however, it is related to pronunciation. For the following *-ing* words, try to figure out what it is about the pronunciation that makes one sentence sound better than the other. To help you figure out the pronunciation trait that is critical for this pattern, the stressed or accented syllable of each word is marked with the symbol ´. Follow the same procedure that you did in choosing the sentence in each sentence pair that sounds better.

List C: Figuring out a pronunciation pattern for the a- prefix
1 a _____ She was discóvering a trail.
   b _____ She was fóllowing a trail.
2 a _____ She was repéating the chant.
   b _____ She was hóllering the chant.
3 a _____ They were figuring the change.
   b _____ They were forgétting the change.
4 a _____ The baby was recognízing the mother.
   b _____ The baby was wrécking everything.
5 a _____ They were décorating the room.
   b _____ They were demánding more time off.

Say exactly how the pattern for attaching the *a-* prefix works. Be sure
to include the three different details from your examination of the
examples in **Lists A**, **B**, and **C**.

In **List D**, say which of the sentences may take an *a-* prefix. Use
your understanding of the rule to explain why the *-ing* form may or
may not take the *a-* prefix.

List D: Applying the a- prefix rule
1 She kept handing me more work.
2 The team was remémbering the game.
3 The team won by playing great defense.
4 The team was playing real hard.
5 The coach was charming.

At various points during the last half century, there have been heated
debates in American society about the linguistic integrity of socially disfavored
language varieties. For example, during the late 1960s and 1970s, there were
many debates in educational circles over the so-called "DEFICIT–DIFFERENCE
CONTROVERSY," with language scholars arguing passionately that dialect
variation was simply a matter of *difference*, not *deficit*, and some educators
arguing that variation from the socially accepted standard constituted a
fundamental deficiency. Three decades later, in the mid-1990s, the debate
flared up again, this time centered on the status of the ethnic variety African
American English, or Ebonics, as it was referred to in this debate. This
time, the controversy even spread as far as a Senate subcommittee hearing
on the topic and state legislation about the legitimacy of this variety in a
school setting.

When dialect differences involve groups unequal in their power relations,
it is quite common for the PRINCIPLE OF LINGUISTIC SUBORDINATION to come

into operation (Lippi-Green 1997). According to this principle, the speech of a socially subordinate group will be interpreted as linguistically inadequate by comparison with that of the socially dominant group. Linguists, who study the intricate patterning of language apart from its social evaluation, stand united against any definition of dialect as a corrupt version of the standard variety. Thus, a resolution adopted unanimously by the Linguistic Society of America at its annual meeting in 1997 asserted that "all human language systems – spoken, signed, and written – are fundamentally regular" and that characterizations of socially disfavored varieties as "slang, mutant, defective, ungrammatical, or broken English are incorrect and demeaning."

When the term "dialect" is used to refer to a kind of corrupt English, it obviously carries very strong negative connotations, as many of the popular uses of dialect do. A clause such as "but it's a very colorful way of speaking" in Quote 2 may soften the negative associations, but such statements must be made explicit to mitigate the commonly held assumption that some dialects aren't as good as others. With or without qualification, the popular use of the term dialect carries connotations ranging from mildly to strongly negative.

Finally, the term "dialect" is sometimes used to refer to a specific, socially disfavored variety of English. A person speaking a recognized, socially stigmatized variety of English may be said to speak "the dialect" (Quote 4). Such designations have, for example, been used to refer to the speech of low-income African Americans or rural Appalachians as a kind of euphemistic label for this variety. With the definite article, the term "the dialect" functions more like a proper noun than in the generic, neutral sense in which the term is used by linguistic scientists. Notice that people would not refer to a socially acceptable variety of standard English as *the* dialect.

1.3 Dialect Myths and Reality

What do these popular uses of the term "dialect" say about the general public's perception of dialect, especially as it differs from the neutral technical definition presented earlier? As the preceding discussion points out, there is a popular mythology about language differences that is at odds with the linguistic facts about language diversity. The following are some of these myths, as they contrast with linguistic reality:

MYTH: A dialect is something that *someone else* speaks.
REALITY: Everyone who speaks a language speaks some dialect of the language; it is not possible to speak a language without speaking a dialect of the language.
MYTH: Dialects always have highly noticeable features that set them apart.

REALITY: Some dialects get much more attention than others, but the status of a dialect is unrelated to public commentary about its special characteristics.

MYTH: Only varieties of a language spoken by socially disfavored groups are dialects.

REALITY: The notion of dialect exists apart from social status or evaluation; there are socially favored as well as socially disfavored dialects.

MYTH: Dialects result from unsuccessful attempts to speak the "correct" form of a language.

REALITY: Dialect speakers acquire their language by adopting the speech features of those around them, not by failing in their attempts to adopt standard language features.

MYTH: Dialects have no linguistic patterning in their own right; they are deviations from standard speech.

REALITY: Dialects, like all language systems, are systematic and regular; furthermore, socially disfavored dialects can be described with the same kind of precision as standard language varieties.

MYTH: Dialects inherently carry negative social connotations.

REALITY: Dialects are not necessarily positively or negatively valued; their social values are derived strictly from the social position of their communities of speakers.

Though most dialect myths involve negative connotations, there are occasional positive connotations, though these are often based on idealized, rather romanticized notions of "quaint" or "pure" or "authentic" dialects. For example, some people believe that dialects in historically isolated regions, such as those in the Appalachian Mountains and in the islands along the Southeastern coast of the United States, preserve Elizabethan or Shakespearean English. Though older forms of English sometimes endure in these varieties, they are constantly undergoing change as well. In fact, we have found that some aspects of isolated dialects may change more rapidly than more widely dispersed, mainstream language varieties. Language is a dynamic phenomenon, and the only static variety of language is, in reality, a dead one.

As we see, the popular uses of the term "dialect" strongly reflect the attitudes about language differences that have developed in the United States over the centuries. For this reason, some groups of educators and language scientists prefer to avoid the use of the term dialect, using terms such as "language difference," "language variety," or "language variation" instead. Regardless of the label, however, we still have to confront the significant discrepancy between the public perception of linguistic diversity and the linguistic reality. In fact, given popular attitudes about dialect diversity, there is a good chance that whatever euphemism we use will eventually take on the kinds of pejorative connotations that are associated with the current popular uses of the term dialect. Throughout this book, we will use the term dialect in its linguistically neutral sense and confront the issue of public education about language diversity as a separate matter. Educating the public about language variation is an enormous challenge, and we will return to this matter in our final chapter. For the time being, it is sufficient to set forth the technical and popular uses of the dialect label and see how its popular uses have come to reflect some predominant attitudes about dialect diversity in American society.

1.4 Standards and Vernaculars

In the preceding discussion, it was difficult to avoid some reference to the dialect of English often referred to as STANDARD AMERICAN ENGLISH. The notion of a widespread, normative variety, or "standard dialect" is an important one, but it is not always easy to define in a precise way, especially for English. In some countries, such as France and Spain, language academies have been established and these institutions are responsible for determining what forms are considered acceptable for the normative "standard." They determine, for example, what new words are allowed to be included in official dictionaries and what grammatical forms and pronunciations are included as standard. In the United States we do not have such an institution, and various attempts to establish this type of agency have failed (Heath 1976). Labels such as standard English and popular terms such as "correct English" or "proper English" are commonly used but not without some ambiguity. At best, we can discuss how the notion of standard English is used and then offer a reasonable definition of the term based on how it seems to operate in our society.

Exercise 2

Common popular labels for what we call standard English are "correct English," "proper English," "good English," and "grammatical English." What do these labels tell us about the public perception of standard dialects in terms of the myths about dialects we discussed above? What do they say about the ideology that informs the interpretation of dialects in our society? By LANGUAGE IDEOLOGY here, we mean ingrained, unquestioned beliefs about the way the world is, the way it should be, and the way it has to be with respect to language. What implications do these terms have for those dialects that are considered "corrupt," "bad," or "ungrammatical" versions of the standard?

Before we get too far into this discussion, we should note that whether or not there are specific institutions set up to guide the establishment of a standard variety, language standardization of some type seems inevitable. Ultimately, we can attribute this to underlying principles of human behavior in which certain ways of behaving (dressing, speaking, treating elders, and so forth) are established as normative for the society.

As a starting point, it is helpful to distinguish between the operation of standard English on a formal and informal level. In formal standardization, language norms are prescribed by recognized sources of authority, such as grammar and usage books, dictionaries, and institutions like language academies. In the United States, we don't have a language academy, but we have many grammar and usage books that people turn to for the determination of standard forms. The key words in this definition are "prescribed" and "authority" so that the responsibility for determining standard forms is largely out of the hands of most speakers of the language. Whenever there is a question as to whether or not a form is considered standard English, we can turn to authoritarian guides to usage. If, for example, we have a question as to where to use *will* and *shall*, we simply look it up in our usage guide, which tells us that *shall* is used for first person questions (*Shall I go?*) and *will* is used in other contexts (*He will go*). At that point, the question of a particular usage is often settled.

FORMAL STANDARD ENGLISH, or PRESCRIPTIVE STANDARD ENGLISH, tends to be based on the written language of established writers and is typically codified in English grammar texts. It is perpetuated to a large extent in formal institutions, such as schools, by those responsible for English language education. It also is very conservative and often resistant to changes taking place within the language. For some features, the prescribed usage will border on obsolescence. For example, the subjunctive use of *be* in sentences such as *If this be treason, I am a traitor* is a structure that is largely obsolete, yet this use can still be found in some prescriptive grammar books. Similarly, the maintenance of the singular form of *data* as *datum*, or even the *shall/will* distinction, has largely disappeared from spoken language, but it is still prescribed in many usage guides and maintained in written language. Without an official agency responsible for the maintenance of a uniform formal standard English in the United States, there will be some disagreement among prescriptive grammarians, but in most cases, there is fairly strong agreement. As set forth, formal standard English is most likely to be exemplified in impersonal written language and the most formal kinds of spoken language occasions, especially where spoken language has been written first.

If we took a sample of everyday conversational speech, we would find that there are virtually no speakers who consistently speak formal standard English as prescribed in the grammar books. In fact, it is not unusual for the same person who prescribes a formal standard English form to violate standard usage in ordinary conversation. For example, one of the prescribed formal standard English rules prohibits the use of a pronoun following a subject noun, as in *My mother, she took me to the movies*, and many teachers will correct children who use this form. Yet we have documented these same teachers using sentences such as *The students who returned late from recess yesterday and today, they will have to remain after school* within a few minutes of correcting children for using similar types of sentences. The point of these illustrations is not to expose as hypocrites those who assume responsibility for perpetuating standard English norms, but to show that the prescribed formal variety is, in reality, not always maintained consistently in natural spoken language. Does this mean that standard English does not exist in our society, and that we should stop talking about this variety as if it were a real entity? On the contrary, there is plenty of evidence that people in our society make judgments about other people's speech, including an evaluation of standardness, based on everyday, natural speech. So there appears to be another, more informal level, of standardness that operates in American society.

INFORMAL STANDARD ENGLISH, without recourse to prescriptive authority, is much more difficult to define than formal standard English, and a realistic definition will have to take into account the actual kinds of assessments that members of American society make as they judge other speakers' standardness. As a starting point, we must acknowledge that the informal notion of standard English exists on a continuum, with speakers ranging along the continuum between the standard and nonstandard poles. Informal standard English is a continuous rather than categorical notion and speakers may be judged as more or less standard. For example, speakers may be placed at different points on a standard–nonstandard continuum as in figure 1.1, with Speaker **A** using few, if any, nonstandard forms, and Speaker **E** using many.

Ratings of standardness not only exist on a continuum; they can be fairly subjective as well. Based on different experiences as well as different regional and social dialect backgrounds, one listener may rate a particular speaker as standard while another listener rates the same speaker as nonstandard. For example, a Northern-born middle-class African American might rate a Southern white as nonstandard, while a native of the region might rate the same speaker as a standard speaker. By the same token, a person from the Midwest might rate a native of New York City as nonstandard while

```
              A      B    C      D    E
Standard ------|----------|----- |----------|-------|------ Nonstandard
```

Figure 1.1   A continuum of standardness

another New Yorker might rate the same speaker as standard. Further, preconceptions and prejudices about how different groups of people are expected to speak come into play as well. For example, researchers (e.g. Williams 1973) have shown that people may judge the *same voice* as "standard" or "nonstandard" depending on which video image it is paired with (e.g. a European American vs. African American face).

Though there is certainly a subjective dimension to the notion of standardness, there is, at the same time, a consensus in rating speakers at the more extreme ranges of the continuum. Thus, virtually all listeners will rate Speaker **A** in figure 1.1 as a standard English speaker and Speaker **E** as a nonstandard English speaker. On the other hand, there might be considerable difference in the ratings which Speakers **B** and **C** receive in terms of a simple classification into standard or nonstandard categories. Furthermore, we have found that the classification of speakers at the extreme poles of the continuum (such as Speakers **A** and **E**) tends to be consistent regardless of the socioeconomic class of the person making the judgment.

Classifications of standardness will also be somewhat flexible with respect to the specific features of the regional variety being judged. Thus, the *r*-less pronunciations which characterize Eastern New England or Southeastern American pronunciation (as in *cah* for *car* or *beah* for *bear*) may be judged as standard English, as will the *r*-ful pronunciations that characterize certain other dialects. And people may be judged as standard English speakers whether they *go to the beach*, *go to the shore*, or *go to the ocean* for a summer vacation. On this informal level, standard English is a pluralistic notion, at least with respect to pronunciation and vocabulary differences. That is, there are regional standards recognized within the broad and informal notion of standard American English. For example, there are regional standards for the South, for the Midwest, and for New England, though they may differ in terms of the particular items included in each standard.

What is it about a speaker's dialect that is critical in determining whether the speaker will be judged as standard or nonstandard? There is no simple answer to this question, and people tend to give overall impressions, such as "quality of voice," "tone of expression," or "correct grammar," when they are asked to explain their judgments of standardness and nonstandardness. Despite the vagueness of such responses, there do seem to be a few relatively specific criteria that people use in judging a person's speech as standard. For one, standard American English seems to be determined more by what it is *not* than by what it is. To a large extent, American English speech samples rated as standard English by a cross-section of listeners exhibit a range of regional variation in pronunciation and vocabulary items, but they do *not* contain grammatical structures that are socially stigmatized. If native speakers from Michigan, New England, and Arkansas avoid the use of socially stigmatized grammatical structures such as "double negatives" (e.g.

They didn't do nothing), different verb agreement patterns (e.g. *They's okay*), and different irregular verb forms (e.g. *She done it*), there is a good chance they will be considered standard English speakers even though they may have distinct regional pronunciations. In this kind of assessment, informal standard English is defined in more of a negative than a positive way. In other words, if a person's speech is free of socially disfavored structures, then it is considered standard.

The definition of informal standard English as a variety free of stigmatized features tends to be supported by an additional observation about Americans' attitudes toward dialects. For the most part, Americans do not assign strong positive, or prestige, value to any particular dialect of American English. The basic contrast in the US exists between negatively valued dialects and those without negative value, not between those with prestige value and those without. Curiously, Americans still assign positive value to British dialects, which are not even viable options for wide-scale use in the United States and Canada. It is difficult to say exactly why Americans look upon British English so favorably, but one possibility is a lingering colonial effect, thus showing the enduring influence of traditional language attitudes a couple of centuries after the US gained its independence from British rule. Americans, in commenting on different dialects of American English, are much more likely to make comments about nonstandardness ("That person doesn't talk correct English") than they are to comment on standardness (e.g. "That person really speaks correct English"). The notion of standard English is certainly operative in American society on an informal level, but it differs considerably from the formal standard English norm that is often taught as *the* standard. For the purposes of our discussion throughout this book, we will refer to this more informal definition of the standard language rather than the formal one, since it is the informal version that has a more direct bearing on our everyday lives.

Exercise 3

There are a couple of levels of standards that seem to be noticeable to people when they listen to speech. We don't usually comment on informal standard English, but we may comment on a person's speech if it is nonstandard. It is, however, possible to call attention to speech because it sounds too formal or "proper." Forms that are too standard for everyday conversation are sometimes referred to as SUPERSTANDARD ENGLISH. In the following sets of sentences, identify which sentences characterize (1) nonstandard English, (2) informal standard English, and (3) superstandard English. What forms in the sentences are responsible for your assessment? Are there any sentences you're not sure about? Why?

1. a He's not as smart as I.
   b He's not so smart as I.
   c He ain't as smart as me.
   d He not as smart as me.
2. a He's not to do that.
   b He not supposed to do that.
   c He don't supposed to do that.
   d He's not supposed to do that.
3. a I'm right, ain't I?
   b I'm right, aren't I?
   c I'm right, am I not?
   d I'm right, isn't I?
4. a If I was going to do that, I would start right now.
   b If I were going to do that, I would start right now.
   c Were I to do that, I would start right now.
   d I would start right now, if I was going to do that.
5. a A person should not change her speech.
   b One should not change one's speech.
   c A person should not change their speech.
   d A person should not change his or her speech.

Why do people sometimes comment about other people's speech because it sounds too proper?

1.5 Vernacular Dialects

At the other end of the continuum of standardness is nonstandardness. Varieties that seem to be typified by the use of nonstandard forms are often referred to as VERNACULAR DIALECTS. The term vernacular is used here simply to refer to varieties of a language that are not classified as standard dialects. It is used in much the same way that the term *vernacular language* is used to refer to local or native languages of common communication which contrast with the official language of a multilingual country. Other researchers may refer to these vernacular varieties as NONSTANDARD DIALECTS or nonmainstream dialects, but we have chosen to use the term *vernacular* because it seems more neutral than these alternatives.

As with standard dialects of English, there are a number of different social and regional factors that go into the labeling of a vernacular, and any attempt to define a vernacular dialect on a single dimension is problematic. Ultimately, each dialect is delimited according to a complex array of factors, including matters related to social class, region, ethnicity, situation, and so forth. Furthermore, vernacularity, like standardness, exists on a continuum so that particular speakers may exhibit speech which is more or less vernacular. Thus, Speaker D in figure 1.1 may or may not be classified as a vernacular dialect speaker, but we can expect a consensus of people (from the same and different dialects) to recognize Speaker E as a representative of some vernacular variety. Nonetheless, it is possible for both vernacular and non-vernacular speakers of English to identify paradigmatic speakers of vernacular varieties in a way that is analogous to the way that we can identify representatives of standard dialects.

Unlike standard dialects, which are largely defined by the *absence* of socially disfavored structures of English, vernacular varieties seem to be characterized by the *presence* of socially conspicuous structures – at least to speakers of informal standard English who do not typically use them. In other words, vernacular varieties are the converse of standard dialects in that an assortment of marked nonstandard English structures sets them apart as being vernacular. Although each vernacular dialect seems to have its own core of vernacular structures, we have to be careful saying that all speakers of a given variety will exhibit these core features. Not all speakers of a given dialect necessarily use the entire set of structures associated with their dialect, and there may be differing patterns of usage among speakers of the variety. In fact, attempts to isolate *the* common core of structures for a particular vernacular often lead to heavily qualified, imprecise descriptions. Such qualification is typified in the attempt of Walt Wolfram and Donna Christian to delimit "Appalachian English."

> There may be some question as to whether it is justifiable to differentiate an entity such as AE [Appalachian English] from other (equally difficult to define precisely) varieties of American English, particularly some of those spoken in the South. Quite obviously, there are many features we have described which are not peculiar to speakers within the Appalachian range. On the other hand, there also appears to be a small set of features which may not be found in other areas. Even if this is not the case, we may justify our distinction of AE on the basis of the combination of features. . . . Fully cognizant of the pitfalls found in any attempt to attach terminological labels to the varieties of English, we shall proceed to use the designation AE as a convenient, if loosely-defined notion. (Wolfram and Christian 1976: 29–30)

Language scholars sometimes have difficulty defining the set of features that uniquely distinguishes a given vernacular variety, but it is easy to demonstrate that both professionals and non-professionals identify and classify quite accurately speakers representing the vernacular pole on the continuum. Vernacular dialects are identifiable entities in American society, despite our inability to come up with precise sets of structures characterizing them. As we make our way through our description of the dimensions of American English dialects, we will discuss a number of the specific factors that go into more precise definitions of these dialects.

We can summarize the features that set apart standard dialects and vernacular dialects as follows:

> FORMAL STANDARD: applied primarily to written language and the most formal spoken language situations; objective standards prescribed by language "authorities"; standards codified in usage books, dictionaries, and other written texts; conservative outlook on language forms.
>
> INFORMAL STANDARD: applied to spoken language; determined by actual usage patterns of speakers; listener judgment essential in determining socially acceptable norms; multiple norms of acceptability, incorporating regional and social considerations; defined negatively by the avoidance of socially stigmatized linguistic structures.
>
> VERNACULAR: applied to spoken language; determined by usage patterns of speakers; listener judgment essential in determining social unacceptability; usually defined by the presence of a set of socially stigmatized linguistic structures.

Since both formal and informal standard varieties are usually associated with socially favored, mainstream groups, they are socially respected in American society, but since vernacular varieties are associated with socially disfavored groups, they are not considered socially respectable. This association, of course, simply reflects underlying values about different social groups in our society and is hardly dependent on language differences alone.

Before concluding our discussion of definitions of "standard" and "vernacular," it is important to note that notions of standardness and prestige can operate quite differently in different societies. Although the US doesn't really have one single language variety that is accorded great social prestige, there are prestige varieties in some other countries and other societies, and these varieties may or may not be used as widespread norms or "standards." For example, Classical Arabic is not widely used in everyday communication in the Arabic-speaking world; instead, there exist a number of national and regional standards that are used in communicative interactions where a widespread norm is needed (e.g. in business situations). In such cases the standards may actually be somewhat devalued rather than socially favored (as in the US), since they do not correspond with the prestige variety. Hence, the widespread standards in use in the Arabic-speaking world tend to be considered "lesser" forms of the language than classical Arabic, despite their widespread usage. Even in Great Britain, where "proper" British English, or "Received Pronunciation" (RP), seems the logical choice as a standard variety for daily interaction, evidence indicates increasing usage of several widespread standards that are quite different from RP and which do not have the same prestige value (e.g. Britain 2001; Milroy and Gordon 2003: 88–115).

1.6   Labeling Vernacular Dialects

Although the choice of a label for a particular vernacular dialect such as African American English or Appalachian English may seem relatively unimportant, it can become a very important consideration when the broader social, political, and cultural considerations associated with naming are taken into account. For example, in the past half century, the vernacular dialect associated with African Americans has had the following labels, given here in approximate chronological sequence: *Negro Dialect, Substandard Negro English, Nonstandard Negro English, Black English, Afro-American English, Ebonics, Vernacular Black English, African American (Vernacular) English*, and *African American Language*. And believe it or not, this is not a complete list. On one level, one can correlate some of these name changes with changes in names for ethnic groups themselves that have taken place in American society. But there are also more subtle dimensions, such as the choice between African American Language versus African American English. In this instance, the term "language" is used because of the legitimacy ascribed to languages as opposed to dialects. Furthermore, there are often strong affective associations related to particular labels. For example, the label *Ebonics*, originally introduced in the early 1970s, gained great notoriety in the mid-1990s in connection with a highly publicized resolution by the Oakland Unified School District Board of Education. As a result of the controversy, the label evoked many negative comments and derogatory parodies. In contrast, the synonymous terms typically used by linguists, African American English or African American Language, do not typically evoke such parodies. Labels are always tricky because it can be difficult to delimit their referents in a precise way and because they may carry such strong affective connotations. Terms for vernacular dialects, like other aspects of behavior, do not exist in an ideological vacuum and often reflect underlying attitudes about sociolinguistic asymmetries and linguistic sub-ordination, as well as the social inequities underlying this subordination.

In this text, we use the term AFRICAN AMERICAN ENGLISH (often abbreviated AAE) to refer to that variety spoken by and considered to be a key part of the ethnic heritage and cultural identity of many people of African descent in the US. The term actually encompasses a number of sub-varieties, since there is variation in African American English based on region, social class, and style, among other factors. We choose this label chiefly because of its neutrality and its widespread usage in current linguistic scientific studies, while recognizing that other labels may be equally appropriate, or perhaps more so, for different purposes (e.g. for promoting African American cultural heritage or sociopolitical equality). Our choice of label should not be taken as any sort of statement regarding whether AAE should be considered a "language" or a "dialect," since the distinction between "language" and "dialect" cannot be made on purely linguistic grounds but is intricately tied to sociopolitical and sociocultural considerations. In addition, decisions as to whether a particular variety constitutes a language in its own right can change over time. For example, in recent decades in the former Yugoslavia, Serbo-Croatian, once regarded as a single language, has come to be regarded as at least three separate languages: Serbian, Bosnian, and Croatian, largely as a result of recent political rather than linguistic changes.

Parallel to the term "African American English," we use the term "African American" to refer to people of African descent in the US, most often those with historic or cultural ties to the slave trade. It is not easy to determine the precise population(s) covered by the label "African American." For example, it is unclear whether the term should be applied to recent immigrants from Africa and their families; it is also not clear whether it includes those from North Africa (e.g. Egypt) or only those from Sub-Saharan Africa. In addition, many African Americans self-identify as "Black" rather than, or in addition to, "African American." Further, the classification of particular people as "African American" may be different in different regions or among different social groups and may change over time; and people may even feel different degrees of "African-American-ness" in different situations – for example, when talking with family members about ethnically sensitive issues vs. participating in a classroom discussion about linguistics with people of various ethnicities.

Another label employed widely throughout this text is EUROPEAN AMERICAN, used to refer to speakers popularly labeled "White" in American society. The term "White" defies precise definition and indeed often seems to be a catch-all to refer to anyone who does not consider themselves, or is not considered by others, to have a marked "ethnic" identity. In reality, everyone is of *some* ethnicity. It's just that many people of European descent, especially of British or Northern European descent, have been dominant in American society for so long that they have come to be seen (or to uphold themselves) as the "default" or "normal" group (e.g. Hill 1998) against which everyone who is different must be compared (and, sadly, often judged lacking). The widespread belief that European Americans are not "ethnic" parallels in many ways the belief, in discussions of language and gender, that only women's gender matters and that men's linguistic and other behavior is "neutral" rather than influenced by gender in any way (see chapter 8). To the extent that we can apply any degree of precision to the term "European American," we intend it to refer to those people in US society of British or Continental European (especially Northern European) descent who would label themselves or be labeled by others as "White." When a group identifies itself with an ethnic label (e.g. Jewish American), we will use that term when relevant to the discussion at hand (but see, e.g., Modan 2001 on the complex and shifting relation between "Jewishness" and "Whiteness"). Again, "European American" is no easier to define than "African American," and again the definition is relative in that who is considered "White" can change over time or vary according to a variety of factors such as region, class, and speech situation. As will be made evident in the following chapters, there is no single European American English any more than there is a single African American English. In fact, research indicates that European American varieties differ more widely from one another than do the different varieties of African American English.

Labels for other ethnic and social varieties of English are introduced in subsequent chapters with definition and discussion where appropriate. Despite the prominence of the Black–White distinction in American society historically and currently, America has always been a country of rich ethnic and social diversity, and it is important to recognize and gain greater understanding of the many other cultures and language varieties that have shaped American society and continue to shape it today.

Exercise 4

Consider how the Hispanic or Latino population does or does not fit into the above discussion of ethnic labeling. For example, do they fit the designation "European American" as defined and discussed above? It is interesting to note, in this connection, that in the Southwestern US, Latinos and Latinas are often referred to as Chicanos or Chicanas and White people are typically referred to as Anglos. Who might and might not fit into the category of "Anglo" and why?

1.7 Why Study Dialects?

There are a number of reasons why the study of dialects is an attractive field of inquiry. First, our natural curiosity is piqued when we hear speakers of different dialects. If we are the least bit interested in different manifestations of human behavior, then we are likely to be intrigued by the facets of behavior revealed in language. The authors have become accustomed to, if somewhat wary of, the responses of people at casual social gatherings when people find out that we study dialects. Such responses range from challenges to identify where people originally come from (guaranteeing instant credibility) to the question of why particular groups of speakers talk as they do (usually a forewarning of an opinionated explanation to follow). Furthermore, it is not uncommon to encounter individuals from varied walks of life who profess an interest in dialects as a "hobby" simply because dialects are so fascinating to them. The positive side to this curiosity is that the study of dialects can often sell itself; the negative side, as discussed earlier, is that a corresponding set of attitudes and opinions about American dialects makes it difficult to deal with information about them in a neutral way. In one form or another, most professional students of dialects have simply cultivated the natural interest that resides within us all.

As a manifestation of human behavioral differences, dialects may be studied because they provide the opportunity to extend social science inquiry into language, a quite natural application for fields such as history, anthropology, sociology, psychology, and geography. Thus, one of the most extensive series of studies ever conducted on the dialects of American English, the *Linguistic Atlas of the United States and Canada*, carefully charted the geographical distribution of various forms in American English as a kind of dialect geography; in fact, studies of this type are often referred to as LINGUISTIC GEOGRAPHY. At the same time, these studies attempted to trace the English settlement patterns of America through language differences, as a kind of history. Further, these studies noted the distribution of forms in different social categories of speakers as a kind of sociology. It is easy to see how dialect differences can be seen as a natural extension of a number of different fields within the social sciences since these differences are so integrally related to all aspects of human behavior.

Other studies have shown how the cultural and historical heritage of particular cultural groups has been maintained through their dialects, such as the cultural detachment historically linked with regions such as Appalachia and the island communities along the Eastern seaboard of the United States – for example, Tangier Island off the coast of Virginia, the Outer Banks off the coast of North Carolina, or the Sea Islands along the South Carolina and Georgia coast. From this perspective, interest in dialects may derive from a basic concern with humanities studies such as folklore, history, and English. The US government agency the National Endowment for the Humanities has been a primary source of financial support for dialect surveys over the years, along with the National Science Foundation.

Motivation for studying dialects may naturally go beyond "objective" social science inquiry and the description of different social and ethnic heritages. In some cases, dialect differences may be studied as a part of growing self- or group awareness. Thus, members of a particular social group may seize upon language differences as a part of their identity and sense of place. It is no accident that language and gender issues have become an important topic in the last several decades, as attention has been drawn to gender-differentiated social roles and asymmetrical power relations based on sex and gender in our society. Similarly, a rise of interest in African American English coincided with the general development of cultural consciousness in other spheres of life in the late 1960s and early 1970s. The emphasis on the identificational issues surrounding English dialect variation might strike members of the majority population or socially dominant cultural groups as somewhat overstated, until we realize how central language is to the identification of self and group. Issues of nationalism and identity often come to a head over language, as demonstrated by the attention paid to the issue of French versus English in Canada. In a similar way, the status of the Dutch-based language Afrikaans in South Africa is hardly a simple language issue; it reflects deeper issues related to political and ethnic self-determination. In these cases, the conflicts are not about language *per se*, but the power of language to serve as a proxy for broader sociopolitical and cultural issues. The transparency of language as cultural behavior makes it an ideal stage for acting out much more fundamental issues and conflicts among different groups in society.

A review of the development of the English language in the United States shows that the notion of American English itself was strongly tied to nationalism historically. Noah Webster, the parent of generations of English dictionaries, issued the declaration that "as an independent nation, our honor requires us to have a system of our own, in language as well as government" and that "a national language is a bond of national union." In this context, studying American English as compared with British English might be motivated by a feeling of patriotism and loyalty to the United States. It is easy to compile an extensive list of cases in which nationalism and group consciousness movements were motivating factors for studying languages and dialects.

At the other end of the spectrum, the study of dialect differences might be justified on a linguistic theoretical basis. Scholars may examine language variation in an effort to understand the basic nature of language as a cognitive and human phenomenon. This theoretical concern may range from the investigation of how language changes over time and space to how language reflects and affects the cognitive capabilities of a speaker of a language. In this context, the examination of dialects may provide an essential and unique database. William Labov, one of the pioneers in modern sociolinguistics, articulated a linguistic scientific motivation for studying dialects in the published version of his doctoral dissertation, *The Social Stratification of English in New York City*, when he stated that "my own intention was to solve linguistic problems, bearing in mind that these are ultimately problems in the analysis of social behavior" (Labov 1966: v–vi). Empirical data from the study of dialects thus may contribute to our understanding of some central issues concerning the nature of language variation. For example, data from the study of variation within language increase our understanding of the kinds and amount of variation which may be contained within a single language and those which may not.

Finally, there is a practical, applied motivation for studying dialects. Many students in education and the health professions have become interested in dialects because of the "usefulness" of the information as it relates to another primary activity such as teaching or service delivery. Virtually all fields of education focused on language-related activities, including reading, language arts, and language service professions such as speech and language pathology, have recognized the need to understand both general principles governing language differences and specific descriptive details of the dialects characterizing students. In fact, in one case of litigation that took place in Ann Arbor, Michigan, in 1979, the judge ordered teachers to attend workshops on dialects because of the potential impact of such information on the interpretation of reading behavior by vernacular-speaking students. Similarly, a widely publicized resolution adopted by the Oakland School Board in 1996 maintained that an understanding of the vernacular variety spoken by African Americans should be used as an important bridge for teaching proficiency in standard English. In the early 2000s, several widely publicized cases of "linguistic profiling" once again raised the issue of discrimination based on dialect differences (Baugh 2003). Speakers identified as African American over the telephone were informed that apartment vacancies were already filled, while European American callers were invited to visit the advertised vacancies. Such cases remind us that dialect discrimination in one form or another is still a social and legal problem in American society. Dialectologist Dennis Preston (back cover of Lippi-Green 1997) goes so far as to observe that "the 'dialectists' among us have done the same sorts of damage to individual advancement and self-esteem that racists and sexists have done."

After reading the previous paragraphs, we might wonder if there is any justifiable reason for not studying dialects. The glib answer to this question is, "Probably not!" However, when we consider the full range of reasons for studying dialects, as well as the fact that there is a rich historical tradition underlying each motivation, it is easy to see why there are scholars who feel that knowledge about dialects should be a central component of our educational process, as fundamental as any other traditional topic covered in our education.

Exercise 5

On a personal level, consider which of the above motivations matches your interest most closely. Is there more than one reason that appeals to you? Rank in terms of priority the reasons given above as they relate to your interest (basic curiosity, social science inquiry, humanities study, personal and group identity, linguistic study itself, the application of knowledge about dialects to another primary field). Are there other reasons you can think of for studying dialects? Has the need to study dialects been oversold? Why or why not?

1.8 A Tradition of Study

There is a longstanding tradition of collecting and studying data on variation in English, guided by the variety of motivations cited above. As we already mentioned, some of the earliest collections of American English were concerned with those aspects of American English that set it apart from British English, particularly with respect to vocabulary. Vocabulary is one of the most transparent ways in which dialects differ, and vocabulary studies are a common way in which dialect differences are profiled. Typical of relatively early works on dialect differences was John Pickering's 1816 work entitled *A Vocabulary, or Collection of Words and Phrases which have been Supposed to be Peculiar to the United States of America to which is Prefixed an Essay on the Present State of the English Language in the United States*. Some of the early studies of the dialect structures of American English *vis-à-vis* British English were based largely on vague impressions, but others represented fairly meticulous and exhaustive approaches to the cataloging of dialect differences. In addition, politicians and social leaders often became involved in language issues. For example, Benjamin Franklin suggested an early spelling reform, and John Adams proposed an academy for establishing an American standard as differences between British and American English began to emerge and the social and political implications of this divergence were considered.

As the United States became securely independent, the focus changed from the relationship between American and British English to the diversity within American English itself. The American Dialect Society was formed in 1889 for "the investigation of English dialects in America with regard to pronunciation, grammar, phraseology, and geographical distribution" (Grandgent 1889). This concern with geographical distribution coincided with a period of fairly widespread migration and resettlement and was motivated by a strong historical rationale, as dialectologists began to fear that the original American English dialects would fade away as old boundaries to intercommunication were erased. As we shall see later, this has hardly been the case, and some modern dialect boundaries still reflect the earliest European American settlement patterns. The initial hope of the American Dialect Society was to provide a body of data from which a dialect dictionary or series of linguistic maps might be derived. A considerable amount of data towards this end was published in the Society's original journal, *Dialect Notes*, but it was not until 1928 that a large-scale systematic study of dialect geography was undertaken, titled the *Linguistic Atlas of the United States and Canada*. Along with the historical goals already mentioned, this survey aimed to correlate dialect differences with different social classifications, an incipient stage in the development of a field of study that would blossom fully several decades later. A comprehensive set of *Linguistic Atlas* surveys for different areas of the United States and Canada was proposed and the initial survey of New England undertaken. As one of the nation's initial areas of settlement by English speakers, New England was a logical starting place, given the project's focus on historical settlement patterns. Fieldworkers combed the region looking for older, lifetime residents from whom they might elicit particular items of pronunciation, grammar, and vocabulary. Quite typically, the fieldworkers ended up recording up to ten or twelve hours of elicited forms. Of course, in the early stages these recordings consisted of on-the-spot phonetic transcriptions without the aid of any mechanical recording equipment. Some of this work is still ongoing, despite some criticism of the techniques for gathering data and the approach to describing language variation that were the basis of these studies.

Over a century after the establishment of the American Dialect Society, one of its major goals is finally being realized, namely, the publication of the *Dictionary of American Regional English* (Cassidy 1985; Cassidy and Hall 1991, 1996; Hall 2002). Four volumes, covering the letters A–Sk, have now appeared, with the completion of the six-volume work projected by the end of the first decade of the twenty-first century. This much-heralded, comprehensive work dates its modern history to 1962, when Frederic G. Cassidy was appointed general editor. It taps a wealth of data sources, including its own extensive dialect survey of the United States, the various *Linguistic Atlas* projects, and the publications of the American Dialect Society, among others. The American Dialect Society remains a small but active organization concerned with language variation in American English. Each year in January, when it announces its annual "Word of the Year" award, the organization receives a few minutes of national media attention. Its regular publication of the quarterly journal, *American Speech*, has been a staple of dialectology for more than three-quarters of a century. This journal balances the traditional focus on regional variation with a more current emphasis on social, ethnic, and gender-based variation in a readable format.

Beginning in the 1960s, research on dialects in the United States started focusing more specifically on social and ethnic variation in American English than on regional variation. Part of this emphasis was fueled by a concern for language-related social problems, particularly problems related to educational issues concerning America's lower social classes. Some linguistic descriptions of vernacular dialects such as African American English and Appalachian English became the basis for programs which sought to remedy educational inequalities. The use of sociolinguistic data and engagement of sociolinguists in addressing social and educational problems remains a continuing concern. For some investigators, however, following the pioneering work of Labov, the fundamental nature of linguistic variation as a theoretical issue in linguistics became a rationale for sociolinguistic inquiry. Although some current investigators motivate their dialect studies exclusively on a theoretical basis, the more typical rationale combines theoretical and applied or social perspectives. Since the 1970s there has been an unprecedented proliferation of studies of vernacular varieties of English. In fact, one comprehensive bibliography of African American English (Brasch and Brasch 1974) listed over 2,400 entries related to this variety over three decades ago. Another annotated bibliography of Southern American English (McMillan and Montgomery 1989) listed over 3,800 works, the majority of which relate to the vernacular dialects of the South. The range of vernacular dialects considered over the past several decades has been extended to include both urban and rural varieties of American English, as well as English varieties developed from contact situations with other languages. Both newly developing and older, vanishing varieties of English are included in this focus. Indeed, no vernacular dialect seems safe from descriptive scrutiny, and no social or ethnic group is assured of sociolinguistic anonymity given the current state of dialectology in the United States.

Methods of data collection and the kind of data considered necessary for adequate analysis have also shifted drastically during the past several decades. Spontaneous, casual conversation has become a key source of data for analysis, replacing the earlier emphasis on direct probes to elicit particular forms. Some fairly creative techniques were devised to enhance the possibility of recording good "naturalistic" data, aided by advancing technology in audio and video recording equipment. In addition, more careful and systematic attention has been given to an array of social and interactional factors, ranging from the social relationships and practices of groups and individuals to the social and sociopsychological factors that affect speech in unfolding conversational interaction. Such developments naturally were aided by perspectives from other fields in the social sciences such as psychology, anthropology, and sociology. In addition, researchers in recent decades have been making increasing use of data from various media sources (e.g. film, internet), as well as compiling and utilizing large computer-searchable data collections.

Advances in the analysis of data now incorporate more rigorous quantitative methods, including the use of state-of-the-art automated search engines, statistical procedures, and mapping techniques. At the same time, increasing emphasis is now being placed on developing and implementing qualitative methodologies that will yield results superior to those achieved by impressionistic observations and anecdotal evidence concerning the patterning of isolated language forms. A traditional dialectologist, frozen in the time frame of a half century ago, would hardly recognize what constitutes dialect study today. The underlying motivations for studying dialects in the present day may be well established in the historical record, but the field has undergone some profound changes in its focus and methods. Finally, current dialect study is characterized by more of an "entrepreneurial" spirit than in the past. Specialists in different areas of dialect study have carved out productive and useful niches for the application of information gleaned from the study of dialects, ranging from dialect training programs for actors projecting different regional and social roles to consultation services offering the analysis of language features for various legal purposes. And the range of applications for dialect study continues to expand.

1.9   Further Reading

Bauer, Laurie, and Peter Trudgill (eds.) (1998) *Language Myths*. New York: Penguin. This collection of articles exposes the kinds of myths about language and language diversity that are perpetuated in popular culture. Among the myths relevant to this book (each discussed in its own chapter) are "New Yorkers can't talk properly," "Black Americans are verbally deprived," "Southern speech is slovenly," and "Shakespearean English is spoken in the mountains."

Baugh, John (1991) The politicization of changing terms of self-reference among American slave descendants. *American Speech* 66: 133–46. The author considers the evolution of changing terms of self-reference among African Americans and the sociopolitical context of dialect labeling. This article should be read along with a companion article in the same issue by Geneva Smitherman titled "What is Africa to me? Language and ideology, and African American?" (*American Speech* 66: 115–32).

Labov, William (1972d) The logic of nonstandard English. Chapter 5 in *Language in the Inner City: Studies in the Black English Vernacular*. Philadelphia: University of Pennsylvania Press, 201–40. This influential article, which appears as a chapter in Labov's *Language in the Inner City*, deals with basic misconceptions about vernacular dialects. Historically, it constituted a critical argument for the linguistic integrity and conceptual adequacy of vernacular dialect. It has been reprinted in numerous anthologies, including the *Atlantic Monthly* (June 1972) under the title "Academic ignorance and Black intelligence."

Lippi-Green, Rosina (1997) *English with an Accent: Language, Ideology, and Discrimination in the United States.* New York/London: Routledge. Lippi-Green offers an insightful description of linguistic subordination that ranges from language ideology in the United States to institutional and personal discrimination based on language differences.

Mencken, H. L. (1962) *The American Language: An Inquiry into the Development of English in the United States*, Supplement I. New York: Alfred A. Knopf. The initial chapters of Mencken's classic work, chapters 1 through 4 in particular, provide an intriguing account of the early developments of American English, with rich references to early commentary about this emerging variety by politicians and general observers of language. Although the commentary is now dated, it is still worthwhile reading from a historical vantage point.

2

Why Dialects?

Most people find dialects intriguing. At the same time, they have lots of questions about them and often have strong opinions as well. Probably the most common question we encounter about the status of American dialects, especially from journalists, is, "Don't you think dialects are dying, due to television and the increasing mobility of the American population?" Certainly, advances in transportation and media technology have radically compressed the geography of the United States and opened up new worlds of communication and cultural connections over the last century. But the fact of the matter is that American dialects are hardly endangered. Indeed, there is even evidence that some types of dialect differences are actually intensifying rather than receding, and it is difficult to imagine the English language without its array of dialects. Regardless of how we may personally feel about the virtue of dialect differences, the reality of regional and social dialects in American society is that they are alive and well. In fact, we would boldly venture to say that as long as the English language exists, it will be full of dialect diversity.

We may start our explanation of dialects by asking the question, "Why are there so many dialects in the first place?" What are the factors that lead to language differences, and why does dialect diversity persist in the face of mass communication, increased mobility, and growing cultural homogenization? In our efforts to answer these questions, we consider both social and linguistic factors. Socially, we look to the same types of factors that account for general regional and behavioral differences among people, whether these differences are in style of dress, architecture, or other cultural traits. Linguistically, we look to the way we produce and perceive language as well as how individual language features are organized into coherent systems. These linguistic and social factors may come together in countless ways, resulting in a wide variety of dialects. In the following sections, we examine some of the historical, social, and linguistic considerations that help explain the development of dialect variation.

2.1 Sociohistorical Explanation

One side of the explanation for dialects is found in the social and historical conditions that surround language change. At the same time that language operates as a highly structured communicative code, it also functions as a kind of cultural behavior. It is only natural, then, that social differentiation of various types should go hand-in-hand with language differences. Dialects are most likely to develop where we find both physical and social separation among groups of speakers. In the following sections, we discuss some of the chief social, cultural, and psychological factors that set the stage for dialect differentiation.

2.1.1 Settlement

One of the most obvious explanations for why there are dialects is rooted in the settlement patterns of groups of speakers. The history of American English does not begin with the initial arrival of English speakers in the Americas. Some of the dominant characteristics still found in varieties of American English can be traced to dialect differences that existed in the British Isles before the British colonization of America began. Others can be traced to varieties that arose in language contact situations in areas such as the Caribbean and the west coast of Africa. The earliest English-speaking inhabitants in America came from different parts of the British Isles, where dialects were already in place. Many emigrants from Southeastern England originally established themselves in Eastern New England and Tidewater Virginia. Others, from northern and western parts of England, situated themselves in the New Jersey and Delaware area. In addition, emigrants of Scots Irish descent from Ulster, Northern Ireland, set up residence in Western New England, upper New York, and many parts of Appalachia. From these points, the population fanned westward in a way that is still reflected in the dialect configuration of the United States today. The major dialects of American English were focused around population centers established by emigrants, such as Boston, Richmond, and Charleston. Notice, for example, how the configuration of the dialects of the Eastern United States we give in chapter 4 (figure 4.2) still reflects the distribution of early British habitation in the New World.

Settlement generally takes place in several distinct phases. In the initial phase, a group of people moves to an area where there are attractive environmental qualities. The immigrants bring with them the culture of their origin. In the next phase, available land is occupied, and a new cultural identity emerges, as a cohesive society develops in the region. The creation of this new culture is often accompanied by the elimination of established cultures and ways of speaking. For example, in the process of forging an "American" culture out of various European cultures, colonists overwhelmed numerous Native American cultures – and languages. Today, there exist very few Native American languages, and numbers of speakers are dwindling rapidly. This is not to say that Native American languages played no part in the development of American English dialects; but the Native American languages that the original European emigrants encountered when they first arrived in North America were almost completely supplanted by varieties of English, as well as other European languages such as Spanish.

In the third phase of settlement, regional populations define roles for themselves with respect to wider social groupings. The response to national commerce and culture becomes an important part of the definition of the localized population, as it maintains and adjusts aspects of its dialect in shaping a distinctive identity.

The forerunners of the dominant cultural group in a given region typically establish cultural and linguistic boundaries that persist in time, although the original features that characterize each area may change in a number of ways, and other features may take their place. Much has changed in English over the centuries of its existence in America, but the initial patterns of habitation by English speakers from various parts of the British Isles, as well as by emigrants and enslaved peoples who spoke languages other than English, are still reflected in the patterning of dialect differentiation in the United States today. The durable imprint of language structures brought to an area by the earliest groups of people forging a new society in the region is referred to as the FOUNDER EFFECT. For example, the use of an -*s* ending on verbs with plural subjects, as in *The dogs barks*, in varieties of Southern Appalachian speech today, is probably attributable to a founder effect from the English variety of the Ulster Scots. Though it is sometimes difficult to sort out founder effects centuries after the establishment of a new settlement in a region, there is little doubt that the earliest peoples in new settlements can have a lasting effect on the language legacy of a region.

2.1.2   Migration

Once primary population centers are established, dialect boundaries will often follow the major migratory routes from these areas. Thus, the dividing lines between the traditional dialects of American English (see figure 4.2) reflect both original colonization and migratory flow. It is no accident that many of the current dialect boundaries of American English show an east–west fanning pattern, since this was the pattern of westward migration from the earliest points of English-speaking settlement along the east coast. For example, a major dialect boundary runs across the state of Pennsylvania, separating the so-called North from Midland dialect. North of the line, speakers distinguished between the pronunciations of *horse* and *hoarse* and *which* and *witch*; south of the line, they did not. These pronunciation patterns went along with a number of traditional vocabulary differences such as the use of *pail* versus *bucket*, *teeter-totter* versus *seesaw*, and *stoop* versus *porch*. In the trough of the northern boundary through Pennsylvania and the southern boundary running through Delaware and Maryland a major early migration route existed. The high-density east–west flow of early colonizers in the North and Midland regions is still reflected in major interstate highway routes that run through the area. Major population centers within this Midland region carved out their own cultural and linguistic niches rather than simply conforming to the patterns that characterize the Midland in general, but the evidence of early routes of movement is still unmistakable in the present configuration of American English dialects.

The primary east–west migratory pattern reflects the movement of speakers of European descent, but other groups show different patterns. For example, African American migratory patterns are primarily south to north, emanating from different points in the rural South. African American speakers from South Carolina and North Carolina migrated northward along a coastal route into Washington, DC, Philadelphia, and New York. The migratory route of inland African Americans from the Deep South, on the other hand, led into Midwestern areas such as St Louis, Chicago, and Detroit. The vernacular dialects of eastern coastal cities such as Washington, DC, versus those of Midwestern cities such as Chicago still reflect some differences attributable to these different paths of migration, cutting across the east–west routes that typified European American migration. We also have to keep in mind that current and future migrations may eventually erase some of the long-established dialect lines. For example, Southern dialect areas may soon be altered if non-Southerners continue pouring into Southern cities as they have in recent years. Some dialect areas of Southern Florida have already been altered by the influx of people from the Northeast who brought their dialects with them, while the dialects of some Southern cities are beginning to show signs of leveling, or becoming less regionally distinctive, as Northern industries and population groups move to these cities in increasing numbers.

2.1.3   Geographical factors

Geography often plays a role in the development of dialects, not because of topography *per se*, but because rivers, lakes, mountains, valleys, and other features of the terrain determine the routes that people take and where they settle. Major rivers such as the Ohio and Mississippi played an important role in the development of American English dialects, as the British and other Europeans established inland networks of commerce and communication. It is thus not surprising that a major boundary runs along the course of the Ohio River. On the other hand, the Mississippi River, running a north–south route, deflected the westward migration of Midland populations northward, creating a discontinuous boundary between the Northern and Midland dialect areas which is still in place to some extent today.

Terrain that isolates groups also can play a critical role in the development of dialects. For example, African Americans living in the Sea Islands off the coast of South Carolina and Georgia and European American residents of the Outer Banks islands of North Carolina historically have been isolated from mainland speakers and their language varieties. In both cases, distinctive varieties of English were fostered in these out-of-the-way island settings. However, the two varieties were quite different from one another, because the first non-indigenous inhabitants of each island community spoke very different varieties to begin with. The Outer Banks dialect is characterized by the retention of a number of features from earlier versions of English, including such unusual lexical items as *mommuck*, meaning "to harass or bother", and *quamish*, meaning "sick in the stomach". On the Sea Islands, a language preserving features of original contact between English speakers and speakers of various African languages was perpetuated. This language, known as GULLAH, historically has been quite different not only from European American varieties but also from mainland varieties of African American English. Of course, both Gullah and Outer Banks English have also changed over the centuries, but these changes have not always paralleled changes taking place in mainland varieties of American English. Thus, their current distinctiveness is perpetuated by different patterns of change as well as the retention of forms brought to each area in the early days of British colonization and the formation of the US as an independent nation.

When we talk about the significance of geographical boundaries, we are really talking about lines of communication and the fact that discontinuities in communication develop between communities due, in part, to geographical conditions. The most effective kind of communication is face-to-face, and when groups of speakers do not interact on a personal level with one another, the likelihood of dialect divergence is heightened. Combined with various other sociological conditions, natural boundaries provide a firm foundation for the development and maintenance of dialect differences.

2.1.4   Language contact

Contact with speakers of other languages often takes place during the course of the establishment of new settlements and subsequent migration from these initial settlements, and this contact can influence dialect development. For example, in the seventeenth century, American English was influenced by Native American languages from the Algonquian, Iroquoian, and Siouan language families. Lexical items from various Native American languages made their way into general American English, such as *moccasin*, *raccoon*, and *chipmunk*. Today, there are still hundreds of regions and towns that bear names derived from Native American languages; however, there is little ongoing language influence. In the eighteenth century, American English was influenced by French, which gave the language such words as *bureau*, *depot*, and *prairie*. German gave American English *delicatessen*, *kindergarten*, and *hamburger*, while early Spanish contact gave it *canyon*, *rodeo*, and *patio*. All of these items are now in such widespread use across the varieties of American English that they are no longer considered dialect-specific features.

In areas where contact with languages other than English has been intensive and localized, borrowings from these languages may remain restricted to a given dialect. For example, in New Orleans, where French influence historically has been particularly strong, we find such dialect-specific terms as *lagniappe* "a small gift or bonus" or *boudin* "pork sausage". Interestingly, *lagniappe* itself is a mixture of several borrowings. Originally, it comes from the Quechua (Native American) term *yapa*, which was borrowed into Spanish as *la ñapa* and finally into French as *lagniappe*. Other localized terms include such German words as *stollen* "a kind of fruit cake" in Southern Pennsylvania and the Spanish term *arroyo* "a kind of gully" in the Southwest. In many cases, lexical borrowings simply reflect cultural borrowings; thus, English speakers in New Orleans have borrowed a number of terms from Cajun French which pertain to Cajun cooking, while Southwestern varieties of English now incorporate a number of lexical items from Spanish which relate to ranching practices.

Exercise 1

Following are some words that are borrowed from French, Spanish, and German. For the most part, these words are regionally restricted to areas where extensive contact with native speakers of one of these languages took place. Identify the language that each of the words comes from, as well as the region where you would expect to find the item.

coulee, arapajo grass, serape, schnickelfritz, cuartel, pumpernickel, zwieback, levee, rathskeller, pirogue

Do you know the meanings of all of the above words? Which ones give you the most difficulty? Why?

The impact of language contact on American English is perhaps most obvious in terms of vocabulary words, but there have been other kinds of influences as well. Certain suffixes have been borrowed from other languages, such as German *-fest* in words like *songfest*, *slugfest*, and *gabfest*, and the French suffix *-ee*, as in *draftee*, *enlistee*, and *trainee*. (Note that *-ee* is simply a feminine ending in French, as is *-ette* in both English and French.) In Southeastern Pennsylvania, with its heavy influx of German settlers, the use of the sentence structure *Are you going with?* for *Are you going with me/us?* is most reasonably accounted for by tracing it to the German construction *Gehst du mit?*, literally "Are you going with?" And in the South, the absence of the *be* verb in sentences such as *They in the house* or *We going to the store* among both African Americans and European Americans is most likely due to the influence of the language variety spoken by peoples of African descent early in the history of the United States. We will discuss in more detail the various contributions of different language groups to the formation of American English in chapter 4.

Historical patterns of conquest, colonization, migration, and language contact are important factors in the development of dialect differences, but they are not the sole considerations. Groups of speakers who share a common background in terms of these factors still manage to differentiate themselves from one another. This is because there are sociological and psychological bases for talking differently that have to be recognized along with historical, geographical, and demographic factors.

2.1.5   Economic ecology

How people earn their living often goes hand-in-hand with how populations are distributed geographically and culturally. In the United States, there is a full complement of ecologically based occupations, including fishing in coastal areas, coal mining in the mountains, and farming in the plains. Different economic bases not only bring about the development of specialized vocabulary items associated with different occupations; they also may affect the direction and rate of language change in grammar and pronunciation. The traditional distinction between the rural, agriculturally based lifestyle that historically has characterized much of the United States and the urban, industrialized focus of the nation's major population centers is reflected in dialect differences on all levels of language organization.

In American society, metropolitan regions typically have been centers of change, while rural locales have been slower to change. This difference in the speed with which cultural innovations are adopted encompasses linguistic innovations as well. Many older language features, such as the *a-* prefix in *She was a-hunting and a-fishing* or the *h* in *Hit's nice out today*, are now retained only in rural areas. If dialectologists want to observe whether an older form of English is still in use in a particular area, they will typically seek out older, life-time residents of rural areas; and if they want to see if a recent language change has been adopted, they will seek out younger speakers from metropolitan or suburban areas. Originally, urban–rural distinctions in this country had a strong economic base. Today, however, these distinctions carry a host of social and cultural meanings besides particular ways of making a living, all of which may be conveyed by the different language varieties. Sometimes, widespread language changes may originate in rural areas if the social meanings attached to rural forms become important to people in urban and suburban areas. Rural language features are often associated with a long-established heritage in a given area, and such associations may become important if a formerly isolated dialect area is suddenly faced with an influx of outsiders. For example, as we shall see in chapters 4 and 5, the rural Southern form *fixin' to*, as in *She's fixin' to go to church now*, has recently spread from rural to urban areas in Oklahoma and Texas in the face of mass migrations into the state by non-Southerners.

2.1.6 *Social stratification*

Social stratification is a fact of life in American society. We may debate the number of distinct classes or the basis for their delineation, but in reality social status differences cut across virtually all regional varieties of American English. Members of different social classes distinguish themselves from one another in a whole range of social behaviors, including the type of language they use, whether they reside in a Southern community like Anniston, Alabama, a large Northeastern metropolitan area like New York City, or a California city like Los Angeles. In fact, it is difficult to talk about regional dialect differences in American English without qualifying our discussion in terms of social status considerations. For example, when we talk about rural Appalachian English features such as *hit* for *it* or *a-hunting and a-fishing*, we have to be careful to note that these features are used at different rates among different social groups in Appalachia and may not even be used at all by those of higher social or cultural status. It is also important to note that there are a number of features of English language variation, such as the use of "double negatives" (for example, *She ain't been nowhere*), different irregular verb forms (for example, *She done it*), and doubly marked comparative forms (for example, *more bigger*), whose distribution among various populations is best explained by starting with considerations of social status difference. In other words, these features tend to be found among lower-status speakers in all dialect regions rather than being confined to speakers in particular areas.

Social status differences play a role not only in language variation across space but also in language change over time. It is sometimes assumed that language change begins in the upper classes, perhaps because speakers in this social stratum feel a need to distance themselves as far as possible from the lower classes who continually strive to emulate them. One linguist even went so far as to say that language change is reducible to the "protracted pursuit of the elite by an envious mass, and consequent 'flight' of the elite" (Fischer 1958: 52). However, numerous sociolinguistic studies have shown that there are a number of social and psychological factors that bring about language change besides social status differences. In addition, as we will see in chapter 6, most language changes in progress which have been studied in detail actually originate in middle rather than upper or lower social class groups. Though it is difficult to determine the social class and other social group divisions that are most relevant to a particular community, especially in American society, where social class divisions tend to be more fluid than in some other countries and societies (for example, the United Kingdom), social class differences do play a major role in the patterning of language variation and change and must be taken into account in our exploration of American English dialect variation.

Sometimes, it is believed that extremely small communities that are isolated from the mainstream population are free of social class differences. While this may be true to an extent, our studies of several small rural communities in the Southeastern and Mid-Atlantic coastal regions of the US have shown that, despite a lack of obvious differences in social status, such as type of home or dress, people who live in small communities nonetheless distinguish themselves socially from other community members in a number of ways, including how much property they own, how much they travel, what their family lineage is, and how they use language. Thus, it seems that no matter how small and seemingly homogeneous the community, the role of locally constructed social status differences can never be entirely discounted.

2.1.7 Social interaction, social practices, and speech communities

Who people talk to on a regular basis is an important factor in the development of dialect differences. Interactional patterns exist on a couple of levels. First, there are broad patterns of intercommunication and population movement that affect the patterning of dialects. A city like Washington, DC, is very different from a city like Charleston, West Virginia, in terms of population movement and, hence, conversational contact. In fact, in Washington, DC, there is so much movement into, out of, and through the region that it is common to assume that "everybody is from someplace else," an assumption that makes defining the local dialect norm rather difficult. People in the area are often unsure of what a "native Washingtonian" is even supposed to sound like, and the socially dominant population groups in the area have adopted a non-Southern dialect norm, though the areas surrounding Washington, DC, are quite Southern and there are neighborhoods within DC with Southern-based dialects as well. On the other hand, in Charleston, West Virginia, where population movement is more limited by comparison, people do not have nearly as much difficulty distinguishing a native from a non-native. Broadly based patterns of communication among speakers of various dialects have played and continue to play a major role in the development of American regional dialects.

On another level, we can talk about communication networks in terms of individual patterns of interaction, or SOCIAL NETWORKS. At this level, we are concerned with such issues as what kinds of people the residents of a given community tend to interact with most often on a daily basis: Do they communicate most regularly with family, neighborhood friends, and friends of friends; or are there patterns of sustained contact with people outside the immediate circle of acquaintances? When we examine social networks, we are concerned with the DENSITY and MULTIPLEXITY of speakers' social interactions. By density, we mean the extent to which members of a social network all interact with one another. If everybody knows everybody else in the network, it is a HIGH-DENSITY network; if not, it is LOW-DENSITY. Multiplexity refers to the extent to which people interact with the same people in different spheres of activity, for example, in work, in leisure activities, and in the neighborhood. Those in MULTIPLEX NETWORKS interact with the same people in different social arenas while those in UNIPLEX NETWORKS interact with different sets of people in different social spheres. Researchers have shown that social network density and multiplexity can have a significant impact on dialect maintenance and change. In particular, speakers in high-density, multiplex networks tend to maintain localized, vernacular language varieties far more tenaciously than speakers in uniplex, low-density networks, who are quicker to adopt language features from outside their local communities.

In addition to looking at people's patterns of interaction, we also need to investigate why people come together as they do – that is, what sorts of activities people join together to participate in, and what these social practices reveal about people's values, as well as the role of language in shaping and projecting these values. In this regard, we can investigate dialect variation from the perspective of the COMMUNITY OF PRACTICE (Eckert and McConnell-Ginet 1992), where community of practice is defined as "an aggregate of people who come together around some enterprise" and which is "simultaneously defined by its membership and the shared practices in which that membership engages" (Eckert 2000: 35). In other words, when considering people's communities of practice, the focus shifts from pre-established *structures*, whether the small-scale structures of localized social networks or large-scale structures like social class groups, to the ongoing social *practices* through which social structures are sustained and changed. In addition, communities of practice are defined in terms of people's subjective experiences and senses of belonging rather than the external criteria often used to delimit social group memberships (e.g. type of residence, income level) or determine the strength of an individual's social network ties (e.g. number of workmates who live in one's neighborhood). Communities of practice are also viewed as dynamic and fluid rather than as static entities, and individuals are seen as active agents in the construction of individual and group identity, rather than simply as passive respondents to the social situations in which they find themselves (e.g. the social class group to which they belong).

Through looking at individualized, localized practices rather than simply at social structures, we can begin to understand not only what sorts of language patterns correlate with which groups but also *why* people use the language features they do. For example, in conducting a study of a small African American community in the Smoky Mountain region of Appalachia, Christine Mallinson and Becky Childs (2005) found that the linguistic practices of women in the community could only be explained in terms of the different communities of practice in which the women participated. One group, the "church ladies," engaged in practices such as church-going and other activities associated with cultural conservatism and "propriety." The other primary group, the "porch sitters," engaged in regular socializing on one group member's porch, where they would listen to music and engage in other activities indicative of affiliation with more widespread African American culture, especially youth culture. Such patterns of practice help explain why the "porch sitters" showed high usage levels for features of African American English, while the "church ladies" showed low usage levels for these features and instead used features associated with the local European American variety, as well as more features of standard American English.

Another term associated with the study of dialect variation in its social context is SPEECH COMMUNITY. One of the pioneers of modern sociolinguistic study, William Labov, has defined the speech community as a group of people with shared norms, or common evaluations of linguistic variables (1966, 1972b). This is a fairly good working definition for our purposes, but it is important to understand it correctly and to recognize the difficulties involved with even such a seemingly straightforward definition (Patrick 2002). When we talk of "shared language norms," we do not mean that everyone in a speech community speaks exactly the same way, or even very similarly, only that they orient toward the same language norms. For example, in an early sociolinguistic study of the Lower East Side of New York City, Labov (1966) showed that the people in his study used certain language features at quite different rates depending on their social class and how formally they were speaking. However, the community as a whole was uniform in that there were regular patterns of language variation by social class groups, with higher classes showing higher usage levels for standard features and lower-class groups showing higher levels for vernacular features. In addition, the study participants indicated a uniform evaluation of features as prestigious vs. stigmatized, since they showed uniform patterns of variation across speech styles – namely, increasing usage levels for prestige features and decreasing levels for stigmatized ones as they spoke more and more formally, no matter what social class they belonged to. And even individuals in the community who showed overt resistance to the shared norms of the wider community still made reference to these norms in discussing and using language, and so could be considered to be a part of the speech community as well. For example, Labov discusses the case of a young man who overtly stated his rejection of standard norms in favor of New York City vernacular features. However, the young man's comments showed that he was still very aware of the community's general evaluation of standard vs. vernacular dialect forms, and his patterns of usage in different speech styles indicated that he did indeed get somewhat more standard as he got more formal in style, despite his best efforts to be as vernacular as possible.

Despite the seeming utility of Labov's definition, a number of issues arise when we attempt to delimit a "speech community" in order to conduct a sociolinguistic study of our own. For example, should we as researchers apply external, "objective" criteria in delimiting a community, or should we allow our definition of the community to emerge as we study particular populations and come to realize how they themselves demarcate their communities? On a related note, should we start by identifying a particular social unit and seeing how they use language, or should we start with the particular language variety we're interested in, and then see who uses it and how they are tied together socially? Further, there are questions of size and uniformity. Can we really talk about a very large social aggregate like the Lower East Side of New York City, or perhaps a city like Charleston, South Carolina, as a single unified community with a shared set of norms, or is it more likely that different sub-populations have different norms for language use and other social behaviors? For example, vernacular dialects have many positive associations for the people who use them, and it is not necessarily the case that speakers of such varieties really do believe that standard varieties are actually "better," especially not in all speech situations. In this regard, it may be best to view the "speech community" as more of a multi-layered than unitary construct, since people have affiliations at different levels, ranging from various communities of practice, neighborhood communities, concentrated larger population groups (e.g. a city population), and even broadly based regional groups (e.g. US Southerners). In this sense, a resident of Charleston, South Carolina, may be affiliated with an individualized set of communities of practice, some of which extend beyond Charleston or South Carolina, at the same time that he or she is affiliated with a particular neighborhood group that may be based on ethnic and family ties as well as geographic proximity. This same person may also have a loose affiliation with the city as a whole, as well as the broadly based "Southern community" that extends well beyond the city and state.

Finally, in considering the various intersecting communities of which all speakers are necessarily a part, we need to question whether we should take a "top–down" approach, in which we begin by focusing on large social aggregates such as cities or regions, or a "bottom–up" approach, in which we begin by studying individuals and their various interconnections. As we will see in the chapters to follow, it may be best if we work "back and forth" between the individual and the community, and between the social and the linguistic, as we study the interrelation of language and community. For example, Labov began his study of New York City by first applying social criteria to the identification of a particular group as a "community." He then narrowed this group down through linguistic criteria, selecting only native speakers of the New York City English varieties he was particularly interested in studying. Finally, though his focus was on community patterns of language variation and change, he did not neglect individuals and included in his studies investigations of individual speech patterns in different stylistic contexts, as well as individual speakers' comments about stigmatized vs. prestigious language features. In more recent work (e.g. Labov 2001b), he relies even more on detailed studies of individuals, including individual personality traits and social networks, in seeking to understand the large-scale patterns of variation and change that characterize particular dialect regions or concentrated population groups. Speakers necessarily use language features that reflect their multi-layered and overlapping interactions, affiliations, and orientations, and in addition use features with a variety of social associations to help shape social groups and social meanings in their daily conversational interactions.

Exercise 2

Based on the previous discussion, describe the kinds of social interactions and levels of communities in which you currently participate, ranging from your specific communities of practice to your affiliation with more broadly based communities. Do you consider these various communities to be "speech communities"? Why or why not? What is the most narrowly defined, and the most broadly defined, community in your experience?

2.1.8   Group and individual identity

People often want to be considered as part of a particular social group, and so they project their identity with this group in a number of ways, including "talking like" other members of the group. Sometimes, group membership is voluntary and negotiated by the individual and the various groups to which they seek to belong, and sometimes it is rooted in established social structures (e.g. class or gender groups) and is not completely a matter of choice – or at least very easy choice. The linguistic means for conveying association with a particular group may range from the relatively superficial adoption or heightened use of a couple of language features to the use of entire pronunciation and grammatical systems. For example, teenagers may adopt some "slang" lexical items in order to distinguish themselves from adult speakers, while members of a particular ethnic group may project their group membership via a complex array of grammatical, phonological, and lexical structures. In a groundbreaking study of language variation and change in Martha's Vineyard, a historically isolated island community off the coast of Massachusetts, Labov demonstrated how members of established island families heightened their usage of certain unusual vowel sounds in order to distinguish themselves from the increasing numbers of tourists on the island. We have found similar patterns of selective heightening in the use of traditional dialect features in our investigations of Ocracoke Island, North Carolina, which is also witnessing an influx of tourists and new residents after generations of seclusion.

In American English, the various social meanings associated with ethnic and regional varieties may force speakers to choose between "fitting in" and "talking correctly." Thus, some features of African American English or Latino English may be associated with ethnic solidarity at the same time as they are socially stigmatized by the mainstream culture. Similarly, Appalachian English is associated with a rural, stigmatized vernacular at the same time that it may be associated with people's sense of cultural identity. Faced with the dilemma of choosing between group solidarity and social sanction by outside, mainstream groups, it is not uncommon for speakers of vernacular dialects to attempt a kind of dialect balancing act. For example, native speakers of a vernacular dialect in Western Arkansas who have moved away and now speak more standardly may feel constrained to shift to some degree back to the native dialect when visiting with family back home. If they fail to do so, not only will they fail to fit in with family members but their relatively standard speech patterns may even be interpreted as a kind of symbolic rejection of family ties. An individual's dialectal range is often related to flexibility in terms of balancing considerations of status and solidarity. Some speakers of American English dialects are amazingly adroit at balancing two dialects in order to live in two different worlds – the world of in-group identity and the world of mainstream social expectations. Others are not as successful in shifting their dialects, or choose not to conform to local or wider societal expectations, and so may be rejected by their local in-group or suffer the scorn of wider society.

Group affiliations are not the only symbolic meanings associated with language differences; there may also be strong associations with character attributes. For example, when listeners hear a Southern accent, not only do they identify the speaker as being from a Southern dialect region, but they may also unconsciously assign a set of character attributes to the speaker. These traits may range from positive qualities such as warmth and hospitality to negative attributes such as backwardness and ignorance. Similarly, speakers of varieties associated with lower classes or with certain minority ethnic groups are often considered to be tough and street-smart at the same time as they are held to be poor and uneducated. Because of the association of dialect features with character traits, speakers may use language to project personal qualities in addition to group membership status. For example, a European American teenager who wants to be "cool" may adopt features of African American English, while used car salespeople may intensify their usage of Southern vernacular speech when talking with customers or making a television commercial in order to convey authenticity and honesty. In addition, as people use language features in shaping and projecting who they are or how they wish to appear in particular situations, they subtly shape the personal and social associations of these features by bringing different features together in their own unique ways.

Conversely, speakers may avoid features associated with characteristics that they do not wish to project. For example, speakers may refrain from using vernacular features such as double negatives because they do not wish to be considered "uneducated." In place of these vernacular features, speakers will adopt features of standard varieties of English, not necessarily because they wish to project membership in the middle and upper classes who use more standard English but because they wish to project the character traits associated with standard English in American society – competence, intelligence, and achievement. It is, in fact, possible to be unintelligent but "talk smart" and, conversely, to be smart but "talk dumb." When the first author of this book gives class lectures using some nonstandard features of English, some students consider him to be unintelligent because of his speech patterns. He has, for example, had students confide to him (after completing the course) that they initially had trouble believing that he could be a competent teacher and still "talk like that." Of course, we realize that there may be other factors that cause students to doubt this professor's intellectual abilities, but language no doubt plays a part in students' assessments of his character.

It is important to bear in mind that an individual speaker does not always seek to project the same set of personal characteristics through language. Rather, a speaker may project different traits at different moments during the course of daily conversational interaction. For example, we may normally use standard language forms while at work to project an air of authority and competence, but we may switch into more vernacular speech when gossiping with a co-worker to indicate solidarity and informality. Thus, language enables speakers to project and shape facets of identity on a number of different levels, ranging from their affiliation with certain well-established social groups (e.g. gender or ethnic groups) to their association with particular character traits – for example, toughness vs. warmheartedness, or simultaneous toughness *and* warmheartedness. At the same time, we regularly and continuously shape our identities to suit our various conversational purposes. Identity is not static but is continually shaped and reshaped from moment to moment, and as we progress through life; and a large portion of our identity construction (perhaps all of it, according to some scholars) is done through our manipulation of language features.

2.2 Linguistic Explanation

The other side of explaining language differences relates to the structure of language. It is sometimes assumed that the dialects of a language may differ in unrestricted and random ways. This is not true. Instead, the evidence from actual dialect divergence indicates that there are underlying principles of language variation and change that guide the ways in which the dialects of a language may differ from each other. Different kinds of social pressures may lead to the acceptance or rejection of potential changes, but the language changes themselves will follow certain orderly principles of language patterning.

As a starting point, we need to understand that all languages are dynamic systems undergoing constant change. Certainly, the language Shakespeare used in his plays is different from today's English, as was the English of the Elizabethan period compared to a period several centuries earlier. In fact, the English language has changed so much in the course of history that scholars have divided it into different types of English: Old English, which was spoken from about 600 to 1100, Middle English, spoken from 1100 to 1500, Early Modern English, spoken from 1500 to about 1800, and Modern English, which is what we speak today. To illustrate the dramatic changes that have taken place in the language over time, consider the following excerpt from the Lord's Prayer, as it appeared at four different time periods:

Old English (about 950 AD):
Fader urer ðu bist in heofnas, sie gehalgad noma ðin.

Middle English (about 1350 AD):
Oure fadir Þat art in heuenes, halwid be Þi name.

Early Modern English (about 1550 AD):
O oure father which arte in heven, hallowed be thy name.

Modern English (about 1985 AD):
Our father who is in heaven, may your name be sacred.

The English language today is also undergoing change, and people several centuries in the future will look back on the English of this period as "archaic," just as we look at the English of several centuries ago. In fact, the only languages not undergoing change are dead languages – that is, languages with no native speakers, such as classical Latin.

Under constant linguistic pressure to change, some groups of speakers adopt certain changes while others hold out against them. If a new language feature continues to be used by a certain group but not by others, then a dialect difference is born. And if differing patterns of change by different groups of speakers go far enough, dialects may split into separate languages, particularly if contact between the groups is severed. Of the approximately 6,000 languages in the world today, the overwhelming majority developed into separate languages in precisely this way. The dialects of English also have the potential to split into separate languages, though it is questionable whether or not this could actually happen in an era of increasing cultural globalization as well as of the spread of the English language throughout the world. Nonetheless, we must admit the linguistic possibility of such radical differentiation, since language change is ever-present in living languages.

Languages are intricately patterned systems. Furthermore, the patterns within each language system are constantly being adjusted and readjusted on the basis of how the particular system is organized, resulting in language changes. These kinds of innovations are called CHANGES FROM WITHIN, because they take place apart from the influence of other languages. Changes may also originate from contact with other languages or dialects. Structures may be borrowed from other varieties, or preexisting structures may be altered by their contact with the structures of a neighboring language variety. Features may also be entirely subsumed by those of competing language varieties. When changes take place due to language contact, they are referred to as CHANGES FROM OUTSIDE. Although we distinguish the two sources of change, they often work hand-in-hand, since the internal structure of a language system may dictate what items from outside will be adopted, and how.

It is noteworthy that some language changes leading to dialect differentiation look very similar to the types of variation that speakers show when they are in the process of acquiring a language – whether the language is their native tongue or another language. For example, in some vernacular dialects of English, it is common for speakers to pronounce *th* sounds as *d* or *t*, so that words like *this* and *with* are pronounced as something like *dis* and *wit*. This process of changing *th*'s to other sounds is also common in the speech of people who are learning English as a second language; for example, a non-native speaker may say *tink* or *sink* for *think*. In addition, we find that children who are acquiring their first language produce the *th* sound relatively late in the acquisition process.

Unfortunately, the similarities that people have noticed among dialect features and some features of first and second language acquisition have sometimes led to the erroneous conclusion that vernacular dialects are nothing more than underdeveloped versions of language. In reality, the features that characterize both language acquisition and the linguistically based language changes that lead to dialect differentiation are simply the result of natural processes that have to do with how language is articulated, how it is perceived, and how it is organized and processed in the human mind. Standard language varieties sometimes resist the natural pressure of these processes, because language standards tend to be based on the preservation of conservative forms. This leads to a resistance to some of the natural changes that might take place otherwise.

The fact that dialect differences often have to do with the underlying principles of human language organization also helps explain why we sometimes find that dialects having no apparent contact with one another share features. For example, the use of *was* with all types of subjects (as in *we was* or *they was*), the formation of plurals such as *oxes* and *deers*, and the dropping of final consonants in words like *test* and *desk* (*tes'* and *des'*) are common to Latino English vernacular varieties in California, Native American English vernacular varieties spoken on reservations in the Southwestern United States, African American English vernacular varieties spoken in Northern urban areas, and many European American English vernacular varieties throughout the US. Such similarities exist even among groups that have never had significant contact with one another. Why is it that certain structures are so widely distributed among some vernacular varieties? As we said above, the answer lies in the way language is cognitively organized and in the processes of physical production and perception. At this point, we look at some of the processes and organizing principles that help account for the systematic ways in which the dialects of America differ from each other.

2.2.1   Rule extension

As we stressed in chapter 1, every language and dialect is governed by an intricate set of unconscious patterns or "rules" that dictate when we use certain forms and when we don't. Sometimes these rules correspond to the patterns of standard English and sometimes they don't. For example, when we say a simple phrase such as *the blue house*, we are conforming to a rule of English that dictates that adjectives such as *blue* must precede nouns like *house*. We know that this is a language *rule* and not simply "common sense," because there are a number of languages in which a different pattern is in operation. For example, the rule for adjective placement in Spanish positions adjectives after nouns, as in the Spanish phrase *la casa azul*, which literally translates as "the house blue". One of the principles that leads to language change is a universal preference for language rules that are as general as possible. Over time, a language rule of limited application may be extended to more situations and apply to a broader set of items. This process is known as RULE EXTENSION. For example, a longstanding rule of English involves the use of one form of the personal pronoun for subjects (for example, *I walk, we walk, she walks*) and a different form when the pronoun serves as the object of a verb or preposition (for example, *Pat saw me* or *Terry gave the book to her*). Over the centuries, English speakers have expanded the use of pronouns so that they may appear in object case even when they are not acting as objects. Thus, we frequently hear sentences such as *It's me* for "It is I" and *Me and Charlie went to the store* for "Charlie and I went to the store", even though grammar books caution us against such uses. In fact, this rule extension has become so much a part of our unconscious language knowledge that many of us feel as though we are speaking very unnaturally indeed when we try to abide by the "grammar rules" by saying things like *It is I* or *This is she*.

Rule extension also affects pronunciation patterns. For example, we have mentioned that some dialects, such as British English and traditional Eastern New England English, are characterized by the loss of *r* in certain positions in words and sentences, as in *pahk* for "park" or *cah* for "car". Unexpectedly, speakers of such "*r*-less" dialects often insert "extra" *r*'s, called INTRUSIVE *r*, in places where speakers of most English varieties would not have *r*, as in a phrase such as *the idear of it* for "the idea of it". In British English and some *r*-less varieties of American English, these extra *r*'s are actually the result of rule extension. *R*-dropping is governed by a rule where *r*'s at the ends of words are dropped only when the next word begins with a consonant but are retained when the next word begins with a vowel. In a sentence such as *Park the car by the house*, the final *r* in *car* would be dropped, because the next word begins with a consonant (*cah by*). However, in a sentence such as *Park the car over there*, the final *r* in *car* would be pronounced because the following word begins with a vowel (*car over*). This rule has been extended to apply to words which never really ended in *r* but which seem as if they did because they end in a vowel sound, just like *r*-less *car* (*cah*) or *far* (*fah*). Thus, a word like *idea* is now pronounced as *idear* when it comes before a vowel-initial word, as in *the idear of it*, just as *cah* is pronounced as *car* before a vowel in *car over there*. And just as *cah* is pronounced as *cah* when it comes before a consonant (*Park the cah by the house*), *idea* is pronounced simply as *idea* when it occurs in a similar environment (*the idea behind it*). In some varieties, *r* may even be added to vowel-final words at the end of sentences, as in *I got the idear*, in a further extension of the *r*-insertion pattern.

The rule that states "add *r* on to vowel-final words (including *r*-less words like *cah*) when they come before words beginning with a vowel" operates in a subtle way and often goes unnoticed by outside observers, who may mistakenly assume that speakers of *r*-less dialects *always* drop word-final *r*'s and *always* add *r*'s to the ends of vowel-final words like *idea*. However, close examination reveals that *r*-lessness and *r*-insertion are actually intricately patterned – and that these two seemingly opposing pronunciations are the result of a single language rule whose operation has been gradually extended over time. Rule extension is one of the natural linguistic tendencies that leads to language change and dialect differentiation.

2.2.2   Analogy

The tendency for languages to become as regularly patterned as possible also underlies another common mechanism of language change, ANALOGY. In the study of language, analogy refers to the process of taking language forms that are similar in some way – for example, in meaning or function – and making them more similar in form based on an existing pattern. In English, most plural nouns are formed by the addition of an -*s* to a noun, with the exception of a small set of nouns such as *oxen* and *deer*. It is common for speakers of vernacular dialects to regularize these irregular plurals, producing forms such as *oxes* and *deers*. This regularization takes place via analogy: Because the plural meaning is almost always indicated by -*s* or -*es*, speakers alter the form of irregular plural words so that the plural meaning corresponds with the -*(e)s* ending in these cases as well.

There are two types of linguistic analogy. The first type is called FOUR-PART or PROPORTIONAL ANALOGY. This type of analogy involves changing the form of words that derive their meaning in an irregular way so that they conform to the shape of words that derive this meaning in a more regular or predominant way. This change process can be expressed as a four-part relationship:

$$x \text{ is to } x' \text{ as } y \text{ is to } y' \text{ OR } x : x' :: y : y'$$

Plugging the language forms into the formula, we get such forms as:

cow : cows :: ox : oxes
cow : cows :: sheep : sheeps

Four-part analogy also underlies the regularization of irregular past and participle verb forms that we often find in vernacular dialects. For example, we may hear speakers who say *knowed* for *knew* or *growed* for *grew*. The analogical formula in this case is:

walk : walked :: grow : growed

The other type of linguistic analogy is called LEVELING. Leveling involves taking a grammatically conditioned set of forms – for example, the different forms a verb may take when used with different subjects – and making the forms more similar or identical. For example, consider the subject person and number set, or PARADIGM, for the verb *to be* in standard English. Two paradigms for subject–verb agreement with *be* are given below, one for present tense and one for past:

Present		*Past*	
I am	we are	I was	we were
you are	you (pl.) are	you were	you were
she/he/it is	they are	she was	they were

The person–number sets for present and past *to be* are both highly irregular, with different forms for both singular and plural subjects and for the different singular subjects. Speakers of vernacular dialects may regularize or "level" these irregular paradigms, producing sets such as the following:

I is	we is	I was	we was
you is	you (pl.) is	you was	you was
she/he/it is	they is	she was	they was

Sometimes, the basis on which speakers level verbal paradigms may vary, so that differences among vernacular dialects result. In the standard English paradigm for past tense *to be*, the form is changed based on the distinction between singular and plural; *was* is used for singular subjects and *were* is used for plural ones. (The exception, second person singular *you*, was, in fact, once a plural pronoun, so it is a vestige of this earlier distinction that makes it an exception in modern-day English.) In some coastal dialect areas of North Carolina, Virginia, and Maryland, it is common for speakers to regularize past tense *to be* based on whether the sentence is an affirmative or negative one. The form *were* is thus used in negative sentences, as in *I weren't there* or *They weren't home*, whereas *was* or the standard *was/were* alternation is used for affirmative sentences, as in *We was there* or *He was home*. We therefore have the following paradigms:

Affirmative		*Negative*	
I was	we was (were)	I weren't	we weren't
you was (were)	you was (were)	you weren't	you weren't
she was	they was (were)	she weren't	they weren't

Exercise 3

For each of the following examples, state whether the regularization is due to four-part analogy or leveling.

1 This class is even badder than the last one.
2 Joe helped hisself to more mashed potatoes.
3 He just don't understand me.
4 Kate brung me a present.
5 The deers ate all of our vegetables in the garden.
6 She weren't there yesterday.
7 That's the beautifulest cat I've ever seen.

Sometimes, four-part analogy may be based on patterns that do not follow the dominant or most common pattern, such as the *-(e)s* plural ending or the *-ed* past tense ending. For example, some vernacular dialects may use *brang* or *brung* as the past tense of *bring*, by analogy to forms such as *sing/sang/sung* and *ring/rang/rung*. This type of change is known as MINORITY PATTERN ANALOGY, since it involves reshaping irregular forms on the model of a minor pattern rather than a more predominant one, such as the *-ed* past tense ending. Although it may seem as if speakers are not really regularizing anything but merely substituting one irregular form for another when they say *brung* for *brought*, in reality, this change is a regularization of sorts, since the *sing/sang/sung* past tense pattern is more common in English than the very limited *bring/brought/brought* pattern.

Occasionally, minority pattern analogy does result in what we might call "irregularization." For example, the past tense of *dive* historically is the regular form *dived*. However, in many American English varieties, it is being replaced with *dove*, by analogy to forms like *drive/drove* and *ride/rode*. Similarly, we occasionally find "irregularization" of plural forms. For example, the form *dwarves* is newer than *dwarfs* and was most likely created via minority pattern analogy with forms such as *elf/elves* and *wolf/wolves*. The word *dwarf* commonly co-occurs in fairy tales with the words *elf* and *wolf*, an incidental fact that may have inadvertently aided the progression of this particular analogy.

For the most part, though, the predominant movement is toward regularization rather than irregularization, and whenever new words enter the language – or old words take on new meanings – they are almost always given regular plural and past tense forms. Thus, we do not hear *netwrought* for *networked*, *flew out* for *flied out* (in baseball), or *kang* for *kinged*, as in *She kinged me in checkers*.

It is important to understand that analogical change does not represent imperfect learning or language decay. If it did, then we would have to say that today's standard English is actually quite a decrepit language, since many standard forms are the result of analogical changes that took place centuries ago. For example, in Middle English, there were just as many plurals that ended in *-n* or *-en* as with *-(e)s*. In fact, the *-(e)n* ending was so commonplace that some plurals were regularized to *-(e)n* from *-s*; for example, the plural of *shoe*, which originally ended in *-s*, became *shoon*. Gradually, however, almost all Middle English *-(e)n* plurals were regularized to *-(e)s*. Although *oxen* remained *oxen*, *kine* became *cows* and *shoon* reverted to *shoes*. This regularization took place through the same process of analogy that gives us socially stigmatized forms such as *oxes* and *deers* today; it just so happens, however, that most of the plural forms that were regularized during the transformation from Middle English to Modern English gained social acceptance, while forms like *oxes* and *deers* have yet to do so. The social acceptability of forms has nothing to do with the forms *per se*. Rather, forms are assigned "acceptability" in an arbitrary way. For example, if a Modern English speaker were to regularize the plural of the rodent known as a *mouse* as *mouses*, the form would be considered unacceptable. At the same time, if a speaker pluralizes a computer *mouse* as *mouses*, the regularized form is perfectly acceptable. In fact, if a computer technician were to use *mice* for *mouses* in a sentence such as *Everyone in our office got new mice for their computers*, the form would sound quite odd indeed. Judgments of social acceptability in language don't make a lot of linguistic sense despite lofty claims about their logicality.

As it turns out, a large number of formerly irregular verb forms have found their way into standard English as regular verbs. For example, *help* once had such irregular past tense forms as *healp* and *hulpon*, while the past tense of *work* was *wrought*. In addition, although verbs used to show person–number distinctions in the past tense, these distinctions have been completely lost in all English verbs except *to be*. Even verbs with irregular past tense forms, such as *thought* or *sang*, show the same form for all persons and numbers in the past tense and so can be considered to be "regular" in at least one way. Furthermore, changes resulting from minority pattern analogy sometimes make their way into standard English. For example, the past tense of *ring* was originally *ringed* but was later changed to *rang* on the basis of analogy with *sing/sang/sung*.

Again, the only thing separating verb forms like *helped* and *rang* from forms like *knowed* and *brang* is social acceptability; all of these regularized verbs are perfectly well-formed words, from the point of view of linguistic structure, and all resulted from the application of very natural processes of language change. From a strictly linguistic standpoint, the designation of regularized forms as "standard" vs. "nonstandard" is completely arbitrary. From a sociological perspective, of course, it is no accident that the forms associated with socially favored groups become established as standard forms while those associated with low-status groups remain nonstandard.

2.2.3 Transparency and grammaticalization

At first glance, it seems that rule extension and analogy will cause the English language to just keep getting simpler and simpler over time and that eventually we won't have to worry about such matters as irregular verb forms or subject–verb agreement. However, the tendency for speakers to make things as easy as possible on themselves cognitively is counterbalanced by the need to ensure that meaning distinctions are as clear as possible. The need to make meanings obvious is sometimes referred to as the TRANSPARENCY PRINCIPLE. This principle ensures that certain grammatical distinctions are formed and preserved in obvious ways, and it may also lead to the introduction of some new grammatical distinctions. For example, the same speakers who eliminate subject–verb agreement marking on past tense *be* would never eliminate the marking of negatives (e.g. *I was/ I wasn't*) and in fact may enhance the marking of negativity in a couple of different ways. We saw earlier that instead of altering verb roots for different subjects, a vernacular dialect of English may use different roots for affirmative and negative forms, as in the use of *was* for affirmative sentences and *weren't* for negative ones, as found in some dialects along the Southeastern coast. In addition to an *-n't* negative ending, Southern American *can* vs. *cain't* may be distinguished by the vowel; the vowel of *can* rhymes with *fan* and the vowel of *cain't* rhymes with *faint*. Similarly, in many vernacular dialects, speakers use *am/is/are* in affirmative sentences and the distinct form *ain't* in negative ones.

Speakers may also use so-called "double negatives" to ensure that listeners pick up the negative meaning of their utterances, as in *I didn't do nothing* for "I didn't do anything". In fact, vernacular dialects often attach a negative marker to every indefinite element in a sentence, as in a sentence such as *I ain't never learned nothing from nobody*. For this reason, linguists prefer the term MULTIPLE NEGATION or NEGATIVE CONCORD (that is, negative agreement) to "double negatives," since we often find more than two negative markers per sentence. Linguistically, the attachment of the negative element on indefinite forms throughout the sentence makes negation more transparent than in its standard English counterpart where it can only be attached at one point.

Not only may meaning distinctions be doubly marked, but new grammatical markers may be created, often out of existing language material. Linguists refer to the process whereby a meaning becomes linked to a particular grammatical structure as GRAMMATICALIZATION. For example, in some varieties of Southern American English, speakers may string together two or more helping verbs, such as *might* and *could*, in order to convey a meaning which is slightly different from that of either *might* or *could*. Thus, a sentence such as *I might could go with you* doesn't mean either *I might go* or *I could go* but instead means something like *I may be able to go with you but I'm not really sure*. In other words, the use of these double helping verbs, technically called DOUBLE MODALS, lessens the force of the verbs in a way that a single modal does not. This meaning is uniquely marked by the double modal in Southern vernacular dialects; in other regions, this meaning would have to be conveyed by substantially rewording the original sentence.

Another Southern American helping verb form, or AUXILIARY, that serves to convey a distinctive meaning is the word *liketa*, as in *It was so cold out there, I liketa died*. Historically, *liketa* comes from *like to have* and seems simply to have been equivalent in meaning to *almost*. However, in some American dialects that use this form today, *liketa* is now a single element, not a phrase, and the meaning has been altered in a subtle way, so that *liketa* refers not only to things that almost took place in real life but to things that were narrowly avoided in a figurative sense. Thus, when a speaker utters the sentence, *It was so cold, I liketa froze*, she is not conveying that she was in any real danger of freezing but only that she was very, very cold. This construction may be referred to as "avertive liketa" to capture the distinctive meaning now associated with this form.

A final example of a meaning difference conveyed through the different use of verb forms or auxiliaries is the use of *be* by speakers of vernacular varieties of African American English in sentences such as *He always be coming to school late*. In these cases, *be* is used to indicate a habitual or ongoing state, so that *be* would be used in a sentence like *She always be going to school* but not in a sentence like **She be going to school right now*, since the latter indicates a one-time activity rather than a habitual one. It is a common misperception among speakers of other varieties to assume that speakers of African American English simply use *be* instead of the standard English forms *am, is,* or *are*. In reality, *be* is used only in certain types of sentences that signify habituality. In other types of sentences, speakers of African American English use *am, is,* or *are* (*He is coming to school right now*) or no form of *be* at all (*He coming to school right now*). Thus, *be* in African American English, like *might could* and *liketa* in Southern English, specifies a distinctive meaning.

Because tendencies such as adding new meaning distinctions are in competition with principles that seek to eliminate "extra" linguistic markers of meaning, language change may follow very different paths, depending on which type of principle wins out in a given instance. More importantly, we see that the seeds of dialect differentiation are planted deep within the language system itself. And when we set these changes in language within a social system that influences whether a certain language change will be adopted or not, the potential for the wide divergence of dialects over time and place becomes very great indeed.

Exercise 4

Consider several uses of the form *done* in some vernacular dialects of English, as illustrated in the following sentences.

1 They *done* their homework last night.
2 They *done* what they said they would do.
3 She was *done* with her homework.
4 Are you *done* with your homework yet?
5 They *done* ate all of the food in the refrigerator.
6 They *done* finished all of their homework.
7 They *done* did their homework last night.
8 They *done done* their homework last night.

What kinds of verb forms (for example, past tense) are covered by the form *done*? Do you think that the use of *done* in sentences like *They done ate all of the food in the refrigerator* involves a unique, grammaticalized use of *done* as an auxiliary or helping verb? Why or why not? If so, what do you think its distinctive meaning is?

2.2.4   *Pronunciation phenomena*

The language-internal principles that we have so far discussed tend to affect
the formation of words and the structure of sentences. There are also
a number of natural processes that lead to pronunciation changes and
subsequent dialect differentiation. These processes have to do with several
different factors, especially with how language sounds are produced and
perceived and how they are organized into systems. These processes are
commonplace and operate in regular ways. There are a couple of other
pronunciation-related processes that are not as common and which operate
more sporadically. We will talk about these latter processes once we have
discussed the more regular processes.

Articulation-related changes
It is a physiological fact that some language sounds are more difficult to
articulate than others because they involve more complex movements of the
tongue or other organs of speech or involve more intricate coordination
among the various articulators such as the tongue, the lips, and vocal cords.
For example, the slightly different but related sounds that occur at the
beginning of the words *think* and *these* happen to be quite difficult to
produce and therefore are relatively rare in the languages of the world. This
is why, as we mentioned earlier, native speakers of English acquire these
sounds late in their language development and adult second language learners
or vernacular dialect speakers often use other sounds in place of these
sounds. For example, second language learners may use *t* or *s* for *th* (as in
tink or *sink* for "think"), while native speakers of vernacular varieties may
use *t* or *f*, as in *wit* or *wiff* for "with". Thus, some dialect differences in
pronunciation are the result of using more "natural" language sounds than
those that are difficult and relatively "unnatural" to pronounce.

Other articulation-related pronunciation changes involve altering sounds
when they occur in certain sequences, following certain natural tendencies
of human language production. One very common change is for neighboring
sounds to become more similar to one another, a process known as ASSIMI-
LATION. Some pronunciations that derive from assimilation are so widespread
that they have nothing to do with dialect divergence; they are simply a part
of the English language. For example, the prefixes meaning "not" which we
find on the words *impossible*, *illogical*, and *irregular* all derive from the same
in- prefix (as in *inexcusable*). In each case, however, the pronunciation (and
spelling) of the *n* has been altered to make it more like the first sound in the
word to which it attaches: In the first case, *n* becomes *m* because both *m* and
p are produced by putting both lips together; in the second and third cases,
the *n* has become completely assimilated to the following *l* and *r* by turning
into the same language sound.

Other pronunciations that result from assimilation are confined to certain regional or social dialects. For example, it is common for speakers of Southern American English to pronounce words such as *wasn't* and *business* as *wadn't* and *bidness*. The reason that the *z* sound in the middle of these words is changed to *d* is because it occurs next to *n*. Both *n* and *d* are language sounds that are produced by fully blocking the airflow in the mouth (although air escapes through the nose with *n*). The *z* sound, however, is unlike these sounds, because it is produced with only partial air blockage (as evidenced in the buzzing we hear when *z*'s are produced). When we change *z* to *d*, we are changing it to a sound in which airflow is completely blocked in the mouth, just like *n*. Even though at first glance *d* doesn't seem any more similar to *n* than *z*, a close examination of articulatory processes reveals that changing *z* to *d* before *n* really is a process of assimilation.

Another process affecting sounds is WEAKENING. Weakening involves producing sounds that involve less blockage of airflow in the mouth and is especially likely to occur when sounds occur next to other sounds that involve little or no obstruction of the airflow, particularly vowels. It is important to remember that when linguists refer to the process of "weakening," they are not making a value judgment about the worth of a particular sound or sound system but are simply referring to how strongly the airflow is blocked in the mouth when a given sound is produced. The sound systems of all languages and dialects contain both strong and weak sounds; in fact, all vowels are inherently "weak" sounds, since they involve no blockage of airflow in the mouth whatsoever. Furthermore, all sound systems are subject to weakening processes regardless of their social valuation.

A given consonant may weaken in various ways, leading to differentiation among dialects. For example, when speakers of American English produce the *t* that occurs in the middle of words like *butter* and *better*, they almost always weaken it to a *d*-like sound. This sound is actually a quick tap, called a FLAP, of the tip of the tongue to the roof of the mouth rather than a full-fledged *d* sound. Speakers of some varieties of British English may also weaken *t*'s in the middle of words; however, they do so in a different way. Instead of pronouncing *t* as a flap, they pronounce it as a slight "catch" in the throat, which sounds almost as if they are leaving out the *t* entirely, as in *bo'l* for *bottle*. This "catch," called a GLOTTAL STOP, is actually a quick closing and reopening of the vocal cords. It is found in some varieties of American English, particularly some types that are spoken in New York City, as in the pronunciation of the *tt* of *bottle* or *little* with a glottal stop, and also happens to be found in the middle of the phrase *uh oh*. It is not an easy sound to describe on paper, however, because English has no letter for it. Phonetically, the sound is indicated as [ʔ], a question mark without a period.

Not only may sounds be weakened, but they may be completely lost when they occur in certain sequences. It is common, for example, for speakers to omit consonants when several of them cluster together in a row, since such clusters are "unnatural." There is a natural principle of human language organization that holds that consonants should alternate with vowels rather than cluster together without intervening vowels. Most English speakers tend to drop at least one consonant from the clusters that occur at the ends of plural words like *sixths*, *tempts*, and *tests*; and they also sometimes leave off the final consonant in non-plurals such as *test*, *friend*, or *desk*. This is particularly likely to occur in informal speech and when the word following the cluster begins with a consonant, as in *des' by the window* for "desk by the window." Speakers of some vernacular varieties have extended this process of word-final consonant loss so that they may drop final consonants before vowels as well as consonants, as in *des' over there* for "desk over there." Consonant loss of various types is so commonplace that it is even an integral part of formal standard English. For example, the "silent" *k* at the beginning of *knight* and *knee* used to be pronounced, as did the *gh* at the end of *knight* (with *gh* being pronounced as something like the final *ch* in German *Bach* or Scottish English *loch*).

Another way to eliminate consonant clusters is to break them up by inserting vowels. Thus, speakers of some vernacular varieties say *deskes* or *desses* for *desks* as well as *athuhlete* for *athlete*. Consonants are sometimes inserted into words as well, though this process does not have to do with cluster simplification but with the overlap of articulatory gestures that occur in quick succession. For example, it is very common for speakers to insert *d*'s between *n*'s and *r*'s, which is why the Old English word for *thunder*, *þunrian*, gradually became *thunder* (and why children often refer to Donner and Blitzen as Donder and Blitzen). Occasionally, the "extra" consonants that we find in vernacular dialects are the result of such insertion, as, for example, when speakers of some varieties pronounce *chimney* as *chimbley*. Most often, however, the additional consonants we sometimes find in vernacular dialects represent retentions of sounds that were lost in other English varieties, including standard English. For example, when older rural Southern speakers say *hit* for *it*, they are not inserting an *h* but rather preserving a pronunciation that goes all the way back to the Old English period.

Some pronunciation changes have more to do with how sounds are perceived by listeners than how they are pronounced. For example, people often pronounce *et cetera* as *eksetera*, not necessarily because the latter is any easier to say but because *et cetera* sounds like *eksetera* (or even *extra*) in fast speech. As with articulation-based language change, perception-based changes are commonplace in mainstream varieties of English as well. For example, the reason why some words ending in *augh* and *ough*, as in *laugh* and *rough*, are today pronounced with a final *f* is that the sound originally indicated by the final *gh* (which we have already described as similar to the *ch* in Scottish English *loch*) is readily misperceived as *f*.

Sound systems

One very important class of pronunciation changes relates to how sounds are organized into systems rather than how individual sounds or strings of sounds are produced or perceived. We already noted that some sounds that seem initially to be quite different (e.g. *z* and *d* as in *wasn't* vs. *wadn't*) are actually very similar in terms of how they are produced in the mouth. If we examine our language closely, we also find that some sounds that we perceive to be the "same" are actually produced somewhat differently. For example, the *p* that occurs in words like *pit* and *pot* is produced with a distinct puff of air, called ASPIRATION, following the sound, while the *p* in *spit* and *spot* is not. We can test this for ourselves by loosely holding a thin piece of paper close to our lips and uttering the words *pit* and *spit* in succession. Notice how much the paper moves for *pit*, while it barely moves at all for *spit*. Thus, the two types of *p*'s, which we consider to be the same, are actually not the same at all. In fact, there are languages, such as Thai or Hindi, in which the two *p*'s are considered to be two different language sounds; and there is even a separate phonetic symbol for each type of *p*: [pʰ] represents aspirated *p* (as in *pit*), while [p] stands for unaspirated *p* (as in *spit*).

In essence, the main thing separating sounds which are considered to be the "same" from those that are held to be "different" is whether or not the sounds can be used to make a meaning difference in the language. Thus, in English, *d* and *z* are different language sounds because they can be used to distinguish a word like *dip* from a word like *zip*. Conversely, [p] and [pʰ] are not two different sounds, because there is no word [pɪt] (as opposed to [pʰɪt]) that has a meaning different from "pit". In Thai, however, word pairs with [p] and [pʰ] abound. For example, *paa* means "forest" while *pʰaa* means "to split".

When two sounds can be used to make meaning differences, they are called PHONEMES. Linguists indicate that a given sound is considered to be phonemic in a particular language by enclosing it in slashes (e.g. /p/, /b/); if they are concerned merely with the physical sound itself rather than its meaningful status in a sound system, they enclose the sound in square brackets (e.g. [p], [pʰ]). Even though sounds that are considered to be different phonemes, or different meaningful sounds, may sometimes be produced rather similarly (as with [z] and [d] in English), it is very important for languages to keep different phonemes different enough so that listeners can recognize them as different. Sometimes, when a sound takes on a new pronunciation, it becomes very similar to the sound of another phoneme and so the latter sound is changed as well in order to ensure that the two sounds remain distinct enough to convey meaning differences. This process of CHAIN SHIFTING is most likely to affect vowels, since vowels are differentiated from one another chiefly by differences in the height of the tongue and how far forward in the mouth the tongue is during the production of the sound. Consonants, on the other hand, are differentiated by where the tongue comes into contact with the inside of the mouth, how completely the tongue blocks airflow, whether or not air comes out of the nose during the production of the sound, and whether or not the vocal cords vibrate when the sound is produced.

Because vowels are not as clearly distinct as consonants, if one vowel is even slightly altered in pronunciation, then it begins to sound like vowels that are produced with similar tongue positioning. If speakers still hope to preserve a meaning distinction or phonemic distinction between this altered vowel and "neighboring" vowels, then the neighboring vowels will have to be altered in pronunciation as well. In turn, these alterations lead to further alterations, and a sort of "domino effect" may result. We will discuss chain shifts in more detail in chapters 3 and 5. For now, all we need to know is that such shifts are commonplace and once led to a sweeping change in the pronunciation of all long vowels in English. For example, words with the vowel sound of *name* used to be pronounced with the vowel of *father*, words with the vowel of *beet* were pronounced with the vowel of *bait*, while those with the vowel of *time* were pronounced with the vowel of *team*. Chain shifts are also under way currently in American English dialects; in fact, they are proceeding quite differently in different areas of the country, leading to increased dialect differentiation rather than the decreased differentiation we might expect in the face of mass communication and improved methods of transportation. We will discuss these current chain shifts in chapter 5.

Sporadic sound changes

Finally, we should mention sound changes that do not necessarily operate in neat, systematic ways but are more sporadic in nature. Among these are changes involving making sounds more unlike each other rather than more like each other and changes involving the reordering of sounds within a word. The first type of change, called DISSIMILATION, often affects sounds which are not immediately adjacent and seems to affect mostly *r* and *l* sounds: It is rather difficult to pronounce words when they contain a number of *r*'s or *l*'s, and so speakers may leave out some of these sounds or even change *r*'s to *l*'s and vice versa, in order to create a more "balanced" word. The pronunciation of *corner* as *co'ner* in some Eastern US dialects, in which the first *r* has been deleted, results from dissimilation, as is the pronunciation of *colonel* as *kernel*, where the first *l* has been changed to an *r*. These pronunciations are general and widespread, but sometimes dissimilation is confined to certain regional or social varieties. Despite how common dissimilation is, it does not always operate in a regular way in the dialects of English; it affects some words but leaves other very similar words untouched. Thus, while many speakers say *lib'ary* for "library", nobody ever says *cont'ary* for "contrary", even though the structures of the two words are very much alike.

Another process that affects words sporadically is the reversal or transposition of sounds, or METATHESIS. Again, this process has led to a number of pronunciation changes that are fully accepted as part of mainstream English and, again, it often involves *l*'s and *r*'s, particularly *r*'s. For example, words such as *bird*, *first*, and *third* used to be *bryde*, *frist*, and *thridde*, respectively, in Old English. Nowadays, metathesis is responsible for a couple of dialect differences, including the highly stigmatized pronunciation of *ask* as *aks* by speakers of vernacular varieties of African American English, as well as some other vernacular dialects. Interestingly, the *ask/aks* alternation goes all the way back to Old English, when it represented a regional rather than ethnic dialect variation.

Syllable structure considerations
Often, sounds are added, deleted, or moved around in order to create syllables that conform to a general language preference for consonants and vowels to alternate with one another in sequences. The most natural syllable is one consisting of a single consonant plus a single vowel, as in *me* or *ma*. Syllables that end in a consonant, as in *man* or *bad*, are not too difficult to pronounce either; but once consonants begin clustering at the ends of syllables or at the beginning, speakers begin omitting consonants or inserting vowels. Thus, a word such as *test* becomes *tes'*, while *athlete* becomes *athuhlete*, with a vowel breaking up the *th-l* consonant sequence. Similarly, speakers may move sounds around so that words consist of simple syllables of the form consonant + vowel (CV). For example, the stigmatized pronunciation of *nuclear* as *nukular* is the result of moving the *l* to break up a consonant cluster and to give us three CV syllables in a row.

It is important to keep in mind that, just as with the word formation and sentence structure change processes we discussed above, the pronunciation changes that lead to dialect differentiation do not always represent simplifications. In other words, it is not the case that vernacular varieties have "simpler" sound systems than standard varieties. Although such processes as consonant cluster reduction and the pronunciation of *th* as *d* or *t* may technically be described as simplifications, other processes, such as the chain shifting of vowels or certain cases of metathesis, do not produce structures that are simpler in any way. In addition, we must bear in mind that even seemingly straightforward simplification may take many forms. For example, speakers who seek to reduce the consonant cluster in *tests* may say *tesses* or *tess*, with the double *s* in the latter word representing a single *s* that is lengthened in duration. Because the natural principles that guide pronunciation change do not always produce simpler forms and because natural

changes may proceed in very different directions in different areas or among
speakers of different social and ethnic groups, the potential for the development of dialect differences in pronunciation is very great indeed.

2.2.5   Words and word meanings

So far, in our discussion of the principles underlying language change and
dialect differentiation, we have not yet mentioned lexical and semantic
differences – that is, differences in words and word meanings. One of the
most noticeable differences is the different vocabulary words we find in
different language varieties. We are all familiar with the fact that speakers
in different parts of the country use different words to refer to various
foods and drinks; for example, we may have heard the words *soda*,
pop, *cola*, and *tonic* being used to refer to a particular kind of carbonated
beverage, as well as such terms as *sub*, *hoagie*, *grinder*, and *hero* to refer
to a submarine sandwich. One of the main reasons why we find such wide
differentiation in dialect words has to do with one of the most basic facts
that underlies human language: The relationship between the sounds
that make up a given word and the meaning or meanings associated with
this word is essentially arbitrary. That is, there is no one "true" name for
a given object or idea. Thus, even a common, everyday substance like
bread is associated with quite different words in different languages; for
example, *bread* is *pain* in French and *chleb* in Russian. Similarly, different
dialects of a single language may use quite different words to refer to one
and the same item.

Word meanings can also be complex and change: A given word may have
not only a central, core meaning but also a host of peripheral meanings and
associations that make it difficult to pin down the meaning of the word with
precision. Sometimes, two dialect areas may share a word, but speakers in
each area may have chosen a different sub-meaning as the word's central
meaning. For example, we have encountered the unusual word *mommuck*
in several of the dialect areas we have investigated in North Carolina. In the
Outer Banks, the word means "to harass or bother", as in *Don't mommuck
me; I've had a hard day*. However, in Robeson County in the Southeastern
mainland portion of the state near the South Carolina border, *mommuck* has
a slightly different meaning, "to make a mess of", as in *He mommucked up
his homework*. Clearly, the two meanings are related; speakers in each dialect
area have simply seized on a different facet of the word's overall meaning as
the word's principal meaning. Interestingly, *mommuck* can be traced back at
least as far as Shakespeare's day, when it had yet another meaning: "to tear
or shred", as in *He mommucked his shirt in a fit of rage*. Thus, we see that
word meanings can shift, sometimes rather drastically, over time as well as

over space. We will discuss various ways in which MEANING SHIFT can occur in chapter 3.

Another reason why we have different words in different language varieties has to do with factors that lie outside the linguistic system itself. Sometimes, speakers need different words because they have to – or want to – talk about different things not shared by other groups. Thus, it is not surprising that there are many terms for marine-related items and activities in coastal areas such as the Chesapeake Bay area of Maryland and Virginia that are not shared with speakers in Ohio or Montana or even in inland regions of coastal states. For example, coastal residents may make reference to a *peeler crab* for "a crab that is shedding its shell in preparation for growing a new and larger one", a *buckram* for "a crab with a crinkly hard shell", a *bait box* for the section on the bottom of the crab pot where bait is placed, and so forth. On the other hand, people who live in non-coastal areas have no occasion to talk about such details of crabs. Similarly, we find different food-related terms in different areas simply because the foods people eat vary greatly from region to region. Even within a single dialect area, we find lots of variation in what people talk about. Some of these terms will be related to occupation, but others will pertain to cultural activities and general lifestyle differences.

Exercise 5

Think about some of the local activities or situations that might set apart the local neighborhood, community, or region where you live. Are there any terms that would be known by local residents but not necessarily by those outside the area? For example, are there particular lexical items that might denote cultural activities or other aspects of the lifestyles typical of the community? How might these terms contribute to the notion that every community seems to have its own dialect?

When speakers encounter items or concepts for which their language or language variety currently has no term, they come up with terms to describe these activities. They may simply make up, or COIN, the word, such as the term *zhush* for "fluff up or primp" or *SARS*, the acronym for "severe acute respiratory syndrome", a medical condition that surfaced at the turn of the twenty-first century. New words may also be created out of existing language resources. There are a number of different ways of doing this, which we will discuss in more detail in chapter 3. One of the most common processes in English is COMPOUNDING, or putting two existing words together to get a new term whose meaning may be completely unrelated to the meanings of the original words. The Southern American term *hushpuppies*, which refers to bite-sized pieces of deep-fried cornmeal batter, is an example of a compound word, as in the Eastern coastal term *breakwater*, which refers to a barrier which prevents water from eroding coastal land or to the process of erecting such barriers. Finally, as we discussed earlier in this chapter, terms for regionally or culturally specific items or concepts may be borrowed from other languages. Early in the history of American English, borrowings came from Native American, European, and African languages; nowadays, borrowings may come from just about any language in the world.

As with new pronunciations, word-formation processes, and sentence structures, it is difficult to predict which new lexical items will be widely adopted and which will remain restricted to particular groups of speakers. However, we do know that many of today's common English words started out as dialect-specific items and then spread across dialects to the point where they have become identified as common English vocabulary items. For example, the words *bisque* "a cream soup", *cruller* "a type of doughnut", and *ranch* all began as regionally restricted terms but are now part of the general word stock of English.

By the same token, there are also present-day items that were once in widespread usage but have since retracted to regional usage only. For example, the use of *garret* for "attic", or *yonder* for "over there" in rural Southern dialects are local retentions of older items which were once in much wider use in the English language. When a particular group of speakers does not participate in a change taking place elsewhere in the language, the result may be the retraction of a general English vocabulary word to dialect-specific status.

2.3   The Final Product

Linguistic and social factors do not work in isolation in the formation of dialects. Rather, dialects are affected by a complex array of factors in various combinations. It is often difficult to determine with precision the role of a particular linguistic or social factor in the formation of a given dialect. This uncertainty, however, does not detract from the highly structured nature of the resultant variety or from the significant roles that dialect differences can play in society.

Perhaps the best analogy we can draw for the creation of a dialect is the preparation of a special meal prepared by an experienced home cook. Starting with a number of separate ingredients and working mostly by "feel" or "instinct", the cook combines differing amounts of various items using several different techniques. The cook may alter the basic composition of the dish by adding "just a pinch" of this or "a touch" of that. The resultant dish turns out to be a delicious concoction when prepared by the cook, but it is extremely difficult to replicate. Similarly, dialects are formed when sociohistorical and linguistic factors come together in combinations and proportions that are sometimes difficult to specify exactly. The resultant language product – the dialect – turns out to be a unique variety whose distinctive flavor would be lost if it were mechanistically constructed of precise portions of readily identifiable linguistic and sociohistorical ingredients.

2.4   Further Reading

Chambers, J. K. (2003) *Sociolinguistic Theory*, 2nd edn. Oxford: Blackwell. Chapters 2–4 in this book discuss many of the traditional demographic and interactional factors used in sociolinguistic description and explanation, whereas chapter 5 discusses some of the linguistic factors that give rise to linguistic variation.

Chambers, J. K., Peter Trudgill, and Natalie Schilling-Estes (eds.) (2001) *Handbook of Language Variation and Change*. Oxford: Blackwell. This collection has extensive, critical discussions of many of the factors affecting dialect variation that are introduced in this chapter. For example, entire chapters are dedicated to constructs such as identity, communities of practice, the speech community, and so forth. This is an excellent resource for those interested in more detailed discussion of fundamental social and linguistic factors in language variation.

Hock, Hans Henrich, and Brian D. Joseph (1996) *Language History, Language Change, and Language Relationship: An Introduction to Historical and Comparative Linguistics*. Berlin/New York: Mouton de Gruyter. This book provides a comprehensive introduction to the linguistic principles that guide language change. Of particular interest are chapters 4 through 9, in which the principles of phonological, morphosyntactic, lexical, and semantic change are discussed. The book provides plenty of examples from English at various stages in its historical development and so is especially relevant to students interested in variation and change in English.

Labov, William (1972b) *Sociolinguistic Patterns*. Philadelphia: University of Pennsylvania Press. This is a classic collection of William Labov's pioneering works in the establishment of modern sociolinguistic study. Several chapters in this collection, particularly chapters 1, 4, 5, and 7, reveal how the processes of linguistic change interact with social forces in the development and continued delimitation of the varieties of English. A more complete and current version of the linguistic and social principles of language change for graduate students in linguistics and sociolinguistics is found in Labov's two volumes, *Principles of Linguistic Change*, vol. 1: *Internal Factors* (1994) and *Principles of Linguistic Change*, vol. 2: *Social Factors* (2001b).

3
Levels of Dialect

Dialect differences can be manifested in a number of different ways. For example, they may involve the use of different words for the same item, as in the use of *sub*, *hoagie*, *hero*, or *grinder* for a sandwich made on a long roll with cheese, meat, and vegetables such as lettuce, tomatoes, and onions. They may also involve the pronunciation of the same word in different ways. For example, in some dialects the vowels in word pairs like *dawn* and *Don* are pronounced the same, while in other dialects, they are pronounced differently. Dialect differences may also involve the way words are put together into sentences, as in *The house needs painted* vs. *The house needs painting*, and even how language is used in carrying out social routines, such as greeting people with *Hi*, *Hey*, *Yo*, or *S'up*.

Languages are patterned on several different levels, and each of these is subject to dialectal variation. These levels include the LEXICON, the vocabulary of a language; PHONOLOGY, the sound system of a language; GRAMMAR, the formation of words and sentences; SEMANTICS, the meanings of words; and PRAGMATICS, the use of language forms to perform different functions. We are not surprised to find dialect differences on all of these levels; what is of more interest is how these differences are distributed among different groups of people and the social meanings they carry in our society. In this chapter, we examine some dialect differences on each of these different levels and consider how these differences are viewed in American society.

3.1 Lexical Differences

One of the most obvious levels of dialect variation is the lexicon, or vocabulary, of a language. Most of us can remember times when our failure to recognize a word used by some regional or social group resulted in confusion, if not outright communication breakdown. We may have been surprised when we traveled to different places in the United States and ordered a *soda*, only to find that we received different drinks in different regions – for example, a simple carbonated drink in Philadelphia and a carbonated drink with ice cream in it in Chicago. Or we may have been surprised to discover that different people were referring to the same kind of animal when they talked about *mountain lions*, *cougars*, and sometimes even *panthers*. And many parents have shaken their heads in dismay when their teenagers described an extraordinary event or object as *tight*, *dope*, or *ill*. Just about everyone has a collection of favorite anecdotes about lexical differences among the dialects of English.

As we mentioned in chapter 2, there are a number of different ways in which lexical differences can manifest themselves. Because the relationship between a real-world object and the word used to describe it is almost always arbitrary, we often find that different labels are used to describe the same object (or idea) in different dialect areas. For example, *green beans* and *string beans* are simply different labels for the same vegetable, while *sneakers*, *tennis shoes*, *gym shoes*, and *running shoes* refer to the same basic type of athletic shoe when worn as casual footwear. We also find different words because we find diverse objects and activities in different regions. People who live in coastal areas routinely use a number of marine-related terms that those who live in inland areas away from the water may never have heard. The multitude of lexical items that arise in different dialect areas may spring from any of a number of word-formation processes. We have already mentioned in chapter 2 that new words may be completely made up, in a process known as COINING; in addition, they may be borrowed from other languages or created out of already existing words. In table 3.1 there is a list of some of the ways in which new words can be created. These words may be associated with social groups or regional groups of various types, including groups who share a particular interest. A new word typically starts out with a restricted range of usage; if it persists only among a regional or social subset of speakers, it becomes established as a dialect form, but if it spreads across a wide range of English dialects, then it may become part of the English language as a whole. Table 3.1 illustrates both broad-based and dialectally restricted items as developed through the different processes available for new word creation.

Not only do dialects use different words, but they may use the same words with different meanings. Meanings are flexible and transitory, and they may change in a number of ways over time and place. Dialect differences result when a meaning changes in one way in a particular region but in some other way, or not at all, in other dialect areas. In one common type of change a word may BROADEN or NARROW its meaning. For example, when the word *barn* was brought from Britain to America, it was used to refer to a building that was used only for storing grain. Its meaning was gradually

Table 3.1 Some of the ways in which new words can be created

Process	Definition	Examples
compounding	two or more existing words are combined to form a new word	*in-group, honeysuckle, breakwater, fatback*
acronyms	new words are formed by taking the initial sounds or letters from existing words	*radar* (**r**adio **d**etecting **a**nd **r**ange) *WASP* (**W**hite **A**nglo **S**axon **P**rotestant) *UN* (**U**nited **N**ations)
blending	parts of two words are combined to form a new word	*smog* (smoke/fog) *brunch* (breakfast/lunch) *sitcom* (situation/comedy) *broasted* (broiled/roasted)
clipping	words are formed by shortening existing words	*gas* (gasoline) *dorm* (dormitory) *'za* (pizza)
conversion	words are shifted from one part of speech to another without any change in their form	*run* (as a noun in "They scored a run") *tree* (as a verb in "They treed a cat") *breakwater* (as a verb in "Everything around the island is breakwatered.")
proper names	proper nouns, which refer to a specific person, place, or thing, are changed into common nouns, which refer to a general class of items	*jello, frigidaire, xerox*
borrowing	words from other languages are incorporated into the language or dialect	*chipmunk* (Ojibwa) *delicatessen* (German) *arroyo* (Spanish)
folk etymology	words are altered to make their meanings more transparent	*cold slaw* (from *cole slaw*), *old timers' disease* (from Alzheimer's disease)
back formation	shorter words are created from longer words based on the removal of what appears to be an affix but is in reality part of the original word	*burgle* from *burglar*, *orientate* from *orientation*, *conversate* from *conversation*
recutting	words are reanalyzed into component parts which differ from the original parts	*an apron* (from *a napron*), *-aholic*, as in *workaholic* (from *alcohol + ic*), *a whole nother* (from *an + other*)
derivation	words are created through the addition of a derivational affix	*bewitched* from *bewitch + ed*

broadened so that it could be used to refer to a building for storing all sorts of farm-related items, including animals and machinery. However, this broadening took place only in America, resulting in a lexical difference between America and Britain; in Britain, *barn* still means a storage place for grain. Other broadenings that have occurred in the history of English affected such familiar words as *holiday* (originally "holy day", a day of religious significance), *butcher* (originally, "slaughterer of goats"), *companion* ("someone with whom you share bread"), *bird* ("young bird"), and *drive* ("to drive an animal"). And broadening still occurs today. One prominent case is the broadening of brand names, which originate as labels for products manufactured by one particular company but may develop into more general terms for certain types of products. Americans throughout the country use *kleenex* to refer to facial tissues of any type and *xerox* to refer to photocopying in general, no matter what brand of machine they use. On a more dialectally restricted level, speakers in the American South may refer to all refrigerators as *frigidaires* or to all brands of dark-colored carbonated beverages as *cokes* or *Co-Colas*.

Narrowings are also commonplace on both a regional and national level. For example, the word *meat* once referred to food in general but now refers to only one type of food. Similarly, the word *deer* referred to any type of animal, and the word *girl* could once be used to refer to a child of either sex. As with broadenings, some narrowings affected American English but left British English untouched. For example, the word *corn* in Britain is still used to refer to any type of grain, while its meaning has narrowed to refer to only one specific type in America. Innumerable English words have narrowed or broadened in meaning over time, and this is an ongoing process.

Another type of change is MEANING SHIFT, or a change in the primary meaning of a word, often in the direction of one of the word's sub-meanings. One of the most noteworthy historical examples of meaning shift involves the word *bead*. Originally, this word meant "prayer", but it came to refer to a particular type of jewelry because rosary beads were often worn in the Middle Ages while saying prayers. Other shifts include *knight* (originally, "young person"), *nice* (originally "ignorant"), and even *pen* (from the Latin *penna* "feather"). Some meaning shifts involve FIGURATIVE EXTENSION, or metaphorical extension, in which the use of a word is extended so that it can refer to items that are very different from those originally referred to, based on a common meaning feature shared by the two classes of items. For example, the term *submarine*, which literally refers to an underwater boat, has been figuratively extended to apply to a type of sandwich that is similar in shape to the seagoing vessel. Similarly, the word *offshore*, which literally means "located off the coast", can be used on the coast of North Carolina to refer to people who are crazy or silly – that is, *outlandish*, a figurative extension that is more commonly used in inland locations to refer to such people. There are many instances of "new meanings for old words" across the dialects of English, although in many cases speakers may be completely unaware of the fact that the words they use in daily conversation originally had quite different meanings from the ones they have today.

Exercise 1

Following are some sets of lexical items that reflect the cross-dialectal vocabulary differences we find in the regional dialects of American English. For each set of words, first attempt to determine whether the different terms are the result of the broadening or narrowing of a general English word or of lexical innovation. If the word represents an innovation, which of the processes discussed above (e.g. compounding, borrowing, etc.) were used to create the word? Are there cases which seem to involve figurative extension?

1   baby's breath/chalkweed/mist "a type of plant, gypsophila"
2   bathroom, restroom, washroom, toilet "toilet facilities in a public place"
3   sneakers, running shoes, tennis shoes, gym shoes, runners "athletic shoes as casual footwear"
4   earthworm/angleworm/fishing worm/night crawler "a type of worm used in fishing"
5   metro/underground/subway "underground railway system"
6   cashier/check-out/register "place where you pay in a store"
7   ATM/bank machine/cash machine/guichet "machine that performs banking services"
8   lowland/low ground/bottom land/savannah "land that usually has some standing water with trees or bushes growing on it"
9   snap beans/string beans/green beans "a type of vegetable with a stringy fiber on the pods"
10   beltline, beltway, loop, perimeter "a road that encircles a metropolitan area"

The inventory of lexical differences across the dialects of American English covers a wide range of categories, and the number of dialectally restricted words runs well into the thousands. In the questionnaire for eliciting items in the *Dictionary of American Regional English*, some 41 different categories of lexical difference are outlined. Topography, food, furniture, animals, and equipment related to rural occupations lead the list, but the range of possible differences is virtually unlimited and encompasses many terms for physical and emotional states as well as those for concrete items. More current lists of regionally restricted lexical items (Boberg forthcoming) tend to focus on fast foods, technology, and transportation, following some of the cultural changes that have taken place in the last century.

In the preceding discussion, we focused on lexical differences in so-called CONTENT WORDS – words that refer to objects, ideas, events, or states in the real (or imagined) world. There are also differences pertaining to FUNCTION WORDS such as prepositions (e.g. *in, on, under*) and articles (e.g. *the, a/an*), items more likely to indicate grammatical information than semantic content. In many cases, differences in function words are confined to particular phrases. For example, different prepositions may be used in the phrase *sick to/at/in/on one's stomach* and *of/in the morning* (as in *We drink coffee of the morning*), while different articles may appear in a sentence such as *I've got a/the toothache*. In other cases, the difference involves the use or non-use of a function word in a particular type of construction. Thus, speakers in some dialect areas will say *She lives in Coal City* while others say *She lives __ Coal City*. Since content words far outnumber function words, dialect differences involving function words are not as common as those involving content words, but some of the function word differences can be quite important in distinguishing varieties from one another.

In most instances, the kinds of lexical differences we have discussed above are considered to be regional curiosities, and little significance in terms of social status or personal worth is attached to them. Lexical differences do carry social associations on other dimensions, such as urban vs. rural or "modern" vs. "old-fashioned," but people are not usually socially stigmatized purely on the basis of saying *soda* versus *pop*, or *sneakers* versus *tennis shoes*. TABOO WORDS, which are popularly known by such labels as "four-letter words," "swear words," or "curse words," constitute an exception to this observation. These items certainly stigmatize their users in particular social situations, but in American society, these items are viewed more in terms of socially appropriate behavior than of social group differentiation. Speakers of any social class or ethnic group may be considered ill-mannered if they use these terms in inappropriate circumstances. In addition, the use of these terms by females traditionally was considered inappropriate under *any* circumstance, though this has changed, at least in some segments of American society. All dialect groups recognize taboo terms, although the conventions for usage may differ to some extent from group to group, as may the classification of particular terms as taboo items. The use of *bloody* as an intensifier (e.g. *Where's the bloody car?*) is considered acceptable, if odd, in American English but is quite offensive to British English ears, while the word *tits* to refer to female breasts is not nearly as unacceptable in some rural American dialects as it is in non-rural dialects.

Some sets of vocabulary items are associated with groups of speakers who share a particular interest rather than with regional or sociocultural groups of speakers. These interests may range from technical or academic fields such as computer programming or linguistics to recreational activities like football, aerobics, or popular music. Any novice computer user who is looking for *user-friendly documentation* on how to set up *email filters* to avoid getting too much *spam* is well aware of the specialized vocabulary that has grown up around computer technology. Sometimes a beginning computer user may confront so many technical terms in a single sentence as to make it practically incomprehensible. Similarly, a casual observer of a Sunday afternoon football game may have no idea what is meant when they are told that "The Giants' *nickel defense sacked* the Cowboys' *quarterback* in the *shotgun formation* with a *safety blitz*." Such specialized vocabularies, or JARGONS, cut across all types of social groups and arise via the same processes of word formation and meaning change that give rise to regional, social class, ethnic, and gender-based lexical differences. In popular culture, the term "jargon" is sometimes used by confused or annoyed observers to refer to vocabulary which seems to be purposely obscure. However, what may be incomprehensible "mumbo-jumbo" to outsiders may simply be a necessity for precise, detailed communications among those who are involved in a specific field.

A more deliberately secretive jargon, such as a special vocabulary used by criminals, is referred to as an ARGOT (pronounced as *are-got*). A few dialectologists and lexicologists have become outstanding specialists in the vocabulary of various "underworld" groups, although there are certainly special fieldwork problems associated with the investigation of such communities of practice. Such study might, however, be a convenient fieldwork project for a wayward linguist who has been sentenced to spend time in prison.

3.2   Slang

Slang is one of those terms that gives dialectologists fits. In popular culture, the label is used freely to refer to everything from the general use of a vernacular dialect (e.g. "They don't speak standard English; they speak slang") to specialized vocabulary words that are technically considered jargon (e.g. "Computer people use a lot of slang") to individual words that are socially stigmatized (e.g. "*Ain't* is a slang word"). The rather loose, imprecise way the term *slang* is often used has caused many dialectologists to shy away from using this label at all. As one dialectologist put it, "Until slang can be objectively identified and segregated or until more precise subcategories replace the catchall label SLANG, little can be done to analyze this kind of lexis" (McMillan 1978: 146). The *Dictionary of American Regional English* explicitly rejects the use of this label because it is "imprecise" and "too indefinite" (Cassidy 1985: xvii). At the same time, some dictionary-makers, or LEXICOGRAPHERS, do employ the term to mark dictionary entries, with varying degrees of reliability among them. In addition, there exist special dictionaries devoted to slang, such as the *Historical Dictionary of American Slang* (Lighter 1994, 1997), *Slang U!* (Munro 1989), and *Slang and Sociability: In-Group Language Among College Students* (Eble 1996), as well as numerous web sites that feature many words that are considered to be slang.

From a strictly linguistic standpoint, words are words, and those that are labeled as slang are formed linguistically no differently from any other lexical item. In fact, many slang terms are simply common lexical items that are recycled with new meanings; for example, terms like *cool, sweet, ill, fresh,* and *tight* for "exceptionally good" are all common adjectives in English with non-slang uses. From the perspective of language as a kind of social behavior, however, there does seem to be a group of "slang" words that have a special status in American culture. What distinguishes these items is their sociopsychological role rather than their linguistic composition. As Connie Eble, one of the leading experts on college slang, puts it, "Slang is vocabulary with attitude" (2004: 382). The notion of relegating some words to this special status has been around a long time (over 2,000 years, according to some records), and serious sociolinguists and psycholinguists can hardly afford to dismiss this specialized use of items on the basis of a "lack of precision." Several dialectologists and lexicographers (Chapman 1986, 1995; Lighter 1994, 1997; Eble 1996, 2004) have devoted themselves to the careful collection and description of slang terms of various types, and we are now beginning to understand more fully the specialized role that these items fulfill for different groups in our society.

Part of the problem with defining slang comes from the fact that terms appear to be classified as slang based on a *set* of characteristics rather than a single criterion. Furthermore, some terms appear to fit the slang designation better than others. Just about everybody would agree that a phrase like *out to lunch* for "uninformed or oblivious" is a slang item and that *uninformed* is not, but a term like *dense* seems to fall between the extremes.

One of the essential traits of slang is its association with informality. Granted that formality and informality are not always easy to define in themselves, there are some social situations that are fairly readily identified as formal or informal. In situations that we intuitively feel are informal, we find that formal words simply sound "wrong" or inappropriate while the opposite is true in situations we consider formal. Slang items are always found at the informal end of the continuum. A person who is rather slow-witted or oblivious to his or her surroundings might be described variously as *incognizant, unenlightened, unaware, blind, dense, clueless, spacey,* or *out to lunch* but the social occasions considered appropriate for these different items differ drastically. Imagine how a student would feel if he or she walked out of a meeting with an academic advisor who had just accused him or her of "spacing" on a major exam – or how a teenager would feel if her or his best friend referred to a friend as "incognizant" or "unwitting" during a lunchtime conversation. In each case, the terms used would be considered inappropriate because slang terms such as *spacing* are reserved for informal occasions while formal terms such as *incognizant* are more appropriate for use on formal, serious occasions than in casual conversation among peers. Words classified as slang carry strong informal overtones.

Another attribute of slang is its potential for indicating a special familiarity with a group outside of the mainstream adult population. An item like *ill* for "exceptionally good" is not only marked as informal, it is also associated with speakers who fall within a relatively narrow age range and who are considered to be "less responsible" than the adult members of society. Similarly, word usages associated with minority ethnic groups might be labeled slang, such as the terms *brother*, *bro*, *sister*, and *girl* as used by African Americans with a special in-group meaning to refer to other African Americans (e.g. *He's a brother*). One slang specialist (Chapman 1986: xi) notes that "the black influence on American slang has been more pervasive in recent times than any other ethnic group in history." In part, this is because the vocabulary from non-mainstream cultures often strikes members of mainstream culture as novel, rich, and imaginative (Eble 2004: 383).

Slang items are also often cultivated in the context of close-knit peer groups, and the idea that the particular use of a term might be difficult for outsiders to understand may make it even more appealing as a symbol of in-group membership. This is one reason why teenagers and college students, with their emphasis on peer-group relationships, are often the primary source of new slang terms. That adults and people in other locales are totally unfamiliar with these terms is hardly a problem – in fact, a group of teenagers may revel in the restricted sphere of usage of their terms. Not all items classified as slang have strong group identity associations, but many of the most recognizable cases of slang do.

Another characteristic of slang relates to its role as a special kind of synonym. Slang terms typically have well-known, neutral, conventional synonyms. English speakers who use *kick the bucket* for "die", *toasted* for "drunk", or *dope* for "exceptionally good" generally know that there is a neutral, alternate term but choose not to use it. Psychologically, or, more properly, psycholinguistically, the slang term is thus viewed as an intentional replacement, or a "flouting," of the conventional, more neutral term that might have been used. Listeners presume that a person who uses *out to lunch* is deliberately choosing not to use a conventional term such as *unaware* and that a speaker who uses *barf, puke, ralph, yak,* or *worship the porcelain goddess* instead of *regurgitate, vomit,* or *throw up* is making a deliberate choice. On one level, slang projects a deliberate sense of irreverence or defiance of proper behavior.

Finally, we should observe that slang items are often perceived as having a short life span. Certainly, some slang items are short-lived, particularly those associated with localized or temporary social groups. But many items have considerable staying power. For example, *dough* for "money", *cram* for "study intensely for a short period of time", *smooth* for "excellent", and *flunk* for "fail" have been around since at least the turn of the twentieth century – much longer than many terms that have been adopted as conventional words of English. The senior author remembers using the term *cool* as a teenager and thinking that it would probably not last very long – an early precursor to an impending career in sociolinguistics, no doubt. More than four decades later, he was surprised to elicit the same term when he asked a group of college students to give him the latest terms for describing something exceptionally good. Nonetheless, in popular culture, slang tends to be viewed as ephemeral and destined to be short-lived. In fact, this perception, real or imagined, may actually contribute to the designation of items as slang in the first place. Some items have persisted as slang terms for quite a long time and show no signs of fading out or becoming part of mainstream English. It is impossible to predict which of today's slang words will become part of the lexical stock of mainstream English, which will die, and which will remain "slangy" for years to come. Only time will tell if a term will catch on and become a stable part of the language or whether it will fall by the wayside along with other short-lived slang items.

The definition of slang which we have presented may seem somewhat imprecise, particularly if we are looking for a single criterion for definitively separating slang from non-slang items. However, we have to keep in mind that slang tends to exist on a continuum and that, to some extent, one person's slang may be another person's conventional lexical item. Some items, characterized by extremes in terms of the attributes mentioned above, are considered slang by virtually all English speakers, while others, which possess some but not all of these attributes, are of more indeterminate status. So far, we have yet to find a native speaker of American English who does not consider items like *ill* or *dope* for "excellent" to be slang, but there is much more latitude in the classification of other items, such as *rip off* for "steal" or *buck* for "money". The items *ill* and *dope* are closely associated with non-mainstream, in-group usage in informal settings. On the other hand, a term like *rip off* for "steal" is relatively informal and not associated with a particular in-group; it is now used in some relatively neutral contexts. Furthermore, *rip off* has been around for quite a while, while *buck* for "dollar" was first attested in 1856. Situated between slang and conventional lexical items are items that are sometimes referred to as COLLOQUIAL – that is, items that share the attribute of informality with slang but are not closely associated with in-group identity or with flouted synonymy. While all slang terms are probably colloquial, not all colloquialisms are slang. Of course, the distinction between colloquialism and slang is not always discrete, especially considering that the definition of "slang" cannot be pinned down with precision.

Exercise 2

Rate the following items in terms of how strongly you feel that each constitutes a "slang" item. Use a three-point scale, where 3 is the highest (you have a strong feeling that the item is slang) and 1 is the lowest (you don't believe that the item is slang). For example, an item like *dope* for "excellent" might be given a rating of 3 while *great* would be given a 1.

1 chicken "afraid"
2 zilch "nothing"
3 buck "dollar"
4 out to lunch "unaware"
5 frisk "search"
6 ill "excellent"
7 awesome "excellent"
8 neat "excellent"
9 stupendous "excellent"
10 cool "excellent"

What is it about these items that determines your rating? In your response, you should consider the factors of informality, in-group association, existence of neutral synonyms, and anticipated life span.

3.3 Phonological Differences

Like lexical differences, phonological variation among the dialects of English can be highly noticeable. Listeners are quick to hone in on the distinctive vowel sounds associated with "the Southern drawl," the "broad *a*" and "dropped *r*" of Boston speech, or the "dropped *g*" of *swimmin'* for *swimming* in vernacular dialects across the country. At the same time, some differences in phonology are quite subtle and may not be noticeable to casual observers

– or even to the speakers who use them – although they still serve to set apart different dialects. Phonological patterns can be indicative of regional and sociocultural differences, and a person who has a good ear for dialects can often pinpoint a speaker's general regional and social and ethnic affiliation with considerable accuracy based solely on phonology. Even in today's increasingly interconnected world, the use of a few critical pronunciation cues can narrow down a person's place of origin to at least a general region of the United States, if not to the precise county of origin.

There are several ways in which phonological differences may be manifested in the dialects of American English. One of the most striking differences involves the pronunciation of various vowel sounds. As discussed in chapter 2, it is quite possible for a sound to be pronounced in a number of different ways but still be considered a single meaningful sound or phoneme. Thus, *p* may be produced as the [p] of *spit* or [pʰ] of *pit* in English, but both of these pronunciations, or variants, are considered to represent the phoneme /p/. In sociolinguistic study, the term VARIANTS simply refers to different ways of saying the same thing, whether different ways of pronouncing the same sound, different ways of forming the same construction, or different words for the same item or concept. And a given phoneme can have many more than two variants. For example, most varieties of English have a vowel phoneme represented as /ɔ/, as in *bought*, *cough*, and *raw*, but the way this phoneme is produced varies widely. In some regions, it may sound similar to the vowel in *book* and *look* (phonetically [ʊ]), while in others it sounds like the vowel in *father* or *cot* (phonetically [ɑ]).

As we discussed in chapter 2, a pronunciation difference in one vowel often sets off a kind of domino effect in related vowel sounds, resulting in a wholesale vowel shift or CHAIN SHIFT. In order to investigate vowel shifts in more detail, we need to understand how various vowels are produced in the mouth. Vowels are differentiated from one another along several dimensions: the height of the tongue in the mouth when the vowel is produced, how far forward or backward the tongue is, how much muscle tension is involved, and whether or not the lips are rounded during the production of the vowel. We can obtain a convenient picture of where the tongue is positioned during the production of various vowels by drawing a chart in which the roof of the mouth is located along the top, the front of the mouth on the left-hand side, and the back of the mouth on the right. The result is a chart such as that in figure 3.1. Note that the chart is not drawn as a square because the space in our mouths is more trapezoidal in nature.

Figure 3.1 indicates that each vowel has its own "space," referred to as PHONETIC SPACE, within the vowel trapezoid. The notion of phonetic space is important because the shift of one vowel in phonetic space often has an effect on adjacent vowels. As one vowel moves phonetically closer to a nearby vowel (e.g. [æ] may move forward and upward, into the "territory"

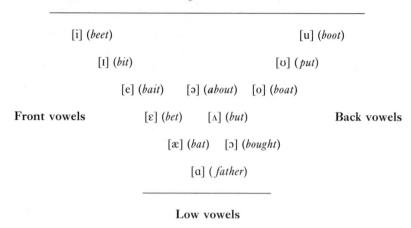

High vowels

[i] (*beet*)   [u] (*boot*)

[ɪ] (*bit*)   [ʊ] (*put*)

[e] (*bait*)   [ə] (*about*)   [o] (*boat*)

Front vowels   [ɛ] (*bet*)   [ʌ] (*but*)   **Back vowels**

[æ] (*bat*)   [ɔ] (*bought*)

[ɑ] (*father*)

Low vowels

Figure 3.1   A chart of American English vowels according to tongue position

of [ɛ]), the second vowel may shift its phonetic value to ensure that the two vowels remain phonetically distinct enough to make meaningful distinctions in words – that is, to remain distinct phonemes. This second movement may trigger the movement of a third vowel, and thus a whole sequence of movements may be set in motion. For example, there are currently some dialects of American English in which the lowering and fronting of /ɔ/ to [ɑ], so that a word like *caught* sounds like *cot*, has triggered the fronting of /ɑ/ to near [æ], so that *lock* sounds almost like *lack*. This shift in turn is causing /æ/-words (e.g. *bat*, *lack*) to sound more like /ɛ/-words (e.g. *bet*, *wreck*) – or even /e/-words (e.g. *bait*, *lake*) so that words such as *bag* and *bad* may sound something like *beg* and *bed* (or even *bade*). This vowel movement or VOWEL ROTATION, illustrated in figure 3.2, is part of a vowel shift pattern currently taking place in the Northern US, particularly in large cities such as Chicago, Detroit, and Buffalo. We will discuss this shift in more detail in chapter 5, as well as a couple of other important vowel shifts that are currently taking place in American English dialects.

Chain shifting has also played a large part in the historical development of English. In fact, if it weren't for a major chain shift which took place from around 1450 to 1650, today's English would sound more like the English of Chaucer's time than the English we are used to hearing today. For example, words with "i" vowels (as in *time*) would be pronounced with "ee" sounds (phonetically [i]), as they were in Middle English (and as they still are in a number of continental European languages); words with "ee" spellings would be pronounced with [e] rather than [i] (thus, *meet* would

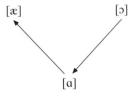

Figure 3.2   An illustration of chain shifting in the low vowels of American English

sound like *mate*); while words with "ou" (as in *house*) would be pronounced with [u] (as in *hoos* for *house*). In fact, we can still hear some of these old pronunciations in some dialect areas in the British Isles; for example, some Scots English speakers may say *hoos* for *house* or *neet* for *night*. In the United States, there are isolated pockets, for example along the Southeastern coast and in the Appalachian Mountains, where a few older speakers still pronounce *anyhow* as *anyhoo*.

There are several English vowel sounds that we haven't included in the chart in figure 3.1: /ai/ as in *time*, /au/ as in *down*, and /ɔi/ as in *boy*. These sounds, called DIPHTHONGS, are each made up of two different vowel sounds and are pronounced by gliding from one sound into the other. The /ai/ diphthong is produced by gliding from [ɑ] as in *father* (or from a somewhat fronter low vowel: [a]) to the [i] of *beet* or [ɪ], of *bit*; /au/ is produced by gliding from [ɑ] or [a] to the [u] of *boot* or the [ʊ] of *put*; and /ɔi/ is produced by gliding from [ɔ] as in *bought* to the vowel of *beet* [i] or *bit* [ɪ]. In each case, the first element of the diphthong is called the NUCLEUS, since it is the central part of the vowel, and the second element is called the GLIDE, since speakers "glide" up to this vowel in producing the diphthong. Not all speakers of American English pronounce these diphthongs exactly as we have just described; in fact, differences in diphthongs can be highly salient in terms of delimiting different dialects. For example, Southern Americans are perhaps more well known for their pronunciation of /ai/ as [ɑː] or [aː] (where the colon indicates lengthened duration), as in *tahm* for *time*, than for any other dialect feature. The pronunciation change affecting /ai/ in Southern speech is referred to as UNGLIDING or MONOPHTHONGIZA-TION, since speakers who say [taːm] for *time* (/taim/) have taken the /ai/ diphthong – a two-part vowel – and turned it into a one-part vowel by leaving off the /i/ glide, or at least drastically shortening it. The /ɔi/ diphthong may also be unglided in some Southern varieties, as in [bɔːl] for *boil*, and /au/ may be subjected to the same fate as well. In particular, in Pittsburgh, Pennsylvania, the ungliding of /au/, as in something like *dahntown* for *downtown*, is so distinctive that it is often cited as one of the defining features of the dialect known as "Pittsburghese." We discuss Pittsburghese in more detail in chapter 5.

A slightly different type of ungliding occurs in areas of the Midwest where English has been influenced by Scandinavian languages. In most dialects of American English, tense vowels such as /e/ and /o/ are actually produced with a slight glide, as in something like [eɪ] for /e/ and [oʊ] for /o/. However, in parts of the Midwest, particularly the northern Midwest, /e/ and /o/ may be pronounced without the glide, as in the stereotypical pronunciation of the next-to-last syllable of *Minnesota* as *soht* – that is, with a longer, unglided /o/ vowel. This ungliding may also be found in a few other regionally restricted dialect areas, such as Charleston, South Carolina.

Along the Southeastern coastal area, extending from the Eastern Shore of Maryland down through the Outer Banks of North Carolina, there is an unusual /au/ sound in which the glide of the vowel sounds more like the [i] of *beet* rather than [u] of *boot*. Thus, we may hear pronunciations such as *hace* [hæɪs] for *house* or *dine* [daɪn] for *down*. In fact, outsiders hearing this pronunciation often confuse the word *brown* with *brain* and *down* with *dine*.

The pronunciation of the nucleus of a diphthong may also serve to distinguish dialects from one another. For example, the nucleus of /ai/ in some regions may be pronounced more backed and raised in the mouth so that it sounds something like (though not identical to) the /ɔɪ/ of *boy* than the /ai/ of *buy*. Residents of the Outer Banks islands off the coast of North Carolina are so well known for this production, as in *toid* for *tide* or *toim* for *time*, that they are often called – and call themselves – "hoi toiders" for "high tiders." This pronunciation is found in coastal areas such as the Outer Banks and Tangier and Smith Islands in the Chesapeake Bay, but it is also found in some isolated inland areas of the South as well. It is also found to a lesser extent in New York City English and a few other locations, though it doesn't seem to be as noticeable in these areas as along the Southeastern and Mid-Atlantic coast.

In other dialect areas, such as Philadelphia, /au/ may be pronounced with an [æ] nucleus, as in the vowel of *bat*, rather than an [a] or [ɑ], so that a word like *down* is pronounced as [dæʊn], while in an area such as Tidewater Virginia (and in many parts of Canada), /au/ is pronounced with an "uh" ([ə]) nucleus, so that a phrase such as "out and about" may come out sounding more like "oat and a-boat," at least to the casual listener. As we can see, there are lots of dialect differences that may affect the diphthongs of English, including differences in the pronunciation of both the nucleus and the glide. A partial list of some of these differences is given below.

Differences in the production of the nucleus
- Backing, raising of the nucleus of /ai/ in *tide* [tɔid] (Outer Banks of North Carolina; Charleston, South Carolina)
- Fronting and raising of the nucleus of /au/ in *mouth* [mæʊθ] (e.g. Philadelphia, Pittsburgh, other regions)

- Raising of the nucleus of /au/ in *out* [əut] (e.g. Ontario, Canada; Tidewater Virginia)
- Raising of the nucleus of /ai/ in *price* [prəɪs] (Tidewater Virginia; Canada)

Differences in glide production
- Ungliding of diphthong in tide [tad] (e.g. South)
- Ungliding of diphthong in *price* [pra:s] (e.g. Highland South, Texas South)
- Ungliding of diphthong in *down* [da:n] (e.g. Pittsburgh)
- Ungliding of diphthong in *boil* [bɔ:l] (e.g. parts of the South)
- Ungliding of vowel in *goat* [got] (e.g. parts of Minnesota, Wisconsin; Charleston, South Carolina)
- Ungliding of vowel in *face* [fes] (e.g. parts of Minnesota, Wisconsin; Charleston, South Carolina)
- Fronting of the glide in *mouth* [maɪθ] (e.g. coastal Maryland, Virginia, North Carolina)

Sometimes, when a vowel moves into the phonetic space of another vowel, the tendency to preserve distinctiveness does not come into play, and the two vowels simply end up sharing the same phonetic space. When this happens, the distinctiveness between the two vowels is lost, and we say that a MERGER has occurred. One of the most noticeable and most widespread mergers currently taking place in American English dialects is the merger of /ɔ/ and /ɑ/, so that the vowels in word pairs such as *caught/cot*, *hawk/ hock*, and *Dawn/Don* now sound alike. As we will discuss in chapter 5, the area affected by this merger is quite large and is growing rapidly, spreading from centers such as western Pennsylvania to encompass a vast portion of the American West. This merger is so commonplace that it may soon be considered part of mainstream or standard English rather than a regional variation. In fact, the second author of this book was surprised to find that a group of college students she was teaching refused to believe that /ɔ/ and /ɑ/ are considered to be two different phonemes in English. Apparently, these students had never even heard the vowels pronounced differently, let alone produced them that way themselves.

In many instances, a merger only takes place in restricted phonetic contexts. Sounds are highly sensitive to their phonetic context, including the sounds they occur next to, the positions they occupy in words, and whether or not they occur in accented, or stressed, syllables. It is quite common for a merger to take place in one phonetic context but not in another. In one well-known case, the /ɪ/ and /ɛ/ vowels are merged, but only when the following segment is a nasal sound such as [n]. Thus, in many Southern American dialects, there is no contrast between items such as *pin* and *pen* (with both usually pronounced as [pɪn]) or *tinder* and *tender*. In these same dialects, the vowels in word pairs like *pit* [pɪt] and *pet* [pɛt] actually remain distinct, even though caricatures of Southern speech by outsiders may erroneously depict all [ɪ]'s and [ɛ]'s as sounding the same. Similarly, speakers of many US dialects do not distinguish between *morning* and *mourning*, and speakers of some dialects do not distinguish between *sure* and *shore*. In these cases the critical phonetic environment for the merger is the following [r]. Other mergers are not confined solely to one particular phonetic context but are nonetheless more likely to occur in one environment than in other places. For example, the merger of the /ɪ/ of *pill* with the /i/ of *peel* in Southern American English is more likely to take place before [l] than in most other contexts. Similarly, the merger of the /u/ in *fool* with the /ʊ/ of *full* which is affecting some Northern and Southwestern varieties only takes place before [l], as does the merger of the vowels in word pairs such as *bail* and *bell* or *whale* and *well*. In American English, vowels that are followed by nasal sounds such as [m] and [n] and liquid sounds like [r] and [l] are more prone to merger than vowels in other phonetic environments. For example, in many dialects of English, the vowels of *merry*, *Mary*, and *marry* are all merged before *r*, whereas in at least one dialect (Philadelphia), the vowels of *merry* and *Murray* are merged while the vowels in *Mary* and *marry* remain distinct. Following is a partial list of some mergers that characterize varieties of American English:

Mergers in American English dialects
- /ɔ/ and /ɑ/, as in *Dawn* and *Don* (Western Pennsylvania, gradually fanning out to encompass much of the Western US)
- /ɪ/ and /ɛ/ before nasals, as in *pin* and *pen* (South)
- /i/ and /ɪ/, especially before [l], as in *field* and *filled* (South; sporadically elsewhere)
- /e/ and /ɛ/ before [l], as in *sale* and *sell* (South; sporadically in Northern areas)
- /u/ and /ʊ/, as in *pool* and *pull* (South; sporadically in Northern areas)
- /e/, /ɛ/, and /æ/ before /r/, as in *Mary*, *merry*, *marry* (many areas of the US, including the South)
- /hy/ and /y/ in *Hugh* and *you* (New York City, Philadelphia; sporadically elsewhere)
- /hw/ and /w/ in *which* and *witch* (throughout much of the United States)

The last two mergers in the above list involve glides rather than vowels. Glides are intermediate sounds between consonants and vowels.

Exercise 3

As noted, one of the interesting cases of vowel merger before [r] involves the vowels of the words *merry*, *Mary*, *marry*, and *Murray*, or *berry*, *beary* (acting like a bear), *Barry*, and *bury*. Ask several people who come from different regions of the country to pronounce these items and observe which items are pronounced the same and which are pronounced differently. What patterns of merger and distinction do you observe? What other sets of items fall into this general pattern? Can you identify any correlation between dialect region and the patterns of merger and non-merger in the speech of those you question?

There are also cases in which differences between consonants may be eliminated, or NEUTRALIZED. One classic case of neutralization is so-called "*g*-dropping." When the nasal segment represented phonetically as [ŋ] (often spelled "ng") occurs at the end of a word in an unstressed syllable (as in *fighting*), it can be produced as the sound [n] (*fightin'*). This process makes the final nasal segment of *taken* [tekɪn] and *takin'* [tekɪn] or *waken* [wekɪn] and *makin'* [wekɪn] phonetically the same. Unfortunately, the popular term "*g*-dropping" to describe this process is somewhat misleading, since the process really involves the substitution of one nasal sound for another rather than the loss of a sound.

In many Southern dialects, the [z] and [ð] sounds in words such as *wasn't* and *heathen* become [d] before nasal sounds, resulting in pronunciations such as *wadn't* and *headn*. Thus, we can say that the contrast between [z] and [ð] is neutralized before nasals in these varieties. And, of course, there is the stereotypical *dese*, *dem*, and *dose* for *these*, *them*, and *those*, in which [d] and [ð] are neutralized word-initially, as well as the neutralization in some vernacular dialects of [f] and [θ] in word-final position, as in *roof* for *Ruth*. While there are a number of cases of neutralization across dialects, the phonetic contexts in which these processes occur are usually highly restricted. Many cases of consonant neutralization result from the way in which sounds are pronounced when they occur next to each other rather than to how sounds are organized into systems.

The kinds of differences illustrated so far all concern instances in which a sound in one dialect corresponds to a different sound in another variety. As we discussed in chapter 2, there are also instances where sounds are added or deleted, affecting the basic sequencing of sound segments. The addition and deletion of sounds, like neutralization, has to do with how sounds are pronounced when they occur in a particular sequence or with the arrangement of sounds into syllables rather than with overall changes in the organization of sound systems. Thus, addition and deletion processes tend to be restricted to certain phonetic contexts as well. For example, there are a number of dialects in which [r] and [l] may be deleted, as in *ca'd* [kɑd] for *card* or *he'p* [hɛp] for *help*. However, this deletion occurs only when the [r] or [l] follows a vowel; further, [l] is fully deleted only when it follows a vowel and precedes a LABIAL consonant – that is, one which is articulated using the lips, such as [p] or [f], as in *he'p* [hɛp] for *help* or *woof* [wʊf] for *wolf*. In other post-vowel environments (e.g. *cold*), [l] is likely to be weakened, or pronounced in a more vowel-like way, but it will not be completely absent. Deletion may also be contingent upon where a particular sound occurs in a word or whether the sound occurs in a stressed or unstressed syllable. For example, the deletion of the [w] sound of the word *one* in a phrase such as *young 'uns* "young ones" or *second 'un* "second one" is contingent upon the [w] being in word-initial, unstressed position.

Other cases of deletion have to do with how sounds are arranged into syllables. As discussed in chapter 2, it is not very "natural" for syllables to contain groups or clusters of consonants, and so these clusters tend to get reduced. Thus, speakers of practically all varieties of American English tend to reduce the final consonant clusters in words such as *west* [st], *find* [nd], *act* [kt], or *cold* [ld] to a single consonant, as in *wes'* [s], *fin'* [n], *ac'* [k], and *col'* [l] – particularly when speaking in informal style. Speakers of relatively standard varieties tend to restrict this process to instances in which the word following the cluster begins with a consonant (e.g. *Wes' Point, col' cuts*). On the other hand, speakers of some vernacular dialects may reduce the cluster regardless of the following segment (e.g. *Wes' End, col' outside*).

In another process relating to the sequencing of syllables, unstressed syllables at the beginning of words may be deleted, resulting in such pronunciations as *'lectricity* for *electricity* or *'member* for *remember*. There are also cases in which the number of syllables in words differs across dialects because of the deletion or insertion of vowels within the word. *Tire* and *fire* are two-syllable sequences in some dialects (i.e. [taɪːɚ], [faɪːɚ]) but single syllables in others. For example, in a number of Southern varieties, *tire* and *fire* may be pronounced as *tar* and *far*. Similarly, an item like *baloney* consists of three syllables for most English speakers (*ba-lo-ney*) but only two syllables for some other speakers (*blo-ney*).

As mentioned above, one of the most important differences between Southern and non-Southern dialects involves the absence of the [ɪ] glide on the /ai/ diphthong, so that words like *ride* and *time* are pronounced as *rahd* [raːd] and *tahm* [taːm] in Southern American varieties. Conversely, Southern American English is also distinguished from other varieties by the addition of a glide to some vowels which are not typically glided in non-Southern varieties. In some cases, the addition of this glide actually leads to changes in syllable structure. In most non-Southern varieties, words such as *bed* and *Bill* consist of only one syllable. However, in some Southern dialects, the vowels in these words are given such a prominent glide that the words sound almost like two-syllable sequences, as in *beyud* [bɛyəd] for *bed* and *Biyul* [biyʊl] for *Bill*. According to some researchers, the diphthongization, or BREAKING, of vowels is actually becoming more prominent in Southern varieties at the same time as it continues to be absent from non-Southern dialects (e.g. Feagin 1987; Labov 1994).

Finally, we should mention the potential for pronunciation differences that have to do with such matters as the intonational contours of sentences, the stress patterns of words, and the timing of syllables. These differences are referred to as SUPRASEGMENTAL or PROSODIC differences, since they involve overarching "melodic" considerations rather than individual sound segments and their arrangement into syllables. Although prosodic differences have been studied in far less detail than segmental differences, newer advances in technology allow for more precise measurement of these prosodic dimensions of speech. For example, several studies (Foreman 2000; Wolfram and Thomas 2002; Thomas and Reaser 2004) have shown that speakers of African American English tend to use more "pitch accents" (i.e. greater prominence on stressed syllables) and a wider pitch range than speakers of European American varieties. In addition, speakers of African American English (especially males) also seem to use a falsetto or very high pitch register more frequently than speakers of European American varieties. However, as with other phonological differences among dialects, differences in prosodic or suprasegmental features tend to be gradient rather than absolute, and so we cannot really say that certain groups of speakers have a "wide" pitch range while others have a "narrow" range, but only that certain groups have a wider range than others.

Variations in the stress patterns of words, mostly related to individual lexical items, also serve to separate the dialects of American English. For example, depending on what regional dialect they speak, people may stress either the first or second syllable in items such as *Júly/Julý*, *hótel/hotél*, and *théater/theáter*. Speakers may also give different rhythmic patterns to syllables and phrases according to what dialect they speak. For example, Spanish-influenced varieties of American English are sometimes characterized by what is referred to as "syllable-timed rhythm," where each syllable in a phrase such as *in the garden* is pronounced with equal length. On the other hand, speakers of most other American English dialects tend to have "phrase-timed rhythm," in which syllables which are more strongly stressed (e.g. the first syllable of *gárden*) are held longer than other syllables in the phrase. Computer-aided studies of speech timing (Fought and Fought 2003; Carter 2004), however, show that these differences are also gradient and that Spanish-influenced varieties of English are differentiated from other English dialects by the degree to which they use syllable-based timing vs.

stress-based timing rather than the use vs. non-use of one timing system or the other.

There are also varieties that exhibit a generalized lengthening of syllables. For example, evidence indicates that speakers of Southern American varieties tend to prolong vowel sounds for a slightly longer time than speakers of other varieties. This difference in vowel duration may be partly responsible for the popular perception that Southerners speak "slower" than most non-Southerners. However, we have to keep in mind that not all Southerners speak slower than all non-Southerners; in fact, there are some Southerners who speak faster than non-Southerners. Further, the subtle speech-rate differences that do exist between Southern and non-Southern varieties are often exaggerated in popular characterizations of Southern speech, most likely because speakers of Southern American English are often stigmatized as "dumb" and "uneducated" and thus "slower" than speakers of non-Southern varieties. Although speech-rate features are often very noticeable to casual observers of language variation, dialectologists and sociolinguists have only begun studying them systematically, and there is still a good deal of work to do in sorting out linguistic fact from popular stereotypes.

Although there may be some social stigma attached to certain pronunciation differences, phonological dialect differences, particularly vowel differences, are usually considered to be matters of curiosity rather than grounds for condemnation. Speakers may comment on the *o* of Wisconsin speech or the "broad *a*" of Boston as regional peculiarities without attaching particular social stigma or prestige to them. Consonantal differences are more apt to be socially diagnostic than vowel differences and may even lead to the stigmatization of speakers as "stupid" or "uneducated," as in the case of *dese*, *dem*, and *dose* for *these*, *them*, and *those*; *baf* for *bath*; and *takin'* for *taking*. While phonological differences may be of relatively little importance in terms of social prestige, they do play a central role in terms of regional identity. Thus, Southerners are more readily identified as Southerners by their /ai/ vowels than by any other single dialect feature, and Southerners themselves have come to take pride in their distinctive pronunciations as a badge of their unique regional identity and cultural heritage.

In terms of the principles governing the organization of language systems, it is difficult to explain why certain pronunciation changes take place in some regions or among some social groups and why other changes take place elsewhere. For example, it is hard to explain why Pittsburgh adopted the *dahntahn* pronunciation for *downtown* or why residents of Tangier and Smith Islands in the Chesapeake Bay adopted a pronunciation for *brown* that makes it sound like *brain* to outsiders. However, once a given pronunciation takes hold, it may persist for quite a long time as a symbolic marker of regional or social group identity.

3.4 Grammatical Differences

Grammatical variation may be discussed in terms of two types of language organization. One level, called MORPHOLOGY, relates to the way in which words are formed from their meaningful parts, or MORPHEMES. A word such as *girls* consists of two morphemes, the noun *girl* and the plural suffix *-s*; a word such as *buyers* consists of three morphemes, the verb *buy*, the agentive suffix *-er*, which changes a verb into a noun, and the plural suffix *-s*. Suffixes such as *-er*, which change the part of speech, or grammatical class, of the word to which they attach, are referred to as DERIVATIONAL suffixes. Endings such as the plural *-s* which do not alter the basic grammatical class and which serve to augment rather than change meaning are referred to as INFLECTIONAL suffixes. English has a relatively small set of inflectional suffixes, consisting of plural *-s*, (e.g. *girls*, *houses*), possessive *-s* (e.g. *John's hat*, *the girl's hat*), third-person present tense *-s* (e.g. *She runs*), past tense *-ed* (e.g. *John guessed*), participle *-ed* (e.g. *He has helped*), progressive *-ing* (e.g. *He is running*), and the comparative and superlative endings *-er* and *-est* (e.g. *smaller*, *smallest*).

Inflectional morphemes in English are susceptible to language variation in two ways, both of which make perfect sense in terms of the principles of language organization we presented in chapter 2, particularly the principle that states that language patterns should be as regular and straightforward as possible. In some cases, this principle leads to the loss of inflectional morphemes, whereas in other cases it leads to the creation of different forms. For example, some vernacular varieties, such as vernacular forms of African American English, are characterized by the loss of the third-person singular *-s* suffix (e.g. *She run* vs. *She runs*). This loss is the result of regularization: In modern English the third-person singular verb form is the only one that takes any suffix at all in the present tense. If we eliminate this *-s* ending, then all present tense verbs now have exactly the same form, no matter what subject we use them with (except *to be*, which is more irregular than other verbs). This regularization is illustrated below:

Standard English		Vernacular variety	
I run	we run	I run	we run
you run	you (pl.) run	you run	you (pl.) run
he/she/it runs	they run	he run	they run

Vernacular African American English also exhibits the absence of the *-s* possessive ending, as in *John hat* vs. *John's hat*. In this case, the ending has been lost because, in essence, it is a redundant marker; the positioning of *John* and *hat* is sufficient to indicate that *John* stands in a possessive relationship to *hat*. Similarly, in some Southern rural varieties, the plural

-*s* ending may be absent from nouns indicating measurement (e.g. *Go about four mile up the road*) but only when the plural noun is preceded by a quantifier (a word indicating a specific or general quantity such as *four, many*, or *some*), since it serves as a clear marker that the following noun is plural, thus making the -*s* ending superfluous.

Making language forms as regular and straightforward as possible also sometimes leads to the addition of inflectional endings. For example, in order to regularize the irregular person-number set, or paradigm, of possessive pronouns (*mine, yours, hers/ his/ its, ours, yours, theirs*), speakers of vernacular dialects may add various inflectional endings to some of the pronoun forms, as illustrated below:

Standard English		*Vernacular variety I*		*Vernacular variety II*	
mine	ours	mines	ours	mine	ourn
yours	yours (pl.)	yours	yours	yourn	yourn
hers/his/its	theirs	hers/his	theirs	hern/hisn	theirn

Finally, regularization may lead to the use of different inflectional markers in different dialects rather than to the differential presence or absence of such markers. For example, the irregular plural ending -*en* in *oxen* may be regularized to -*es* in vernacular varieties, while irregular past tense verbs may be marked with the regular -*ed* suffix (e.g. *throwed* vs. *threw*) rather than by a vowel difference as in standard varieties.

Morphological differences that are due to regularization carry a great deal of social significance in American society, and listeners draw sharp distinctions between vernacular and standard speaking groups on the basis of the use or non-use of regularized morphological forms. In part, the prominence of regularized morphological forms may be attributed to the fact that all speakers have an unconscious inclination to regularize irregular forms. This tendency is overcome only by paying special attention to the irregular forms, which must be learned by rote since they are not as linguistically "natural" as regularized forms. This focused attention on learning these forms subsequently makes them sensitive to social marking. In other words, because speakers of standard varieties may have struggled to learn irregular forms such as *oxen* and *thought* during their school years, they will be quick to notice when regularized forms are used and just as quick to stigmatize speakers who use them.

Furthermore, we have to keep in mind that not all vernacular word-formation processes are the result of regularization or simplification. As discussed in chapter 2, there is a tendency to mark forms as clearly as possible so that listeners will pick up on all intended meanings. This tendency competes with the tendency toward regularity and simplicity of language form. Thus, vernacular word-formation processes may involve complications as well as simplifications, and vernacular speakers may sometimes use inflectional endings where they are not strictly "needed," just to ensure that meanings are clear. For example, speakers of some vernacular varieties may "double mark" comparative and superlative adjectives, as in *more farther* or *most fastest*, and highly vernacular speakers may even double mark plurals, as in *feets* or *woodses*. We also have to keep in mind that speakers of vernacular varieties may sometimes retain morphological markings which have been lost in standard varieties through processes of regularization and simplification. For example, speakers of some historically isolated Southern varieties such as Appalachian English may retain an *a-* prefix on *-ing* verbs (*She was a-huntin' and a-fishin'*) even though this prefix, which used to indicate ongoing action, has long since vanished from standard varieties of English.

We summarize below some of the morphological features of various dialects in the US, as introduced in this section and in chapter 2.

Regularized forms
- Absence of inflectional morphemes
  - Third-person singular -*s* absence; e.g. *He go* (African American English)
  - Possessive -*s* absence; e.g. *the man hat* (African American English)
  - Plural -*s* absence; e.g. *five mile* (Southern vernacular dialects)
- Addition of inflectional endings
  - Possessive pronouns; e.g. *mines* (African American English; selected vernacular dialects); *hisn* (southern Appalachian dialects)
- More transparent forms
  - Double-marked comparatives and superlatives; e.g. *most beautifulest* (most vernacular dialects)
  - Marking of second-person plural forms; e.g. *y'all* (Southern dialects); *you'ns* (southern Appalachian dialects, Pittsburgh dialect); *youse/youse guys* (Northern dialects, especially Northeastern)
  - Retention of *a-* prefix; e.g. *a-huntin' and a-fishin'* (Appalachian English)

The other major level of grammatical organization, SYNTAX, refers to the arrangement of words into larger units such as phrases or sentences. As with morphology, we find that the tendency toward making meaning differences transparent may lead to dialect differentiation in syntax. For example, it is common for speakers of vernacular varieties to use auxiliary, or helping, verbs to give verbs special meanings that can only be indicated in standard varieties through adding a good bit of additional material to the sentence, if the meaning can be conveyed at all. Vernacular varieties may be characterized by special auxiliaries such as COMPLETIVE *done*, as in *He done washed the clothes*, HABITUAL *be*, as in *Sometimes my ears be itching*, and AVERTIVE *liketa*, as in *It was so cold, I liketa froze.* If speakers of standard varieties wish to convey the meanings indicated by these special auxiliaries, they must resort to complex constructions such as *He washed the clothes and has now completely finished washing them, Sometimes my ears itch and sometimes they don't,* and *It was below freezing outside, so I could have frozen in theory, but I was in no real danger.* Auxiliaries may also cluster together in different ways to convey special meanings. Thus, DOUBLE MODALS (e.g. *might could*) are commonplace in Southern varieties and serve to convey a meaning of lessened intensity. For example, a sentence such as *I might could go* indicates that the speaker may be able to go but isn't quite sure.

Other verb-related differences in syntactic structure have to do with the types of structures that can co-occur with particular verbs. For example, some verbs take a particular kind of object in one dialect and a different kind of object, or no object at all, in another dialect. Thus, some vernacular dialects of English use the verb *beat* without an object (e.g. *The Cowboys beat*), whereas other varieties only use it with a direct object – that is, as a TRANSITIVE VERB (e.g. *The Cowboys beat the Giants*). In a similar vein, the verb *learn* in some dialects may co-occur with a subject indicating the person who is conveying knowledge to someone else, as in *The teacher learned me my lesson.* In other dialects, including standard varieties, *learn* can take as its subject only the person or people who are the recipients of the knowledge, as in *The students learned the lesson*; otherwise, the verb *teach* must be used. Although the reduction of the *teach/learn* pair to *learn* alone is highly stigmatized, there are other verbs indicating similar relationships of converseness which have been reduced to a single verb with little or no negative social repercussion. For example, the verb *rent*, as in *The landlord rented an apartment to me* and *I rented an apartment from the landlord,* was originally used only with subjects indicating the recipient of the item of property, as in the latter example above. The reciprocal verb *let* was used when the subject indicated who was bestowing the item, as in *The landlord let the apartment to me.* Interestingly, speakers of British English still use the *let/rent* distinction, even though *rent* alone is quite "proper" according to the rules of standard American English.

In another case of dialect differentiation based on the types of structures that can co-occur with particular verbs, we find that the verb *need* may co-occur with either *-ing* or *-ed* verbs, depending on the dialect area. In most of the US, *need* takes an *-ing* complement, as in *The car needs washing.* However, in some areas, most notably Western Pennsylvania and Eastern Ohio, *need* takes an *-ed* verb, as in *The car needs washed.* The *need* + verb + *-ed* pattern is also found in some areas of the British Isles, particularly Scotland. Although using an *-ed* verb with *need* may sound awkward or even "wrong" to speakers who use *-ing* with *need,* there is nothing intrinsically more "correct" or more logical about using the *-ing* form. This is evidenced in the fact that there is a verb which is very similar to *need* – namely, *want* – which takes an -*ed* rather than -*ing* complement in all US dialect areas (e.g. *I want the car washed*). Interestingly, though, there are parts of England, including parts of the Midlands and North, where *want* takes -*ing* (*I want the car washing*), thus demonstrating that -*ed* with *want* is no more "correct" than -*ing* with *need*.

Another type of syntactic variation involves patterns of AGREEMENT among different elements in a sentence. Agreement relations can be seen as either co-occurrence relations or as the "double marking" of meaning. For example, in standard varieties of English, we say that third-person singular present tense verbs must "agree" with their subjects (e.g. *She runs five miles every day*) because whenever a third-person singular subject occurs, it must co-occur with the -*s* form of a verb. However, the -*s* marker also represents a "double marking," in the sense that we can clearly tell that a sentence has a third-person singular subject without the -*s* marker on the end of the verb simply by looking at the subject itself.

Agreement patterns between subjects and verbs in English have changed substantially during the course of the history of the language. In particular, there has been a longstanding movement toward reducing the extent of agreement. In standard varieties of English today, the only agreement marking with almost all present tense verbs is the third-person singular -*s* (or -*es*, as in *goes*) which we have just been discussing. In the past tense, of course, there is no agreement marking at all, since we use the same verb ending (-*ed*) no matter what subject the verb occurs with (e.g. *I/you/she/we/they walked*). In Old and Middle English, however, there were agreement endings for use with first, second, and third person subjects, as well as for use with both singulars and plurals and for both past and present tense verbs. This complex agreement system eventually developed into today's simpler system. Today, there are only a couple of verbs that still show slightly more complicated patterning in the present tense – namely, *be*, which is clearly highly irregular, and *do*, whose third-person singular form, *does*, has a different vowel sound in addition to an -*es* ending. In the past tense, only *be* remains irregular, since it has two forms, *was* and *were*.

Among speakers of vernacular dialects, there is a strong tendency to continue the tradition of eliminating complications and irregularities in the English subject–verb agreement system. This tendency may be manifested in several different ways, including the frequent use of *don't* with third-person singular subjects in vernacular dialects throughout the US (e.g. *He don't like me anymore*), the regularization of *be* (e.g. *We was going to the store*), and the absence of the third singular -*s* form, as discussed above (e.g. *She walk a mile every day*).

Other vernacular subject–verb agreement patterns have to do with the retention of historical agreement patterns. For example, in varieties such as

Appalachian English and Outer Banks English, speakers often use -*s* endings with third-person plural subjects (e.g. *People goes, The boys works in the store*) as well as with third-person singular subjects. Although a structure such as *people goes* is highly stigmatized, it is not the result of ignorance of the standard English subject–verb agreement pattern; nor does it represent a lack of subject–verb agreement. Rather, it is a retention of a pattern that was commonplace and, indeed, perfectly acceptable, a couple of centuries ago in such varieties as Scots-Irish English, spoken in the province of Ulster in what is now Northern Ireland.

As with a number of other language structures we have looked at thus far, we find that the use of the -*s* verb ending with third-person plural subjects shows a rather intricate patterning that may not be evident at first glance. Speakers who use -*s* in the third-person plural do not use it with all third-person plural subjects to an equal extent. Rather, the -*s* ending is used more frequently with certain types of subjects, including so-called collectives. Collectives are nouns that identify some sort of group or collection. They may be fairly specific, as in *government, family*, or *team*; or they may refer to more general collections of people or objects, as in *people, some of them*, or *a lot of them*. Because each of these words and phrases refers to one group composed of a number of members, there has always been a certain amount of uncertainty as to whether collective nouns should be treated as singular or plural. Some varieties, including standard American English varieties, classify them as plural and so use them with plural verbs, as in *people go*. Others classify them as singular and thus use them with verbs ending in -*s*, as in *people goes*. Neither agreement system can really claim to be the definitive, "correct" form, however. This is evidenced in the fact that, although general collectives such as *people* are considered to be plural in standard American English (e.g. *People are visiting*), there are some specific collectives which are held to be singular (e.g. *The government was debating the issue; The team was winning*). Interestingly, these specific collectives are considered to be plural in standard British English (*The government were debating; The team were winning*), a variety which is certainly highly regarded for its "correctness." Thus, we see that subject–verb agreement patterns, which we often consider to be based on rigid, inflexible rules, are not even consistent across current standard varieties of English, let alone in vernacular varieties or in a single variety over the course of time. This is an important realization indeed, considering that many speakers of American English believe that "standard" subject–verb agreement patterns are inflexible and permanent.

Syntactic agreement relations may affect other elements of a sentence besides subjects and verbs. In particular, the "double negatives" we discussed in chapter 2 (e.g. *I didn't do nothing*) may be viewed as "negative agreement" as well as double marking, since double negation, or, more properly, multiple negation, involves using indefinite forms (e.g. *nothing* rather than *anything*) which agree with the negative form of the verb. Many distinctive dialect differences in syntax involve agreement patterns between words or morphemes, and they are among the most evident social markers within American English.

Finally, syntactic differences may involve the basic linear arrangement of words in phrases or sentences. Although there is considerable variation across languages with respect to the sequencing of different types of phrases within sentences, there is relatively little variation of this type within English itself. Nonetheless, there are a few occasions where the ordering of elements within sentences varies across regional or social dialects. For example, the ordering of words in questions may vary, as in *What that was?* vs. *What was that?* Similarly, the placement of adverbs may differ slightly in different dialects, as in *We'd all the time get into trouble* vs. *We'd get into trouble all the time.* Given the possibilities for sequencing differences in sentences, however, these differences play a relatively minor role in the differentiation of American English dialects. Some of the major syntactic differences in the dialects of American English are summarized in the following list:

Special auxiliaries
- Completive *done*; e.g., *She done ate the food* (Southern vernacular dialects)
- Habitual *be*; e.g. *Sometimes they be acting weird* (African American English)
- Avertive *liketa*; e.g. *He liketa died* (Southern vernacular dialects)
- Remote time *béen*; e.g. *I béen met her a long time ago* (African American English; see chapter 7)
- Double modals; e.g. *They might could do it* (Southern dialects)

Co-occurrence patterns with verbs
- Transitive–intransitive; e.g. *The team beat* (African American English)
- Reciprocal verbs; e.g. *The teacher learned me what I needed to know* (some vernacular dialects)
- Participle forms; e.g. *The cars needs washed* (Midland)

Agreement patterns
- Negative agreement (multiple negation); e.g. *They didn't do nothing to nobody* (Most vernacular dialects)
- Subject–verb agreement with *be*; e.g. *We was there* (most vernacular dialects)
- Past tense *be* in negative sentences; e.g. *I weren't there* (Southeastern and Mid-Atlantic coastal vernacular dialects)
- Inflectional *-s* on third-person plural verbs; e.g. *The dogs barks* (Southern rural dialects, Appalachian English)

Linear order
- Adverb placement; e.g. *We're all the time in trouble* (Southern rural dialects)
- Question formation; e.g. *What that is?* (African American English)

As we see in this list, some of the dialect differences in syntax converge with other kinds of processes such as regularization. The absence of a verbal suffix in a sentence like *She go home* is a kind of regularization that relates to agreement. Similarly, regularization of past tense *be* to *was* is a change related to agreement.

Exercise 4

The following sentence pairs represent different kinds of syntactic variation as discussed above. These types include the following: (1) the use of auxiliaries or verbal markers to give verbs special meanings (e.g. the use of double modals or avertive *liketa*), (2) co-occurrence patterns with verbs (e.g. whether or not a verb needs an object), (3) agreement patterns (e.g. agreement between subjects and verbs), and (4) variation in the linear order of structures (e.g. *He's all the time talking*). Identify the type of syntactic variation in the following sentence pairs or sets of sentences according to the categories set forth above. For example, a sentence pair such as *The Rams beat/The Rams beat the Cowboys* would be classified as type 2 in this classification, since the variation relates to whether or not the verb *beat* takes an object. In your description of each difference, be as specific as possible about the variation you observe.

1   *Did ever a stray animal come to your house?/Did a stray animal ever come to your house?*
2   *Some people makes soap from pig fat/Some people make soap from pig fat.*
3   *They started to running/They started a-running/They started running.*
4   *There's six people in our family/There're six people in our family.*
5   *They made him out the liar/They made him out to be the liar.*
6   *We once in a while will have a party/We will have a party once in a while/Once in a while we will have a party.*
7   *The dog ugly/The dog's ugly.*
8   *The man béen met him/The man met him a long time ago.*

3.5 Language Use and Pragmatics

Knowing a language involves more than knowing the meanings of the words and the phonological and grammatical structures of the language. In every language and dialect, there are a variety of ways to convey the same information or accomplish the same purpose, and the choice of *how* to say something may depend upon *who* is talking to *whom* under *what* social circumstances. The term PRAGMATICS is used to refer to how language is used in context to achieve particular purposes. One important concept in the study of pragmatics is the SPEECH ACT, which refers to an utterance that accomplishes a social action, such as requesting, making a promise, complimenting, or apologizing.

Speakers of all languages and dialects are quite capable of performing the same basic kinds of speech acts – directing, requesting, apologizing, and so forth – but how these speech acts are carried out and the conditions under which they are considered to be appropriate varies considerably across cultural groups. Statements may be strong and direct or they may be softer and less direct. For example, consider the range of sentences that might be used to direct a person to take out the garbage.

Take out the garbage!
Can you take out the garbage?
Would you mind taking out the garbage?
Let's take out the garbage.
It would be nice if someone would take out the garbage.
The garbage sure is piling up.
Garbage day is tomorrow.

Each of these sentences may be used to accomplish the goal of getting a person to take out the garbage. However, the sentences show varying degrees of directness, ranging from the direct command at the top of the list to the indirect statement at the bottom of the list. The sentences also differ in terms of their relative politeness and situational appropriateness. For example, a person of superior status (e.g. parent, supervisor) might use the most direct form when speaking with a subordinate, whereas a person of subordinate status would not typically have the option of using a direct command with someone in a higher social position. Knowledge of when and how to use certain forms is just as important for communication as the literal understanding of structures and words, and the failure to abide by cultural conventions for language use can have severe implications for how people are perceived within and across social groups.

Different social and cultural groups often have contrasting expectations about the appropriate use of direct or indirect expressions. Working-class African American parents have sometimes been observed to be more direct than European Americans in speaking to children, especially in correcting them. For example, a working-class African American parent or teacher might use a direct order in directing a child who has strayed: "Get back here, Melvin!" In a similar situation, however, a European American teacher might attempt to accomplish the function of getting the child to return to the group by saying, "Melvin, you need to stay with the group" or "Melvin, would you like to stay with the group?" Because indirectness has come to be valued in some settings, such as the school or workplace, teachers have been taught that "I like the way Jeffrey is keeping his eyes on the blackboard" is better than "Look at what I'm writing on the chalkboard, Kim." Contrasting expectations about directness may lead to misunderstandings across different groups. Children who are accustomed to a more direct style of adult communication may, for example, misconstrue indirect commands as less serious than their more direct counterparts and thus consider compliance optional. On the other hand, children who are used to more indirectness may feel threatened or intimidated by adults who consider directness to be the appropriate norm for directives with children.

Studies show that women in positions of authority in the workplace are often expected to be more indirect in their instructions to workers than male authorities and that conflict arises when women do not meet expectations of indirectness (Tannen 1995). Thus, women who use direct commands may be given such negative labels as "pushy" or even "bitchy," whereas men who are direct in their instructions to workers may be labeled simply as "aggressive" or "demanding," words which are far less negative than "pushy" and may even be considered positive. In matters of directness vs. indirectness, expectations for gender-appropriate behavior may play a more important role than differing norms across different ethnic, social class, or regional groups, although all these factors tend to intersect in quite complex ways in determining the "appropriate" degree of directness or indirectness for any given speech act.

Related to the issue of cultural differences in directness is the distinction between literal and non-literal language use. For example, a statement such as "What are you doing?" can have both a literal and a non-literal interpretation. It may be interpreted literally as a request for explanation among workers who are performing a task together. However, if a teacher or parent utters this sentence upon entering a classroom full of misbehaving children, it is not intended to be a literal request for information but an indirect directive to get the children to stop misbehaving. In fact, if the children were to respond to the question as if it were a literal request (e.g. by answering "We're throwing things at each other"), this might evoke a more direct reprimand, perhaps about the inappropriateness of the response itself (e.g. "Don't act smart!").

Conventions for interpreting statements as literal or non-literal vary considerably among different social and cultural groups, as does the value accorded to literal vs. non-literal language use. For example, Shirley Brice Heath (1983) found that European Americans in one particular working-class community valued perfectly factual children's stories more highly than African Americans in the same community, who placed higher value on stories embellished by non-literal language use, including invented quotations. This contrast contributed to the negative valuation of African American children by schoolteachers, since storytelling conventions in the classroom setting were largely reflective of mainstream, European American values regarding literalness. Conventions regarding literal meaning can also vary within ethnic groups, based on such factors as gender. For example, Marjorie Harness Goodwin (1990) noticed that whereas pre-adolescent African American boys frequently referred to their abilities and actions in exaggerated terms, African American girls of the same age criticized each other for bragging. In some cultural groups, not only is exaggerating one's abilities considered inappropriate, but even making literal statements about one's personal qualities is considered to be "bad manners," since it is expected that personal strengths will be downplayed, in keeping with a value on personal humility. Thus, we see that underlying cultural values often enter into the determination of situational appropriateness concerning literal and non-literal meaning, as they do for directness and indirectness.

Unfortunately, we have a tendency to become so accustomed to our own community's norms for carrying out speech acts that we fail to notice when contrasting conventions within another group might be interfering with communication. Our initial reaction is to interpret differences in language use based on our own group's conventions. For example, we interpret more directness than we are accustomed to as rudeness and less literalness as deceitful. Conversely, we interpret more indirectness than we are used to as a sign of weakness and more literalness as a lack of tact.

Although there are many types of language-use differences, a couple of areas are particularly sensitive to variation. One involves ADDRESS FORMS – that is, the titles and names speakers use when referring to the people they are talking to, such as the use of *Mr* or *Ms* with a last name or the use of a first name only. Considerations of social status, age, ethnicity, gender, age, familiarity, formality, and so forth all come into play when determining the form of address that is appropriate for a particular person in a given situation, but in many instances these diverse social factors can be reduced to the dimensions of power and solidarity. Loosely defined, "power" refers to how much control conversational participants have over each other, while "solidarity" refers to how much intimacy there is between addressors and addressees. Different regional and social groups weigh power and solidarity differently in determining appropriate address forms, and thus speakers in these groups may use quite different forms to address a single individual in a given social setting. For example, many middle-class European Americans treat social status as more important than age in their choice of address forms, so that an older person working as a laborer may be addressed by his or her first name by a younger person. Conversely, speakers in many other ethnic communities in America consider age to take precedence over social status, and so younger speakers would address an older laborer by title and last name.

There are various combinations of titles and names that may be used in addressing people, including some that are unique to specific regions. In the South, a wide range of adults are addressed with the respect labels *Sir* and *Ma'am*, including parents, whereas in the North only a few adults with special status are addressed by these forms. Similarly, although non-Southerners tend to think of titles such as *Mr*, *Mrs*, and *Ms* as indicative of unequal power relations, Southern speakers may use *Mr* or *Miss* with a first name to indicate special closeness. For example, young children or subordinate workers may address Marge and Walt Wolfram as *Miss Marge* and *Mr Walt*. In some situations, such address forms suggest a sort of extended kinship relationship, so that children of Marge and Walt's close friends might address the couple as *Miss Marge and Mr Walt* but only until the children reach adolescence. Such terms have also been used traditionally in the South by long-term domestic help in addressing their bosses in the home. In the North, the terms *aunt* and *uncle* may be used to indicate figurative kinship relationships with close friends of parents, including godparents.

Dialect differences in address forms are frequently judged as "rude" or "polite" by speakers from outside a particular regional or social group, and those who use inappropriately "familiar" forms are held to be "rude," while those who use inappropriately "formal" terms are considered to be insincerely deferential, or overly "polite." In reality, of course, different address forms are simply reflective of different conventions for "appropriate" language use.

Exercise 5

One of the regional and cultural differences in language conventions is sometimes referred to as "Southern politeness." Can you think of language use conventions that might be included under this rubric? Are there differences in politeness conventions, address forms, directness, literalness, and so forth that might account for the perception that Southerners are more polite than Northerners? Think of concrete examples of language usages that might be a reflection of regional and cultural differences in norms for interacting with strangers and friends. To what extent do you think that the notion that Southerners are more polite than Northerners is a valid interpretation of differences in language use conventions?

Related to address forms are conventions for greeting and leave-taking, which involve ritualized forms that are not to be interpreted literally. In most cases, greeting routines simply involve rote memorization of a limited set of formulaic exchanges and an understanding of the appropriate circumstances for their use. Thus, the appropriate response to "What up?" or "S'up?" when used as a greeting among African American speakers is simply a rote response such as "Nothing to me" rather than a literal or spontaneous response such as, "A number of students are currently on their way to class, and you and I are talking." Similarly, speakers learn to respond to the greeting "What's up?" with "Not much," even if they are undergoing dramatic, life-changing experiences, just as they learn to reply to "How ya doing?" with "Fine," even if they are currently feeling miserable. Of course, greeting routines may vary across different settings. Greetings themselves may range from *Yo* in Northern cities such as New York and Philadelphia to *Howdy* in some parts of the South (e.g. parts of Texas) to *Hey* in other parts of the South (e.g. North Carolina). Telephone greetings are also different from face-to-face encounters, and those accompanying service exchanges (e.g. between service provider and customer/client) are different from greetings between friends. For our purposes, however, it is most important to recognize that greeting routines are sensitive to regional, ethnic, gender, age, and status differences in American society. Although greetings are highly ritualized and are not meant to be taken literally, their social significance in establishing interactional relationships may be highly significant.

Similarly, conversational closings carry great social weight at the same time that their informational content is highly limited. Speakers do not simply turn away from each other abruptly and without explanation when ending a cooperative conversation. First of all, a participant may "pass" a potential turn in the conversation by saying something like "OK," "Well," or "So." This signals a desire to end the conversation, which may be accepted or rejected by the other participants. Then a speaker engages in one of several leave-taking routines, including offering a compliment (e.g. "It was nice to talk to you"), providing a "reasonable" excuse for terminating the conversation (e.g. "I'll let you get back to your work now," "I've got a meeting in five minutes"), or making reference to a future meeting ("See you later"). We typically cannot say things such as "This conversation is boring, so I'm leaving" (as someone once did to the senior author) or "I'd rather be talking to Dave than you," even if such a feeling represents the real reason for closing a conversation. As with other areas of language use, conventions for "appropriate" leave-taking may vary from group to group. Thus, it is not surprising that an older speaker expecting a conventionalized and relatively formal parting statement such as "I enjoyed talking with you" may interpret a younger speaker's innovative and informal closing, "I'm outty" as rude and inappropriate.

Failing to recognize conventional cues for closing a conversation can lead to some awkward situations, and someone who is talking with speakers from a different cultural group may not be able to figure out the appropriate moment for leave-taking or how to allow the other speakers to exit the conversation gracefully. Even within a single culture, there are vast differences in how conversations are closed. For example, many of us have come across speakers who do not seem to be able to pick up on any of our cues that we wish to terminate a conversation, even though they may share a common cultural background with us. Knowing how to close off a conversation is just as important as knowing how to start one, and those who fail to do so "appropriately" may be subject to the same sort of social censure as those who use the "wrong" address forms or give commands which are unexpectedly direct or indirect.

Topics of conversation also may differ according to the social or regional group of the participants involved. The determination of "safe" topics of discussion varies according to situational context and social relationships among speakers. A middle-class European American might consider a question like "What do you do for a living?" as an appropriate conversational opener at a casual social gathering, but the same question might be considered inappropriate by some minority groups in the same situation, who may interpret this as an indirect and inappropriate request for information about status. The appropriateness of direct questions about income and cost (e.g. house, car, etc.) may also vary from group to group. Regional and social groups may also differ in the amount of "small talk" that is appropriate before getting to the heart of the interaction. For example, "small talk" may be an important preliminary to getting down to business in some Southern areas or among some Latino/a groups but is not considered to be necessary by speakers in some other regions. Conventions for raising new topics and continuing with old ones also vary across groups. Some groups expect speakers to respond to all new topics raised in a conversation, while in other groups conversational participants may simply pass over a new topic without comment and without giving offense.

As with differences in other areas of language use, cross-regional and cross-cultural differences concerning conversational topics may lead to misunderstandings and negative evaluations of speakers from cultural groups other than one's own. However, we must bear in mind that a difference such as the use of more "small talk" than we are accustomed to does not necessarily mean that a speaker is "beating around the bush." Nor does less small talk mean that speakers are overly cold and businesslike. Rather, such differences are often simply reflective of differences in cultural conventions for the appropriate use of language in its social setting.

Once a topic is chosen and a conversation initiated, then matters of conversational "turn-taking" arise. Knowing when it is acceptable or obligatory to take a turn in a conversation is essential to the cooperative development of discourse. This knowledge involves such factors as knowing how to recognize appropriate turn-exchange points and knowing how long the pauses between turns should be. It is also important to know how (and if) one may talk while someone else is talking – that is, if conversational *overlap* is allowed. Since not all conversations follow all the rules for turn-taking, it is also necessary to know how to "repair" a conversation that has been thrown off course by undesired overlap or a misunderstood comment.

Cultural differences in matters of turn-taking can lead to conversational breakdown, misinterpretation of intentions, and interpersonal and intergroup conflict. For example, people from cultural groups accustomed to relatively long pauses between turns (e.g. Native American English speakers in the Southwest) may feel that they have been denied their fair share of the conversational "floor" when they are talking with people who are used to shorter pauses, because the short-pause speakers always step in and speak before the long-pause people. To further complicate matters, another feature of long-pause conversational style is a prohibition against overlapping talk. Those who do not allow overlapping conversation may feel interrupted by speakers from groups who are used to conversational overlap, such as Jewish speakers in New York City. Conversely, those who are accustomed to their listeners' interjecting comments while they are speaking may feel that those who fail to do so are not showing enough involvement in the conversation and are unenthusiastic about the subject matter.

One particular type of overlapping talk found among a wide range of social and regional groups is BACKCHANNELING. Backchanneling involves interject-ing small utterances such as *Mmmhmm*, *Uh-huh*, *Yeah*, and *Right* – or even just nodding the head – into the conversation in order to let the current speaker know that he or she may continue speaking. Different groups naturally vary in terms of the kinds of reinforcement offered to speakers by their listeners, and sometimes these differences may lead speakers to feel that their conversational contribution is not being appreciated (when there is too little backchanneling) or that their listeners are displaying insincere interest in what they have to say (when there is too much or the wrong kind of backchanneling). If listeners do not display appropriate variation in backchanneling signals (e.g. alternating between *Right*, *Yeah*, and *Mmmhmm*), then the message conveyed by the signals will be one of lack of support for the current speaker rather than increased support. Thus, if we are talking with someone who simply keeps repeating *Mmmhmm* with the same basic intonation, we will most likely come to the conclusion that this person is bored by what we are saying.

Since the 1970s, gender-based differences in turn-taking and overlapping talk have been studied in detail. The results of these studies clearly defy the widespread stereotype in American culture that women talk more than men (e.g. James and Drakich 1993). Research shows that in mixed-sex conversation, men tend to take more speaking turns than women; they also "hold the floor" longer than women. It is not as clear whether men interrupt more than women, partly because it is not easy to define what constitutes an interruption. As we have just discussed, many cases of conversational overlap are supportive rather than disruptive. Further, women's and men's patterns for language use can be quite different in different societies, communities, and settings, and it is impossible to make blanket statements about "women's language use" vs. "men's language use." We will discuss gender and language variation in more detail in chapter 8.

Exercise 6

Think of some types of behaviors you have observed among members of a social group other than your own that have made you uncomfortable or that you have considered offensive. Classic cases might involve talking with someone of a different gender, service encounters at stores, cross-ethnic encounters, and so forth. What kinds of language use tend to go along with the behaviors that have bothered you? In what ways might language-use conventions contribute to your impression? What is different about the conventions of your cultural/dialectal group compared to the other group? Are there aspects of your perception that, upon further reflection, might simply be related to how you interpret the language routines of other cultural groups rather than the intentions of the speakers? Are there aspects related to what you *expect* of certain social groups vs. what individual speakers actually *do*?

As we have seen, there are a number of different rules or conventions that govern our conversational format and interactional style. Furthermore, there are a variety of factors that have to be considered, ranging from broad-based cultural values about who can talk to whom about what, to minute details concerning how certain subtle intentions may be expressed in a given community. Given the number and significance of the factors that enter into the selection of strategies for carrying out conversation, the likelihood of misinterpretation is almost staggering. Certainly, there are many shared language-use conventions across the varieties of American English, but there are also important differences among groups that can lead to significant misunderstandings across regional and social dialects.

The acknowledgment of language-use differences as a legitimate domain of dialect studies is relatively recent compared to the traditional focus on language form (i.e. lexical items, pronunciations, grammatical structures), but the social significance of language-use differences should not be underestimated. In fact, some of the major areas of social dissonance and conflict among different social and ethnic groups in American society are directly tied to people's failure to understand that different groups have different language-use conventions.

3.6   Further Reading

American Speech. A publication of the American Dialect Society. Tuscaloosa: University of Alabama Press. This quarterly journal contains articles on all levels of dialect differences in American English dialects, balancing more technical treatments of dialect forms with shorter, non-technical observations. A regular section entitled "Among the New Words" contains lists of lexical items that have been innovated in the different ways discussed above.

Cassidy, Frederic G. and Joan Houston Hall (general editors) *Dictionary of American Regional English*, vols. 1–4 (1985, 1991, 1996, 2002). Cambridge, MA: Harvard University Press, Belknap. Four volumes of this exhaustive dictionary of regional lexical items have now been published, covering the letters A–Sk, with the final two volumes to be published in the next decade. The introductory articles in Volume 1, by Frederic Cassidy and James Hartman, set forth some of the major phonological and grammatical processes that have led to differences in American English dialects.

Eble, Connie (2004) Slang. In Edward Finegan and John R. Rickford (eds.), *Language in the USA*. Cambridge: Cambridge University Press, 375–86. This chapter provides a succinct, thoughtful account of the nature of slang and its social functions in society, based on years of collecting slang terms from college students and from considering both the linguistic formation and social functions of these specialized terms. Other helpful readings and web addresses are provided in this article.

Goodwin, Marjorie Harness (1990) *He-Said-She-Said: Talk as Social Organization among Black Children*. Bloomington: Indiana University Press. This description of adolescent African American speech combines an in-depth conversational analysis of speech with more broadly based ethnographic studies of the speech community.

Labov, William (1994) *Principles of Linguistics Change*, vol. 1: *Internal Factors*. Oxford: Blackwell. This is a major descriptive and theoretical work setting forth the principles governing vowel shifts in the English language. The technical description presumes advanced linguistic knowledge. Up-to-date information on Labov and his colleagues' continuing research on the vowel systems of American English can be obtained by consulting the following web address: http://www.ling.upenn.edu/phono_atlas/home.html (accessed 20 December 2004).

Lighter, Jonathan E. (1994) *Historical Dictionary of American Slang*, vol. 1: *A–G*. New York: Random House. This book provides a list of slang terms, with historical derivations, in dictionary format.

Morgan, Marcyliena (2002) *Language, Discourse and Power in African American Culture*. Cambridge: Cambridge University Press. This description of language use in the African American community includes discussions of language use conventions, discourse patterns, and language ideologies. The focus is on language function rather than language form.

Tannen, Deborah (1984) *Conversational Style: Analyzing Talk Among Friends*. Norwood, NJ: Ablex. This book provides an engaging introduction to differences in language use conventions (e.g. turn-taking patterns) in different cultural groups, and the misinterpretations and conflicts that can result when groups with different conventions come into contact. It is approachable for non-experts as well as of interest to experts in variation in language form who want to learn more about discourse-level variation across dialects.

Thomas, Erik R. (2001) *An Acoustic Analysis of Vowel Variation in New World English*. Publication of American Dialect Society 85. Durham, NC: Duke University Press. Though technical in detail, this work represents the most thorough presentation and discussion of the phonetics of English vowels presented to date.

Wolfram, Walt, and Natalie Schilling-Estes (1997) *Hoi Toide on the Outer Banks: The Story of the Ocracoke Brogue*. Chapel Hill: University of North Carolina Press. This book, designed for non-experts, provides an in-depth description of the lexical, phonological, and grammatical features of one American English dialect, with numerous examples and discussions of the processes that led to the formation of these features.

4

Dialects in the United States: Past, Present, and Future

As shown in chapters 2 and 3, the formation of dialects involves a complex array of historical, social, and linguistic factors. Furthermore, dialects are not static, discrete entities; they constantly interact with one another and undergo change over time and place. In an important sense, dialects simultaneously reflect the past, the present, and the future. The present configuration of American dialects is still very much in touch with past boundaries, and their future development no doubt will build on present dialect contours. Dialects mark the regional and cultural cartography of America as well as any other cultural artifact or practice, and there is no reason to expect that they will surrender their emblematic role in American life in the near future – despite popular predictions and persistent rumors that American English is heading towards homogenization.

In this chapter, we briefly consider the evolution of the dialects of American English from their inception to their current course of development. In the process, we will see that American dialects still reflect some of the influences of the dialects brought by the original English-speaking colonists, the so-called founder effect we described in chapter 2. At the same time, they reflect the history of contact with speakers of other languages. In addition, they have undergone many innovations that continue to set various dialects of American English apart from one another – and from other varieties of English throughout the world.

In the process of its development, American English has evolved through a number of different stages, from the simple transplantation of a wide range of British dialects to the Americas to the internal diversification of dialects within America. Edgar Schneider (2003) suggests that there are five stages that can be applied to the spread of English to different locations across the world, including its movement to and development within the United States. In the initial phase, the FOUNDATION STAGE, English is used on a regular basis in a region where it was not used previously. In this stage, often typified by colonization, speakers come from different regional backgrounds and do not behave linguistically in a homogeneous way. In the second phase, called EXONORMATIVE STABILIZATION, communities stabilize politically under foreign dominance – historically mostly British – with expatriates providing the primary norms for usage. In the next phase, NATIVIZATION, there is a fundamental transition towards independence – politically, culturally, and linguistically, and unique linguistic usages and structures emerge. An important part of this phase is the differentiation of the language variety of the newly independent country from its linguistic origins or homeland. In the fourth phase, known as ENDONORMATIVE STABILIZATION, the new nation adopts its own language norms rather than adhering to external norms, while in the final phase, DIFFERENTIATION, internal diversification takes over and new dialects evolve on their own, usually quite differently from how language change is proceeding in the former homeland. Each phase in this cycle is characterized by a set of cultural and political conditions that coincide with linguistic changes, reflecting the close association that often exists between language and nationhood, especially in Western industrialized societies. In such a progression, we see how language variation in the United States has developed from its initial roots in the English language of the early British colonists to its current state in which the dialects of American English are viewed as the regional and cultural manifestations of diversity solely within America.

4.1   The First English(es) in America

When the first successful English settlement was founded in Jamestown, Virginia, in 1607, British English was quite different from what it is today. American English, of course, was non-existent. As we mentioned in chapter 2, scholars refer to the language of this time period – the language of Shakespeare and the Elizabethan era – as Early Modern English, to distinguish it from today's English (Modern English or Present-Day English) as well as from the English of Chaucer's day (Middle English, spoken from about 1100 to 1500) and from even earlier varieties of the language (Old English, *c*.600–1100). Not only was Early Modern English in general quite different from today's language, but there was also quite a bit of variation within the language at that time. Since the beginnings of English, there have been numerous distinct dialects within the British Isles, dialects that arose and were continually enhanced by longstanding lack of communication between speakers of different dialect areas. Furthermore, the notion of a unified "standard" language was not firmly established until around the mid-eighteenth century so that there was no social pressure to try to erase dialect differences. These differences in earlier varieties of British English had a profound effect on the development of the dialects of the United States, since people from different speech regions tended to establish residence in different regions of America. In fact, some of today's most noticeable dialect differences can still be traced directly back to the British English dialects of the seventeenth and eighteenth centuries.

Contrary to popular perceptions, the speech of the Jamestown colonists more closely resembled today's American English than today's standard British speech, since British English has undergone a number of innovations which did not spread to once-remote America. For example, even though Shakespearean actors, speaking in "proper" British style, pronounce words such as *cart* and *work* as *caht* and *wuhk* (that is, without the *r* sounds), many of Shakespeare's contemporaries would have pronounced their *r*'s, just as do most Americans today. Similarly, the early colonists would have pronounced the /æ/ vowel in words like *path*, *dance*, and *can't* as the low front vowel [æ] (as in *cat*), just as Americans do today, even though British standards now demand a sound similar to the [ɑ] of *father*.

In addition to pronunciations, there are certain words and word meanings that have been handed down to today's Americans by the first colonists, despite the fact that British speakers have long since abandoned them. For example, Americans can use the word *mad* with its early meaning of "angry", while British speakers can only use it to mean mentally unbalanced. Americans can also use the word *fall* to refer to the season which follows summer, but British speakers only use the term *autumn*, even though both terms coexisted for centuries in Britain. There are also a few syntactic structures that have been preserved in American English that were lost from British English. The American use of *gotten*, as in *Has he gotten the mail yet?*, is an older form, supplanted in Britain by *got* (*Has he got the mail?*); further, the British use of *done* in a question–answer pair such as *Did you leave your wallet in the car?/ I might have **done*** arose after English had sunk its roots in American soil. Thus, Americans reply to questions such as the above with *I might have* or *I might have **done** so* but never with *I might have done*, a distinct British-ism.

Many of the early colonists in the Jamestown area – that is, Tidewater Virginia – came from Southeastern England, the home of Britain's cultural center, London. These speakers would have spoken varieties of English that were quite close to the emerging London standard rather than the more "rustic" varieties spoken in outlying areas such as Northern and Southwestern England. The fact that Tidewater Virginia was long associated with "proper" British speech led to one of its chief defining characteristics, the loss of *r* after vowels and before consonants in words such as *cart* and *work*. Even though, as we mentioned above, English was largely *r*-pronouncing, or *r*-ful, in the early seventeenth century, the loss of *r*, or *r*-lessness, was not uncommon in Southeastern England at this time. It gradually gained prestige in this region and finally became a marker of standard British speech, a development which most likely had occurred by the mid-eighteenth century or so. As *r*-lessness was gaining in prestige in England, colonists in Tidewater Virginia were building a prosperous society based on plantation agriculture. The aristocrats of this region, descended from fairly *r*-less Southeastern English speakers, maintained strong ties with the London area and its standard speakers, and so *r*-lessness was established in lowland Virginia. This is in sharp contrast to the piedmont and mountain regions to the west of the Tidewater, and indeed to most varieties of American English today, which are *r*-ful rather than *r*-less. Most of the English speakers who established residence in the uplands of Virginia, more than a hundred years after the founding of Jamestown, were vernacular speakers from Britain's *r*-pronouncing regions or were descended from these speakers. In particular, the *r*-pronouncing Scots-Irish from Ulster in Northern Ireland were to have an enormous impact on the speech of the Virginia colony and on American English in general. We will discuss the contribution of the Scots-Irish to American English momentarily.

Another reason for the *r*-ful character of upland Virginia speech is that this region was subject to more dialect mixing than the Tidewater area, which remained relatively homogeneous for a number of generations. When a number of different dialects come into contact with one another, differences among the varieties may be ironed out. For some reason, most likely the preponderance of Scots-Irish settlers in the American colonies, the reduction of dialect differences in early America tended to produce *r*-ful rather than *r*-less speech, even if a number of settlers in "mixed" areas initially brought *r*-less speech with them. Finally, speakers in upland Virginia (as well as other *r*-pronouncing regions, which we will discuss below) were *r*-ful because they did not maintain as much contact with Britain as their neighbors to the east. Settlers in the piedmont and mountain regions tended to establish small farms rather than large plantations and to lean toward democracy rather than aristocracy. In addition, they were less wealthy than plantation owners and were not able to afford luxuries such as travel or schooling in London.

As in Tidewater Virginia, speakers of "proper" Southeastern England speech were prevalent in Eastern New England, beginning with the founding of the Massachusetts Bay Colony in 1620. Thus, Eastern New England became an *r*-less dialect area as standard or "proper" British English moved toward an *r*-less norm, in contrast with neighboring dialect areas such as Western New England (west of the Connecticut River Valley) and New York State, which became *r*-pronouncing regions for the same reasons that upland Virginia did: (1) settlement by *r*-pronouncing speakers; (2) the reduction of dialect differences in the face of dialect contact and language contact; and (3) relative lack of contact with London as compared with speakers in Eastern New England. To this day, Eastern New England survives as an *r*-less island in the midst of a sea of *r*-fulness. The strongly *r*-less character of New England speech is evidenced in the fact that it is often caricaturized through phrases such as "Pahk the cah in Hahvahd Yahd" for "Park the car in Harvard Yard." Interestingly, one of the most stereotypically *r*-less regions in this country, New York City, as demonstrated in phrases such as "toity-toid street" for "thirty-third street," began life as an *r*-ful speech area. In fact, it wasn't until at least the mid-nineteenth century that *r*-lessness, which spread into the city from New England, was firmly established there. Today, *r*-lessness is receding sharply in New York City English, as well as in Eastern New England and Tidewater Virginia. Regions traditionally characterized by *r*-less speech are depicted in figure 4.1.

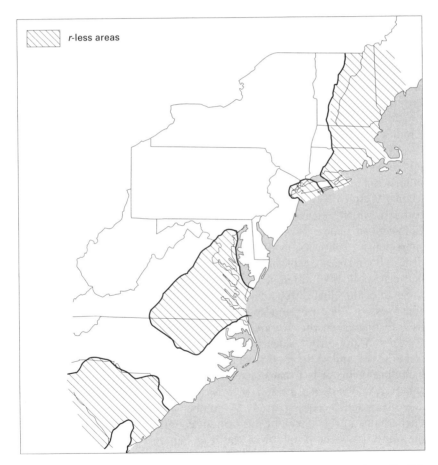

Figure 4.1 Traditional regions of *r*-lessness and *r*-fulness in American English (adapted from Kurath and David 1961: map 32)

Exercise 1

In the decades following World War II, *r*-lessness has been receding
sharply in the US. What do you think the reason for this decline
might be? Consider caricatures of New York City and Boston speech
(e.g. *toity-toid street* "thirty-third street", *pahk the cah* "park the car")
as you shape your answer. Compare the decline of *r*-lessness in the
US with its historical rise and continued maintenance in British speech.
What do the changing patterns of *r*-fulness and *r*-lessness in America
and Britain tell us about the inherent value (linguistic and/or social)
of particular dialect features?

Following the establishment of the Massachusetts Bay Colony, a number
of other important settlements were founded in the mid- to late seventeenth
century. These include several settlements in the Connecticut River Valley
area beginning in 1635, as well as settlements in the Hudson River Valley,
including what was later to become New York City, beginning in the 1640s.
In addition, Providence, Rhode Island, was established in 1638 by several
families from the Massachusetts Bay Colony who were dissatisfied with the
severity of religious and social practices in Salem and Boston. While Boston
was to become the cultural and linguistic center of Eastern New England,
influencing speech patterns throughout Massachusetts and up into lower
Maine, Western New England would develop its own characteristic speech
patterns, which radiated outward from the initial settlements in the lower
Connecticut Valley. Further, Rhode Island would persist as a dialectal
subregion for centuries, evidence for the strong and enduring character of
dialect boundaries established in an era of minimal intercommunication
between speakers of different areas, including even neighboring regions.

Some of the chief differences between traditional Eastern New England
and Western New England speech derive from cultural differences that
have distinguished the two areas since their initial settlement by English
speakers. Many early residents of Eastern New England made their living
from the sea, and so the traditional dialect is rich with nautical terminology,
including such words as *nor'easter*, which refers to a storm from the north
and east, and *lulling down* and *breezing up*, used, respectively, to refer to
decreasing and increasing winds. A number of these nautical terms have
their origins in the speech of the western counties of England rather than
the southeast, since people from the seagoing west were frequent settlers
along the coastal areas of early America.

Far to the south of New England, the Tidewater Virginia speech area
also shares important connections with Western England, particularly the

southwestern counties. Even today, there are portions of the Tidewater, chiefly along its easternmost edge, whose speech is quite different from general Tidewater English. For example, there are strong pockets of *r*-fulness in the midst of an otherwise *r*-less speech area. Most likely, the easternmost portion of the Tidewater derives its character from relatively heavy settlement by speakers from Southwestern England, a region characterized by strong *r*-fulness, among other features. In addition, people who made their living via maritime activities rather than plantation agriculture did not have the strong ties with "proper" (*r*-less) British speech that plantation owners did. The highly distinctive speech of the Delmarva Peninsula, the Chesapeake Bay Islands (including Tangier Island, Virginia, and Smith Island, Maryland), and the Outer Banks islands of North Carolina is to this day far more reminiscent of the speech of Southwest England than of the Southeastern English from which Tidewater English proper is descended.

As we move inland, traditional regional dialects tend to be characterized by a preponderance of farming terms rather than nautical words. Thus, the traditional Western New England dialect is replete with terms pertaining to an agricultural lifestyle, in contrast with neighboring Eastern New England speech. Of special interest are terms that relate to localized farming practices. For example, a *stone drag* refers to a piece of equipment used for extricating stones from the rocky New England soil, while the term *rock maple* refers to the sugar maple, an important source of income for early farmers in Western New England.

The traditional speech of rural New York State is also replete with localized farming terms. However, its overall character is rather different from the speech of neighboring Western New England, due in part to the influence of Dutch and German on speakers. The Dutch had control of the Hudson Valley area until 1644, when the British took over; in addition, a huge influx of Germans began pouring into New York and Pennsylvania in the early eighteenth century. The Dutch and German influence on traditional New York speech is evidenced in terms such as *olicook* "doughnut" (from Dutch *oliekoek* "oil cake") and *thick milk* "clabber" (from German *dickemilch* "thick milk"), which remained current in the region through the early years of the twentieth century. In recent years, most of these words have faded out of use or have spread far beyond the region (e.g. *cruller* "doughnut", from Dutch *krulle* "curly cake") and so no longer serve as markers of New York speech. In fact, the only Dutch and German terms that truly remain intact in the region are place names such as *Brooklyn* and *Harlem* (from Dutch *Breukelyn* and *Haarlem*, respectively). At the same time, many current place names reflect the names for the original Native American groups in these areas: for example, Merrimac, Nabasset, and Cochituate in Massachusetts (as well as the name of the state of Massachusetts itself); and Tappahannock, Wicomico, and Massaponex in Virginia.

Exercise 2

Using an appropriate map or maps, examine the place names found in two states from different regions of the United States. To what extent do you see the influence of different language groups in these place names? Cite the influences of at least several groups of inhabitants, including Native Americans. If you aren't sure about the etymology of the place name, you might try looking at the web site for the town or region; such web sites often give information on the origins of local place names.

Another of the nation's earliest cultural and linguistic centers was Philadelphia, established in the 1680s by Quakers under the leadership of William Penn. The Quaker movement was organized in Northern England and the northern Midlands, and so Philadelphia was, from the first, far less like Southern England in its speech habits than New England. Also prevalent in Philadelphia from its earliest days were emigrants from Wales and Germany. Almost immediately, the Germans, many of whom were of the Moravian, Mennonite, and Amish sects, began moving westward into Pennsylvania and began developing their own distinctive culture and language, Pennsylvania Dutch. This language is not really Dutch but rather a unique variety of German which developed in the New World, partly in response to speakers' contact with English and partly as a result of longstanding isolation from European German varieties. One of the most important groups to settle in early Philadelphia was the Scots-Irish. In 1724, thousands of Scots-Irish arrived in Delaware and then proceeded northward into Pennsylvania, New York, and New England. The initial wave of immigration was followed by numerous others throughout the course of the eighteenth century. Immigration reached its peak in the 1770s but persisted well into the twentieth century.

The Scots-Irish were descendants of Scots who had emigrated to Ulster in the north of Ireland at the beginning of the seventeenth century in order to seek economic gain and to escape discrimination and persecution at the hands of the English. At the time of the initial migrations to Ulster, Scots English was more distinct from London speech than today's highly distinctive Scots English is from standard British English, or RP (Received Pronunciation). The English spoken in Scotland in the early seventeenth century tended to become less distinctive as the centuries passed; however, the old, highly distinctive speech tended to be preserved in Ulster, since the Scots-Irish did not maintain much contact with Scotland, or with England. Thus, the variety of English that the Scots-Irish brought to America in the early eighteenth century was a rather archaic form of Scots English. It was little influenced by Irish English, since most Irish people in the Ulster area spoke the Irish language (also known as Irish Gaelic) rather than English. Among its other characteristics, Scots-Irish was strongly *r*-ful, and as it established itself in America, it successfully resisted the incursion of *r*-lessness via such cultural centers as Boston and Richmond. At the time of the American Revolution, the Scots-Irish speech variety was already having an enormous impact on the development of American English: It is estimated that around 250,000 Scots-Irish had migrated to America by 1776 and that fully one in seven colonists was Scots-Irish at this time. The impact of the Scots-Irish would only strengthen over time. From their initial settlement areas, particularly Pennsylvania, the Scots-Irish and their descendants would spread throughout the Mid-Atlantic states and the highlands of the American South; and their influence can even be felt throughout the Northern and Western US, where *r*-ful speech predominates to this day, despite the fact that *r*-lessness now dominates in Great Britain. Eventually, some two million immigrants of Scots-Irish descent made their way to America during the eighteenth, nineteenth, and twentieth centuries.

As early as the 1730s, the Scots-Irish began moving westward into the heart of Pennsylvania, where they encountered the Pennsylvania Dutch. From these colonists the Scots-Irish picked up such German terms as *sauerkraut* and *hex*; in addition, they borrowed the musical instrument known as the dulcimer, which would later become a trademark of Scots-Irish culture in the Southern highlands, as well as the German-style log cabin, a hallmark of American pioneer culture throughout the frontier period. Because the Germans had already claimed much of the prime farming land in Pennsylvania, the Scots-Irish quickly turned toward the hill country. As early as the 1730s, they began traveling southward down the Shenandoah Valley in the western part of Virginia. From there they fanned out into the Carolinas, Kentucky, and Tennessee, bringing with them enduring features of speech. A number of features of the Midland and Southern highland dialect regions are traceable to the persistent influence of the Scots-Irish, including the use of *till* to express time (e.g. *quarter till four*), constructions such as *the car needs washed*, and the use of *want* plus a preposition, as in *the dog wants in*. In addition, the Midland feature known as "positive anymore" is of Scots-Irish origin as well. "Positive anymore" refers to the use of *anymore* in affirmative construction to mean something like "nowadays", as in *There sure is a lot of traffic around here anymore*. By 1776, there were already several thousand Scots-Irish living in Eastern Kentucky and the Tennessee Valley, and they continued to pour into the area throughout the Revolutionary War.

As the Scots-Irish established a culture revolving around small, independent farms in the highland South, they remained relatively separated from the plantation culture that was flourishing in the lowland South. We have already mentioned one major center of plantation culture, the lower Virginia area, especially Richmond. The most important center, however, was Charleston, South Carolina, established in 1670. From the beginning, Charleston was a far more heterogeneous speech area than Richmond. Its original settlers were English, Irish, and Welsh; these were quickly followed by such widely varied groups as Huguenots from France, Dutch people from Holland and New Amsterdam, Baptists from Massachusetts, Quakers from Louisiana, and a number of Irish Catholics. Slaves imported from the west coast of Africa to work in South Carolina's booming rice plantations also constituted an important group of settlers. Among the most important planters were a group of Barbadians, who established plantations to the north of Charleston and initiated an active trade with the West Indies that was to play a vital role in the formation of the language and culture of Charleston. Very quickly, Charleston's booming rice-based economy led to its establishment as the largest mainland importer of African slaves. As early as 1708, its population included as many Blacks as Whites, and by 1724, there were three times as many Blacks as Whites.

The early development of African American speech in the American South has been intently studied and hotly debated by linguists for decades. The slaves who were brought to the New World spoke a number of different African languages. As often happens when speakers of different languages are brought together, some New World slaves developed a modified language, based on English, in order to communicate with one another and with their White owners. This modified language, called a PIDGIN, eventually developed into a CREOLE. "Pidgin" is the linguistic term for a simplified language created for limited purposes, often business-related, among speakers of different languages. Pidgins often develop into creoles, or full-fledged languages for use in all communicative contexts. Often, the vocabulary of a creole comes from the language of the most powerful group, while the grammar derives largely from the linguistic processes common in language contact situations. For example, a creole language called Gullah or Geechee (in the local vernacular) developed in the Sea Islands area of coastal South Carolina and Georgia, due in large part to the high proportion of Black to White speakers in this area. It has also been speculated that a creole was spoken in the inland Plantation South, but this has been strongly debated. Gullah is still spoken by African Americans in the Sea Islands area and is the only English-based creole that has survived continuously in the US since colonial times. It is closely related to the creoles of the Caribbean. Further, it seems to bear relation to such West African creoles as Krio, spoken in Sierra Leone. It is believed by some that Gullah is a remnant of a once-widespread Black creole that developed into African American English, preserved through the longstanding isolation of its speakers. We discuss the origins of African American English in more detail in chapter 7, when we consider a fuller range of possibilities regarding the early development of this language variety.

The influence of Charleston speech, both White and Black, quickly spread throughout the lowlands of South Carolina and into Georgia, where settlement was halted for a number of decades at the Ogeechee River, the borderline between colonial and Native American territory. Florida was not as heavily influenced by the Charleston hub in the colonial years as the rest of the Lower South, since it was under Spanish rule until the early nineteenth century and was not subject to extensive settlement by English speakers until relatively late. For the most part, the English that radiated outward from Charleston was *r*-less, just like the plantation speech centered around the Tidewater Virginia settlement hearth. At the same time, traditional Charlestonian speech, particularly in the pronunciation of its vowels, developed as a distinct dialect, different even from other dialects of the South, and the remnants of this distinctiveness are still evident today (Baranowski 2004).

One final center of early settlement in America that played a role in shaping its dialect landscape was New Orleans. The construction of New Orleans by the French began in 1717, but it was some years before significant numbers of settlers could be persuaded to live in this swampy, humid area. The earliest settlers were, of course, French, with an admixture of German. Slaves from Africa and the West Indies were also among the earliest inhabitants, although New Orleans plantations were never as prosperous as those of the Atlantic colonies. Blacks in the New Orleans area developed their own creole language, based on French rather than English, which is the ancestor of today's Louisiana Creole. The year 1765 marks the arrival of another very important cultural group in Louisiana, the Acadians, or 'Cajuns. The Acadians were a people of French descent who had been deported from the Canadian settlement of Acadia (now Nova Scotia and New Brunswick). They brought with them a variety of French that was quite different from and more archaic than the Parisian French of the mid-1700s. Today the speech variety of the Acadians in Louisiana survives in a variety of English known as Cajun English, which we discuss in more detail in chapter 6. Spain took over control of New Orleans in 1763, but the impact of the Spanish language on this speech region has always been very slight, with the French influence far outweighing that of any other linguistic group, as evidenced in such regional terms as *lagniappe* "a small gift", as well as terms of French origin that originated in this region but later spread throughout the US, such as *bisque* "a cream soup" and *brioche* "a kind of coffee cake". In 1803, New Orleans passed into American hands, and settlers of British descent finally began inhabiting the region in significant numbers. This strong English presence in New Orleans, however, came far too late to erase the heavy French influence, which is now finally fading from New Orleans speech.

4.2   Earlier American English: The Colonial Period

In the previous section, we showed the dialect influence of five primary cultural hearths established early in the history of colonial America: Jamestown, Boston, Philadelphia, Charleston, and New Orleans. All of these regions had emerged by the time of the Revolutionary War. Some of the most distinctive dialects in the United States were already developing at this early date, though they might not have been recognized as such until much later. To a large extent, the period leading up to the Revolutionary War was more focused on how "Americanisms" in English were differentiating it from British English, as is often the case during the nativization phase of English spread.

When the Thirteen Colonies became the United States, there were already clear indications that American English was becoming a separate linguistic entity from British English. We have already hinted at the changes that took place in American English due to contact with various foreign languages. Earlier American English was influenced by French in the New Orleans area, Spanish in Florida, German in Pennsylvania and New York, and by West African languages such as Mande, Mandingo, and Wolof throughout the Lower South. And, of course, it was influenced by the numerous Native American languages spoken by the indigenous inhabitants of the Americas. As we discussed in chapter 2, American English acquired such terms as *raccoon*, *hominy*, and *bayou* (from Choctaw *bayuk* "a small, slow-moving stream", through New Orleans French) from various Native American languages, including languages of the Algonquian, Muskogean, Iroquoian, Siouan, and Penutian families. However, the influence of Native American languages in today's America is best attested in the hundreds of current place names in the United States that come from the original inhabitants of these regions.

In addition, the development of English in America was affected by contact between speakers of language varieties that originated in different parts of the British Isles, including such varieties as Southeastern English, Southwestern English, the Midland English of the Quakers, Scots English, Scots-Irish, and even Irish and Scots Gaelic. For example, such words as *shenanigan* "trickery, mischief", *smithereens*, and *shanty* most likely come from the Irish language, although their etymologies are not completely certain. In addition, general American usages such as *He's in the hospital* (compare the British *He's in hospital*) and Appalachian English *He's got the earache* "He has an earache" may be the result of transfer from the Irish language to English, since early Irish English speakers in America tended to use definite articles in a number of constructions where speakers of other English varieties would omit them.

Language and dialect contact were not the only factors responsible for the creation of a uniquely American brand of English. When early emigrants arrived in America, they encountered many new objects, plants, animals, and natural phenomena for which they had no names. Some names they borrowed from other languages, particularly Native American languages such as those of the Algonquian family, but other labels were innovated using the resources of the English language. For example, *seaboard*, *underbrush*, and *backwoods* are all compounds which were created in America; in addition, some existing words were given new meanings to better suit the American landscape. Thus, *creek*, which originally meant "small saltwater inlet" (still a current meaning in Great Britain and parts of the Southeastern US coast), came to be used in America to refer to any sort of small stream, in particular a freshwater stream. Proof that English in America very quickly became distinct from British English is found in the fact that, as early as 1735, British people were complaining about American words and word usages, such as the use of *bluff* to refer to a bank or cliff. In fact, the term "Americanism" was coined in the 1780s to refer to particular terms and phrases that were coming to characterize English in the early US but not British English.

A number of innovations that distinguish American from British English were undertaken quite self-consciously by early Americans, who wanted to indicate their political separation from Britain through their language. For example, Thomas Jefferson was a frequent coiner of new words (*belittle*, for instance, is an invention of his), while Benjamin Franklin was a staunch advocate of spelling reform for American English. The greatest champion of this cause, however, was the early American lexicographer Noah Webster, who gave Americans such spellings as *color* for *colour*, *wagon* for *waggon*, *fiber* for *fibre*, and *tire* for *tyre*.

Despite resistance to British English in early America, there is no doubt that British norms continued to exert considerable influence in American for quite some time. The transition from British-based, external norms to American-based, internal norms was not a rapid, seamless one. In fact, there is reason to wonder how complete it has been even centuries after independence. For example, British English is still viewed as more standard or prestigious than American English throughout the world – and also by many Americans themselves. Furthermore, the spread of *r*-lessness throughout the South and in New England was almost certainly due in part to emulation of British standards. In addition, other sweeping changes in British English which took place during the Early Modern English period occurred in America as well. For example, *thee* and *thou* were replaced by *you* in both Britain and America at this time (though they still persist in some English dialects), and third-person singular *-eth* (e.g. *He maketh me to lie down in green pastures*) was replaced by *-s* on both sides of the Atlantic as well.

One of the questions that comes up with respect to earlier American English is the extent to which the leveling of the different dialects brought from the British Isles took place. Certainly, some of these differences were reduced as American English nativized, and some features became quite widespread, rather than confined to only a few regions or settlement groups. For example, the use of third-person plural *-s* in sentences like *The dogs barks a lot* became fairly widespread among earlier varieties of American English even though it was a regional British trait associated primarily with Northern England to begin with. Although there are certainly many cases in which distinctive features of regional British dialects were leveled and some cases in which localized British dialect traits became part of generalized American English, there is also evidence that regional varieties of English arose relatively early in the history of the United States, in many cases as a direct result of regional dialect differences brought over from the British Isles, and that these differences have been maintained since their initial establishment. As noted above, a number of Scots-Irish traits were documented relatively early in the Midland dialect area and restricted to that region from that time forward. And the regional use of *weren't* in sentences such as *It weren't me* was largely confined to Southeastern coastal areas relatively early and has remained regionally restricted to this day. Earlier dialect influence seems evident in the traditional dialect map given in figure 4.2, one of the first systematically compiled maps of dialect areas in the United States. The data for the map were gathered from older speakers in the 1930s and 1940s. Though the data thus represent the speech of people who learned their varieties of English in the second half of the nineteenth and early twentieth centuries, their connection to the original settlement patterns seems apparent. For example, the map indicates the early influence of the Boston (Northern) and Philadelphia (Midland) linguistic and cultural hubs, as well as the outward spread of distinctive varieties from these central points.

Although American English shared innovations with British English and instituted its own language changes, the traditional dialects of American English are rather conservative in character when compared with standard British English. Interestingly, this is particularly true of the two dialect areas that once kept pace with changes in British English more than the rest of the country, New England and the South. For example, these two dialect areas are still typified by lexical items from Elizabethan and even earlier English. Thus, in New England we may still hear terms such as the

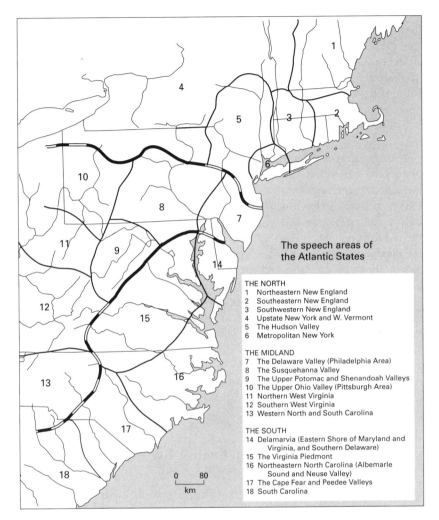

THE NORTH
1   Northeastern New England
2   Southeastern New England
3   Southwestern New England
4   Upstate New York and W. Vermont
5   The Hudson Valley
6   Metropolitan New York

THE MIDLAND
7   The Delaware Valley (Philadelphia Area)
8   The Susquehanna Valley
9   The Upper Potomac and Shenandoah Valleys
10 The Upper Ohio Valley (Pittsburgh Area)
11 Northern West Virginia
12 Southern West Virginia
13 Western North and South Carolina

THE SOUTH
14 Delamarvia (Eastern Shore of Maryland and
      Virginia, and Southern Delaware)
15 The Virginia Piedmont
16 Northeastern North Carolina (Albemarle
      Sound and Neuse Valley)
17 The Cape Fear and Peedee Valleys
18 South Carolina

The speech areas of the Atlantic States

Figure 4.2   Dialect areas of the Eastern United States: a traditional view (from Kurath 1949: figure 3; reprinted by permission of the University of Michigan Press)

fourteenth-century word *rowan* ("a second crop grown in a hayfield which has been harvested"), while in the South we may hear such fifteenth-century terms as *foxfire* (a phosphorescent light caused by fungi on decaying wood), *kinfolk* (family, relatives), and *liketa* "almost" (*He **liketa** broke his neck*). The Midland dialect area has long been more innovative than its neighbors to the north and south, chiefly because immigrants from the

British Isles, Europe, and points beyond continued to pour into this area long after New England and the South were effectively settled. The fact that New England and the South are partners in linguistic conservatism is evidenced in the fact that the two regions traditionally have shared a number of dialect features, despite their geographic distance from one another. For example, the two regions share such older lexical items as *piazza* "porch" (an early borrowing from Italian) and such pronunciation features as *r*-lessness. As we have mentioned above, *r*-lessness was at one time an innovative feature in American English, but it is now receding sharply.

It seems apparent that the seeds of regional speech were sown early in the history of English in the United States, and regional distinctions have remained surprisingly intact over several centuries, notwithstanding the effects of leveling. Even when traditional dialect features are lost, they may be supplanted by new features whose distribution follows the same lines as the old features, thus preserving the dialect boundary. Whereas many terms associated with old-fashioned methods of farming have understandably passed out of the New England lexicon, some newer terms pertaining to newer lifestyles, such as the use of *rotary* for "traffic circle", *parkway* for a divided highway with extensive plantings, or *wicked* as a general intensifier (e.g. *He's wicked crazy*) are largely confined to the traditional New England dialect region. Such regionally confined terms, according to Craig Carver, offer "proof that dialect expressions inevitably spread or die out, but that dialect boundaries remain relatively stable and alive" (1987: 32). We will discuss the fate of traditional dialect regions in the US in more detail in the final section of this chapter and in the following chapter.

4.3   American English Extended

Just as initial British and Continental European settlement patterns along the Eastern Seaboard dictated the dialects of the East Coast, so too did these initial dialect boundaries play a large role in determining the dialect landscape of the interior of the US. For the most part, European settlers and their descendants tended to move directly westward as America expanded, so that Northern states in the interior tended to be inhabited by speakers from New England and New York, the middle states to be inhabited by Midland speakers, and the Southern states by Southerners. The dialect areas that resulted from this settlement pattern are shown in figure 4.3, one of the most commonly cited maps of American dialects (Carver 1987). This map is based on lexical differences. Later, we present a map based on current phonological differences that shows considerable overlap with this map.

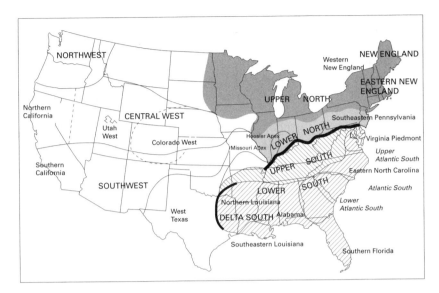

Figure 4.3   The major dialect areas of the United States: a revised perspective (from Carver 1987: 248; reprinted by permission of the University of Michigan Press)

The map clearly portrays the primarily westward flow of dialect expansion in the United States. In the latter half of the eighteenth century, Europeans and their descendants in New England and New York began pushing westward beyond New York into Ohio, driven by overcrowding, high land prices, steep taxes, and the extreme religious and social conservatism of the Northeast. The northeastern corner of Ohio, called the Western Reserve, became an important region of New England speech and was to remain for many years a sort of dialect island in a state largely dominated by Southern and Midland dialects. The opening of the Erie Canal in 1825 deflected migrations from New York and New England from the Ohio River Valley to the Great Lakes, reinforcing the linguistic insularity of the Western Reserve and populating Michigan. After 1833, thousands of people came to Detroit by regular steamer service, fanning out from there into Michigan and Northern Illinois. By 1850, most of lower Michigan had been settled by New England farmers.

For the most part, Indiana was bypassed by New England settlers, who were swayed by reports of high land prices and undesirable living conditions. Some of the earliest settlers of European descent in neighboring Illinois were miners, who flocked to the northwestern portion of the state beginning in 1822. Chicago began to be transformed from a small settlement to one of the nation's greatest cities in the 1840s, when steamboats began bringing settlers on a regular basis. By 1850, European American settlement in Illinois was firmly established. Europeans and people of European descent also pushed into Wisconsin in the early years of the nineteenth century; most came to this state from New England, but there was also an important contingent of settlers from Western Europe, including Norway, Ireland, and especially Germany.

In general, then, the northern US is largely a region of New England expansion. It forms a large dialect area which is extremely unified through the easternmost portion of the Dakotas and is referred to simply as the North by traditional dialectologists but as the Upper North by Carver (1987). Traditional dialect items characterizing the North were phonological features such as the different pronunciation of the vowels in *horse* [hɔrs] and *hoarse* [hors], the use of [s] rather than [z] in *greasy*, and the pronunciation of *root* with the same vowel as that used in *put* rather than the vowel of *boot*. Traditional lexical items which typify Northern speech include the use of *pail* (vs. *bucket*) and *eaves* or *eavestrough* for *gutter*. Grammatical features include items like *dove* as the past tense of *dive* and phrases such as *sick to/at the stomach* (vs. *sick in/on the stomach*). In the next chapter, we see how the Northern Cities Vowel Shift has become a prominent dialect trait now setting apart many metropolitan areas of the North from other dialect regions.

Although the map in figure 4.3 shows New England and Eastern New England as subregions of the North, other dialect geographers classify these two areas as separate from the Northern dialect area, a region roughly equivalent to Carver's Upper North. This region draws its dialectal distinctiveness, in part, from the numerous non-English-speaking Europeans who were among its earliest non-native inhabitants, particularly in the northernmost section of the region. In fact, the 1860 Census (the first to record origin of birth) shows that 30 percent of those living in Minnesota, Wisconsin, and northern Michigan were born outside the US, a higher percentage than almost anywhere else in the US at that time.

On dialect maps based on traditional dialect features, such as Carver's map in figure 4.3, a discontinuity in the primary boundary separating the North from the Midland occurs at the Mississippi River, along the Illinois–Iowa border. This is because the Mississippi facilitated south-to-north migration into Iowa, creating a sort of "dialect fault line." Beyond the Mississippi, the cohesiveness of the North weakens significantly, due to the ever-widening sphere of influence of Midland speech varieties as one proceeds westward.

The westward expansion of the American Midland was accomplished chiefly by three groups of speakers: those from the Upper South, the Mid-Atlantic states, and the New England/New York dialect area. For the most part, the three streams remained separate, at least up to the Mississippi River, giving rise to a three-tiered settlement and dialectal pattern, most notable in Ohio, Indiana, and Illinois. Settlers from the Upper South had pushed into the heart of Tennessee and Kentucky by the latter part of the eighteenth century and from there continued into Southern Missouri and Northern Arkansas. In some places, heavy concentrations of Southern settlement extend beyond the boundaries of the Southern Midland (or the Upper South, in Carver's terms), forming anomalous dialect pockets called APEXES. The best known of these is the HOOSIER APEX, a pocket of Southern speech in lower Indiana and Illinois; in addition, the encroachment of Southern speech into Missouri is considered to constitute another dialectal apex.

Also pushing westward along with Upper Southerners were settlers from the Mid-Atlantic, chiefly Pennsylvania and Maryland, who traveled along the Ohio River and the National Road (a road that extended from Cumberland, Maryland, to Southern Illinois, the precursor of today's US 70), settling in Ohio, Indiana, and Central Illinois. Subsequently, they pushed on into Southern Iowa, Missouri, and other points west of the Mississippi, where they fanned out broadly to encompass portions of states as far north as North Dakota and as far south as Oklahoma. Besides Upper Southern and Midland speakers, there were also a limited number of speakers from New York and New England who settled in the Midland. However, they tended to confine themselves to the northern portions of this dialect area, in effect pushing the bounds of the Northern dialect area southward rather than contributing substantially to the character of the Midland dialect.

At the same time that the Northern and Midland dialect boundaries were being extended westward, the South was expanding as well. Several dialect lines were laid in Georgia, since settlement was halted at the Ogeechee River for a number of decades until 1805 and at the Chattahoochee for a number of years beginning in the 1830s. Alabama is also sometimes considered a separate subdialectal area, since it was settled rather late in comparison with the majority of the South and since its settlers tended to be from both Lower and Upper Southern dialect regions. However, Mississippi is Lower Southern in character. Southern Oklahoma and Texas are Southern as well, though Central Texas has developed its own brand of Southern speech, probably due in large part to Texans' strong sense of cultural distinctiveness from the rest of the US. As we noted above, most of Florida forms a separate subregion, as does the delta area in Southern Louisiana.

As the English language was transported westward in America, dialect mixing intensified, and American English became more and more different from English in the British Isles, where mixing did not occur on as grand a scale. At the same time, the leveling out of dialect differences within the

US increased, as speakers from different dialect areas came into increasing contact with one another, particularly speakers in the ever-expanding Midland dialect region. Another factor that had some impact on the development of American English in the nineteenth century and beyond were the numerous foreign immigrations that took place during the nineteenth and early twentieth centuries. Millions of Irish people poured into America, mostly via New York, in the 1830s and 1840s. The Germans came in even greater numbers in the 1840s and 1860s, along with more than five million Italians, who came to America between 1865 and 1920. In addition, there were several other groups who immigrated in significant numbers, including about three million Jews from Eastern and Central Europe who came to the US between 1880 and 1910, and nearly two million Scandinavians, who arrived in the 1870s. German had considerable influence on American English, since Germans were one of the largest immigrant groups to come to America (with more than seven million having arrived since 1776). Thus, we find in today's American English not only German-derived vocabulary items (e.g. *delicatessen*; *check*, from German *Zech* "bill for drinks") but also sentence structures (e.g. *Are you going with?* in some regions) and word formations (e.g. the *-fest* ending of *gabfest*, *slugfest*, etc.).

A large majority of the non-English immigrants who came to the US in the nineteenth century settled in the North and Midland portions of the country rather than in the South, which further intensified dialect differences between Southern and non-Southern speakers. However, Southern American English had already been heavily influenced by such languages as French in the New Orleans area, Spanish in Florida and Texas, and Native American and West African languages throughout the entire region. In addition, there were several important German settlements in the South, including in the western parts of Virginia and neighboring West Virginia, as well as in the San Antonio–Austin–Houston area of Texas.

4.4   The Westward Expansion of English

While immigrants were pouring into the US in the nineteenth century, all sorts of Americans were pushing westward toward the Pacific Coast, particularly after the California Gold Rush of 1849. Although traditional dialect boundaries break down in the Western US, there are several long-standing dialect areas in the West, and newer dialects have arisen here as well. The most coherent of these are the Northwest and Southwest, as indicated again in figure 4.3. The Northwest encompasses the entire state of Washington as well as most of Oregon and Western Idaho. The Southwest spans more than a thousand miles, from West Texas to Southern California, and can be broken down into two subdialects, one centered in Southern California and the other in Texas. Both areas had long been dominated by Spanish speakers, first under Spanish and Mexican rule and then under the US government. The influence of Colonial Spanish on the speech of the Southwest is pervasive to this day, chiefly in the lexicon, which is replete with such terms as *corral*, *canyon*, and *fiesta*, all three of which, of course, are now part of general American English.

Southern Texas remains largely Spanish-speaking to the present, particularly south of the San Antonio River. East Central Texas (which we will call simply Central Texas) was heavily populated by English-speaking settlers after 1836, when Texas became an independent republic. The southern portion of Central Texas received a large influx of English speakers from the Gulf States (Alabama, Mississippi, and Louisiana), while northern Central Texas was populated by many English speakers from the Upper South, especially Tennessee, Kentucky, Missouri, and Arkansas. Settlement by English-speaking peoples in West Texas took place somewhat later than in East Texas, essentially as an extension of settlement in the north central part of the state.

English-speaking settlers did not begin arriving in Southern California until the 1850s, but by the 1880s Los Angeles had become a thriving population center with a wide sphere of cultural and linguistic influence. Northern California received its first major influx of English speakers in 1849, with the advent of gold fever, and migrations to the famed mining region became even heavier after 1869, when the Transcontinental Railroad was completed. The Pacific Northwest forms a relatively coherent dialect area and is centered on the Portland district. The earliest English speakers in the Northwest were the British, who had settled in the Puget Sound area of Washington by 1828. Following closely on their heels were trappers and traders from New England. These people were so prevalent on the Oregon coast, even as early as the latter years of the eighteenth century, that Native Americans in the area once referred to all White people as "Bostons." Following the establishment of a successful American settlement in Northwestern Oregon in 1843, English-speaking settlers began arriving in the Northwest in large numbers, at first from the Ohio Valley states and Tennessee, and later from Missouri, Illinois, and Iowa. In addition, there was a significant Scandinavian presence in the region from the end of the nineteenth century.

The New Englanders who populated the Pacific Northwest during its earliest decades of English-speaking settlement brought with them a number of Northern dialect features which persisted into the early twentieth century, including lexical items such as *gunny sack* for "burlap bag" and pronunciation features such as the use of a British-like *a* vowel in words such as *path* and *grass*. This latter is now an archaic feature in the US and is largely confined to portions of Eastern New England and certain highly localized areas of the Pacific Northwest. In contrast, the Southwest has little Northernism, particularly in the immense area dominated by the Texas hub. The persistence of New England speech features as far west as Washington and Oregon is testament to the enduring character of the dialect boundaries established in the earliest decades of English in the New World.

At the same time, some newer dialect areas in the West are now becoming more distinctive from other varieties of American English. For example, West Coast speech increasingly is characterized by the fronting of back vowels, so that the vowel of *boot* sounds more like *biwt* and *good* sounds more like *gid*. Southern California is apparently leading the way with this language change. Similarly, the use of so-called UPTALK – that is, rising or "question" intonation on declarative statements – is now becoming a prominent trait of West Coast dialects ranging from Los Angeles to Portland. Though once associated with the "Valley Girl" talk of teenage girls in the San Fernando Valley area of California, uptalk has spread far beyond its apparent West Coast origins and is now prevalent in the speech of young people of both sexes in many parts of the US. We thus see that some innovations in American English are now actually spreading from West to East rather than following the traditional East to West flow. Furthermore, in some regions, features with originally regional associations are coming to be used to convey social or cultural distinctions. For example, residents of urban areas in Arizona tend to use West Coast vowel pronunciations, while Arizona ranchers use more Southern vowel features. Most likely, the differing pronunciation patterns are due to each group's sense of cultural distinctiveness from the other and their desire to project these differences in speech and other social behaviors. A focus on the original development of English on the West Coast may reflect a westward expansion of the traditional dialects of the Eastern US, but a contemporary perspective shows that some regions on the West Coast are forming their own dialect niches and even initiating changes that are becoming widespread throughout American English.

4.5 The Present and Future State of American English

Finally, we examine the current dialect contours of the US and their future path of development. As we have already mentioned, the traditional dialect boundaries of the US, particularly those in the Eastern US, were drawn based on information from linguistic surveys that were conducted in the 1930s and 1940s. Since most of the speakers surveyed were older, the patterns reflect dialect divisions in the late nineteenth and very early twentieth centuries, when these speakers' speech patterns were established. Thus, one cannot simply assume that the dialect boundaries depicted in figure 4.2 were still firmly in place in the 1940s and beyond. The boundaries depicted in figure 4.3, based on data gathered between 1965 and 1970 in addition to the earlier data (Carver 1987), suggest that dialect divisions may not have changed greatly in the first half of the twentieth century. However, the data from the latter half of the twentieth century do suggest that some dialect areas are losing the distinctiveness that they still possessed in the early part of the century while other areas may be developing new dialect traits that set them apart.

As we consider the extent to which the traditional dialect landscape has been altered over the past century, and particularly in more recent decades, we must bear in mind that a number of important sociohistorical and sociocultural changes have taken place since the initial linguistic surveys were conducted in the US. Among the important changes are the following: (1) changing patterns of immigration and language contact; (2) shifting patterns of population movement; (3) changing cultural centers; and (4) increasing interregional accessibility.

During the twentieth century, immigrants continued to pour into America. Many were members of the same cultural groups who came in large numbers in the nineteenth century (e.g. Germans, Italians, Irish), while others were new to the US or arrived in significant numbers for the first time. The languages brought by these new immigrant groups affected general American English, as did the languages of previous generations of immigrants. These languages may also serve as bases for the creation of new sociocultural varieties of English. Hispanic English is now so widespread in such states as Florida, Texas, and New Mexico, as well as a number of major cities throughout the country, that there are now recognized varieties of Hispanic English. Although Spanish influence on English is longstanding, this influence was not pervasive enough to lead to the formation of a distinctive dialect of English until recent decades, when new influxes of Spanish-speaking peoples began arriving in large numbers. For example, Mexican Americans now form the biggest minority group in Texas, and they are the majority ethnic group in two of Texas's five biggest cities: San Antonio and El Paso. In Florida, most Hispanics are of Cuban ancestry, although a number of Puerto Ricans and Central Americans have also settled in the state. And Southeastern states such as Georgia and North Carolina have had large waves of Latino immigrants within just the last decade. Many continue to speak Spanish, whether as their sole language or in addition to English or other languages. Others speak primarily English. Often, they speak a variety of English that was influenced by Spanish earlier in the course of its development, even though they themselves do not use

Spanish as their primary language (or may not even speak it at all). We will discuss some of the traits of Hispanic varieties of English in more detail in chapter 6.

Other immigration patterns are more limited to particular historical events, but they may also have their linguistic effect. For example, a variety of Vietnamese English arose following the extensive migration of Vietnamese into the US after the fall of Saigon in the mid-1970s. In regions where it has been studied (e.g. Houston, Texas, and Arlington, Virginia) this variety has been found to be characterized by features such as the use of unmarked past tense forms (e.g. *When we were children, we go to the market with our mothers*) and extensive consonant cluster reduction (e.g. *wes'* for *west* or *fin'* for *find*). However, it is unclear whether these traits will persist into the future. Other varieties of English may be in formation among other recent immigrants from Asia, for example, among the Hmong in St Paul, Minnesota.

In addition to the changing patterns of cultural contact that result from new patterns of immigration, we also find changing cultural relations among members of different ethnic groups who have long resided in America. The desegregation of ethnic communities is an ongoing process in American society which continually brings speakers of different ethnicities into closer contact with one another. The expected result of this interethnic contact is the erosion of ethnic dialect boundaries; however, research indicates that ethnolinguistic boundaries can be remarkably persistent, even in the face of sustained daily interethnic contact. This is largely because ethnic dialects are an important component of cultural and individual identity. Furthermore, our own research on interethnic dialect contact has shown that even when speakers do cross ethnic dialect lines by adopting features from other ethnic groups, they may subtly alter the adopted features in order to convert them into markers of their own ethnolinguistic identity. In chapter 6 we discuss two instances of this phenomenon, the case of Cajun English and the case of Lumbee Native American English.

Not only are speakers coming into contact with different cultural and linguistic groups through immigration and desegregation, but we also find that cross-cultural and cross-dialectal mixing results when large populations of speakers migrate from one region of the country to another. Historically, the significant migrations of English-speaking people in the US have run along east–west lines, but in the twentieth century there was major population movement along north–south lines as well. For example, beginning in the post-World War I years, large numbers of rural southern African Americans began migrating northward into such major cities as Chicago, Detroit, and New York. As we mentioned in chapter 2, there were two streams of northerly migration: African Americans from such states as North and South Carolina tended to migrate along a coastal route to Washington, DC, Philadelphia, and New York, while those from the Deep South tended to migrate via a Midwestern route into St Louis, Chicago, and Detroit. There are some subtle dialect lines that seem to mark these routes of migration. For example, speakers of African American English (AAE) in Midwestern cities are less likely to use [v] for voiced *th* [ð] in items such as *bruvver* "brother" and *smoov* "smooth" than their counterparts in Eastern Seaboard locales such as Philadelphia and New York. In more recent decades, however, there has been a movement of African Americans back to the South, indicating something of a reversal of the population movement of the early and mid-twentieth century, a trend that has extended into the twenty-first century.

For the most part, it seems that the descendants of the African Americans who migrated northward following World War I, particularly those of the working class, have remained relatively isolated from surrounding White speakers, and so there has been little cross-assimilation between African American and European American speech varieties in America's large northern cities. Only in certain cultural areas has AAE made a large impact on European American English. For example, because popular music has been heavily influenced by African Americans, so too has its lexicon, as evidenced in the widespread usage of such AAE-derived terms as *jazz*, *riff*, and *jam* for older generations and *rap* and *hip hop* for younger ones. In addition, youth culture in America relies heavily upon African American music, fashion, and ways of speaking. Linguists debate whether non-native speakers of AAE can really "pick up" the dialect, using all of its (unconscious) rules correctly; however, there is no denying that adolescents and young adults all over the nation (and across the world) can be heard to use certain AAE lexical items, set phrases, and specific pronunciations, whether or not they have managed to integrate these various features into a consistent language system. Further, we have to bear in mind that people use features of other dialects for a variety of social reasons (e.g. "fitting in," performing, "being cool"), and linguistic "accuracy" may have very little bearing on achieving these goals. We discuss the linguistic and social aspects of using non-native dialects, or CROSSING, in more detail in chapter 9.

In recent decades, the American South has witnessed a large influx of European American speakers from Midland and Northern dialect areas, who are settling there in increasing numbers due to factors that range from economic opportunity to desirable climate. It is unclear at this point exactly how great an impact the speech of these non-Southerners has had or will have on the traditional Southern dialect. At first glance, the effect seems enormous indeed, especially in areas such as Miami, Florida; Houston, Texas; and the Research Triangle Park area of North Carolina, where Southerners are overwhelmed by non-Southerners to such a degree that it is becoming increasingly rare in these areas to locate young people with "genuine Southern accents." However, there are factors that work to counter the dialect inundation that may result from such linguistic SWAMPING. For example, Southerners have long viewed their dialect as a strong marker of regional identity and often even as a source of cultural pride, and such feelings about a speech variety may certainly help preserve it, even in the face of massive linguistic pressure from outside groups. For example, Guy Bailey and his colleagues (Bailey, Wikle, Tillery, and Sand 1993) have found that some Southern dialect features in Oklahoma, including the use of *fixin' to* (as in *She's fixin' to go to the races*), have persisted and even spread in the face of increasing settlement within the state by non-Southerners. Furthermore, heavy use of *fixin' to* correlates with regional pride, as measured in people's responses to the survey question, "Is Oklahoma a good place to live?" Thus, it seems that *fixin' to* carries strong symbolic meaning as a marker of regional identity; this symbolic meaning may play a key role in the form's ability to stay afloat in the face of linguistic swamping.

If indeed only those dialect forms that carry special social significance are likely to be retained in the face of pressure from outside dialects, perhaps the true result of linguistic swamping in the American South will be neither the complete loss of Southern speech varieties nor their preservation in "pure form." Rather, the result may be a sort of linguistic FOCUSING, in which a few highly noticeable dialect features are retained while other, less "important" features are readily relinquished. Such linguistic focusing may give the appearance that a particular dialect is becoming more rather than less distinctive from surrounding varieties as it struggles against competing varieties. In reality, though, only a few of its features are distinctive; it just so happens that these features are extremely conspicuous and readily serve to make listeners "sit up and take notice."

A third type of sociocultural change that has affected America over the last couple of centuries is the shifting of cultural and economic centers. As Americans began leaving rural areas in large numbers for the economic opportunities offered by the nation's large cities in the early twentieth century, older and newer metropolitan areas took on increased significance. Today, these metropolitan areas are the focal points for many current linguistic innovations. In the process, dialect features that were formerly markers of regional speech have been transformed into markers of social class, ethnicity, or urban–rural distinctions. For example, some of the Southern regional features which form part of AAE (e.g. *r*-lessness, the pronunciation of *time* as *tahm*) became markers of ethnic rather than regional identity in the large northern cities to which AAE was transplanted. Similarly, it has been shown that as Europeans in the Midwestern cornbelt leave their farms for the economic opportunities of the city, they are bringing with them certain linguistic innovations that characterize rural speech. They then use these rural language features as a symbolic means of asserting their belief in rural values and a rural lifestyle even though they are surrounded by urban culture and dialect forms in the midst of the big-city atmosphere. Further, the English varieties developed by the immigrant groups who poured into America in the nineteenth century came to serve as markers of intra-city ethnic identity rather than as indicators of European (or other) nationality *per se*; in addition, these speech varieties also often came to serve as indicators of lower-class status, as did AAE and other varieties whose roots are in rural dialects.

Another change in the linguistic landscape brought about by increasing urbanization is the loss of much of the traditional vocabulary, largely rural in nature, whose distributional patterns underlie the traditional dialect map. However, as we discussed above, the loss of traditional dialect terms does not necessarily entail the erasure of dialect boundaries. Although many traditional rural terms have disappeared from the New England dialect area, a number of new terms have come into the dialect, and these follow the same dialect boundaries as the older words.

The final type of change we must bear in mind is the ever-widening network of transportation and intercommunication that has spread across the US landscape throughout the later twentieth century and is still spreading in the current one, providing ready access to even the remotest of speech communities. The development of major interstate highways in the mid-twentieth century, as well as the paving of roads and building of bridges broke down formidable geographic barriers, and once-remote regions have been transformed into havens for tourists and other outside visitors. Cable and satellite television, mobile telephones, and internet communications are bringing Americans from across the country into closer communicative contact than ever before. Just a few years ago it was hard to imagine that we might contact a participant in a study in a remote mountain or island community by e-mail or Instant Messenger to ask follow-up question after an interview, but such is the nature of present-day communication networks – and sociolinguistic fieldwork.

One of the most important linguistic consequences of this increasing contact has been the emergence of the phenomenon we now call DIALECT ENDANGERMENT. As some of the more remote areas of the nation are opened to intercommunication with the outside world, their distinctive language varieties, fostered in isolation and spoken by relatively small numbers of people, may be overwhelmed by encroaching dialects. Such a fate is currently befalling a number of islands on the Eastern Seaboard that have become increasingly accessible to tourists and new residents during the latter half of the twentieth century. For example, our in-depth studies of islands on the Outer Banks of North Carolina and in the Chesapeake Bay indicate that some of these dialects are in a MORIBUND, or dying, state. We have also seen dramatically different responses to dialect endangerment, ranging from the rapid decline of a traditional dialect within a couple of generations of speakers to the intensification of dialectal distinctiveness. Thus, while some dialect areas of the Outer Banks in North Carolina are rapidly losing most of their traditional dialect features, residents of Smith Island, Maryland, in the Chesapeake Bay, are actually escalating their use of distinguishing dialect features. As the traditional maritime trade in Smith Island declines, more and more islanders are moving to the mainland. Thus, even though the dialect is intensifying rather than weakening, it is in danger of dying out through sheer population loss. Most likely, this intensification is due to an increasing sense of solidarity as fewer and fewer islanders remain to follow the traditional Smith Island way of life.

The fact that different communities may have such different responses to moribund dialect status underscores the need to examine ecological, demographic, economic, and sociocultural factors in examining the course of language change, not only with respect to endangered dialects but with respect to language change in general. These situations also raise cautions about predicting the fate of dialects in a given community, since there are so many different intersecting factors that come into play, ranging from the nature of linguistic structures to the sociopsychological disposition of the community with respect to its traditional lifestyle, including its dialect.

Though the ultimate fate of American English dialects in the new millennium is often debated in public and by the media, it is hardly an issue to linguists. Current dialect surveys based largely on phonological systems, in particular, vowel systems, rather than on isolated lexical items and scattered pronunciation details indicate that American dialects are alive and well – and that some dimensions of these dialects may be more prominent than they were in the past. The key figure in current pronunciation-based dialectology is William Labov. Using data from a telephone survey (called TELSUR) conducted in the 1990s, Labov and his associates have determined that the three major dialect divisions indicated by early dialect geographers (e.g. Kurath 1949) still seem to be in place. A dialect map based on the results of the TELSUR survey is given in figure 4.4.

Although the exact path followed by Labov's dialect lines differs slightly from Kurath's, the basic separations in the East and Midwest are still between a Southern dialect area, a Midland region (characterized by the merger of the [ɔ] and [ɑ] vowels in word pairs such as *Dawn* and *Don*), and a Northern area, which Labov calls the Northern Cities area, since the pronunciations that characterize this region are most prominent in the region's large cities. In addition, we see that some new dialect regions seem to have arisen. As we discussed in section 4.4, the West has become a distinctive region, and some West Coast dialects are even leading the spread

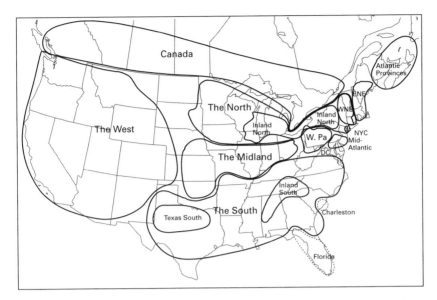

Figure 4.4 Dialect areas of the United States, based on telephone survey data (from Labov, Ash, and Boberg 2005; reprinted by permission of Mouton de Gruyter, a division of Walter de Gruyter GmbH & Co.)

of certain dialect features across the US. For example, the use of *be like*, or *go* to introduce quoted speech or indicate what the speaker was thinking at the time (e.g. *So he goes, "What are you doing tonight?" and I was like, "Give me a break!"*) most likely started in Southern California just a few decades ago, but today it is used not only throughout North America but in Britain, Australia, and New Zealand as well. Furthermore, as we have mentioned, "uptalk," in which question-like intonation is used on statements, seems to be diffusing in the United States from the West Coast eastward. Labov further indicates that the basic dialect divisions may actually be intensifying rather than weakening. As we will discuss in more detail in chapter 5, it appears that the vowel systems that characterize the Northern Cities and the South are becoming more distinct from one another, as well as from the intervening Midland area.

Clearly, new dialects must be included along with the old when we consider the contemporary state of dialects in the United States. Dialect difference in America is by no means a thing of the past, and there is every indication that the boundaries whose foundations were laid when the first English colonists arrived in Jamestown in 1607 will continue to exist in some form long into the current millennium.

Exercise 3

Given the fact that television and other forms of mass media now expose speakers to all sorts of dialects, particularly the American standard, why do the basic dialect divisions in the US appear to be holding steady and perhaps even strengthening? Why do you think television and the internet have little effect on core dialect differences, despite the popular perception that the mass media serve as the primary culprit in the erosion of longstanding dialect boundaries?

4.6 Further Reading

Carver, Craig M. (1987) *American Regional Dialects: A Word Geography*. Ann Arbor: University of Michigan Press. Based on data from linguistic surveys conducted under the aegis of the *Linguistic Atlas of the United States and Canada* in the 1930s and 1940s and the *Dictionary of American Regional English* in 1965–70, Carver carefully delineates the dialects of American English, eliminating the "Midland" area established by traditional dialect geographers. His discussions of dialect areas and dialect features are interwoven with a detailed account of the dialect history of the US. A number of illustrative maps are provided.

Downes, William (1998) Rhoticity. In *Language and Society*, 2nd edn. London: Fontana, 133–75. This chapter provides a detailed discussion of the history and current status of *r* in British and American English dialects. Of particular interest is Downes's discussion of the viewpoints of several researchers regarding the disputed history of *r*-lessness in the United States.

Kurath, Hans (1949) *Word Geography of the Eastern United States*. Ann Arbor: University of Michigan Press. In this work, Kurath presents what has come to be regarded as the traditional dialect map of the United States. Subsequent dialectologists have made slight revisions to this map, but Kurath's original lines, for the most part, remain intact, and his work remains historically significant.

Labov, William, Sharon Ash, and Charles Boberg (2005) *The Atlas of North American English*. New York/Berlin: Mouton de Gruyter. This work presents the results of the most comprehensive and current survey of American English dialects, as delimited by their phonological systems. Interactive CD-ROMs with extensive sound files help illustrate many of the features discussed in the book.

Montgomery, Michael (2004) Solving Kurath's puzzle: Establishing the antecedents of the American Midland dialect region. In Raymond Hickey (ed.), *The Legacy of Colonial English*. Cambridge: Cambridge University Press, 410–25. This article provides an informed discussion of issues surrounding the formation of the Midland dialect of American English, with a discussion of specific retentions, modifications, and losses of structures from Ulster English. It also points out the complexities involved in making these assessments.

Schneider, Edgar W. (2003) The dynamics of new Englishes: From identity construction to dialect birth. *Language* 79: 233–81. This article offers an excellent outline of the sociopolitical, sociopsychological, and sociolinguistic traits associated with the progressive stages of English language diffusion throughout the world. Case studies of the spread of English into many locations world-wide, including the United States, give insight into the social and linguistic dynamics of earlier American English.

5

Regional Dialects

The investigation of the regional dialects of American English has been a major concern for dialectologists and sociolinguists since at least the early part of the twentieth century, when the *Linguistic Atlas of the United States and Canada* was launched and dialectologists began conducting large-scale surveys of regional dialect forms. Although the traditional focus on regional variation took a back seat to concerns for social and ethnic dialect diversity for a couple of decades, there has been resurgent interest in the regional dimension of American dialects. This revitalization was buoyed by the publication of different volumes of the *Dictionary of American Regional English* (Cassidy 1985; Cassidy and Hall 1991, 1996; Hall 2002), and more recently, by the publication of *The Atlas of North American English* (Labov, Ash, and Boberg 2005).

Linguists have long debated the precise place of regional dialect studies in the overall investigation of language variation, given the fact that traditional studies have concentrated on the geographical distribution of individual words as opposed to overall patterns of language organization. The focus on cartographic plotting as opposed to linguistic patterning has led some to the conclusion that regional dialect study is really a branch of geography rather than a kind of linguistic inquiry. Certainly, studies of regional language variation may be informed by models and methods from the fields of cultural and historical geography, but there is no inherent reason why the study of regional variation in language cannot mesh models from geography with the rigorous study of linguistic patterning. In fact, linguists have historically turned to regional dialect diversity in search of answers to fundamental questions about language patterning and language change. By the same token, the study of regional dialects profits from the precise structural description of forms that detailed linguistic study provides. Some recent studies of language variation have neatly integrated models from these distinct vantage points in insightful and informative ways. In this chapter, we consider various methodologies for studying regional variation, as well as models that apply to the spread of linguistic forms over time and space.

5.1 Eliciting Regional Dialect Forms

The traditional approach to charting regional dialect patterns starts with the elicitation of diagnostic dialect forms from speakers representing local communities within a broader geographical area. In most major projects conducted under the aegis of the *Linguistic Atlas of the United States and Canada*, targeted areas constituted major regions of the United States, such as New England, the Upper Midwest, the Gulf States, and so forth, but studies run the full gamut of regional size, including state surveys or even subdivisions within states.

Traditional questionnaires can be quite exhaustive and may take hours to administer as each possible dialect form is probed. For example, the questionnaire used for the *Dictionary of American Regional English* (*DARE*) contains over 1,800 questions in all. The actual questions used to elicit forms may vary, depending on the item. Typical elicitation frames include the following:

1 Labeling Based upon a Description of an Item
    e.g. *What do you call a small amount of food that's eaten between meals?*
        What do you call the heavy metal pan that's used to fry foods?
2 Labeling an Item Present at the Scene
    e.g. *What do you call that piece of furniture you're sitting on?*
        What time is it in this picture?
3 Completing Incomplete Phrases or Sentences
    e.g. *When your skin and eyeballs turn yellow, you're getting* _____.
        When a pond or lake becomes entirely covered with ice, you say it's _____.
4 Listing Topical Inventories of Items
    e.g. *What kinds of wild flowers do you have around here?*
        What kinds of snakes do you have around here?

The aim of elicitation is simply to get subjects to offer the variant they would normally use, without biasing their choice by suggesting a variant of the item in the elicitation frame. A fieldworker's notes may include the variant offered by the subject in response to a particular question frame, appropriate notes about reactions to forms, familiarity with alternative forms, and any other relevant observations. In figure 5.1, we have excerpts from the fieldnotes of a leading American dialectologist, Raven I. McDavid, Jr. The interview was conducted in 1946 in Charleston, South Carolina, with

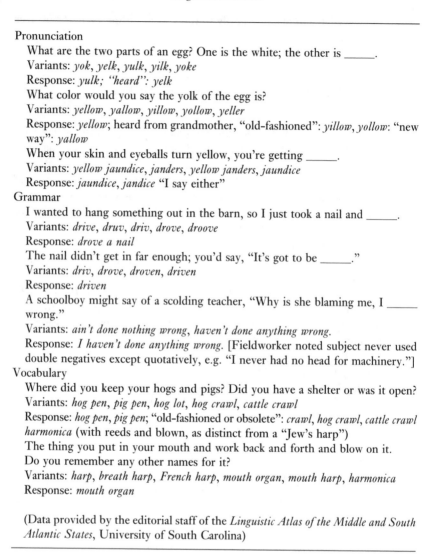

Pronunciation

 What are the two parts of an egg? One is the white; the other is _____.
 Variants: *yok, yelk, yulk, yilk, yoke*
 Response: *yulk; "heard": yelk*
 What color would you say the yolk of the egg is?
 Variants: *yellow, yallow, yillow, yollow, yeller*
 Response: *yellow*; heard from grandmother, "old-fashioned": *yillow, yollow*: "new way": *yallow*
 When your skin and eyeballs turn yellow, you're getting _____.
 Variants: *yellow jaundice, janders, yellow janders, jaundice*
 Response: *jaundice, jandice* "I say either"

Grammar

 I wanted to hang something out in the barn, so I just took a nail and _____.
 Variants: *drive, druv, driv, drove, droove*
 Response: *drove a nail*
 The nail didn't get in far enough; you'd say, "It's got to be _____."
 Variants: *driv, drove, droven, driven*
 Response: *driven*
 A schoolboy might say of a scolding teacher, "Why is she blaming me, I _____ wrong."
 Variants: *ain't done nothing wrong, haven't done anything wrong.*
 Response: *I haven't done anything wrong.* [Fieldworker noted subject never used double negatives except quotatively, e.g. "I never had no head for machinery."]

Vocabulary

 Where did you keep your hogs and pigs? Did you have a shelter or was it open?
 Variants: *hog pen, pig pen, hog lot, hog crawl, cattle crawl*
 Response: *hog pen, pig pen*; "old-fashioned or obsolete": *crawl, hog crawl, cattle crawl*
 harmonica (with reeds and blown, as distinct from a "Jew's harp")
 The thing you put in your mouth and work back and forth and blow on it.
 Do you remember any other names for it?
 Variants: *harp, breath harp, French harp, mouth organ, mouth harp, harmonica*
 Response: *mouth organ*

(Data provided by the editorial staff of the *Linguistic Atlas of the Middle and South Atlantic States*, University of South Carolina)

Figure 5.1 Samples from a *Linguistic Atlas* worksheet

a white female, age 69, who was an artist and author as well as a member of the highest social class in the community. The excerpt includes sample questions designed to elicit pronunciation, grammar, and lexical forms as contained in the fieldwork manual used by each fieldworker in the survey.

 The existence of an established dialect survey questionnaire format also provides a convenient basis for comparing dialect surveys in different communities and in the same community at different points in time. For example, in *American Regional Dialects: A Word Geography* (1987), Craig Carver compares a set of items elicited in the New England area in the *DARE* surveys of the 1960s with items elicited in surveys of the same area conducted in connection with the *Linguistic Atlas of the United States and Canada* project, launched in 1929. He concludes that "despite enormous changes in the distribution and currency of the regional vocabulary during the middle third of the twentieth century, these subregions [of New England] and their particular dimensions have remained intact" (1987: 51). Likewise, Ellen Johnson, in *Lexical Change and Variation in the Southeastern United States* (1996), compares items in similar populations across a 55-year time span to show how the dialect vocabulary of the Southeastern United States has shifted over time. She shows further that various cultural and social variables such as education level, rurality, and age have remained fairly constant in their effect on the lexicon as it has changed during this period.

Exercise 1

Following are some dialect variants, including pronunciation, grammar, and vocabulary items. For each of the items, construct reasonable question frames that would enable a fieldworker to elicit the items without using the item itself in the question. Try your questions on some speakers and evaluate the relative success of your frames. What kinds of items seem the easiest to elicit, and what items the most difficult?

Pronunciation
1 The production of the vowel in *ten* and *tin*.
2 The production of the first vowel in *ferry*, *fairy*, and *furry*.
3 The production of the vowel in *caught* and *cot*.

Grammar
1 The plural form of *deer*.
2 The past tense and participle form (e.g. *has_____*) of *creep*.
3 The use of indefinite forms in a negative sentence (e.g. *He didn't go anywhere/nowhere*).

Lexical
1 The use of the term *frying pan*, *skillet*, *spider*, etc.
2 The use of *ATM/bank machine/cash machine/guichet*.
3 Distinctions between different shades of purple in the color spectrum.

5.2 Mapping Regional Variants

Once the data have been collected from community representatives, the different variants for each item are plotted on a map in some fashion. Typically, distinct symbols are used to indicate different variants. In a classic example of this cartographic method, from Hans Kurath's *A Word Geography of the Eastern United States* (1949: fig. 66), the distribution of *pail* and *bucket* is charted for subjects interviewed in the 1930s and 1940s as part of the initial phase of the *Linguistic Atlas* project. In the map in figure 5.2, the larger symbols indicate that four or more subjects in a community used the variant in question.

Charting the variants for each item and community on a map was originally done by hand, a time-consuming task that required careful attention to cartographic detail. In more recent years, this process has been aided immeasurably through the use of software that can generate these cartographic plots automatically. Plotting programs allow researchers not only to plot their data more quickly and accurately but to display their data in a variety of formats. In figure 5.3, we provide a computer-generated map of the same data captured in figure 5.2. The plotting includes four degrees of probability shading for the elicitation of the *pail* variant, with the darkest squares showing the highest probability that speakers will use the term *pail* (75–100 percent) and the white squares showing the lowest probability (0–25 percent) that this term will be elicited. In current dialect mapping, probabilities are often preferred over depictions of the simple use or non-use of forms, because they more accurately reflect the tendencies when variable data are involved.

Plotting programs such as the one used to produce figure 5.3 are now readily available to researchers. It is also possible to generate maps of particular regional dialect features from certain web sites, for example the web site for the *Linguistic Atlas of the Middle and South Atlantic States* (http://hyde.park.uga.edu/lamsas/lingmaps.html). National maps for distinctive vowel traits can be found at http://www.ling.upenn.edu/phono_atlas/home.html.

Computerized cartographic methods were first used in connection with the *DARE* surveys beginning in the early 1960s. In figure 5.4 is a comparison of a computer-generated map from *DARE* and a conventional, hand-drawn map. An added wrinkle in the *DARE* map is its proportional display of states on the basis of population density, rather than geographical area. With this type of display, a state such as Texas is not nearly as large as New York, even though it is much more expansive geographically, since New York has a higher proportion of the population of the United States than Texas. By comparison with the traditional spatial map, the proportional

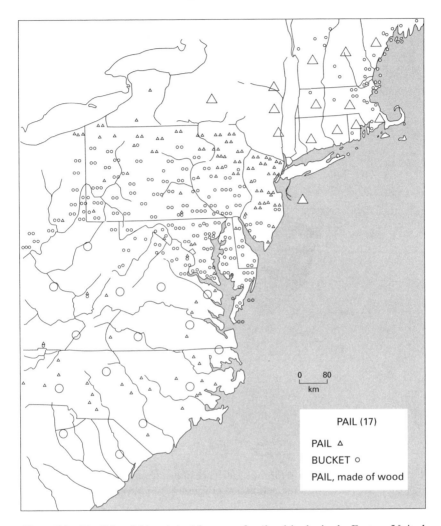

Figure 5.2   Traditional *Linguistic Atlas* map of *pail* and *bucket* in the Eastern United States (from Kurath 1949: figure 66; reprinted by permission of the University of Michigan Press)

map seems distorted, but it adds the important dimension of population distribution to the consideration of regional variation. As we shall see when we discuss dialect diffusion later in this chapter, population density can be an important factor in the regional spread of dialect variants.

The development of computerized cartographic techniques certainly has gone a long way towards reducing the time-consuming and painstaking

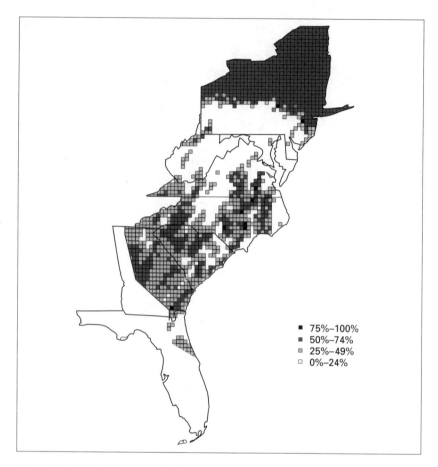

Figure 5.3   Probability map for the occurrence of *pail* (from Kretzschmar 1996: 32, figure 14. Reprinted with the permission of Cambridge University Press)

work once involved in mapping patterns of geographical distribution and has made cartographic plotting readily accessible to a wide audience of researchers and students.

5.3   The Distribution of Dialect Forms

For some items that are characteristic of certain regions, the distribution of dialect forms shows a GROUP-EXCLUSIVE pattern in which communities in

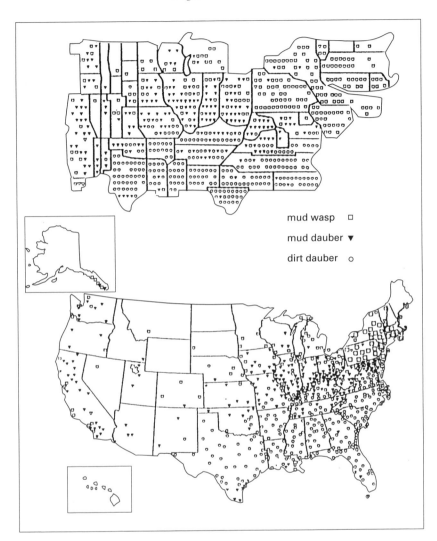

mud wasp ▫

mud dauber ▼

dirt dauber ○

Figure 5.4   Comparison of *DARE* map and conventional map of dialect variants (from Cassidy 1985: xxix, figure 7; © 1985 by the President and Fellows of Harvard College, reprinted by permission of Harvard University Press)

one area use one variant while those in another region use a different one. For example, in the map of *pail* and *bucket* displayed in figure 5.3, you can trace a line of demarcation that sets apart southern and northern regions of Pennsylvania: South of the line *bucket* is used and north of the line *pail* is used. When the distribution shows a fairly clear-cut demarcation, a

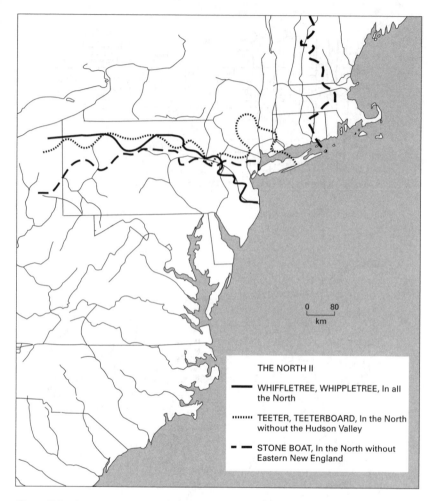

Figure 5.5   Sample of a bundle of isoglosses (from Kurath 1949: figure 5A; reprinted by permission of the University of Michigan Press)

line indicating the boundaries of the different variants, an ISOGLOSS, may be drawn.

Isoglosses set apart zones of usage in a very discrete way, but not all patterns of usage are as clear as that delimited for the use of *pail* and *bucket* in Pennsylvania in the 1930s and 1940s. In many cases, variants are more interspersed, making it difficult to draw a meaningful isogloss. Thus, in the South, there are pockets of usage for *pail* in Virginia, North Carolina, and Georgia. Furthermore, there are often TRANSITIONAL ZONES, where the variants coexist, so different speakers might use different variants, or individual speakers may use both. In fact, transitional zones are more typical than the abrupt pattern of distribution implied by isoglosses, especially in more densely populated areas. Isoglosses are certainly useful in indicating the outer boundaries of regional usage patterns, but they must be used with important qualifications. Isoglosses often represent ideal rather than real patterns of delimitation, a "convenient fiction existing in an abstract moment in time" (Carver 1987: 13).

In a microscopic view of regional variation, each boundary line between two different forms for a given item indicates a different dialect area, but this reduces the definition of regional dialect to a trivial one. When the overall responses to dialect questionnaires are considered, different isoglosses may show similar patterns of delimitation. These clusters, or BUNDLES OF ISOGLOSSES, are usually considered significant in determining regional dialect areas. For example, when the isogloss for *pail* vs. *bucket* is considered along with those for *whiffletree, teeter/teeterboard*, and *stone boat*, the isoglosses tend to coincide, as shown in figure 5.5.

Predictably, major regional areas are typically determined by having larger bundles of isoglosses than minor dialect areas. Using this approach, the initial phase of the *Linguistic Atlas* survey of the Eastern United States ended up proposing several major regional dialects and some minor dialect areas. For example, Kurath, in his *Word Geography of the Eastern United States* (1949), presented a map of major and minor areas that became the standard representation of regional dialects along the Eastern Seaboard for almost a half century. As we discussed in chapter 4, this map delimits three major regional areas, the North, the Midland, and the South, with a number of subregional dialects for each major area. This map is reprinted as figure 5.6.

A number of direct quantitative measures have been proposed for determining the relative significance of isogloss bundles. One of the more systematic and comprehensive analyses of regional dialects using isogloss patterning is found in Carver's *American Regional Dialects: A Word Geography* (1987), which is based primarily upon lexical data (800 lexical items with regional distribution) taken from the files of *DARE*. Carver's analysis uses the notion of ISOGLOSSAL LAYERING to determine major and minor regional varieties. The term LAYER, taken from physical geography, is used to refer to a unique set of areal features, but the importance of this concept lies in the fact that it is used to capture overlap and divergence in regional dialects by examining levels of layering rather than independent sets of isogloss bundles. The most concentrated regional dialect area, where the greatest number of regionally specific features are present, is the PRIMARY DIALECT AREA. In SECONDARY and TERTIARY dialect areas, there are progressively fewer of these dialect features. For example, the core of the Northeast American English dialect has 20 to 24 words from Carver's inventory of

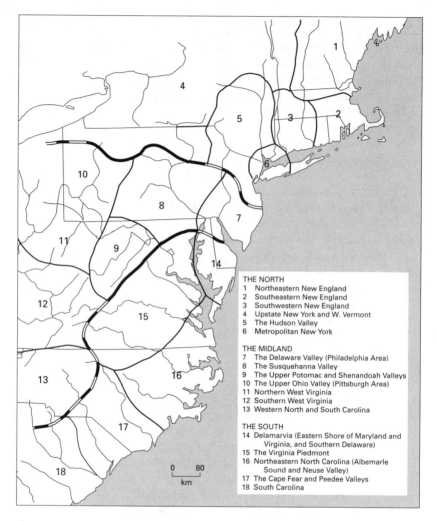

Figure 5.6 Dialect areas of the Eastern United States, based on *Linguistic Atlas* isoglosses (from Kurath 1949: figure 3; reprinted by permission of the University of Michigan Press)

regional lexical items, whereas secondary layers have only 15 to 19, and so forth. While this approach does not eliminate some of the basic problems with isoglosses already pointed out, it captures the hierarchical nature of overlap and divergence in regional varieties. As an example of layering, Carver's (1987) analysis of the extension of the Northern dialect area into the Northwestern United States is given in figure 5.7. The areas labeled as

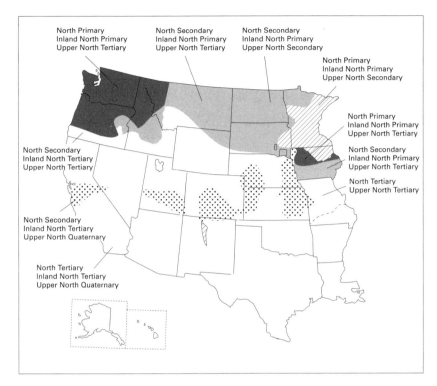

North Primary
Inland North Primary
Upper North Tertiary

North Secondary
Inland North Primary
Upper North Tertiary

North Secondary
Inland North Primary
Upper North Secondary

North Primary
Inland North Primary
Upper North Secondary

North Primary
Inland North Primary
Upper North Tertiary

North Secondary
Inland North Tertiary
Upper North Tertiary

North Secondary
Inland North Primary
Upper North Tertiary

North Tertiary
Upper North Tertiary

North Secondary
Inland North Tertiary
Upper North Quaternary

North Tertiary
Inland North Tertiary
Upper North Quaternary

Figure 5.7   An example of dialect layering in the Northwestern United States (from Carver 1987: 214; reprinted by permission of the University of Michigan Press)

primary represent the core areas of the westward extension of Northern and Inland Northern dialect features, whereas the secondary and tertiary areas represent less concentrated layers of these extensions.

Layering can also be represented hierarchically. For example, Carver's Western dialect layers can be presented in the form of a hierarchical tree, as in figure 5.8.

The fact that lexical variation is so often used as a primary basis for regional dialects has been a major source of contention among students of language variation. For example, Carver's regional analysis is based exclusively on lexical differences. Some linguists have maintained that lexical differences are among the most superficial types of linguistic structure, and therefore among the least reliable indicators of dialect areas. However, it should be noted that Carver's lexical boundaries correlate well with boundaries arrived at independently in cultural geography, including areas delimited by such features as particular architectural styles, religion, political ideology,

Layer
West

Regions

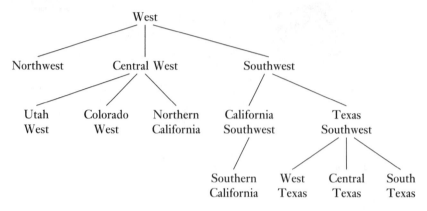

Figure 5.8   An example of dialect layering in the West, represented hierarchically (from Carver 1987: 243; reprinted by permission of the University of Michigan Press)

and a number of other culturally significant variables. Thus, lexical items, regardless of their linguistic status, serve as indicators of more broadly based cultural and historical foundations upon which regional dialects rest, and they should not be dismissed as insignificant.

Many phonological variables show regional variation in a way that parallels with, or, in some cases, departs from the patterns shown for lexical items. Figure 5.9 shows the regional patterning of the merger of the vowels in words such as *cot* and *caught* and *Don* and *Dawn*, based on the telephone survey conducted by William Labov and his associates in the 1990s (Labov, Ash, and Boberg 2005). The merger of the distinction between these vowels is currently one of the major phonological variables differentiating regional varieties of American English.

As with lexical variables, we may expect a kind of regional isogloss layering for phonological variables. We may, for example, expect to find a core Southern or core Northern area, where the highest concentration of specific phonological features is found, and secondary and tertiary zones surrounding these primary areas.

Some phonological features that help define dialect regions involve single items, such as the pronunciation of *greasy* as [grisi] in the North and [grizi] in the South or the pronunciation of *aunt* and *ant* as distinct ([ant] vs. [ænt]) or homophonous items ([ænt]). Ultimately, though, regional pronunciations

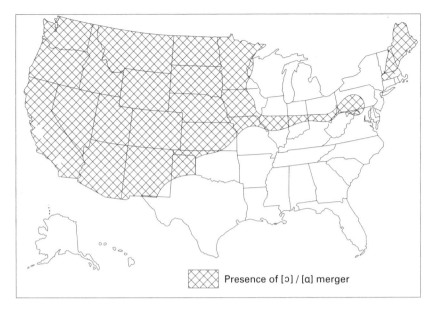

Presence of [ɔ] / [ɑ] merger

Figure 5.9 The three dialect areas of the United States as indicated by the distribution of the [ɔ]/[ɑ] merger

are best viewed in terms of entire sound systems, or sets and subsets of sounds that work together, particularly sets of vowel sounds. As we mentioned in chapters 3 and 4, investigations of vowel systems conducted in the past couple of decades (Labov 1994; Labov et al. 2005) have revealed that there are several major systematic changes currently under way in the US, and each delimits a major dialect area.

One pattern of change is called the Northern Cities Vowel Shift. As Labov (1994: 177–201) describes this change pattern, or vowel rotation pattern, the low long vowels are moving primarily forward, and then upward, and the short vowels are moving downward and backward. For example, a vowel like the /ɔ/ in *coffee* is moving towards the /ɑ/ vowel of words like *father*. The /ɑ/ vowel, in turn, moves towards the /æ/ of *bat*, which then moves upward towards the vowel /ɛ/ of *bet*. At the same time, the /ɛ/ vowel of words like *bet* moves backward towards the /[ʌ]/ vowel of *but*, which is then pushed backward. Diagrammatically, the shift may be represented as in figure 5.10. Recall that the vowels are arranged so that vowels produced with greater tongue height appear at the top of the chart, and those produced with greater fronting of the tongue appear on the left. For convenience, "key words" in terms of idealized standard American English

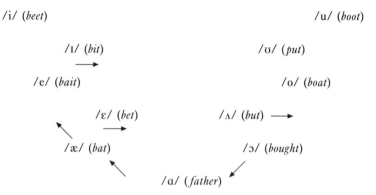

Figure 5.10   The Northern Cities Vowel Shift (adapted from Labov 1991)

phonemes are given. The arrows indicate the direction in which the vowels are moving, based on Labov's characterization of this shift pattern.

Regionally, the vowel rotation pattern depicted in figure 5.10 starts in Western New England and proceeds westward into upstate New York; the extreme northern portions of Ohio, Indiana, and Illinois; Michigan; and Wisconsin. It is more concentrated in the larger metropolitan areas. More advanced stages of this change can be found in younger speakers in the largest metropolitan areas in this Northern region, such as Buffalo, Cleveland, Detroit, and Chicago.

Exercise 2

Identify in the following list of words those items that would be involved in the Northern Cities Vowel Shift. Is the vowel of the word involved in the low long vowel rotation (e.g. *coffee, bat*) or the short vowel shift (e.g. *bit, but*)? Three answers are possible: (1) the vowel is *not* involved in the Northern Cities Vowel Shift, (2) the vowel is involved in the *low long* vowel rotation, (3) the vowel is involved in the *short* vowel rotation.

1	*beet*	6	*stack*
2	*step*	7	*loft*
3	*pat*	8	*top*
4	*look*	9	*cut*
5	*tip*	10	*rope*

As the Northern Cities Vowel Shift spreads across the northern portion of the US, researchers continue to track its progress, not only in geographic space but also across social groups and age groups. In addition, not all researchers are in agreement that the pattern in figure 5.10 tells the whole story, and there may be other vowel movement patterns that are also an important part of dialect change in the Northern US (e.g. Gordon 2001a, 2001b). However, there is no question that sweeping pronunciation changes have been taking place over the course of at least the past several decades – and that these changes are proceeding in quite different directions from the vowel shift patterns affecting the rest of the nation, including the next major shift we discuss, the Southern Vowel Shift.

In the SOUTHERN VOWEL SHIFT, the short front vowels (the vowels of words like *bed* and *bid*) are moving upward and taking on the gliding character of long vowels. In standard American English, a vowel like the long *e* of *bait* actually consists of a vowel nucleus [e] and an upward glide into an [ɪ], so that it sounds more like *bay-eet*. A vowel like the short *e* [ɛ] of *bet* does not have this gliding character, at least not in the idealized standard variety. In the Southern Vowel Shift, the vowel of *bed* moves up toward [e] and takes on a glide, becoming more like *beyd* [beɪd]. Meanwhile, the nuclei of the front long vowels (the [i] of *beet* and [e] of *late*) are moving somewhat backward and downward while preserving their diphthongal or gliding character, and the back vowels are moving forward. The rotational patterns that characterize the Southern Vowel Shift are indicated in figure 5.11.

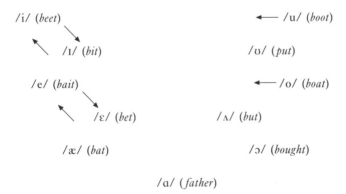

Figure 5.11   The Southern Vowel Shift (adapted from Labov 1991)

Exercise 3

Identify in the following list of words those vowels that would be
involved in the Southern Vowel Shift. Is the vowel of the word
involved in (1) the short vowel shift (e.g. *bid*, *bed*), (2) the long vowel
shift (e.g. *beet*, *late*), or (3) the back vowel shift (e.g. *boat*, *boot*)?

1	*lid*	6	*loop*
2	*rate*	7	*wrote*
3	*leap*	8	*bought*
4	*red*	9	*shed*
5	*keep*	10	*rid*

Because the Southern Vowel Shift and Northern Cities Vowel Shift
involve very different rotation patterns, the two broad varieties characterized by these vowel shifts are becoming increasingly different from one
another. In fact, this differential rotation is the major reason why many
dialectologists now claim that Southern and Northern speech are currently
diverging rather than converging. Regionally, the distribution of the Southern
Vowel Shift is largely confined to the Southern dialect area depicted in both
traditional and more current dialect maps (e.g. Carver's map in figure 4.3,
Labov et al.'s map in figure 4.4). Core and secondary areas within this broad
region may be defined in terms of differing stages in the progression of the
shift – very similarly to how Carver defines primary, secondary, and tertiary
dialect areas on the basis of differing degrees of lexical similarity. Also, it
appears that the Southern Vowel Shift is more advanced in rural areas of
the South than in metropolitan areas. This is largely because Southern
speakers in metropolitan areas are influenced by the speech of non-
Southerners to a greater degree than are Southerners in rural locales. Thus,
the focal area of change for the Southern vowel system is the converse of
that observed for the Northern system, in which changes radiate outward
from, and are most advanced in, urban areas rather than rural locations.

Exercise 4

Identify whether the vowels in the following words are involved in the
Northern Cities Shift or the Southern Vowel Shift. In some cases,
the same vowel may be involved in either the Northern Cities Shift or
the Southern Vowel Shift, but the rotation will be in quite different

directions. There are three types of answer: (1) Northern Cities Shift, (2) Southern Shift, and (3) both the Northern Cities and the Southern Shift, but rotating in different directions. In cases where the same vowel is subject to both the Northern and Southern Shift, identify the direction of the rotation for each shift. You might try producing some of these vowel differences, especially if you know someone who is a good model for the particular shift.

1	*bed*	6	*lost*
2	*cap*	7	*give*
3	*pop*	8	*leap*
4	*lock*	9	*kid*
5	*loop*	10	*said*

Another major dialect region is defined chiefly by its lack of participation in the sweeping rotations of either the Northern Cities or Southern Vowel Shift. In this region, the vowel /æ/ of *bat*, a pivotal vowel in the Northern Cities Shift, is relatively stable, and there is a merger of the low back vowel /ɔ/ (as in *caught*) with the low back/central vowel /ɑ/ (as in *cot*). The approximate area encompassed by this LOW BACK MERGER has already been set forth in figure 5.9. It appears that this merger radiates from three centers. One is in Eastern New England, near the Boston area, which extends well to the north but not very far to the south. Another center is found in Western Pennsylvania which extends to the northern boundary of the traditional Midland area east of the Mississippi River. The third area covers most of the American West, with a transitional area running through Wisconsin, Minnesota, Iowa, Missouri, and Kansas, and then southward to the southernmost portions of New Mexico and Arizona. In the West, the low back vowel merger is more of a rural than a metropolitan phenomenon, as indicated by the fact that speakers in Los Angeles and the Bay area are not nearly as consistent in their merger as speakers in rural areas.

The major dialect regions that emerge based on systematic vowel changes actually approximate the traditional Northern, Southern, and Midland regions as defined chiefly in terms of lexical variation. Further, phonologically based dialect areas encompass areas that are "exceptional" in terms of their vowel shift patterns, just as the traditional North, South, and Midland contain pockets of lexical nonconformity. Thus, whether or not we view the dialect areas of the US in terms of vocabulary or phonology, major metropolitan areas such as New York City and Philadelphia constitute exceptions to the dialect rule; in fact, large cities such as these seem to comprise their own dialect regions.

Exercise 5

Can you think of other examples in which a particular regional pronunciation only seems to affect one word, as with *aunt/ant* and *greasy/greazy*? (Hint: Consider the way natives of a particular city or state may pronounce its name). There are some linguists who would say that pronunciation differences in *greasy/greazy* and *aunt/ant* are actually lexical rather than phonological differences, since they affect only one item and are not the result of general phonological processes. Do you agree?

Grammatical variation can also be represented in ways similar to the phonological and lexical distributions displayed above, although these kinds of isoglosses are less commonly found in the dialect literature. In most cases, geographical studies of grammatical variables have been limited to morphological variants, such as past tense forms of irregular verbs like *dive* (*dove* or *dived*) or different prepositional uses such as *sick to/at/on my stomach*. Most of these cases surveyed in regional dialect studies focus on single forms in grammar rather than general rules. This is not to say that there is no geographical distribution of syntactic patterns, but simply to note that most surveys focus on individual items rather than overarching grammatical patterns.

As an example of regional distribution in syntax, consider the use of *anymore* in affirmative sentences such as *They watch mostly DVDs anymore*. In contexts such as this one, *anymore* means something like "nowadays." This regionally based pattern departs from the general English pattern in which *anymore* can only be used with negative sentences such as *They don't go to the movies anymore* or in questions such as *Do they go to the movies anymore?* The regional distribution of positive *anymore* runs a distinct Midland course though Central Pennsylvania, Ohio, and Indiana and westward into Missouri, Utah, and a number of other Western states. It is also found in mountainous regions of the South (which form part of the Midland dialect area, according to the traditional dialect divisions of Kurath 1949). It does not appear that Northern and Southern dialect areas use the form at all, unless they have been particularly influenced by Scots-Irish. We thus see a persistent founder effect in the regional distribution of this construction.

As we saw in chapter 3, the analysis of dialect differences may focus on lexicon, phonology, grammar, or language use. While lexical and phonological levels have been investigated from a regional perspective, pragmatic features (e.g. address forms, forms for various speech acts) have not been investigated in a systematic way by dialect geographers. It is possible, however, for regional language use differences to be plotted on a map in a way parallel to regional differences in lexical and phonological features. From such a perspective, one could potentially draw an isogloss between certain address forms associated with "Southern politeness" and forms more common in the Midland or North (e.g. the use of *ma'am* and *sir* vs. people's first names), just as readily as between regions characterized by different vowel shift patterns.

5.4 Dialect Diffusion

How do dialect features spread from one place to another? What mechanisms promote or inhibit the spread of dialect forms? Is there a general model of dialect DIFFUSION that accounts for the spread of dialect variants? These are the kinds of questions that often occupy dialectologists and historical linguists as they attempt to explain the spread of dialect forms in time and space.

From one perspective, the regional distribution of language features may be viewed as the result of language change through geographical space over time. A change is initiated at one locale at a given point in time and spreads outward from that point in progressive stages so that earlier changes reach the outlying areas later. This model of language change is referred to as the WAVE MODEL, in which a change originating at a given locale at a particular point in time spreads from that point in successive layers just as waves in water radiate out from a central point of contact when a pebble is dropped into a pool of water.

As a hypothetical example of how the language-change process proceeds, let us assume that there are three linguistic innovations, or rule changes, within a language: R1, R2, and R3. We assume further that all three changes originate at the same geographical location, the FOCAL AREA for the language change. Each one starts later temporally than the other, so R1 is the earliest innovation, R2 the next, and R3 the third. This relation is given in figure 5.12.

At Time 1, R1 is present at the location where the change originated but not in outlying areas. At Time 2, R1 may have spread to an outlying area while another innovation, R2, is initiated in the focal area. At this point, both R1 and R2 are present at the focal site, R1 alone is present in the immediately outlying area, and neither R1 nor R2 may have spread to an area further removed from the focal area. At Time 3, the first change, R1, has spread to the more distant area, but not the later changes, R2 and R3. In this hypothetical pattern of diffusion, we see that the successive dialect areas marked by isoglosses reflect successive stages of language change over

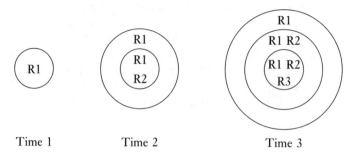

Figure 5.12　Wave model of language change in time and space

time. The spread of dialect forms that follows such a straightforward time and distance relation is sometimes referred to as CONTAGIOUS DIFFUSION.

Although dialect diffusion is usually associated with linguistic innovations among populations in geographical space, a horizontal dimension, it is essential to recognize that diffusion may take place on the vertical dimension of social space as well. In fact, in most cases of diffusion, the vertical and horizontal dimensions operate in tandem. In a population with different social class groups, a change will typically be initiated within a particular social class and spread to other classes from that point, even as the change spreads in geographical space. For example, sociolinguistic researchers such as Labov (1966, 1972b) have shown that much change in American English is initiated in upper working- and lower middle-class groups, as defined by various socioeconomic measures, and spreads from these groups to other classes. (See chapter 6 for more on defining "social class" and delimiting class groups, as well as the spread of language change through social space.)

In the spread of regional dialects, it is quite possible for an innovative form to skip an area which is isolated for physical or social reasons. Most often such areas are geographically distant from focal areas, but sometimes, physical barriers to communication, such as mountainous terrain or bodies of water, may block the spread of a change from a relatively nearby focal point. Prime examples of such areas historically include some of the southern mountain ranges of Appalachia and some of the islands along the Atlantic coast, such as Tangier Island, Virginia, Smith Island, Maryland, and the Sea Islands off the coast of South Carolina and Georgia. It is, however, wrong to equate varieties that retain some older forms of the language with dialects frozen in time, as in the popular mythology that people on the Eastern Shore of Maryland, on the Outer Banks of North Carolina, or in the mountains of Appalachia speak "pure Elizabethan English." While such varieties certainly may not have participated in some of the changes that characterize surrounding dialects, ongoing changes take place in these varieties as well. However, the changes may be of a different type or occur at a different rate than those occurring in less isolated populations.

Social and demographic factors such as social and cultural separation may similarly play a significant role in the rate and direction of change. Thus, many working-class African Americans in Northern metropolitan areas within the United States maintain some older Southern rural dialect forms such as the production of *ask* as *aks* or the use of completive *done*, as in *Kim done took out the trash*, despite the fact that they are a couple of generations removed from their Southern roots. Patterns of ethnic and social segregation have, in fact, inhibited significant changes such as the Northern Cities Vowel Shift from greatly affecting inner-city African American communities, which may remain immune to such changes while maintaining a Southern-based vernacular dialect.

As noted above, a number of qualifications need to be made with respect to the simple wave model of dialect diffusion captured in figure 5.12. In fact, this model rarely works out neatly or symmetrically. Because of various physical, social, and psychological factors, the direction of spread can take a variety of configurations. According to Everett Rogers (1995), a leading researcher in the general diffusion of cultural innovation, at least five factors influence the diffusion of customs, ideas, and practices: (1) the phenomenon itself, (2) communication networks, (3) distance, (4) time, and (5) social structure. Although linguistic structures are inherently quite different from some other types of phenomena, such as technological innovations, they are subject to many of the same factors influencing diffusion in general. A full set of sociocultural and physical factors affects dialect diffusion just as it does other types of cultural innovation. Thus, a wave model of dialect diffusion which considers only distance and time in accounting for dialect diffusion is too simplistic in accounting for the facts of dialect spread.

A GRAVITY MODEL or HIERARCHICAL DIFFUSION model (Trudgill 1974) often provides a better picture of dialect diffusion than a simple wave model. According to this model, which is borrowed from the physical sciences, the diffusion of innovations is a function, not only of the distance from one point to another, as with the wave model, but of the population density of areas that stand to be affected by a nearby change. Changes are most likely to begin in large, heavily populated cities which have historically been cultural centers. From there, they radiate outward, but not in a simple wave pattern. Rather, innovations first reach moderately sized cities that fall under the area of influence of some large, focal city, leaving nearby sparsely populated areas unaffected. Gradually, innovations filter down from more populous, denser areas to less densely populated areas, affecting rural areas last, even if such areas are quite close to the original focal area of the change. The spread of change is thus like skipping a stone across a pond rather

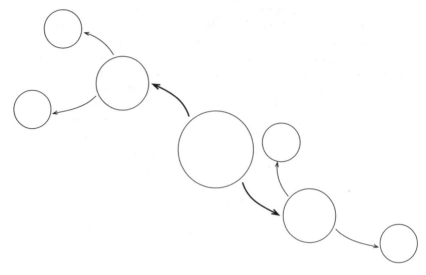

Figure 5.13   Hierarchical model of dialect diffusion

than like that of dropping a stone into a pond, as with the wave model. Figure 5.13 illustrates such a model. Note that larger circle sizes indicate higher population density.

The reason linguistic and other innovations often spread in a hierarchical pattern is due to the fact that there is greater interpersonal contact among places with larger populations, and heavy contact across different population groups strongly promotes the diffusion of innovations. At the same time, diffusion varies based on the distance between locales – that is, interaction diminishes as the distance between two population centers increases. This interplay between the population density of two areas and the distance that separates them parallels the effects of density and distance on gravitational pull – the amount of influence two physical bodies exert upon one another – according to the physical scientific gravity model.

A number of American dialect studies reveal patterning in which linguistic innovations "skip" from one population center to another, leaving rural areas unaffected until the final stages of the change. For example, several features of the Northern Cities Vowel Shift spread from Chicago to outlying areas in a hierarchical pattern – for example, the raising of the /æ/ vowel in words like *tag* and *bad*, so that these words sound similar to *teg* and *bed*, and the fronting of the /ɑ/ vowel in words like *lock* and *top*, so that they sound more like *lack* and *tap*. In fact, Robert Callary (1975) showed that the extent of /æ/ raising in words like *tag* correlated neatly with community size, so that the larger the community, the greater the incidence of vowel raising. In general, /æ/ raising and the other features of the Northern Cities Vowel Shift are centered in large Northern metropolitan areas. Intervening rural areas are not affected, and some inner-city ethnic communities are also unaffected by these changes. In most cases of hierarchical diffusion, the spread of innovation is from relatively large regional centers to smaller, more localized towns. When changes actually do proceed strictly from larger cities to smaller, we have so-called CASCADE DIFFUSION.

The gravity model takes into account the factors of distance and communication networks as a function of population density, but it still doesn't recognize the role of other social structures and physical factors in the spread of dialect forms. For example, a change may reach a smaller city before a slightly larger area, perhaps for geographic reasons, such as difficult terrain, or for social and demographic reasons, such as a high concentration of a certain social class in a given city. The social and demographic characteristics of a region may serve as even stronger barriers to or promoters of change than its geographic features. Changes do not spread evenly across all segments of a population, since some demographic groups are simply more resistant to or accepting of change in general, or to certain specific changes, than others. Labov's research (1966, 1972b, 2001b) indicates that members of "upwardly mobile" social classes, such as upper working- and lower middle-class groups are quicker to adopt innovations than members of other classes. Studies also show that women are often among the leaders in certain kinds of language change and that younger speakers are generally quicker to adopt new speech forms than older members of a given community. Thus, it is essential, in tracking the spread of a change, to investigate the usage of a form, not only across different regions, but across different age groups, gender groups, and socioeconomic classes.

In examining diffusion, it is also necessary to include a closer look at local communication networks. The results of social network studies show that, in general, populations whose social networks involve frequent, prolonged contact with the same small peer group in a number of social contexts are more resistant to linguistic innovations than are populations whose social ties are looser (Milroy 1987; Milroy and Gordon 2003: 116–35). In other words, speakers with dense and multiplex networks are not as quick to adopt new language features as those whose communications are spread out among many people of different social groups.

In examining the effect of local social networks on the spread of linguistic innovations, we find that the first people to adopt changes, called INNOVATORS, are those with loose ties to many social groups but strong ties to none, since strong ties inhibit the spread of change. In order for the changes adopted by the innovators to make their way into more close-knit groups, they need to be picked up by so-called EARLY ADOPTERS – people who are central figures in tightly knit groups but who are willing enough to take risks to adopt change anyway, perhaps for reasons of prestige. Because these early adopters are well regarded in their social groups, the changes they adopt are likely to be picked up by other members of these groups, thereby diffusing through a large segment of a population (Labov 2001b).

Language change is not, however, simply a by-product of interactional patterns and demographic characteristics. As we saw in chapter 4, the social meanings attached to dialect features and community attitudes about language may have a profound effect on the spread of language change. For example, Guy Bailey, Tom Wikle, Jan Tillery, and Lori Sand (1993) have shown that, although some linguistic innovations in Oklahoma (e.g. the merger of [ɔ] and [ɑ] in word pairs such as *hawk* and *hock*) have spread throughout Oklahoma in the expected hierarchical pattern, other features, most notably the use of the special modal *fixin' to*, as in *They're fixin' to go now*, displayed exactly the opposite diffusion pattern. That is, *fixin' to* initially was most heavily concentrated in the rural areas of the state. After World War II, it began to spread to larger population centers and has now reached the state's most urban areas. Bailey, Wikle, Tillery, and Sand explain this CONTRAHIERARCHICAL pattern of diffusion by pointing to the fact that *fixin' to* is regarded as a marker of traditional Southern speech. In the face of large influxes of non-Southerners into the state, *fixin' to* has spread from the rural areas where it traditionally has been most heavily concentrated into urban areas as speakers throughout the state seek to assert their Southern identity. Forms such as the merger of [ɔ] and [ɑ], on the other hand, are markers of urbanization and sophistication, and so they spread outward from cities into rural areas. We see, then, that the social meanings attached to linguistic forms can drastically affect the process of linguistic diffusion. Linguistic markers of local identity may be of such importance over a widespread region that once-rural forms actually take root and spread, effectively reversing the usual direction of linguistic diffusion.

We have noted several overall patterns of diffusion in the preceding discussion: CONTAGIOUS DIFFUSION, in which dialect features spread in a wave-like pattern, primarily as a function of distance rather than population density; HIERARCHICAL or CASCADE DIFFUSION, in which the diffusion proceeds from larger populations down through smaller ones, bypassing intervening rural areas; and contrahierarchical diffusion, in which dialect forms spread from more sparsely populated rural areas to larger urban areas. All three patterns can even co-exist in a given area. The survey of Oklahoma speech conducted by Bailey et al. (1993), for example, shows cascade diffusion for the [ɔ] and [ɑ] merger, contrahierarchical diffusion for the spread of *fixin' to*, and contagious diffusion for the merger of [ɪ] and [ɛ] in words like *field* and *filled* or *kill* and *keel*. Quite obviously, the social meaning of different dialect forms has to be considered along with geographical, demographic, and interactional factors in explaining patterns of dialect diffusion.

5.5 Perceptual Dialectology

We have seen that there are a variety of approaches to charting regional patterns of dialect production. However, we have yet to consider people's untrained perceptions regarding regional dialect variation, or where speakers themselves draw mental dividing lines between dialects. The consideration of speakers' subjective viewpoints, commonly referred to as PERCEPTUAL DIALECTOLOGY (Preston 1989, 1991, 1996), adds an important perspective to understanding and interpreting dialect differences. This approach is also sometimes referred to as FOLK DIALECTOLOGY, since it focuses on people's "commonsense" beliefs and subjective mental categories rather than spoken language data. However, such beliefs and mental representations are important to linguistic scientists, since they may play an important role in shaping language variation and change across regional and social space.

In the most straightforward procedure for determining people's "mental dialect maps," study participants are simply asked to draw, on a blank or minimally detailed map, lines around regional speech zones. Instructions that guide such drawings involve eliciting people's perceptions of the boundaries of Southern and Northern speech areas. These lines can then be traced on to digitized pads and software can then be used to generate composite maps of various types based on drawings from a large number of respondents. In figure 5.14 we show a map of generalized speech regions in the US generated from the drawings of 147 respondents from Southeastern Michigan who were simply asked to draw dialect boundaries for the continental United States. The legend accompanying the map indicates the percentage and the number of respondents who drew the particular region indicated on the map. For example, 94 percent of the respondents drew a region identified as the South, whereas only 16 percent drew a West Coast and an East Coast dialect region, indicating the prominence of the Southern dialect region in the minds of the respondents.

Differences in mental maps may correlate with a range of respondent attributes such as region, age, social class, ethnicity, gender – the same social factors shown to be relevant in the patterning of variable dialect productions. For example, respondents from Southeastern Michigan and Southern Indiana draw very similar Southern dialect regions. However, there seems to be a "home region effect" that influences how each group draws their Northern and Southern Midland boundaries, with each group drawing a larger dialect boundary around their home region.

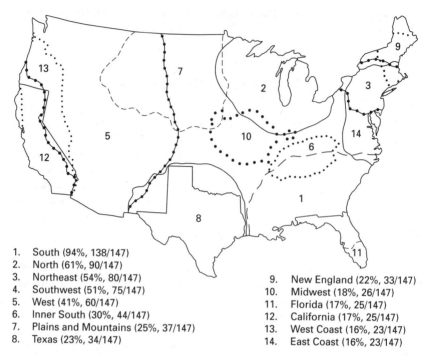

1. South (94%, 138/147)
2. North (61%, 90/147)
3. Northeast (54%, 80/147)
4. Southwest (51%, 75/147)   9. New England (22%, 33/147)
5. West (41%, 60/147)   10. Midwest (18%, 26/147)
6. Inner South (30%, 44/147)   11. Florida (17%, 25/147)
7. Plains and Mountains (25%, 37/147) 12. California (17%, 25/147)
8. Texas (23%, 34/147)   13. West Coast (16%, 23/147)
                                   14. East Coast (16%, 23/147)

Figure 5.14 Perceptual map of American English dialects, Southeastern Michigan respondents (from Preston 2003: 242; reprinted by permission of Duke University Press)

These maps are supplemented by people's evaluative judgments of different regional dialects, elicited through instructions such as "Rank the states on a scale of 1 to 10 showing where the most correct and the most incorrect English are spoken," "Rank the states showing where the most pleasant and unpleasant English are spoken," and "Rank the states showing where English is most and least like your own variety." For example, New York City and the South tend to be ranked as "most different" by respondents from Michigan and Indiana. New York City and the South were also ranked as "most incorrect" by these same respondents. But all is not lost; for some Southern respondents, Southern dialect is rated high on a scale of pleasantness, showing people's complicated and sometimes somewhat contradictory reactions to regional speech varieties.

In earlier research on the sensitivity to the North–South dimension in US English, Preston asked respondents to listen to the voices of nine speakers from locations that extended from Saginaw, Michigan, in the north to Dothan, Alabama, in the south (figure 5.15). All of the speakers were

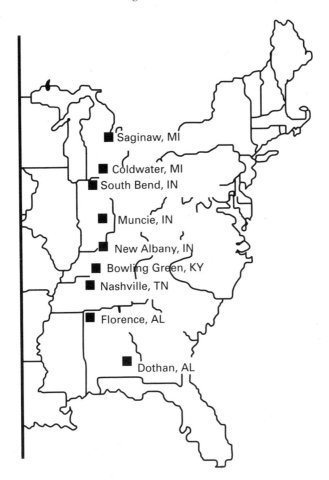

Figure 5.15   Home sites of the nine voices played in the identification task (from Preston, personal communication)

male, European American, middle-aged and middle-class, and all speech samples were devoid of all dialect-specific features except pronunciation. The respondents, from southernmost Indiana and southeastern Michigan, were asked to match these voices (played in scrambled order) with their sites. The results are shown in figure 5.16. In the figures for Indiana and Michigan the voices shaded the same were not statistically different from one another in their site assignments.

For both groups of judges, although there are apparently three degrees of distinctiveness, perhaps a North, Midlands, and South, there is confusion in the placement of voices from the northern and midland regions.

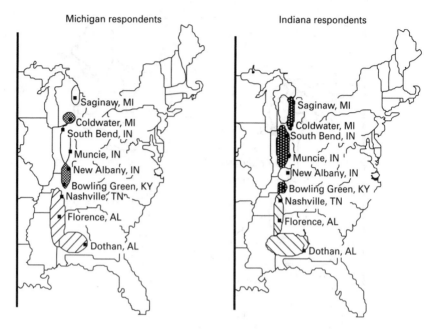

Figure 5.16 Responses of Michigan and Indiana listeners to regional voices (from Preston, personal communication)

Respondents from Michigan find the Coldwater, Michigan, speaker to be no different from the more southern voices of the New Albany, Indiana, and Bowling Green, Kentucky, speakers. The Indiana speakers hear their own area, New Albany, as being no different from the northernmost sites (Coldwater and Saginaw, Michigan), and they find Bowling Green, Kentucky, no different from the four northernmost sites, although distinct from their own. For both Michigan and Indiana respondents, however, as the shading in both maps shows, there is no difference in the ratings of the three southernmost voices. The distinctiveness of southern speech appears to be paramount in perception studies, and its distinctiveness appears to be related to prejudices against it, although, as noted above, southerners often find their speech pleasant if not correct.

Listener reactions may also focus on specific dialect features, such as particular vowel pronunciations. In one experiment (Wolfram, Hazen, and Schilling-Estes 1999), listeners reacted to the production of the vowel of *caught* as produced by speakers from different regions: (1) New York City, where the vowel is relatively high and followed by a schwa-like glide, as in something like *cuaht* [ɔə]; Eastern New England, where the vowel is merged with the vowel of *cot* [ɑ]; (3) rural Southern North Carolina Piedmont, where it is pronounced with a glide that makes it sound more like *cawut* [ao]; and (4) the Outer Banks of North Carolina where the vowel is unglided as in *coht* [ɔ] and sounds much like the traditional British production. Listeners were asked to rate the productions of the four speakers from the most to the least Southern-sounding on a four-point scale, and from the most to the least Northern-sounding. Predictably, the rural Southern Piedmont production was rated by far as the most Southern and the least Northern, but the Outer Banks production was rated as among the least Southern productions. In fact, some listeners noted that the Outer Banks production sounded British rather than American, a finding confirmed by a group of native speakers of British English who also rated Outer Banks speakers as non-American.

Analyses of listeners' reactions to different productions can become quite sophisticated, thanks to computer software and hardware that allows for various kinds of experimental manipulations of speech, including speech synthesis. For example, it is possible to alter just the production of a particular vowel while keeping the rest of the utterance constant so that the specific contribution of a vowel production to listeners' reaction can be teased out. Experimentation of this type has advanced our understanding of the role of vowel production in listeners' judgments of regionality as well as the interaction of regionality with social factors, including speaker ethnicity. For example, perception tests indicate that the fronting of the vowel in *boat* so that it sounds more like *bewt* is strongly associated with European American speech in the American South and that African Americans who use this feature are regularly identified as being European American rather than African American (Torbert 2004). In contrast, the fronting of the vowel in *boot*, so that it sounds more like *biwt* is not as strongly associated with European American ethnicity, and African Americans with this feature tend to be identified correctly as African Americans. This indicates that the fronted productions of these two vowels, both common in many Southern-based speech varieties, have quite different ethnic associations. Careful perceptual studies hold promise for sorting out the effects of subtle nuances of vowel production on listeners, and for determining the relative saliency of different phonetic factors in marking regional and ethnic identity.

5.6   Region and Place

Region is more than physical location; it also has social meaning in terms of grounding people's identities in localized communities. Dialect may symbolically mark people's regional and social identity in a way that is similar to other kinds of cultural behaviors associated with social grouping.

For example, dialect may be used to distinguish between insiders and out-siders, may emblematically mark social place, and may help construct a sense of local community. As one Lumbee Indian from Robeson County, North Carolina, put it, "When you hear the [Lumbee] dialect, no matter where you are, you know it's somebody from home." In relating his dialect to "home," this speaker was not so much referring to physical location or region *per se*, though that was part of it, but to local cultural "place." In marking local identity through dialect, the precise regional distribution of dialect forms may not be nearly as important as how strongly particular features figure in people's social construction of community.

The use of regional dialect features in the city of Pittsburgh, in South-western Pennsylvania, is a good example of how dialect can be used in the construction of local identity (Johnstone and Kiesling 2001). Many people in this region think that there is a distinctive dialect spoken in this region, which they refer to as "Pittsburghese." This construct is an important reference point in talking about Pittsburgh and its residents and in dis-tinguishing Pittsburghers from outsiders. Not only is the dialect a common topic of conversation, but Pittsburghese has become a commercial com-modity, and is showcased on T-shirts, postcards, and other souvenir items. Typical features associated with Pittsburghese are lexical items such as *gumband* "rubberband", *nebby* "nosy", *slippy* "slippery", and *redd up* "clean up". Pronunciation features include the pronunciation of the "ow" vowel in words like *downtown* as more of an "ah," so that *downtown* sounds like *dahntahn*; the merger of certain vowels before *l*, so that a word like *steal* sounds like *still* (and the local football team, the Pittsburgh Steelers, is called the Pittsburg *Stillers*); and the merger of the vowels in *cot* and *caught*. Grammatical features include the use of *yinz* (or *you'ns*) for the second person plural pronoun (*y'all* in the American South); the use of an *-ed* verb with *need*, as in *the shirt needs ironed*; and the use of *whenever* to mean *when*, as in *Whenever he finally died he was 90*. With the possible exception of the pronunciation of *downtown*, none of these is unique to Pittsburgh. For example, *redd up* is used from central Pennsylvania well into midland Ohio, *yinz* and *whenever* for *when* are used in various regions of Appalachia, and the merger of the vowels in *cot* and *caught* is common throughout much of the Western United States. Notwithstanding their actual geographical distribution, items like *dahntahn*, *Stillers*, and *yinz* have been appropriated as localisms and signify people's pride in being residents of Pittsburgh, and in the working-class or "blue-collar" character of the community. Over the last several decades, Pittsburghese has become as much a part of local identity as any other physical landmark or cultural artifact. We thus see that the distribution of dialect features in physical space may be quite different from the role that they play in people's construction of cultural place. As the study of regional dialect variation moves forward, researchers must consider not only how regional features are distributed geographically, but how these features become reference points for charting social and regional identities.

5.7 Further Reading

American Speech. A publication of the American Dialect Society. Tuscaloosa: University of Alabama Press. Articles on various dimensions of regional variation are regularly published in this quarterly journal. Readers may refer to periodically published indices for studies of particular structures and regions.

Bailey, Guy, Tom Wikle, Jan Tillery, and Lori Sand (1993) Some patterns of linguistic diffusion. *Language Variation and Change* 5: 359–90. This article uses data from the Survey of Oklahoma Dialects (begun in 1991) in order to demonstrate that linguistic innovations are diffusing throughout Oklahoma in a variety of patterns, including hierarchical, contrahierarchical, and contagious. A number of illustrative maps are included.

Johnstone, Barbara, Neeta Bhasin, and Denise Wittofski (2002) "Dahntahn" Pittsburgh: Monophthongal /aw/ and representations of localness in Southwestern Pennsylvania. *American Speech* 77: 148–66. This article provides a discussion of the historical development and current use of the *ah* pronunciation in *downtown* as a crucial part of the Pittsburghese dialect, as revealed in conversational speech and films.

Kretzschmar, William A., and Edgar W. Schneider (1996) *Introduction to Quantitative Analysis of Linguistic Survey Data.* Thousand Oaks, CA: Sage Publications. This book provides an introduction to the quantitative analysis of linguistic survey data, using data from the *Linguistic Atlas of the Middle and South Atlantic States* (*LAMSAS*) to illustrate analytical techniques. The description includes an account of how *LAMSAS* was reconceived in terms of computerized methods of dialect mapping.

Labov, William, Sharon Ash, and Charles Boberg (2005) *The Atlas of North American English.* New York/Berlin: Mouton de Gruyter. This work presents the results of the most comprehensive and current survey of the regional varieties of American English, as delimited by phonological systems. Interactive CD-ROMs with extensive sound files help illustrate many of the features discussed in the book.

Preston, Dennis R. (1996) Where the worst English is spoken. In Edgar W. Schneider (ed.), *Focus on American English.* Amsterdam/Philadelphia: John Benjamins. This article discusses the rationale for and provides a guide to the procedures used in perceptual dialectology, with focus on people's mental pictures of regional dialect boundaries and their evaluative judgments of regional varieties.

Thomas, Erik R. (2002) Sociophonetic applications of speech perception experiments. *American Speech* 77: 115–47. This article provides a review of so-called socioperceptual studies, or experimental studies that test people's perceptions of various regional, social, and ethnic speech varieties, as well as their perceptions of the speakers who use them. The concluding section of the article offers practical guidelines for conducting perception experiments.

Web sites

http://www.ling.upenn.edu/phono_atlas/home.html (accessed January 1, 2005). This site reports on the continuing progress of Labov et al.'s ongoing telephone survey of dialects in the United States (TELSUR), which is based primarily on phonological data.

http://hyde.park.uga.edu/lamsas (accessed December 20, 2004). This site provides various reports on regional dialect variation based on data from the *Linguistic Atlas of the Middle and South Atlantic States*. Included are numerous maps generated with state-of-the-art cartographic plotting software. The site also provides a useful comparison of current and older methods of analysis in lexical dialect geography.

6

Social and Ethnic Dialects

In many respects, the social implications of socially and ethnically based differences in language are much graver than differentiation along regional lines. Regional differences are often interpreted by the American public as matters of quaint curiosity and charming intrigue, but the stakes are much higher when it comes to socially and ethnically related differences. On the basis of these differences, speakers may be judged on capabilities ranging from innate intelligence to employability and on personal attributes ranging from sense of humor to morality.

The social class dimension of dialect has long been recognized in the study of American English, though it was typically assigned a secondary role in large-scale regional surveys. The *Linguistic Atlas of the United States and Canada* distinguished three social categories based on the fieldworker's overall impression of the participant. Type I subjects were those the fieldworker classified as having "little formal education, little reading and restricted social contacts," Type II were those with "better formal education (usually high school) and/or wider reading and social contacts," and Type III were those with "superior education (usually college), cultured background, wide reading and/or extensive social contacts" (Kurath 1939: 44). Many surveys of regional structures in this tradition are qualified by phrases such as "used primarily by Type I informant" or "found only among Type III informants," in recognition of the interaction of social status and regional variation.

Over the past half-century, the concern for status- and ethnicity-based differences in language has become a primary rather than a secondary focus in many dialect studies, and the study of SOCIOLECTS and ETHNOLECTS has become a specialization within sociolinguistics. In the process, this focus has redefined the scope of American dialectology in important ways.

6.1 Defining Class

Studies that correlate linguistic behavior with social stratification must be grounded in the classification of speakers on the basis of social divisions of various types. Impressionistically, this classification seems fairly straightforward. Some people in our society have social prestige, power, and money, and others have little of these commodities. Few people would disagree about the social status classification of individuals who possess these attributes to an extremely high or extremely low degree. We would hardly mistake a chief executive officer of a major corporation who resides in a spacious house in a wealthy neighborhood for an uneducated, unskilled laborer from the "wrong side of the tracks." The reality of social stratification seems obvious, but identifying the precise traits that define social status differences in a reliable way is not always that simple. Ultimately, social class distinctions seem to be based upon status and power, where, roughly speaking, status refers to the amount of respect and deference accorded to a person and power refers to the social and material resources a person can command, as well as the ability to make decisions and influence events (Guy 1988: 39). For the social science researcher, the challenge is to translate these abstract concepts into objective, measurable units that can be correlated with linguistic variation. Different kinds of procedures have been used with varying degrees of success in an attempt to capture the construct of "social class."

The traditional sociological approach to social status differences is to isolate a set of objective, readily observable socioeconomic characteristics that can be used to rank individuals in some way. Typical variables include occupation, level of education, income, and type of dwelling, with ranked levels within each variable. For example, occupations may be scaled based on categories such as the following:

Rank occupation
1   Major professionals
    Executives of large concerns
2   Lesser professionals
    Executives of medium-sized concerns
3   Semi-professionals
    Administrators of small businesses
4   Technicians
    Owners of very small businesses
5   Skilled workers
6   Semi-skilled workers
7   Unskilled workers
    (from Shuy, Wolfram, and Riley 1968: 12)

Similar kinds of scales are set up for other social characteristics such as education, housing, and income, and different weightings may be assigned to variables if one trait is considered more significant than another. For example, occupation may be weighted more heavily than education or residency in computing a socioeconomic status score. The overall ranking obtained from combining scores for the different variables is the SOCIO-ECONOMIC STATUS, usually abbreviated simply as SES. Although this kind of ranking system results in a continuous scale, it is possible to divide the distribution of scores into discrete social status groupings of some type, with attendant labels such as upper-class, middle-class, working-class, and so forth. Groupings may be made on a fairly simple, arbitrary basis (for example, dividing the total range of scores into four equal sub-ranges and assigning class labels), or they may be based upon more sophisticated statistical analyses of the clustering of scores distributed on the scale, thus reflecting more natural divisions in the sample population.

In recent years, SES scales have been subject to critical scrutiny, as social scientists realized that most of them are subtly grounded in the values of mainstream, socially dominant groups. For example, researchers investigating language and gender have pointed out that females traditionally have been grouped into socioeconomic categories based on the characteristics of husbands, fathers, or other male "heads of household," often with wildly misleading results (e.g. Eckert 1989b). In addition to the biases contained in such measures, it must be admitted that they selectively focus on superficial indices that are presumed to reflect underlying behavioral and attitudinal differences that are the core of sociocultural differences.

Exercise 1

Most people can think of individuals who are exceptions to the rule when it comes to the link between language variation and objective socioeconomic measures. That is, a person assigned a low SES rating may speak like one typically associated with a high SES rating, or the converse. What kinds of factors may account for such discrepancies? Do you think that such discrepancies invalidate the general correlation of language variation with SES scores based on objective measures? Why or why not?

As an alternative to strict reliance on objective measures of social status assigned by an outside social scientist, one can rely upon community members to make judgments about status differences. Under this approach, members of a community are rated by other community members in terms of certain imputed status traits. Is a person from the "upper crust" or the "wrong side of the tracks"? Typically, communities have designations for particular subgroups in terms of the social status hierarchy, and these can be tapped to determine class distinctions. In this way, researchers avoid imposing predetermined categories that may not be relevant to the community under study and also may come closer to uncovering the beliefs and behaviors underlying social class distinctions. However, this more subjective approach to social classification is not without its own problems. For example, different pictures of social class may emerge from representatives of different segments of the community, both on an individual and a class level. The lower classes may, for example, perceive social class structure very differently from the upper classes.

Furthermore, the view of class presented here, which is based on analyses of Western society, emphasizes shared evaluations and notions of prestige. That is, it is assumed that all social groups share certain expectations for appropriate and desirable behavior and view increases in social status as positive and desirable. Under this view, sometimes referred to as the CONSENSUS MODEL of social class, individual competition is emphasized over conflicts between classes. But it is also possible to view class differences as conflicts between those who control resources and means of production and can live off the profits of the workers – the bourgeoisie – and the workers who earn the profits for those in power. Under the CONFLICT MODEL, class differences are viewed as the consequences of divisions and conflicts between the classes; in turn, linguistic differences are seen as a reflection of the interests of different classes and conflicts between classes. Accordingly, the standard–vernacular dichotomy may be viewed as the symbolic token of a class struggle, and vernacular speech is seen as a symbolic expression of alienation from the upper classes with whom the lower classes are in conflict.

6.2   Beyond Social Class

Ideally, a valid assessment of social class differences should combine both objective and subjective measurements of many types of behaviors and values, but this is often easier said than done. Even if this were always possible, it would not assure a neat fit between social status or class differences and language variation. There are other demographic factors that intersect with social class, including region, age, gender, and so forth; there are also factors besides status differences pertaining to community life and relationships that are essential in accounting for language variation. One of the important correlates of linguistic difference may relate to the so-called

LINGUISTIC MARKETPLACE – that is, the extent to which a speaker's economic activity necessitates the use of a particular language variety. People in certain occupations tend to use standard varieties more often than members of the same social class who hold other occupations. For example, teachers, salespeople, or receptionists, who are expected to conform to public expectations of standardness, may be more standard in their language than their SES peers in other occupations that are not as closely linked to the use of standard language forms. David Sankoff and Suzanne Laberge (1978) show that, in at least some communities, a person's LINGUISTIC MARKET INDEX, a ranking assigned to speakers based upon descriptions of their socioeconomic life histories, may correlate with the use of standard vs. nonstandard language features more closely than traditional social status designations.

Another parameter that intersects with social class relates to SOCIAL NETWORK, as introduced in chapter 2. Within a given social class or status classification there may be important differences in interactional activity which correlate with language differences. For example, closed social networks that are characterized by repeated interactions with the same people in a number of spheres of activity (e.g. work, leisure, and church) tend to correlate with a greater concentration of localized, vernacular dialect features than do open social networks where people interact with a wide scope of people in different circumstances. Similarly, the COMMUNITY OF PRACTICE as described in chapter 2 may have more bearing on speakers' linguistic usages than their place in an objectively defined social order. In addition, attention to the practices in which people regularly engage may help explain why speakers use certain language features vs. others in their construction of individual and group linguistic styles. In many cases, locally meaningful social groups and practices correlate with linguistic variation more neatly than traditional macro-level social category classifications such as class. For example, Penelope Eckert's work with teenagers in the Detroit suburbs (1989a, 2000) shows that the students' own social distinctions (chiefly between *jocks* and *burnouts*) are much more relevant than social class designation. Similarly, Norma Mendoza-Denton (1999) shows that local social categories, including gang affiliation, are crucial to the full description and explanation of language variation in the California high school population she studied. Problems in the neatness of fit between social class and language, then, are not simply problems with defining social class and grouping people into appropriate categories, although these problems certainly exist. Instead, many of the difficulties with the straightforward correlation of social status with language variation relate to the ways in which social characteristics, relationships, and practices interact with each other in their effect on linguistic variation. Local social distinctions, group dynamics, and personal presentation have to be taken into account along with conventional status measures in accounting for language variation.

6.3   The Patterning of Social Differences in Language

According to popular belief, dialect patterns are quite simple: The members of one social group always use a particular dialect variant while members of a different group use another one. For example, under this view, vernacular dialect speakers always pronounce -*ing* words such as *swimming* as *swimmin'* and use multiple negatives such as *They didn't do nothing*, while speakers of standard varieties never use these forms. However, this "all or nothing" perspective often obscures the actual ways in which dialect forms are used and distorts the picture of language variation.

The pattern of dialect distribution which most closely matches the popular perception of dialect differences is referred to as GROUP-EXCLUSIVE usage, where one community of speakers uses a feature but another community never does. In its ideal form, group-exclusive usage means that all members of a particular community use a certain feature whereas no members of other groups ever use it. This ideal pattern, however, is rarely if ever manifested in American English dialects. The kinds and levels of social groupings that take place are just too complex for language patterns to work out so neatly. In many cases, linguistic distinctions between groups exist on a continuum rather than in discrete sets. For example, a certain group may use a certain amount of -*in'* for -*ing* while another group still uses -*in'*, but at a different rate. Furthermore, the definition of a social group is usually multidimensional rather than unidimensional, based, as it is, on a range of factors such as social class, ethnicity, gender, age, patterns of interaction, common practices, etc. And, as we have seen, dialects are constantly undergoing change – change that is distributed unevenly even within a seemingly unified community. For example, quotative *be like* (e.g. *She's like, "Where are you going?"*), a relatively recent innovation in American English, can be found even in small, fairly isolated communities, but it is found generally only among younger speakers.

The essential aspect of group-exclusive dialect forms is that speakers from other groups do not use these forms rather than the fact that all the members of a particular group use them. Not all people who are native to Pittsburgh use *you'ns* and *gumband*, but it is a safe bet that someone who is native to San Francisco or Seattle does not use these forms. Group-exclusive usage is therefore easier to define negatively than positively. Viewed in this way, there are many dialect features on all levels of language organization that show group-exclusive distribution. On a phonological level, many of the regional vowel productions presented thus far, such as the pronunciation of the vowels in *caught* and *cot* as the same vowel or the pronunciation of the /ai/ in *time* as [a] (as in *tahm*), show group-exclusive distribution across regions. There are similar examples in morphology, such as the absence of the *-s* plural on nouns of weights and measures as in *four acre, five pound*, and the pluralization of *you* as *youse, y'all*, or *you'ns*. In syntax, the use of positive *anymore* in *They go to the movies a lot anymore* and verbal complements such as *The kitchen needs remodeled*, or *The dog wants out* are examples of group-exclusive usage patterns, while in the lexicon there are numerous examples such as *gumband* for *rubberband, garret* for *attic, juvember* for *sling shot*, as well as thousands of words found in the *Dictionary of American Regional English* (1985–2002).

In contrast to group-exclusive forms, GROUP-PREFERENTIAL forms are distributed across different groups or communities of speakers, but members of one group are more likely to use the form than members of another group. For example, highly specific color terms (e.g. *mauve, plum*, etc.) are often associated with women as opposed to men, at least among middle-class European American speakers in the United States, but there are certainly many men who make similar distinctions, and, of course, there are women who do not use such refined color designations. The association of a finely graded color spectrum with women is statistically based, as more women make these distinctions than men. We thus refer to the use of highly specific color terms as a group-preferential pattern rather than a group-exclusive one. We would not expect group-preferential patterns to be as socially meaningful as group-exclusive dialect features, although popular stereotypes of group-preferential dialect patterns sometimes treat them as if they were, in fact, group-exclusive. The popular characterization of vernacular speakers as saying *dese, dem*, and *dose* is a case where the stereotype of group-exclusive behavior actually obscures a fairly complex pattern that is really group-preferential – and also highly variable.

The careful examination of usage patterns shows that social groups are often differentiated on the basis of how frequently speakers use particular forms rather than whether or not they use the forms at all. In other words, individual speakers within groups may fluctuate in their use of variants, sometimes using one form and sometimes using an alternate. For example, consider the following excerpt showing the fluctuation of *-ing* and *-in'* within the speech of a single speaker during one stretch of conversation.

> We were walk*in'* down the street and we saw this car go*ing* out of control. The driver looked like he was sleep*ing* at the wheel or someth*in'*. The next thing I knew the car was turn*in'* around and just spinn*ing* around. I thought the car was com*in'* right at me and I started runn*in'* like crazy. I was so scared, think*ing* the car was gonna hit me or someth*in'*.

In the ten examples of the form *-ing* in this passage, four cases end in *-ing* and six in *-in'*. According to the linguistic pattern or "rule" for this process, which states that *-ing* in unstressed syllables may become *-in'*, all ten cases of *-ing* should be realized as *-in'*, yet only six of them occur as *-in'*. This kind of variation, where a speaker sometimes produces one variant and sometimes an alternate one, is referred to as INHERENT VARIABILITY. This term reflects the belief, common among sociolinguists, that this fluctuation is an internal part of a single linguistic system and not the result of importations from another dialect. It seems very unlikely that the speaker fluctuating between *-ing* and *-in'* is switching between two dialects, one exclusively using *-ing* and another exclusively using *-in'*. Nor is the speaker shifting between two different styles within the interview. Instead, the speaker is using a single dialect system – one with two variants of this ending – and simply fluctuates in the use of the variants. This kind of fluctuation has long been recognized within linguistics, where certain processes are considered "optional" because they may or may not be applied. For example, there is an optional process that permits a speaker to place the particle *up* after a noun phrase rather than directly after the verb, so that *She looked up the number* may alternatively be realized as *She looked the number up*. Linguists do not typically say that each of these sentences belongs to a distinctly different dialect, and that a speaker switches between the dialects. Instead, we say that both of these sentences are options within a single system. Similarly, we may say that the *-in'* and *-ing* forms are alternating variants within one system for most English speakers.

One of the important discoveries to emerge from the detailed study of dialects over the past several decades, particularly social dialects, was that dialects are sometimes differentiated not by the discrete, or categorical, use or non-use of forms, but by the relative frequency with which different variants of a form occur. In fact, it can be shown for a number of phonological and grammatical features that dialects are more typically differentiated by the extent to which a particular feature occurs, its relative frequency, rather than by its complete absence or categorical presence.

Table 6.1 displays the frequency levels of *-in'* for *-ing*, a phonological variable, and the syntactic variable of pronominal apposition (e.g. *My mother, she's coming to school* as opposed to *My mother's coming to school*) in four different social status groups of Detroit speakers (adapted from Shuy, Wolfram, and Riley 1967). Although the figures represent the mean scores for each social group, all of the individual speakers also exhibit variability between *-ing* and *-in'*, as well as between *my mother, she* . . . and *my mother.* . . . Frequency levels were computed for individual speakers by first noting all those cases where a form like *-in'* might have occurred – namely, in unstressed syllables ending in *-ing*. Then, the number of cases in which *-in'* actually occurred was counted. For example, in the sample passage given above, there are ten cases where *-in'* could have occurred, but only six of them, or 60 percent, were actually produced with the *-in'* form. This tabulation procedure follows a fairly standard format for

Table 6.1   Frequency of a variable phonological feature and a variable grammatical feature in four different social groups in Detroit

	Upper middle class	Lower middle class	Upper working class	Lower working class
Mean percentage of -*in'* forms	19.4	39.1	50.5	78.9
Mean percentage of pronominal apposition	4.5	13.6	25.4	23.8

Adapted from Shuy, Wolfram, and Riley (1967)

determining frequency levels of dialect forms, which can be indicated in the simple formula:

$$\frac{\text{No. of cases where a given form occurs}}{\text{No. of cases where the form might have occurred}} \times 100$$

In other words, we calculate the proportion of actual cases out of potential cases (i.e. 0.6) and multiply by 100 to arrive at a percentage score (60 percent).

The fact that there is fluctuation between forms such as -*ing* and -*in'* does not mean that the fluctuation is totally random or haphazard. Although we cannot predict which variant might be used in a given instance, there are factors that can increase or decrease the likelihood that certain variants will occur. These factors are known technically as CONSTRAINTS ON VARIABILITY. The constraints are of two major types. First, there are various social factors such as social class (as in table 6.1) which systematically correlate with an increase or decrease in the frequency level of usage. In other words, looking at table 6.1, we can say that a speaker from the lower working class is more likely to use both -*in'* for -*ing* and pronominal apposition than speakers from other classes.

Not all linguistic structures correlate with social status differences in the same way. Different linguistic variables may align with given social status groupings in a variety of ways. For example, consider the ways in which two linguistic variables are distributed across four different social strata within the African American community of Detroit, Michigan. These variables are third-person singular suffix absence (e.g. *She go to the store* for *She goes to the store*) in figure 6.1 and *r*-lessness (e.g. *bea'* for *bear*) in figure 6.2.

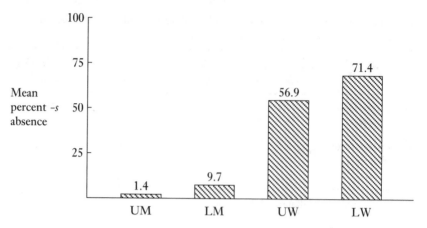

UM = upper middle class; LM = lower middle class; UW = upper working class; LW = lower working class.

Figure 6.1   Third-person singular -*s*/-*es* absence: an example of sharp stratification

In figure 6.1, the linguistic variation correlates with certain discrete social strata. The middle-class groups show very little -*s*/-*es* absence whereas working-class speakers show significant levels of -*s*/-*es* absence. The distribution of -*s*/-*es* use shows a wide separation between middle-class and working-class groups and is therefore referred to as a case of SHARP STRATIFICATION. On the other hand, the distribution of *r*-lessness in figure 6.2 indicates a pattern of GRADIENT or FINE STRATIFICATION, in which the relative frequency of *r*-lessness changes gradually from one social class to the adjacent one.

In the examples given in figures 6.1 and 6.2, sharp stratification is illustrated by a grammatical variable and gradient stratification by a phonological one. Although there are exceptions, grammatical variables are more likely to show sharp stratification than phonological ones. This underscores the fact that grammatical features are typically more diagnostic of social differences than phonological ones with respect to the standard–nonstandard continuum of English.

Stable linguistic variables defined primarily on the standard–nonstandard continuum of English tend to be sharply stratified, whereas linguistic features undergoing change often exhibit gradient stratification. This is due, in part, to the role of social class in language change within a community. As we discuss in the next section, change tends to start in a given social class and spread from that point to adjacent social classes. The kind of correlation that exists between social status and linguistic variation may thus be a

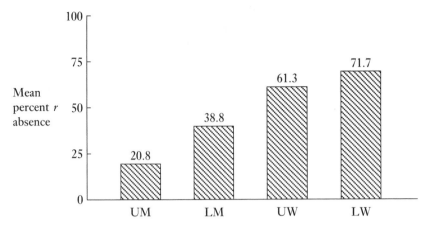

UM = upper middle class; LM = lower middle class; UW = upper working class; LW = lower working class.

Figure 6.2 Postvocalic *r* absence: an example of gradient stratification

function of both social and linguistic considerations. There is no single pattern that can be applied to this co-variation.

Since there are different patterns of correlation between social stratification and linguistic variation and many ways of differentiating social groups besides traditional measures of socioeconomic status, it is sometimes difficult to answer the question of how many social dialects there are in English. On one level, this question is best answered by examining the social stratification of particular linguistic variables. From this perspective, the answer may range from two, for a sharply stratified variable that shows a basic dichotomy between two broadly defined social groups, through six or seven varieties for finely stratified features. For linguistic variation showing a correlation with two basic social groups, the popular perception that there are two social dialects – namely, a standard and a vernacular – may be matched by the reality of social stratification. However, for other variables, multi-layered social dialect differentiation is indicated. It is important to understand that both continuous and discrete patterns of sociolinguistic variation may simultaneously exist within the same population.

6.4 Linguistic Constraints on Variability

Not all of the systematic influences on variation can be accounted for simply by appealing to various social factors. There are also aspects of the linguistic system itself that may affect the variability of particular forms. Particular types of linguistic contexts, such as the kinds of surrounding forms or the larger units in which the form occurs, may also influence the relative frequency of occurrence. Because the linguistic influences on variation operate apart from the social factors that correlate with variability, these are sometimes referred to as INDEPENDENT LINGUISTIC CONSTRAINTS on variability.

The effect of linguistic factors can best be understood by looking at a particular case of phonological variation. Consider the process of word-final consonant cluster reduction that may affect sound sequences such as *st*, *nd*, *ld*, *kt*, and so forth. When this process operates, items such as *west*, *wind*, *cold*, and *act* may be pronounced without the final member of the cluster, as *wes'*, *win'*, *col'*, and *ac'*, respectively. The incidence of cluster reduction is quite variable, but certain linguistic factors systematically favor or inhibit the operation of the reduction process. These factors, or constraints, include whether the following word begins with a consonant or a vowel (more precisely, a non-consonant) and the way in which the cluster is formed.

With respect to the sound that follows, the likelihood of reduction is increased when the cluster is followed by a word beginning with a consonant. This means that cluster reduction is more frequent in contexts such as *west coast* or *cold cuts* than in contexts like *west end* or *cold egg*. An individual speaker might, for example, apply consonant cluster reduction in 75 percent of all cases when the cluster is followed by a word beginning with a consonant (as in *wes' coast*) but show only 25 percent consonant cluster reduction when the cluster is followed by a non-consonant (as in *wes' end*). The important observation is that reduction may take place in both kinds of linguistic contexts, but it is regularly favored in those contexts where the word following the cluster begins with a consonant.

Exercise 2

In the following passage, tabulate the incidence of cluster reduction for all the underlined word-final clusters. Observe whether the cluster is reduced or not, as indicated by the phonetic content in the brackets following the underlined cluster. For example, gue*st*[s] would indicate a reduced item since the final [t] has been omitted, and gue*st*[st] would not. For the sake of the exercise, ignore consonant clusters that are not underlined. Tabulate the items by setting up two columns, one for clusters followed by consonants and one for clusters followed by non-consonants. Items at the end of a sentence should be considered to be followed by non-consonants. For each cluster, first identify whether it is followed by a consonant or non-consonant and then enter it under the relevant category and identify in some way whether it is reduced or non-reduced. After extracting the first couple of items, your tabulation sheet might look like the following:

Clusters followed by a consonant	*Clusters followed by a non-consonant*
<u>0</u> e.g. be<u>st</u>[st] movie	<u>0</u> e.g. mo<u>st</u>[st] of
<u>1</u> e.g. la<u>st</u>[s] year	<u>1</u> e.g. coa<u>st</u>[s]. It
. . .	. . .

<u>1</u> = reduced cluster
<u>0</u> = unreduced cluster

After you have finished entering all the items under the appropriate category, calculate the percentage of cluster reduction for each category by dividing the total number of clusters in the category into the number of clusters that are actually reduced, and multiply by 100. This will give you a percentage of cluster reduction for clusters followed by consonants and clusters followed by non–consonants. What can you say about the influence of the following context on cluster reduction based on this calculation?

Passage for word-final cluster reduction tabulation

La<u>st</u>[s] year I saw the be<u>st</u>[st] movie. It seemed silly but it was serious too. It was about this detective who lived in California, but he traveled up and down mo<u>st</u>[st] of the coa<u>st</u>[s]. It seemed like he was always one step ahead of the cops and one step behi<u>nd</u>[n] the bad guys at the same time. Nobody really liked him, and it seemed like he was almo<u>st</u>[s] killed every time he left the house. Mo<u>st</u>[s] of the time, he was running from both the criminals and the police. In fa<u>ct</u>[kt] both sides were totally confused by him.

One time, the police set up a scam bu<u>st</u>[s] by pretending to smuggle in some drugs off the coa<u>st</u>[st]. When they smuggled the stuff inla<u>nd</u>[n] they wanted to sell it to the dealers. But the detective wasn't told so he thought it was a chance for a real bu<u>st</u>[st] on the dealers. Ju<u>st</u>[s] as he jumped in to make an arre<u>st</u>[s] a couple of dealers showed up, and he had to a<u>ct</u>[k] like he was one of them. So the police thought he was part of the dealers and the dealers thought he was part of the police. Both sides jumped in and he was trying to a<u>ct</u>[k] as if he was with the other side. He told a policeman to go along with him 'cause he was making a bus<u>t</u>[st] and he told a drug dealer to go along with him and he would get the drugs. Both sides were so confused by him they jus<u>t</u>[s] went along with the a<u>ct</u>[kt] and followed his lead. As it turned out, some of the police had gone underground[n] and some of the dealers had turned evidence to the police. He was so confused himself he didn't know who to arres<u>t</u>[st]. Finally, he jus<u>t</u>[s] left both groups shooting at each other. He jus<u>t</u>[s] couldn't figure out who was bad and who was good.

Cluster reduction is also influenced by the way in which the cluster is formed. Clusters that belong to a single morpheme, as in the case of root words such as *wind* and *guest*, are more likely to undergo reduction than clusters that are created through the addition of an *-ed* suffix, as in *guessed*, which ends phonetically in [st] ([gɛst]), and *pinned*, which ends in [nd] ([pɪnd]). Again, fluctuation between reduced and full pronunciation takes place with both types of clusters, but reduction takes place more frequently when the cluster is an inherent part of a word rather than the result of *-ed* suffix addition.

When we compare the relative effect of different linguistic factors on the cluster reduction pattern, we find that some linguistic influences are greater than others. In some dialects of English, the influence of the following segment (consonant vs. non-consonant) is more important than the cluster formation type (not *-ed* vs. *-ed* cluster). Differences in the relative effect of linguistic constraints may be likened to the relative effect of different social factors, where, for example, social group membership, age, and gender may all influence the relative incidence of cluster reduction, but not in equal proportions.

In some cases, linguistic constraints on variability can be ordered differently across varieties of English. Table 6.2 presents a comparison of word-final cluster reduction for some different dialects of English, based upon a sample of speakers in each population. As seen in this table, all of the varieties of English represented here show clusters to be systematically influenced by the following phonological context and the cluster formation type, but the relative influence of the constraints may differ. In some cases, such as standard English and Appalachian Vernacular English, the influence of the following consonant is more important than the cluster type, whereas in other cases, such as Southern European American working-class speech and Southern African American working-class speech, the cluster type is a more important constraint than the following phonological context.

The analysis of linguistic constraints on variability can get much more sophisticated than the frequency tabulations and comparisons introduced here, as there now exist computerized statistical procedures for determining

Table 6.2   Comparison of consonant cluster reduction in representative vernacular dialects of English

Language variety	Followed by consonant		Followed by non-consonant	
	Not -ed % reduced	-ed % reduced	Not -ed % reduced	-ed % reduced
Standard English	66	36	12	3
Northern Anglo American working class	67	23	19	3
Southern Anglo American working class	56	16	25	10
Appalachian working class	74	67	17	5
Northern African American working class	97	76	72	4
Southern African American working class	88	50	72	36
Chicano working class	91	61	66	22
Puerto Rican working class (NYC)	93	78	63	23
Italian American working class (Boston)	67	39	14	10
Native American Puebloan English	98	92	88	81
Vietnamese English	98	93	75	60

From Wolfram (1986)

the probabilistic effects of different kinds of constraints on variable linguistic processes such as consonant cluster reduction. These programs can take the analyst well beyond the level of precision provided through raw tabulations. For our purposes here, however, it is sufficient to recognize the fundamental insights about the nature of linguistic variation that have come from these systematic approaches.

First, we see that dialect differences are sometimes reflected in quantitative differences rather than qualitative differences. Thus, in describing a dialect, we must be careful to note ways in which it differs quantitatively from other varieties as well as ways in which it differs qualitatively. We must also recognize that there are important constraints on the relative incidence of dialect forms based upon linguistic structure, as particular contexts and constructions will favor or inhibit the occurrence of a particular linguistic variant. It is also important to take these systematic effects into account in the description of language variation. When we talk about the absence of the copula in varieties such as African American English or Southern European American English, for example, it is important to note that this phenomenon is much more common in contexts in which general American English has *are* (e.g. *You ugly*, *They ugly*) than those in which it has *is* (e.g. *He ugly*, *The bird ugly*), even though copula absence may be observed in both types of contexts.

Finally, our studies show that not all linguistic constraints have equal weight, as their effects may be ordered with respect to each other. In other words, some constraints are more important than others in their relative effect on the fluctuation of forms. The investigation of linguistic constraints on variability reveals the subtle and complex ways in which dialect differences are systematically structured. This complexity is, of course, a far cry from the common popular perception that dialects are rather haphazard and that vernacular speakers randomly "drop consonants" when they talk.

6.5   The Social Evaluation of Linguistic Features

Although no linguistic features are *linguistically* better or worse than any other features, it is not surprising that the social values assigned to certain groups in society will be associated with the linguistic forms used by the members of these groups. If, for example, Southerners are viewed as stupid, then the merger of *pin* and *pen* associated with Southern speech will be taken as a sign of this stupidity, since people assign their perceptions of social groups to the distinctive language patterns used by the members of those groups.

SOCIALLY PRESTIGIOUS variants are forms that are positively valued through their association with high-status groups as linguistic markers of status, whereas SOCIALLY STIGMATIZED variants carry negative connotations through their association with low-status groups. In grammar, most prestige forms are related to prescriptive norms of standardness or even literary norms. For example, the use of *whom* in **Whom** *did you see?* or the placement of *never* in **Never** *have I seen a more gruesome sight* might be considered prestige variants in some social contexts. Apart from these somewhat special cases, it is difficult to find clear-cut cases of prestige variants in American English on the grammatical level of language, particularly in the grammar of ordinary conversation.

Examples of prestige variants are also relatively rare in phonology. The use of an "unflapped" *t* in words like *better* or *latter* (e.g. [bɛtəʴ] as opposed to [bɛDəʴ]) as used by a select group of "Brahmin" dialect speakers found in the Boston metropolitan area may be an example of a prestige variant, as would some other phonological characteristics of this dialect, but this is a fairly isolated, somewhat unusual situation. The pronunciations of this restricted prestige dialect are modeled more on standard British English, or Received Pronunciation, than on American English. The fact that an external norm serves as a model for prestige in this instance is actually a commentary on the relative absence of prestige variants in American English dialects. That a British dialect is still held in such esteem a couple of centuries after America gained independence from British rule also may speak to the lingering sociolinguistic effects of colonialism. In some regions, the pronunciation of *either* as [aɪðəʴ] instead of [iðəʴ] or the pronunciation of *vase* as [vaz] vs. [ves] may be associated with high status, but these relate to the pronunciation of single lexical items rather than phonological systems and are therefore more properly considered lexical than phonological variants.

For present-day American English, the vast majority of socially diagnostic structures exist on the axis of stigmatization rather than the axis of prestige. Classic illustrations involving grammatical features include the familiar cases of multiple negation (e.g. *They **didn't** do **nothing***), regularized past tense verb forms (e.g. *He **knowed** they **were** right*), and different subject–verb agreement patterns (e.g. *We **was** there*). Stigmatized phonological features include *-in'* for *-ing* (e.g. *stoppin'*, *swimmin'*), [d] or [t] for *th* (e.g. [dey] *they*, [tɪŋk] *think*). There are also lexical shibboleths such as *ain't*. Unlike prestige variants, it is relatively easy to come up with examples of stigmatized variants for different levels of linguistic organization. This distribution pattern was, in fact, part of the rationale that led us to conclude in chapter 1 that standard American English is more adequately characterized by the absence of negatively valued, stigmatized items than by the presence of positively valued, prestige items.

It is important to understand that stigmatized and prestigious variants do not exist on a single axis in which the alternative to a socially stigmatized variant is a socially prestigious one, or vice versa. The absence of multiple negation, for example, is not particularly prestigious; it is simply not stigmatized. Similarly, the non-prestigious variant for *either* [iðəʴ] is not necessarily stigmatized; it is simply not prestigious. In fact, there are very few cases in American English where a socially prestigious variant is the alternate of a socially stigmatized one.

As discussed in the preceding section, it is important to keep in mind that the patterning of socially diagnostic structures is not an all-or-nothing pro-position; it is often a matter of relative frequency that determines the social valuation of a form. For example, all English speakers use *-in'* for *-ing* to some extent, with those of lower social status using more *-in'*, the stigmatized variant, than those of higher status, who use *-in'* to a lesser extent. However, there is little stigma attached to the relatively low usage levels for *-in'* in higher-status groups, as opposed to the negative valuation attached to the higher usage levels for *-in'* among lower-status speakers.

The discussion of the social evaluation up to this point has been undertaken from the vantage point of those who place high value on the widespread, institutional language norms established by higher-status groups. These norms are overtly perpetuated by the agents of standardization in our society – teachers, the media, and other authorities responsible for setting the standards of linguistic behavior. These norms are usually acknowledged across a full range of social classes on a community-wide basis. Linguistic forms that are assigned their social evaluation on the basis of this widespread recognition of social significance are said to carry OVERT PRESTIGE. At the same time, however, another set of norms may exist, related to solidarity with more locally defined social groups irrespective of their social position. When forms are positively valued apart from, or even in opposition to, their social significance for the wider society, they are said to carry COVERT PRESTIGE. In the case of overt prestige, the social valuation lies in a unified, widely accepted set of institutional norms, whereas in the case of covert prestige, the positive social significance lies in the local culture of social relationships. It is possible for a socially stigmatized variant in one setting to have covert prestige in another. A young person who adopts vernacular forms in order to maintain solidarity with a group of friends clearly indi-cates the covert prestige of these features on a local level even if the same features stigmatize the speaker in a wider, mainstream context such as school. The notion of covert prestige is important in understanding why vernacular speakers do not rush to become standard dialect speakers, even when these speakers may evaluate the social significance of linguistic variation in a way that superficially matches that of their high-status counterparts. Widely recognized stigmatized features such as multiple negation, nonstandard subject–verb agreement, and different irregular verb paradigms may function at the same time as positive, covertly prestigious features in terms of local norms.

In recent years, the maintenance or even heightening of vernacular language features among non-mainstream speakers has been viewed in terms of power as well as prestige. For example, Scott Kiesling (1996) points out that working-class men may use vernacular variants as a means of projecting economic power rather than covert prestige, since working-class men traditionally have held occupations associated with physical toughness and "manliness" (and hence vernacular language features) rather than with advanced education. We discuss this alternative view in more detail in chapter 8.

The social significance of language forms changes over time, just as linguistic structures themselves change. It may be difficult for present-day speakers of English to believe that linguistic shibboleths such as *ain't* and multiple negation were once socially insignificant, but the historical study of the English language certainly supports this conclusion. Furthermore, shifts in social significance may take place from generation to generation. As William Labov (1966: 342–9) has shown, for New York City, the social significance of postvocalic *r* (as in *cart* or *farm*) has shifted during the past 50 years. For the older generation, there is very little social class stratification for the use of postvocalic *r*, but younger speakers show a well-defined pattern of social stratification in which the presence of *r* (e.g. *cart*) is more highly valued than its absence (e.g. *caht*). Similarly, as we saw in chapter 4, postvocalic *r*-lessness in Southern speech was once a prestigious pronunciation, following the model of British English. However, the valuation of *r*-less speech has changed over the decades, and today it is working-class rural groups in the South who are most characteristically *r*-less rather than metropolitan upper-class speakers. Because *r*-lessness used to carry prestige, we find that older, upper-class groups in some regions of the South retain a high incidence of *r*-lessness; however, younger upper-class speakers tend to pronounce their *r*'s. At the same time, younger, rural working-class speakers may be relatively *r*-less, thus uniting older metropolitan and younger rural speakers in *r*-lessness. The social valuation accorded to regional variables can shift fairly abruptly.

The social significance of linguistic variables may also vary from region to region. As a native Philadelphian, the first author grew up associating the pronunciation of *aunt* as [ant] with high-status groups. In his own working-class dialect, [ænt] was the normal pronunciation, and *aunt* and *ant* were homophones in his dialect. He was quite shocked to discover later in life that the pronunciation of *aunt* he considered to be prestigious and even "uppity" was characteristic of some Southern dialects regardless of social status, including highly stigmatized varieties such as vernacular African American English. Meanwhile (actually a couple of decades later), the second author grew up in a Southern dialect area assuming that [ant] was a highly stigmatized pronunciation associated with vernacular rather than standard dialects. In a similar vein, postvocalic *r*-lessness may be associated with the prestigious Boston Brahmin dialect or the RP (Received Pronunciation) English of the British Isles at the same time as it is socially disfavored in other settings, such as present-day New York City.

Although some socially diagnostic variables have regionally restricted social significance, other variables may have general social significance for

American English, in that a particular social evaluation holds across regional boundaries. Many of the grammatical variables mentioned above have this type of broad-based significance. Virtually every population in the United States that has been studied by sociolinguists shows social stratification for structures like multiple negation, irregular past tense verb forms, and subject–verb agreement patterns. On the whole, phonological variables are more apt to show regionally restricted social significance than are grammatical variables. This is due to the fact that grammatical variables have been ascribed the major symbolic role in differentiating standard from vernacular dialects. Phonological variables show greater flexibility, as they are more likely to be viewed as a normal manifestation of regional diversity in English. As noted earlier, this is particularly true in the case of vowel differences.

There are several different ways in which speakers within the sociolinguistic community may react to socially diagnostic variables. Speakers may treat some features as SOCIAL STEREOTYPES, where they comment overtly on their use. Items such as *ain't*, "double negatives," and "*dese, dem,* and *dose*" are features of this type. Stereotypes can be local or general and may carry either positive or negative connotations. Items like *ain't* and *dese, dem,* and *dose* are widely recognized as "bad grammar," while features like the pronunciation of *high tide* as something like "hoi toid," which characterizes the speech of coastal North Carolina, are strongly stereotyped but only locally. Further, the latter feature carries positive associations in that it is often associated with "British English" or "Shakespearean English." However, it still qualifies as a stereotype because it is the subject of overt commentary.

As with other kinds of behavioral stereotyping, we have to be careful to differentiate the actual sociolinguistic patterning of linguistic stereotypes from popular beliefs about their patterning. These beliefs are often linguistically naive, although they may derive from a basic sociolinguistic reality. For example, people tend to believe that working-class speakers always use the stereotypical *dese, dem,* and *dose* because they are too lazy to exert the effort required to produce them "correctly." They also think that working-class speakers always use these forms and that middle-class speakers never do. These beliefs are not supported empirically. Furthermore, stereotypes tend to focus on single vocabulary items or selective subsets of items rather than more general phonological and grammatical patterns. For example, speakers may focus on a single lexical item like *ain't* or the restricted pronunciation pattern involving *tomatoes* and *potatoes* in which *'maters* and *'taters* is stigmatized and *tomahtos* and *potahtos* is prestigious. Finally, we have to understand that popular explanations for sociolinguistic differences are often rooted in the same type of folk mythology that characterizes other types of behavioral stereotyping and therefore must be viewed with great caution.

Another role that a socially diagnostic feature may fill is that of a SOCIAL MARKER. In the case of social markers, variants show clear-cut social stratification, but they do not show the level of conscious awareness found for the social stereotype. Various vowel shifts, such as the Northern Cities Vowel Shift discussed in chapter 5, seem to function as social markers. There is clear-cut social stratification of the linguistic variants, and participants in the community may even recognize this distribution, but the structure does not evoke the kind of overt commentary and strong value judgments that the social stereotype does. Even if participants don't talk about these features in any direct manner, there are still indications that they are aware of their existence at an unconscious level. This awareness is often indicated by shifts in the use of variants across different styles of speaking. Although we will take up the notion of speech style more fully in chapter 9, we may anticipate our discussion by noting that the incidence of prestigious variants tends to increase and the use of stigmatized variants to decrease as we use more formal speech styles. For example, a speaker who is conversing with an employer during a business meeting will use more *-ing* pronunciations in words like *working* and *running* but will use more *-in'* when talking with friends over lunch.

The third possible sociolinguistic role which a socially diagnostic feature may fill is that of a SOCIAL INDICATOR. Social indicators are linguistic structures that correlate with social stratification without having an effect on listeners' judgment of the social status of speakers who use them. Whereas social stereotypes and social markers are sensitive to stylistic variation, social indicators do not show such sensitivity, as shown by the fact that levels of usage remain constant across formal and informal styles. This suggests that the correlation of socially diagnostic variables with social status differences operates on a more unconscious level than it does for social markers or stereotypes. Although social indicators have been identified for some communities of English speakers (Trudgill 1974: 98), practically all of the socially diagnostic variables in American English qualify as social markers or stereotypes rather than indicators. One possible exception involves variants associated with the earliest stages of vowel shifts, such as the Northern Cities Vowel Shift. When such vowel shifts begin, the use of new vowel pronunciations tends to correlate with social class differences but does not yet show any correlation with stylistic differences. This is particularly true of the backing of the vowel of *bed*, which moves closer to the vowel of *bud* and the subsequent backing of *bud* so that it moves closer to the vowel of *bought*. As these changes proceed, the new pronunciations will become social markers, and some of them may even attain the status of a stereotype, but they start out simply as social indicators.

6.6   Social Class and Language Change

One of the important contributions of the study of social dialectology has
to do with the roles that different social classes play in language change.
Language change does not take place simultaneously on all different social
strata; instead, it originates in a particular social group and then spreads
from that point to other strata, just as regional dialect change typically starts
in a focal area and spreads outward from that point.

What social classes are most likely to start language change? The popular
view assumes that the upper classes originate change and that other social
classes follow their lead. The model of change showing the elite leading
the masses seems intuitively satisfying, but turns out to be somewhat
mistaken. In reality, as we have mentioned in previous chapters, the lower
social classes are much more responsible for language change than they
have been given credit for. Furthermore, extremes in the social strata, for
example, the highest and the lowest social classes, tend to be peripheral
to the origin of change; it is the social classes between the extremes that
bear the major responsibility for change. The middle-status groups tend
to have the strongest loyalty to their local communities so they are more
sensitive to local innovation. Further, those in middle–class groups also
have connections to speakers in outside groups who may serve as models
for language change. According to Gregory Guy (1988: 58), the highest
social groups are not as likely to identify with local communities, while the
lowest social groups have neither strong affinity to their local community
nor broader community allegiance.

In order to understand the role of social class in language change, it is
essential to understand the distinction between changes that take place
below the level of conscious awareness, so–called CHANGES FROM BELOW, and
those that take place above the level of consciousness, or CHANGES FROM
ABOVE. Although this distinction often happens to coincide with change
in terms of social class in that the lower social classes are more likely to be
active in changes from below and the upper classes in changes from above,
the fundamental distinction refers to the level of consciousness, not social
class. Many of the phonological changes in American English, particularly
those involving vowel systems, are changes from below, or at least start out
as changes from below. Changes from above tend to reflect a movement
away from socially stigmatized features or toward external prestige forms
that become the model to emulate. For example, the adoption of *r*-lessness
in the late eighteenth and early nineteenth centuries by some regional varieties
in the United States, based on the external, British prestige norm, is an
example of change from above. Conversely, and somewhat ironically, the
increased use of postvocalic *r* in New York City in recent decades on the

basis of dialect models outside of the area is also a change from above, but in this instance the model is other dialects of American English.

The spread of new forms through the population is only one side of language change. The other side concerns *resistance to change*. Whereas change is certainly natural and inevitable, some social groups may differentiate themselves by withstanding changes taking place in other social groups. As presented in chapter 2, many changes that occur in language involve making language systems as orderly as possible, such as the regularization of irregular grammatical paradigms. For the most part, it is the lower classes that adopt these changes initially and the upper classes that tend to resist them. The regularization of irregular plurals (e.g. *sheeps*, *oxes*), irregular reflexives (*hisself*, *theirselves*), and irregular verbs (e.g. *knowed*, *growed*) in the grammar – attributable to natural forces from within the grammatical system – are certainly changes in the English language that are witnessed to a greater degree in the lower classes than in the upper classes. These changes, along with a number of natural phonological changes noted in chapter 2, have made some headway in the lower classes but are resisted by the upper classes in spite of their linguistic reasonableness. It is the upper classes who have the most investment in maintaining the language as it is; the lower classes have less investment in maintaining the current state of linguistic structures. Accordingly, more conscious attention by the upper classes is given to withstanding potential changes conveniently put forth by the lower classes, even if these changes are natural adaptations of the linguistic system. Only a change in the social valuation of forms can result in the adoption of linguistically natural but socially stigmatized forms by the upper classes.

Exercise 3

In referring to the rodent *mouse*, the plural form *mouses* rather than *mice* is highly stigmatized. At the same time, when referring to computers the plural of *mouse* is usually the regularized form *mouses*, as in *We bought new mouses for all of the computers in the lab.* How might you explain the differential social valuation of these forms? What does this say about language innovation and social valuation?

An important principle of sociolinguistic stratification involves the inhibition of natural linguistic changes by high-status groups. By resisting the changes that occur in lower-status groups, the social stratification of linguistic differences is maintained and even heightened. The bottom line is that higher-status groups do not want to be mistaken for lower-status groups in language any more than they do in other kinds of behavior. Thus, high-status groups often suppress natural changes taking place in lower-status groups to keep their sociolinguistic position intact. In many respects, then, the social differentiation of language in American society is typified by the resistance to proposed changes initiated by the lower classes by a steadfast upper class rather than the initiation of change by the upper classes and subsequent emulation of these changes by the lower classes.

6.7　Ethnicity

Although the correlation of ethnicity with linguistic variation is indisputable, the precise contribution of ethnic group membership to the overall configuration of a dialect or ethnolect is not always simple to identify. Nominal classification of some people into ethnic categories in our society appears to be straightforward on the surface, but in reality it is quite difficult to capture the sociocultural factors that constitute ethnicity. What is popularly identified as "ethnicity" may be difficult to separate from other social factors such as region, social class, and language background. For example, the popular notion of Jewish English has a strong regional association with New York City English; similarly, what is identified as African American English is strongly linked to social status, age, and Southern regional English. A variety such as Chicano English in the Southwest, on the other hand, is often linked with bilingualism even though many of the features of this language variety are now maintained by monolingual speakers. Notwithstanding these kinds of qualifications, it is apparent that "in communities where the local lore acknowledges more than one ethnic group, we would expect ethnicity to be a factor in linguistic variation" (Laferriere 1979: 603).

　The definition of an ethnic group usually involves the following kinds of parameters (from the National Council of Social Studies, Task Force on Ethnic Studies 1976): (1) origins that precede or are external to the state (e.g. Native American, immigrant groups); (2) group membership that is involuntary; (3) ancestral tradition rooted in a shared sense of peoplehood; (4) distinctive value orientations and behavioral patterns; (5) influence of the group on the lives of its members; and (6) group membership influenced by how members define themselves and how they are defined by others. This is an expansive set of parameters, but even this definition does not always lead to clear-cut ethnic categorization. In some cases, self-reported definition turns out to be stronger in determining a person's ethnicity than any of the parameters set forth in the institutional definition.

Notwithstanding the problems involved in teasing out the variable of ethnicity, there is ample evidence that ethnicity can be a key component in the definition of some English varieties. The literature on American English dialects thus includes descriptions of varieties labeled Italian English, Jewish English, Irish English, German English, Puerto Rican English, Chicano English, American Indian English, Vietnamese English, and, of course, African American English, which we take up separately in the next chapter. The extent to which ethnicity *per se* contributes to the definition of dialect in these accounts, however, varies greatly, as does the degree of dialectal distinctiveness. Several surveys (Gold 1981; Steinmetz 1981; Bernstein 2003) of research on Jewish English, for example, concluded that this variety could be distinguished from others solely on the basis of a restricted set of lexical differences, a small inventory of phonological differences related to vowels and intonation, isolated grammatical features, and several aspects of conversational style. By contrast, there are entire books describing the phonological and grammatical features that set African American English apart from other dialects (e.g. Labov 1972a; Baugh 1983; Rickford 1999; Green 2002), as well as separate books devoted exclusively to the lexicon of African American English (Smitherman 1994) and language-use conventions in the black community (e.g. Smitherman 1977; Kochman 1981; Morgan 2002). By comparison, Latino English is still underrepresented (see section 6.8), despite the fact that this is now the largest minority group in the US.

Ethnic groups tend to form subcultures within the larger culture, and part of the distinctiveness of these subcultures may be constructed through the use of linguistic forms. However, the role of linguistic distinctiveness in determining cultural distinctiveness varies greatly from subculture to subculture, depending on the social position of various ethnic groups in American society. Though we might hypothesize that the greater the isolation of an ethnic group from the mainstream of society, the greater its linguistic distinctiveness will be, there are so many other intersecting factors and sociohistorical considerations that this simple principle rarely works out very neatly. Ethnicity does not stand alone in its correlation with language variation; it invariably interacts with a wide array of other social and sociopsychological variables and is embedded within an intricate set of sociocultural relationships, processes, and identities.

There are several different kinds of relationships that may exist between ethnicity and language variation. For ethnic groups that maintain a language other than English, there is the potential of language TRANSFER from another language that is stabilized, or FOSSILIZED, and integrated into an English variety associated with members of the ethnic group. By transfer, we mean the incorporation of language features into a non-native language based on the occurrence of similar features in the native language. For example,

Marion Huffines (1984, 1986, 2002) notes that the English of Pennsylvania Germans in Southeast Pennsylvania is characterized by items that seem to be direct translations of German into English, such as the use of *all* ("all gone") in *He's going to have the cookies **all**, what for* ("what kind of") in *I don't know **what for** a car you had*, and *sneaky* ("finicky about food") in *I'm kind of sneaky when it comes to meat like that*. Similar transfer can be found in phonological features, including the DEVOICING of word-final stops, so that a word like *bad* sounds more like *bat*, and the use of falling rather than rising intonational contours at the ends of questions.

In a similar way, the use of *no* as a generalized tag question (e.g. *You go to the movies a lot, **no**?*) in some Chicano communities in the Southwest may be attributable to transfer from Spanish, as can such phonological features as the merger of *ch* /č/ and *sh* /š/ (e.g. *shoe* as *chew* [ču], *chain* as *Shane* [šen]), the devoicing of /z/ to [s] (e.g. *doze* as *dose* [dos], *lazy* as *lasy* [lesi]), and the merger of /i/ and /ɪ/ (e.g. *pit* as *peat* [pit], *rip* as *reap* [rip]) (Peñalosa 1980; Santa Ana 1993). In many cases, the language features are directly traceable to transfer from Spanish. In some cases, though, the transferred feature has fossilized and been perpetuated so that speakers of Chicano English varieties may use these features even if they are not native speakers of Spanish (Galindo 1987; Fought 2003).

While some of the characteristics of the English dialects associated with particular ethnic groups may be attributable to transfer from a non-English language, others derive from more generalized strategies related to the acquisition of English as a second language rather than specific language structures carried over from another language. It is not uncommon, for example, to find the absence of marked tense forms (e.g. *Yesterday he play at the school*) among English varieties that originated among non-native speakers, including varieties of Native American English and Vietnamese English (Wolfram 1984, 1985; Leap 1993).

The tricky question regarding structures traceable to language contact is determining whether the form is simply a transitional one, which will be eliminated as soon as English becomes the native language of a generation of speakers, or whether the form will be retained and perpetuated as a distinct part of the dialect to be carried forth by subsequent generations. Hindsight seems to be the only way we can answer this question satisfactorily. In some cases, an item traceable to a language contact situation may be retained, but in a redefined form. For example, studies of Native American English in the Southwest indicate that tense unmarking is maintained by successive generations, but it has now become restricted to constructions marking habitual activity (e.g. *Before, we eat at home a lot, but now we don't*). Only the study of an ethnic English variety over several generations of speakers can ultimately determine which of the characteristics derived from second-language acquisition will be integrated into the ethnic variety and which will be cast aside. Older speakers from Vietnam now living in various communities in the US (e.g. Washington, DC, Houston, Los Angeles) exhibit extensive tense unmarking, but it is still to be determined if this feature will be maintained as part of a "Vietnamese English." To make this ultimate determination, we must look at current and future generations of speakers who learn English as a first language.

All transfer from other languages is not readily transparent, as the effects of a heritage language may be quite subtle. Labov thus observes that vowel patterns for the Jewish and Italian communities in New York City do not coincide with those of other New Yorkers, and that this may be due to the effect of the non-English languages spoken by previous generations of Italians and Jewish people. Similarly, some speakers of Latino varieties show subtly different pronunciations for vowels such as the [o] of *coat* and the [u] of *boot* from surrounding European American speakers even when Spanish is no longer their primary language. Although the vowels of these ethnic group members ultimately may be traced to their heritage language backgrounds, the route of influence is not nearly as direct as the kind of transfer referred to above. This, however, does not diminish the impact of ethnicity on language variation. Labov thus concludes that for the New York City vowel system "ethnic differentiation is seen to be a more powerful factor than social class differentiation, though both exist in addition to marked stylistic variation" (1966: 306).

The restructuring of an item from another language may not only involve linguistic adjustment; it also may involve adjustment in the form's social associations. Items like *chutzpah* "impudence, guts", *schlep* "haul, take", and the expression *I need this like a hole in the head* all can be traced to Yiddish, but they have quite different social and ethnic associations. For example, the ethnic associations of *chutzpah* are quite strong, and those who are not part of the Jewish community would only use the term as a borrowed item from that culture. The use of *schlep* is less exclusively embedded in the Jewish community, although it still has an ethnic association; it is now an integral part of regionally situated "New Yorkese." The expression *I need this like a hole in the head*, directly translated from a Yiddish expression (Gold 1981: 288), is the least ethnically associated of these items and is not nearly as regionally restricted as an item like *schlep*. We see, then, that ethnic association is often a relative matter and that other social and regional factors intersect with ethnicity in varying degrees.

Finally, we must recognize that ethnically correlated variation need not be traceable to previous language background at all. Some ethnic associations simply reflect patterns of assimilation and isolation with respect to more widespread regional and social dialects. For example, Martha Laferriere (1979) shows ethnic correlations for Italian, Irish, and Jewish speakers in Boston with reference to the local pronunciation of *-or* in words like *form*, *short*, and *horse*. The usual pronunciation of the vowel in these items among non-Italians in Boston who speak fairly standard English is similar to the [ɔ] of *dog* or *law* in some other regions, but the vernacular Boston pronunciation involves lowering the tongue more toward the [ɑ] vowel of *father* so that *short* is pronounced more like *shot* [šɑt] and *corn* more like *con* [kɑn]. (Remember that this region is largely an *r*-less dialect area to begin with.) Jews most closely follow the standard European American pattern (i.e. [šɔ(r)t], [kɔ(r)n]), followed by the Irish and then the Italians, who are most apt to use the lower vowel found in the vernacular pattern. These ethnic groups also reflect different stages with respect to the current change taking place in the pronunciation of the vowel. The Jewish community has virtually completed a change toward the Boston standard pronunciation (using the higher vowel [ɔ]), followed by the Irish who are in the middle of the change, and the Italians, who are just beginning a change toward the standard production.

Ethnic group association also varies by linguistic feature. Whereas Italians and Jews do not participate in the typical New York pattern with respect to some vowels, they participate fully in the New York pattern of *r*-lessness. Similarly, the Italian, Irish, and Jewish communities in Boston participate in many of the linguistic characteristics of the regional variety in a way that is indistinguishable from other Bostonians at the same time that these ethnic communities distinguish themselves in their realization of a particular vowel.

In the next sections, we consider language variation for three different ethnic groups that represent diverse sociolinguistic situations. First, we consider the case of Latino or Hispanic English, which is associated with a large, broadly distributed ethnic group living under a variety of sociolinguistic conditions throughout the US. Then we consider the case of Cajun English in Southern Louisiana, a variety associated with a widely recognized, regionally concentrated cultural group that developed under a particular set of sociohistorical circumstances. Finally, we describe the case of Lumbee English, which is linked to a relatively unknown, localized Native American group in the Southeast. The case of African American English will be discussed separately in the next chapter.

6.8   Latino English

The case of *Latino English*, or *Hispanic English*, illustrates the wide range of circumstances and the complexity of the issues related to ethnolinguistic variation in American English. Peoples descended from the Spanish have populated the Americas since the fifteenth century and are second only to Native Americans in their continuous habitation in the New World. Many Latinos are of diverse ancestry, descended from Europeans, people indigenous to the Americas, and, in some cases, Africans. At the same time, Spanish speakers are currently the largest group of recent immigrants to the United States mainland. During the 1990s, the Hispanic population increased by over 50 percent, and since the 2000 Census, it has grown nearly four times faster than the US population. In the process, Hispanics have replaced African Americans as the largest minority group in the US, with a population now totaling nearly 40 million. Latino English variation ranges from the speech of long-term, regionally established English monolinguals of Latin American descent to that of first-generation speakers of limited English proficiency, with a full range of bilingualism in between. Accordingly, language differences in English may vary from structures characteristic of the initial stages of second language acquisition to durable ethnolinguistic features now only remotely associated with Spanish.

To some extent, the issue of ethnic labeling, including appropriate terms for ethnic varieties of English, reflects the diversity of situations involving speakers whose heritage language is Spanish. For Southern California alone, Carmen Fought (2003: 17) observes a range of terms for those of Latin American descent, as well as opinions about these terms, with the terms Chicano, Latino, and Mexican American strongly preferred over Hispanic, which is described as a "White person's word." Nevertheless, Hispanic seems to be an acceptable supra-regional term used most notably in national Spanish-language television programming and, for some, may imply a sense of cohesion for a group with diverse ethnic and cultural backgrounds. In some regions of the US, *Latino* and *Hispanic* seem to be used interchangeably, while the label "Mexican" is socially stigmatized to the point of becoming a taboo term. In New York City, the blended term *Nuyorican* refers to a New Yorker of Puerto Rican heritage and *Dominican Yorker* is used for a New Yorker of Dominican Republic heritage, signifying a kind of cultural syncretism or blending. We see, then, that labeling a variety associated with a Spanish–English contact situation can become a sociolinguistic issue in its own right, sensitive to region, sociopolitical context, and ideology. The labeling issue is further complicated by the fact that terms such as *Chicano English* and *Latino English* use the masculine suffix *-o* to refer to the speech of both men and women, thus raising issues about the use of masculine grammatical forms for generic reference (see chapter 8).

Exercise 4

A number of terms have been used to identify the variety of English spoken by Spanish-heritage residents in the US. In some respects, the shifting labels are similar to the situation related to African American speech. In chapter 7, we list the labels used for African American English over the past four decades; these include Negro Dialect, Non-standard Negro English, Black English, Vernacular Black English, Afro-American English, Ebonics, African American (Vernacular) English, and African American Language. In what ways are the issues of labeling Latino varieties similar to and different from those used in labeling the speech of African Americans?

The issue of ethnolinguistic variation is complicated by settlement history, region, and social circumstance. The Southwestern US has been the home of Mexican Spanish speakers for centuries now; in fact, California and Texas did not become states of the USA until the mid-nineteenth century and New Mexico and Arizona did not become states until the twentieth century. Urban areas of the Northeast such as New York City and Hartford, Connecticut, have had stable populations from Puerto Rico for several generations, while Southern Florida, particularly Miami, has been the home of Cuban refugees for a half-century. More recently, however, some of these areas have experienced so much immigration from other Latin American countries that the Latino communities have become quite diverse there.

In the Midwest, Chicago has had a long history of migrants from Mexico and Puerto Rico. Meanwhile, some rural and urban regions in the Southeast, Midwest, and Northwest are witnessing a wave of immigrants from Central America for the first time. Differences in settlement history, social conditions, and community dynamics make it virtually impossible to describe a generic dialect of "Latino English"; local communities and individuals define their ethnolinguistic identity in a wide assortment of ways. Spanish-influenced English varieties may be linked through a common heritage language, one that also includes quite diverse dialects, but there is no unified core variety of Latino English in the US that necessarily shares a common set of linguistic traits.

6.8.1   Chicano English

The sociolinguistic situation involving Latinos in the Southwest, particularly in the border states of Texas, California, Arizona, and New Mexico, has been developing for centuries. English varieties spoken in this region are most commonly referred to as *Chicano English*, though the term has been defined in various ways. Most current researchers (Santa Ana 1993; Mendoza-Denton 1997; Fought 2003) define Chicano English as a vernacular variety that has been influenced by Spanish but it is not dependent on bilingualism *per se*. Otto Santa Ana (1993: 15), for example, limits the term Chicano English to a variety "spoken only by native English speakers," noting explicitly that it "is to be distinguished from the English of second-language learners."

As with other English dialects linked to ethnic group membership, it is necessary to debunk a set of myths associated with the variety. Fought (2003: 3ff.) describes four myths associated with Chicano English, some of which are similar to the kinds of general myths about dialects that we discussed in chapter 1:

MYTH: Chicano English is spoken by people whose first language is Spanish, which introduces mistakes into their English.

REALITY: Many speakers of Chicano English are monolingual in English and learn this variety like native speakers learn any other vernacular variety of English. Though influenced by Spanish contact historically, Chicano English exists independent of bilingualism.

MYTH: Chicano English is the same as "Spanglish."

REALITY: Though codeswitching, popularly referred to as *Spanglish*, is a natural part of bilingualism, it is separate from, and should not be confused with, Chicano English.

MYTH: Chicano English is a dialect used primarily by gang members and not used by middle-class Latinos and Latinas.

REALITY: Chicano English is used by speakers that may cut across a range of social and cultural groups. It is defined mainly by a set of phonological, grammatical, and lexical features rather than social division.

MYTH: Chicano English is merely incorrect grammar.

REALITY: Chicano English is a separate variety of English with highly organized linguistic patterns. Its interpretation as "incorrect grammar" derives from the principle of linguistic subordination (see chapter 1), and has no basis in linguistic reality.

Sociolinguists have described a number of phonological and grammatical features in Chicano English (Bayley and Santa Ana 2004; Santa Ana and Bayley 2004). As with other socially and ethnically diagnostic linguistic variables, they interact with sociohistorical, sociocultural and sociopsychological factors, as discussed in chapter 2. A number of the traits associated with Chicano English relate to vowels. Though these traits can be traced to the effects of the original contact situation involving Spanish and English, they are fully integrated into the English variety and no longer depend on bilingualism. Children who learn English as their first language acquire the vowel traits of Chicano English in a social setting where this ethnic dialect is the vernacular norm. One prominent feature has to do with the degree to which vowels are reduced. In most varieties of English, the vowel in unstressed syllables is reduced to a schwa-like quality, so that, for example, *because* sounds like *buhcause* [bəkɔz] and *today* like *tuhday* [tədei]. However, speakers of Chicano English are more likely to produce a non-reduced vowel closer to [i] or [u] than to schwa [ə], as in *beecause* [bikɔz] or *tooday* [tudei]. In another subtle distinction, the vowels of words like *beet* and *boot* also may not be as glided as they typically are in most varieties of English, where *beet* is actually pronounced more like *bieet* [phonetically [bɪit]) and *boot* as *buoot* (phonetically [bʊut]). Another vowel trait is the merger of the vowels in words like *beet* and *bit* or *sheep* and *ship* into a single sound that falls somewhere between [i] and [ɪ] phonetically. The resulting pronunciations may sound similar to the merger of both of these vowels into *ee* [i] often heard in the speech of native Spanish speakers in the early stages of learning English; however, the sound in these words in Chicano English may be slightly different. For example, Mendoza-Denton (1999) found that some teenage girls in her study pronounced *-ing* as more like "-eeng" [iŋ] to signal greater social distance from European Americans and from Chicanas who associated with them. We see, then, that features originally associated with learning English as a second language may be restructured into symbols of identity in terms of different groups of Chicanas and Chicanos as well as non-Chicano groups.

With respect to consonants, there is a tendency to produce the *th* of words like *then* and *think* as stops produced with the tongue tip touching the back of the teeth. In this respect, Chicano English is not different from many vernacular dialects of English, but the frequency of the process may be greater than in some other vernacular varieties. Consonant clusters at the end of words also may be reduced (e.g. *west end* as *wes' en'*) more frequently than they are in other vernacular dialects of European Americans.

In some respects, the prosodic features of rhythm and intonation may be among the most distinctive traits of Chicano English, though they are also more difficult to describe in precise detail than consonant and vowel segments. The timing of syllables tends to be more SYLLABLE-TIMED than PHRASE-TIMED, in that each syllable occurs at roughly equivalent intervals. By contrast, timing in standard English is dictated by the stressed syllables within a phrase, which are more prominent and of longer duration than other syllables. For example, in the phrase *in the gárden*, the syllable *gár* is held longer and the other syllables reduced in length in general American English. In Chicano English, on the other hand, the duration of the syllables is more evenly distributed. This difference, however, is a relative rather than an absolute one. The intonation patterns of sentences in Chicano English may also be different from those associated with other varieties of American English, so that declarative statements sometimes sound more like questions than statements to the uninitiated listener. Of course, as we saw in chapter 4, the use of rising intonation on declarative sentences, or UPTALK, is becoming more prevalent in many American varieties, and so this difference between Chicano English and other varieties is eroding slightly.

Although most of the traits mentioned above are due to direct or indirect influence from earlier Spanish–English contact situations, it would be wrong to assume that all of the features of Chicano English are the result of language contact. In Southern California, younger speakers of Chicano English combine traits deriving from language contact with those of the emerging California vowel system, such as the fronting of vowels in words like *boot* to *biwt* and *boat* to *bewt* (Fought 2003).

The grammar of Chicano English is a combination of features that includes general structures shared by a wide range of vernacular English varieties, structures resulting from the Spanish–English contact situation, and items shared with neighboring regional and social dialects. For example, the leveling of past tense *be* in *We was there*, multiple negation in *She ain't been nowhere*, and irregular past forms in *Yesterday he come to visit* are features of vernacular English dialects throughout the US and elsewhere. At the same time, the use of prepositions such as *on* in sentences like *She's on fifth grade*, or *for* in sentences like *She told the truth for she won't feel guilty* are traceable to transfer from Spanish–English language contact. The adverb *barely* for "just recently" in a sentence like *I barely broke my leg* seems to blend the meaning of the Spanish adverb *apenas* "scarcely, hardly" and a related meaning for *barely* in English sentences such as *Don't leave yet, you barely got here* in a somewhat novel way (Fought 2003).

Grammatical influence from neighboring dialects is reflected in the fact that young Chicano English speakers in Southern California may freely use the habitual form of *be* (e.g. *The news be showing it too much*), now stereotypically associated with African American English, alongside the innovative use of quotative *be like* and *be all* in sentences such as *She's like, "You don't leave the house"* or *He's all, "I'm working for you"* associated stereotypically with Southern California Valley Girl Talk and now in more widespread usage in the US, especially among younger speakers. Though a dialect combining features derived from Spanish–English contact with features associated with younger European Americans and African Americans in California may seem somewhat peculiar to outsiders, in reality all dialects combine features from the sources available to them. In the case of Chicano English in California, the resultant variety is a distinctive, regionally situated variety of English that is, among other things, symbolically linked to ethnic group membership.

6.8.2　The range of Latino English

Chicano English in Southern California is only one of the Spanish-related varieties of English in the US; in fact, it is just one of the varieties of Chicano English used in the Southwest. There are a number of Latino communities in different parts of the US that construct their ethnolinguistic identities in different ways, both in terms of their own sense of group identity and in terms of their relation to surrounding non-Latino communities. The situation involving communities in Southern Texas (Galindo 1987; Bayley 1997), for example, is somewhat different from that in Southern California, and the situations involving the diverse Latino communities in New York City and communities of Cuban heritage in Southern Florida are even more distinctive from that characterizing Chicano English on the West Coast.

A study of first-generation Puerto Rican adolescents in New York City conducted several decades ago (Wolfram 1974b) indicated that some Puerto Rican teenagers who had extensive contacts with African Americans assimilated features from this variety, such as habitual *be*, the absence of the copula in *He ugly*, and third-person singular *-s* absence in *She like to act*. Even those teenagers who had limited social interaction with African Americans showed some indirect assimilation, although this group did not typically use core features of vernacular African American speech such as habitual *be* and inflectional *-s* absence. At the same time, their speech showed features attributable to influence from Spanish–English contact. What this earlier study failed to recognize, however, was the developing influence of the local regional dialect on this variety, including the adoption of New York City postvocalic *r*-lessness (*fea'* for *fear*) and the imprint of the more general New York City vowel system on Puerto Rican English. As indicated in a symbolic way in labels like *Nuyorican*, a sociocultural and ethnolinguistic blend may now be associated with New York Latino English. Thus, Michael Newman (2003) reports an example in which a teenage Nuyorican rap artist uses the phrase "I'm gonna spin you like a dreidel," referring to a top used in Chanukah celebrations; meanwhile, his Latino classmate often says, "What the schmuck!" as an expression of surprise (with *schmuck* being a Yiddish-derived word associated with New York Jewish English). Obviously, such speakers are borrowing liberally from local varieties while maintaining some traits that continue to mark them as Latinos. Based on research in Philadelphia, Shana Poplack (1978) suggests that gender also may be an important factor in the acquisition of local dialect features. In a study of sixth grade Puerto Rican boys and girls, she found that the girls were more likely to acquire traits of the local Philadelphia vowel system associated with European Americans than boys, who were more likely to acquire features associated with African American English.

Although stable communities have existed in some regions for centuries, other locations in the US, particularly the Southeast, Upper Midwest, and Northwest, are just beginning to experience the emergence of Latino communities. In these circumstances, there is a steady stream of new immigrants who come directly from their country of origin with little proficiency in English. Thus, they acquire English exclusively in regionalized contexts in the US. Spanish remains the dominant native language in the emerging community, and most speakers remain quite proficient in Spanish, even children born in the US. These circumstances are quite different from the kinds of situations we described above, but they offer an opportunity to examine the dynamics of new dialect formation in progress. Important questions about these situations involve the extent to which speakers acquire the local dialect features of neighboring English-speaking communities as they learn English, and how they mix these traits with structural transfer from Spanish and generalized second language learning phenomena. There may also be differences in the acquisition of the local dialect features of neighboring ethnic groups based on regional setting (urban vs. rural), population ecology (e.g. size of the community, percentage of Latinos, etc.), the language–contact relationship between Spanish and English, and community-based cultural values.

The examination of emerging Latino/a communities in rural and urban areas of North Carolina indicates that these situations are both similar to and different from the kinds of situations described above (Wolfram, Carter, and Moriello 2004). Speakers in these Latino/a communities show a wide range of proficiency in English, and many of the traits associated with second language acquisition are pervasive in the English of these communities as well. At the same time, there is evidence of local dialect influence. For example, the adoption of lexical items associated with longstanding local communities, such as the Southern second-person plural pronoun *y'all* and the Southern auxiliary *fixin' to*, as in *He's fixin' to be there* may occur relatively early in the acquisition of English, while speakers still have heavily accented pronunciations. The adoption of local phonology is much more complicated and sensitive to various demographic and sociocultural factors. This process is illustrated in our examination of the production of the /ai/ diphthong in words like *time* and *ride* in two Latino communities in different locales in North Carolina, one in the metropolitan area of Raleigh and a rural community about 50 miles from Raleigh. In many Southern dialects, /ai/ is largely unglided, as in *tahm* for *time* or *rahd* for *ride*. In our study, we found that the adoption of the Southern unglided pronunciation by Latino speakers was affected by a number of social factors, including degree of rurality, length of speakers' residency, sociocultural values, and their relationship to the non-Latino community. Though neither Latino community showed the wholesale adoption of the unglided Southern variant, the rural Latino speakers were more inclined to unglide the vowel of *time* and *ride* than their urban counterparts. The role of individuals' constructions of personal and group identity in the process of dialect acquisition was demonstrated vividly in one sociolinguistic interview conducted with two siblings, an 11-year-old girl and her 13-year-old brother (Moriello and Wolfram 2003). Their parents came from Mexico, but the children lived their entire lives in North Carolina. The sister only had one case of unglided /ai/ in her entire interview, whereas her brother unglided well over half of his /ai/ diphthongs, showing a marked difference between the two siblings in the production of this Southern pronunciation. This difference is most likely explained by the fact that the adolescent boy identifies strongly with the local non-Latino "jock" culture, setting him apart from his sister, who is more oriented toward mainstream school values of academic achievement. Thus, we see that individual choice, gender roles (and expectations for "appropriate" gendered behavior), and other social factors may lead to quite different outcomes in terms of the adoption of local dialect features, as speakers mold their identities in relation to those around them and for themselves. In this respect, the varieties of Latino English are no different from those that are shaped in other sociolinguistic situations.

6.9   Cajun English

Whereas Latino English covers a wide variety of sociolinguistic situations united by a shared language heritage, the case of Cajun English involves a variety associated with a specific cultural group who live, for the most part, in Southern Louisiana. Though knowledge of Cajun culture is often superficial and based on stereotypes, most Americans have heard of the Cajuns. As mentioned in chapter 4, the term *Cajun*, derived from the word *Acadian*, refers to the descendants of a group of French Canadians from Nova Scotia, formerly Acadia, who colonized the Bayou Teche area of Louisiana in the 1760s. Many French were forced to leave Acadia when they would not pledge allegiance to the British rule established there at the time. Emigrants left for various destinations that extended from French-ruled Caribbean islands to the coastlines of the US, including Southern Louisiana. They often settled in isolated pockets where they could maintain the French language and practice the Catholic religion, setting them apart from neighboring groups. The marshy terrain of Southern Louisiana created by the offshoots and the overflow of the many lakes and rivers, referred to as the *bayou*, also fostered their cultural and linguistic separateness.

Several varieties of French existed during this period in Southern Louisiana, including Acadian French and a French-based creole language. A CREOLE LANGUAGE is a contact language whose vocabulary comes primarily from one language, called the LEXIFIER language, and whose grammar is composed partly of structures from the other contact language(s) and structures common in language contact situations. In this case, the creole arose from contact between the Acadians, other groups of French speakers already in Louisiana, Native Americans, slaves from Africa and the Caribbean, and Spanish-speaking Isleños from the Canary Islands, as well as other European immigrant groups, creating a contact situation that gave rise to a French-based Creole. Though varieties of French were maintained in the region for a couple of centuries, English has now replaced French as the dominant language in most Cajun communities – and the primary source for "sounding Cajun."

There are a number of features that are associated with Cajun English, most of which are traceable to its French language heritage. Some features now extend well beyond Cajun culture and have become part of a more broadly based regional dialect of the area. Terms like *lagniappe* "something extra" and *boudin* "a seasoned pork and rice sausage", for example, are now associated with general Southern Louisiana speech regardless of ethnicity.

A set of phonetic traits is among the most salient characteristics of Cajun English (Dubois and Horvath 1998a, 1998b, 1999, 2003; Melançon 2001). Whereas most American English speakers produce vowels in words like *late* and *boat* with a glide at the end of the vowel so they sound more like *layeet* [leɪt] and *bowuut* [boʊt], respectively, these glides may be eliminated in Cajun English. This is similar to the production of the corresponding vowels in French, though this trait is found in speakers who are monolingual English speakers as well as those who are native Cajun French speakers. The diphthong /ai/ of *time* and *light* is also unglided (e.g. *tahm*, *laht*), a transfer feature from French that is, at the same time, quite similar to the surrounding regional variety of Southern English. There is also heavy nasalization on vowels before nasal segments, so that words like *man* and *bone* sound like the nasalized vowels associated with the French pronunciation of *n* when it is not followed by a vowel (e.g. *pain* "bread", *bon* "good"). Consonants such as *p*, *t*, and *k* may be produced without the aspiration, or puff of air, that usually accompanies their pronunciation in English, so that the word *pat* sounds more like *bat* and *coat* sound more like *goat* to outsiders. In addition, interdental fricatives in words like *think* and *that* are stopped, as in *tink* and *dat*. Though lots of dialects exhibit stopping of *th* at the beginning of words, stopping in all positions (e.g. *broder* for *brother* and *teet* for *teeth*) is distinctive, as is the extensive stopping of the voiceless *th* in words like *think* and *thank*. Practically all of these features can be traced to influence from the French varieties that have been dominant in some rural Louisiana jurisdictions, or *parishes*, until recent generations.

In grammar, Cajun English shares a number of features with other vernacular dialects of English, such as multiple negation (e.g. *They didn't want no schooling*), different uses of irregular verbs in past tense (e.g. *She seen it; She brung it*), and past tense *be* leveling (e.g. *We was there*). The grammar of Cajun English is also characterized by features associated with learning English as a second language, such as the use of past tense with infinitives (e.g. *They wanted to drank*) and progressives without *-ing* (e.g. *I kept drank*). Distinguishing constructions such as *making groceries* for "buying groceries" and *getting down* for "getting out" of a vehicle are also traceable to influence from French (Dubois and Horvath 2003). There are also a number of traits that align Cajun English with Southern European American and African American vernaculars such as copula absence (e.g. *She nice; They from around here*) and verbal *-s* absence (e.g. *She go with it*) (Dubois and Horvath 2003).

At one point, the features of Cajun English were viewed simply as reflections of transfer effects from French. However, as the heritage language associated with Cajun culture has receded, Cajun English has become the primary linguistic symbol of Cajun identity. Megan Melançon (2001: 32) thus notes that "to be a Cajun these days, the necessary and sufficient condition seems to be that you must speak Cajun English." The emblematic role now assumed by Cajun English is illustrated dramatically by the changes in the use of linguistic features taking place across different generations of speakers. If the occurrence of features in the English of Cajuns were simply due to French influence, we would expect a steady decrease in their use across different generations of speakers, as English replaces French. We would expect the oldest speakers, for whom English was learned as a second language, to have a high incidence of transfer features from French; we would expect middle-aged speakers, who learned English along with Cajun French, to have a lower usage level; and we would expect the youngest generation of speakers, who are English-dominant, to have the lowest levels of usage. But Sylvie Dubois and Barbara Horvath's (1998a, 1998b, 1999) study of three generations of Cajuns shows that this is not necessarily the case. In examining usage levels for several phonological features, including the stopping of interdental fricatives, as in *tink* for *think*, the lack of aspiration on *p*, *t*, and *k*, and heavy nasalization on words like *man* and *pin*, Dubois and Horvath found that some features showed a steady decline across age groups, but others did not. Instead, some features showed a curvilinear, or v-shaped, pattern of usage across the three generations of speakers, in which the youngest group of speakers was more like the oldest group than the middle group, which showed reduced levels of usage. The unaspirated production of *p*, *t*, and *k*, for example, showed a progressive decrease in usage across the three generations of speakers, but the stopping of interdental fricatives and strong nasalization showed a reversal in usage rather than a progressive decline.

The pattern of usage shows that some of the features associated with the traditional Cajun French accent are being recycled and intensified in the dialect of English that is becoming increasingly associated with Cajun identity. The forms produced by the older generations of speakers can be attributed to a transfer effect, but they play a very different role for younger speakers, for whom French is not a dominant language. The resurgence of these features is linked to the Cajun cultural renaissance that has been taking place over the last several decades, even as the traditional heritage language has been receding. Dubois and her colleagues (Dubois and Melançon 2000; Dubois and Horvath 1998a, 1998b, 1999, 2003) note that Cajun identity, once disparaged and actively suppressed in schools and other institutions, is now socially and economically advantageous, and younger Cajuns can now express overt pride in their Cajun identity. However, there are complex age, gender, and social network effects on the revitalization of Cajun identity and Cajun English. While older men and women show very similar usage levels for Cajun English features, middle-aged and younger men are more likely to use features associated with Cajun French influence than their female counterparts. Further, young men in open social networks rather than closed networks lead the revival for most linguistic features. The male lead in recycling features may be explained in terms of the gendered nature of the cultural renaissance. Since the hallmarks of today's Cajun culture stem from traditional male activities, including hunting, fishing, performing Cajun music, and cooking special feast-day foods, Cajun identity is strongly associated with Cajun men, not only among Cajuns themselves but in the eyes of tourists and other non-Cajuns who pay to see performances and eat foods traditionally associated with Cajun male culture. As Dubois and Horvath observe (1998a: 185), "The young men are the ones who benefit the most from the change in attitudes to all things Cajun and they are the heirs of Cajun identity."

Cajun English shows how an ethnic group can reallocate some of the language structures originally associated with a heritage language to a variety of English. It further demonstrates how once-stigmatized, accented features can be recycled and reinterpreted to serve as symbolic tokens of cultural identity. At the same time, it indicates the complexity of such processes and the array of social and linguistic factors that may affect them, including social networks, gender roles and gender-based activities, and the commodification of cultural identity. While many people might have predicted the recession of Cajun French in Southern Louisiana a half-century ago, few anticipated the cultural renaissance that would lead to a corresponding linguistic resurgence of accented features to highlight a distinct, ethnically based variety of English.

6.10   Lumbee English

Lumbee English is a language variety uniquely associated with a particular
Native American group in the rural Southeast. Like Latino English, there is
a wide range of variation in the English of Native Americans based on region,
sociohistorical circumstances, and local social context. In some areas of the
Southwestern US, where indigenous Native American languages are still
spoken, transfer from the heritage language and generalized second language
acquisition structures still may be prominent in Native American varieties
of English. Structural traits from heritage languages may also be incorporated
into the English of Native Americans whose first or only language is English,
paralleling the situation described in the previous sections. In addition,
William Leap (1993) suggests that in some parts of the western US there
may even be a kind of pan-Indian variety of English that developed partly as
a result of the (often forced) cultural segregation of Native Americans, and
partly as a result of the establishment of a few centralized boarding schools
to which Indians from different tribal groups were sent well into the twentieth
century. Of course, there are Native Americans whose English is virtually
indistinguishable from regional varieties associated with the dominant,
European American population, as is the case for many Eastern Band
Cherokees who live in the Smoky Mountains by the Tennessee–North
Carolina border. Younger monolingual Cherokees in this region simply
acquire the regional variety of Appalachian English associated with White
European American speakers, though there are some middle-aged speakers
who still may show subtle residual effects from their Cherokee language
background. However, these effects are often so subtle that they would not
generally be noticed by outside listeners (Anderson 1999).

Even when we consider the broad spectrum of variation in Native
American English, Lumbee English seems to be set apart. Though the
Lumbee are the largest Native American group east of the Mississippi
River, with over 55,000 members now registered on the tribal rolls, they are
surprisingly unknown outside of Southeastern North Carolina. Over 45,000
Lumbee live in Robeson County, North Carolina, located on the South
Carolina border in the southeastern part of the state, giving the county by
far the largest Native American population of any rural county in the
Eastern United States. Within Robeson County, the Lumbee are the largest
ethnic group, including approximately 40 percent of the county population;
African Americans make up approximately 25 percent, and European Americans the remaining 35 percent. The county population has been tri-ethnic
for a couple of centuries now. In one form or another, ethnic segregation
has existed since the early eighteenth century, and *de facto* segregation among
the three groups is still very evident. Accordingly, three distinct varieties of

English have developed. Local residents listening to anonymous audio samples of speakers can correctly identify the ethnicity of speakers from the three groups about 80 percent of the time (Wolfram, Dannenberg, Knick, and Oxendine 2002).

The Lumbee situation illustrates the social, political, and ideological factors that may impact the development of an ethnic variety. As a Native American group, the Lumbee have an ambiguous status. Though they were recognized as a Native American group in a Congressional Act in 1956, they were explicitly denied entitlements routinely awarded to Native American tribes, such as land and services provided through the Bureau of Indian Affairs. Their ambivalent status in terms of Federal recognition, however, has not affected their resolute sense of Indian identity. As one observer of contemporary Native American life in the US put it: "for as long as any Lumbee can remember, they have possessed an unflagging conviction that they are simply and utterly Indian, a tenacious faith that is troubled only by the failure of most other Americans to recognize it" (Bordewich 1996: 62). To a large extent, their identity is a matter of self-definition, expressed in the oft-repeated phrase, "We know who we are" (Hutcheson 2000).

The ancestral language roots of the Lumbee are a matter of speculation. There are no speakers of any Lumbee heritage language, nor have there been for at least five generations. Furthermore, there is only circumstantial evidence as to what their ancestral language or languages might have been. The absence of a specific Native American language lineage is also, no doubt, part of the reason that the Lumbees' Native American status has been questioned; if they could be linked to a single Native American language, they would be recognized as an authentic Indian tribe without question. The sociohistorical and archeological evidence suggests that the Lumbee came from a multi-tribal aggregate, with Iroquoian (particularly Tuscarora), Siouan (particularly Cheraw) and even Algonquian languages providing formative influence. The English variety they have developed in the local context of Robeson County, however, shows how an ethnic variety can be constructed independently of a language contact situation involving a heritage language. Detailed descriptive study of Lumbee Vernacular English (Dannenberg 2002; Wolfram et al. 2002) highlights a dialect created from various input English dialect sources and from innovation within the community of speakers. For example, Lumbee English retains an older use of *be* rather than the use of the perfect form *have* in constructions, such as *I'm been to the store* for *I've been to the store*. Lumbee English speakers also regularize to *were* rather than *was* in negative sentences such as *I weren't there* or *She weren't here*. Neither of these features is found to any extent in neighboring European American and African American vernacular varieties, though regularization to *weren't* is a well-attested trait among coastal dialects of North Carolina.

The grammatical structures of Lumbee English are accompanied by a set of phonological features that seems to be composed of a unique mix of elements of Southern rural inland speech and some vowel traits reminiscent of coastal speech. There is a small set of unique lexical items, such as *ellick* "cup of coffee with cream in it", *on the swamp* "neighborhood", and *brickhouse Indian* "high-status Lumbee"; however, most of the dialect lexicon is shared with other Southern rural varieties. While Lumbee English exhibits a few distinctive dialect traits, it also marks ethnolinguistic distinctiveness by using features from neighboring varieties in unique ways. For example, one of the features characterizing Lumbee Vernacular English is the use of finite *be(s)* in sentences such as *I hope it bes a girl* or *They bes doing all right*. Historically, the European American population in the area, largely of Scots and Scots-Irish descent, used this *bes* form, but this feature is now obsolescent among younger European American speakers. Meanwhile, the neighboring African American community uses *be* to denote habitual aspect, as in *They always be playing* (see chapter 7). Analysis of the speech of Lumbees of different age groups indicates that older speakers do not restrict finite *be* to habitual contexts, but younger speakers are increasingly adapting their use of *be(s)* to habitual contexts, thus indicating increasing alignment with African American English (Dannenberg and Wolfram 1998). At the same time, however, the Lumbee continue to inflect *be* with *-s*, as in *She bes doing it*, even though African American speakers do not typically use this suffix. The end result is a subtly different use of *be*.

The distinctive mix of dialect features in Lumbee Vernacular English shows how a cultural group can maintain a distinct ethnic identity by configuring past and present dialect features in a way that symbolically indicates – and helps to constitute – their cultural uniqueness even though the ancestral language has been completely lost. In the American South, which has been dominated by a bi-racial ideology, the Lumbee have defined themselves as a linguistic other; they are neither White nor Black in their speech (e.g. Schilling-Estes 2000, 2004). The story of Lumbee English shows how language and ethnicity cannot be reduced to a search for the lingering effects of a heritage language. Instead, it demonstrates the linguistic creativity, flexibility, and resiliency of a cultural group that has shaped and reshaped its identity through available linguistic resources, in this case, existing varieties of English brought to the region starting centuries ago. Over the years, their English dialect has become such an integral part of who they are and how they define themselves that the Congressional Act of 1956 that gave the Lumbee their partial recognition notes that "by reason of tribal legend, coupled with distinctive appearance and *manner of speech* [emphasis ours] . . . [they] shall, after the ratification of this Act, be known and designated as the Lumbee Indians of North Carolina."

In the previous sections, we have briefly profiled several cases of ethnolinguistic variation. Many other cases certainly could have been included in a more comprehensive description. The situations we described here are intended only to outline several ways in which language variation can interact with ethnicity. Though ethnicity does not stand alone as an exclusive factor in the maintenance of a dialect, ethnic group membership can be one of the most powerful variables in the development of a language variety. This will be further demonstrated in our discussion of African American English in the next chapter.

Exercise 5

Compare Chicano English, Cajun English, and Lumbee English in terms of their sociohistorical setting, their heritage language background, and how they have constructed their distinct ethnic dialects. In what ways are the local and more broadly based sociopolitical contexts similar and different? How do the varieties compare in terms of the language features associated with each variety?

6.11 Further Reading

Dubois, Sylvie and Barbara M. Horvath (1998a) From accent to marker in Cajun English: A study of dialect formation in progress. *English World-Wide* 19: 161–88. This is one of several articles by Dubois and her colleagues that describe the formation and maintenance of a distinct variety of English symbolically marking Cajun identity. These studies also have important implications for understanding the role of cultural identity and gender in language change.

Fought, Carmen (2003) *Chicano English in Context.* New York/Basingstoke: Palgrave Macmillan. Fought's description of Chicano English covers the wide range of issues related to this variety, from definition and attitudes to description and explanation. It is grounded in extensive fieldwork in Southern California, but the range of issues and comprehensive description presented in a very readable format make this a "must read" for anyone interested in Latino English anywhere in the US.

Labov, William (1972b) *Sociolinguistic Patterns.* Philadelphia: University of Pennsylvania Press. Several of the most influential articles on the interaction of social and linguistic differentiation are included in this collection of Labov's early research studies. These articles set the stage for much of the social dialect research that has taken place over the past several decades.

Leap, William L. (1993) *American Indian English.* Salt Lake City: University of Utah Press. Sections in this overview, which focuses on Native American English varieties in the Southwest, include (1) speaker and structure, (2) Indian English and ancestral language tradition, (3) history and function, and (4) Indian English in the classroom. It is the most comprehensive overview of Native American English varieties currently available.

Santa Ana, Otto (1993) Chicano English and the Chicano language setting. *Hispanic Journal of Behavioral Sciences* 15: 1–35. This article presents an overview of some of the traits of Chicano English as well as the social settings contextualizing this variety.

Schneider, Edgar W., Bernd Kortmann, Kate Burridge, Rajend Mesthrie, and Clive Upton (eds.) (2004), *A Handbook of Varieties of English*, vol. 1: *Phonology*. Berlin/New York: Mouton de Gruyter; and Kortmann, Bernd, Edgar W. Schneider, Kate Burridge, Rajend Mesthrie, and Clive Upton (eds.) (2004), *A Handbook of Varieties of English*, vol. 2: *Morphology and Syntax*. Berlin/New York: Mouton de Gruyter.

(The collections of essays in the companion volumes above contain the most comprehensive descriptions of social and ethnic varieties described in this chapter and the next, including Chicano English, Cajun English, African American English, and other social and ethnic dialects.)

Wolfram, Walt, Clare Dannenberg, Stanley Knick, and Linda Oxendine (2002) *Fine in the World: Lumbee Language in Time and Place*. Raleigh: North Carolina State Humanities Extension/Publications. This book on Lumbee language for general audiences describes the development and current status of the unique English variety spoken by the largest Native American group east of the Mississippi River. It is an extraordinary story of linguistic adaptation and cultural resolve.

7

African American English

AFRICAN AMERICAN ENGLISH (AAE), or more popularly EBONICS, is the paradigm case of ethnicity-based language diversity. It is also the best known and most subject to controversy of any American English dialect. Even its name has become a contentious issue. Among the labels attached to this variety over the past four decades have been Negro Dialect, Non-standard Negro English, Black English, Vernacular Black English, Afro-American English, Ebonics, African American (Vernacular) English, and African American Language. Though it is now popularly referred to as Ebonics, most linguists prefer not to use this label. The term "Ebonics" tends to evoke strong emotional reactions and has unfortunately given license to racist parodies of various types in recent years, so most linguists prefer to use more neutral references like African American English, African American Vernacular English, or African American Language.

The study of AAE dwarfs the study of other social and regional varieties, with more than five times as many publications devoted to it than to any other American English dialect in the past several decades (Schneider 1996). Furthermore, AAE has drawn widespread media attention and public discussion on a number of occasions in the relatively brief history of social dialectology. In the late 1960s, the deficit-difference language controversy discussed in chapter 1 received extensive public discussion, while in the late 1970s a court case over the role of dialect in reading in Ann Arbor, Michigan, received national attention. In the 1990s, the so-called Oakland Ebonics controversy erupted when the Oakland Unified School District Board of Education passed a resolution affirming the legitimacy of AAE as a language system. This situation even resulted in a United States Senate subcommittee hearing on the status of Ebonics in American education. In the first decade of the twenty-first century, several high-profile court cases have featured "linguistic profiling," that is, discrimination based on ethnic voice identification. Speakers identified over the telephone as African American were told that advertised apartment vacancies were filled when they inquired about their availability, whereas their White-sounding counterparts were invited to view the vacant apartments. Such public discussions and disagreements certainly testify to the persistent sociopolitical and educational controversy associated with this variety.

Though linguists naturally affirm the fundamental linguistic integrity of AAE, it is essential to understand how the social valuation of language diversity mirrors the racial inequalities that have characterized American society since the involuntary transportation of Africans to the American continent. Attitudes toward AAE are symbolic of the evaluation of behavior perceived to be associated with African Americans. As Sally Johnson (2001: 599) notes, "It is not language *per se*, but its power to function as a 'proxy' for wider social issues which fans the flames of public disputes over language." AAE continues to be controversial because race and ethnicity in American society remain highly contentious and politically sensitive. No language variety in American society has ever been surrounded by more heated debate, and the controversy does not appear to be subsiding.

In discussing AAE, it is still necessary to start with a disclaimer about language and race. There is no foundation for maintaining that there is a physiological or genetic basis for the kinds of language differences shown by some Americans of African descent. Dialectologists point to cases in which African Americans raised in European American communities talk no differently than their European American peers; conversely, European Americans who learn their language from, and interact primarily with, AAE speakers will adopt AAE features. Yet myths about the physical basis of AAE persist, so that there is a continuing need to confront and debunk claims about language and race. In our ensuing discussion, it should be fully understood that labels such as African American English and European American English refer to socially constructed, ethnolinguistic entities rather than genetically determined language varieties.

There are several major issues related to AAE: (1) the relation of vernacular varieties of AAE to comparable European American vernacular varieties; (2) the origin and early development of AAE; and (3) the nature of language change currently taking place in AAE, including its development into a widely recognized symbol of cultural identity. To a greater or lesser extent, these are the same issues that apply to any sociolinguistic discussion of ethnolinguistic variation, but there are unique controversies associated with AAE because of its particular history and the social roles assigned to African Americans in American society. There are also definitional issues surrounding AAE. For example, are all people of African descent in the US considered to be speakers of AAE, or only those whose native language variety is a vernacular version of AAE that is considered to be different from standard English? Conversely, can people of other ethnicities be considered to be speakers of AAE if they regularly use many or all of the core features of this variety and are more closely integrated into African American culture than European American or other cultures? Such definitional issues defy easy resolution and involve sociocultural and political considerations every bit as much – indeed, more so – than linguistic ones. We will not discuss them in great detail in this chapter but will instead use the working definition of AAE initially set forth in chapter 1: the language variety spoken by many people of African descent in the US and associated with African American ethnic identity and cultural heritage.

7.1 The Status of European American and African American Vernaculars

In its simplest form, the question of Black–White speech relations can be reduced to a question of whether vernacular African American and European American varieties share the same set of linguistic structures. Are there unique features that distinguish vernacular varieties of AAE from comparable European American vernacular varieties in the same regional setting, and if so, what are they?

The matter of the linguistic distinctiveness of speakers of AAE is both simple and complex. Given a randomly selected set of audio recordings whose content contains no culturally identifying material, listeners can accurately identify African American speakers approximately 80 percent of the time. Determining the basis of this identification, however, is not nearly as straightforward as making the categorizations. Linguistically, different levels of language organization may be involved, ranging from minute segmental and suprasegmental phonetic details to generalized discourse strategies and conversational routines. Socially, factors such as listeners' social status, region, and level of education affect their perceptions of ethnic identity, as do interactional factors such as speakers' co-conversationalists and the speech setting. All of these factors enter into ethnic identification based on language, and manipulating the array of linguistic, social, and personal variables in identification experiments greatly affects the likelihood of accurate ethnic identification. Thus, the ethnicity of some African American speakers in certain contexts may be identified correctly less than 5 percent of the time while other speakers are correctly identified more than 95 percent of the time (Thomas and Reaser 2004).

Region and status, along with various other sociocultural attributes, are also important factors in considering structural similarities and differences in African American and European American vernacular varieties. Because AAE is historically rooted in a Southern-based, rural working-class variety, researchers often seek to answer questions of dialectal uniqueness by comparing vernacular AAE with rural Southern European American vernacular varieties. At the same time, the development of AAE into a recognized sociocultural variety in the twentieth century became strongly associated with its use in urban areas in the North.

All dialectologists agree that some features of vernacular AAE are distinct from surrounding European American varieties in Northern urban contexts, but the ethnic uniqueness of vernacular AAE in Southern contexts is more debatable. Though the issue of African American and European American speech relations is still not totally resolved after several decades of heated debate, some agreement is emerging. The following is a partial list of the phonological and grammatical features that are most likely to differentiate vernacular varieties of AAE from comparable European American vernacular varieties. More extensive lists of the dialect traits of AAE (Rickford 1999: 3–14; Green 2002) may include dozens of phonological and grammatical structures, though many of them are shared to some extent with non-African American vernacular varieties. In addition, most likely there are important features on other linguistic levels, including prosodic and pragmatic features, but these have not yet been studied to nearly the same extent as phonological and morphosyntactic ones.

Some distinguishing features of vernacular African American English
    habitual *be* for habitual or intermittent activity
        e.g.   *Sometimes my ears be itching.*
              She don't usually be there.
    absence of copula for contracted forms of *is* and *are*
        e.g.   *She nice.*
              They acting all strange.
    present tense, third-person -*s* absence
        e.g.   *she walk* for *she walks*
              she raise for *she raises*
    possessive -*s* absence
        e.g.   *man_ hat* for *man's hat*
              Jack_ car for *Jack's car*
    general plural -*s* absence
        e.g.   *a lot of time* for *a lot of times*
              some dog for *some dogs*
    remote time stressed *béen* to mark a state or action that began a long time ago and is still relevant
        e.g.   *You béen paid your dues a long time ago.*
              I béen known him a long time.
    simple past tense *had* + verb
        e.g.   *They had went outside and then they had messed up the yard.*
              Yesterday, she had fixed the bike and had rode it to school.

ain't for *didn't*

    e.g.   *He ain't go there yesterday.*
              He ain't do it.

reduction of final consonant clusters when followed by a word beginning with a vowel

    e.g.   *lif' up* for *lift up*
              bus' up for *bust up*

skr for *str* initial clusters

    e.g.   *skreet* for *street*
              skraight for *straight*

Use of [f] and [v] for final *th*

    e.g.   *toof* for *tooth*
              smoov for *smooth*

Even with this restricted list, there are important qualifications. In some cases, it is a particular aspect of the phonological or grammatical pattern rather than the general rule that is unique to AAE. For example, consonant cluster reduction is widespread in English, but in most varieties it applies mostly when the cluster is followed by a consonant (e.g. *bes' kind*) rather than when followed by a vowel. Similarly, we also find plural *-s* absence in some Southern European American varieties, but only on nouns indicating weights and measures (e.g. *four mile, five pound*). In other cases, the difference between the patterning of a feature in vernacular AAE and in a comparable European American vernacular variety involves a significant quantitative difference rather than a qualitative one. For example, the absence of the verb *be* for contracted forms of *are* (e.g. *you ugly* for *you're ugly*) is found among Southern European American vernacular speakers, but it is not nearly as frequent as it is in vernacular AAE.

Exercise 1

In the study of the absence of *be* verb forms (so-called COPULA DELETION) among speakers of vernacular varieties of European American and African American English in the South, the following conclusions were reached:

- Neither European American nor African American speakers delete the copula when the form is *am* (e.g. neither group of speakers uses forms like *I nice*).
- Both African Americans and European Americans delete the copula frequently when the form corresponds to *are* (e.g. *You ugly*), but African Americans have a higher frequency for *are* absence.

- Both European Americans and African Americans delete the copula form *is* when it is followed by the item *gonna* (e.g. *She gonna do it*).
- European Americans show almost no (less than 5 percent) absence of the copula form *is* with forms other than *gonna*, and African Americans show significant frequency levels of *is* absence (for example, 50 percent).

How do these kinds of results show the complexity of the descriptive detail necessary for the resolution of the question of the relationship between African American English and European American language varieties? How would you respond to a person who observed that "copula absence can't be unique to AAE because I hear European American speakers who say things like *They gonna do it right now?*"

Debate over the group-exclusiveness of some AAE structures has continued, and, in some cases, has re-emerged, despite careful study of the present status of AAE in relation to other varieties. For example, research by Guy Bailey and Marvin Bassett (1986) and Michael Montgomery and Margaret Mishoe (1999) shows that the use of uninflected or finite *be* to indicate HABITUAL or intermittent activity (so-called habitual *be*), as for example in constructions like *I be there every day* or *They usually be acting silly*, is found in both European American and African American varieties. At the same time, other investigators have suggested that there are additional forms that may qualify as unique. For example, William Labov (1998) suggests that among the constructions overlooked in earlier descriptions of AAE is a sequence of *be* and *done* together in sentences such as *If you love your enemy, they be done eat you alive in this society*. This construction is often called resultative *be done* in linguistic descriptions of AAE since it indicates that a potential action or condition will lead to some inevitable result. The conditional-resultative meaning, which is often associated with threats or warnings, may be a newer semantic-aspectual development in AAE.

There are also structures in AAE that appear on the surface to be very much like those in other dialects of English but turn out, upon closer inspection, to have uses or meanings that are unique. These types of structures are called CAMOUFLAGED FORMS because they bear surface resemblance to constructions found in other varieties of English even though they are used differently. One of these camouflaged constructions is the form *come* in a construction with an *-ing* verb, as in *She come acting like she was real mad*. This structure looks like the common English use of the motion verb *come* in structures like *She came running*, but research indicates that it actually has a special use as a kind of auxiliary verb indicating annoyance or indignation on the part of the speaker (Spears 1982). The specialized meaning of indignation is apparently unique to AAE.

Another case of camouflaging is found in sentences such as *They call themselves painting the room* or *Walt call(s) himself dancing*. The meaning of this form is quite similar to the standard English meaning of *call oneself* constructions with noun phrases or adjectives such as *He calls himself a cook* or *She calls herself nice* to indicate that someone is attributing qualities or skills to themselves which they do not really possess. Thus, a person who calls him/herself dancing is actually doing a very poor imitation of dancing. The shared counterfactual meaning of the standard English and the AAE constructions obscures the fact that the *call oneself* construction does not typically occur with verb + *-ing* in most dialects of English. European American speakers will, for example, use a sentence like *She calls herself a painter* but not typically *She calls herself painting*, whereas African American speakers are more likely to use both kinds of sentences.

Exercise 2

Studies of vernacular dialects of English have documented the use of *ain't* in a broad range of dialects. Typically, *ain't* is used for *have/ hasn't* as in *She ain't been there for a while* and forms of *isn't* and *aren't*, as in *She ain't home now*. AAE uses *ain't* for *didn't* as well, as in *She ain't do it yet*. The use of *ain't* for *didn't* is rarely included in discussions of the unique features of vernacular AAE. How does this usage compare with other kinds of differences cited above, such as the use of inflectional suffixes or habitual *be*? Would you consider it a "camouflaged form"?

Although the debate over particular structures in considering relations between African American and European American language varieties will no doubt continue, it is fair to conclude that there is a restricted subset of items that is unique to vernacular AAE. The inventory of dialect differences is, however, probably much more limited than originally set forth by some social dialectologists who studied AAE in Northern urban areas a few decades ago. But if significant quantitative differences are admitted to our list of qualitative differences, there may be considerable distinction between comparable European American and African American vernaculars, even in regions within the presumed birthplace of AAE in the rural South. In addition, as mentioned above, there are likely to be important differences on other levels of language organization, including prosodic and pragmatic differences, though these are still under-studied compared to the phonological and grammatical features of AAE.

While it is possible to compare structures used by European American and African American speakers on an item-by-item basis, the picture that emerges from this approach does not fully represent the true relationship between varieties. The uniqueness of AAE lies more in the particular combination of structures that makes up the dialect than it does in a restricted set of potentially unique structures. It is the co-occurrence of grammatical structures such as the absence of various suffixes (possessive, third-person singular, plural -*s*), absence of copula *be*, use of habitual *be*, and so forth, along with a set of phonological characteristics such as consonant cluster reduction, final [f] for *th* (e.g. *baf* for *bath*), postvocalic *r*-lessness, and so forth that best defines the variety rather than the subset of proposed unique features. To find that a structure previously thought to be unique to vernacular AAE is shared by a European American vernacular variety does not necessarily challenge the notion of the uniqueness of AAE as a dialect. Studies of listener perceptions of ethnic identity certainly support the contention that AAE is distinct from comparable European American vernaculars, but researchers are still investigating how to sort out the precise points of this differentiation. Recent experimental investigation by Erik Thomas and Jeffrey Reaser (2004) suggests that phonological rather than grammatical differences, including differences in vowel pronunciation and voice quality, may have as much to do with the perceptual determination of ethnicity as differences in grammatical structures.

Up to this point, we have discussed AAE as if it were a unitary variety in different regions of the United States. We must, however, admit regional variation in AAE, just as we have to admit regional variation within vernacular European American varieties. Certainly, some of the Northern metropolitan versions of AAE are distinguishable from some of the Southern rural versions, and South Atlantic coastal varieties are different from those found in the Gulf region. While admitting these regional variations, it is necessary at the same time to point out that one of the most noteworthy aspects of AAE is the common set of features shared across different regions. Features such as habitual *be*, copula absence, inflectional -*s* absence, among a number of other grammatical and phonological structures, are found in locations as distant as Los Angeles, California, Philadelphia, Pennsylvania, New Haven, Connecticut, Austin, Texas, and Meadville, Mississippi, cutting across both urban and rural settings. The foundation of a core set of AAE features, regardless of where it has been studied in the United States, attests to the strong ethnic association and supraregional dimension of this language variety. There is also a wide range of social class and stylistic variation in AAE; however, variation in this variety by social class has received little systematic study and awaits more detailed investigation.

7.2   The Origin and Early Development of AAE

Although the historical development of AAE has often been linked with the question of its present-day relationship to European American vernaculars, these two issues are not necessarily related. It is, for example, possible to maintain that earlier AAE developed from a radically different language variety but that linguistic accommodation to European American varieties or mixing among varieties has been so complete as to eliminate many of the differences that existed at a prior point in time. Sociolinguistic contact between Whites and Blacks over the generations may have resulted in speakers of both ethnicities picking up features from one another so that the two dialects became very similar. On the other hand, it is possible to maintain that earlier African American and European American varieties in the South were once identical, but that independent dialect innovation, patterns of segregation, and cultural factors related to ethnic identity led to significant dialect divergence. However, whether AAE and European American varieties had quite different histories or developed along very similar lines, it is possible that later developments may have led to the establishment of two similar or quite different varieties. Hence, the question of the historical origins of AAE is not intrinsically tied to a particular position on its current relationship to European American varieties.

There are several major hypotheses about the origin and early development of AAE: the ANGLICIST HYPOTHESIS, the CREOLIST HYPOTHESIS, and the NEO-ANGLICIST HYPOTHESIS. In this section, we review these hypotheses and offer yet another alternative that we will refer to as the SUBSTRATE HYPOTHESIS. The Anglicist hypothesis maintains that the roots of AAE can be traced to the same sources as earlier European American dialects, the dialects of English spoken in the British Isles. Briefly put, this position maintains that the language contact situation of African descendants in the United States was roughly comparable to that of other groups of immigrants. Under this historical scenario, slaves brought a number of different African languages with them when they were transported, but over the course of a couple of generations only a few minor traces of these ancestral languages remained. In effect, Africans simply learned the regional and social varieties of surrounding White speakers as they acquired English. Hans Kurath, a pioneer in American dialectology, noted:

> By and large the Southern Negro speaks the language of the white man of his locality or area and of his education. . . . As far as the speech of uneducated Negroes is concerned, it differs little from that of the illiterate white: that is, it exhibits the same regional and local variations as that of the simple white folk. (Kurath 1949: 6)

From this perspective, differences between AAE and European American varieties that could not be explained on the basis of regional and social factors resulted from the preservation in AAE of British dialect features lost from other varieties of American English. Some of the features mentioned previously, such as habitual *be* and third-person -*s* absence, have been explained on this basis. The pursuit of historical evidence from this perspective involves the scrutiny of earlier British English varieties for features similar to those found in AAE, along with a search for sociohistorical facts that might place the speakers of the potential donor dialects in a position to make their linguistic contributions to people of African descent in North America.

The Anglicist hypothesis, first set forth by prominent American dialectologists such as Hans Kurath (1949) and Raven McDavid (McDavid and McDavid 1951) in the mid-twentieth century, was the prevailing position on the origin of AAE until the mid-1960s and 1970s, when the creolist hypothesis emerged. According to this hypothesis, AAE developed from a CREOLE LANGUAGE developed during the early contact between Africans and Europeans. Those who support the creolist hypothesis maintain that the creole that gave rise to AAE was fairly widespread in the antebellum (pre-Civil War) South (Stewart 1967, 1968; Dillard 1972). They further observe that this creole was not unique to the mainland South but rather shows a number of similarities to well-known English-based creoles in the AFRICAN DIASPORA, or the dispersal of people from Sub-Saharan Africa to other parts of Africa, the Caribbean and North America. These creoles include Krio, spoken today in Sierra Leone and elsewhere on the west coast of Africa, as well as English-based creoles of the Caribbean such as the creoles of Barbados and Jamaica. Creolists further maintain that the vestiges of the creole that gave rise to AAE can still be found in Gullah, more popularly called "Geechee," the creole still spoken by some African Americans in the Sea Islands off the coast of South Carolina and Georgia. It is maintained that this creole was fairly widespread among people of African descent on Southern plantations but was not spoken to any extent by Whites. William Stewart (1968: 3) notes:

> Of the Negro slaves who constituted the field labor force on North American plantations up to the mid-nineteenth century, even many who were born in the New World spoke a variety of English which was in fact a true creole language – differing markedly in grammatical structure from those English dialects which were brought directly from Great Britain, as well as from New World modifications of these in the mouths of descendants of the original white colonists.

Although not all researchers on AAE accepted such a strong interpretation of the creolist hypothesis, many accepted some version of it during the 1970s and 1980s.

Contact with surrounding dialects eventually led this creole language to be modified so that it became more like other varieties of English in a process referred to as DECREOLIZATION. In this process, creole structures are lost or replaced by non-creole features. Decreolization, however, was gradual and not necessarily complete, so that the vestiges of its creole predecessor may still be present in modern AAE. For example, copula absence (e.g. *You ugly*) is a well-known trait of creole languages, so one might maintain that the present-day existence of copula absence in AAE is a vestige of its creole origin. Similar arguments have been made for various types of inflectional -*s* absence (e.g. *Mary go_*; *Mary_ hat*), as well as phonological characteristics such as consonant cluster reduction. However, we are not aware of any serious researchers on AAE who maintain that present-day AAE still qualifies as a genuine creole language.

Both linguistic structures and the social history of Blacks in the antebellum South have been cited in support for the creole origin of AAE. J. L. Dillard's book *Black English: Its History and Usage in the United States* (1972) was quite influential in promoting the creolist hypothesis, although creolists have now engaged in much more detailed and quantitative analysis in support of this hypothesis (Rickford 1999).

Although the creolist hypothesis was clearly the favored position among sociolinguists during the 1970s and 1980s, several new types of data emerged in the 1980s that called this position into question. One important type of data that came to light was a set of written records of ex-slaves. These include an extensive set of ex-slave narratives collected under the Works Project Administration (WPA) in the 1930s (Schneider 1989; Bailey, Maynor, and Cukor-Avila 1991); letters written by semi-literate ex-slaves in the mid-nineteenth century (Montgomery, Fuller, and DeMarse 1993; Montgomery and Fuller 1996); and other specialized collections, such as the Hyatt texts – an extensive set of interviews conducted with Black practitioners of voodoo in the 1930s (Hyatt 1970–8; Ewers 1996). All of these records seem to point toward the conclusion that earlier AAE was not nearly as distinct from postcolonial European American English varieties as would have been predicted under the creolist hypothesis. A limited set of audio recordings of ex-slaves conducted as a part of the WPA in the 1930s (Bailey, Maynor, and Cukor-Avila 1991) also seemed to support this contention.

A different type of data offered in opposition to the creolist hypothesis comes from the examination of Black expatriate varieties of English. For example, in the 1820s, a group of Blacks migrated from Philadelphia, Pennsylvania, to the peninsula of Samaná in the Dominican Republic, where their descendants continue to live in relative isolation and to maintain a relic variety of English (Poplack and Sankoff 1987; Poplack and Tagliamonte 1989). A significant population of African Americans also migrated from the United States to Canada in the early nineteenth century, and some of their descendants have preserved to this day a life of relative isolation in Nova Scotia. The examination of the English varieties spoken by Blacks in these areas by Shana Poplack and Sali Tagliamonte (Poplack 2000; Poplack and Tagliamonte 2001) indicates that these insular varieties were quite similar to earlier European American varieties rather than to a presumed creole predecessor, thus casting doubt on the creole hypothesis.

Finally, closer scrutiny of the sociohistorical situation and demographics of the antebellum South (Mufwene 1996, 2001) has indicated that the distribution of slaves in the Southeastern plantation region of the US was not particularly advantageous to the perpetuation of a widespread plantation creole, as had been postulated by earlier creolists. In fact, the vast majority of slaves lived on smaller farms with just a few slaves per household rather than in the large, sprawling plantations with large numbers of slaves that are sometimes pictured in popular portrayals of the antebellum South. Whereas expansive plantations with large numbers of slaves might be conducive to the development and spread of a plantation-based creole, over 80 percent of all slaves were associated with families that had less than four slaves per household.

The emergence of data from these newly uncovered situations seemed to indicate that earlier African American speech was much more similar to surrounding European American varieties than was assumed under the creolist hypothesis. This conclusion led to the development of the NEO-ANGLICIST HYPOTHESIS (Montgomery et al. 1993; Montgomery and Fuller 1996; Mufwene 1996; Poplack 2000; Poplack and Tagliamonte 2001). This position, like the Anglicist hypothesis of the mid-twentieth century, maintains that earlier postcolonial African American speech was directly linked to the early British dialects brought to North America. However, the neo-Anglicist position acknowledges that AAE has since diverged so that it is now quite distinct from contemporary European American vernacular speech. Poplack asserts that "AAVE [African American Vernacular English] originated as English, but as the African American community solidified, it innovated specific features" so that "contemporary AAVE is the result of evolution, by its own unique, internal logic." Labov (1998: 119) observes: "The general conclusion that is emerging from studies of the history of AAVE is that many important features of the modern dialect are creations of the twentieth century and not an inheritance of the nineteenth."

Despite growing support for the neo-Anglicist hypothesis, it has hardly become a consensus position. Disputes remain over the validity of the data and their interpretation, the exact nature of the language contact situation between Africans and Europeans in the colonies and the early US, and other, more general sociohistorical circumstances that framed the speech of earlier African Americans (Rickford 1997b, 1999; Winford 1997, 1998; Singler 1998a, 1998b). Research on long-term, historically isolated enclave communities of African Americans in such areas as coastal North Carolina (Wolfram and Thomas 2002) and Appalachia (Mallinson and Wolfram 2002; Childs and Mallinson 2004) suggests that earlier African American speech, at least in some regions, converged to a large extent with neighboring European American English varieties. In this respect, the data appear to support the traditional Anglicist and neo-Anglicist hypotheses. But there is also evidence for a durable ethnolinguistic divide that is not generally acknowledged under the Anglicist or neo-Anglicist positions, since some enduring differences between AAE and European American varieties have also been found in these enclave communities. Some of these persistent differences may be attributed to enduring influence from the early contact between African Americans and European Americans. For example, such features as inflectional -*s* absence (e.g. *She go*), copula absence (e.g. *He ugly*), and word-final consonant cluster reduction (e.g. *lif' up* for *lift up*) are common in language contact situations. These features distinguished earlier African American speech from that of its regional European American counterparts and persist to this day in vernacular AAE, despite similarities with respect to other dialect features. Though earlier African American speech may have incorporated local European American dialect features, there thus seems to have been lasting language influence from the earlier language contact situation between Europeans and Africans. Influence from another language or a language contact situation that endures beyond the original contact circumstance is sometimes referred to as a SUBSTRATE EFFECT. The persistence of consonant cluster reduction, inflectional -*s* absence, and copula absence centuries after the original contact situation between Africans and English speakers is probably best considered a substrate effect in AAE.

The SUBSTRATE HYPOTHESIS maintains that even though earlier AAE may have incorporated many features from regional varieties of English in America, its durable substrate effects have always distinguished it from other varieties of American English (Wolfram and Thomas 2002; Wolfram 2003). In this respect, the position differs from the neo-Anglicist position, which argues that earlier AAE was identical to earlier European American English. The substrate effect could have come from the original contact between speakers of African languages and English, whether or not this contact ever resulted in the development of a full-fledged creole language. While the sociohistorical evidence does not support the existence of a widespread plantation creole in the American South, this does not mean that contact with creole speakers during the passage of slaves from Africa to North America could not have influenced the development of earlier AAE. Indeed, extended periods of internment of African slaves along the coast of West Africa and in Caribbean islands such as Barbados before transfer to North America may have resulted in linguistic influence from creole languages – even though a creole most likely was never used extensively among African Americans in the American South. Creole varieties still flourish widely today throughout the Caribbean Islands and in countries such as Sierra Leone and Liberia on the west coast of Africa, and earlier versions of these creole varieties may well have extended some influence over the development of early African American speech in the American South.

Though recent research evidence suggests more regional influence from English speakers than assumed under the creolist hypothesis, and more durable effects from early language contact situations than assumed under the Anglicist positions, we must be careful about assuming that we have the final answer. Given the limitations of data, the different local circumstances under which African Americans lived, and the historical time-depth involved, there will probably always be speculation about the origin and earlier development of AAE. If nothing else, the significant shifts in positions over the past half-century caution against arriving at premature and unilateral conclusions about its origin and early evolution.

7.3   The Contemporary Development of AAE

In many respects, the contemporary development of AAE is as intriguing as its earlier development. Furthermore, questions about its present trajectory of change have now become as controversial as its earlier history. Though the roots of present-day AAE were no doubt established in the rural South, its development into an ethnically distinct variety is strongly associated with its use in Northern urban areas. In fact, descriptive studies of AAE in the 1960s, which helped launch the modern era of social dialectology, concentrated on metropolitan areas such as New York City, Detroit, Los Angeles, Washington, DC, and Philadelphia rather than the rural South where the seeds of this variety were sown.

There are several major factors affecting the recent and continuing development of AAE, including patterns of population movement and matters pertaining to cultural identity. The emergence of urban AAE was in part a by-product of the Great Migration in which African Americans moved from the rural South to large metropolitan areas of the North in the early and mid-twentieth century. However, demographic movement *per se* is not a sufficient explanation for the cultural shift in which urban areas became the contemporary centers of AAE language and culture. In 1910, almost 90 percent of all African Americans in the US lived in the South, and 75 percent of that number lived in communities of less than 2,500. Starting with World War I and continuing through World War II and beyond, there was a dramatic relocation of African Americans as they left the rural South for Northern cities. By 1970, some 47 percent of African Americans lived outside of the South, and 77 percent of those lived in urban areas. More than a third of all African Americans lived in just seven cities – New York, Chicago, Detroit, Philadelphia, Washington, DC, Los Angeles, and Baltimore (Bailey 2001: 66). Large numbers of these African Americans lived under conditions of racial separation, and this separation, coupled with racist ideologies and laws, led to the development of a social environment conducive to the maintenance of a distinct ethnolinguistic variety.

Population movement among African Americans has shifted somewhat in the last several decades, as the movement of Southern African Americans to Northern cities has slowed, and more African Americans move from the inner city to suburban areas, but this has not significantly affected inner-city segregation. The 2000 US Census indicates that approximately 60 percent of all African Americans now live in the non-South and that approximately six million African Americans live in the large metropolitan centers mentioned above. Some of these cities have become even more densely populated by African Americans than they were several decades ago. For example, the city of Detroit is now 83 percent African American (2000 US Census); in the mid-1960s, when the first author of this book conducted his research on the social stratification of AAE in Detroit (Wolfram 1969), it was only 37 percent African American. Furthermore, a half-century ago, the vast majority of middle-aged and elderly African Americans living in Northern urban areas were born in the South; today the majority of African Americans living in Northern cities were born there or in another metropolitan area. At the turn of the twenty-first century, the population demographics of non-Southern urban areas reveal the continued existence of well-established, highly concentrated urban African American populations.

During the latter half of the twentieth century, a couple of noteworthy sociolinguistic developments took place with respect to AAE. First, this variety took on an ethnic significance that transcends regional parameters. That is, there appears to be a SUPRA-REGIONAL NORM for AAE in that it shares a set of distinctive traits wherever it is spoken in the United States. Though AAE is still regionally situated to some extent, some prototypical dialect traits supersede many of the regional boundaries associated with European American dialects. There are several convergent factors that account for this uniformity. As noted previously, a set of common substrate structures from the earliest contact situations provided a linguistic foundation for the development of an enduring ethnolinguistic divide between AAE and local European American vernaculars. In addition, the legacy of slavery, Jim Crow laws, and segregation that most African Americans over the centuries have endured has served to preserve this unique linguistic heritage. At the same time, there is also evidence that speakers of AAE innovated and intensified some dialect structures over the course of the twentieth century.

Patterns of mobility and inter-regional, intra-ethnic social relations helped support the supra-regional base of AAE in the twentieth century. African Americans in isolated rural regions of the South, for example, tend to have more extensive contact with African Americans in urban areas than they did a century ago. In addition, in these rural regions older and younger residents often have different patterns of inter-regional mobility. Elderly residents rarely left the region during the course of their lives, whereas younger residents today travel outside of their local areas on a regular basis and often include visits to larger, more urban areas in their travels. Furthermore, African Americans who move from the rural South often stay connected to their roots through various homecoming events and family reunions that bring together those who live within and outside of the community. Patterns of inter-regional continuity and increased mobility certainly help transmit models for a supra-regional norm.

At the same time, the persistent *de facto* segregation of American society fosters a social environment conducive to maintaining a distinct ethnic variety. As noted, many Northern urban areas are, in fact, more densely populated by African Americans today than they were several decades ago, and the familial and social networks of many urban African Americans include few, if any, European Americans. The lack of regular interaction between African Americans and European Americans in large urban areas provides an ideal context for the growth of ethnolinguistic distinctiveness.

Perhaps more important than population demographics in the development of AAE as a distinctive variety is the fact that African Americans have long had a strong, coherent sense of cultural identity and, in recent decades, have cultivated overt pride in their ethnic identity and rich cultural heritage. In addition, African American culture and language have long had an enormous impact on American popular culture, and on youth culture in general, whether in America or elsewhere in the world. The center of African American youth culture today is primarily urban, and many models for behavior, including language, seem to radiate outward from these urban cultural centers. As Marcyliena Morgan (2001: 205) puts it: "cultural symbols and sounds, especially linguistic symbols, which signify membership, role, and status . . . circulate as commodities."

The growing sense of African American identity and the spread of African American youth culture are bolstered through a variety of informal and formal social mechanisms that range from community-based social networks to media projections of African American speech (Lippi-Green 1997). In addition, part of what it means to speak African American English is the use of features associated with AAE; however, the avoidance of features associated with regional and standard "White speech" is also important. For example, Signithia Fordham and John Ogbu (1986) note that the adoption of standard English is at the top of the inventory of prominent behaviors listed by African American high school students as "acting White." Hence, AAE identity not only concerns the relations, behaviors, practices, and attitudes of African Americans themselves but also so-called OPPOSITIONAL IDENTITY – in other words, how African Americans position themselves with respect to White society.

Studies of vernacular AAE in urban contexts in the last couple of decades seem to show that some structures are intensifying rather than receding and that new structures are developing. For example, the use of habitual *be* in sentences such as *Sometimes they be playing games* seems to be escalating, to the point of becoming a stereotype of AAE. While older speakers in rural areas rarely use this form, some younger speakers use it extensively, especially those in urban settings. Similarly, the narrative use of the auxiliary *had* with a past or perfect form of the verb to indicate a simple past tense action, as in *They had went outside and then they had messed up the yard*, seems to have arisen quite recently and to be on the increase as well. Earlier descriptions of AAE do not mention this feature at all, but more recent descriptions (Rickford and Théberge-Rafal 1996; Cukor-Avila 2001) note that this construction may be quite frequent in the narratives of some pre-adolescents. The fact that this feature is so frequent among pre-adolescents raises the possibility that it may be AGE-GRADED, meaning that young speakers will use the feature less as they become adults; however, this remains to be seen. Furthermore, some of the camouflaged uses such as indignant *come* in *He came here talking trash* seem to be later developments more associated with urban speech.

The change in language observed in a historically isolated community of African American residents in coastal North Carolina illustrates the movement of AAE toward a more supra-regional norm (Wolfram and Thomas 2002). For almost three centuries, a couple of thousand European Americans and African Americans in Hyde County, on the eastern coast of North Carolina, on the Pamlico Sound, lived in this remote marshland community, with regular overland access into the county possible only since the middle of the twentieth century. Elderly African Americans, who traveled little outside of the region, grew up using many of the distinctive features of the regional dialect associated with European Americans while maintaining a core set of AAE features. Over time, however, there has been a reversal in the balance of core AAE features and local regional features in the speech of Hyde County African Americans. Older speakers show moderate levels of core AAE features and extensive use of local dialect features, while younger speakers show a progressive increase in AAE features and a loss of local dialect structures, referred to here as Pamlico Sound features. The trajectory of change with respect to the Pamlico Sound features and core AAE features

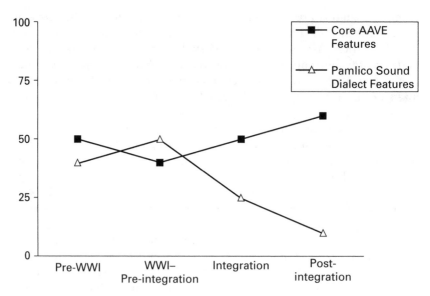

Figure 7.1   Trajectory of language change for African Americans in Hyde County (adapted from Wolfram and Thomas 2002: 200)

in the speech of African Americans of different generational groups in the area, based on our analysis of a number of representative features, is plotted in figure 7.1 (Wolfram and Thomas 2002: 200). Speakers are divided into generational groups based on four important sociohistorical periods: speakers who were born and raised in the early twentieth century up through World War I; speakers born and raised between World War I and school integration in the late 1960s; speakers who lived through the early period of school integration as adolescents; and speakers who were born and raised after legalized institutional integration.

On one level, the explanation of language change over time is based on the local social history of Hyde County, but on another level it appears to be indicative of a more general path of change for rural Southern African American English. The next-to-last group of speakers represents those born in the mid-1950s through the mid-1960s – the group most directly affected by the racial conflict brought about by court-ordered school integration in this county. As children and adolescents, they experienced the social upheaval of school integration first-hand. In this sociopolitical atmosphere, and in the integrated schools that followed, these African Americans actually increased the ethnolinguistic distinction between Whites and Blacks by reducing their alignment with the local dialect and intensifying language norms now associated with vernacular urban AAE. Through the reduction of local dialect features and the intensification of core AAE features, African Americans during the integration and post-integration eras diverged from, rather than converged with, their European American counterparts.

From one perspective, this path of change reveals the limited linguistic effects of institutionally mandated integration. From a different vantage point, however, it indicates the growing consciousness of the role of language in maintaining ethnic identity, even in the face of sociopolitical pressure and legal mandates to integrate. Traditional rural dialects like those spoken on the coast of North Carolina now carry strong associations of White, rural speech. In fact, younger African Americans describe the speech of older Hyde County African Americans as "sounding country" and being "more White" than the speech of younger African Americans. Younger speakers who identify strongly with African American culture vs. "White culture" would therefore be inclined to change their speech toward the more generalized version of AAE – and away from the localized dialect norm. An essential ingredient of the contemporary supra-regional norm for AAE is thus the heightened symbolic role of language as an ethnic emblem of African American culture. This cultural identity would enhance the role of a widespread supra-regional AAE norm *vis-à-vis* regional dialect norms with strong connotations of White speech behavior.

Research evidence shows that the majority of African Americans do not participate in major dialect changes taking place among European American speakers in many areas of the United States. For example, African Americans in Philadelphia are not involved to a significant extent in the evolution of the unique vowel system described for the European American community in this city (Graff, Labov, and Harris 1986). There is also little evidence that the Northern Cities Vowel Shift discussed in chapter 5 is spreading to speakers of AAE in significant numbers in the metropolitan areas affected by this shift. Even in the South, characteristic Southern vowel traits, such as the fronting of back vowels like the [u] of *boot* towards the [i] of *beet*, tend to be primarily found among European Americans, not African Americans. And, while both African Americans and Southern European Americans tend to pronounce /ai/ as [a], as in *tahd* for *tide*, European Americans are much more likely to use the [a] pronunciation before voiceless consonants, as in *raht* for *right* or *laht* for *light*.

We might even cite the role of the media in supporting the development of a supra-regional norm for AAE. Though linguists usually claim that the media play relatively little role in the spread of particular dialect traits because of their impersonal and usually non-interactive nature, media representations may still project a model for African American speech. In TV and the movies, the vernacular speech norm for African Americans tends to be urban and generic rather than rural and local, thus projecting the image of a unified AAE that young African Americans throughout the country can use in constructing their cultural identities as part of the larger community of African Americans.

Like any other variety, AAE is also changing. For example, more recent descriptions of finite *be* show that its meaning may be extending beyond the habitual reference we have noted previously. H. Samy Alim (2001), for example, notes that *be* is commonly used in hip-hop culture in sentences such as *I be the truth* or *Dr Dre be the name* in a way that seizes upon its iconic status as a marker of African American speech. Under earlier analyses, the use of finite *be* in sentences such as the above would have been considered ill-formed in AAE, since finite *be* has tended to be used in this variety to indicate habitual or recurrent activities rather than enduring states. However, such newer usages may signal a shift in the meaning of finite *be* such that it can now be used to indicate not only habituality but also very intense, even super-real, states. This most recent change appears to be taking place in more urban versions of AAE and spreading outward from that point. AAE is changing, as it acquires new forms, loses some older ones, and reconfigures still others.

7.4   Conclusion

AAE is obviously a distinct, robust, and stable socioethnic dialect of English. We have seen that a growing sense of linguistic solidarity and identity among African Americans unifies AAE in different locales. Although it may seem contradictory for the speech of African Americans to be blatantly rejected by mainstream institutions such as schools and professional work-places at the same time that it is supported and embraced by some groups within the community, it is important to remember that different levels of social valuation may exist concurrently for a language variety. As we noted in chapter 6, it is possible for a dialect to be overtly rejected by mainstream institutions while it is covertly valued by those who use it as symbolic of distinctive cultural identity.

At the same time, we have to recognize that not all local situations follow the path of change toward a supra-regional norm that we have outlined here. Comparisons of different local situations involving African Americans suggest considerable variation in patterns of change. In a comparison of four different small communities in locations ranging from the coast of North Carolina to the Appalachian Mountains, we found quite different paths of change. In addition to the pattern of divergence from the local European American dialect toward a supra-regional norm, we found some communities where African Americans and European Americans were converging in their speech. In one case involving a small community of African Americans in Appalachia, researchers found a curvilinear pattern of alignment with the local regional dialect. Middle-aged speakers who had spent time in the city of Atlanta used more AAE features than regional Appalachian speech, while older and younger speakers were quite closely aligned with the local variety associated with European Americans (Childs and Mallinson 2004; Mallinson and Childs in press). Such studies show that we need to be cautious about making unilateral conclusions with respect to change in AAE. Furthermore, these different situations underscore the significance of the social dynamics and the geographical location of local communities in understanding the past and present development of AAE. Original settlement history, community size, local and extra-local social networks, and ideologies surrounding race and ethnicity in American society must all be considered in understanding the changes African American speech has gone through in the past and present.

Finally, we must note that AAE is more than a simple assemblage of linguistic structures of the type that we have described here. Linguists and dialectologists have sometimes focused on structural features of grammar and phonology to the exclusion of other traits that might distinguish groups of speakers from one another. AAE may also encompass culturally significant uses of voice quality and other prosodic features, as well as culturally distinctive pragmatic features such as particular types of conversational routines, including greetings and leave-takings; backchanneling; and narrative styles. Some researchers have maintained that the soul of AAE does not, in fact, reside in the structural features of the language variety but in how AAE is used – that is, in its functional traits. Though great advances have been made in describing the speech of African Americans, fundamental issues of definition still linger, both within and outside of the African American community.

Exercise 3

Linguists have tended to define AAE in terms of the kinds of structural linguistics features we have discussed here. In this connection, consider Salikoko Mufwene's (2001: 353) observation:

> The distinguishing features associated with a referent do not necessarily justify the association nor the naming practice. . . . We should indeed ask ourselves whether we have been consistent practitioners when on the one hand, we argue in theory that it is up to native speakers to determine the affiliation of the language variety they speak and, on the other, we take it upon ourselves to determine who speaks English and who does not on criteria that are far from obvious.

How do you think AAE should be defined? To what extent should the voice of the community be heard in its definition? How important is it to arrive at a consensus definition of this variety?

7.5 Further Reading

Bailey, Guy, Natalie Maynor, and Patricia Cukor-Avila (eds.) (1991) *The Emergence of Black English: Text and Commentary*. Philadelphia/Amsterdam: John Benjamins. This collection of articles focuses on the analysis of the set of WPA recordings with ex-slaves made during the 1930s. The records are a unique and valuable collection, and each author comments on a different aspect of this rich data set. Transcripts of the recordings are also included.

Green, Lisa J. (2002) *African American English: A Linguistic Introduction*. New York: Cambridge University Press. Green offers a thorough overview of the grammar and phonology of AAE, as well as a discussion of the pragmatic and interactional features associated with AAE. Informative chapters on AAE in literary representation, AAE in the media, and the implications of AAE for education give this book broader appeal than most descriptions restricted to linguistic structures.

Lanehart, Sonja L. (ed.) (2001) *Sociocultural and Historical Contexts of African American English*. Philadelphia/Amsterdam: John Benjamins. This work is a collection of articles by experts on various aspects of AAE, ranging from issues of definition and description, to the application of linguistic knowledge to education, to issues of speech and language development and reading. Most of the prominent researchers in the field are represented in this collection. Excellent overviews of the past and present features of AAE in relation to Southern European American English are presented in the articles by Guy Bailey and Patricia Cukor-Avila, while Salikoko Mufwene offers insightful reflections on defining AAE.

Mufwene, Salikoko S., John R. Rickford, Guy Bailey, and John Baugh (eds.) (1998) *African American Vernacular English*. London: Routledge. This collection brings together a set of articles by leading researchers on the history and current state of AAE. The authors consider both historical and descriptive issues pertaining to AAE.

Poplack, Shana, and Sali Tagliamonte (2001) *African American English in the Diaspora*. Oxford: Blackwell. This is the most detailed and careful argument for the neo-Anglicist hypothesis currently available, based on a highly technical, quantitative presentation of variation in the tense and aspect system of black speakers in Nova Scotia and Samaná.

Rickford, John R. (1999) *African American Vernacular English: Features, Evolution, and Educational Implications*. Oxford: Blackwell. This book offers a comprehensive treatment of a wide range of AAE structural features, the historical development of AAE, and the implications of the study of AAE for education. The collection represents over two decades of informed research by one of the leading AAE researchers in the field. Rickford presents a modified creolist position on the origin and early development of AAE.

Rickford, John R., and Russell John Rickford (2001) *Spoken Soul*. New York: John Wiley and Sons. This book is a highly engaging account of AAE for readers with no background in linguistics. The authors consider the history and current status of AAE, as well as its use in literature and the media.

Wolfram, Walt, and Erik R. Thomas (2002) *The Development of African American English*. Oxford: Blackwell. This book provides a description of a unique, insular bi-racial community existing in coastal North Carolina for almost three centuries, with implications for the general development of earlier and contemporary AAE.

8

Gender and Language Variation

One of the most fascinating topics for people interested in language variation is how language varies according to gender. This is also one of the most controversial areas of study. Just as people come to the study of language with many deeply ingrained, often unexamined beliefs about how language operates, or language ideologies (see chapter 1), so too do we hold entrenched ideologies about gender, as well as gender and language. In most societies, it is accepted as a "given" that people can be divided into two basic gender groups, males and females, and that there are clear-cut, stable differences between these groups, many of which are grounded in the "natural" characteristics of the two different groups. This ideology strongly shapes our beliefs about language and gender, and it is very difficult to set aside our preconceived notions in examining how gender and language really operate. Many people, including professional researchers in the field, approach issues of language and gender with the assumption that male and female speech must be very different and that the patterns of difference that we find will be fairly universal, since they are grounded in essential differences between males and females. Further, we tend to interpret any male–female differences we do find in light of our assumptions about the nature of men vs. women. For example, because women in American society are often considered to be less direct and more polite than men, we tend to describe women's speech in these terms. However, in different societies (for example, the Malagasy of Madagascar) women are considered by nature to be *more* direct speakers (Keenan 1974).

As the study of language and gender has unfolded over the past several decades, researchers have increasingly come to realize that female–male language differences are by no means clear-cut and that we find many similarities in speech across gender groups, as well as much diversity within groups. In addition, we often find different patterns of male–female difference in different communities and even in different segments of the population within a single community. The complexity of gender-based patterns of language (and other behaviors) has led researchers to realize that we cannot take gender as a "given," roughly equivalent to biological sex. Instead, gender is a complex social construct that is not readily reducible to a dichotomy between two very different groups (e.g. Eckert 1989b). Further, gender intersects in often complex ways with other social factors such as class, ethnicity, and age. And just as ethnicity-based language differences must be explained in terms of social and cultural factors rather than biological "race," so too must we seek explanation for gender-based language differences in the sociocultural and sociopsychological underpinnings of gender rather than in physiological "sex" or the "natural" attributes of men vs. women. Indeed, as we saw for "race" in chapter 6, "biological sex" itself is socially constructed, since there are in reality a range of physical types that society insists on classifying into one of (usually) two sex groups (Bing and Bergvall 1996; Fausto-Sterling 2000).

There are only a handful of gender-based language differences that have any basis in biology, and even these are altered, often exaggerated, based on people's sociocultural understandings of gender. For example, on average, males talk with a lower pitch than females. This difference is due partly to anatomical differences in the larynx (voicebox) of men vs. women, as well as men's average larger size – but only partly. Research has shown that the male–female pitch difference is typically much greater than simple physiology dictates. In addition, the degree of pitch difference between females and males is different in different cultures (with a greater difference, for example, among women and men in some Asian societies compared with many Western ones). Further, the physical differences affecting pitch in male vs. female speech do not develop until adolescence, yet researchers have shown that little boys and girls begin showing pitch differentiation long before there is any physical reason for them to do so. These illustrations demonstrate that gender-based language differences have much more to do with our societal conceptions of gender than with biological or other inherent differences.

As researchers on language and gender place more emphasis on social constructions of gender, they are coming to realize that there may be more productive and revealing ways to begin our investigations than with the presumption of a fairly clear-cut, dichotomous gender division. Instead of beginning our research with the question "How do men and women talk differently?" or "What gender differences will I find?", we should probably ask more complex questions such as "What sorts of language features do people use to present themselves as women vs. men, or as particular kinds of women or men?", "What if any difference does gender make in this particular situation?", or even "Why does gender make such a difference?" (e.g. Eckert and McConnell-Ginet 2003: 5; McElhinny 2003: 24).

In addition, because gender-based linguistic (and other) practices can vary so much from community to community and from situation to situation, researchers are coming to realize that gender is probably best seen not as an attribute, or something one "has," but perhaps more of a practice, or something one "does," or enacts in daily interaction. People's gendered use of language, and even their very gender identity itself, can change (perhaps subtly) from situation to situation, or at different times in a person's life span. Of course, this is not to say that people are free to do anything they want with gendered language or gender identity in any given interaction. Established gender orders and gender ideologies are strong and act as powerful constraining forces on people's freedom of action. Hence, in studying language and gender, it seems necessary that we have something of a dual focus. On the one hand, we need to take a "close-up" view – to look at particular interactions among members of particular social networks and communities of practice, so that we can gain an understanding of how people use linguistic features to shape gender identity. On the other hand, we need to step back and look at the "big picture" – to look at large-scale patterns of variation across broadly defined social groups such as "women" and "men," or perhaps somewhat more refined groupings such as "heterosexual men" and "gay men," or maybe "women who see themselves as feminine" (however we choose to define such a group) vs. women who see themselves as less so.

In what follows, we look at language and gender study from a couple of different research perspectives, one that grows out of the study of regional and social dialects (as discussed, for example, in chapters 5 and 6), with its "big picture" focus on the quantitative patterning of phonological and morphosyntactic features, and one which focuses on gender differences in patterns of language use, typically from a more "close-up" focus on individual conversational interactions. Our discussion will show that research has progressed from early work in which sex or gender was seen as a clear-cut dichotomous feature, often as a biological "given," through work with a more explicit focus on gender as a social construct which operates differently in different communities, to current work in which gender is seen as practice or performance. In addition, we shall see an increasing focus on combining quantitative and qualitative approaches. In particular, research on language and gender that focuses on the community of practice (see chapter 2) is especially promising in this regard, since it is through the mediating influence of one's various (rather small-scale) communities of practice that individuals relate to large-scale societal structures such as class and gender (e.g. Eckert and McConnell-Ginet 1992; Holmes 1999; Eckert 2000). Following our discussion of *how* members of different gender groups talk, we will look at how members of these groups are talked *about*, as well as efforts to change what are often viewed as sexist language practices. For example, we will consider such matters as the use of GENERIC *HE* (as in *Each student should bring his book*) and the replacement of the *Miss/Mrs* title with *Ms*.

8.1   Gender-based Patterns of Variation as Reported in Dialect Surveys

In early quantitative studies of the regional and social patterning of variation in language, gender was seen as a simple, unchanging attribute, equivalent to biological sex. In addition, it was held to be secondary to social class in its effects on language variation. Further, it was believed that gender-based patterns of variation would be universal, grounded as they were in the "natural" attributes of men and women. Indeed, dialect surveys have revealed some fairly widespread patterns of male–female language difference. These are articulated in William Labov's (1990) three principles regarding gender and language variation:

> Principle I: For stable sociolinguistic variables, men use a higher frequency of nonstandard forms than women.
>
> Principle Ia: In change from above [the level of consciousness], women favor the incoming prestige forms more than men.
>
> Principle II: In change from below, women are most often the innovators.

There are many examples that illustrate Principle I. In one of the earliest studies of sex-based language variation, John Fischer (1958) showed that, among the group of New England children he studied, girls tended to use more word-final *-ing* (as in *swimming*) than boys, who used more of the nonstandard *-in'* variant (as in *swimmin'*). Peter Trudgill (1974) showed similar patterning for *-in'* and *-ing* across sex groups in Norwich, England, as did Barbara Horvath (1985) in her investigation of the cross-sex patterning of *-in'* and *-ing* in Sydney, Australia. Other variables have been shown to pattern in the same way. For example, the first author of this book demonstrated greater use of standard variants by African American women than men for four phonological and four syntactic variables in inner-city Detroit (Wolfram 1969). For example, women used more *th* [θ] than men in items such as *with*, which men tended to produce as *wit* [wɪt] or *wif* [wɪf]. In addition, women produced more postvocalic *r*'s than men as well as less multiple negation (e.g. *I didn't tell you nothing*) and less copula deletion (e.g. *She gonna go now* vs. *She's gonna go now*).

Whereas Principle I deals with women's tendency to use more standard or conservative forms than men, Principles Ia and II indicate that women are also more innovative than men, being the first to adopt incoming prestige forms from outside their local communities as well as linguistic innovations arising from within their own communities. An example of Principle Ia is women's greater use of incoming *r*-ful pronunciations in New York City, as revealed in Labov's classic study of the Lower East Side in the 1960s

(Labov 1966). Illustrations of Principle II date back to even the earliest dialect surveys. For example, Louis Gauchat (1905) showed women adopting new language variants much earlier than men. Subsequent research has confirmed this pattern time and time again (e.g. Labov 1966, 1984; Cedergren 1973) in Western society, and this finding is still being replicated today (e.g. Eckert 2000), though often with important caveats (see below).

While seeming at first glance to provide a neat encapsulation of female–male speech differences, Labov's three principles and the data underlying them bear further investigation. First, it is apparent that the principles embody a contradiction, since they hold that women are at the same time more linguistically conservative and more innovative than men. In addition, even the earliest surveys contain findings that cannot be neatly captured in these principles. For example, studies dating back to Labov (1966) have also shown that female–male differences can be quite different in different speech styles, with women sometimes showing higher usage levels than men for prestige forms in more formal styles but lower levels than men in more casual styles. In addition, Labov (1966) and Wolfram (1969) found different patterns of female–male language difference in different social class groups, with the differences between the sexes being greater in the middle groups than the lowest and highest social classes. Similarly, Ralph Fasold (1968) showed that while Detroit females led males in all social classes in adopting certain vowel innovations, women of a particular social class – namely, the upper working class/lower middle class – were always in advance of both women and men in all other social classes, including both lower and higher classes. Figure 8.1 illustrates this patterning for two innovative vowel pronunciations associated with the Northern Cities Vowel Shift (see chapter 5): the pronunciation of the /æ/ vowel in words like *bat* as more of an *eh* (as in *bet*), and the pronunciation of the /ɔ/ vowel in words like *lock* as more of an [æ] (as in *cat*), so that *lock* sounds like *lack*.

A further difficulty in seeking universal patterns of male–female language difference is that relations may be different at different time periods. For example, in our studies of Ocracoke English on the Outer Banks of North Carolina, we found that the gender-based patterning of at least one vernacular dialect feature, the well-known pronunciation of the /ai/ vowel as more of an *oy* [ɔɪ] (as in "hoi toid" for "high tide"), has changed drastically over time (Schilling-Estes 1999). Among the older speakers we studied, we found nearly identical usage levels by women and men for the "hoi toid" variant. We found more female–male differentiation in middle-aged speakers and even more differentiation among the youngest speakers. Even among speakers in a single age group, we found several different cross-gender patterns of language use. For example, among speakers in the middle-aged group, we found that women used more of the vernacular "hoi toid" pronunciation than some groups of middle-aged speakers. However, there was one group

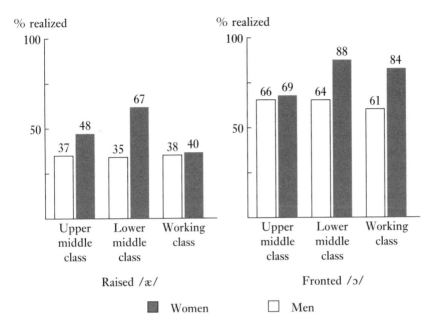

Figure 8.1 /æ/ raising and /ɔ/ fronting in Detroit, by social class and sex (adapted from Fasold 1968)

of men who used more *oy* than older speakers – even though the traditional "hoi toid" variant is, in general, receding in the Ocracoke community. These men are members of the Poker Game Network, a group who project a highly (traditionally) masculine image and who pride themselves on speaking the authentic Ocracoke dialect, or "brogue," as it is often called. Figure 8.2 illustrates the cross-generational and cross-sex patterning of the "hoi toid" vowel in the Ocracoke community.

A similar case of changing gender-based patterns of variation over time is that of the Cajun community studied by Sylvie Dubois and Barbara Horvath (1999), discussed in detail in chapter 6. In this case, older speakers show very little gender differentiation for certain features of Cajun English and middle-aged speakers show some differentiation, but only in the youngest generation do we see the supposedly "universal" pattern in which men use vernacular features at a greater rate than women. Furthermore, the differentiation is strongest for certain network types, since young women in closed networks show higher usage levels for the Cajun features than those in open networks, thus coming closer to young men's higher usage levels for these features.

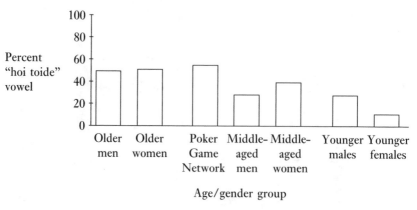

Figure 8.2 The cross-generational and cross-sex patterning of Ocracoke /ai/

Finally, as sociolinguistic research has expanded to include a range of communities beyond those in the United States, as well as to include more investigations focusing on speakers' localized social networks (see chapter 2) rather than larger-scale class divisions, researchers have uncovered a range of different patterns of gender-based variation. They have also uncovered more cases of linguistic differentiation within gender groups as well as between them. For example, sociolinguistic surveys of communities as diverse as Tokyo, Japan (Hibiya 1988), and Puerto Rico (Lopez-Morales 1981) revealed no significant differences between men and women for the language features studied, while network-based studies of communities ranging from the Gullah-speaking community in the Sea Islands area of South Carolina (Nichols 1983) and Belfast, Northern Ireland (Milroy 1987), showed some women using certain vernacular variants at a greater percentage rate than men in their communities. In addition, studies of Arabic-speaking communities in the Middle East have shown men leading women in the use of prestige forms (e.g. Modaressi 1978; Abd-el-Jawad 1987). And Christine Mallinson and Becky Childs (in press) show that there is considerable variation in the use of vernacular forms in women's speech in a small Appalachian African American community based on the two different communities of practice in which the women participate. One group, the "porch sitters," shows high usage levels for features associated with vernacular African American English, while the "church ladies" use higher levels of features associated with neighboring European American varieties, as well as standard American English. So there are lots of different parameters that have to be considered in terms of describing patterns relating to gender and some important qualifications that need to be made with respect to the principles set forth by Labov in terms of language and gender.

8.2   Explaining General Patterns

Along with the search for general patterns of male–female language differ-ence that characterized early studies of regional and social dialects came a search for general explanations. Traditionally, researchers sought explana-tion for women's rather than men's speech patterns, since men's speech was, until only a couple of decades ago, taken to be the "norm" against which other types of speech should be compared. One of the most influential explanations for the general tendencies noted above is the notion that women are more prestige-conscious than men (e.g. Labov 1966; Trudgill 1972), whether by "nature" or due to social circumstances traditionally associated with women's roles and relative status and power in many societies. For example, Trudgill (1972, 1983) proposes several reasons for women's greater concern with prestige. One is the traditional involvement of women in the transmission of culture through childrearing, a process which might heighten the awareness of prestige norms through a desire to pass these norms along to children. Another reason Trudgill offers is the social position of women in most societies, which historically has been less secure than that of men. Given a more insecure social position, women may place more emphasis on signaling social status linguistically. A final reason cited by Trudgill is the different occupational roles of men and women. Men traditionally have been rated by their occupation – by *what they do*. Women, on the other hand, have often been rated to a greater extent by *how they appear*. For example, women are much more frequently complimented on their appearance than are men, in keeping with a value on "looking good." The linguistic "cosmetic" of prestigious language may thus be more important for women than it is for men.

The tendency of males to use more stigmatized features in their speech than females may also be seen in terms of the symbolic value of such features in defining oneself as either masculine or feminine. For example, nonstandard forms may symbolize masculinity and toughness and so may be positively valued by men; at the same time they may be considered inappropriate for use by women, who cannot project toughness if they are to project some measure of feminine identity, at least in a traditional sense.

Labov's and Trudgill's notion that women's linguistic behavior can be explained in terms of their focus on social prestige seems to account for Principles I and Ia, women's greater use of stable standard forms and incoming prestige forms. However, it is a bit more difficult to reconcile with Principle II, women's tendency to adopt innovations that do not carry overt prestige (or stigma) at a greater rate than men. Labov (1984) suggested that innovative variants may carry local prestige (and be too new to have yet acquired stigma) and so be adopted more quickly by women. Later, he also suggested that women's role in childrearing would naturally lead to the prevalence of female-led innovations over those led by males (Labov 1990: 219–20). However, neither explanation seems entirely satisfactory and, indeed, Trudgill (1972) has proposed that it is men rather than women who are more concerned with local prestige (or covert prestige; see chapter 6), suggesting that we need an alternate explanation for Principle II.

Further, as Trudgill (1972) and others have noted, the notion of "prestige" defies easy definition. First, as just mentioned, there may be different types of prestige in a single community, and different segments of the population may orient more toward covert prestige (i.e. the prestige associated with localized values and relationships) than the overt prestige associated with widespread standard language varieties. Secondly, Labov's principles tend to conflate notions of "standard" and "prestige" in a way that may not be appropriate for all communities or cultural groups. We have noted in previous chapters that in the US, standard varieties in widespread usage are at least socially respected, if not necessarily considered especially prestigious. However, in some other societies, standard varieties, or norms in widespread usage, may not necessarily be accorded much respect or prestige. For example, researchers investigating variation in the Arabic-speaking world have pointed out that the prestige variety, Classical Arabic, is quite different from the various "standards" in widespread usage in the Middle East (e.g. Abd-el-Jawad 1987; Haeri 1997). In addition, Lesley Milroy and Matthew Gordon (2003: 100–3) note that even in some Western contexts, including Great Britain, there may exist widespread or supra-local standards that are quite different from the prestige variety of a particular society (Received Pronunciation, in the case of Great Britain). Milroy and Gordon note further that, in many cases, it seems that women lead men in the use of supra-local forms rather than prestigious forms *per se*, and that this generalization may better capture the relation between women, men, and language standards than a generalization based on a simple equation of standard and prestige forms.

Finally, we should be wary of accepting a single general explanation for gender-based patterns of variation, whether based on prestige or any other characteristic, since, as we have seen, gender-based patterns of variation do not turn out to be as general as they at first seem. Further, the fact that gender operates quite differently in different communities indicates that we cannot simply apply explanations based on women's and men's "characteristics." Rather, we must treat gender as the complex social and sociopsychological construct it really is, and must seek explanation in locally relevant gender roles and gender relations, as well as local and individual conceptions of gender identity and gender-appropriate behavior.

8.3   Localized Expressions of Gender Relations

One of the earliest in-depth investigations of the gender-based patterning of language variation in a localized context is Patricia Nichols's study of two traditionally Gullah-speaking communities in coastal South Carolina (Nichols 1976, 1983). One of these groups lived off the coast, in the Sea Islands, while the other lived on the mainland. Nichols focused her study on the use of creole features vs. incoming standard English forms and looked at three features in particular:

1   the use of *to* versus *for* (phonetically [fə]) in infinitive constructions
     e.g.   I come *for* get my coat.
             I come *to* get my coat.
2   third-person singular pronoun *ee* (phonetically [i])
     e.g.   And *ee* was foggy, and they couldn't see.
             And *it* was foggy, and they couldn't see.
3   static locative preposition *to* versus *at*
     e.g.   Can we stay *to* the table?
             Can we stay *at* the table?

While the younger groups of speakers on both the island and the mainland showed women to be ahead of men in their use of standard forms such as infinitive *to* vs. *for* or pronominal *it* vs. *ee*, Nichols found that older women on the mainland actually used more creole features than their male counterparts. That is, the older women on the mainland were more likely to use forms like *for* for *to* or *ee* for *it* than the older males. Nichols attributed these differences to the different occupational and educational experiences of members of each gender group in each different community, particularly the different amounts of exposure to, and need for, the standard language variety that these different experiences entailed. In the mainland group, the older women had less schooling than men, traveled less widely, and were more confined to the immediate community. Hence, they used a higher percentage of localized creole forms than mainland men. For the island group, older men and women had similar educational and occupational experiences and so spoke quite similarly. In contrast, employment patterns were very different for younger men and women, since younger women now had available to them employment opportunities outside the local context, most of which required use of standard English. Young island men, on the other hand, continued to work in the local context, at jobs in which standard English was not needed. Hence, young men retained a higher level of vernacular creole forms while young women adopted more standard features.

Another very important study of the localized workings of language and gender is Penelope Eckert's investigation of the interrelation of linguistic and social patterns in a Detroit-area high school (e.g. Eckert 1989a, 2000). Eckert used both survey and ethnographic (participant-observation) techniques. In this way, she was able to obtain a great deal of linguistic data from different segments of the school population, as well as to investigate localized social and linguistic practices and their meanings in great depth. In addition, Eckert supplemented her in-depth analysis of one particular high school with sociolinguistic surveys of nearby high schools, as well as with information on broadly based speech patterns uncovered by numerous researchers investigating the Northern Cities Vowel Shift (see chapter 5), as well as other features of the Inland North. Like Nichols, Eckert found that gender-based patterns of variation were different for different groups and that these differences could only be accounted for by appealing to localized explanations. In Eckert's case, the relevant groups were the "jocks" and the "burnouts." The jocks were those who oriented toward school and school-related activities, planned to go on to college and to leave the Detroit area. The burnouts were those who oriented toward local urban institutions and activities rather than school and who planned to remain in the Detroit area. While there were certain overall female–male based patterns of language difference across the two social groups, there were also important differences in gender-based patterns within each group, again indicating that gender-based variation defies a single explanation. For example, girls overall tended to show higher usage levels for older changes associated with the Northern Cities Vowel Shift, such as the pronunciation of the /ɔ/ vowel in words like *lock* as something like [æ], so that *lock* sounds almost like *lack*. However, the gender-based patterning of the newer changes (e.g. the pronunciation of a word like *but* as almost like *bought*) was more complex, with burnout girls typically showing higher usage levels for these innovations than burnout boys but jock girls showing lower levels than jock boys.

In seeking explanation for these patterns, Eckert appealed in part to localized patterns of contact and to the symbolic meanings of dialect features. For example, burnout girls and boys had more contact with people from urban Detroit, where the newest language changes were concentrated. Jocks, especially jock girls, had more limited contacts and a more suburban orientation and so were less quick to adopt the language features most associated with urban speech. In addition, jock girls were expected to behave more "properly" and so to avoid forms associated with urban youth speech and its connotations of "toughness" or "coolness."

Eckert also appealed to power relations between the sexes in seeking explanation for her findings, as well as other cases where women seem to show a greater range of linguistic variation than men. She suggests that women make greater use of linguistic resources than men since they must rely on symbolic expressions of worth and symbolic means of attaining power, or SYMBOLIC CAPITAL, since they traditionally have been denied real worth or real capital in most societies (and still are, to a large extent). Hence, the girls in her study use linguistic resources to indicate (and shape) group divisions to a greater extent than do the boys, who can signal group membership more directly through action and who have more access to activities accorded the highest prestige, whether the overt prestige associated with men's varsity sports, or the covert prestige associated with "cruising" and otherwise hanging out in tough urban neighborhoods. Further, Eckert suggests that the girls make greater use overall of some of the older features of the Northern Cities Vowel Shift because these features seem to have taken on a generalized meaning of "expressiveness." And whereas girls rely on linguistic and other forms of expressiveness for their worth, boys, again, can find worth through their actions. Further, "expressiveness" as a social attribute may be less appropriate for boys, who must maintain more of a "cool" or "detached" demeanor.

The fact that girls and women in many communities, including suburban Detroit, coastal South Carolina, and the Lower East Side of New York City, show a wider range variation than boys and men helps explains the apparent contradiction embodied in Labov's principles for the patterning of gender-based language differences: If we group all females together as a single group, then they will be seen to be both more standard and more innovative than men, since women in some social groups and some speech situations (e.g. the island women in Nichols's study, women in careful speech styles) use more standard forms than men, while women in other groups and in other situations (e.g. the mainland women, women in more casual styles) use more vernacular forms. And, as discussed above, we can attribute women's greater use of linguistic variation to a number of factors, including wider contacts, a greater need to signal worth through symbolic means, and, perhaps, greater societal license to display expressiveness (Eckert 2000: 222–6; Eckert and McConnell-Ginet 2003: 266–304).

8.4 Communities of Practice: Linking the Local and the Global

In addition to emphasizing the importance of locally relevant social groups and linguistic meanings, Eckert's study also stresses that it is crucial to look beyond group membership to the practices in which various groups engage. It is only through looking at localized practice that we begin to understand not only what sorts of language patterns correlate with which groups but *why* people use the language features they do. For example, the jocks in

Eckert's study participate heavily in school-related activities associated with middle-class norms and eventual advancement into college and the corporate world. On the other hand, the burnouts engage in activities in the local neighborhood, maintaining and forming the social networks that will form the center of their adult lives as well. Thus, it is no accident that burnouts typically use more features associated with urban speech than jocks, who tend to use features associated with a more suburban lifestyle. In addition, in focusing on people's communities of practice, we begin to understand how individuals' linguistic and other social practices intersect with large-scale patterns and overarching societal institutions such as gender, social class, and ethnicity – in other words, how individuals' everyday linguistic practices reflect, shape, challenge, and perhaps even subvert dominant social orders. As Eckert notes, the individual is not connected independently to their immediate social world (e.g. the world of the high school) or to any of the wider communities to which they can be said to belong (e.g. suburban Detroit, community of women, middle class, etc.) but "negotiates that relation jointly within their communities of practice" (2000: 172).

A number of studies of language and gender in localized communities of practice focus on communities whose participants use linguistic and other resources in the creation and display of gendered identities that do not fit neatly into the dominant gender order in which it is expected that everyone will be either a heterosexual male or heterosexual female. For example, Mary Bucholtz (1996, 1999) shows how a group of "nerd" or "uncool" girls in a California high school use language features as well as other stylistic resources (e.g. clothing styles) to present themselves as "nerds," in conscious opposition to the two different groups of "cool" girls in the school – those who embrace African American youth culture and those who oppose it. For example, the nerd girls consciously avoid using slang terms associated with either of the two cool groups and in addition show lower usage levels for certain vowel changes associated with one of the cool groups. Along with "uncoolness," they also consciously project qualities that are at odds with those expected of women under the dominant gender order: They refuse to wear either the "sexy" or "cute" clothing styles associated with each of the two cool groups of girls and in addition project an image of intelligence through using precise pronunciations and "learned" lexical items.

Other studies demonstrate how men project various types of masculinities, some in accord with the dominant gender order and some in opposition to it. For example, Scott Kiesling (1996, 1998) shows how a group of fraternity men use a single linguistic feature (the pronunciation of word-final *-ing*, as in *swimming*) to project different types of masculine images during fraternity meetings, all associated with power of one sort or another. For example, some men use high levels of *-in'* to project the physical power and hardworkingness of the working-class male, while others use high levels of -*ing* to highlight their structural power, or high position within the fraternity organization. Conversely, Robert Podesva, Sarah Roberts, and Kathryn Campbell-Kibler (2002) show how a male lawyer uses linguistic resources to project a less traditional type of masculine identity, one associated not only with the authoritativeness often traditionally ascribed to men, but also with a gay identity.

Although studies based on communities of practice often involve in-depth analysis of small groups and small samples of language (including, for example, individual stretches of conversation), they nonetheless rely on language patterns revealed in large-scale studies. Although people may mix and match various linguistic features to project individualized or situationally specific meanings and identities, they cannot do so randomly, since linguistic features often derive their social meanings from association with particular groups, or particular situations of use. Hence, for example, the nerd girls in Bucholtz's study draw upon widely known features of standard English in constructing themselves as intelligent, while the pronunciation feature highlighted in Kiesling's study, the alternation between standard -*ing* and vernacular -*in'*, is widely used throughout the English-speaking world to convey formality vs. casualness and standardness vs. vernacularity.

Conversely, researchers conducting broad surveys of particular groups or regions can supplement their survey data with other sources that provide in-depth understanding of local cultural meanings and practices. Thus, for example, though Dubois and Horvath's (1999) primary method was a sociolinguistic survey, they obtained more in-depth sociocultural information about Louisiana Cajuns from several sources, including a sociological survey conducted by Dubois and several other researchers prior to the sociolinguistic survey, numerous previous investigations of Cajun culture by social scientists, observations of the community during the survey process, and the inclusion in the sociolinguistic interview of questions through which they could learn each speaker's individual life history. Hence, in investigating language and gender, it may be best to utilize a combination of quantitative and qualitative methods in order to arrive at an understanding of how people's individual and small group-based gendered practices interact with established gender orders.

Because gender is performed in local settings, in particular interactions, many researchers on language and gender have focused on matters of language use or pragmatics (see chapter 3) rather than the gender-based patterning of phonological and morphosyntactic features. We turn now to an overview of approaches to language and gender that focus on language use. These approaches are often divided into three categories, based on their focus on social and linguistic *deficit*, *difference*, or *dominance* (e.g. Cameron 1996). However, researchers increasingly have been unhappy with these divisions (Eckert and McConnell-Ginet 2003: 1–5; Freed 2003: 701–2). As we shall see, there is necessarily quite a bit of overlap among the three views. In addition, like many studies of language and gender from the dialect survey perspective, all three language-use-based approaches have tended to focus on women and to see only women's language use as "gendered" (rather than "neutral" or "unmarked") and in need of explanation. Further, again like many survey-based studies of language and gender, all three views take as their starting point a binary opposition between males and females, an opposition that is based more on unquestioned ideology than on linguistic and social reality.

8.5   Language-use-based Approaches: The "Female Deficit" Approach

The DEFICIT APPROACH to language and gender studies can be traced at least as far back as the early 1920s, when the renowned linguist Otto Jespersen devoted a chapter of his influential book *Language: Its Nature, Development, and Origin* (1922) to "The Woman." In this chapter, Jespersen claimed that women in a number of cultures throughout the world exhibit speech patterns which differ from those of men and that these differences derive from differences in biological make-up. Among the features of "women's speech" that Jespersen noted were that women have less extensive vocabularies than men, use simpler sentence constructions, and speak with little prior thought. In other words, women's speech was held to be deficient when compared with the male "norm." Some early feminists reacted against the notion that men's language was "normal" language and that women's language was inferior and was to be considered a natural by-product of biological sex. However, Jespersen's ideas remained unchallenged within the field of linguistics for nearly half a century, even though his claims are clearly grounded in the prevailing gender ideologies of his day, and most of the evidence for his claims comes from his examination of portrayals of women in art and literature (which often reflect prevailing ideologies as well) rather than from observations of real-world behavior.

The modern study of language and gender began with the publication of Robin Lakoff's groundbreaking article, "Language and woman's place" (1973; expanded into book form in 1975). Although highly influential, Lakoff's work has been subjected to criticism on a number of grounds. Like Jespersen, Lakoff viewed women's speech as weak in comparison with men's. In addition, she relied on literary texts, casual observation, and reflections on her own linguistic usages rather than large bodies of empirical evidence in forming her generalizations. However, unlike Jespersen, Lakoff was sympathetic to women and maintained that women's deficient speech patterns were not the result of inherent biological or mental deficiency but rather of differential experience. In addition, she hinted that men's greater power in society may be a factor in perpetuating women's weaker use of language. Hence, we see that even from the outset, views based on female deficit, difference, and dominance cannot be neatly separated.

Lakoff noted a number of features that she believed to be characteristic of "women's language," as well as reasons why, in her view, these features render women's language less powerful than men's. We list a few of these features here.

A sampling of "women's speech" features, per Lakoff (1973, 1975)

(1) *Heavy use of "tag questions"*
Lakoff claimed that women use more structures such as, "That sounds OK, **doesn't it?**" than men. The little questions which women often "tag on to" the ends of statements have the effect, Lakoff says, of diminishing the force of the statement; in addition, they convey a lack of confidence, or even a lack of personal opinions or views, on the part of the speaker.

(2) *Question intonation on statements*
Lakoff maintained that women often end statements with the rising intonation that is characteristic of questions rather than with the falling intonation that characterizes assertions. The effect of "question intonation" is similar to that of tag questions, in that it turns utterances into questionable propositions rather than definitive statements.

(3) *"Weak" directives*
According to Lakoff, women tend to frame directives or commands as requests rather than direct commands. For example, women are more likely to get someone to close an open door by saying "Would you mind shutting the door?" than by saying "Shut the door!" Requests, Lakoff maintained, carry less authoritative force than directives which are framed as imperatives.

Exercise 1

In keeping with the notion that women's speech is "less powerful" than that of men, it is often asserted by researchers in language and gender that men interrupt more than women, in order to seize control of conversational interactions. Choose a mixed-sex group (e.g. a class, club meeting) and conduct a simple study of the cross-sex patterning of interruptions during the group meeting. You will need to count how many males and how many females are in the group, since the overall tabulation will have to take into account the proportion of males to females. If the group has a designated leader, do not tabulate the frequency of interruptions by the leader for this exercise (although, as a separate study, it would be interesting to observe the leader's patterns of interruptions, especially as regards the sex of the speaker being interrupted by the leader). You can set up a simple coding sheet something like the following. Be sure to be discreet in recording your tabulations at the scene of the gathering.

Setting: (e.g. discussion group, faculty meeting, etc.)
No. of males present   _____   % of group   _____
No. of females present   _____   % of group   _____
Total participants   _____

	Female	Male
Interruption		

What problems did you encounter in carrying out the project? Do your findings seem to support the notion that men's language is more "powerful" than women's? Do your findings support the idea that interruptions are primarily a strategy for seizing conversational control?

Lakoff's discussion of women's speech features was highly influential and prompted an entire generation of researchers to conduct empirical work on women's language, both in attempts to find support for Lakoff's views and in attempts to prove her wrong. Results of these empirical tests have been mixed. For example, while some studies indicate that women indeed use more tag questions than men in certain contexts (e.g. Crosby and Nyquist 1977), others show that men use more tag questions (e.g. Dubois and Crouch 1975). Thus, as with the gender-based patterning of phonological and morphosyntactic features, gender-based patterns of language use are not as clear-cut as entrenched stereotypes might lead us to believe. Although subsequent scholars have criticized Lakoff for her overgeneralizations, as well as her lack of empirical evidence, Lakoff herself recognized that not all women used all features of women's language in all situations. Further, she did not view her claims as definitive but rather as a starting point for further research, of which there has certainly been a vast amount. Finally, Lakoff's introspective methodology, although unsatisfactory to many researchers in sociolinguistics and other social sciences, fits perfectly well with her early training in formal linguistics, where such methodology is common and does, in fact, yield insight not always available via behavioral observation or experimentation.

Another limitation of Lakoff's work is that it is grounded in the notion that certain language features necessarily connote weakness. Researchers increasingly have come to realize that the social meanings attached to language forms are highly dependent on the social context surrounding the forms and on the interpretation conversational participants choose to give the forms. Thus, one can readily re-interpret so-called "weak" directives as "polite" directives which indicate that those who use them are more attuned to the linguistic and social needs of fellow conversationalists than those who use more direct directives. In addition, while "weak" directives may indeed be indicative of uncertainty in some situations, they may indicate mere politeness in other settings and even hostility or distance in others. For example, a speaker may suddenly start using ultra-polite language forms during a conversation with an intimate friend in order to show anger.

One final concern regarding Lakoff's 1973 article has to do with the broader sociopolitical implications of her perspective. Scholars in the field of language and gender have pointed out that if women consider their language to be weak and inferior, then they will feel pressure to alter their language so it is more like men's language, which is considered to be "strong," or at least free of weakness. Further, Lakoff's views may place pressure on women to "decipher" or "interpret" men's language, with no corresponding pressure on men to learn to correctly understand women's use of language. On the other hand, one cannot ignore power imbalances between men and women, or the speech forms they habitually use, if one wishes to correct those imbalances, as Lakoff was certainly interested in doing.

Not only have researchers cast doubt on the popular belief that women use weaker language than men, but they have also debunked several other widely held stereotypes. For example, many people believe that women talk more than men, a "fact" which is often the subject of humorous – and derogatory – commentary. Thus, husbands often jokingly state that they "can't get a word in edgewise" when their wives are around. However, studies of amount of talk by men and women actually indicate that, in general, men talk more than women. (See James and Drakich 1993, for a summary of the numerous studies that have been conducted on this topic.)

Of course, we have to realize that amount of talk by men and women may be drastically different in different situations, depending on such factors as the topic and setting of the conversation, as well as who is considered to be the authority figure in a given conversational interaction. In addition, amount of talk may be measured in various ways, for example by number of words per conversational turn or by number of minutes per turn, and these different measures may yield quite different results. Despite such important qualifications, however, research simply does not support the popular opinion that women talk more than men.

Another stereotype which has been challenged is the belief, once common among researchers in language and gender, that men interrupt more than women. This belief stems from the notion that men hold more societal and conversational power than women and that interruptions serve as a means of seizing control of conversations. Numerous empirical studies have been undertaken to determine who interrupts more, and, while some of these studies support the belief that men interrupt more than women, others indicate that women interrupt more or, most often, that there is no significant difference in amount of interruptions by men and women. (See James and Clarke 1993, for a summary.)

This wide variation in research results is due to several factors. First, the number of interruptions seems to be dependent not only on who is doing the interrupting but who is being interrupted. For example, women tend to get interrupted more than men by both female and male speakers. In addition, just as with amount of talk, amount of interruption may be measured in various ways, since it can be very difficult to determine exactly what constitutes an interruption and what doesn't. Not all cases of overlapping speech constitute interruption. For example, we may "talk over" someone who is offering an opinion with phrases and responses such as "right" and "ummhmm," but these responses are supportive, whereas true interruptions are considered to be disruptive in some way. Further, the "rules" for what counts as an interruption may be very different in different settings. For example, during an animated family discussion at the dinner table, children may be permitted to engage in overlapping talk to a much greater extent than they would in a setting such as the classroom.

Even utterances that unquestionably serve to interrupt the flow of conversation sometimes have little or nothing to do with conversational dominance. If someone interrupts us in mid-sentence by uttering the cry of "Fire!" we are not likely to interpret the remark as a bid for power; instead we will interpret it as a warning issued out of concern for our safety. Similarly, if someone interrupts us in the middle of an explanation by exclaiming "Oh! Now I get it!" we most likely will interpret the interruption as a positive emotional response to sudden enlightenment rather than as a negative attempt to thwart our explanation. Just as so-called "weak" language features do not always serve to convey weakness, so too do interruptions carry a number of different connotations besides conversational dominance. Thus, there is no clear connection between social dominance and increased interruptions.

8.6   The "Cultural Difference" Approach

As a counter to the view that women's language is deficient compared to men's, a number of researchers maintain that women's language is not inferior but simply different. The CULTURAL DIFFERENCE APPROACH to language and gender is grounded in the belief that women's and men's speech is different because girls and boys in America grow up in essentially separate speech communities, due to the fact that they typically are segregated into same-sex peer groups during the years in which they acquire many of their language-use patterns. This approach is central to the work of a number of researchers, including Deborah Tannen, a sociolinguist who is well known as the author of several best-selling books on language and gender for non-experts, including *That's Not What I Meant! How Conversational Style Makes or Breaks Relationships* (1987) and *You Just Don't Understand: Women and Men in Conversation* (1990).

Tannen seeks to explain the frequent misunderstandings that arise in cross-sex communicative encounters by claiming that women and men have very different notions of how conversations are supposed to work, as well as different expectations regarding the role of conversational interaction in building and maintaining interpersonal relationships. These differences exist because girls and boys spend most of their time in single-sex groups during the stages of their life when most of the rules for interpersonal interaction are being learned. Girls grow up in groups in which heavy emphasis is placed on cooperation, equality, and emotionally charged friendships, and so girls develop conversational styles that are cooperative and highly interactional, with each girl encouraging the speech of others and building on others' communications as she converses. In addition, girls learn to read others' emotions in quite subtle ways, because forming strong friendships is of key importance to them. On the other hand, boys grow up in groups which are hierarchical in nature and in which dominance over others is of central importance. Thus, boys develop conversational styles which are competitive rather than cooperative, and they place a heavy reliance on "proving themselves" through their words rather than on encouraging the ideas of other speakers.

The conversational differences learned in childhood carry over into adulthood, when women and men interact with one another on a frequent basis, and conversational misunderstandings result. For example, if a man dominates a cross-sex conversation, through such means as interruption and lengthy conversational turns, the woman with whom he is conversing may feel that the man doesn't care about her ideas because he doesn't allow her a fair share of talk time. According to Tannen, however, the man may not realize that he has hurt the woman's feelings, because he considers conversations to be contests rather than cooperative exchanges in which each party is to be given an equal chance to be heard. Similarly, because women are more attuned to seeking out the relational implications behind seemingly straightforward factual statements than men, women may feel that men simply "aren't trying" when they fail to understand the underlying meanings behind apparently simple statements. For example, when a woman says to her husband, "I wonder what I should do about that problem at work," she may not be expecting him to respond with directives such as "Quit" or "Put up with it" but with a statement that indicates that he is sympathetic to her feelings of frustration over her job.

Tannen's books have been well received by general audiences, who seem to be glad to have discovered that there are explanations for the miscommunications that they frequently experience in their own cross-sex interactions. At the same time, her works have met with some opposition by researchers. For example, although Tannen admits that her generalizations do not fit all speakers in all situations (Tannen 1990: 13–19), she has been criticized for overemphasizing the differences between women's and men's conversational styles and hence perpetuating the artificial dichotomy between women's and men's language. A number of proponents of the cultural difference theory, including the earliest advocates of this approach (Maltz and Borker 1982), maintain that by the time males and females reach adulthood, their conversational styles are actually quite similar. And even in childhood, it is maintained, similarities in conversational strategies far outweigh differences. For example, it has been shown that girls use the same strategies to win arguments as boys and that they are just as skillful at arguing as boys (Goodwin 1990).

Perhaps the biggest concern with cultural difference approaches such as Tannen's is that they tend to downplay the power relations that underlie the different interactional styles into which boys and girls are socialized (e.g. Freed 2003: 701–2). It is not simply the case that girls are cooperative and boys are competitive because "that's the way things are." Rather, the competitiveness into which boys are socialized stems from male societal dominance – and ensures the perpetuation of such dominance. On the other hand, the cooperativeness and focus on the needs of others into which girls are socialized arises from the subordinate social position of females, who must learn to adjust their actions – and feelings – to accord with those of others because of their own lack of autonomy.

8.7 The "Dominance" Approach

The notion that male–female conversational differences are due to societal power differences between men and women has been termed the DOMINANCE APPROACH. In support of this theory, researchers have pointed out that the features of so-called "male conversational style" almost always seem to be characteristic of speech that is uncooperative or disruptive in some way, a correlation we would not expect if men's conversational differences derived solely from cultural difference rather than cultural dominance (e.g. Henley and Kramarae 1994). Under this view, men take up more conversational time than women, introduce new topics rather than building on old ones, and appear inattentive to the relational implications underlying factual statements, not because they come from a "separate but equal" interactional realm, but because they are clearly *not* the equals of women. Instead, they dominate women, and this dominance pervades their conversational interactions as well as their non-verbal behavior towards women.

Under the dominance theory, not only is the source of female–male miscommunication probed in greater depth than under the cultural difference theory, but the very notion of miscommunication itself is questioned. A number of researchers have suggested that men's "misunderstandings" of women's conversational style are often quite intentional. For example, Penelope Eckert and Sally McConnell-Ginet (1992) suggest that when a man making sexual advances towards a woman interprets her "no" to mean "yes," it is unlikely that he is following a conversational rule he learned in all-male peer groups which states that one accepts sexual advances by pretending to reject them. Instead, "he actively exploits his 'understanding' of the female style as different from his own – as being indirect rather than straightforward" (1992: 467) in order to imbue the woman's response with the meaning that he wishes it to have (see also Kitzinger and Frith 1999). Indeed, men seem to show no difficulty in understanding and even engaging in "female-like" conversational behavior when it suits their purposes. For example, we are all familiar with "sweet-talkers" who engage in highly cooperative conversational interaction with women and display great sensitivity to the emotional and relational meanings underlying women's words in order to win over or seduce the women with whom they are conversing. Thus, it seems that the communicative difficulties that we often find in cross-sex conversations do not stem solely from a genuine inability to understand; rather, they sometimes derive from unwillingness to understand.

As noted above, the deficit, difference, and dominance views are not mutually exclusive. Hence, for example, it is possible to focus on male–female cultural differences while acknowledging that these differences may very well stem from unequal power relations (as Tannen herself acknowledges; 1990: 13–19). In addition, all three views focus on accounting for women's language, with little discussion of the equally gendered nature of men's language. And finally, all three emphasize a simple male–female opposition and downplay the real complexity of gender-based patterns of language use. Because of these limitations, researchers have been moving away from the deficit, difference, and dominance views as originally conceived, in order to focus more fully on how gender as a social construct (rather than dichotomous biological "given") affects language use. Hence, there is an increasing focus on intra-gender difference as well as cross-gender difference. In addition, researchers are paying increasing attention to the contextualized nature of gender-based language patterns, including the interaction of gender with other social categories (e.g. age, ethnicity), with interactional factors such as conversational purpose, and with attitudinal and sociopsychological factors (e.g. one's desire to achieve psychological closeness with or distance from one's co-conversationalists). With this increasing focus on gender as contextually situated, we find increasing focus on gender as performance – that is, as constructed in interactional situations rather than imbued as an attribute.

We see, then, that studies of language and gender that focus on language use (i.e. on the pragmatic or discoursal level of language organization) and studies that focus on the variable patterning of phonological and morpho-syntactic features have gone through common developments and converged around some key notions concerning language and gender, as well as gender itself, that are very different from conceptualizations that existed at the outset of the study of language and gender. Such convergences are not surprising, since both lines of study have influenced one another and in turn have been influenced by developments in the broader field of gender studies. In addition, as mentioned above, researchers in the dialect survey tradition increasingly are incorporating investigations of situated discourses into their investigations, thus further aligning survey approaches with perspectives based on language use.

8.8 Further Implications

Research on language and gender has certainly come a long way since the inception of this field of study in the early 1970s. As work continues, researchers are maintaining their focus on social constructions of gender rather than simply accepting established gender ideologies that place all individuals in all societies into two sharply different gender categories. In addition, researchers recognize the need for more work on how men construct and portray their gendered identities through language, as well as more research on a broader range of populations than those that have formed the focus of most study to date (chiefly English-speaking populations in the Western world). Finally, as researchers pay more attention to how gender is performed in specific interactional contexts, they are increasingly recognizing that gender performance is highly constrained, and that we cannot ignore the role of established gender ideologies and stereotypes in shaping people's speech – as well as shaping research on language and gender. For example, many studies of language and gender still presume from the outset that male–female language differences exist and tend to frame their research questions in terms of this belief.

Not only do researchers need to acknowledge pre-existing beliefs, but we need to treat ideologies and stereotypes as objects of study in their own right, investigating, for example, issues such as people's responses to stereotypes and why stereotypes are so persistent. One interesting answer to the latter question comes from Alice Freed (2003). She suggests that perhaps gender stereotypes are still so strong today, after several decades of feminist activism and scholarship, because traditional gender boundaries are actually blurring, a change which may cause a backlash of heightened insistence on traditional gender divisions. It remains to be seen whether longstanding stereotypes regarding language and gender, and gender itself, will in fact change, but we cannot deny that people's awareness of gendered identity as individually and socially constructed has certainly been heightened thanks to decades of investigation and activism on the part of those who seek change, including an end to the power inequities that are often perpetuated in the name of preserving the established gender order.

8.9 Talking about Men and Women

We have seen that many gender-based patterns of language variation may be grounded in power differences between men and women. It has also been claimed that men's power and women's relative lack of power are encoded – and perpetuated – in how men and women are talked to and talked about. We can examine this claim by looking at some of the traditional differences in how men and women are referred to in American society. In addition, we will consider how language works to perpetuate not only male–female power differences but the very notion of a strict (heterosexual) male–female dichotomy.

8.9.1   Generic he *and* man

The use of the pronoun *he* and its related forms *his* or *him* to refer to a sex-indefinite antecedent (e.g. *If anybody reads this book, he will learn about dialects*) is certainly one of the most often-cited cases of gender bias found in English. It is interesting to note that alternatives to the generic male pronoun such as the use of singular *they* (e.g. *If anybody reads this book, they will learn about dialects*) were quite acceptable during earlier periods of history (Bodine 1975), but these alternatives were gradually legislated out of acceptable usage by prescriptive grammarians. For example, in 1746, the grammarian John Kirby included as one of his "Eighty-Eight Grammatical Rules" the rule that "the male gender was more comprehensive than the female" (quoted in Miller 1994). Even lawmakers spoke out against generic *they* and other alternatives to generic *he*. For example, a law passed by the British Parliament in 1850 stated that "in all acts words importing the masculine gender shall be deemed and taken to include female" (quoted in Miller 1994). It is uncertain exactly when generic *he* arose, but its usage is probably correlated with increased usage of the noun *man* to refer to "humankind," as in *Man shall not live by bread alone* (Smith 1985: 50). Interestingly, in Old English the word *man* really was truly generic and could be used in place of both the feminine *wif* "woman" and the masculine *wer* or *carl* "man" (Frank and Anshen 1983).

The prescriptive use of generic *he* in formal and written English persists despite the widespread use of generic *they* to refer to singular antecedents in informal spoken English, and attempts to use generic *they* in writing continue to meet with steadfast editorial rejection. However, in recent years, grammar books increasingly have been legislating against the use of generic *he*, and many of these books now include sections on how to avoid using generic *he* without "improperly" using generic *they*. For example, students are taught to pluralize sex-indefinite antecedents (*If people read this book, they will learn about dialects*); to use the phrase *he or she* (or *she or he*), as in *If anyone reads this book, he or she will learn about dialects*; or to alternate generic *he* with generic *she* (*If anyone reads this book, he will learn about dialects. The student will thus find that her knowledge of language patterning has been greatly increased*).

Attempts to do away with generic *he* have met with resistance and ridicule for decades, with opponents arguing that the use of generic *he/man* in no way excludes women or obscures their role in society because, by longstanding convention, people readily associate these forms with the meanings "he or she" and "humankind". However, experiments show that, in reality, there is a tendency for readers to associate generic *he/man* with males alone, particularly when the readers themselves are male (e.g. Harrison 1975;

Martyna 1978, 1980). In addition, experiments have shown that the use of generic *he* has a significant impact on readers' comprehension of reading passages, their judgments regarding the personal relevance and worth of a given passage, and their beliefs regarding the gender of the author of the passage (MacKay 1983). For example, it has been shown that men have better comprehension than women when generic *he* is used, while women are more likely to judge that prose containing generic *he* must have been written by a man. Finally, it has been noted that unchecked usage of generic *he* can have far-reaching social implications. For example, it has been shown that women tend to avoid responding to job advertisements containing generic *he*, because they feel that they do not meet the qualifications outlined in the ads (Miller 1994: 269).

8.9.2   *Family names and addresses*

The tradition of family names is another convention that has been cited as an example of how female–male power differences are encoded in language. The traditional adoption by women of the husband's family name may signify "that women's family names do not count and that this is one more device for making women invisible" (Spender 1980: 24). It is also significant that women traditionally have had to use titles that indicate their marital status – that is, *Mrs* or *Miss* – whereas both married and unmarried men are known simply as *Mr.* There have been a number of different interpretations of the sociopolitical significance of this difference, but one of the most prominent is that this pattern indicates that women are defined according to their relationship to men, whereas men are more autonomous in terms of self-definition.

Other issues arise when we consider the linguistic resources available for talking about non-traditional families that exist outside the dominant gender order that maintains that families consist of a heterosexual man, a heterosexual woman, and their biological children. For example, Sally McConnell-Ginet (2004) notes that in institutional contexts such as newspapers, employment policies, and legislation, members of same-sex couples are referred to by such terms as "domestic partner," "life partner," or "long-time companion" rather than "husband," "wife," or "spouse." And even though it could be argued that "husband," "wife," and "spouse" are terms reserved solely for those who are married in the eyes of the law (at the writing of this chapter, same-sex marriage was not legal in most areas of the US), we do find, in these same institutional contexts, such terms as "common-law wife/husband" to refer to members of longstanding heterosexual couples who were never legally married. Further, the term "family" is never used to apply to same-sex couples and their dependants, but only to domestic units headed by heterosexual couples. Thus, it can be argued that existing linguistic practices and policies in the US serve to "police" the dominant gender order, since they serve to relegate non-traditional families to lesser status than traditional ones – and in fact do not really allow us to speak of non-traditional "families" at all.

Other address forms indicate that men typically are more respected and treated with more formality than women. For example, men are more likely to be addressed with formal *sir* than women of comparable status are to be addressed as *ma'am*. Women are also more frequently addressed informally as *dear*, *honey*, and *sweetie* in social contexts where men of comparable status would not be addressed in this way.

8.9.3   *Relationships of association*

As noted above, certain language forms suggest relationships in which women are defined in terms of the men with whom they are associated, whereas the converse does not take place. Associations such as *man and wife*, but not *woman and husband*, or the more common use of the designation *Walt's wife* as opposed to *Marge's husband* have been interpreted as indicative of a relationship between the owner and the owned (Eakins and Eakins 1978). It has even been noted that the conventional placement of male before female in coordinate constructions (e.g. *husband and wife* but not *wife and husband*, or *host and hostess* but not *hostess and host*) indicates a pattern of male precedence. In fact, prescriptive grammarians writing as early as the mid-seventeenth century indicated that the male gender should always be placed first because it is the "worthier" (Spender 1980: 147).

> ### Exercise 2
>
> One of the exceptions to the ordering of masculine and feminine coordinate constructions (e.g. *husband and wife*) is found in the public address salutation, "Ladies and Gentlemen!" How might you explain this apparent exception to the more general pattern of placing the male first? Can you think of any other exceptions to the male-first pattern in coordinates?

8.9.4   *Labeling*

There are many instances of differential labeling that have been offered as evidence that unequal female–male power relations, as well as unequal levels of respect, are encoded in the English language. These include the scope of semantic reference covered by particular words, the emotive connotations of sex-paired words, and the patterns of derivation in lexical items. The age span typically covered by items such as *girl-boy* and *woman-man* illustrates that the semantic range of analogous lexical items is not always comparable for females and males. Older women are much more likely to be referred to as *girls* than older men are to be referred to as *boys*. For example, a person might say, "I met this real nice girl" in reference to a 30-year-old female, but one would hardly say "I met this nice boy" to refer to a 30-year-old male. In virtually every instance of this type, males are referred to as adults much more often than females. Thus, TV announcers may still refer to the NCAA "girls' basketball tournament," while they never refer to the NCAA "boys' basketball tournament," even though both tournaments involve college students roughly between 18 and 22 years of age.

In paired masculine and feminine lexical items, it has been noted that the feminine member of the pair often undergoes SEMANTIC DEROGATION (Schulz 1975). That is, the feminine member of the pair often acquires connotations of subservience or diminished importance, as, for example, in such word pairs as *mister/mistress*, *governor/governess*, and *bachelor/spinster*. In many cases, the feminine item may also acquire connotations of improper sexual behavior, as in the case of *mistress*. Even when feminine items are directly derived from masculine items via the addition of a suffix, as in *bachelorette* or *poetess*, the new word often takes on connotations of lessened significance or respectability. In cases where gender is indicated through the addition of a suffix, the burden is typically carried by the feminine item rather than the masculine (e.g. *Carla* is derived from *Carl* or *Paulette* from *Paul*, etc.), suggesting a male norm for lexical items. Furthermore, one survey of dictionary items (Nilsen 1977) shows that masculine words outnumber feminine words by a ratio of three to one, and masculine words denoting prestige are six times as frequent as feminine words with prestige.

Finally, there are drastic differences in specialized vocabularies that are indicative of the longstanding "double standard" that society has maintained for male and female behavior. For example, Julia P. Stanley (1977) found only 20 items describing promiscuous men (e.g. *animal*, *letch*), some of which even carried some positive connotations, such as *stud* and *Casanova*. By the same token, Stanley stopped counting when she reached 220 labels for promiscuous women (e.g. *whore*, *slut*, *tramp*). There are also comparable disparities in metaphorical labeling, as women tend to be labeled with reference to consumable items such as foods (e.g. *peach*, *sugar*, *cheesecake*, etc.) but men do not (e.g. Hines 1999).

8.10   The Question of Language Reform

The linguistic manifestations of inequality and stereotyping based on sex are hardly disputable. The question that remains is whether changing the language will alter the unequal position of men and women in society or whether achieving increased social equality must precede increased linguistic equality. One answer might be that language simply mirrors sociocultural patterns: If a society treats women as unequal, then language will simply provide the symbolic mechanism for displaying society's underlying discriminatory base. Changing to alternate, more neutral forms will not really stop underlying sex stereotyping, as items characteristically undergo semantic derogation when associated with a feminine referent. After all, at one point, words like *mistress* and *governess* were neutral counterparts of their male equivalents *mister* and *governor*.

Similarly, it has been noted that even in cases of attempted language reform, supposedly non-sexist forms may be altered or used in ways that reflect existing male–female asymmetries rather than challenging them. For example, Susan Ehrlich and Ruth King (1994) and Anne Pauwels (2003) note that while *-person* compounds such as *chairperson* are increasing in usage, they are often not used generically but rather to refer to female chairpersons (with the traditional *chairman* still being used for men). In addition, while *Ms* is certainly growing in popularity as a title for women (e.g. Pauwels 2003), it is not typically used as a replacement for *Miss* and *Mrs* but often as a third term to refer to women who don't quite fit the traditional definitions of *Miss*, a young woman who has never been married to a man, and *Mrs*, a mature woman who is currently married to a man (Pauwels 2003; Fuller 2004). Further, studies of attitudes toward the *Ms* title indicate that it may have acquired some unintended associations over the years. For example, while people do tend to associate *Ms* with such positive attributes as professionalism and independence, at the same time they associate it with women who are less warm and friendly, and less likely to make good wives and mothers (Fuller 2004). Thus, changing language-use patterns may simply be a linguistic cosmetic for the underlying problem of social inequality. From this vantage point, language dutifully follows a symbolic course set for it by the established social system; language can hardly be blamed for the more fundamental social inequity to be confronted.

However, it must be noted that just as language mirrors the prevailing social order, the use of language may reinforce and perpetuate the acceptance of these social conditions. Thus, whereas it may seem pointless to begin using *he or she* in place of generic *he* or to change one's title from *Mrs* or

Miss to *Ms*, we cannot deny that efforts at language reform have raised people's awareness of gender bias in language, even though bias still persists. You may have noticed, for example, that even people who persist in using generic *he* often feel compelled to comment on their reasons for doing so, or to apologize for their usage (Pauwels 2003). In addition, studies indicate that people who do adopt non-sexist usages do so because they are aware of gender bias in language and are committed to change (Ehrlich and King 1994; Pauwels 2003). There is an obvious interdependence between language as a reflection of social differences and language as a socializing instrument. Changing language-use patterns may thus go hand-in-hand with changing social conditions. In other words, language reform may actually serve as an impetus for social change.

While there remains some discussion among linguists and other scholars of language concerning what constitutes "realistic" language reform with respect to sex reference in English, there seems to be a consensus on a number of proposed reforms. In fact, according to Pauwels (2003: 561), "non-sexist language policies are in place in most public-sector and in many large private-sector organizations in English-language countries," as well as a number of European countries and international organizations such as UNESCO. The Linguistic Society of America, the most influential organization for language scholars in the United States, has adopted a clear policy statement regarding non-sexist language usage, which includes the following strategies for avoiding sexist language:

1   Whenever possible, use plurals (*people*, *they*) and other appropriate alternatives, rather than only masculine pronouns and "pseudo-generics" such as *man*, unless referring specifically to males.

2   Avoid generic statements which inaccurately refer only to one sex (e.g. "Speakers use language for many purposes – to argue with their wives . . ." or "Americans use lots of obscenities but not around women").

3   Whenever possible, use terms that avoid sexual stereotyping. Such terms as *server*, *professor*, and *nurse* can be effectively used as gender neutral; marked terms like *waitress*, *lady professor*, and *male nurse* cannot.
    (from the Linguistic Society of America Guidelines for Nonsexist Usage, approved by the LSA Executive Committee, May 1995)

Because guidelines such as the above have been so widely accepted, we don't believe we are being overly optimistic in claiming that most linguists take a strong and unified position favoring non-discriminatory language use.

Exercise 3

A critical notion in debates over reforming sexist language use is the determination of what constitutes "realistic" reform. Suggestions for reform have ranged from fairly radical proposals, such as changing words like *history* to *herstory*, to more modest proposals such as changing address forms (e.g. using *Ms* for women regardless of marital status) and altering generic noun and pronoun reference (e.g. using *people* instead of *man* and *he/she* instead of *he*). Are there any general guidelines we might follow in determining what constitutes a "realistic" reform in this area? For example, one principle might be that we should only change items of clear masculine association. In other words, we know that speakers are apt to associate generic *he* with males, but they may not associate *history* with *his story* (vs. *her story*); thus, we should change generic *he* to something like *he/she*, but we do not need to alter a word like *history*. What general principles can you think of to guide non-discriminatory language use? Are there principles based on practical considerations, such as the likelihood that a change will be adopted? As a point of reference, you might consider an actual set of guidelines set forth by a newspaper, a professional organization, or some other agency.

8.11   Further Reading

Eckert, Penelope (2000) *Linguistic Variation as Social Practice*. Oxford: Blackwell. Already a classic in the field of language variation study, this book represents the culmination of Eckert's many years of sociolinguistic/ethnographic study of language, gender, and social practice in a suburban Detroit-area high school. Eckert describes her study from its inception through her final analyses. In addition, she demonstrates throughout the value of her important insight that the social meaning of large-scale patterns of variation can be fully understood only through in-depth investigation of individuals, communities of practice, and highly localized contexts.

Eckert, Penelope, and Sally McConnell-Ginet (2003) *Language and Gender*. Cambridge: Cambridge University Press. This is an essential textbook for those interested in seeking an authoritative overview of the study of language and gender. Its authors are renowned experts (and innovators) in the field, yet the book is highly readable and engaging to non-experts, including those with little or no background in linguistics. Included are discussions of topics ranging from definitions of "sex" and "gender," gender socialization, gender and language use (i.e. pragmatics and discourse analysis), gender and language variation (i.e. quantitative patterns of variation), gender ideologies, and gender as performance.

Holmes, Janet, and Miriam Meyerhoff (eds.) (2003) *The Handbook of Language and Gender*. Oxford: Blackwell. This comprehensive volume provides an in-depth look at the major issues in the study of language and gender, as well as the history of this field of study. Each chapter is written by an expert on some aspect of language and gender study. Some chapters are perhaps a bit technical for beginners, but many are approachable to novice scholars. Topics covered include the history and theoretical background of language and gender study, negotiating gender relations, notions of authenticity and place, stereotypes and norms, and institutional discourse.

Johnson, Sally, and Ulrike Hanna Meinhof (eds.) (1997) *Language and Masculinity*. Oxford: Blackwell. This collection of articles is devoted to the investigation of men's language as gendered language. Of particular interest to those who are new to language and gender studies is the overview article by Sally Johnson (chapter 1, "Theorizing language and masculinity: A feminist perspective").

Labov, William (2001b) *Principles of Linguistic Change*, vol. 2: *Social Factors*. Oxford: Blackwell. In this book Labov presents his most current thinking on the interrelation of language, gender, and social group (including social class and social networks), with special attention to the interaction of gender and social group in language change. Readers interested in a shorter encapsulation of Labov's views on language, gender, and class may wish to read his earlier article "The intersection of sex and social class in the course of linguistic change" (*Language Variation and Change* 2: 205–54).

Lakoff, Robin (1973) Language and woman's place. *Language in Society* 2: 45–80. Although many of the findings and interpretations in this presentation have been challenged and denounced, this article stands as a pioneering effort in the history of language and gender studies. Some of the observations initially made by Lakoff served to inspire a generation of empirical research on language and gender issues. In addition, Lakoff has often been misinterpreted by those who have not read her original work, and it is imperative for readers interested in the objective assessment of this groundbreaking work to read it for themselves.

Tannen, Deborah (ed.) (1993) *Gender and Conversational Interaction*. New York/Oxford: Oxford University Press. This collection of articles includes a section on competitiveness and cooperation in conversational interaction, a section on the relativity of discourse strategies (such as interruptions and silence), and a very useful section consisting of reviews of the numerous empirical studies that have been conducted on women, men, and interruptions (James and Clarke) and on amount of talk by women and men (James and Drakich).

9

Dialects and Style

Most of us have noticed that people speak very differently on different occasions. For example, we may notice that a friend speaks a certain way when talking with a supervisor in the workplace or with a professor at school but sounds quite different when chatting with friends over lunch or speaking with children at home. We may even notice that we change our own speech when we're in different settings or talking with different people. For example, people who no longer live in their hometown may find themselves switching back into their home dialect when visiting home or even when talking on the phone with a family member back home.

In this chapter, we shift our focus from language variation across different groups of speakers to variation in the speech of individual speakers, or language STYLE. The study of language style is quite important to linguists who study language variation – with good reason. Research has proven that variation in speech style is just as pervasive as regional, social-class, ethnic, and gender-based language variation. There are no single-style speakers. Even speakers who live in relative isolation display a range of speech styles, or a considerable amount of what may be termed STYLE SHIFTING. Thus, if we hope to achieve a full understanding of variation in human language, then we have to include in our investigations not only variation across speakers but variation within individual speakers as well.

9.1   Types of Style Shifting

There are several different types of style shifting that may occur. First, speakers may show shifting usage levels for features associated with different dialects or with different registers. Whereas dialects are language varieties associated with particular groups of speakers, REGISTERS can be defined as varieties associated with particular situations of use. For example, a speaker may show higher usage levels of *-in'* for *-ing* in an informal register than in a more formal one. Speakers may also shift in and out of entire registers and dialects. Thus, a person speaking on the phone to a business colleague may switch quite suddenly from an "adult" register to a "babytalk" register if they are interrupted by pleas from their young child or, perhaps, attentions from a pet. The "babytalk" register encompasses a range of features on different levels of language patterning, including high pitch, exaggerated intonational contours, and the use of words with diminutive /i/ endings (as in *tummy* for "stomach") and double or REDUPLICATED syllables, as in *boo-boo* for "injury" or *din-din* for "dinner". Another readily recognizable register is "legalese," the dense, often incomprehensible prose that typifies legal documents, particularly when you get to the "fine print" section.

As an example of shifting from one dialect to another, a European American teenager may switch from a European American variety into African American English (or at least an approximation thereof) to indicate affiliation with "cool" youth culture. Shifting into a dialect (or language) other than one's "own" is often called CROSSING (Rampton 1995, 1999). However, exactly what it means to "own" a particular dialect (i.e. to have "native" competence in a dialect) and whether it is possible to have more than one dialect as one's "own" are open questions. A final type of style shifting involves shifting in and out of different genres. GENRES are also associated with particular situations of use; however, they tend to be more highly ritualized and formulaic and are often associated with performance or artistic display of some type. For example, preachers may use a specialized "sermon" genre, while a creative writer may write in the genre of the mystery novel or of science fiction.

Since both "genre" and "register" are associated with situations of use, there is no sharp dividing line between them, and what might be classified as a "register" by some scholars may just as easily be termed a "genre" by others. In addition, it is not always easy to determine whether a particular shift counts as a shift in register/genre vs. a shift in dialect variety. For example, in shifting from a casual to a more formal register, speakers whose native dialect is a vernacular variety of African American English may feel that they are shifting both style and dialect in producing a more formal tone. Similarly, it is not easy to determine whether someone is "crossing" into another dialect or merely using *some* of the features associated with another dialect, or even whether a speaker is switching between dialects of one language or from one language to another, a phenomenon typically referred to as CODE SWITCHING. Hence, shifts from African American English into standard (European American) English are sometimes classified as code switching and sometimes as style shifting. In reality, there is no clear dividing line between style shifting and code switching, since, as discussed elsewhere in this book, it is very difficult to determine what counts as a "dialect" of a language vs. a "language" in its own right. We will not explicitly discuss code switching in this chapter. However, many of the issues that pertain to shifting between styles in a single language also apply to switching between different languages. For example, code switching is shaped by many of the same situational factors and speaker motivations that affect stylistic variation.

Style shifts may also involve features on all levels of language use, from the phonological and morphosyntactic features typically studied by researchers interested in the quantitative patterning of social and regional dialect differences, to intonational contours, lexical items, and pragmatic features (e.g. greetings, and politeness formulas), to the way entire conversations are shaped. For example, Deborah Tannen (1984) discusses the different "conversational styles" associated with different cultural and regional groups in the United States, some of which are characterized by a high degree of overlapping talk among speakers and others of which are characterized by very little overlap, and even pauses between speaker turns.

Further, style shifts can involve different degrees of speaker self-consciousness. For example, a student in a college far from her home town may unconsciously shift into her native dialect when holding a phone conversation with friends and family back home, while another speaker may quite self-consciously "cross" into a non-native dialect in order to "perform" the variety for their friends (perhaps to make fun of it), or even use an exaggerated version of their *own* native dialect in a performance situation. Thus, Ryan Rowe (2004) shows how some performers of hip-hop use exaggeratedly high usage levels of some African American English features in their performances when compared with the use of these features in conversation.

Finally, styles may be short-lived, as, for example, in the case of the parent who shifts briefly into "babytalk" register when on the phone with a colleague. They may also be fairly extensive, even becoming part of one's daily routine. Barbara Johnstone (1999) discusses the case of a Texas salesperson who frequently shifts into a "Southern drawl" when talking with potential customers to help her make sales. Style shifts can even be so extensive that they come to characterize particular individuals or groups, so that we can talk about a person's own "unique style" or the group styles associated with the "jocks" and "burnouts" in some US high schools (Eckert 2000).

Exercise 1

Based upon an audio recording of speeches to diverse audiences, examine stylistic variation in the speech of a person well known for the ability to bridge different cultures (for example, Jesse Jackson or Martin Luther King, Jr). Compare speeches made to members of minority cultures with those presented to members of cultural majorities. Are there any qualitative differences in linguistic form (for example, phonology, grammar)? What kinds of differences are there in language-use conventions when different audiences are addressed (for example, speaker–audience interplay, salutations)? Are there particular features with social or situational associations that the speaker might be manipulating (for example, multiple negation)? What kinds of dialect or register features do *not* appear to be manipulated? (For example, are irregular verbs shifted?)

Scholarly interest in language style is probably as old as research on language itself, and research on style may be undertaken from any one of a wide range of perspectives, ranging from the literary analysis of the merits of various artistic styles, to the rhetorical analysis of the effectiveness of different styles for various purposes, to the very practically grounded analysis of spoken and written styles for the purposes of identifying the authors of anonymous communications in connection with criminal investigation (Fitzgerald 2001). Even within sociolinguistics, there have been many approaches to the study of stylistic variation, ranging from early approaches that sought to catalog the wide array of "ways of speaking" of particular cultural groups (e.g. Hymes 1962, 1974) to later work that focused on conversational style as revealed in small stretches of unfolding conversation (e.g. Tannen 1984).

For our purposes, we will focus mostly on the tradition of study associated with the quantitative analysis of social and regional dialect variation. However, as we saw with language and gender studies, researchers increasingly are combining quantitative and qualitative approaches. This makes particular sense in the study of stylistic variation, since there is an intimate connection between individual style and the broader styles associated with particular groups of speakers and speech situations. In order to engage in style shifting, speakers must be aware of the various registers and styles around them, as well as the social meanings associated with each style, and then be able to use features from these various styles in accomplishing their own conversational purposes and presenting themselves as they wish to appear in particular interactions. In the process of combining features from various sources, speakers shape styles, and these new styles in turn might become stylistic norms around which other groups orient. Hence, the up-close investigation of stylistic variation in interaction lends insight into how particular sets of features come to be associated with certain social groups, as well as how varieties may change.

Three major approaches to the quantitative study of stylistic variation have been influential during the past several decades: *attention to speech*, *audience design*, and *speaker design*. We will examine each of these in turn, as well as some of the major research findings from each approach. We will then take a brief look at some further considerations in the continuing study of stylistic variation.

Exercise 2

One of the language registers that has been examined by sociolinguists is the "math register" – the particular use of language associated with mathematics. In the following items, typical of language use in math problems, identify some of the specialized uses of language that might be a part of the math register. What parts of speech seem to be especially affected in this register?

1   Does each real number x have a subtractive inverse?
2   The sum of two integers is 20 and one integer is 8 greater than the other. Find the integers.
3   Find consecutive *even* integers such that the sum of the first and third is 134.
4   Find three consecutive *odd* integers such that the sum of the last two is 7 less than three times the first.
5   From downtown a suburban phone call costs 15 cents more than a local call. One month Dr Thorn's phone bill showed 30 local calls and 42 suburban calls, and the total bill was $14.22. What is the cost of one local call?

In a book on dialect differences and math failure, *Twice as Less: Black English and the Performance of Black Students in Mathematics and Science*, Eleanor Wilson Orr (1987) suggests that the roots of the math difficulties experienced by many working-class African American students are found in the grammatical differences that distinguish vernacular varieties of African American English from standard English. Having examined the typical kinds of language uses in math in the above examples, react to this conclusion. Are there special features of the math register that are common to *all* students studying math? How does the use of language in math differ from "ordinary" language use? Are these differences unique to the field of mathematics? Do you think dialect differences pose special obstacles to learning math? Why or why not?

9.2 Attention to Speech

The ATTENTION TO SPEECH approach holds that speakers shift styles based primarily on the amount of attention they are paying to speech itself as they converse. The more attention they pay to speech, the more formal or standard their speech will become; as they pay less attention to their speech, they become more casual or vernacular. This approach comes from William Labov's studies of language variation and change in the Lower East Side of New York City in the 1960s (Labov 1966, 1972b). Since he was interested in how language changes spread across social groups and different stylistic contexts, Labov devised interview questionnaires that were designed to yield speech affected by differing degrees of attention to speech, in the belief that speakers would move from an informal, casual style to a more formal, standard style as they focused more and more attention on their speech. The bulk of the typical sociolinguistic interview was designed to yield conversational speech, which could be classified as either *casual* or *careful* in style. Casual speech was held to occur in such contexts as extended discussions which were not in direct response to interview questions, remarks by the interviewee to a third party rather than to the interviewer, and discussions of highly emotional topics, such as near-death experiences. Speech was held to be more careful when less emotionally charged topics were discussed or when the interviewee provided direct responses to interview questions. Labov also turned to cues surrounding speech itself, or PARALINGUISTIC CHANNEL CUES, to separate casual from formal speech. For example, features such as increased speech tempo, higher pitch, laughter, and heavier breathing were held to be indicators of a shift into casual style.

In Labov's original study, a third type of stylistic context in the formality continuum was established by including a reading passage as a part of the interview. Labov believed that speakers would use a more formal style in this reading passage than in the conversational interview because reading is usually associated with more formal occasions than speaking. Finally, speakers were asked to read lists of words in isolation. Some of the words were further set apart by being MINIMAL WORD PAIRS – that is, words that are phonetically identical except for one sound. For Labov's purposes, the words in each pair would be pronounced differently in standard American English but might be pronounced the same in New York City speech. For example, one word pair he included was *sauce* and *source*, since these words might be homophonous for *r*-less speakers in New York City; another pair was *god* and *guard*. According to Labov, these latter two tasks should yield highly formal speech, since speakers would be paying increasing attention to *how* they are speaking rather than *what* they are speaking about.

Once interview speech was classified into different styles, Labov then investigated the incidence of certain features of New York City speech in each stylistic context by examining, in each context, the occurrence of a given dialect feature in relation to the number of potential occurrences of the feature. For example, if a speaker uttered 50 words which normally contain *r* after a vowel and before a consonant, as in *weird* or *farm*, and pronounced 20 of these words without the *r*, as in *fahm* for "farm", then the degree of *r*-lessness was said to be 40 percent.

9.2.1 The patterning of stylistic variation across social groups

Labov's studies revealed that, overall, speakers showed quite regular patterns of variation according to stylistic context. Namely, speakers used stigmatized dialect features, such as *r*-lessness, as in "fahm" for *farm*, or *t* for *th*, as in "true" for *through*, at progressively lower frequency levels as they moved from casual style to minimal pair style. This patterning mirrors the patterning of stigmatized features as one moves from the lowest to highest socio-economic class. The intersection of stylistic and social class variation in the use of [t] or [tθ] for *th* in New York City English is depicted in figure 9.1.

Figure 9.1 reveals that social class distinctions in frequency levels for stigmatized features tend to be preserved in each speech style. In other words, although all speakers decrease their use of stigmatized features as they move from casual to formal speech, speakers in lower socioeconomic classes show higher levels of stigmatized features in each speech style than speakers of higher classes.

Sometimes, as speakers become more formal in style, members of some lower social-class groups will actually use stigmatized features at a lower rate (and prestige features at a higher rate) than members of higher social classes. This pattern applies particularly to upper working-class or lower middle-class groups (as defined according to a particular socioeconomic status scale discussed in chapter 2). Labov terms this "cross-over" pattern HYPERCORRECTION, since speakers who exhibit this patterning are speaking in a hyper-"correct" or hyper-standard style. Labov maintained that lower middle-class and upper working-class speakers are more prone to

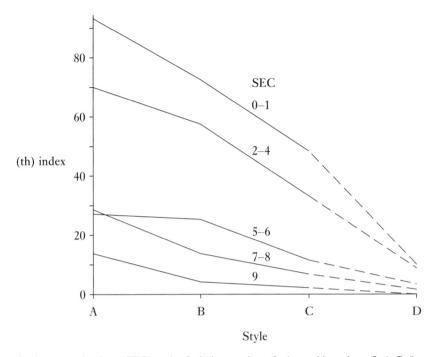

Socioeconomic class (SEC) scale: 0–1, lower class; 2–4, working class; 5–6, 7–8, lower middle class; 9, upper middle class. A, casual speech; B, careful speech; C, reading style; D, word lists.

Figure 9.1 Stylistic and social class differences in [t]/[tθ] usage in New York City English (adapted from Labov 1972b: 113)

hypercorrection than members of other socioeconomic classes because, in his view, they are more concerned with raising their socioeconomic status than members of other class groups. Perhaps this is because members of classes lower than the lower middle and upper working classes cannot envision rising to a higher socioeconomic level, while those in higher classes simply do not have as far to rise. Because of their concern with achieving the next higher level of status, speakers in lower middle-class groups attempt to talk like members of upper middle-class groups. In their attempts, they sometimes go too far and end up utilizing prestige features at a greater rate, or stigmatized features at a lower rate, than those they are trying to emulate. This is particularly likely to occur in formal styles, where the focus on language is greater than in casual styles. Research also suggests that the "cross-over" pattern is most likely to occur with features currently undergoing language change (Labov 1972b: 70–109; Trudgill 1974), such as

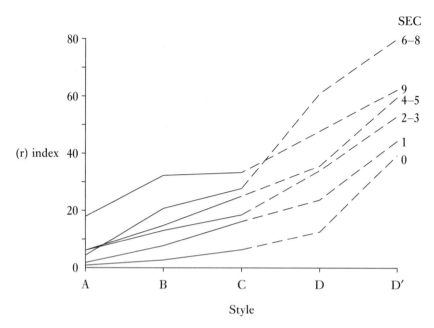

SEC scale: 0–1, lower class; 2–3, working class; 4–5, 6–8, lower middle class; 9, upper middle class. A, casual speech; B, careful speech; C, reading style; D, word lists; D′, minimal pairs.

Figure 9.2 Class and style stratification for postvocalic *r* (adapted from Labov 1972b: 114)

the increasing use of *r*-ful pronunciations (as in *farm* rather than *fahm* for "farm") in New York City in the 1960s. Figure 9.2 depicts hypercorrection in the use of *r*-ful pronunciations in New York City by members of the lower middle class (social classes 4–8). Speakers in this group display a higher rate of usage for this prestigious feature than speakers of the upper middle class (class 9) in the formal "word list" and "minimal pair" styles (styles D and D′).

Another form of hypercorrection involves the use of variants which are not typically found in one's language variety at all, at any percentage rate, as, for example, when a speaker of American English pronounces the "silent" *l* in *salmon* or the *t* in *often*. Hypercorrect pronunciations such as these, based on the spellings of words, are referred to as SPELLING PRONUNCIATIONS.

Hypercorrection can also involve using a feature in linguistic contexts where we do not usually expect it, as for example when a speaker says

Whom is it? or *This is between you and I.* Cases of hypercorrection which involve adding features or extending the boundaries of linguistic patterns are sometimes referred to as STRUCTURAL HYPERCORRECTION, whereas the type of hypercorrection which involves using features at a different rate than expected is known as STATISTICAL HYPERCORRECTION.

Exercise 3

One of the grammatical forms which is most commonly affected by hypercorrection is the reflexive pronoun (e.g. *myself, yourself*). Based on the following examples, identify the reflexive pronoun form most affected by hypercorrection and the types of constructions in which hypercorrect reflexive forms are typically used.

1 David and myself often work together.
2 Please give the ticket to myself.
3 Between Marge and myself, we should be able to raise the kids.
4 This book was really written by the students and ourselves.
5 I arranged for myself to leave early.
6 He brought the project to myself for review.
7 The students often give a party for the other faculty and myself.

In addition to the fact that social class distinctions are usually preserved across speech styles (except in cases of hypercorrection), Labov's studies of speech style also point to several other intriguing patterns. First, as noted by Allan Bell (1984), for any feature that shows differentiation along both social class and stylistic lines, the degree of stylistic differentiation is almost always less than the degree of social class differentiation. For example, if the highest social class in a community shows 20 percent *r*-lessness, as in *fahm* for "farm", and the lowest social class 80 percent (a difference of 60 percent), then the percentage difference in *r*-lessness between the most formal and most casual styles will be less than 60 percent. This patterning suggests that stylistic variation is derivative of social group variation – in other words, that a given feature can be used for stylistic purposes only if it carries some sort of social meaning.

Second, Labov observed that the speech style whose patterning is most regular and most reflective of the general patterning of a given language variety is the casual speech style. For example, in his studies of the vowel system of New York City English, Labov found that speakers' vowel systems in casual speech were more symmetrical and more closely aligned with what he had determined the general New York City system to be than were their vowel systems in more formal speech styles. In other words, speech spoken in casual contexts can be said to more closely approximate the "native" language variety, or the "vernacular," of a given community than speech spoken in other contexts. This view is expressed in Labov's VERNACULAR PRINCIPLE, which holds that "the style which is most regular in its structure and in its relation to the evolution of the language is the vernacular, in which the minimum attention is paid to speech" (1972c: 112). Thus, contrary to popular belief, not only are vernacular dialects not "sloppy" or "lazy" versions of standard varieties, but they actually are *more* regularly patterned than the more self-conscious styles that typify formal, standard speech.

Finally, Labov observed that the New York City vowel system was changing over time and that speakers' vowel systems in casual speech were more similar to the newer New York City vowel system than were their vowels in more formal speech. In other words, in Labov's view, casual speech seems to give a truer picture of language change in progress than more careful speech styles.

Labov's findings have had an enormous impact on sociolinguistic study over the past three decades. However, the methods and theoretical assumptions underlying Labov's approach to stylistic variation have been criticized for a number of reasons. For example, as discussed in chapter 6, researchers have criticized Labov's (and others') reliance on external, "objective" measures for delimiting social class. In addition, notions of prestige and stigma, standard and vernacular defy easy definition, and it may be the case that in some communities, different segments of the population have different notions of prestige, that vernacular features may carry their own prestige, and that features associated with widespread standards are not necessarily particularly prestigious. In addition, Labov's view of stylistic variation as conditioned primarily by attention to speech has been criticized as well. We outline some of the chief criticisms in the next section.

9.2.2   *Limitations of the attention to speech approach*

One of the biggest limitations of Labov's approach to stylistic variation is that, despite its seemingly straightforward methods for delimiting speech style, these methods are actually very difficult to apply in practice. For example, researchers have pointed to the unreliability of Labov's channel cues as indicators of casual speech. In particular, laughter may very well be indicative of increased nervousness (and increased attention to speech) rather than increased relaxation and decreased focus on one's speech. In addition, there is the question of how closely associated with a given stretch of speech a channel cue needs to be in order for the speech to count as truly casual:

Does laughter which comes a few seconds before a given utterance indicate that the utterance is casual, or does the laughter have to occur simultaneously with the utterance?

Another reason Labov's model has been criticized is because of the difficulty of quantifying attention to speech. Experimentation with aural monitoring of speech suggests that there is a covariation of language forms with speakers' ability to hear their own speech. For example, speakers may produce more standard variants when they are able to aurally monitor their own speech than when this ability is blocked via "white noise" fed through headphones. However, while some experiments indicate a correlation between increased aural monitoring and increased use of standard variants (e.g. Mahl 1972), other experiments show just the opposite – that speakers use forms that are *less* standard when they are better able to hear their own speech than when they are forced to speak under "noisy" conditions (e.g. Moon 1991).

In addition, the attention to speech approach has been criticized for its unidimensionality. Under this model, all speech styles must be classified according to the single criterion of degree of formality. This means that sometimes speech styles which we intuitively recognize as quite different must be classed as similar styles. For example, the very different styles that occur when a speaker becomes emotionally involved in a political discussion and when the speaker tells an animated narrative about a near-death experience must be labeled simply as casual or informal style, since, in each case, the speaker is paying a great deal of attention to what they're talking about and little attention to the speech itself.

Further, there are some speech styles that just do not seem to fit neatly along a formality–informality continuum at all. For example, reading styles may not lie on the same plane as spoken styles, and speakers may have special "reading registers" or "listing registers" that they use for the reading passage and word list sections of the interview, and that are very different from any of their formal spoken registers (e.g. Milroy 1987: 100–7). In addition, increased attention to speech does not always go hand-in-hand with increased use of standard or formal features, since speakers might shift into highly vernacular rather than more standard speech when the interview becomes more focused on speech itself, perhaps in an attempt to demonstrate or perform their vernacular variety for the researchers studying it. For example, in our studies of Ocracoke Island, North Carolina, we have found that speakers often "put on" their unusual dialect for the benefit of tourists and prying sociolinguists, even though these speakers may not sound all that unusual in normal conversation. These speakers have even developed several rote phrases which highlight a number of the features of the traditional Ocracoke dialect. For example, one classic phrase, "It's hoi toid on the sound soid" ("It's high tide on the sound side"), showcases the well-known island pronunciation of the /ai/ diphthong in a word like "tide" as more of an "oy" sound (as in "boy"), so that a word like "tide" sounds more like "toid." The phrase also highlights the lesser-known but nonetheless important /au/ vowel, which may be realized on Ocracoke as something like "ey" (as in "hey"), so that a word like *sound* is pronounced as something like *saned*. And despite our best efforts to get people to talk "unself-consciously" during our sociolinguistic interviews with them, some people did give us self-conscious "dialect performances" during their interviews (Schilling-Estes 1998). Further, these performances do show a degree of regular patterning, even though self-conscious speech is held to be less regular than unself-conscious speech under Labov's model. Thus, even when a speaker's attention is sharply focused on speech itself, their speech may not be particularly standard – nor are they intending for it to be.

A final concern has to do with the notion underlying Labov's vernacular principle that each speaker has a single most vernacular or casual style – that is, a language variety that is most "natural" for them. In reality, speakers may use different types of casual, unguarded speech in different settings, or even in a single interaction, depending on such matters as who they're talking with and what they're talking about. For example, a woman at home with her family might not be paying much attention to her speech itself as she talks, but the way she talks in this setting might be very different from how she talks when she's out with a group of friends for the evening (e.g. Hindle 1979). And even in a single sociolinguistic interview with one inter-viewer and one interviewee, we might get different types of casual speech depending on what the topic is. For example, the second author of this book conducted an in-depth study of style shifting in one interview as part of our sociolinguistic study of Robeson County, North Carolina (Schilling-Estes 2004). Both participants were young adult males; the interviewee was a Lumbee Indian (see chapter 6), and the interviewer was an African American. Both participants sounded quite different, yet equally relaxed, when telling humorous stories about the Lumbee's family and when telling stories about common friends at the university they both attended.

Despite the practical and theoretical concerns that have been raised regarding Labov's approach to stylistic variation, Labov and others have demonstrated that speech in sociolinguistic interviews often can be arranged on a continuum from casual to formal using Labov's original criteria, and that the speech styles thus arranged do show regular, direct correlations between casualness and vernacularity, on the one hand, and formality and standardness on the other. For example, Labov showed such correlations in a very large body of data from Philadelphia gathered over the course of a number of years (Labov 2001a). However, it still remains to be demon-strated conclusively that attention to speech is really the key factor in differentiating among speech styles, whether in the sociolinguistic interview or in non-research contexts (e.g. Eckert 2001). For example, when interviewees engage in lengthy discussions about matters not directly related to the inteviewer's questions (i.e. when they go off on a "tangent"), issues of topic control may have more effect on their speech than how much attention they're paying to how they're talking. Similarly, when an interviewee shifts into casual speech in addressing a family member who comes into the room, we can easily view the shift as conditioned by who they're talking to rather than (or in addition to) attention to speech. Indeed, the correlation between stylistic variation and addressee has been seen as so important that it has led researchers, notably Allan Bell (1984), to propose that audience, not attention, is the primary factor affecting stylistic variation.

9.3 Audience Design

In its original formulation (Bell 1984), the AUDIENCE DESIGN approach holds that speakers shift styles primarily in response to their audience. Under this approach, speakers adjust their speech toward their audiences if they wish to express or achieve solidarity with audience members; they adjust away from their audience if they wish to express or create distance. This approach is rooted in a social psychological approach to stylistic variation originally known as SPEECH ACCOMMODATION THEORY (SAT) (Giles 1973; Giles and Powesland 1975; Giles 1984) and now called COMMUNICATION ACCOMMODATION THEORY (CAT) (e.g. Giles, Coupland, and Coupland 1991). According to SAT, style is explained primarily on the basis of a speaker's social and psychological adjustment to the ADDRESSEE – that is, the person(s) being addressed by the speaker. The most common pattern of adjustment is CONVERGENCE, in which the speaker's language becomes more like that of the addressee. The tendency to shift speech toward the addressee is summarized as follows:

> People will attempt to converge linguistically toward the speech patterns believed to be characteristic of their recipients when they (a) desire their social approval and the perceived costs of so acting are proportionally lower than the rewards anticipated; and/or (b) desire a high level of communication efficiency, and (c) social norms are not perceived to dictate alternative speech strategies. (Beebe and Giles 1984: 8)

Put simply, the model is rooted in the social psychological need of the speaker for social approval by the addressee, but the speaker must weigh the costs and rewards of such behavior in shifting speech to converge with that of the addressee.

The other side of the accommodation model is DIVERGENCE, in which speakers choose to distance themselves from addressees for one reason or another. Speakers will diverge linguistically from addressees under the following kinds of conditions:

> [when speakers] (a) define the encounter in intergroup terms and desire positive ingroup identity, or (b) wish to dissociate personally from another in an interindividual encounter, or (c) wish to bring another's speech behavior to a personally acceptable level. (Beebe and Giles 1984: 8)

As we would expect from a model grounded in theories of social psychology, both the motivations of the individual speaker and the social relations among speakers and addressees are central to this explanation for stylistic shifting. A number of different experiments by Giles and others (e.g. Giles, Coupland, and Coupland 1991) have shown how speakers converge, and, in some cases, diverge with respect to speech-related phenomena such as rate of speech, content, pausing, and what is loosely referred to as "accent."

The audience design approach (Bell 1984) extends the speech accommodation model in two very important ways: (1) by articulating in detail the different kinds of audiences that affect speaker convergence/divergence, and (2) by applying Speech Accommodation Theory to the quantitative investigation of specific linguistic variables rather than relying on general discussions of differences in "accent" across speech style. The audience, as defined by Bell, includes not only those directly addressed, or addressees, but also participants of various sorts who are not directly addressed. Speakers make the greatest adjustments in their speech in relation to their direct addressees, but they may also alter their speech based on non-addressed participants, with the degree of adjustment determined by such factors as whether the speaker is aware of the participants' presence and whether participants are ratified (i.e. sanctioned to participate in the conversation). Ratified but non-addressed participants are called AUDITORS, non-ratified parties of whom the speaker is aware are called OVERHEARERS, and other parties – that is, those whose presence is unknown and unratified – are called EAVESDROPPERS. Non-personal factors such as topic and setting may also affect style shifting, but these are held to derive from audience-based considerations, at least in the original formulation of the audience design approach. For example, when speakers discuss a topic such as education, they may commonly shift into more standard speech, but this may be because this topic is associated with a certain type of audience – namely, a high-status, standard-speaking audience – rather than because of the nature of the topic *per se*.

Under the audience design approach, style shifts are usually undertaken in response to elements in the speaker's environment, particularly the

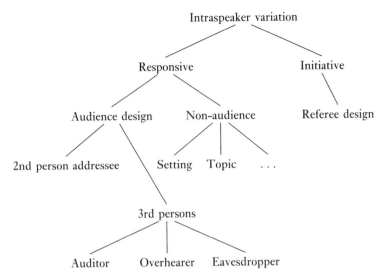

Figure 9.3   Style as audience design (from Bell 1984: 162, figure 6; reprinted with the permission of Cambridge University Press)

make-up of the speaker's audience. However, they may also be initiated from within speakers themselves in an attempt to alter the existing situation. Bell calls such shifts INITIATIVE STYLE SHIFTS. He maintains that they occur when speakers shift their focus from the immediately present audience to an absent person or persons with whom they wish to identify. For example, a speaker who is being interviewed by a standard-speaking linguist may suddenly shift from relatively standard speech into highly vernacular speech because she wishes to identify with fellow speakers in her community rather than with the standard-speaking outsiders whom the linguist represents. The non-present group for whom speakers attempt to adjust their speech when they engage in initiative style shift is called the REFEREE GROUP. REFEREE DESIGN is the term applied to the component of the audience design approach that focuses on these referee groups and initiative style shifting. The basic components of the audience design approach to style shifting are diagrammed in figure 9.3.

9.3.1   The effects of audience on speech style

Bell has conducted detailed studies of style shifting in radio announcers who address a range of audiences and has also compiled evidence from a wide array of language variation studies that demonstrate that speakers do indeed seem to adjust their speech in response to their audiences. In his studies of radio announcers in New Zealand, Bell found that the same announcers used more standard (i.e. British) English when reading the news for a national station but used more features of New Zealand English when reading the news (often from the same script) for a local community station. Further, Nikolas Coupland (1980) showed that audience effects can be pervasive in daily interaction. He studied the speech of an assistant in a travel agency during the course of her work day and found that she too got more or less standard depending on who she was speaking with, including clients, co-workers, and fellow agents at other travel agencies.

In an important study designed to test Bell's model, John Rickford and Faye McNair-Knox (1994) studied stylistic variation in the speech of an African American teenager, whom they called "Foxy Boston," in talking with different interviewers, two African Americans (interviewing as a team) and one European American, at several different time periods. They examined Foxy's and the interviewers' usage levels in each interview for several features of African American English, including invariant *be* (as in *He be talking all the time*), copula absence (e.g. *She nice*), and several types of inflectional -*s* absence (e.g. plural -*s* absence, as in *three cat* "three cats"). In general, as predicted by Bell's model, Foxy did indeed show higher usage levels for the AAE features studied when talking with the African Americans than when talking with the European American. However, there was one interview with the African Americans where Foxy showed relatively low usage levels for invariant *be* and copula absence. In this case, we may need to appeal to the initiative or referee design component of Bell's model, since Foxy's different styles with the same interviewers on two different occasions cannot be the direct effect of audience design. Rickford and McNair-Knox note that the interview in which Foxy uses unexpectedly low levels of AAE features was not as relaxed as the other interviews. In addition, Foxy was going to a predominantly European American high school at the time and had recently attended several motivational programs exposing her to standard American English and its value in "getting ahead." Hence, she may have designed her speech in this interview in terms of a non-present referee group of standard English speakers rather than the present audience of African Americans.

The audience design approach extends the attention to speech approach in a number of ways. First, it applies to a wider range of situations and can be used to investigate style shifting in everyday conversation as well as the sociolinguistic interview. In addition, because it attributes stylistic variation to interspeaker relations rather than individual psychological matters such as attention to speech, it goes some way toward explaining why it is that stylistic and social group variation are so closely intertwined, and why the amount of stylistic variation is typically less than the amount of social class variation. As Bell (1984: 158) notes, "Intraspeaker variation is a *response* to interspeaker variation, chiefly as manifested in one's interlocutors. The fact that style shift falls short of social differentiation . . . reflects the fact that speakers cannot match the speech differences of all their interlocutors – but they can approach them." Further, though both Labov's and Bell's approaches were initially focused on stylistic variation as a responsive phenomenon, Bell did add an initiative component which allows for a degree of speaker agency.

9.3.2   Limitations of the audience design approach

Despite the strengths of the audience design approach, a number of problems have been noted. For example, like the attention to speech approach, the audience design model has been criticized for its unidimensionality, since it attributes nearly all style shifting to a single factor: the make-up of the speaker's audience. Matters such as topic and setting are held to be derivative of audience effects, and even the issue of the different types of relationships that may exist between speakers and audience members (e.g. family, friends, co-workers) is not treated in great detail. Further, even if we agree that audience attributes should be our primary focus, it is not clear *which* attributes speakers accommodate toward or diverge from when they engage in style shifting. As Bell notes, there are three increasingly specific possibilities:

1   Speakers assess the personal characteristics of their addressees and design their style to suit.
2   Speakers assess the general level of their addressees' speech and shift relative to it.
3   Speakers assess their addressees' levels for specific linguistic variables and shift relative to these levels.
    (Bell 1984: 167)

Bell does not attempt to determine definitively which of these three possibilities holds true for most cases of style shifting and in fact maintains that speakers most likely respond to audiences on all three levels when they engage in style shifting. It is quite clear that speakers do indeed respond on level (1). For example, Fasold (1972) noted that the speakers of African American English he studied in Washington, DC, used vernacular variants more frequently with African American than European American inter-viewers, even though most of the African American interviewers were speakers of standard English. However, to say that speakers respond to the personal characteristics of their audience members does not really tell us *what* characteristics they are responding to: When someone speaks in a more vernacular manner with one interviewer than with another, is it primarily because of ethnicity, or perhaps because of some other factor, such as relative age, familiarity (perhaps the interviewee has known one interviewer longer than another), gender, or even how friendly the interviewer is?

It is even more difficult to tease apart levels (2) and (3), since, as Bell puts it, "the general speech impression of level (2) largely derives from the combined assessment of many individual variables" (1984: 168). In the study of "Foxy Boston" discussed above, Rickford and McNair-Knox (1994) found that Foxy seemed to be able to adjust her speech based on her interviewers' general usage levels for the features studied (level 2). However, she did not seem to be able to make more fine-grained adjustments (level 3). Further, Rickford and McNair-Knox note that not all variables seem to stand an equal chance of figuring in style shifting: Features that are used frequently (for example, invariant *be* in vernacular African American English in the 1990s, as in *He always be late for school*) seem to be more likely to be manipulated in stylistic variation than features with a low frequency of occurrence (for example, possessive -*s* absence, as in *Janet book is on the table*).

In our own studies, we have shown that the social meaning of dialect features influences the extent to which they can be used in style shifting. For example, when Outer Banks speakers perform their unique dialect for outsiders, they produce exaggerated versions of the "hoi toid" vowel which is a well-known icon of Outer Banks speech. However, they do not produce exaggerated pronunciations of other, lesser-known vowel sounds that nonetheless are characteristic of traditional regional speech, for example the pronunciation of /au/ as more of an "ey," as in "dane" for *down*. Conversely, residents of Smith Island, in Maryland's Chesapeake Bay, are readily able to manipulate different pronunciations of /au/ in demonstrating and performing their own dialect and other language varieties. However, they do not seem equally able to use /ai/ for stylistic effect. Most likely, this is because it is "ey" for /au/ rather than "oy" for /ai/ that carries the most social meaning on Smith Island, since islanders and others often point to "ey" for /au/ as the most distinctive pronunciation feature of Smith Island speech (Schilling-Estes and Wolfram 1999).

Another limitation of the audience design model is that, in its emphasis on speakers' achieving solidarity with audience members through convergence, it is easy to overlook the fact that there may be any number of linguistic strategies for "identifying with" audience members besides attempting to talk like them. Although Bell has shown that radio announcers may seek solidarity with listening audiences through convergence of speech style, other studies of radio announcers indicate that announcers may achieve solidarity with their audiences through a variety of means (e.g. Coupland 1985, 2001a). For example, an announcer might "grab" their audience by adopting the persona of a well-known cultural figure (whether mythical or real), even though this figure's speech style may be very different from that of either the announcer or the audience. Thus, a radio announcer in a metropolitan area in the American South might perform the dialect of a country farmer to achieve solidarity with a relatively non-vernacular audience, since the announcer and audience share a common image of the "typical" (or stereotypical) rural Southern resident. Further, speakers may use certain pragmatic features that serve to promote closeness between speaker and hearer (for example, politeness markers, "inviting" intonation patterns such as rising intonation on statements) regardless of whether their addressee uses them, or could be expected to, given their demographic characteristics. For example, the particle *eh*, tagged on to the end of sentences such as *Nice day, eh?* functions as a solidarity marker in New Zealand English. In a study designed to test the effects of interviewers' ethnicity and gender on style shifting, Bell and his colleagues (e.g. Bell and Johnson 1997; Bell 2001) found that interviewers used quite high usage levels for *eh* with one particularly hesitant speaker, in order to try to get her to feel more at ease. However, the speaker herself used very little *eh*, and *eh* was not particularly closely associated with her gender or Pakeha (i.e. White) ethnic group.

Perhaps the biggest shortcoming of the audience design approach as originally formulated has to do, not with audience design *per se*, but with referee design. Originally, Bell maintained that initiative shifts were but a small component of the overall picture of style shifting and that most style shifts were based on audience design rather than referee design. In addition, referee design was seen as derivative of audience design, since referee design involves convergence with non-present referee groups – in effect, non-present audience members. However, ongoing study indicates that initiative shifts are far more pervasive than in Bell's original model.

9.3.3 *Newer approaches to audience design*

In recent years, Bell has reworked his approach to stylistic variation, chiefly to give more prominence to initiative style shifting. In fact, he now maintains that not only are initiative shifts every bit as pervasive as responsive ones, but both are always in simultaneous operation (Bell 2001). In addition, the current formulation of the audience design approach places less emphasis on the derivative nature of non-audience effects (e.g. topic and setting), since it is very difficult to demonstrate that audience indeed underlies other types of effects. Furthermore, it has been shown that the effect of topic on stylistic variation is sometimes greater than the effect of audience. For example, Rickford and McNair-Knox (1994) found that, even though Foxy

showed considerable style shifting across interviews with the African
Americans vs. the European American interviewer, she showed even more
stylistic variation within interviews, according to the topic being discussed.
In addition, it is not always easy to view initiative shifts as shifts toward
a non-present referee group, since it is not always clear who such a group
might be. Thus, when speakers in Ocracoke shift into exaggeratedly
vernacular versions of the Ocracoke dialect in the middle of an interview
with a fairly standard-speaking interviewer, this is certainly a case of initiative
style shift. However, it is not clear who the non-present referee group in
this case would be, since no one on Ocracoke uses such exaggeratedly
vernacular speech in non-performative situations.

Finally, in the current formulation of audience design, there is more
recognition of the fact that speakers may employ a range of strategies
besides linguistic convergence to achieve psychological convergence with
their audience. In addition, speakers may have a range of purposes besides
"identifying with" or dissociating from the people they are talking with,
including, for example, getting a hesitant speaker to talk or winning an
argument. In its increasing emphasis on speaker motivation, as well as
initiative shifting, audience design is aligning itself with more recent approaches to stylistic variation that we might call "speaker design" approaches,
following Coupland (1996).

9.4   Speaker Design Approaches

Under SPEAKER DESIGN approaches to stylistic variation, style shifts are viewed,
not merely as a means of responding to the attributes of audience members,
but as a means of projecting one's own attributes – that is, one's personal
identity. It is crucial that we understand that researchers who investigate
speaker design do not view identity merely as the static intersection of
various demographic categories, such as age, social class, and race. Rather,
identity is seen as a dynamic notion that may change from conversational
encounter to conversational encounter, as well as within a single conversational interaction. Thus, a speaker may project one particular identity while
speaking with a small child but quite another identity (or another facet of
a single identity) while reprimanding an employee. It is almost as if we are
acting in a play whenever we engage in conversational interaction, taking on
certain *roles* in certain situations and other roles in others. These roles may
be derived in part from social relations that are relatively permanent, as, for
example, in the case of a mother conversing with her child or a supervisor
talking with an employee. They may also have to do with more transient
expressions of identity, as, for example, in the case of a mother who acts as

playful friend to her child one moment, and so speaks in a lighthearted, conversational style, and as an authority figure the next, when she assumes a commanding tone. In addition, identity is understood to encompass both personal and interpersonal dimensions, since people define themselves in relation to others, and since we may choose to project different aspects of our identity to different types of audiences (e.g. co-workers vs. children). In this regard, personal identity is to be viewed in terms of *relational* as well as *identificational* considerations (Coupland 2001b).

Speaker design-based approaches to stylistic variation have their roots in so-called "social constructionist" approaches to language and society. These approaches are characterized by the belief that language does not simply reflect social structures or social relations among speakers but also plays a crucial role in shaping society. In other words, the language features and patterns a speaker uses are not merely reflective of a set of predefined social groups to which the speaker belongs (e.g. European American middle-class male). Rather, language features and language styles are a vital component of the definition of social groups and social relations. Thus, speaker design-based approaches place less emphasis on social structures than other approaches to language and society and more emphasis on the social practices that go into creating these structures in the first place. In addition, speakers are seen as more proactive than passive. In fact, under speaker design-based views, all style shifts are initiative, even those made in seeming response to a particular situation, since speakers have to choose to conform to the expected norms for that situation rather than to diverge from these norms in some way. As Coupland (2001b: 200) explains, "From a self-identity perspective, shifts that are 'appropriate' are nevertheless creative in the sense that speakers opt to operate communicatively within normative bounds."

In order to investigate speech style as speaker design, researchers are considering a broad range of factors that might influence speakers' stylistic choices, including not only factors external to the speaker, such as audience, topic, and setting, but also such speaker-internal factors as purpose, key, and frame, where "key" is defined as participants' sense of conversational "tone" (e.g. joking vs. serious) and "frame" as participants' sense of what sort of interaction is taking place (e.g. casual conversation, sociolinguistic interview, job interview). For example, we have seen how both the attention to speech and audience design approaches fall a bit short in attempting to explain why an Ocracoke islander might suddenly switch into a dialect performance – i.e. an exaggeratedly vernacular form of their own dialect – in the middle of a conversational interview that is, for the most part, fairly relaxed and casual. Schilling-Estes (1998) examined in depth the dialect performances of one islander, Rex O'Neal, in order to try to determine the factors that might be influencing his shifts into performance speech, including both speaker-external and speaker-internal matters. For the most part, Rex spoke in a fairly relaxed and casual manner with the interviewer, and both participants seemed to view the interview as more of a casual conversation than a formal interview. However, whenever the technical matters of tape-recording had to be attended to (e.g. turning over a tape), Rex suddenly shifted into performance speech. Most likely, this shift in focus to the tape recorder caused the "casual conversation" frame to recede for a few minutes and the "interview" frame to come to the forefront. A typical response to such a frame shift would be for a speaker to shift into more standard speech, since they are suddenly more aware that their speech is being recorded for a group of researchers who intend to analyze it. However, Rex opts for something more creative: He switches into the role of "dialect performer" and proceeds to give the researchers a speech sample that they could not mistake for anything but the "quaint," "exotic" dialect they have come to hear. Thus, Rex's shifts into performance speech are partly a matter of audience design, since they seem to be triggered by a shift in focus from his present co-conversationalists to the researchers who will later listen to his tape-recorded speech. However, they are also a matter of "speaker design," since Rex chooses his own unique response to the shift in audience in order to project the persona that best suits his purposes at the time.

In addition to considering a broad range of factors that might affect stylistic variation, researchers interested in speaker-centered approaches also investigate a wide range of linguistic features, including not only segmental phonological features and morphosyntactic features but also suprasegmental phonological features (e.g. intonational counters), lexical items, pragmatic markers, discourse organization, and even some non-linguistic features. For example, in her study of how students in a Detroit-area high school project and shape group and self-identity, including group and individual style, Penelope Eckert (2000) examined not only a range of language features but also how people's language usages intersected with their use of other stylistic resources such as clothing, make-up, and even body posture. Similarly, Norma Mendoza-Denton (1997) examined how Latina high schoolers use a range of linguistic and extralinguistic features to indicate subtle distinctions in group affiliation. Other recent studies of stylistic variation have examined how features co-occur in shaping various registers (i.e. situations of use). For example, Finegan and Biber (1994, 2001) have conducted large-scale quantitative analyses of co-occurrence patterns for a number of features in registers ranging from written academic prose to casual conversations in search of common properties of the linguistic features that cluster in the different registers.

In addition to investigating a broad range of language features and broad patterns of co-occurrence in registers and in individual and group styles, researchers also conduct narrowly focused investigations of how features co-occur in unfolding discourse in order to gain insight into what sorts of meanings speakers are creating through their various language styles. For example, in the in-depth investigation of an interview between a Lumbee Indian and an African American mentioned above, a range of types of features were investigated, including phonological features (e.g. *r*-lessness, the pronunciation of /ai/ as [aː], as in *tahm* for *time*) and discourse markers indicative of high inter-speaker involvement such as *you know* and *I mean* (Schiffrin 1987). At certain moments in conversation, discourse patterns indicated that the African American interviewer was seeking solidarity with his co-conversationalist and thus using high levels of *r*-lessness and *tahm* for *time* in order to capitalize on the "rural Southern" associations of the features. At other times, however, when discourse patterns indicated more distance between speaker and hearer, the African American seemed to be using these same features to evoke their associations with African American ethnicity, thus highlighting his ethnic distinctiveness from the Lumbee.

The increasing focus on speech styles as proactive rather than simply reactive has led to increasing interest in speech styles that are overtly creative or performative. For example, researchers increasingly are interested in the phenomenon of "crossing," or people's use of language varieties that don't really "belong" to them (e.g. Rampton 1995, 1999), for example, the use of features of African American English by young people of other ethnicities as part of their participation in hip-hop culture. Others continue to investigate people's performance, and often over-performance (i.e. hyper-performance) of their "own" varieties, as for example in the case of the Ocracoke "dialect performer" discussed above, or Coupland's studies of radio announcers who produce exaggerated versions of their own regional vernacular varieties for humorous effect on their radio shows (1985, 2001a). This increasing focus on crossing and hyper-performance has raised interesting issues regarding the "ownership" of language varieties as well as the "authenticity" of particular ways of speaking or otherwise behaving. For example, we have already raised the issue of whether each speaker really has a single most "natural" (i.e. "authentic") vernacular variety that is somehow unaffected by situational factors, or whether it might be more realistic to say that all speech styles are necessarily shaped by contextual factors in some way. In addition, we might question whether it is possible or accurate to say that all speakers have a clearly identifiable regional or ethnic variety that can be neatly demarcated from other varieties, especially in the early twenty-first century as the world's cultures come into increasing contact with one another and people have greater access to a wide range of language varieties and cultural practices (Coupland 2003).

The increasing interconnection among peoples may be leading to increased use of "crossing" and other types of performance speech, as people become more aware of differences among language varieties and of their own varieties as possible objects of display. Sometimes crossing and otherwise "putting on" dialects might be relatively unself-conscious. At other times, however, it can be quite self-conscious indeed. Investigating self-conscious speech styles, as opposed to speech that seems to be unself-conscious, is an important line of inquiry in a research program that views stylistic variation as speaker design or identity performance, since all speech styles are viewed as a part of the ongoing performance of personal and group identity. The view of language (and indeed life) as a performance may be gaining increasing attention in sociolinguistics, but it is certainly nothing new to students of literature, as exemplified in Shakespeare's famous quote: "All the world's a stage, / And all the men and women merely players: / They have their exits and their entrances; / And one man in his time plays many parts, / His acts being seven ages" (*As You Like It* II.vii.139–43).

9.5 Further Considerations

Focusing on stylistic variation as speaker design has certainly increased our understanding of intra-speaker language variation; however, this approach, like the others we have considered, leaves us with a number of questions. First, there is the issue of reliability and reproducibility. Speaker design-based approaches allow for a range of *post hoc* interpretations for any given style shift, since speakers' motivations are not directly observable and can only be inferred. In addition, there is the question of generalizability: Can we determine the personal identificational motivations that underlie stylistic variation in the speech of an individual speaker and then make general statements regarding identity projection and style shifting for an entire community? And is it the case that speakers are free to choose from among an unlimited set of personal identities during the course of their daily communicative interactions? Or, as seems more intuitively satisfying, do we want to maintain that each speaker has a single coherent identity that underpins her or his choice of stylistic varieties (e.g. Bell 2001: 164–5)?

Further, there is the question of whether we can gain a complete view of stylistic variation by focusing solely on individual speakers and highly creative style shifts. Even if intra-speaker variation is largely an individualistic phenomenon, it is necessarily interconnected with inter-speaker variation, since we must use language features and styles that are socially meaningful in some way if we hope to make certain meanings as we shape our individual speech. For example, although we may shift into more standard speech than usual in order to project a highly authoritative individual identity, the authoritative connotations that our highly standard speech carries almost certainly derive from the fact that those with the most authority typically speak standard language varieties, particularly in the formal types of situations where authority is most directly exercised. The fact that stylistic meaning is grounded in social meaning is directly reflected in the quantitative patterning of stylistic variation *vis-à-vis* social class variation, as discussed above: The amount of variation in a given feature across different speech styles is almost always less than the amount of variation in this feature across speakers of different social groups. At the same time, though, stylistic variation works to shape social meaning, and people create new social associations for features through their creative use of these features in different speech styles. Because stylistic variation both reflects and creates social meaning, it seems best studied through a variety of approaches, including quantitative studies of broad correlations between different stylistic contexts and usage levels for particular language features and more qualitatively oriented investigations of the range of factors that contribute to stylistic variation in unfolding interaction (e.g. Bell 2001; Rickford 2001). For example, Eckert (2000) conducts her in-depth investigation of how teenagers in one high school use language features to shape group and individual styles against the backdrop of the broad patterns of language variation that characterize the dialect region in which the high school is situated. Further, her detailed linguistic study is complemented by an in-depth ethnographic study of the practices and meanings that characterize the particular high school she studies, as well as US high schools in general.

Finally, in gaining a full understanding of intra-speaker variation, it is important to focus more attention on what speakers themselves perceive as "style" (e.g. Coupland 1980; Giles 2001). For example, it is unclear whether speakers consider a certain style to be formal because it is characterized by a low percentage of informal variants, such as *-in'* for *-ing* (e.g. *swimmin'* for *swimming*) or for some other reason, such as a relatively flat intonational contour. Similarly, we do not really know exactly how many variants or other features need to cluster together – and how overtly noticeable these features need to be – in order for speakers to view a given speech variety as a separate style or register. The search for the answers to these types of questions is already yielding intriguing findings, and it is certain to add greatly to our ever-increasing understanding of the linguistic, social, and psychological underpinnings of stylistic variation.

9.6 Further Reading

Bell, Allan (1984) Language style as audience design. *Language in Society* 13: 145–204. This article is one of the most comprehensive attempts to explain the dynamics of style shifting. As indicated in the title, Bell's approach gives primacy to the speaker's audience in its account of stylistic variation.

Eckert, Penelope (2000) *Linguistic Variation as Social Practice.* Oxford: Blackwell. This book is essential reading for anyone interested in current approaches to quantitative sociolinguistics, including, crucially, the intersection of quantitative and qualitative approaches. It is recommended as further reading in several of our chapters for its in-depth exploration of the interrelation between language variation, social group, and social practice, as well as the relation between intra- and inter-speaker variation and between stylistic variation and language change. Eckert presents her analyses of these broad topics against the backdrop of her sociolinguistic/ethnographic study of a suburban Detroit-area high school.

Eckert, Penelope, and John R. Rickford (eds.) (2001) *Style and Sociolinguistic Variation.* Cambridge/New York: Cambridge University Press. This edited collection brings together state-of-the-art investigations of stylistic variation by a number of experts from a variety of perspectives, including anthropological and social psychological perspectives, in addition to the range of sociolinguistic approaches outlined above. Readers are referred in particular to Nikolas Coupland's chapter titled "Language, situation, and the relational self: theorizing dialect-style in sociolinguistics" for in-depth discussion of "speaker design" approaches to stylistic variation.

Labov, William (1972b) *Sociolinguistic Patterns.* Philadelphia: University of Pennsylvania Press. Chapter 2 in this collection describes a classic department store experiment carried out in New York City in which "casual" stylistic responses are contrasted with "emphatic" ones. It is worth reading for the ingenuity of the field technique. Chapter 3 reports one of the earliest attempts to incorporate stylistic variation into the study of social dialectology. The approach to stylistic variation set forth in this chapter has heavily influenced quantitative sociolinguistic approaches to stylistic variation, although researchers now typically use more comprehensive approaches.

Rampton, Ben (1995) *Crossing: Language and Ethnicity among Adolescents.* London: Longman. In this work, Rampton presents the first in-depth study of "crossing," or the use of language varieties other than one's "own." Rampton explores various purposes for, and effects of, crossing, including establishing identity with another cultural group or redefining boundaries between cultural groups. In addition, he demonstrates that crossing may have important implications for the study of second-language learning, language change in multi-ethnic communities, and language change in general. Crossing is further explored in depth in a special issue of the *Journal of Sociolinguistics* (volume 3.4, 1999) guest-edited by Rampton, titled *Styling the Other.*

Rickford, John R., and Faye McNair-Knox (1994) Addressee- and topic-influenced style shift: a quantitative sociolinguistic study. In Douglas Biber and Edward Finegan (eds.), *Sociolinguistic Perspectives on Register.* New York: Oxford University Press, 235–76. The authors of this article conduct a thorough and thoughtful investigation of variation in the speech of an individual speaker of African American English according to addressee, topic, and other factors, in order to test the predictions of Bell's audience design approach to stylistic variation. The authors are also careful to investigate linguistic as well as possible social constraints on variation, in order to determine when the speaker's patterns of variation are indeed due to social factors and when they are simply a by-product of the linguistic factors that affect variation (see chapter 2).

Schilling-Estes, Natalie (1998) Investigating "self-conscious" speech: The performance register in Ocracoke English. *Language in Society* 27: 53–83. This article
examines performance speech in the Outer Banks island community of Ocracoke,
North Carolina. In particular, it provides an in-depth look at the speech performances of one islander from the perspectives of acoustic phonetics, quantitative
sociolinguistics, and discourse analysis.

10

On the Applications of Dialect Study

10.1 Applied Dialectology

Although the study of dialects is fascinating in its own right, many people still ask a basic utilitarian question: "What good is all this information about dialects anyhow?" Educators, for example, may want to know what value such information has in teaching basic educational skills, or parents may want to know how this information is relevant to their children's development. Further, political leaders often want to know how issues of linguistic diversity bear on fundamental issues related to a nation's social and political welfare.

The relatively short history of social dialectology has shown that it is quite possible to combine a commitment to the objective description of sociolinguistic data and a concern for social issues relating to dialect. According to William Labov (1982), there are two primary principles that may motivate linguists to take social action, namely, the PRINCIPLE OF ERROR CORRECTION and the PRINCIPLE OF DEBT INCURRED. These are articulated as follows:

Principle of error correction
A scientist who becomes aware of a widespread idea or social practice with important consequences that is invalidated by his [*sic*] own data is obligated to bring this error to the attention of the widest possible audience. (Labov 1982: 172)

Principle of debt incurred
An investigator who has obtained linguistic data from members of a speech community has an obligation to use the knowledge based on that data for the benefit of the community, when it has need of it. (Labov 1982: 173)

There are several outstanding instances in the history of social dialectology where these principles have been applied. In the 1960s, sociolinguists in the United States took a strong pro-difference stance in the so-called DEFICIT–DIFFERENCE CONTROVERSY that was taking place within education and within speech and language pathology (Baratz 1968; Labov 1969). Consonant with the principle of error correction, sociolinguists took a united stand against the classification and treatment of normal, natural dialect differences as language deficits or disorders. Sociolinguists led the way in pushing for a dialect-sensitive definition of normal language development, although the practical consequences of this definition are still being worked out in many clinical and educational settings (Wolfram, Christian, and Adger 1999).

In keeping with the principle of debt incurred, social dialectologists also rose to the occasion in a legal case referred to as the *Ann Arbor Decision* (1979). Linguistic testimony was critical to the judge's ruling in favor of the African American children who brought suit against the Ann Arbor, Michigan, Board of Education for not taking their dialect into account in reading instruction. In effect, the judge ruled that the defendants had failed to take appropriate action to overcome language barriers, in violation of federal anti-discrimination laws. In compliance with the judge's ruling, a series of workshops was conducted to upgrade awareness about language variation and to demonstrate how to apply sociolinguistic expertise in reading instruction.

Linguists were also quite active in their support of the resolution by the Oakland Unified School District Board of Education in 1996 and 1997, affirming the legitimacy of African American English as a language system. Linguists attempted to explain to the American public why such a resolution was appropriate and even testified on behalf of the Oakland School Board at a US Senate subcommittee hearing on the status of this variety and its role in education.

Linguists have also been active in recent cases of LINGUISTIC PROFILING, in which speakers identified as African American or Latino on the basis of their telephone voice were subjected to discrimination. Linguist John Baugh (2003) of Stanford University, for example, has been involved in several highly publicized legal cases in which speakers identified as African American over the telephone were informed that apartment vacancies were already filled while European American callers were invited to visit the advertised vacancies. Such cases show that there is ample opportunity for sociolinguists to combine their objective examination of language variation with a social commitment to apply their knowledge to fundamental social and educational problems.

There is another level of social commitment that sociolinguistic investigators might strive for with respect to the communities where they conduct their dialect research. This level is more proactive, in that it involves active pursuit of ways to return linguistic favors to the community. It is articulated in the PRINCIPLE OF LINGUISTIC GRATUITY (Wolfram 1993a: 227).

Principle of linguistic gratuity
Investigators who have obtained linguistic data from members of a speech community should actively pursue positive ways in which they can return linguistic favors to the community.

Collaborative partnerships with communities may range from volunteer service in community organizations to the production of language-related products on behalf of the community.

In this and the final chapter, we will take up several different areas of APPLIED DIALECTOLOGY. First, we examine the issue of dialect diversity and language assessment, one of the most critical areas for the application of dialect knowledge. Then we examine the issue of teaching standard English, a persistent concern raised by educators when confronted with dialect diversity. In the final chapter, we consider the application of information about dialects to language arts, including reading and the representation of dialects in literature. We discuss the impact of dialects not only upon the development of particular skills such as reading and writing, but also in terms of collaborative dialect awareness programs that focus on promoting an understanding of and appreciation for language variation on a local level and beyond.

10.2   Dialects and Testing

The importance that mainstream American society places upon testing is fairly obvious; in fact, standardized testing probably could be added to the small list of inevitable obligations in our society, such as paying taxes. Many standardized tests attempt to measure students' knowledge of language directly, but language issues with respect to testing extend considerably beyond test items focused on language *per se*. The language in which directions are given, the language register used to measure knowledge in other content areas, and even the language used in interactions between test administrators and test takers raise sociolinguistic issues regardless of the subject area. No area of testing is really free of language-based concerns.

A sociolinguistic perspective may be applied to three critical dimensions of testing: (1) the definition of "correctness," or the normative linguistic behavior that serves as a basis for evaluating responses to test items; (2) the way in which language is used as a medium to measure different kinds of knowledge and skills; and (3) the sociolinguistic situation or context in which testing takes place. The first area involves an understanding of dialect differences since standardized tests use norms taken from some dialect of English, usually the standard dialect. The second area more typically involves an understanding of specialized language uses in testing, since language is necessarily used to convey instructions and provide responses. The third area involves more broadly based issues of language socialization and underlying values about language use. All three dimensions may play a significant role in students' overall test performance, although notions of "correct" vs. "incorrect" structural forms tend to be the most transparent in considering dialect differences and testing.

The definition of "correct," or normative, responses is essential to success in most types of standardized tests. In some cases, definitions of linguistic correctness are based upon response data collected from sample populations used to standardize testing instruments – traditionally middle-class majority populations who use a variety of standard English. In other cases, the definition of correctness is not based on data obtained from sample populations at all, but is based instead upon the opinions of pre-scriptive language authorities who determine what the ideal standard form is to be – usually formal standard English as discussed in chapter 1. There is considerable latitude in classifying "incorrect" responses, but the traditional notion of correctness used in standardized testing instruments is often restricted to items characterizing a standard dialect in its real or ideal state.

10.2.1 Language achievement

One of the clearest examples of the impact of dialect differences on stand-ardized test instruments comes from the kinds of achievement tests given to students at regular intervals in their educational progress. For example, consider how the notion of incorrectness is defined in several examples taken from the "Language Use" section of an achievement test. The examples in this case come from a disclosed version (that is, a test no longer in use and in the public domain) of the *California Achievement Test* given to third-graders. The directions for choosing a response instruct the student simply to identify the item in the brackets that "you think is correct."

(1) Beth $\left\{ \begin{array}{c} \text{come} \\ \underline{\quad} \\ \text{came} \end{array} \right\}$ home and cried.

(2) Can you $\left\{ \begin{array}{c} \text{went} \\ \underline{\quad} \\ \text{go} \end{array} \right\}$ out now?

$$(3) \quad \text{When} \begin{Bmatrix} \text{can} \\ \\ \text{may} \end{Bmatrix} \text{I come again?}$$

In each of these three cases, the "correct" form is the standard English form. The incorrect choice, or "distractor," may involve several different kinds of responses. In question (1), the choice is between a standard dialect variant and a vernacular dialect variant. The use of the "bare root form" *come* as an irregular past tense form is quite common in a number of vernacular dialects (e.g. *Beth come home and cried*), whereas *came* is the standard dialect past tense form. In this sentence, incorrect is simply defined as a vernacular dialect form.

In sentence (2), the choice is between a form which is acceptable in both standard and vernacular dialects and one that is also unacceptable in both standard and vernacular varieties. In other words, *Can you go out now?* is a well-formed standard and vernacular dialect form and *Can you went out now?* is unacceptable in both varieties as well. In this case, the option is between a linguistically well-formed, or GRAMMATICAL, sentence and a linguistically ill-formed, or UNGRAMMATICAL, sentence, regardless of the dialect.

The differentiation between a correct and incorrect response in sentence (3), unlike (1) and (2), seizes upon the distinction between a formal, pre-scriptive standard variant and an informal standard one. In informal spoken standard English, most speakers would say *When can I come again?* since present-day English uses the modal *can* to refer to both capability and per-missibility. In the case of sentence (3), the contrast is therefore between an ideal, conservative form (*may*) and an informal spoken standard English form (*can*).

What do these different notions of correctness and incorrectness mean for speakers of different dialects, in particular, for speakers of vernacular vs. standard dialects? For sentence (1), vernacular speakers relying on unconscious knowledge, or LINGUISTIC INTUITIONS, of their language rules may choose the "incorrect" response, whereas a standard speaker relying on this same type of knowledge would make the "correct" selection. In this regard, an awareness of the rules of vernacular dialects, such as those found in the Appendix, can help us understand why vernacular speakers might systematically select "incorrect" answers. In order to make the "correct" choice for this sentence, the vernacular speaker must make a counter-intuitive linguistic choice and select a socially acceptable structure instead of a linguistically well-formed vernacular structure. In this respect, we see that there may be very different tasks involved in responding to this item for a native vernacular dialect speaker and a native standard English speaker. Perhaps more importantly, the confusion between linguistic acceptability and social acceptability brings us back to the erroneous assumption about vernacular dialects widely held in some educational circles: Forms that do not agree with the rules of standard English violate fundamental rules of linguistic well-formedness – that is, they are "ungrammatical." We see that this myth about the nature of dialect differences, discussed originally in chapter 1, has worked its way into the institutionalized definition of correctness built into standardized language achievement tests.

For sentence (2), reliance upon knowledge of language rules should result in a correct response for both the vernacular and standard speaker, other things being equal, since the incorrect item is linguistically ungrammatical across dialects. For sentence (3), however, reliance upon such knowledge would lead to an incorrect response by both a vernacular and a standard speaker, since the item involves a prescribed formal structure which is not a regular part of informal standard or vernacular varieties. In this case, both standard and vernacular test takers would have to resort to explicitly learned knowledge about formal standard English to obtain the correct response.

A survey of representative language achievement tests given to students in early schooling shows that many of the test items focus on the first notion of correctness – the simple distinction between vernacular and standard dialect forms. In the *California Achievement Test* from which the examples above were taken, 14 out of 25 total sentences in the section titled "Language Usage" focus exclusively on this distinction. The distinction between formal and informal standard (sentence (3) above) is not as critical in early achievement testing, but it becomes much more prominent as students proceed to the higher levels of education; for example, it is rampant in tests such as the *Scholastic Aptitude Test*.

Exercise 1

The following are some additional items from an achievement test. Identify the focus of each item in terms of the three dimensions of correctness discussed above: (1) standard vs. vernacular sentence structure, (2) grammatical vs. ungrammatical structure regardless of dialect, and (3) formal standard English vs. informal standard English sentence structure.

1   My sister $\left\{ \begin{array}{c} am \\ is \end{array} \right\}$ six years old.

2   She will give me $\left\{ \begin{array}{c} them \\ these \end{array} \right\}$ dolls.

3 I $\begin{Bmatrix} \text{shall} \\ \\ \text{will} \end{Bmatrix}$ go there tomorrow.

4 I $\begin{Bmatrix} \text{am} \\ \\ \text{are} \end{Bmatrix}$ a good pupil.

5 There $\begin{Bmatrix} \text{was} \\ \\ \text{were} \end{Bmatrix}$ no ducks on the lake.

6 Is George going to eat with $\begin{Bmatrix} \text{us} \\ \\ \text{we} \end{Bmatrix}$?

7 Father and $\begin{Bmatrix} \text{they} \\ \\ \text{them} \end{Bmatrix}$ are going on a trip.

The examination of standardized language achievement tests clearly shows that such tests are often heavily weighted toward the recognition of standard English forms. Assessing whether or not a student can recognize standard English is not, in itself, an issue, especially if an educational system incorporates the systematic introduction of the standard dialect into its educational curriculum. It is, however, problematic as an overall measure of "achievement," since it may measure different things for different groups of speakers. For a standard speaker, an achievement test may measure what the student, for the most part, already brings to school from the home community – inner language knowledge of the standard dialect. For a student from a vernacular dialect introduced to the standard dialect, it actually may measure an aspect of achievement – the ability to recognize standard English forms after the student has been introduced to them in the classroom. The underlying problem, then, is in the comparison of standard and vernacular speakers as if both groups started from the same linguistic baseline.

One of the recurring questions about language tests of all types is the matter of CONTENT VALIDITY: Does the testing instrument measure the content area it claims to measure? As we have seen, a test might measure quite different language capabilities for different dialect groups. Thus, vernacular speakers who have learned to recognize some forms in the standard dialect may have made significant educational progress yet still score well below standard English speakers who get credit for achievement when they are simply resorting to language knowledge they brought to school to begin with. Those who construct such tests and those who interpret the scores of these tests must be careful to determine what the test actually measures in relation to what it claims to measure, particularly since "language usage" tests so often emphasize the standard–vernacular distinction.

10.2.2   *Speech and language development tests*

As children develop, they are routinely assessed in a number of areas of behavior, including language. The purpose of such testing is fairly straightforward – to determine if children are acquiring their language at a normal rate of development. All children in the US are screened for language development before entering public school for the first time, and, on that basis, they are recommended for more extensive diagnosis and subsequent classification as "normal" or "disordered." If they are judged as disordered, they are typically enrolled in a speech and language therapy program, so that the consequences of the diagnostic procedure can be quite significant. Because of such wide-scale assessment of children, many formal standardized test instruments have been developed to measure the normalcy of linguistic development. Unfortunately, the definition of normal development traditionally has been based upon the norms of the standard English-speaking population, as middle-class samples of children typically have been used to arrive at developmental norms.

Defining normative responses exclusively in terms of standard English structures holds considerable potential for DIALECT DISCRIMINATION, where a normative response in a vernacular English dialect is erroneously classified as an unacquired standard English form. For example, various popular tests of language development (e.g. the *Clinical Evaluation of Language Fundamentals-Revised* [*CELF-R*], and the *Test of Language Development* [*TOLD*]) use a type of sentence-completion task called "grammatic closure" to determine children's mastery of English morphology. In this assessment procedure, the examiner points to appropriate pictures while reading a statement, stopping at the point where the child is to fill in the missing word(s). For example, the child may be shown two pictures, one with one bed and another with two beds, while the examiner says, "Here is a bed, and here are two _____." The child then completes the utterance, with a correct response in this case considered to be the plural form *beds*. In scoring the test according to the procedures set forth in most test manuals, standard English forms are considered as "correct" responses. Many of the items inadvertently focus on differences between standard and vernacular dialect forms. For example, if vernacular-speaking children are given a stimulus such as "This is a foot. Here are two _____," they might legitimately respond *foots* or *feets*, applying a regularization process that characterizes their dialect. However, since the scoring only recognizes *feet* as a correct response, the authentic dialect response would be considered incorrect. Similarly, given a stimulus such as "The boy is opening the gate. The gate has been _____," speakers who respond with *open* rather than *opened* because of the application of the consonant cluster reduction process discussed in chapter 3 would be penalized despite their use of a dialect-appropriate form. As with the achievement tests discussed above, an understanding of dialect differences reveals that many of the forms scored as "incorrect" constitute linguistically well-formed structures in terms of vernacular dialect norms.

Exercise 2

Below are five more items from a grammatic closure subtest. Based upon the kinds of dialect rules found in the appendix, predict which of these items might have legitimate dialect alternates. What are the variant dialect forms? Refer to the dialect rules in the Appendix in your responses. In each case, the response(s) considered correct according to the test manual is (are) given in italics.

Item 9. The boy is writing something. This is what he *wrote/has written/did write*.

Item 15. This horse is not big. This horse is big. This horse is *bigger*.

Item 19. This is soap, and these are *soap/bars of soap/more soap*.

Item 22. Here is a foot. Here are two *feet*.

Item 29. The boy has two bananas. He gave one away and he kept one for *himself*.

In some cases, the effects of imposing standard norms of development on vernacular speakers can be quite severe. For example, in the case of one grammatic closure subtest, over 20 of the 33 items have legitimate dialect variants. If the test is scored at face value, a normally developing child who uses dialect variants where possible would look like a linguistically delayed standard English speaker. A normally developing ten-year-old vernacular speaker may, in fact, be assessed as having the linguistic development of a child less than five years of age. On the basis of such a discrepancy between chronological and mental age, vernacular-speaking children commonly have been enrolled in therapy, even though they are developing quite normally in terms of their community dialect. The stakes for the assessment of children's language development can be quite severe if legitimate dialect differences are not recognized for language development tests. Fortunately, more speech and language development tests now include alternative response forms so that vernacular speakers can be given credit for forms that are dialectally appropriate, thanks to the application of findings from dialect studies. And there are now even a couple of tests that are specifically designed to test normal language development in terms of vernacular norms. Nonetheless, on a practical level there has been some resistance to an informed socio-linguistic perspective on testing and the consideration of dialect variants as "correct" responses. Change is taking place, but not quite as fast as most applied sociolinguists would like to see it proceed.

10.2.3   Predicting dialect interference

The type of language analysis typically used to determine the specific impact of dialect diversity on the assessment of language development is called CONTRASTIVE LINGUISTICS. In its simplest version, contrastive linguistics places the rules of language variety X and language variety Y side by side and, on the basis of comparing similarities and differences in the systems, highlights areas of potential conflict for a speaker of X confronted with the norms of Y. This is the procedure we employed above when we compared the correct responses of a test normed on standard English speakers with the rules of vernacular varieties and determined where alternate responses might be expected due to differences between systems. Over the past two decades, a number of major language assessment instruments have been examined from this perspective. However, it is necessary to balance ideal-ized predictions of dialect interference with actual studies of speakers' per-formance. In ERROR ANALYSIS, which is based on the analysis of actual rather than idealized performance, some of the predicted structures show up much more frequently than others. Furthermore, there are some "incorrect" responses that may be attributed to dialect differences in an indirect way. And there may be items that turn up that are not predictable based upon a simple side-by-side comparison of language varieties.

There are a couple of reasons why not all predicted dialect variants may occur in the assessment procedure. Many of the predicted dialect alternates may be variable structures rather than categorical ones, as discussed in chapter 3. For example, we might predict plural -s absence for AAE speakers in a formal test, but vernacular speakers typically show plural absence levels of only 10 to 20 percent when actual levels of absence are tabulated in relation to those cases where a plural form might be absent. Certainly, we would expect this inherent variability to have an effect on test responses; presumably, a low-frequency dialect item will have a lower probability of occurring than a high-frequency one. It is also possible that the formality of the testing situation may bring forth responses not directly predictable, as speakers may shift away from their native forms in erratic ways. For example, test takers sensitive to the social stigmatization of a vernacular verb agreement pattern such as *We was there* might compensate by extending *were* usage beyond its specified limits, thus using constructions such as *I were there* in a testing situation even though they would not use such structures in everyday speech. For most American dialects, *I were* follows neither standard nor vernacular dialect rules; US vernacular dialects typically level to *was* for both *was* and *were*, not to *were* for *was* and *were*. This is a case of hypercorrection, as discussed in chapter 9, most likely due to the formality of the testing situation. Indirectly, we may attribute this usage to the vernacular dialect, but not as a case of simple transfer of a vernacular dialect form to the standard dialect.

Although all predicted dialect forms will not occur in an actual test, studies of the incidence of dialect forms in relation to predicted forms indicate that these dialect variants may still account for a significant portion of "incorrect" responses.

10.3   Testing Language

The concern for dialect differences in language testing actually raises deeper questions about the conventional tests used to assess language capability. Most standardized language assessment instruments focus on restricted domains or levels of language, raising the question of content validity mentioned earlier. In the case of tests constructed to assess language development, we may ask if the selective language capability measured by the instrument adequately represents the language content it proposes to measure. For example, consider how a traditional assessment instrument like the *Peabody Picture Vocabulary Test* (*PPVT*) measures a particular aspect of "word knowledge." In the *PPVT*, "knowing a word" is defined by the test taker's ability to associate a word label given by a test examiner with a picture of the object or activity, given a multiple choice of pictures (e.g. "Show me *toboggan*"). This notion of word knowledge involves a passive recognition task limited to items that are sometimes culturally specific and dialectally restricted. From a broader linguistic perspective, however, knowing a word involves at least the following: (1) syntactic constraints – how to use the word in phrases and sentences; (2) semantic constraints – knowing appropriate ideas conveyed by the word and how the word relates to associated ideas; (3) stylistic constraints – knowing appropriate settings and styles of speaking for using the item; (4) morphological information – knowing what words the item is related to and how it attaches to other forms; (5) pragmatic constraints – for example, knowing what the word presupposes and implies; and (6) phonological information – knowing how the word is pronounced.

Compared to the expansive linguistic nature of word knowledge, the *PPVT* measures a very restricted aspect of knowledge.

Many language assessment instruments focus on the more superficial aspects of language rather than the underlying categories and relationships that constitute the deeper basis of language organization. Word inflections (e.g. plural suffixes, possessive suffixes) and more superficial grammatical structures (e.g. the *be* copula, negative indefinite forms) are often examined rather than the deeper conceptual basis of language capability such as the underlying categories of negation, possession, and identity. The limitations of traditional tests in this regard raise concerns about using such instruments for any speaker, but their impact is even more significant given the ways in which the dialects of English typically differ from each other. Most comparisons of vernacular and standard varieties of English indicate that the majority of differences are found on the more superficial levels of language organization. The deeper the language level, the more similar the different dialects of English tend to be. We therefore may offer the following hypothesis about language testing and dialect differences:

> The more superficial and limited the scope of language capability tapped in a testing instrument, the greater the likelihood that the instrument will be inappropriate for speakers beyond the immediate population upon which it was normed.

This hypothesis has important implications for vernacular dialect speakers, who are often not represented adequately in norming samples. Though some research on more universally applicable language tests is taking place, it is still in its incipient stage.

10.3.1 Using language to access information

Although differences in linguistic form are the most obvious dimension of dialect differentiation in standardized testing, dialect differences also come into play when subject areas other than language itself are being examined. All tests are replete with language-based tasks that range from interpreting test directions to determining appropriate strategies for arriving at correct responses. Since language is used as a medium for providing and tapping data in a broad range of content areas, sociolinguistic differences may therefore affect the results of tests which, at first glance, have very little to do with language.

Test directions call for the establishment of a common frame of reference for test takers. Obviously, the desired goal of directions is clarity – the unambiguous understanding of what activity is to be performed by all test takers. It cannot be assumed, however, that all test takers interpret directions in the same way, despite the fact that methods of standardization can sometimes be quite elaborate. Even the most "simple" and "obvious" directions may be laden with the potential for misinterpretation. This misinterpretation may involve a particular item or the overall format in which directions are presented. For example, our observation of a simple instruction to "repeat" a sentence shows the word *repeat* to have different possible interpretations. In some communities, we have found that this simple direction may be interpreted as a paraphrasing task rather than a verbatim repetition task. We found that some children embellish stimulus sentences such as *The car is in the garage* by paraphrasing it, so that the original sentence might be rendered as *That little bitty car just sitting in the garage*. Children are attempting to succeed at the task, but their creative paraphrase in this instance only leads to reduced scores, since tests are based on the assumption that "repeat" is to be interpreted as verbatim repetition.

There are many ways of testing students' skill and knowledge levels, and most standardized tests rely upon special language uses to access the desired information. In fact, close scrutiny of the language of testing suggests that there is a special language register that guides those who write test items. In part, the language of test taking is based on a version of formal written language, but it is often more than that. For example, a "question" may be defined as an incomplete declarative statement, as in the following: "To prevent scum from forming in a partly used can of paint, one should _____" (from *Arco's Practice for the Armed Forces Tests* 1973: 23). In addition to the specialized definition of a question as a completion task, the impersonal pronoun *one* and the infinitive at the beginning of the sentence set apart this sentence from everyday language usage. Note how this sentence differs from a common everyday question such as "What do you do if you want to keep scum [i.e. *skin* in some dialects] from forming in a can of paint that's been opened?"

Exercise 3

Consider the following questions, taken from previous versions of training manuals for the Armed Forces Vocational Aptitude Battery and the *Scholastic Aptitude Test*. First translate these items into ordinary spoken language style. Compare your spoken language version with the formal test version of the question and note the kinds of differences between the two types of language use. What differences may be attributable to the conventional distinction between spoken and written language and what usage patterns seem peculiar to the way language is used in test questions?

1 When measuring an unknown voltage with a voltmeter, the proper precaution to take is to start with the . . .
2 When a certain pitcher contains three cups of water, the pitcher contains half its capacity.
3 It can be inferred from the passage that all of the following are characteristic of the author's grandmother EXCEPT . . .
4 Unlike a patient with Wernicke's aphasia, a patient with Broca's aphasia can do which of the following?

In some cases, the language register of testing may even use sentence structures that are "ungrammatical" in ordinary language use. For example, the specialized use of verb + *-ing* forms in a frame such as "*Show me digging!*" (from the *Peabody Picture Vocabulary Test*) is not a grammatical sentence in spoken or written standard English. In its grammatical form, this sentence would have to be formed something like "*Show me [a picture of] somebody [who is] digging!*" Examples of unique formats for asking questions accumulate fairly rapidly when actual language usage in formal testing instruments is examined.

Along with the specialized registers of language used in testing, it is important to understand that many tests rely upon particular METALINGUISTIC TASKS, that is, special ways of organizing and talking about language apart from its ordinary uses for communication. These peculiar ways of using and referring to language may be critical to obtaining the relevant data for measurement. For example, it may be necessary for test takers to complete metalinguistic tasks involving word replaceability and opposition (i.e. selecting the correct antonym) in order to access their mastery of word knowledge. There is certainly ample indication that all individuals can give approximate definitions or uses of words, but this does not necessarily involve word replaceability or opposition. In natural language use, words are more likely to be defined through examples in which the words are used appropriately. In addition, notions such as synonymy (sameness) and antonymy (opposition) may be interpreted in several different ways in natural language use even though they are considered to have only one "correct" interpretation in the testing situation. Thus, antonymy may legitimately be interpreted as "very different from" rather than "in direct opposition to," so that *tall* and *far* might be considered opposites just as readily as *tall* and *short*.

In a similar way, the special use of rhyming or minimal word pairs (i.e. where the words sound alike except for one sound difference, such as *pit* and *pet*) to tap a person's ability to decode letters in reading or spelling involves skills that have little or nothing to do with decoding *per se*. Yet, it is common for reading and spelling tests in the early grades to use such tasks to measure decoding capability, as in "Find the word that rhymes with *sad*" or "Find the word that sounds the same as *too*." Minimal word pairs and rhymes, of course, may be different across dialects. We have already seen that *pin* and *pen* are homophonous rather than a minimal word pair in Southern dialects; *fine* and *mind* rhyme in some dialects; and in the native Philadelphia dialect of the first author, *bad* rhymes with *mad*, but not with *sad*. The particular metalinguistic tasks used to determine decoding capability may turn out to be just as significant, and, in some cases, a more significant stumbling block in testing than transparent structural dialect differences, although the effects of the former may be more subtle and indirect than the effects of the latter.

10.3.2 The testing situation

Although the consideration of broad-based social situations might seem somewhat removed from the discussion of dialect structures in testing, we must remember that dialects are ultimately embedded in sociocultural differences. Tests do not take place in a contextually neutral social setting, although many tests implicitly make this assumption, or at least assume that it is possible to control the social situation so tightly that unwanted background factors do not influence performance in a significant way.

Testing calls for the test taker to enter the experimental frame created by the test constructor and administrator. If the test taker is unable or unwilling to "play the experimental game," the measurements resulting from the test cannot be valid. Test takers bring with them values and assumptions about language use, and different cultural orientations yield differences in language use in the test situation. For example, language usage may be guided by the status relationship between the test administrator and test taker. One ethnographic study of a rural African American Southern community concludes that "experience in interacting with adults has taught him [i.e. the child] the values of silence and withdrawal" (Ward 1971: 88), values commonly expressed in the working-class dictum that "children should be seen and not heard." This cultural orientation toward language interaction with adults may influence how a child responds to an adult administrator; it may also determine a child's willingness to ask questions about directions when confused. Culturally determined responses and interactional patterns may ultimately end up affecting test scores, although such influences are considerably more difficult to pin down specifically than are structural dialect differences. Regardless of the pervasive influence of culturally determined language-use patterns, the experimental frame of testing may assume, and indeed demand, that participants divorce themselves from cultural orientations about status relationships, interactional norms, and the role of language use just for the sake of the test.

Labov (1976) has pointed out that some of the most innocuous-appearing procedures for eliciting data (for example, eliciting spontaneous conversation) may be fraught with sociolinguistic values. For example, a friendly invitation by an adult to a child to "tell me everything you can about the fire engine on the table" is laden with values about verbosity (the more you tell the better), obvious information (describe the object even though you know the adult knows all about it), and consequences about information sharing (what a child tells the adult will not be held against the child). Values about language use, however, are particularly difficult to change merely for the purpose of entering an experimental frame. For example, Shirley Brice Heath (1983) reports that "labeling" obvious information, objects, and activities (e.g. responding to questions such as "What is this?" or "What are they doing?" when the questioner already knows the answer) is a sociolinguistic routine quite common in some communities but not in others. Thus, speakers from different communities might relate to this common "teacher routine," sometimes used in informal language assessment procedures, in quite different ways.

Exercise 4

The following are some hints for taking a test, found in a US Department of Labor guide on tests. Examine these hints in terms of the social situation surrounding the testing environment. What kinds of social factors might affect the outcome of the test? What do these factors have to do with the capability being tapped in a test? Do any of the hints involve underlying assumptions about language?

1 Get ready for the test by taking other tests on your own.
2 Don't let the thought of taking a test throw you, but being a little nervous won't hurt you.
3 Arrive early, rested, and prepared to take the test.
4 Ask questions until you understand what you are supposed to do.
5 Some parts of the test may be easier than others. Don't let the hard parts keep you from doing well on the easier parts.
6 Keep time limits in mind when you take a test.
7 Don't be afraid to answer when you aren't sure you are right, but don't guess wildly.
8 Work as fast as you can but try not to make mistakes. Some tests have short time limits.

10.3.3   The language diagnostician

Specialists such as speech and language pathologists and English/language arts teachers often have little alternative but to assess the language capabilities of their clients or students. How can these professionals arrive at an authentic picture of the language of those who do not come from standard English-speaking communities? The answer to this question involves acquiring a knowledge base founded in descriptive sociolinguistics and applying this information to diagnostic procedures in a practical way. As a starting point, such professionals must *know the descriptive linguistic characteristics of the local communities they serve.* A language specialist in Southern rural Appalachia must know the linguistic structures characterizing this community, just as a language specialist in a Northern African American urban context should know the dialect characteristics of this community. While descriptive sociolinguistic profiles of different communities are certainly not complete, there are now a number of dialect overviews available to specialists. In most cases, however, these general descriptions still need to be supplemented by active observation of the sociolinguistic particulars of local communities. The serious language diagnostician really needs to observe community language behavior as well as to read available sociolinguistic profiles.

In cases where the selection of formal test instruments is outside the diagnostician's control, there is a need to bring sociolinguistic information to bear on subjects' responses. More than once, specialists have bemoaned the fact that they thought a particular language assessment test was unfair to vernacular dialect speakers but that they had no choice but to administer it. In these situations, it is necessary to be able to identify those particular linguistic responses that might be attributable to dialect differences and how these responses might affect the score. Of course, this kind of analysis can only be conducted when item-by-item responses are made available to the language specialist.

Where possible, language specialists should also *experiment with the administration of required standardized tests in a nontraditional, or nonstandardized manner.* A test can be given in standardized format first, then given in a way that might provide the client or student an opportunity to perform at a maximal level. Instructions can be reworded, additional time for responding can be given, and additional props can be used, among other nonstandard administration options. Where possible, it is also important to *ask test takers why particular responses were chosen.* Practitioners who do this may find the explanations quite insightful, often revealing different kinds of sociolinguistic processing. Some "wrong" answers turn out to be quite reasonable when the test taker explains how the answer was obtained.

When tests are given in a nonstandardized manner, this must be reported for the record, so that both a standard and alternative score are included in any report of the test, along with an explanation of how the scores were obtained. Such reports may provide important information on how different sociolinguistic tasks are interfering with the valid interpretation of test results.

In reality, it is not possible to obtain a full picture of language capability on the basis of formalized assessment instruments, since so many of these tests measure limited, superficial aspects of language ability. *Formal measures of language ability must be complemented with assessment strategies more focused on underlying language capabilities in realistic communicative contexts.* In some professions, such as speech and language pathology, there is increasing emphasis on the use of a language sample in assessment. As defined in this discipline, a LANGUAGE SAMPLE consists of data on language collected through natural conversational interviews instead of a technique in which language items are directly elicited. Such interviews are typically conducted by the diagnostician, but there is no reason why they cannot be conducted just as effectively by community members of some type (e.g. parents, peers, or other appropriate members of the community). Using language data from such interviews, those who devise and administer tests should be able to move away from more superficial aspects of language form toward a focus on underlying aspects of the communicative message. As mentioned previously, such an approach is less likely to penalize the vernacular dialect speaker, since the vast majority of structural dialect differences involve the relatively superficial levels of grammar and phonology. In their extensive study of children acquiring AAE, Ida Stockman and Fay Vaughn-Cooke (1986) found very few differences from standard English speakers when the focus is upon underlying semantic content categories and relationships rather than surface grammatical form. For example, whereas the possessive meaning may not be indicated by a surface morpheme (i.e. -'s) in vernacular constructions such as *woman_ dress* ("woman's dress") or *Terry_ hat* ("Terry's hat"), the collocation of nouns certainly indicates the underlying category of "possession" quite adequately. This model neutralizes the effect of dialect in the assessment of language capability. It also provides a baseline for distinguishing those normally developing speakers of vernacular African American English from the small percentage of speakers who are genuinely disordered in their language development in terms of community language norms.

Finally, *it is essential to complement the assessment of language capabilities with ethnographic information about language use in a natural setting.* How is language used in a natural setting with peers, family members, and other community participants? To some extent, such information may be obtained by questioning relevant community participants. Since it is the community that sets norms, the community's perspective on speech may be critical for obtaining a true profile of language capability. But more than simple questioning of community members is involved if a true picture of language is to emerge. There is a sense in which the diagnostician must become an active observer of how language is used in its social settings – in the playground, on the bus, and in the classroom with teachers and other students. How does the student use language to communicate and interact socially? Whereas an ethnographic perspective may take a language diagnostician considerably beyond the clinic or classroom setting, it is imperative to extend the context of language observation if an accurate profile of language capability is to emerge. The insights from direct observation of everyday activities may not be as readily quantifiable as data obtained from standardized formal instruments, but they are invaluable for a true picture of language capability.

10.4   Teaching Standard English

Few people would deny that there are some social and educational advantages in knowing standard English. Nonetheless, the topic of spoken standard English is controversial for a number of reasons. Furthermore, the issue of teaching standard English often serves as a proxy for deeper feelings about educational and cultural diversity. Can a delicate balance between the "appropriate" uses of a vernacular and standard dialect be achieved? What happens when speakers of vernacular dialects must confront the standard variety? Can standard English really be taught effectively in an educational setting, and if so, how? Given the nature of the issues surrounding standard English, it is not surprising that discussions of this topic can become quite heated. In the following discussion, we examine some of the major issues involved in teaching and learning spoken standard English and set forth some of the conditions for successful pedagogy.

10.4.1   What standard?

We already noted in chapter 1 that the notion of standard American English operates on both a formal and informal level. The formal standard is codified, prescriptive, and relatively homogeneous, whereas the informal standard is more subjective, somewhat flexible, and tends to exist on a continuum. It also may be quite regionalized, so that the informal standard English of Seattle, Washington, is quite different from that of Charleston, South Carolina. Obviously, the formal standard is easier to define than the informal one, since we can appeal to established sources such as usage guides and established authorities on the English language. The sphere of usage for the formal standard, however, is relatively restricted and largely confined to writing and specialized public presentations. On the other hand, the notion of an informal standard is more widely applicable, and relevant to the vast majority of everyday language interactions. Furthermore, it is the informal standard, rather than the formal one, that most consistently governs people's everyday evaluation of the social significance of dialect differences.

Given the heterogeneity of spoken standards, we may ask if there is any way we can unify this notion, at least for instructional purposes. In an effort to unify the notion of spoken standard English, the British linguist Peter Strevens, in the article "Standards and the standard language" (1985), separates ACCENT, which refers to features of phonology, from other levels of dialect. He notes that accent is highly localized and variant, whereas other components of a language, particularly grammar, are less localized and less variant in terms of social norms of standardness. Once accent is eliminated from the definition of the standard language, he maintains that there is one standard that may be paired with any local accent. According to this definition, standard English has no local base, and is the "only dialect which is neither localized in its currency nor paired solely with its local accent" (Strevens 1985: 6).

There is certainly some merit to the separation of phonology from other aspects of dialect when talking about standard English, but Strevens's proposal oversimplifies the issue. For one, there are aspects of pronunciation alone that may mark a person as a vernacular speaker, such as the frequent use of *d* for voiced *th*, the stereotypical *dese*, *dem*, and *dose* pattern, and the use of *t* for voiceless *th*, as in *trow* for *throw* or *tink* for *think*. In fact, we have cases where speakers are classified as nonstandard on the basis of phonology alone. By the same token, one locale's normative grammar may sometimes be considered nonstandard in another context. Thus, the use of double modals, as in *You might could do it*, is fairly widespread among native residents of the Carolinas regardless of social class, yet it is considered quite nonstandard in non-Southern contexts. And there are certainly grammatical differences between standard American and standard British English (e.g. American English "the government is . . ." vs. British English "the government are . . ."), so even a rough working definition of standard English based solely on grammatical features would differ somewhat from country to country as well as across different regions of the US. So we see that phonology is not always excluded from the definition of the spoken standard, nor is grammar always generally applicable in judging standards across different regions. On the whole, however, grammar is less flexible than phonology across regional standard varieties, but it is a matter of degree rather than kind.

A couple of terms often used in reference to spoken standard English in the United States are STANDARD AMERICAN ENGLISH (SAE) and NETWORK

STANDARD. The designation SAE is often used to distinguish this variety from other Englishes used throughout the world, such as standard British English (so-called Received Pronunciation, or RP), Australian English, and so forth. It is the variety that is aimed at when teaching American English to speakers of other languages and is the model most often used as the basis for teaching standard forms to vernacular speakers. The Network Standard simply seems to be a concrete example of SAE; it is the model aimed for by TV and radio announcers whose audiences are national in scope, in much the same way that BBC English has traditionally been an instantiation of RP in the British Isles. National network newscasts are probably the prime example of network standards, though, in reality, newscasters show some range in their pronunciation and occasionally their syntax as well.

What exactly do people mean when they refer to SAE and Network Standard? They typically refer to a variety of English devoid of both general and local socially stigmatized features, as well as regionally conspicuous phonological and grammatical features. This, however, does not eliminate dialect choices altogether. We have repeatedly noted that it is impossible to speak English without speaking some dialect of English. In those cases where dialect choices have to be made, the guiding principle calls for the selection of a form that will be least likely to call attention to itself for the majority of speakers outside of the area because of its dialect uniqueness. Items that have distinct regional connotations are therefore to be avoided in striving for SAE. Of course, the determination of what features are least likely to call dialect attention to themselves is somewhat subjective and tends to be a relative rather than absolute matter.

For example, speakers attempting to achieve the SAE pronunciation of the vowel in items like *caught* and *fought* would typically avoid a raised vowel quality (something closer to the [ʊ] of *put*) or a lowered quality (something like the [ɑ] of *father*), since these are likely to be dialectally marked. In actual network announcing, however, the latter pronunciation is apparently becoming more acceptable, as the LOW BACK MERGER of *caught* and *cot* spreads among American dialects. Whatever the case, the choice of the pronunciation is hardly "dialect-free." Given the alternative pronunciations, the [ɑ] pronunciation is now becoming the least likely to call attention to its regionality. In this regard, entire dialect areas may be considered to be more marked than others, so that a widespread regional variety (e.g. Southern, New England) may be singled out as dialects to be avoided in striving for the SAE ideal.

The attempt to "deregionalize" speech to achieve SAE or Network Standard is, of course, easier said than done, and most speakers considered representatives of SAE still retain vestiges of their regional dialect. A simple comparison of nightly news programs will reveal that some network announcers are better than others at disguising their native regional dialect heritage; however, discerning dialectologists can usually still identify traces of regionality in pronunciation and lexical choice. In many cases, those who aspire to acquire this ideal standard have worked very hard to eliminate the most regionally obtrusive features. Manuals of instruction and so-called "accent reduction" training are available to help attain this goal, but in most instances, success in the SAE ideal is a matter of degree.

Contrary to popular opinion, SAE is fairly limited in terms of the occasions and professions that call for its usage; it is also quite restricted in terms of who routinely uses it. On most speaking occasions, REGIONAL STANDARD ENGLISH is more pertinent than SAE, although the notion of regional standards certainly receives much less public attention than SAE. Regional standard English simply refers to the variety implicitly recognized as standard for speakers in a given locale. This variety may contain regional features, particularly in pronunciation and vocabulary, but also some features of grammar and language use. At the same time, the regional standard differs from the regional vernacular in that it avoids socially stigmatized features of English. Most typically, it is associated with middle-class, middle-aged educated native English speakers of the region. In the local context, these speakers would be rated as standard English speakers by community members from different social strata within the community.

In a Southern setting such as Memphis, Tennessee, the regional standard may include a number of Southern regionalisms, such as the lack of contrast between [ɪ] and [ɛ] before nasals in *pin* and *pen*, the monophthongization of /ai/ in *time* or *side*, plural *y'all*, personal dative pronouns, as in *I got me a new outfit*, and so forth. The standard Philadelphia, Pennsylvania, variety would not, of course, have any of these features but might include the local "broad *a*" pronunciation (i.e. [ɛə] or even [ɪə] in items like *bad* and *pass*), the vowel [i] in items such as *att*[i]*tude* vs. *att*[ə]*tude* or *magn*[i]*tude* vs. *magn*[ə]*tude*), positive *anymore* (e.g. *Anymore we watch DVDs rather than go to the movies*), and the absence of the pronoun in personal *with* phrases (e.g. *Are you coming with?*), among other features. In both locales, the standard dialects would share the avoidance of a general set of socially stigmatized features such as multiple negatives and different irregular verbs (e.g. *They seen it, They brang it to the picnic*), and so forth.

Regional standards are not necessarily transferable, so that the standard dialect for Memphis might not be considered standard in the context of Philadelphia, and vice versa. To a large extent, the acceptance of a regional standard outside of its indigenous locale is tied in with attitudes and stereotypical views of the region by speakers from other regions. Thus, the regional standard of Memphis, as a Southern-based dialect, and Philadelphia, located in the New York–Philadelphia dialect corridor, would be considered inappropriate outside of these regions. This follows from the generally held opinion in the US that New York and the South are the regions where the "worst" English is spoken (Preston 1996). The difficulty in transferring regional standards has sometimes concerned educators who wish to teach a standard English, but it is doubtful whether SAE can replace regional standard varieties on a broad scale. One reason for this is that those who strongly influence the perpetuation of language, such as schoolteachers and social and political leaders, tend to model their speech on regional standards rather than SAE. Furthermore, in recent decades, many leaders, including even national leaders such as US presidents, have begun using Southern standard speech norms rather than a more "regionally neutral" variety in their public addresses, and so serve as highly visible role models for students as they learn to use English "well" or "effectively." We will have more to say about the conflict between regional standards and SAE when we discuss the practical considerations for instructional programs in standard English. At this point, it is sufficient to understand the types of standard English relevant to the discussion of spoken language standards in an educational context.

10.4.2   Approaches to standard English

There are basically three different philosophical positions on the teaching of standard English. One position maintains that standard English should be taught as a REPLACIVE DIALECT, supplanting the dialect of vernacular-speaking students. This position, sometimes referred to as ERADICATIONISM, is the one manifested by educators who "correct" the nonstandard dialect forms of their students. Traditionally, much of the motivation for this position has been based on the conviction that vernacular dialects are simply linguistic corruptions of standard English, following the popular mythology we discussed in chapter 1. A more enlightened sociolinguistic viewpoint, however, still might maintain that the realities of present-day American society confer social stigma on speakers of a vernacular dialect in the mainstream linguistic marketplace, so even if a vernacular dialect is linguistically equal, it is socially unequal. Therefore, the vernacular variety should be replaced with the more socially acceptable, mainstream variety.

Another position on teaching standard English maintains that it should be taught as an ADDITIVE DIALECT rather than a replacive one. This position is referred to as BIDIALECTALISM, by analogy with bilingualism, in which two separate languages are maintained. An educational curriculum with this goal is geared toward maintaining both standard and vernacular varieties for use in different social situations. For many community contexts, where the vernacular serves important functions of social solidarity, the vernacular would be available, and for more formal, mainstream marketplace functions, the non-stigmatized standard variety would be available. Like the eradicationist position, the bidialectalist position recognizes the social stigmatization of vernacular dialects, but it rejects the notion that the vernacular dialect is an inferior linguistic system that needs to be replaced. Instead, it advocates the use of two different systems for different purposes within and outside the local community.

A more extreme position rejects the obligation to learn spoken standard English at all, maintaining that both the eradicationist and bidialectalist positions stand too ready to accommodate the dialect prejudices of American society. Rather than focusing on teaching standard English as a replacive or additive dialect, the DIALECT RIGHTS position devotes attention to attacking the underlying ethnocentrism and prejudice that are at the heart of dialect intolerance. In 1974, a subdivision of the nation's largest and most influential organization of English teachers, the National Council of Teachers of English (NCTE), adopted a quite strong position on students' dialect rights, as follows:

> We affirm the students' right to their own patterns and varieties of the language – the dialects of their nurture or whatever dialects in which they find their own identity and style. Language scholars long ago denied that the myth of a standard American dialect has any validity. The claim that any one dialect is unacceptable amounts to an attempt of one social group to exert its dominance over another. Such a claim leads to false advice for speakers and writers, and immoral advice for humans. A nation proud of its diverse heritage and its cultural and racial variety will preserve its heritage of dialects. We affirm strongly that teachers must have the experiences and training that will enable them to respect diversity and uphold the right of the students to their own language. (Committee on College Composition and Communication Language Statement 1974: 2–3)

Predictably, such a forceful position statement turned out to be quite controversial. A number of discussions from within and outside NCTE have attacked this position, and subsequent discussion has attempted to modify it and clarify the meaning of critical phrases such as "the rights of students to their own language." Recent discussions within NCTE have, however, reaffirmed this position.

While the dialect rights position may seem idealistic, it rightly points to the unequal burden placed upon vernacular speakers. The burden of adjustment is placed squarely upon the linguistic shoulders of vernacular speakers, when there should be an equally strong moral responsibility placed upon the mainstream population to confront its prejudices and respect dialect differences for what they are – a natural manifestation of cultural and linguistic diversity.

The dialect rights position may be morally right, but there is another issue to be confronted. Whether we like it or not, some type of language standardization seems inevitable in large diverse societies whose members must communicate with one another no matter what their dialect background. Standard languages exist throughout the world, not just in the United States or other English-speaking areas (Fasold 1984). Given the fact that some kind of language standardization seems bound to persist in English, as in other languages, the crux of the standard English debate ultimately seems to involve balancing the existence of dialect diversity with the maintenance of some sort of norm for wider communication.

10.4.3 Can standard English be taught?

The previous discussion ignored a practical but essential factor in the consideration of teaching standard English – the prospects for success. Is it really possible to teach spoken standard English on a broad-based scale? No one denies that there are individual cases in which people from vernacular-speaking backgrounds learn standard English, but there is no indication that this is happening for large groups of students in American schools. Furthermore, it may be questioned whether the majority of these individual success stories can be attributed to specific instructional programs. In one form or another, the educational system has been attempting to impart standard English to its students for a long time, without apparent widescale success.

Why is it that so many students from vernacular-speaking backgrounds seem to be immune to efforts to teach them standard English? Although this question cannot be answered definitively, a couple of reasons for the resistance can be offered. Probably the most essential explanation is a sociopsychological one. Dialect is an integral component of personal and social identity. Despite the mainstream stigmatization of vernacular dialects, these varieties may carry strong positive connotations for individuals and local groups. The acquisition of spoken standard English simply cannot be isolated from its social ramifications, as the acquisition of some other types of academic knowledge may be. There is an important difference between learning a set of facts about math or science, for example, and learning a standard English language structure. When peer influences dictate vernacular dialect use in the projection of group solidarity, the use of standard English may lead to an identity crisis. Notwithstanding that there are different contexts in which standard and vernacular varieties may be appropriate, students are still often called upon to choose symbolically between one or the other, sometimes right in the classroom. For many students, group reference norms simply overrule the mainstream values of the classroom. Furthermore, a large part of in-group identity is often oppositional identity, or the positioning of oneself as the opposite of what one is not, including positioning oneself as someone who does not use standard English. For example, Signithia Fordham and John Ogbu (1986) showed that the adoption of standard English was at the top of the list of behaviors associated with "acting White" among African Americans in the urban high school they studied. This kind of oppositional identity, in which African Americans avoid conduct with strong associations of White behavior, may thus be an important part of the explanation for the rejection of a standard English. To use standard English among vernacular-speaking peers may be an open invitation to ridicule by other students. In fact, we have collected many personal anecdotes about students being put down by their peers for using the standard variety, even in the context of the classroom.

There is also a dimension of language learning that helps explain why standard English forms may be difficult even for the most motivated students who want to learn the standard variety. When two cognitive systems are highly similar, with minor differences, it is sometimes difficult to keep the systems apart. In such cases of overwhelming cognitive overlap, more careful attention to the small differences is required – especially if one language has already been thoroughly habituated. In some ways, it may be easier to work with language systems that are drastically different. Naturally, dialectologists tend to emphasize differences rather than similarities between dialects, but in reality, standard and vernacular dialects show only minor structural differences, and these differences may be difficult for the learner to sort out.

Once a linguistic structure is entrenched, it is difficult to break out of the pattern without paying focused attention to its details. The special attention needed to do this, referred to as MONITORING, is actually somewhat unnatural, given the fact that we do not ordinarily have to think about the structures of language in order to speak a language. In fact, excessive monitoring has its own set of problems. Excessive monitoring can be disruptive to the normal fluency of relatively unmonitored speech, where we focus on the content of our conversation rather than the structures we are using.

It may well be that the major issue surrounding standard English instruction is not whether it should be offered to those who want to learn it, but rather how it should be taught. Are there conditions and methods that might be used to teach it effectively? These conditions should offer students a reasonable chance of succeeding at the same time as they remain faithful to the fundamental sociolinguistic premises underlying dialect diversity.

As a preliminary consideration, *the teaching of standard English must take into account the group reference factor*. The available evidence on second-language and second-dialect learning suggests a strong dependency on the sociopsychological factor of group reference for success. Speakers who desire to belong to a particular social group will typically learn the language of that desired group, whereas those with no group reference can be stubbornly resistant to change. Thus, vernacular speakers will best achieve success if their social orientation is geared toward a standard English-speaking group.

The group reference dimension may be the most essential of all the factors affecting the learning of standard English, but it is also the most difficult to program into pedagogical materials. Values relating to social group membership and social aspirations are typically not under the control of the educational system, and efforts to motivate students in terms of vague future employment opportunities, one of the commonly cited reasons for knowing standard English, are often made in vain. Remember that the positive values of the standard dialect in mainstream culture are countered with a competing set of values for the vernacular – values that are often a lot more compelling for an adolescent than the pronouncements made by a classroom teacher. Programs with realistic hopes of success therefore have to mold peer and indigenous community influence into a constructive force endorsing the standard variety. This is, of course, easier said than done, but there may be some situations within the everyday lives of an indigenous peer group in which the use of standard English is advantageous, and these must be highlighted in outlining a rationale for the use of the standard variety. In effect, standard English needs to serve some fairly immediate instrumental role.

At the very least, an instructional program in standard English should involve an honest, open discussion of the values of both vernacular and standard varieties of American English and some relevant, concrete scenarios that might underscore the utility of being able to command both types of varieties. The key here is to stress that there may be immediate needs for standard English as well as the vernacular variety. Such discussions may seem to be mere preliminaries to actual instruction, but students must feel within themselves, and reinforce in one another, that standard English serves some useful purpose in their lives. The reasons for learning standard English must be examined closely from the perspective of the student, and, in some cases, such instruction could even be offered as an optional program for those students who feel a need for it.

Exercise 5

Think of some reasons why a junior high school student might want to know standard English apart from reasons given by traditional educators. Try to put yourself in the place of a junior high school student who is not really thinking about future educational success and distant employment opportunity. What might standard English do for students right now, in terms of people they interact with? Looking at it from such a vantage point, what do you conclude about the utility of standard English at this point in the students' lives?

Once a program in standard English is adopted, *the goals for teaching standard English should be clearly recognized in the instructional program*. There are obviously quite different goals that might be incorporated into a standard English program, ranging from the ability to use standard English in a restricted real-world context (e.g. service encounters, job applications and interviews, interactions with respected community leaders) to the ability to use both standard and vernacular English in a full set of conversational encounters. The goals of a particular program should be integrated into the materials, and the pedagogical strategies should be consistent with these goals. If, for example, the stated goal of a program is functional bidialectalism in which both the standard and vernacular are maintained to serve different social purposes, then the materials should integrate this perspective pedagogically in a meaningful way. The program should incorporate some language scenarios that start with the vernacular and move to the standard variety and others that start with the standard and move to the vernacular. In this regard, it is noteworthy that many current instructional programs explicitly state the goal of bidialectalism as an educational objective but never support the notion with truly bidialectal instructional materials. Just as there are social contexts in which standard English may be more useful, there are contexts in which vernacular dialects serve essential social functions, and the existence of these differential social contexts must be squarely faced and made evident in the materials if they are to capture the real-life significance of dialects in students' lives. A creative instructor may choose to have students engage in role-playing or to participate in real-life activities that reveal the value of dialectal diversity. The bottom-line consideration, however, is a program in which underlying educational goals and pedagogical strategies are in harmony.

Another principle that must be considered in teaching standard English is *the need to couple information about the nature of dialect diversity in American society with pedagogical instruction in standard English*. Given the level of misinformation and dialect prejudice existing in our society, there is a strong need to incorporate basic sociolinguistic information into instructional materials. This information should include some basic notions of the nature of dialect diversity, as well as an introduction to the historical and sociolinguistic facts that lead to the development of dialects. Students should know that the reason they are learning standard English is not related to the inherent inadequacy of their linguistic system or their presumed failure to learn "the English language." In all fairness, they have a right to understand that all dialects, including their own vernacular dialect, are intricately patterned, and that the dialects of English differ from each other in systematic ways. Students can never gain genuine linguistic self-respect unless they realize the sociopolitical basis of dialect inequality rather than simply assuming that the basis for dialect differences lies in some inherent linguistic deficiency.

An understanding of basic sociolinguistic principles related to dialect differences can do several things for a student. First, it can provide a proper perspective on dialect diversity to counteract the popular misconceptions that presently abound. Instructors are just as fully obligated to present factual information about languages and dialects as they are to provide students with accurate information about such subjects as chemistry and biology. A second reason for incorporating information about the nature of dialect diversity into standard English instruction is related to its inherent interest level. Learning about dialect differences piques a natural curiosity about cultural differences. Presented properly, language variety is a fascinating subject in its own right. Whether or not students choose to learn standard English, they deserve the opportunity to learn about the nature of American English dialects as a part of general education. It is not a frivolous or tangential study, but one which presents a unique laboratory for scientific inquiry as well as social science and humanities study. We discuss the rationale for studying dialects in more detail in chapter 11. Third, there is now some indication that students who feel more positive and confident about their own dialect are more successful in learning the standard one. So there is also a pedagogical reason for presenting to students an accurate perspective on their own dialect.

Another consideration in teaching standard English is *the focus on systematic differences between standard and nonstandard English forms.* Teaching standard English is not identical to teaching a foreign language, where a speaker starts with no background knowledge of the language. We have already noted that the similarities between the dialects of English far outnumber the differences, and this fact cannot be ignored in instructional materials on standard English. Given the similarities and differences between standard and vernacular forms, it seems reasonable to organize materials in such a way as to highlight this systematic relationship between standard and non-standard forms. Students do not need to learn the "English language"; they need to learn some standard English correspondences for particular socially stigmatized forms. Materials should take into consideration the systematic differences between standard and nonstandard correspondences, including the nature of the differences, the relative social significance of the differences, and even how frequently particular stigmatized forms might be expected to occur. In other words, the program should take advantage of current socio-linguistic descriptions of vernacular dialects. This contrastive base should underlie all programs for teaching standard English regardless of the type of instructional method used.

Although dialectologists tend to focus on the structural linguistic differences between standard and vernacular varieties, the teaching of standard English cannot be limited to grammatical and phonological structures. *Conventions for language use also enter into the consideration of standard English,* and this dimension must be incorporated into an effective program of instruction in standard English. In fact, many of the concerns about language expressed by those in the workplace turn out to be focused on *how* language is used rather than on *what* particular structures are used. For example, how people answer the telephone or engage in service encounters in the workplace is a vital concern to employers, and such matters often become central issues in cross-cultural and cross-regional interactions. Regional and social differences in conventions for communicative encounters tend to bear greater responsibility for interpersonal conflict than linguistic structures *per se*, so that discussions of these conventions have to be included in standard English instruction along with more narrowly defined linguistic structures. Conventional language routines such as greetings, leave-taking, turn-taking, and so forth, as well as particular speech acts such as denial, refusal, and so forth, have to be considered as important components of programs that teach standard English. To underscore the significance of these conventions in the workplace, we often ask educators and employers which is preferable, a person who responds to an inquiry about a boss's whereabouts by saying, "She's not here. What do you want, anyhow?" or a person who replies with, "I'm sorry, she not in now. She be back this afternoon." In practically every case, people prefer a person who comes across as "polite but vernacular" to one who uses standard English forms without adopting the appropriate conventions for carrying out various mainstream language functions. A program for teaching standard English probably cannot be very successful without considering the broader conventions of language use and behavior. Such a program may move closer to prescribing "appropriate" appearance and behavior than some sociolinguists feel comfortable with, but in order to fully understand the overall context in which standard English exists, one cannot naively disregard the full set of behavioral complements that go along with language form, including norms for carrying out various communicative functions.

Exercise 6

Suppose you were asked to design a standard English program specifically for receptionists whose primary responsibility is to answer the telephone and take messages. What particular functionally based routines and specialized language-use conventions have to be included in this program? Are there any particular structural features that you might anticipate occurring fairly regularly in such a situation? In order to answer these questions, you will have to envision the kinds of interactions that ordinarily occur in this interactional situation. Better yet, try observing some actual telephone conversations between receptionists and clients in order to accumulate real data.

In determining standard English norms, it is important to point out that *the standard variety taught in an instructional program should be realistic in terms of the language norms of the community.* We have pointed out repeatedly that the definition of spoken standard American English is a flexible one, sensitive to regional variation, stylistic range, and other social variables. The notion of general standard American English is not going to prove very useful to a classroom of students who speak Texas Southern or Eastern New England dialects in varying degrees of vernacularity, particularly if this class is likely to be instructed by a teacher who speaks a standard version of the local regional variety. It seems ludicrous for an instructor in the South to attempt to get schoolchildren to make the distinction between [ɪ] and [ɛ] in *pin* and *pen* if the instructor, a standard Southern dialect speaker, does not maintain the distinction. Similarly, we have witnessed a New England speaker pontificating about the need to "put in your *r*'s" while pronouncing the phrase without the postvocalic *r* (i.e. saying [az] for *r*'s). Apart from the difficulty instructors may have in teaching students to use dialect features they do not use themselves in their regional standard, it seems futile to attempt to rid vernacular speakers of local standards on a widescale basis. There is very little realistic hope of success for a program in Knoxville, Tennessee, which sets out to make standard English speakers sound as if they come from Midland Ohio. And the few speakers who might successfully complete such a program would obviously run the risk of coming across as pretentious and "phony" in their native region.

The admission of local standard norms in a program of instruction does not necessarily rule out generally applicable materials, since there are many aspects of social differentiation in grammar that cut across regional varieties. A focus on local norms, however, implies that the vernacular items selected for replacement by standard features should represent the broadest-based socially stigmatized items possible. At the same time, the instructional program should allow for regional flexibility. This flexibility will naturally be greatest with respect to pronunciation, but it may also apply to some dimensions of grammar, vocabulary, and language use as well.

Finally, materials in standard English instruction *should take into account our current understanding of how a second dialect is acquired.* At this point, there is considerable debate about how a second dialect is acquired, as well as the extent to which an alternate dialect can actually be mastered once the native dialect has been acquired. Our knowledge about acquiring a second language is much more advanced than our knowledge of second-dialect acquisition, so that we might turn to studies of second-language acquisition for models. In doing so, however, we must keep in mind the clear-cut differences that exist between second-language and second-dialect acquisition. Programs for teaching a standard dialect have been heavily influenced by second-language instructional models and methods in recent decades, but most standard English materials have not kept up to date with the rapid development of second-language acquisition models in very recent years. For example, many current standard English programs rely heavily on contrastive drills – that is, drills which highlight the sometimes subtle differences between standard and vernacular varieties. One such is a discrimination drill in which a standard structure is contrasted with a nonstandard one so that students can clearly detect the difference between the standard and nonstandard variant. Sentence pairs are given, and subjects are asked simply to identify the sentences as the same or different. A typical drill for the third-person singular -*s* ending would look something like the following:

Stimulus pair	Student response
She works hard. She work hard.	different
She play after school. She play after school.	same
She comes home late. She comes home late.	same

For a motivated student, this kind of drill certainly raises the level of consciousness about the structural differences between standard and nonstandard variants. There are, however, some practical and theoretical concerns that have to be raised about these kinds of drills. On a practical level, they can be very boring, and students lose interest rapidly unless they are highly motivated to begin with. In fact, such exercises tend to be more effective with motivated adults than they are with schoolchildren unless they are creatively packaged in some way. Even when complemented with higher-interest activities, the routine of the drills can become monotonous quite quickly.

Research in second-language acquisition also indicates that contrastive drills are not necessarily a very effective language-learning strategy. In this regard, an important distinction is made between language acquisition and language learning (Krashen 1982). LANGUAGE ACQUISITION involves tacit or implicit knowledge of language rules and tends to come forth automatically, whereas LANGUAGE LEARNING involves the explicit knowledge of rules, which tends to come forth under certain conditions associated with increased awareness or monitoring of speech. Acquisition, rather than learning, leads to fluency in a second language, and too much explicit learning of language rules can, in fact, interfere with second-language fluency, as a speaker may tend to "overmonitor" speech. The difference between language learning and language acquisition seems to have important implications for second-dialect acquisition. Contrastive drills tend to rely upon explicit learning rather than the tacit rule knowledge characteristic of acquisition. The drill approach may serve a person adequately when speech is being heavily monitored, as in language testing or deliberative writing, but it may break down in less monitored, more natural situations. Thus, a heavy dose of more naturalistic uses of language that incorporates standard English forms might prove to be more effective in the acquisition of standard English than reliance upon the kind of explicit learning that takes place in structural drills. Of course, we cannot assume that acquiring a second dialect is identical to acquiring a second language, and it may well be that the over-whelming similarities of two dialect systems leave little alternative but to focus on the finer points of differentiation that are targeted through these kinds of drills.

Unfortunately, we do not have exhaustive research data on the ideal conditions under which a standard variety is acquired as a second dialect. Case studies of native vernacular speakers who have acquired a standard variety, however, underscore the motivational factor rather than pedagogical technique, and the set of strategies that has been shown to lead to successful acquisition ranges from "immersion" in a standard English-speaking context, mimicry of personal and impersonal standard English models, explicit drill techniques, and even traditional prescriptive "correction."

We also do not have solid research data on the optimal age for learning another dialect. Some programs, taking a cue from the apparent naturalness of second-language acquisition during the pre-adolescent period, feel that standard English instruction should focus on children in their early years of schooling. Certainly, there is evidence that native-like control of a language, particularly with respect to phonology, is realistically achieved only prior to the "critical period" of development, the prepubescent period. The study of second-dialect acquisition shows a similar cut-off period for dialect shift, although some adjustment apparently takes place after this period. At the same time, there is evidence that standard English grammar certainly can be acquired after this period, and selective changes in socially stigmatized phonological features can also take place. Thus, the CRITICAL AGE HYPOTHESIS, which maintains that true language mastery can only take place during the prepubescent age period, is not nearly as relevant for the acquisition of standard English as for the acquisition of another language or even another regional variety of English.

A strong argument against teaching standard English in the earliest years of a child's education comes from the social and psychological considerations examined in this chapter. Children may learn some standard English forms when presented with them in primary education, but will these forms persist in the face of strong peer pressure as these children move into adolescence? There is a good chance that the speech of a student's peers will pre-empt other considerations in the formative adolescent years of dialect development, regardless of what took place in school prior to this time.

Some sociolinguists feel that success in teaching spoken standard English will only come if and when a person realizes the utility of this dialect on a very personal level. In most cases, this heightened personal awareness of the uses of standard English in the broader linguistic marketplace does not take place until early adulthood. After years of investigating students' progress in informal and formal programs to teach spoken standard English, there is still no evidence that this variety can really be imposed against a student's will. Nonetheless, where there's a will, there are probably a number of different ways to attain this dialect goal. Thus, the role of instructional programs in the acquisition of standard English seems to be to facilitate the process for motivated students by providing systematic and relevant opportunities to move toward the desired standard English goal. This observation is not meant to dismiss the many well-intended programs that currently exist, but simply to place them in their proper perspective. A guaranteed pedagogical strategy has not yet emerged in teaching standard English. We would, however, expect a reasonable instructional approach to be consistent with the fundamental sociolinguistic premises that we have discussed at various points in this book.

10.5   Further Reading

Adger, Carolyn T., Donna Christian, and Orlando Taylor (eds.) (1999) *Making the Connection: Language and Academic Achievement among African American Students.* Washington, DC: Center for Applied Linguistics. This collection of essays based on a conference related to the Oakland Ebonics controversy includes articles ranging from assessment issues to reports on programs for teaching standard English.

Adger, Carolyn T., and Natalie Schilling-Estes (2003) *African American English: Structure and Clinical Implications.* Rockville, MD: American Speech-Language-Hearing Association. This manual and interactive CD-ROM is intended for speech-language pathologists and educators who wish to incorporate an informed perspective on African American English, as well as dialect diversity in general, into language assessment and language arts instruction. Included are video exercises on identifying vernacular dialect features.

Fasold, Ralph (1990) *The Sociolinguistics of Language.* Oxford: Blackwell. The final chapter of this book, "Some applications of the sociolinguistics of language," covers a number of educational implications that result from the consideration of language variation. The approach to the application of sociolinguistic knowledge is quite similar to that found in this treatment.

Labov, William (1976) Systematically misleading data from test questions. *Urban Review* 9: 146–69. In this article on the general question of language assessment and cultural and linguistic divergence, Labov examines the broad sociolinguistic context of interviewing and the interpretation of test data.

Milroy, James, and Lesley Milroy (1999) *Authority in Language: Investigating Standard English* (3rd edn.). London/New York: Routledge. This book offers historical and contemporary commentary on the problem of prescription and "correctness" in English. The presentation shows how the notion of standard language has affected a wide range of practical matters in society.

Terrell, Sandra L. (ed.) (1983) *Nonbiased Assessment of Language Differences: Topics in Language Disorders*, No. 3. Rockville, MD: Aspen. This special issue of the periodical *Language Disorders* is devoted to the question of assessing the language capabilities of linguistically diverse populations in a non-biased manner. The articles are of most immediate concern to speech and language pathologists involved in assessing vernacular dialect speakers, but also have broader application.

Wolfram, Walt, Donna Christian, and Carolyn Adger (1999) *Dialects in Schools and Communities*. Mahwah, NJ: Lawrence Erlbaum. This work directly deals with the most common educational concerns about dialects and standards, including dialect and writing, dialect and reading, and dialect and classroom behavior. It is intended primarily for practitioners who confront the practical manifestations of dialect divergence in an educational context.

11

Dialect Awareness: Extending Application

In this final chapter, we continue our discussion of the applications of dialect study by examining the effects of dialect differences on reading and writing. We also consider the use of dialects in literature, or *literary dialect*, one of the longstanding uses of written dialect. We conclude our discussion by considering the role of dialect study in general education, including both formal and informal venues. We examine in particular how dialect researchers may work collaboratively with local communities in establishing dialect awareness programs. As used here, a DIALECT AWARENESS PROGRAM refers to activities that are intended to promote an understanding of, and appreciation for, language variation. Following the principle of linguistic gratuity introduced in chapter 10, we maintain that these programs should be proactive and collaborative, as linguists work with community members and educators to foster an understanding of the role of dialect in community life.

11.1   Dialects and Reading

There are many factors that correlate with reading achievement, ranging from students' nutritional problems to the number of books in the home and the level of parental education. Among these potential factors is the spoken dialect of the reader. Given the fact that reading failure correlates with vernacular-speaking populations, it is important to understand how language variation may relate to the reading process. It is also important to understand how reading specialists, teachers, and other practitioners can benefit from knowledge about dialect differences.

One process in reading that may be affected by dialect is DECODING. By decoding, we mean the process whereby written symbols are related to the sounds of language. In English, of course, this process refers to the ways in which the letters of the spelling system, or orthography, systematically relate to the English sound system, along with ways in which syntax and morphology are represented in writing. Whereas different approaches to reading rely on decoding skills to varying degrees, and some approaches de-emphasize a basic decoding model of reading, reliance to some extent on the systematic "sounding out of letters," referred to as the PHONICS approach, has been utilized for over half a century now. As students proceed in the acquisition of reading skills, the significance of decoding may diminish drastically, but it is still a rudimentary skill that plays a significant role in the beginning stages of many reading programs.

A reading teacher engaged in decoding tasks with students must recognize that there are systematic differences in the symbol–sound relationships from dialect to dialect. For example, consider how a speaker of a vernacular dialect might decode the passage: "There won't be anything to do until he finds out if he can go without taking John's brother." A modified orthography is used here to indicate the pronunciation differences for the vernacular speaker.

An example of vernacular dialect decoding
Deuh won't be anything to do until he *fin'* out if he can go wi*f*out taki*n'* John_ bro*v*uh.

We see that decoding differences affect a number of symbol–sound relationships in the example, such as the initial consonant of *there*, the final consonant of *find*, the *th* of *without*, the *th* and final *r* of *brother*, and so forth (e.g. Labov 2001c). These differences are no more significant than variant regional decodings of the vowel *au* of *caught* (e.g. [ɔ] or [a]) or the *s* of *greasy* (e.g. [s] or [z]), except that they involve a couple of socially disfavored variants. Differences in decoding become a problem only if an instructor does not recognize dialectally appropriate sound–symbol relationships and classifies these differences as errors in decoding rather than legitimate variants in production. Imagine the confusion that might be created for a dialect speaker if an accurate dialect decoding such as the pronunciation of the *th* as [f] or as [v] in *without* and *brother*, respectively, is treated as a problem analogous to the miscoding of *b* as [d] or *sh* as [s]. The potential impact of dialects on the decoding process can be minimized if reading instructors are able to separate dialect-appropriate renderings of sound–symbol relationships from genuine miscodings of sound–symbol relationships such as the pronunciation of *d* as [b].

The next version of the passage considers the possible mismatch between dialect-based grammatical differences and the standard English grammar of reading texts.

An example of grammatical mismatch in written text and spoken vernacular dialect

It won't be *nothing* to do till he find_ out *can he* go without taking John_ brother.

The use of existential *it* for *there*, multiple negation in *won't be nothing*, the absence of inflectional -*s* in *find_*, and the inverted question order of *can he go* are all instances of mismatch between the spoken vernacular variety and the written word that might occur if the reader were processing the language in a vernacular dialect.

From the standpoint of simple linguistic processing, it is reasonable to hypothesize that the greater the mismatch between the spoken and written word, the greater the likelihood that processing difficulties will occur in reading. But the real issue is whether dialect differences are great enough to become a significant barrier to linguistic processing. At this point, there are no carefully designed experimental studies that have examined this important research question in detail, but several observations are relevant. First of all, there is some indication that vernacular dialect speakers are capable of processing most spoken standard English utterances whether or not they produce this variety themselves. In other words, they have receptive if not productive ability in standard English. Although receptive and productive capability in language may not transfer to the reading process in the same way, we would certainly expect considerable carryover from this receptive capability in spoken standard English to the reading process, which is itself a receptive language activity.

It is also erroneous to assume that standard English speakers confront written language that is identical to the way they speak, and that vernacular speakers do not. In reality, all readers encounter written text that differs from spoken language to some extent. Even in early reading, sentences with adverbial complements before verbs, such as *Over and over rolled the ball* or *Up the hill she ran* represent a written genre that differentiates written from spoken language for all speakers of English regardless of dialect background.

Admittedly, the gap between written language and spoken language will be greater for vernacular dialect speakers than it is for speakers of standard varieties. But is this gap wide enough to cause processing problems on the basis of linguistic differences alone? Again, carefully controlled experimentation designed to resolve this issue is lacking. However, we are reminded of the fact that there are situations in the world where the gap between spoken dialect and written text is quite extensive but does not result in significant reading problems. In northern Switzerland, for example, texts are written in standard German although much of the population speaks Swiss German, yet the Swiss population does not reveal significant reading failure.

Although it is difficult to measure "degree of dialect difference" in a precise way, Swiss German is certainly as different from standard written German as many vernacular dialects of English are from standard written English. Pointing to linguistic mismatch as the primary basis for reading failure among vernacular speakers thus seems suspect. Differences in the written and spoken language may have to be taken into account by an aware reading instructor, but it is doubtful that the neutralization of these differences in reading material would alleviate the reading problems associated with various vernacular-speaking populations.

Another area of language variation that may have an impact on the reading process involves the broader sociolinguistic base of language, including differences in cultural background. Even proficient readers of English – including graduate students – may make glaring mistakes in comprehension when they read a text that presumes intimate knowledge of a different cultural background or setting (Steffensen, Joag-dev, and Anderson 1979). In most current models of the reading process, the application of background knowledge is essential for comprehension. Readers need such background in order to derive meaning by inference; they may also need to apply knowledge about the world in order to process some literal content. For example, imagine the differences in how a third grader from California and one from New York City might interpret the following passage on the age of giant redwood trees. Incidentally, this item appeared in a previous version of the *Metropolitan Achievement Test* designed for third graders.

They are so big that roads are built through their trunks. By counting the rings inside the tree trunk, one can tell the age of the tree. (from Meier 1973)

Some of the children in New York who read this passage conjured up fairy-tale interpretations of this passage that included, among other things, pictures of golden rings floating around inside trees. The fairy-tale interpretation was certainly fostered by images of cars driving through giant holes in trees. On the other hand, children who live near a redwood forest in California would interpret the passage quite differently, since its literal content would match their knowledge of the world. There is certainly the potential for students to expand their range of experience through reading, but background information is also critical for comprehension. Thus, community-specific language and cultural experiences may actually affect reading comprehension in subtle but important ways.

Finally, we need to remember that dialect differences may have an effect on the assessment of reading skills. Early-level reading tests are particularly susceptible to the impact of dialect because they often rely on metalinguistic tasks that are sensitive to dialect-specific decoding differences. For example, the use of tasks involving minimal word pairs (i.e. pairs of words that differ from one another by only one sound) or rhyming tasks to measure decoding skills might result in misclassifying cases of dialect-appropriate symbol–sound relationships as incorrect responses. Consider the following test items taken from an actual reading achievement test that includes word pairs as part of an attempt to determine early readers' specific decoding abilities.

Choose the words that sound the same:
pin/pen
reef/wreath
find/fine
their/there
here/hear

For speakers of some vernacular varieties, all of these items might legitimately sound the same. The "correct" responses, however, would be limited to *their/there* and *here/hear*, based upon a Northern middle-class dialect norm. An informed perspective on language variation must therefore consider the ways in which reading skills are measured in testing along with dimensions by which reading skills are acquired.

11.1.1   Dialect readers

At one stage in the consideration of dialects and reading, it was proposed that "dialect readers" be used in teaching vernacular-speaking children to read. A DIALECT READER is a text that incorporates the grammatical forms typical of a vernacular-speaking community. For example, the following passages, taken from the *Bridge* reading materials developed by Gary C. Simpkins, Charlesetta Simpkins, and Grace Holt (1977), contrast vernacular African American English and standard English versions of a passage.

Vernacular African American English version
No matter what neighborhood you be in – Black, White or whatever – young dudes be having they wheels. Got to have them. Well, anyway, there happen to be a young brother by name of Russell. He had his wheels. Soul neighborhood, you know. He had this old '57 Ford. You know how brothers be with they wheels. They definitely be keeping them looking clean, clean, clean.

Standard English version
Young guys, Black or White, love their cars. They must have a car, no matter how old it is. James Russell was a young man who loved his car like a baby loves milk. He had an old blue and white '59 Chevrolet. He

spent a great deal of time keeping his car clean. He was always washing and waxing it. (taken from Rickford 1997a: 179)

Limited experimentation with dialect readers has shown that students tend to make gains in traditional reading achievement levels when using dialect readers as opposed to conventional reading materials (Rickford and Rickford 1995). For example, Gary C. Simpkins and Charlesetta Simpkins (1981) reported that students using the *Bridge* materials far exceeded the gains of students using regular reading materials on a standardized reading test (6.2 months of gain for a four-month period vs. 1.2 months for a four-month period for those using the regular reading materials).

Notwithstanding some positive results of preliminary studies, dialect readers have proven to be highly controversial. One reason for the controversy relates to the deliberate use of socially stigmatized language forms in written material. This tactic is viewed by some as a reinforcement of nonstandard dialect patterns, thus flying in the face of traditional mainstream, institutional values endorsing standard dialects. Another reason for the controversy is the fact that this approach singles out particular groups of readers for special materials, namely, those who speak vernacular dialects. This selective process may be viewed as patronizing and, ultimately, racist and classist educational differentiation.

From a sociolinguistic vantage point, the use of dialect readers seems to be based on three assumptions: (1) that there is sufficient mismatch between the child's system and the standard English textbook to warrant distinct materials, (2) that the benefits of reading success will outweigh any negative connotations associated with the use of a socially stigmatized variety, and (3) that the use of vernacular dialects in reading will promote reading success. We have already considered whether the mismatch between spoken and written language is a significant problem; at this point, there simply is no good evidence for this strong position. Given children's socialization into mainstream attitudes and values about dialects at an early age, there is also little reason to assume that the social and psychological benefits of using a vernacular dialect would outweigh the disadvantages. In fact, the opposite seems to be the case, as children reject nonstandard forms in reading, and parents and community leaders rail against their use in dialect readers. Although preliminary research has indicated some gains for children given these materials (Rickford and Rickford 1995), large-scale, substantive research on dialect readers is lacking. Due to the continuing controversy surrounding the use of dialect primers, this alternative now has been largely abandoned, although John Rickford and Angela Rickford (1995) have called for renewed and more extended experimentation with dialect readers.

Although there are some essential ways in which dialect may affect reading, most current approaches downplay simple linguistic differences as a primary factor in accounting for the high levels of reading failure found among vernacular-speaking populations. Instead, cultural values about reading, socialization into reading as a significant social and individual activity, and the mismatch between students' interests and the content of reading material have been considered more essential factors in accounting for high failure rates among non-mainstream populations. Focus on these other variables does not, however, excuse reading instructors from understanding the ways in which dialects may affect reading and from taking these factors into consideration in teaching literacy skills to speakers of vernacular dialects. In addition, ethnic and social class discrimination are unfortunately still rampant in American society, and such discrimination almost certainly has a bearing on how well members of disadvantaged groups fare in school and later life.

11.2   Dialect Influence in Written Language

When a rural schoolchild in Central Pennsylvania writes a sentence like *Cow feed don't have jagers* ("Cow feed doesn't have thorns in it") or a phrase like *the corn got all* ("The corn is finished"), spoken language is reflected in writing. The word *jagers* (perhaps spelled more appropriately as *jaggers*) is a dialect term in this region for "thorns" and other objects capable of causing scratches. Similarly, the use of *don't* with a third-person singular subject is a common vernacular agreement pattern, and the use of *got all* is a regional expression traceable to the influence of Pennsylvania German in the area (Wolfram and Fasold 1974: 205). Obviously, spoken language can have some influence on written language. However, the relationship between spoken and written language is not always as simple and direct as examples of this type might lead us to believe. Writing, after all, is more than a simple reflection of spoken language, and very few people actually write exactly as they talk. With respect to dialects, the important question is how language variation may be manifested in written language style.

Though it seems apparent that spoken language may influence writing, it is not always as easy to sort out cases of spoken language influence from matters pertaining to the acquisition of writing skill in general, for speakers of all varieties. As we shall see below, we need to appeal to some general principles related to the process of acquiring writing skills as well as knowledge about dialects in order to explain some of the patterns of nonstandard writing. One of the interesting findings about dialect and writing relates to the relative frequency with which certain nonstandard forms occur in the speech of vernacular-speaking students. For example, Marcia Farr-Whiteman (1981) identifies a few nonstandard structures that occur relatively frequently in writing and some others that occur infrequently, at least at certain stages in the process of acquiring writing skills. Among those forms frequently found in a sample of writing by eighth-grade students are the following: (1) verbal -*s* absence (e.g. *She go_*), (2) plural -*s* absence (e.g. *four mile_*), (3) possessive -*s* absence (e.g. *John_ hat*), (4) -*ed* absence resulting from consonant cluster reduction (e.g. *Yesterday they miss*), and (5) copula *is* and *are* absence (e.g. *We going to the game*). On the other side of the ledger are nonstandard structures that appear relatively infrequently, including multiple negation, the use of *ain't*, and habitual *be*. In spelling, the orthographic reflection of *f* for *th* (e.g. *baf* for *bath*) and postvocalic *r* absence (e.g. *ca* for *car*) were also relatively rare in writing compared with their incidence in speech.

A partial explanation of the different frequency levels we find for different vernacular features in writing may relate to the social evaluation of forms. Items that are highly stigmatized and that affect relatively small sets of items are apparently the first to be corrected during the course of a child's schooling. By the time students are in eighth grade, as they were in the Farr-Whiteman study, shibboleths of nonstandard usage such as *ain't* may have been purged from writing. There is, then, a dimension of social evaluation that enters into the explanation of why some nonstandard structures are more susceptible to reflection in writing than others.

One of the most revealing aspects of spoken and written language relationships in the Farr-Whiteman study involves the comparison of the relative frequency of nonstandard forms in speech vs. writing, tabulated for both European American and African American vernacular dialect speakers. In figure 11.1, the incidence of verbal -*s* and plural -*s* absence in spoken (S) and written (W) language is summarized for 32 European American and African American eighth graders in Southern Maryland.

Figure 11.1 indicates relationships between spoken and written language that go beyond a simple DIRECT TRANSFER MODEL. Under the transfer model, the occurrence of a form in writing which is matched by one in the spoken dialect is interpreted as a direct carryover from a spoken language pattern to written language. That is, there is a straightforward causal relationship between spoken and written language variation. The figures in 11.1 do not support a simple version of this model. For example, European Americans have a higher frequency of verbal and plural -*s* absence in their written language than in their spoken language. This pattern would hardly be predicted on the basis of their spoken language, since the European American speakers do not have appreciable levels of suffix -*s* absence in their speech. Furthermore, we would normally expect a lower incidence of a socially stigmatized feature in the formal context of a written school essay than in spoken language.

Differences in the relative occurrence of suffixes in spoken and written language are also shown for the African American sample. Plural -*s* absence

% absent

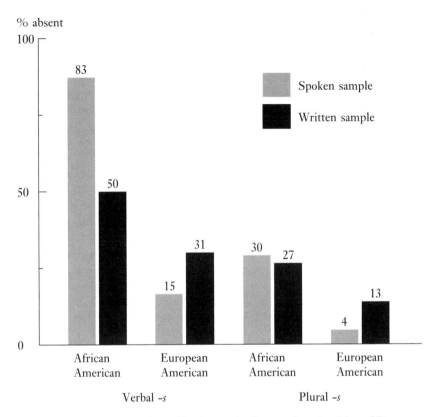

Figure 11.1 Percentage of -*s* suffix absence in the speech and writing of European Americans and African Americans (adapted from Farr-Whiteman 1981: 158)

in spoken AAE is relatively infrequent compared to verbal -*s* absence, yet both types of suffix absence are relatively high in writing.

The pattern of suffix absence in writing is further confirmed by a pattern found for consonant cluster reduction. In writing, word-final cluster reduction affecting -*ed* forms (e.g. *miss* for "missed") is much more frequent than it is for clusters that are part of the same morpheme (e.g. *mis* for "mist"), quite the reverse of what it is for spoken language. As Farr-Whiteman (1981: 160) puts it, "these features (plural -*s*, verbal -*s*, and consonant -*ed*) seem to be omitted in writing at least in part simply because they are inflectional suffixes." In this regard, we note that inflectional suffixes are typically redundant markings, and that most words may stand as independent items in writing apart from the suffix. In other words, *miss* alone is a whole word whether or not the -*ed* is added; *mis* for *mist*, however, cannot stand alone in this way. All writers of English, regardless of their native dialect, seem to reveal some instances of suffix omission in the process of learning the written form of the language.

While generalized processes pertaining to the developmental stages of writing may affect all writers to some extent, this does not nullify the effect of dialect on writing. Some forms may still be directly attributable to the spoken dialect; other spoken language forms, however, combine with different principles of writing to account for nonstandard written language forms. Inflectional -*s* absence may be revealed as part of the natural process of learning how to write regardless of the spoken dialect, but speakers of a dialect with substantial levels of suffix absence still tend to show a higher incidence of suffix omission in writing than writers of other dialects. The point that needs to be emphasized here is that dialect definitely can influence writing, but it is not solely responsible for the occurrence of nonstandard forms.

Writing failure, like reading failure, is a complex issue that goes far deeper than surface differences in dialect forms. Nonetheless, a writing instructor who is aware of the way in which dialect may be manifested in writing is certainly in a better position to improve writing skills than one who has no awareness of potential spoken language influences on the written medium.

Exercise 1

In the following sample composition, there are two types of digression from standard written English. First, there is a set of errors related to the mechanical conventions of written language. These include various mistakes in the application of arbitrary punctuation conventions and some types of spelling errors (e.g. *to* vs. *too*, *fair* vs. *fare*). The second set of nonstandard writing forms may reflect the influence of spoken language by a speaker of a vernacular dialect. Based on your knowledge of vernacular dialect features, differentiate the "error" types, labeling mechanical problems as **Type I** errors and spoken language influence as **Type II**. In the case of those forms classified as **Type II**, indicate what vernacular dialect feature may be the source of the spoken language influence. You may need to consult the Appendix of distinguishing dialect features for this exercise.

I tel you bout me and my fren basebal team. wen we together we do all kinds of things he play basketball and I play basebal. Las yere I seen the basketbal teme play and it look like I didnt have a chanc of making it. Im a prety good baseball player tho and the coch knowed it. James the best player we miss him when he couldnt play last weak.

11.3   Written Dialect

Not only do dialect forms sometimes inadvertently appear in writing, but they may also be used deliberately in various forms of writing. Writers have attempted to portray characters through dialect for centuries. Such portrayals can be found everywhere from the daily comic strips in most newspapers to respected literary works going back as far as Chaucer. The representation of dialect in American literature arose, for the most part, in the nineteenth century and is now quite common in modern literature and other written materials depicting the regional, social, and ethnic backgrounds of different characters.

There are a number of reasons why an author might want to represent some aspect of dialect in a literary work. In one tradition, dialects have been used for parody or comic effect, to poke fun at a character portrayed as culturally unsophisticated or uneducated. This tradition is manifested in various comic-strip characterizations of hillbilly speech, Ebonics, or Spanglish that belittle the speakers of these varieties. Parodies of these types are referred to as MOCK LANGUAGE or JUNK LANGUAGE, since their intent seems to be to ridicule or deride the language of the particular social group (Hill 1995). For example, over 200 billboards along Interstate Route 95 on the East Coast feature a cartoon character, Pedro, in an oversized sombrero who entreats drivers in "Mexican Speak" to stop at a tourist stop along the South Carolina–North Carolina border called "South of the Border." These advertisements include statements that clearly play off racist stereotypes about Mexican Americans and others of Hispanic descent, including, for example, "No Monkey Business, Joost Yankee Panky" or "Too Moch Tequila?" (accompanying an upside-down billboard sign). Since the so-called Ebonics controversy of the late 1990s, Mock Ebonics has been quite rampant in comic strips, on internet sites, and even in various opinion columns in newspapers (Ronkin and Karn 1999) that use caricatures of AAE. For example, *De Ebonic Lectric Library O De Classicks* is an internet site that offers translations of selected classic works of Western literature into AAE, for example, *The Ebology of Blato: Socradees Defense* ("The Apology of Plato: Socrates' Defense"). These translations wrongly depict the dialect as a disordered, illegitimate version of English. Such written representations seize on the stereotype that varieties like AAE represent out-group, inferior behavior, in effect, "reproducing racism in everyday life" (Ronkin and Karn 1999: 361).

Exercise 2

Collect some examples of Mock Dialect from the internet. One can find lots of examples of this type by using a search engine simply to find sites on "Ebonics" or "Spanglish." Although these sites may seem, at first glance, to be innocent fun and entertainment, what is the underlying language ideology represented in these caricatures? Do linguists who rail against such parodies take themselves too seriously? Why or why not?

In another, quite different tradition, dialects are used in literary works to represent the voices of characters from different regional and social backgrounds. It would be incongruous for Mark Twain's Huckleberry Finn to speak like a citified standard English-speaking adult when the perspective being developed is that of a rural Southern adolescent. The development of a local character may come, in part, from the regional dialect. There is an established literary tradition for these kinds of representations; however, they do raise the issue of linguistic subordination we discussed in chapter 1. Regional characters who speak vernacular dialects are often portrayed as unsophisticated, ignorant people inferior to those who speak standard varieties of the language, in effect, perpetuating stereotypes about language differences and linguistic subordination. There are, however, cases in which authors use local dialect to portray speakers as wise, trustworthy local characters who are the direct opposite of suspicious outsiders who speak standard English. Such use of dialect is found, for example, in the works of the Southern writer, Lee Smith (e.g. 1983, 1988), who often uses Appalachian dialect in her novels.

Dialect writing may also be used by an author to portray identity and voice. The poet Paul Laurence Dunbar, for example, wrote about one-fourth of all his poems in a vernacular dialect at the turn of the twentieth century, projecting a vernacular voice to express the conditions and experiences of Black life in America at the time. Such texts are sometimes referred to as SPEAKERLY TEXTS because they project the vernacular speech of the author in writing and thus mediate between traditional vernacular speech and written standard English (Gates 1988). In these texts, narrators act as if they are speaking to their audience rather than writing for them. Zora Neal Hurtson's classic novel, *Their Eyes Were Watching God,* and Alice Walker's *The Color Purple* are examples of speakerly texts that project an effective Black voice in the writing.

There even are a few African American scholars who sometimes write academic text in dialect. For example, Geneva Smitherman's *Talkin' and*

Testifyin' (1977), an academic book about African American English that strongly endorses its usefulness as a communicative system in the African American community, deliberately sprinkles the text with doses of written AAE. The written code switching into AAE at various points emphasizes important features of this dialect in a way that underscores the effectiveness and legitimacy of the variety. We see, then, that different authors use dialect for purposes that range from mocking parody to character development to cultural and personal voice. The appropriateness of dialect in a particular literary work has to be evaluated in terms of what the writer is trying to accomplish through the representation of dialect rather than the use of written dialect *per se*.

The representation of literary dialect is actually quite tricky from the perspective of dialectology. Dialectologists are often concerned with linguistic accuracy, but authors typically have other goals in mind that are related to the development of character and voice. To accomplish such goals, authors must strike a balance between presenting a credible version of a dialect, writing readable text, and fulfilling their literary intentions. A completely faithful rendition of a dialect in phonetic detail would probably be incomprehensible to most readers and would be out of keeping with the author's goals in using dialect to develop character or create a distinctive and effective voice.

There are, of course, different levels of language variation that may be captured in literary dialect, but the most difficult level to represent is phonology, which must be reflected through spelling modifications. Given the many obstacles to representing dialect phonology through spelling, most writers have resorted to a tradition that relies heavily on a selective and somewhat arbitrary set of spelling changes.

One of the traditional ways of representing dialect in spelling is through EYE DIALECT. Eye dialect typically consists of a set of spelling changes that have nothing to do with the phonological differences of real dialects. In fact, the reason it is called "eye" dialect is because it appeals solely to the eye of the reader rather than to the production of items, since it does not really capture any phonological differences. The spellings of *was* as *wuz*, *does* as *duz*, *excusable* as *exkusable*, or *wunce* for *once* do not represent any known aspect of phonological variation; these changes are just different ways of spelling common words to convey the impression that their speaker is an uneducated vernacular speaker.

Certain changes in spelling conventions may, on the other hand, be used to portray real phonological variation between a standard dialect and a vernacular or regional variety. A writer who spells *them* as *dem*, *fellow* as *feller*, *first* as *fust*, or *itch* as *eetch* is attempting to convey phonological differences in which a sound is changed (e.g. *them* becomes *dem*, *itch* becomes *eetch*), a sound is added (*fellow* becomes *feller*), or a sound is lost (*first* becomes *fust*) in a non-mainstream variety. Consonant changes are relatively easy to portray in writing but vowels are difficult, given the small phonetic details often involved in differentiating dialects. Furthermore, symbol–sound correspondences tend to be more varied for vowels than they are for most consonants. Nonetheless, writers may effectively use the spelling *ee* for *eetch* to symbolize the [i] rather than the [ɪ] sound usually associated with the *i* spelling (e.g. *bit*, *mitt*). Certain changes based on fairly widespread patterns of sound–symbol correspondence of this type have become fairly traditional in literary texts (e.g. *u* to symbolize a central vowel, as in *tuck* for *took*). Other cases exemplify specially created conventions for dialect writing. For example, an apostrophe is usually used in dialect writing to indicate that a sound or a syllable has been left out in the dialect by comparison with the standard variety, so that *mo'* for *more*, *ac'* for *act*, *'cause* for *because*, and *'cept* for *except* would all indicate an "absent" sound or syllable.

Of course, literary spelling conventions do not always differentiate clearly between eye dialect and real dialect differences, sometimes combining both conventions within the same word. Dialect spellings such as *wunst* for *once* and *'nuff* for *enough* combine eye dialect (the *wu* . . . of *wunst* and the . . . *uff* of *'nuff*) with genuine pronunciation differences, namely, the intrusive *t* of *once* and the deleted word-initial syllable of *enough*. For descriptive and practical reasons, it is virtually impossible to be faithful to dialect pronunciation in writing, although there are certainly different degrees of accuracy that distinguish writers.

In principle, it should be easier to represent dialect grammar and vocabulary than phonology, and some authors choose to represent dialect by ignoring phonology and concentrating on particular grammatical structures and vocabulary items. As it turns out, however, writers range widely in how accurate their portrayals of dialect grammar and vocabulary are, since these portrayals require a high degree of familiarity with the descriptive details of the dialects being depicted in order to remain faithful to the actual spoken dialects. Many writers resort to using a restricted set of grammatical and lexical features rather than attempting to use a comprehensive set of structures based upon dialectological study. Consequently, many writers often lapse into stereotypes based upon a mixture of personal experience and a conventional set of structures taken from other authors' literary representations of dialect. Even for writers quite familiar with the representative dialects, it is virtually impossible to be completely faithful to a dialect in writing. This is especially true when we consider the variable dimension of dialects as discussed in chapter 3.

Based upon descriptive accounts of various dialects, as well as knowledge of the author's spoken variety and how he or she might "translate" spoken language into written form, it is quite possible for a dialectologist to evaluate how accurately different varieties are represented in literary works. For example, it is possible to evaluate the literary representation of regional dialects found in *The Adventures of Huckleberry Finn* (Rulon 1971) based upon descriptive knowledge of the dialects Twain intended to represent in his characters. It is also possible to compare how different writers represent the same dialect, as Constance W. Weaver (1970) has done for the literary representations of AAE in several different works. Detailed tabulations of dialect features that include both a qualitative and quantitative dimension show considerable variation and degrees of faithfulness among authors. Some authors are obviously more skilled at portraying dialect details than others. For example, although Claude Brown's (1965) portrayal of AAE in *Manchild in the Promised Land* shows discrepancies between his literary representation and the dialect as it is typically used in Northern urban communities, the author manipulates the relative frequency of nonstandard structures in the main character's passage from adolescence to adulthood and in shifting between different speaking styles in a subtle but effective way, according to Weaver's (1970) sociolinguistic analysis.

As we consider the question of accuracy in literary dialect, we also have to consider the matter of artistry. Just as writers of literature do not necessarily seek to portray people exactly as they exist in real life, so too is it sometimes necessary for artistic purposes to depart from complete accuracy in dialect representation. Sometimes this departure is based on sheer practicality. As we have been discussing, it is impossible to portray every dialect detail on all levels and still end up with a text that is readable to the non-linguist. At other times, departures from dialect accuracy may be undertaken for effect. For example, just as descriptive detail pertaining to a character's physical appearance or surroundings may be downplayed at moments where other matters are more crucial, so too are there moments where obtrusive dialect differences must take a back seat to other facets of character or plot development. Thus, it is not always the case that apparent dialect "inaccuracies" from a sociolinguistic point of view necessarily reflect a lack of knowledge about dialect patterning or an inability to portray these patterns on the part of the writer who uses dialect in literary texts. In fact, an exclusive focus on linguistic accuracy in dialect representation probably misses the primary point of most literary dialect – to develop local characters and present spoken voice through written text.

Exercise 3

Examine the following passage from Richard Wright's *Native Son.* The passage portrays the vernacular dialect of an African American preacher. Answer the following questions, based on the passage, which is taken from page 263 of a 1961 publication of this work. The original work was published in 1941.

1   What forms seem to be simple examples of eye dialect?
2   What cases of spelling change represent actual phonological differences?
3   What kinds of grammatical details are included in the passage?
4   Are there phonological and grammatical differences that you might expect but do not appear in the passage?

> fergit ever'thing but yo' soul, son. Take yo' mind off ever'thing but eternal life. fergit what the newspaper say. Fergit yuh's black. Gawd looks past yo' skin 'n inter yo' soul, son. He's lookin' at the only parta yuh tha's *His*. He wants yuh 'n' He loves yuh. Give yo'se'f t' 'Im, son. Lissen, lemme tell yuh why yuh's here; lemme tell yuh a story tha'll make yo' heart glad.

How does the author use dialect to portray the voice of the African American preacher? What effect does the use of dialect have in this instance? How important is dialect accuracy in this portrayal?

11.4   Proactive Dialect Awareness Programs

It is easy to argue that educational practitioners who deal with dialectally diverse groups of students should know something about the dialects of their students. But what about such knowledge for the students themselves? And what about dialect awareness for community members who are no longer involved in formal education? We maintain that both formal and informal educational programs on dialects hold appeal for all sorts of people in the community, from elementary school students to retired citizens with an interest in local customs and history. In the following sections, we discuss dialect awareness programs in both formal and informal education contexts, focusing on community-based programs.

Most educational systems claim to be committed to a search for fundamental truths about matter, nature, human society, and human culture. When it comes to dialects, however, there is an educational tolerance of misinformation and folklore that is matched in few subject areas. Remember, from our original presentation in chapter 1, that there is an entrenched mythology about dialects that pervades our understanding of this topic, particularly with respect to the nature of standard and vernacular varieties. In its own way, the popular understanding of dialects is probably akin to a modern geophysicist's maintaining that the planet Earth is flat. Furthermore, the factual misinformation is not all innocent folklore, as we saw in our discussion of dialects and testing. At the very least, then, the educational system and society at large should assume responsibility for replacing the entrenched myths about dialects with factual information about the authentic nature of dialect diversity.

Operating on erroneous assumptions about language differences, it is easy for students and community members to fall prey to the perpetuation of unjustified stereotypes about language as it relates to class, ethnicity, and region. Equity in education is hardly limited to how educators view students. It also affects how students feel about other students and themselves. Students who speak mainstream varieties may view their vernacular-speaking peers as linguistically deficient, just as the broader-based educational system often does. Worse yet, the stereotypes that evolve from the myths about dialects affect how people view themselves, so that vernacular speakers may actually come to view their own linguistic behavior as proof that they are just as "stupid" as their language varieties are held to be.

From a humanistic standpoint, dialect awareness programs help us understand similarities and differences in human behavior. They also offer an opportunity to see how language reflects and helps shape different historical and cultural developments. In this context, it is somewhat surprising that the current emphasis on multicultural education in the US has, for all practical purposes, excluded the study of linguistic diversity, since language is often an integral part of people's cultural identity. For example, many communities and schools have special programs related to Black History Month each February, but the language history of Black Americans tends to be excluded from such presentations. Understanding language differences as a manifestation of cultural and historical differences provides an important rationale for studying the nature of dialect differences on a formal and informal level.

There is another rationale for examining dialect differences related to the nature of intellectual inquiry. The study of dialects affords us a fascinating window through which we can see how language works. Certainly, an important aspect of understanding language in general, and the English language in particular, is the development of an appreciation for how language changes over time and space and how various dialects arise. Studying dialects formally and informally provides a wealth of information for examining the dynamic nature of language. Given people's inherent interest in dialects, this type of study has great potential for piquing students' and community members' interest in how language works. Furthermore, the inner workings of language are just as readily observed in examining dialects and their patterning as through the exclusive study of a single standard variety.

The study of dialects offers another enticement. Language, including dialects, is a unique form of knowledge in that speakers know a language simply by virtue of the fact that they speak it. Much of this knowledge is not on a conscious level, but it is still open to systematic investigation. In examining dialect differences, students can hypothesize about the patterning of language features and then check these hypotheses by carefully studying and describing a set of data on people's actual usage patterns. This process is, of course, a type of scientific inquiry. Such a rationale for studying dialects may seem a bit esoteric at first glance, but hypothesizing about and then testing language patterns is quite within the grasp even of younger students. In fact, we have led classes of students in the middle elementary grades through the steps of hypothesis formation and testing by using exercises involving dialect features. The exercise on *a*-prefixing that was included in chapter 1, for example, actually comes from an eighth-grade curriculum on dialects that we have taught in North Carolina for over a decade now. Students inductively learn how to formulate and test hypotheses at the same time as they learn about the intricate nature of patterned dialect differences.

Finally, there is a utilitarian reason for studying dialects. Information about dialects should prove helpful to students as they work to develop the language skills required as a part of the educational process, including the use of the standard variety. Vernacular dialect speakers may, for example, apply knowledge about dialect features to composing and editing skills in writing. We have personally witnessed students, who studied third-person singular -*s* absence in a unit on dialects, transfer this knowledge to their writing when called upon to write standard English. The studying of various dialects hardly endangers the sovereignty of standard English in the classroom. In fact, if anything, it enhances the learning of the standard variety through heightened sensitivity to language variation.

11.5   A Curriculum on Dialects

Although it is beyond the scope of this book to present actual lesson plans for a curriculum on dialects, it is reasonable to introduce some of the major themes that might be covered in such a unit of study, especially since dialect study is a relatively novel idea at the elementary and secondary levels of education. Our own experimentation has focused on a middle-school curriculum bridging social studies and language arts, but similar units can be designed for other levels of K–12 education as well.

A unit on dialects needs to focus on the fundamental naturalness of dialect variation in American society. Students should confront stereotypes and misconceptions about dialects, and this is probably best done inductively. An easy method of doing this involves having students listen to representative speech samples of regional, class, and ethnic varieties. Students need to hear how native standard English speakers in New England, the rural South, and urban North compare to appreciate the reality of diverse regional spoken standards, just as they need to recognize different vernacular varieties in these regions. And students in "standard"-speaking regions need to consider some of the features of their own dialect as it compares with others in order to understand that everyone really does speak a dialect. Although most tape-recorded collections of dialect samples are personal ones that are not commercially available, a growing inventory of video productions can be used to provide an entertaining introduction to dialects while, at the same time, exposing basic prejudices and myths about language differences.

It is also important for students to examine cases of dialect variation from their own community and beyond as a basis for seeing how natural and inevitable dialects are. For starters, students should at least be able to offer regional names for short-order, over-the-counter foods and drinks (e.g. *sub/hoagie/hero*, etc.; *soda/pop*, etc.), as well as local transportation (e.g. *beltline, beltway, loop, perimeter*, etc. for "road encircling a metropolitan area"). Virtually all communities have some local and regional lexical items that can be used as a starting point for examining dialect diversity. For example, in some of our dialect awareness materials, we have developed exercises on lexical items such as the following, which comes from a curriculum for middle-school students in North Carolina. For this particular curriculum, lexical items are introduced in a series of vignettes from videos that include Outer Banks speech on the North Carolina Coast, Appalachian English in the western part of the state, and Lumbee Native American English in the Southeastern part of the state, among others.

Dialect words in North Carolina

Following are some words introduced in the different videos on the dialects of North Carolina: Outer Banks dialect, Mountain dialect, and the Lumbee dialect of Robeson County. Fill in the blanks in the following sentences with the appropriate dialect word.

airish	boomer	buck	doast	ellick
gaum	goaty	juvember	meehonky	mommuck
on the swamp	poke	plumb	quamish	sigogglin
slick cam	touron	token	yonder	young 'uns

1 They used a _____ for target practice.
2 That _____ is from New Jersey.
3 That place sure was smelling _____ .
4 Put those groceries in a _____ and I'll take them home.
5 When I got up this morning it was right _____ outside.

6   You could find it way back _____.
7   They're always together because he's his _____.
8   At night we used to play _____.
9   The ocean was so rough today I felt _____ in my stomach.
10 Last night she came down with a _____.
11 I saw a _____ in the field last night and it scared me.
12 They worked so hard that they were _____ wore out.
13 Last night a _____ got in the attic.
14 They live over there _____.
15 If I don't have some _____ I'm going to fall asleep.
16 The road going up there sure is _____.
17 She used to _____ him when he was a child.
18 It sure was _____ on the sound without any wind.
19 Don't _____ up the radiator with that stuff.
20 _____ don't act like they used to back then.

Some of the dialect words are used on the Outer Banks, some are used in the mountains, and some used mostly by the Lumbee Indians in Robeson County. Some words are also shared by different groups of speakers. List the words that are used by each group as well as those that are shared by groups.

[ANSWERS: 1 *juvember* "slingshot"; 2 *touron* "tourist" (Outer Banks); 3 *goaty* "foul smelling" (Outer Banks); 4 *poke* "bag" (shared); 5 *airish* "breezy, cool" (shared); 6 *yonder* "far away" (shared); 7 *buck* "good friend" (Outer Banks); 8 *meehonky* "hide and seek" (Outer Banks); 9 *quamished* "sick" (Outer Banks); 10 *doast* "flu" (shared); 11 *token* "ominous sign of danger" (shared); 12 *plumb* "completely" (shared); 13 *boomer* "red squirrel" (Mountain); 14 *on the swamp* "neighborhood" (Lumbee); 15 *ellick* "coffee" (Lumbee); 16 *sigogglin* "crooked" (Mountain); 17 *mommuck* "hassle" (shared); 18 *slick cam* "very calm" (Outer Banks); 19 *gaum* "mess" (shared); 20 *young 'uns* "children" (shared)]

Students themselves can take an active role in constructing dialect vocabulary exercises by helping to collect local lexical items. Though the list of lexical items cited above may seem esoteric to readers in different regions, all areas have distinctive lexical items that can be seized upon in constructing such exercises. In the process, students learn to document and compile dialect items and determine the ways in which their local dialect is similar to and different from other varieties. In fact, in our studies of lexical items, community members have often taken leading roles in the collection and compilation of community-based lexical inventories. Certainly, such collections underscore the naturalness of dialect diversity and seize upon the natural curiosity that all people seem to have concerning "different word uses."

Another essential type of activity concerns learning about the true nature of the patterning of dialects. As we saw in chapter 1, the popular stereotype is that various dialects, particularly vernacular varieties, are simply imperfect attempts to speak the standard variety. In addition, people tend to think of "grammar rules" as prescriptive dicta that come from books rather than from natural language usage. An inductive exercise on the systematic nature of dialects, such as the *a*-prefixing exercise in chapter 1, can go a long way toward dispelling such notions. It also can set the stage for generating a non-patronizing respect for the complexity of systematic differences among dialects. The advantage of the *a*-prefixing exercise in particular is that it involves a form whose patterning is intuitive to both those who use the form in their vernacular dialect and those who do not (Wolfram 1982). This fact makes the exercise appropriate for students regardless of their native dialect. Exercises of this type are an effective way of confronting the myth that dialects have no rules of their own; at the same time, such exercises effectively demonstrate the underlying cognitive patterning of language.

The following is an example of a dialect patterning exercise that illustrates how students can uncover the intricate patterns that underlie dialect forms. This exercise involves the well-known merger of the vowels [ɪ] and [ɛ] in items like *pin* and *pen* in Southern dialect areas.

A Southern vowel pronunciation

In some Southern dialects of American English, words like *pin* and *pen* are pronounced the same. Usually, both words are pronounced as *pin*. This pattern of pronunciation is also found in other words. **List A** has words where the *i* and *e* are pronounced the **SAME** in these dialects.

List A: i *and* e *pronounced the same*
1   *tin* and *ten*
2   *kin* and *Ken*
3   *Lin* and *Len*
4   *windy* and *Wendy*
5   *sinned* and *send*

Although *i* and *e* in **List A** are pronounced the **SAME**, there are other words where *i* and *e* are pronounced differently. **List B** has word pairs where the vowels are pronounced **DIFFERENTLY**.

List B: i *and* e *pronounced differently*
1   *lit* and *let*
2   *pick* and *peck*

3   *pig* and *peg*
4   *rip* and *rep*
5   *litter* and *letter*

Is there a pattern that can explain why the words in **List A** are pronounced the **SAME** and why the words in **List B** are pronounced
DIFFERENTLY? To answer this question, you have to look at the
sounds that are next to the vowels. Look at the sounds that come after
the vowel. What sound is found next to the vowel in all of the examples
given in **List A**?

Use what you know about the pronunciation pattern to pick the word
pairs in **List C** that are pronounced the **SAME** and those that are
pronounced **DIFFERENTLY** in some Southern dialects. Mark the word
pairs that are pronounced the same with <u>S</u> and the word pairs that are
pronounced differently with <u>D</u>.

List C: same or different?
1   *bit* and *bet*
2   *pit* and *pet*
3   *bin* and *Ben*
4   *Nick* and *neck*
5   *din* and *den*

Exercise 4

Work through the following exercise as if you were a student in a
dialect awareness program. What might a student learn about grammatical rules pertaining to vernacular dialects from this exercise? The
exercise is from Wolfram and Reaser (2004).

Plural absence on nouns

In English, we form a regular plural by adding an *-s* sound, so that we
say *one dog* but *two dogs* or *a cat* but *two cats*. In some rural dialects
of the South, there is a set of nouns that do not take *-s* endings. **List
A** gives some of the nouns that do not need to add a plural *-s*. As
you look at the sentences in **List A**, answer the following questions:

- What kinds of things do the nouns in **List A** refer to? Is there a
  common topic for these nouns?
- What kinds of words occur before the noun?

List A: nouns without plural -s
1 We caught *two hundred pound_* of flounder.
2 How *many bushel_* does he have?
3 There are *two pint_* sitting in the back yard.
4 There are *lots of gallon_* of water.
5 They have *three acre_* for building.
6 It's about *six mile_* up the road.

List B: nouns with plural -s
In **List B** the nouns in the sentences MUST take a plural *-s* ending. What is the difference in the type of nouns in **List A** and **List B** that might explain why some nouns MUST have the *-s* and why others do not need it? Look at the differences in the meaning of the nouns in **List A** and **List B**.

1 We caught *two hundred cats.*
2 How *many dogs* does he have?
3 There are *two chickens* sitting in the back yard.
4 They have *lots of ponies* down below.
5 They have *three sisters.*
6 It's about *six teachers.*

In **List C** the same nouns of **List A** are given, but as they are used in **List C** they MUST have the *-s* plural. What is the main difference that can explain when the *-s* is needed and when it is not needed?

List C: when the plural -s needs to be present
1 We had *pounds* of flounder that spoiled.
2 Sometimes people use *bushels* instead of *pounds.*
3 The *pints* of ice cream are in the freezer.
4 We had *gallons* of water in the skiff.
5 The best *acres* are owned by the government.
6 The beautiful beaches go for *miles.*

After examining the three lists of words, you should be able to figure out the rule or pattern for leaving off the *-s* plural. The rule has two parts. One part has to do with the meaning of the noun and the other part has to do with the kind of word that modifies the noun.

• State the exact pattern for *-s* plural absence based on your analysis of the nouns in **Lists A, B,** and **C.**

- Say which of the nouns in **List D** must have the *-s* and which do not need the *-s* ending and say why. If you have stated the rule for plural *-s* correctly, you should be able to do this without guessing.

List D: predicting -s *plural absence*

1 She had three pound_ of fish left.
2 She had pound_ of fish left.
3 It's forty inch_ to the top.
4 It's inch_ to the top.
5 There are six cat_ in that yard.
6 There are cat_ in the yard.

In these types of exercises students learn how linguists collect and organize data to formulate rules. Such exercises also provide students with a model for analyzing data that they might collect from their own community. In the best-case scenario, students should record language data, extract particular examples from the data, and formulate linguistic rules themselves. In this way, students may learn on a first-hand basis about examining language in a scientific way.

In addition to seeing dialect study as a kind of scientific investigation, students should be encouraged to see how dialect study merges with the social sciences and the humanities. Dialect study can be viewed from the perspective of geography, history, or sociology; it also can be linked with ethnic or gender studies. Thus, the examination of dialect differences offers great potential for students to probe the linguistic manifestations of other types of sociocultural differences. For example, a student or group of students interested in history may carry out independent research to determine the contributions of various historical groups to a particular locale by research-ing the migratory routes of the first English-speaking inhabitants of the area and showing how settlement history is reflected in the dialect. Similarly, students interested in sociology may examine group differences (e.g. age, status) in a community as manifested in language. Students may further probe the linguistic manifestations of in-group behavior by examining the way new vocabulary items are created and diffused in a group of speakers who share a common interest. The ways in which new words are formed, as discussed in chapter 3, can be examined through the investigation of the jargon surrounding some specialized activity (e.g. electronic mail, playground basketball) or through the investigation of slang as used by peer cohorts who hang out at the mall just as readily as it can through the study of how mainstream words have developed. Students can even create a new slang term and follow its spread among their peers to observe the social dynamics of language.

While it is possible to develop specific lessons relating dialect study to social science and the humanities, the true value of broad-based approaches to dialect study is realized by allowing groups of students to examine complementary topics and by having the groups share their investigations with other class members. There are a number of creative ways in which students can examine how language and culture go hand-in-hand.

It is also important for students to reflect on how they use language in different situations, and why. The following exercise (from Wolfram and Reaser 2004) focuses on style shifting in general and the uses of African American English in particular. It is used in connection with a video vignette in which African Americans discuss the demands placed on them to shift their language based on different situations.

You will see a vignette about the language experience of African Americans from the documentary *Voices of North Carolina*. Before you watch the video answer the following questions:

1   Do you ever feel that you have to change the way you speak? Why?
2   When you change your speech, is it mostly conscious or unconscious? That is, do you have to think about it or does it just happen naturally?
3   List 5 situations where you are likely to change your speech. Rank these situations from 1 to 5, with 1 being the situation where you have to be most careful about the way you speak and 5 being the situation where you can be most casual.

Now we will watch the video. As you watch, think about the following questions:

4   Could you hear differences in the speech of individuals in different situations?
5   Are these African Americans aware of the fact that they change their speech or not?
6   Why do you think that they feel as though they must change their speech in different situations?

As we have mentioned, one of the greatest advantages of a curriculum on dialects is its potential for tapping the language resources of students' indigenous communities. In addition to classroom lessons, students can learn by going into the community to collect live dialect data. In most cases, the language characteristics of the local community should make dialects come alive in a way that is unmatched by textbook knowledge. Educational models that treat the local community as a resource to be tapped rather than a liability to be overcome have been shown to be quite effective in other areas of language arts education, and there is no reason why this model cannot be applied to the study of community dialects. A model that builds upon community strengths in language, even when the language is different from the norm of the mainstream educational system, seems to hold much greater potential for success than one that focuses exclusively upon language conflicts between the community and school. In fact, the community dialect may just turn out to be the spark that ignites students' interest in the study of language arts, social studies, or history. The study of dialects can, indeed, become a vibrant, relevant topic of study for all students, not just for those who choose to take an optional course on this topic on a post-secondary level.

11.6   Community-based Dialect Awareness Programs

In the previous section, we examined the role of dialect studies in formal education. In this section, we turn to the role of dialect awareness in the broader context of the community. There are a number of relationships and roles that dialectologists can assume with respect to the communities in which they conduct their research. Deborah Cameron and her associates define several different kinds of relationships between researchers and those they are researching, including ADVOCACY RESEARCH and EMPOWERING RESEARCH (Cameron, Fraser, Harvey, Rampton, and Richardson 1992). Advocacy-based research is characterized by a "commitment on the part of the researcher not just to do research on subjects but research *on* and *for* subjects" (Cameron et al. 1992: 14). Empowering research is research *on*, *for*, and *with* the community, and is guided by several underlying considerations that include the following:

(a)   Persons are not objects and should not be treated as objects.
(b)   Subjects have their own agendas and research should try to address them.
(c)   If knowledge is worth having, it is worth sharing (Cameron et al. 1992: 22–4). (i.e., researchers should seek to share their insights into the language and community they are studying with community members, as well as to discuss with community members how they as researchers have learned from the community.)

Though such ideals are rarely achieved practically in research, sharing knowledge and using linguistic information to address some of the needs and desires of the communities who provide data for our research studies is becoming an increasing concern in the study of language variation. As John Rickford (1999: 315) puts it:

> The fundamental rationale for getting involved in application, advocacy, and empowerment is that we owe it to the people whose data fuel our theories and descriptions; but these are good things to do even if we don't deal directly with native speakers and communities, and enacting them may help us to respond to the interests of our students and to the needs of our field.

Dialectologists are not in a position to make decisions about how a dialect should be used in a given community, or whether it should be used at all (e.g. in the case of an endangered dialect). However, they can work with community members: (1) to ensure that the dialect is documented in a valid and reliable way, (2) to raise the level of consciousness within and outside the community about the current and possible future state of the dialect, and (3) to engage representative community agents and agencies in an effort to understand the historic and current role of dialect in community life.

Our personal involvement with local communities in North Carolina and elsewhere has involved projects that range from dialect exhibits in museums to the production of documentaries, CDs, trade books, and workshops for the general public. For example, the first author and his associates constructed a permanent exhibit on Lumbee English for the Museum of the Native American Resource Center in Pembroke, North Carolina. We also produced a video documentary on Lumbee English titled *Indian by Birth: The Lumbee Dialect* (Hutcheson 2000) that aired on the North Carolina affiliate of PBS. The first author and his associates wrote a book for non-expert audiences that presents the language history of the Lumbee and the development of Lumbee English (Wolfram, Dannenberg, Knick, and Oxendine 2002). Further, we produced *A Dialect Dictionary of Lumbee English* with a community member as the lead author (Locklear, Schilling-Estes, Wolfram, and Dannenberg 1996) and participated in a number of public education activities related to Lumbee language on a local level.

Similar community-based projects have been carried out now in several different communities where we have conducted research, including oral history projects that extend our collaborative partnerships beyond the scope of our linguistic research. For example, in one community project, researchers produced a documentary featuring flood stories related to a devastating hurricane that destroyed the entire town in 1999 (Grimes and Rowe 2004). Such activities involve key community members and local institutions such as museums, civic organizations, and governing councils in an effort to raise awareness about local language history and customs. In some communities, our work has been highly collaborative and visible on a public level with strong public support from local community members.

11.7   Scrutinizing Community Partnerships

Collaboration with local communities in dialect awareness programs may involve social, educational, and economic alliances. While few linguists are, in principle, opposed to giving back to the communities in which they conduct their research and to establishing collaborative relationships with these communities, we must admit that notions such as "linguistic gratuity" and "collaboration" are not unproblematic. At the very least, we need to be aware of some of the issues that underlie alliances between researchers and research communities, with an eye towards establishing parameters that might guide researcher–community partnerships with respect to dialect awareness programs. From the outset, there may be questions about the community's need for sociolinguistic information. Sociolinguists' focus on language differences is typically viewed as an oddity in most communities, whose primary concerns are more likely to be economic and social. There is also the underlying question of motive. Most sociolinguists promote an agenda of social and educational change that is at odds with mainstream language ideology (i.e. the ideology that standard English is "better" than vernacular varieties). The "sociolinguists-know-best" agenda may be antithetical to the community's desired goals with respect to language, particularly in cases where language difference is viewed as an obstacle to be overcome rather than an integral part of cultural heritage.

In addition, researcher–community partnerships involve issues of power and authority. Although the members of a research team may take on a variety of roles and relationships with community members – for example, visitors, researchers, friends – deep down, their primary role is really that of university-based language experts. This role carries with it an associated set of privileges and opportunities, as well as some drawbacks. For example, community members do not immediately welcome strangers based on academic credentials or expert status. In fact, such credentials are typically more of an obstacle to be overcome than an asset in establishing partnerships. Specialized language expertise establishes the basis for an asymmetrical relationship where the researcher is cast as the "authority" and those being researched as "non-experts."

Issues of authority also impact matters of "ownership" with respect to linguistic knowledge. We have found that community members do sometimes assert their expert status regarding their local language, especially in matters involving the lexicon. Thus, for example, they sometimes challenge our definitions of their "dialect words," and a few community members have even taken it upon themselves to collect sets of words and sayings on their own. However, no community member has yet challenged us on our grammatical or phonological descriptions. Though we view the involvement of community members in the collection and presentation of lexical items as a good sign, we have tended to reserve the right to make final decisions about items to be included or excluded, as well as item definitions, in our published "dialect dictionaries," based on our "expert" status. For example, we have sometimes chosen to exclude lexical items offered by community collectors, based on our knowledge of the wide distribution of these forms beyond the local community. However, this decision is questionable, since obviously, the items provided by community members must carry some importance for them, even if they do not fit our "scientific" definition of what counts as a "local" word.

Issues also arise concerning which particular language-related issues should be highlighted in the dialect awareness materials we produce with community members. For example, in researching speech on the Outer Banks island of Ocracoke, North Carolina, we were concerned about the moribund status of the dialect and therefore stressed a theme of dialect endangerment, not only in our academic publications, but in our dialect awareness materials as well (Wolfram and Schilling-Estes 1997). However, ethnographic interviews with islanders regarding cultural identity and dialect recession (McClive 1995) indicated that few islanders actually associated the dialect directly with "genuine" islander identity and that island residents did not necessarily share our concern for the recession of the dialect. The fact of the matter is that language issues are simply not paramount to islanders, who are much more concerned about economic and environmental issues such as property taxes, excessive development, and ecology.

One of the riskier matters concerning dialect awareness programs involves cooperation with the media. As Sally Johnson (2001: 592) notes, "scientists themselves have much to learn from the reception of their ideas by those outside their area of expertise," including their reception by the media. On a number of occasions, the first author introduced journalists to community residents who were quite friendly and helpful to the media personnel. His rationale in involving the media in some of the community programs has been to promote awareness of the true nature of dialect diversity, as well as of the value of dialects as part of community heritage, among as wide an audience as possible. However, there are no guarantees of how the media might portray communities and their language. For example, a couple of newspaper stories produced by media personnel were based on erroneous assumptions and even stereotypes. On one occasion, a BBC correspondent in search of Elizabethan English on Ocracoke proposed getting some residents to read Shakespeare on camera. Although we strongly advised him *not* to ask islanders to do so, we later came upon one of our island friends, Rex O'Neal, standing on the dock in front of the television camera reading Shakespeare. On the one hand, we had a good laugh, especially at Rex's parody of a melodramatic Shakespearean actor, complete with a contrived British accent. On the other hand, we had to admit that we probably played into the hands of those who perpetuate stereotypes about Outer Banks English and other isolated varieties as "true Elizabethan English," in our zeal to publicize the unique language heritage of Ocracoke.

Presentation issues are closely related to issues of representation, that is, how the local dialect is characterized and perhaps even made into a commodity, or commodified. How should we depict dialect in portrayals intended for non-expert audiences? In most cases, sociolinguists tend to portray more marked and vernacular versions of dialect – the more "exotic" and historically older forms of language variation – in their representations to wider audiences, including, sometimes, audiences of linguists. At the same time that we are careful in our classrooms and textbooks to stress that dialect features are usually variable rather than categorical, and that features are shared among dialects, in creating dialect awareness materials we run the risk of creating oversimplified dialect caricatures that downplay the authentic complexity of variation in the communities we are portraying. The general public is not the only population that may have a tendency to create stereotypes. As Rickford (1997a) points out, the themes that researchers highlight in their presentations may serve to reinforce or even create new kinds of stereotypes about language and life in vernacular dialect communities. One of the stereotypes that linguists have to guard against is the BASILECTAL STEREOTYPE, where vernacular dialects are portrayed in their maximally vernacular form rather than in their full complexity.

In researcher–community collaboration, we can expect to encounter conflicting beliefs and values about language that may differentiate community members from the professional linguists who study them. As professional linguists, we are quite prepared to counter popular beliefs about the systematic patterning of vernacular dialects and the logic of these dialects in the name of the principle of error correction. But how do partnerships really work when community members and linguistic researchers enter into a partnership with different belief systems about cultural as well as linguistic diversity? How do we present findings that might describe what we as researchers view as racist, classist, or sexist attitudes among community members as a part of the essential social background for understanding language variation in the community when the researcher is committed to sharing information with community members? Is it ethical for a dialect awareness program to modify information for different audiences in order to "protect" our collaborative interests? These are difficult questions with no easy answers, but they affect the sharing of knowledge and researcher–community partnerships in significant ways. The sharing of information, as well as the very definition of "information" or "knowledge," has to be negotiated between researchers and community members when researchers work in partnership with communities to help meet the needs and desires of the community, as well as the goals of the researchers.

Finally, there is the issue of profit, including monetary profit as well as less tangible value. Who really profits from our participation in the community? Though linguists may not profit greatly in an economic sense from research conducted in a given community, or from the production of dialect awareness materials such as video documentaries, we can hardly claim that there is no profit motive at all, at least not if one views less tangible gains in terms of monetary metaphors. Linguists profit greatly from the communities researched – with respect to professional advancement, publications records, and even in recognition from community or other organizations for proactive involvement with local communities (Rickford 1997a: 184).

Though we may feel that awareness about dialect diversity is heightened through active involvement in the community, we need to ask whether the partnership yields mutual benefit or simply represents the imposition of a sociolinguistically oriented political and cultural agenda on the community. Clearly, many issues need to be contemplated before rushing into researcher–community partnerships: the application of the linguistic gratuity principle, and the implementation of dialect awareness programs on a community level. Nonetheless, it seems that giving back to communities in some form is a good and proper thing to consider when we have mined the community's linguistic resources to our advantage. The development of dialect awareness programs for and with the community being researched represents a special opportunity for sharing information and working with host communities. At the same time, we need to be aware of the kinds of issues that arise in the implementation of these programs and honestly confront these concerns about researcher–community relations.

The study of language variation starts with a natural curiosity about the way language reflects human behavior. In the final analysis, we can seize on this natural curiosity as a basis for working with communities as we come to understand – and celebrate – language diversity as an integral part of community heritage and individual and cultural identity. Helping people develop an appreciation for dialect diversity seems to be the least we can do as dialect researchers who profit greatly from studying the rich variety of dialects and languages that lend so much to the cultural landscape of American society.

11.8 Further Reading

Cameron, Deborah, Elizabeth Fraser, Penelope Harvey, M. B. H. Rampton, and Kay Richardson (1992) *Researching Language: Issues of Power and Method.* London: Routledge. This collection of articles represents a thoughtful discussion of the relationships between researchers and the communities they research, raising some important questions about the power and responsibility of researchers.

Farr, Marcia, and Harvey Daniels (1986) *Language Diversity and Writing Instruction*. Urbana, IL: National Council of Teachers of English. This reasoned treatment offers a theoretical framework, along with practical suggestions for educators who wish to improve the writing skills of students from vernacular-speaking communities.

Rickford, John R. (1997) Unequal partnership: Sociolinguistics and the African American speech community. *Language in Society* 26: 161–98. Rickford discusses the responsibility of linguists to consider ways in which they can serve the communities that have provided rich data for descriptive and theoretical research.

Rickford, John R., and Angela Rickford (1995) Dialect readers revisited. *Linguistics and Education* 7: 107–28. This article discusses a recent attempt to experiment with dialect readers. It also reviews some previous experimentation with such readers and concludes that their abandonment was premature and empirically unwarranted.

Wolfram, Walt (2004) Dialect awareness in community perspective. In Margaret C. Bender (ed.), *Linguistic Diversity in the South: Changing Codes, Practices, and Ideologies*. Athens, GA: University of Georgia Press, 15–36. This article discusses ethical considerations in language awareness programs and considers a couple of case studies of community-based, collaborative projects.

Wolfram, Walt, and Natalie Schilling-Estes (1997) *Hoi Toide on the Outer Banks: The Story of the Ocracoke Brogue*. Chapel Hill: University of North Carolina Press. This book is written for non-experts, including tourists on the Outer Banks, residents of the local community, and other readers curious about Outer Banks dialects. The final chapter details the community-based collaborative dialect awareness programs that have been implemented in the Ocracoke community and the Ocracoke school.

Web site

http://www.ncsu.edu (accessed January 3, 2005). The web site of the North Carolina Language and Life Project, housed at North Carolina State University, provides extended samples of curricular materials as well as links to educational materials related to dialect awareness.

Appendix: An Inventory of Distinguishing Dialect Features

The following inventory summarizes many of the dialect features of American English mentioned in the text, as well as some features not covered. It is limited to phonological and grammatical features. For each of the features, a brief general comment is given about the linguistic patterning of the feature, as well as a statement about its dialect distribution. We emphasize items that are socially significant in terms of the standard–vernacular continuum rather than those that are strictly regional, although many of the features are both socially and regionally meaningful. To the extent possible, traditional orthography is used in representing forms, but this is not possible in all cases. Exhaustive descriptions of a full range of North American English dialects are found in Kortman et al. (2004) and Schneider et al. (2004). More comprehensive descriptions of Southern American English vernaculars are found in works such as Bailey (2001) and Cukor-Avila (2001), and more extensive descriptions of Appalachian English are found in Wolfram and Christian (1976) and Montgomery and Hall (2004). Descriptions of African American English (AAE) structures are found in Rickford (1999) and Green (2002). In our discussion of dialect features, we often use the term GENERAL AMERICAN ENGLISH as a basis of comparison. This term is used simply to refer to varieties of English that are not characterized by the particular dialect trait under discussion. Though this use is related to the term "standard English," it avoids some of the value judgments often associated with the label "standard." Furthermore, in many cases, differences between dialects may be equally standard (or nonstandard), so that the distinction between standard and vernacular is not always appropriate.

Phonological Features

Consonants

Final cluster reduction

Word-final consonant clusters ending in a stop can be reduced when both members of the cluster are either voiced (e.g. *find, cold*) or voiceless (*act, test*). This process affects both clusters that are a part of the base word (e.g. *find, act*) and those clusters formed through the addition of an *-ed* suffix (e.g. *guessed, liked*). In general American English, this pattern may operate when the following word begins with a consonant (e.g. *bes' kind*), but in vernacular dialects, it is extended to include following words beginning with a vowel as well (e.g. *bes' apple*). This pattern is quite prominent in AAE and English-based creoles; it is also common in dialects of English that retain influence from other languages, such as Latino English, Vietnamese English, Hmong English, and so forth. It is not particularly noticeable in other American English dialects.

Plurals following clusters

Words ending in *-sp* (e.g. *wasp*), *-sk* (e.g. *desk*), and *-st* (e.g. *test*) may take the "long plural" *-es* (phonetically [ɪz]) plural in many vernacular varieties, following the reduction of their final clusters to *-s*. Thus, items such as *tes'* for *test* and *des'* for *desk* will be pluralized as *tesses* and *desses*, respectively, just as words ending in *-s* or other *s*-like sounds in general American English (e.g., *bus, buzz*) are pluralized with an *-es* ending (*buses, buzzes*).

In some rural varieties of English such as Appalachian and Southeastern coastal varieties, the *-es* plural may occur even without the reduction of the final cluster to *-s*, yielding plural forms such as *postes* and *deskes*. Such forms are considerably rarer in AAE and seem to be a function of hypercorrection, in which speakers who formerly produced *desses* for *desks* simply add the *k* while retaining the long plural *-es*, resulting in forms like *deskes*.

Intrusive t

A small set of items, usually ending in *-s* and *-f* in the standard variety, may be produced with a final *t*. This results in a final consonant cluster. Typical items affected by this process are *oncet* [wʌnst], *twicet* [twaɪst], *clifft*, and *acrosst*. Intrusive *t* is primarily found in Appalachian varieties and other rural varieties characterized by the retention of older forms.

A quite different kind of intrusive *t* involves the "doubling" of an *-ed* form. In this instance, speakers add the "long past form" *-ed* (phonetically [ɪd]) to verbs that are already marked with an *-ed* ending pronounced as *t* (e.g. [lʊkt] "looked"). This process yields forms such as *lookted* for *looked* and *attackted* for *attacked*. In effect, the speaker treats the verb as if its base form ends in a *t* so that it is eligible for the long past form that regularly is attached to verbs ending in *t* or *d*.

th *sounds*

There are a number of different processes that affect *th* sounds. The phonetic production of *th* is sensitive to the position of *th* in the word and the sounds adjacent to it. At the beginning of the word, *th* tends to be produced as a corresponding stop, as in *dey* for *they* ([d] for [ð]) and *ting* for *thing* ([t] for [θ]). These productions are fairly typical of a wide range of vernaculars, although there are some differences in the distribution of stopped variants for voiced vs. voiceless *th* ([ð] vs. [θ]). The use of *t* in *thing* (voiceless *th*) tends to be most characteristic of selected European American and second-language-influenced varieties, whereas the use of *d* in *they* (voiced *th*) is spread across the full spectrum of vernacular varieties.

Before nasals (*m*, *n*, *ng*), *th* participates in a process in which a range of fricatives, including *z*, *th*, and *v*, may also become stops. This results in forms such as *aritmetic* for *arithmetic* or *headn* for *heathen*, as well as *wadn't* for *wasn't*, *idn't* for *isn't*, and *sebm* for *seven*. This pattern is typically found in Southern-based vernacular varieties, including Southern European American and African American vernacular varieties.

In word-final position and between vowels within a word (that is, in intervocalic position), *th* may be produced as *f* or *v*, as in *efer* for *ether*, *toof* for *tooth*, *brover* for *brother*, and *smoov* for *smooth*. This production is typical of vernacular varieties of AAE, with the *v* for voiced *th* [ð] production more typical of Eastern vernacular varieties. Some Southern-based European American dialects, as well as some varieties influenced by other languages in the recent past, also have the *f* production in *tooth*.

Some restricted varieties use a stop *d* for intervocalic voiced *th* as in *oder* for *other* or *broder* for *brother*, but this pattern is much less common than the use of a stop for *th* in word-initial position.

r *and* l

There are a number of different linguistic contexts in which *r* and *l* may be lost or reduced to a vowel-like quality. After a vowel, as in *sister* or *steal*, the *r* and *l* may be reduced or lost. This feature is quite typical of traditional Southern speech and Eastern New England speech. It is a receding feature of Southern European American English, especially in metropolitan areas.

Between vowels, *r* also may be lost, as in *Ca'ol* for *Carol* or *du'ing* for *during*. Intervocalic *r* loss is more socially stigmatized than postvocalic *r* loss and is found in rural, Southern-based vernaculars.

Following a consonant, the *r* may be lost if it precedes a rounded vowel such as *u* or *o*, resulting in pronunciations such as *thu* for *through* and *tho* for *throw*. Postconsonantal *r* loss may also be found if *r* occurs in an unstressed syllable, as in *p'ofessor* for *professor* or *sec'etary* for *secretary*. This type of *r*-lessness is found primarily in Southern-based varieties. Before a bilabial sound such as *p*, *l* may be lost completely, giving pronunciations like *woof* for *wolf* or *hep* for *help*. Again, this is characteristic only of Southern-based varieties. Other regional dialects (e.g. Pittsburgh, Philadelphia) sometimes vocalize *l* after a vowel to the point where it is almost indistinguishable from a vowel, thus making the words *vow* and *Val* sound the same.

Sometimes *r*-lessness causes one lexical item to converge with another. Thus, the use of *they* for *their* as in *theyself* or *they book* apparently derives from the loss of *r* on *their*, even though speakers who currently use *they* in such constructions may no longer associate it with *r*-less *their*.

There are also occasional instances in which an intrusive *r* may occur, so that items such as *wash* may be pronounced as *warsh* and *idea* as *idear*. Certain instances of intrusive *r* are the result of a generalized pronunciation process, whereby *r* can be added on to the ends of vowel-final words (e.g. *idear*), particularly when these words precede vowel-initial words (*the idear of it*). Other cases (e.g. *warsh*) seem to be restricted to particular lexical items and are highly regionally restricted as well.

Initial w *reduction*

In unstressed positions within a phrase, an initial *w* may be lost in items such as *was* and *one*. This results in items such as *She's* [šiz] *here yesterday* for *She was here yesterday* and *young 'uns* for *young ones*. This appears to be an extension of the process affecting the initial *w* of the modals *will* and *would* in standard varieties of English (as in *he'll* for *he will*, or *she'd* for *she would*). This process is found in Southern-based vernaculars.

Unstressed initial syllable loss

The general process of deleting unstressed initial syllables in informal speech styles of general American English (e.g. *'cause* for *because*; *'round* for *around*) is extended in vernacular varieties so that a wider range of word classes, for example, verbs such as *'member* for *remember* or nouns such as *'taters* for *potatoes*, and a wider range of initial syllable types (e.g. *re-* as in *'member* for *remember*, *su-* as in *'spect* for *suspect*) are affected by this process.

Initial h *retention*

The retention of *h* on the pronoun *it* [hɪt] and the auxiliary *ain't* [heɪnt] is still found in vernacular varieties retaining some older English forms, such as Appalachian English and Outer Banks English. This form is more prominent in stressed positions within a sentence. The pronunciation is fading out among younger speakers.

Nasals

There are a number of processes that affect nasal sounds; there are also items that are influenced by the presence of nasals in the surrounding linguistic environment.

One widespread process in vernacular varieties is so-called "*g*-dropping," in which the nasal [ŋ], represented as *ng* in spelling, is pronounced as [n]. This process takes place when the *ng* occurs in an unstressed syllable, as in *swimmin'* for *swimming* or *buyin'* for *buying*. Linguists refer to this process as "velar fronting" since it involves the fronting of the velar nasal [ŋ], produced toward the back of the mouth, to [n], a more fronted nasal sound.

A less widespread phenomenon affecting nasals is the deletion of the word-final nasal segment in items such as *man*, *beam*, and *ring*, particularly when the item is in a relatively unstressed position within the sentence. Even though the nasal is deleted, the words still retain their final nasal character, because the vowel preceding the *n* has been nasalized, through an assimilation process common to all varieties of English. Thus, *man*, *beam*, and *ring* may be pronounced as *ma'* [mæ̃], *bea'* [bĩ], and *ri'* [rĩ], respectively, with the vowel carrying a nasal quality. Most frequently, this process affects the segment *n*, although all final nasal segments may be affected to some extent. This process is typical of AAE.

The phonetic quality of vowels may be affected before nasal consonants, as in the well-known merger of the contrast between [ɪ] and [ɛ] before nasals as in *pin* and *pen*. Some Southern dialects restrict this merger to a following *n*, whereas others extend it to following *m* (e.g. *Kim* and *chem*) and [ŋ] as well.

Other consonants

There are a number of other consonantal patterns that affect limited sets of items or single words. For example, speakers have used *aks* for *ask* for over a thousand years and still continue to use it in several vernacular varieties, including vernacular AAE. The form *chimley* or *chimbley* for *chimney* is also found in a number of Southern-based vernaculars. The use of *k* in initial *(s)tr* clusters as in *skreet* for *street* or *skring* for *string* is found in vernacular AAE, particularly rural Southern varieties. Such items are usually very noticeable and tend to be socially stigmatized, but they occur with such limited sets of words that they are best considered on an item-by-item basis.

Vowels

There are many vowel patterns that differentiate the dialects of English, but the majority of these are more regionally than socially significant. The back vowel [ɔ] of *bought* or *coffee* and the front vowel [æ] of *cat* and *ran* are particularly sensitive to regional variation, as are many vowels before *r* (e.g. compare pronunciations of *merry, marry, Mary, Murray*) and *l* (compare *wheel, will, well, whale,* etc.). Although it is not possible here to indicate all the nuances of phonetic difference reflected in the vowels of American English, several major patterns of pronunciation may be identified.

Vowel shifts

There are several shifts in the phonetic values of vowels that are currently taking place in American English. The important aspect of these shifts is the fact that the vowels are not shifting their phonetic values in isolation but as rotating systems of vowels. As noted in the text, one major rotation is the NORTHERN CITIES VOWEL SHIFT. In this rotation, the phonetic values of two series of vowels are affected; the low long back vowels are moving forward and upward, and the short front vowels are moving downward and backward. For example, the /ɔ/ vowel, as in *coffee*, is moving forward toward the /ɑ/ of *father*. The low vowel in a word like *pop* or *lock*, in turn, moves towards the /æ/ of *bat*, so that outsiders sometimes confuse *lock* with *lack*. The /æ/ of *bat*, in turn, moves upward toward the vowel /ɛ/ of *bet*. At the same time, another rotation moves the short vowel /ɪ/ of *bit* toward the /ɛ/ of *bet*. The /ɛ/, in turn, moves backward toward the mid vowel of *but* /ʌ/, which is then pushed back. Short vowels and long vowels tend to rotate as different subsystems within the overall vowel system. Diagrammatically, the shift may be represented as shown in figure A.1. In this chart, front vowels appear to the left of the chart and high vowels towards the top. For convenience, "key words" in terms of idealized standard American English phonemes are given. The arrows point in the direction of the phonetic rotations taking place in the shift.

Regionally, the pattern of vowel rotation represented in figure A.1 starts in Western New England and proceeds westward into the northern tier of

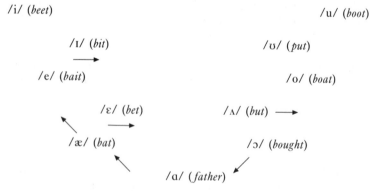

Figure A.1   The Northern Cities Vowel Shift (adapted from Labov 1991)

Pennsylvania; the extreme northern portions of Ohio, Indiana, and Illinois; Michigan; and Wisconsin. It is concentrated in the larger metropolitan areas. More advanced stages of this change can be found in younger speakers in the largest metropolitan areas in this Northern region, such as Buffalo, Albany, Cleveland, Detroit, and Chicago. Minority groups in these metropolitan areas tend not to participate in this phonetic shift.

The SOUTHERN VOWEL SHIFT is quite different from the Northern Cities Vowel Shift. In this rotation pattern, the short front vowels (the vowels of words like *bed* and *bid*) are moving upward and taking on the gliding character of long vowels. In general American English, a vowel like the long *e* of *bait* actually consists of a vowel nucleus [e] and an upward glide to [ɪ], whereas a vowel like the short *e* [ɛ] of *bet* does not have this gliding character, at least not in the idealized standard variety. In the Southern Vowel Shift, the vowel of *bed* takes on a glide, becoming more like *beyd* [bɛɪd]. Meanwhile, the long front vowels (the vowels of *beet* and *late*) are moving somewhat backward and downward, and the back vowels (the vowels of *boot* and *boat*) are moving forward. This phonetic rotation is illustrated in figure A.2.

Low back vowel merger
One of the major regional pronunciation processes affecting vowels is the merger of the low back vowel /ɔ/ and the low back/central vowel /ɑ/. This merger means that word pairs like *caught* and *cot* or *Dawn* and *Don* are pronounced the same. This regional merger radiates from several areas, one in Eastern New England, centered near the Boston area, one centered in Western Pennsylvania in the Ohio Valley, and one covering a large portion of the American West, excluding major metropolitan areas such as Los Angeles and San Francisco.

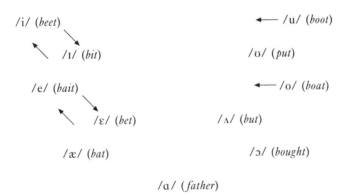

Figure A.2 The Southern Vowel Shift (adapted from Labov 1991)

Other vowel mergers
There are a number of vowel mergers or "near mergers" that take place
when vowels occur before certain kinds of consonants. The following mergers
may occur before *r*, *l*, and the nasal segments (*m*, *n*, *ng*).

- /ɔ/ and /ɑ/, as in *Dawn* and *Don* (Western Pennsylvania, Eastern
  New England, much of the Western US)
- /i/ and /ɪ/, as in *field* and *filled* (South; sporadically elsewhere)
- /e/ and /ɛ/ before /l/, as in *sale* and *sell* (South; sporadically
  elsewhere)
- /u/ and /ʊ/, as in *pool* and *pull* (South; sporadically elsewhere)
- /e/, /ɛ/, /æ/ before /r/, as in *Mary*, *merry*, *marry* (many areas of
  the US, including the South)
- /ɪ/ and /ɛ/ before nasals, as in *pin* and *pen* (South)

Different dialects naturally may be distinguished by the kinds of mergers in
which they participate. Thus, some varieties in the South and some other
areas of the United States merge the vowels of *Mary*, *merry*, and *marry*,
while the regional dialect of Southeastern Pennsylvania and New Jersey that
encompasses Philadelphia merges *merry* and *Murray* at the same time that it
keeps these items distinct from *Mary* and *marry*.

Other dialects may be characterized by vowel shifts in which a vowel
moves so close to another vowel that speakers from other dialect areas may
think the two sounds have merged. In reality, a subtle distinction between
the two sounds is maintained. For example, the backed and raised /ai/
vowel of the Outer Banks of North Carolina in words like *tide* may seem
quite similar to /ɔi/ (as in *boy*), but it is maintained as distinct. Similarly,
the /ɪ/ vowel (as in *bit*) may be raised so that it sounds almost like /i/ (as
in *beet*), particularly before palatals such as *sh* and *tch*, so that people may
hear *feesh* for *fish* and *reach* for *rich*. Just as with /ai/ and /ɔi/, though,
a distinction between /ɪ/ and /i/ is preserved. This near merger is also
found in some mainland Southern varieties, including the Upper Southern
variety of Appalachian English. Isolated varieties may also retain a lower
vowel production of /æ/ before *r* so that *there* may sound like *thar* and
bear like *bar*.

æ raising
The vowel of words such as *back* or *bag* may be raised from its typical
phonetic position so that it is produced closer to the [ɛ] of *beg* or *bet*. The
feature is found in a number of Northern areas and is an integral part of the
Northern Cities Vowel Shift.

Variants of au

The vowel nucleus of words like *out*, *loud*, and *down* may be produced in a number of different ways. In one pronunciation, which is sometimes referred to as CANADIAN RAISING because of its prominence in certain areas of Canada, the nucleus of /au/ is pronounced as a mid central rather than low vowel, so that a phrase such as *out and about* sounds like *oat and aboat* [əʊt n əbəʊt]. This pronunciation is found in coastal Maryland, Virginia, and North Carolina, as well as some scattered dialect regions in Northern areas. Other dialect areas (e.g. Philadelphia) pronounce /au/ with a fronted nucleus [æ], as in [dæʊn] for *down*; and there is at least one dialect area (Pittsburgh) where /au/ may be produced with little or no glide as well, as in *dahntahn* for *downtown*.

In a somewhat different production, the glide of /au/ may be fronted as well as the nucleus, so that *brown* [bræɪn] may actually be confused with *brain* and *house* [hæɪs] may be confused with *highest*. This production is concentrated in the coastal dialects of the Mid-Atlantic and Southeastern US, such as those of Smith Island and Tangier Island in the Chesapeake Bay and the North Carolina Outer Banks.

Variants of ai

Several different processes may affect the diphthong /ai/ in words such as *time*, *tide*, and *tight*. The [ɪ] glide which forms the second half of this diphthong (made up of [a] + [ɪ]) may be lost, yielding pronunciations such as [tam] for *time* and [tad] for *tide*. This glide loss, or UNGLIDING, is characteristic of practically all Southern-based vernaculars and is not particularly socially significant in the South. The absence of the glide is more frequent when the following segment is a voiced sound (e.g. *side*, *time*) than when it is a voiceless one (e.g. *sight*, *rice*), and only certain European American Southern varieties exhibit extensive ungliding of /ai/ before voiceless sounds.

Another process affecting some varieties of American English involves the pronunciation of the nucleus of /ai/ as a mid central rather than low vowel, so that *tide* and *tight* may be produced as [təɪd] and [təɪt]. This process often parallels the raising of the nucleus of /au/ and is also referred to as Canadian Raising because of its widespread presence in Canada. In the US, this type of /ai/ raising is found in the Tidewater Virginia area and other Eastern coastal communities. It is especially common before voiceless sounds (e.g. [təɪt] "tight").

The nucleus of /ai/ may also be backed and/or raised (that is, /ai/ is pronounced as something like [ʌˀɪ]) so that it sounds quite close to the /ɔi/ of *toy* or *boy*. This backing and raising is associated with the Outer Banks of North Carolina, where speakers are referred to as "hoi toiders" for *high tiders*. A few other dialects of American English use a backed nucleus for

/ai/, including New York City English and some mainland Southern varieties. For other differences in vowel nuclei and glides, see chapter 3.

Final unstressed ou
In word-final position, general American English *ow*, as in *hollow* or *yellow*, may become *r*, giving *holler* or *yeller*, respectively. This "intrusive *r*" also occurs when suffixes are attached, as in *fellers* for *fellows* or *narrers* for *narrows*. This production is characteristic of Southern mountain varieties such as those found in Appalachia or the Ozarks, although it is found to some extent in rural varieties in the lowland South as well.

Final unstressed ə *raising*
Final unstressed *a* (phonetically [ə]), as in *soda* or *extra*, may be raised to a high vowel [i] giving productions such as *sody* (phonetically [sodi]) and *extry* [ɛkstri]). Again, this production is found in rural Southern vernaculars.

ire/our *collapse*
The sequence spelled *ire*, usually produced in general American English as a two-syllable sequence which includes the [aɪ] diphthong (i.e. [taɪ.ɚ] "tire"; [faɪ.ɚ] "fire"), can be collapsed into a one-syllable sequence when /ai/ is unglided to [a]. This process yields pronunciations such as *far* for *fire* and *tar* for *tire*. It affects not only root words like *fire* but also /ai/+ *er* sequences formed by the addition of an *-er* suffix, as in *buyer* [bar]. A similar process affects *-our/-ower* sequences which phonetically consist of a two-syllable sequence involving the [aʊ] diphthong and *r*, as in *flower* [flaʊ.ɚ] or *hour* [aʊ.ɚ]. These sequences may be reduced to a single syllable, so that *flower* sounds like *fla'r* [flar] and *hour* like *a'r* [ar].

Grammatical Features

The verb phrase

Many of the socially significant grammatical structures in American English varieties involve aspects of the verb phrase. Some of this variation is due to the principles of readjustment discussed in chapter 2, but there are also some items that have their roots in the historical origins of different dialect varieties.

Irregular verbs
There are five ways in which irregular verbs pattern differently in standard and vernacular dialects of English. For the most part, these different patterns

are the result of analogy, but there are also some retentions of patterns that have become obsolete in standard varieties. These differences are as follows:

1 past as participle form
   I *had went* down there.
   He may *have took* the wagon.
2 participle as past form
   He *seen* something out there.
   She *done* her work.
3 bare root as past form
   She *come* to my house yesterday.
   She *give* him a nice present last year.
4 regularization
   Everybody *knowed* he was late.
   They *throwed* out the old food.
5 different irregular form
   I *hearn* [heard] something shut the church house door.
   Something just *riz* [rose] up right in front of me.

Dialects vary according to which of the above patterns they exhibit. The majority of vernaculars in the North and South indicate patterns 1, 2, and 3. Some rural vernaculars in the South may exhibit pattern 5 in addition to the first three. Varieties subject to the influence of second-language-learning strategies will often reveal a higher incidence of regularization pattern 4 than other varieties.

Co-occurrence relations and meaning changes
There are a number of different types of constructions that can vary from dialect to dialect based on the types of structures that can co-occur with certain verbs. There are also meaning changes that affect particular verbs. These constructions and meaning changes include the following types:

1 shifts in the transitive status of verbs (i.e. whether or not the verb must take an object)
   If we *beat*, we'll be champs.
2 types of complement structures co-occurring with particular verbs
   The kitchen *needs remodeled*.
   The students *started to messing* around.
   I'll *have* him *to do* it.
   The dog *wanted out*.
   Walt *calls himself dancing*.
3 verb plus verb particle formations
   He *happened in* on the party.
   The coach *blessed out* [swore at, yelled at] his players.

4   use of progressive with stative verbs

> He *was liking* the new house.
>
> She *was wanting* to get out.

5   verbs derived from other parts of speech (e.g. verbs derived from nouns)

> Our dog *treed* a coon.
>
> We *doctored* the sickness ourselves.

6   broadened, narrowed, or shifted semantic reference for particular verb forms

> He *carried* her to the movies.
>
> My kids *took* the chicken pox when they were young.
>
> I been *aimin'* to [intending] go there.

For the most part, differences related to meaning changes and co-occurrence relations have to be dealt with on an item-by-item basis. All vernaculars, and many regional varieties, indicate meaning shifts and co-occurrence relations not found in standard English to any great extent.

Special auxiliary forms

There are a number of special uses of auxiliary forms that set apart vernacular dialects of English from their standard counterparts. Many of these auxiliaries indicate subtle but significant meanings related to the duration or type of activity indicated by verbs, or "verb aspect."

Completive done

The form *done* when used with a past tense verb may mark a completed action or event in a way somewhat different from a simple past tense form, as in a sentence such as *There was one in there that done rotted away* or *I done forgot what you wanted*. In this use, the emphasis is on the "completive" aspect or the fact that the action has been fully completed. The *done* form may also add intensification to the activity, as in *I done told you not to mess up*. This form is typically found in Southern European American and African American vernaculars.

Habitual be

The form *be* in sentences such as *Sometimes my ears be itching* or *She usually be home in the evening* may signify an event or activity distributed intermittently over time or space. Habitual *be* is most often used in *be* + verb *-ing* constructions, as in *My ears be itching*. The unique aspectual meaning of *be* is typically associated with AAE, although isolated and restricted constructions with habitual *be* have been found in some rural European American varieties. In recent stylized uses often associated with hip-hop culture, the form has been extended to refer to intensified stativity or super-real status, as in *I be the truth*.

Be + s

In some restricted parts of the South (e.g. areas of the Carolinas where the historic influence of Highland Scots and Scots-Irish is evident), *be* may occur with an *-s* third-person suffix as in *Sometimes it bes like that* or *I hope it bes a girl*. However, *bes* is not restricted to contexts of habitual activity and thus is different from habitual *be* in AAE. *Bes* is also distinguished from *be* in contemporary AAE by the inflectional *-s*; further, *bes* is a receding form, while *be* in AAE is quite robust and escalating.

Remote time béen

When stressed, *béen* can serve to mark a special aspectual function, indicating that the event or activity took place in the "distant past" but is still relevant. In structures such as *I béen had it there for years* or *I béen known her*, the reference is to an event that took place, literally or figuratively, in some distant time frame. This use, which is associated with vernacular AAE, is dying out in some varieties of this dialect.

Fixin' to

The use of *fixin' to* (also pronounced as *fixta*, *fista*, *finsta*, and *finna*) may occur with a verb with the meaning of "about to" or "planning to". Thus, in a sentence such as *It's fixin' to rain*, the occurrence of rain is imminent. In a construction such as *I was fixin' to come but I got held up*, the speaker is indicating that he or she had intended to come. This special use of *fixin' to* is found only in the South, particularly in the South Atlantic and Gulf states.

Indignant come

The use of the form *come* as an auxiliary in sentences such as *She come acting like she was real mad* or *He come telling me I didn't know what I was talking about* may convey a special sense of speaker indignation. It is a CAMOUFLAGED FORM, in the sense that it appears to be much like a comparable general American English use of *come* with movement verbs (e.g. *She came running home*), but it does not function in the same way as its standard counterpart. It is found in AAE.

A- *prefixing*

An *a-* prefix may occur on *-ing* forms functioning as verbs or as complements of verbs as in *She was a-comin' home* or *He made money a-fishin'*. This form cannot occur on *-ing* forms that function as nouns or adjectives. Thus, it cannot occur in sentences such as *He likes a-sailin'* or *The movie was a-charmin'*. The *a-* is also restricted phonologically, in that it occurs only on forms whose first syllable is accented; thus, it may occur on *a-fóllowin'* but not usually on **a-discóverin'*. As currently used by some speakers, the *a-* prefix may be used to indicate intensity, but it does not appear to have any unique aspectual marking analogous to habitual *be* or completive *done*. It is associated with vernacular Southern mountain speech but is found in many other rural varieties as well. To a lesser degree, an *a-* prefix also can be attached to other verb forms, such as participles in *She's a-worked there* or even to simple past forms as in *She a-wondered what happened*.

Double modals
Double modals are combinations of two MODAL verbs, or verbs expressing certain "moods" such as certainty, possibility, obligation, or permission. Possible combinations include *might could, useta could, might should, might oughta*, and so forth. Sentences such as *I might could go there* or *You might oughta take it* are typically Southern vernacular structures; in Northern varieties, modal clustering occurs only with *useta*, as in *He useta couldn't do it*. Double modals tend to lessen the force of the attitude or obligation conveyed by single modals, so that *She might could do it* is less forceful than either *She might do it* or *She could do it*. In some Southern regions, double modals are quite widespread and not particularly stigmatized.

Liketa *and* (su)poseta
The forms *liketa* and *(su)poseta* may be used as special verb modifiers to mark the speaker's perceptions that a significant event was on the verge of happening. *Liketa* is an AVERTIVE, in that it is used to indicate an impending event that was narrowly avoided. It is often used in a figurative rather than literal sense; for example, in a sentence such as *It was so cold, I liketa froze to death*, the speaker may never have been in any real danger of freezing, but the use of *liketa* underscores the intensity of the condition. *(Su)poseta*, in sentences such as *You (su)poseta went there*, parallels the general American English construction *supposed to have*.

Quotative be like *and* go
Over the past few decades, the use of *be like* and *go* to introduce a quote (e.g. *So she's like, "Where are you going?" and I go, "Where do you think?"*) has shown phenomenal growth. Once associated with Valley Girl talk in California, it is now used throughout North America, as well as the British Isles, Australia, and New Zealand. It is also now used in a wide variety of vernacular varieties, even some situated in comparative cultural or regional isolation. Because of its relatively recent expansion, it is much more common

among speakers born after the 1960s than those born earlier, though it is now even being adopted by some older speakers. Some speakers of AAE may still use *say* to introduce a quote, as in *I told him, say, "Where you going?"* but its use is rapidly receding. In fact, quotative *be like* is taking over in AAE as it is in other dialects. Quotative *be like* can also be used in a somewhat more figurative sense, to introduce an imagined quote, or what the speaker was thinking rather than literally saying at the time, as in *I was like "What is wrong with you?"* A related form is quotative *be all*, as in a sentence such as *I was all, "What's going on?"*

Absence of be *forms*

Where contracted forms of *is* or *are* may occur in general American English, these same forms may be absent in some vernacular varieties. Thus, we get structures such as *You ugly* or *She taking the dog out* corresponding to the general American English structures *You're ugly* and *She's taking the dog out*, respectively. It is important to note that this absence takes place only on "contractible" forms; thus, it does not affect *they are* in a construction such as *That's where they are*, since *they are* cannot be contracted to *they're* in this instance. Furthermore, the absence of *be* does not usually apply to *am*, so that sentences such as *I ugly* do not occur. The deletion of *are* is typical of both Southern European American and African American varieties, although the absence of *is* is not very extensive in most European American vernaculars. A more general version of *be* absence – that includes *am* and past tense – is sometimes found in varieties developed in the process of learning English as a second language.

Subject–verb agreement

There are a number of different subject–verb agreement patterns that enter into the social and regional differentiation of dialects. These include the following:

1. agreement with existential *there*
   There was five people there.
   There's two women in the lobby.
2. leveling to *was* for past tense forms of *be*
   The cars was out on the street.
   Most of the kids was younger up there.
3. leveling to *were* with negative past tense *be*
   It weren't me that was there last night.
   She weren't at the creek.
4. leveling to *is* for present tense forms of *be*
   The dogs is in the house.
   We is doing it right now.

5 agreement with the form *don't*
   She don't like the cat in the house.
   It don't seem like a holiday.
6 agreement with *have*
   My nerves has been on edge.
   My children hasn't been there much.
7 *-s* suffix on verbs occurring with third-person plural noun phrase subjects
   Some people likes to talk a lot.
   Me and my brother gets in fights.
8 *-s* absence on third-person singular forms
   *The dog stay_* outside in the afternoon.
   *She usually like_* the evening news.

Different vernacular varieties exhibit different patterns in terms of the above list. Virtually all vernacular varieties show patterns 1, 2, and 5 above (in fact, standard varieties are moving towards the pattern found in 1), but in different degrees. The patterns illustrated in 6 and 7 above are most characteristic of rural varieties in the South, and that in 8 is most typical of vernacular AAE. The leveling of past *be* to *weren't* in 3 appears to be regionally restricted to some coastal dialect areas of the Southeast such as the Eastern Shore of Virginia and Maryland, and the Outer Banks of North Carolina.

Past tense absence
Many cases of past tense *-ed* absence on verbs (e.g. *Yesterday he mess up*) can be accounted for by the phonological process of consonant cluster reduction found in the discussion of phonology. However, there are some instances in which the use of unmarked past tense forms represents a genuine grammatical difference. Such cases are particularly likely to be found in varieties influenced by other languages in their recent past. Thus, structures such as *He bring the food yesterday* or *He play a new song last night* may be the result of a grammatical process rather than a phonological one. Grammatically based tense unmarking tends to be more frequent on regular verbs than irregular ones, so that a structure such as *Yesterday he play a new song* is more likely than *Yesterday he is in a new store*, although both may occur. In some cases, both phonological and grammatical processes operate in a convergent way.

Tense unmarking has been found to be prominent in varieties such as Vietnamese English and Native American Indian English in the Southwest. In the latter case, unmarking is favored in habitual contexts (e.g. *In those days, we play a different kind of game*) as opposed to simple past time (e.g. *Yesterday, we play at a friend's house*).

Historical present
In the dramatic recounting of past time events, speakers may use present tense verb forms rather than past tense forms, as in *I go down there and this guy comes up to me.* . . . In some cases an -*s* suffix may be added to non-third-person forms, particularly with the first person form of *say* (e.g. *so I says to him* . . .). This structure is more prominent in European American vernaculars than in AAE.

Perfective be
Some isolated varieties of American English may use forms of *be* rather than *have* in present perfect constructions, as in *I'm been there before* for "I've been there before" or *You're taken the best medicine* for "You have taken the best medicine". This construction occurs most frequently in first-person singular contexts (e.g. *I'm forgot*) but can also occur in the first-person plural and in second-person contexts as well (e.g. *we're forgot, you're been there*). Occasionally, the perfect tense can even be formed with invariant *be*, as in *We be come here for nothing* or *I'll be went to the post office*. Perfective *be* derives from the earlier English formation of the perfect with *be* rather than *have* for certain verbs (e.g. *He is risen* vs. "He has risen"). In most cases, it is a retention of the older pattern.

Adverbs

There are several different kinds of patterns affecting adverbs. These involve differences in the placement of adverbs within the sentence, differences in the formation of adverbs, and differences in the use or meaning of particular adverbial forms.

Adverb placement
There are several differences in terms of the position of the adverb within the sentence, including the placement of certain time adverbs within the verb phrase, as in *We were all the time talking* or *We watched all the time the news on TV*. These cases do not hold great social significance and are not particularly socially stigmatized. More socially marked is the change in order with various forms of *ever*, as in *everwhat, everwho*, or *everwhich* (e.g. *Everwho wanted to go could go*). These are remnants of older English patterns and are mostly dying out.

Comparatives and superlatives
Most vernacular varieties of English indicate some comparative and superlative adjective and adverb forms that are not found in standard varieties.

Some forms involve the regularization of irregular forms, as in *badder* or *mostest*, while others involve the use of *-er* and *-est* on adjectives of two or more syllables (e.g. *beautifulest*, *awfulest*), where the standard variety uses *more* and *most*. In some instances, comparatives and superlatives are doubly marked, as in *most awfulest* or *more nicer*. As we discuss in chapter 2, both regularization and double marking are highly natural language processes.

-ly *absence*

In present-day American English, some adverbs that formerly ended in an *-ly* suffix no longer take *-ly*. Thus, in informal contexts, most general American English speakers say *They answered wrong* instead of *They answered wrongly*. The range of items affected by *-ly* absence can be extended in different vernacular dialects. These items may be relatively unobtrusive (e.g. *She enjoyed life awful well*) or quite obtrusive (e.g. *I come from Virginia original*). The more stigmatized forms are associated with Southern-based vernacular varieties, particularly Southern mountain varieties such as Appalachian and Ozark English.

Intensifying adverbs

In some Southern-based vernaculars, certain adverbs can be used to intensify particular attributes or activities. In general American English, the adverb *right* is currently limited to contexts involving location or time (e.g. *He lives right around the corner*). However, in Southern-based vernaculars, *right* may be used to intensify the degree of other types of attributes, as in *She is right nice*. Other adverbs, such as *plumb*, serve to indicate intensity to the point of totality, as in *The students fell plumb asleep*. In some parts of the South, *slam* is used to indicate "totality" rather than *plumb*, as in *The students fell slam asleep*; *clean* may be used in a similar way in other areas, including some Northern dialects (e.g. *The hole went clean through the wall*). The use of *big* in *big old dog*, *little* in *little old dog*, and *right* in *It hurts right much* also function as intensifiers in these varieties.

A special function of the adverb *steady* has been described for AAE. In this variety, *steady* may be used in constructions such as *They be steady messing with you* to refer to an intense, ongoing activity.

Other adverbial forms

There are a number of other cases in which the adverbial forms of vernacular varieties differ from their standard counterparts. Some of these involve word class changes, as in the use of *but* as an adverb meaning "only," as in *He ain't but thirteen years old*, or the item *all* in *The corn got all* ("The corn is all gone/finished"). In many Midland dialects of American English, *anymore* may be used in positive constructions with a meaning of "nowadays," as in *She watches a lot of videos anymore*.

Some vernacular dialects contain adverbial lexical items not found at all in standard varieties, for example, adverbs of location such as *yonder*, *thisaway*, *thataway*, and so forth (e.g. *It's up yonder*, *It's thisaway, not thataway*). Other adverbial differences come from the phonological fusion of items, as in *t'all* from *at all* (e.g. *It's not coming up t'all*), *pert' near* (e.g. *She's pert' near seventy*), or *druther* (e.g. *Druther than lose the farm, he fought*). In parts of the South historically influenced by Scots-Irish, the adverb *whenever* may be used to indicate a one-time event (e.g. *Whenever he died, we were young*) rather than habitually occurring events (e.g. *Whenever we dance, he's my partner*), as it does in most general American varieties. Again, such differences must be considered on an item-by-item basis.

Negation

The two major vernacular negation features of American English are the use of so-called "double negatives," or the marking of negative meaning at more than one point in a sentence, and the use of the lexical item *ain't*. Other forms, resulting directly from the acquisition of English as a second language (e.g. *He no like the man*), are found in the speech of people learning English as a second language, but these do not seem to be perpetuated as a continuing part of the vernacular English variety of such speakers once they have completed their transition to English. An exception may be the negative tag *no* as found in some Hispanic English varieties, as in *They're going to the store, no?*

Multiple negation
There are four different patterns of multiple negative marking found in the vernacular varieties of English:

1　marking of the negative on the auxiliary verb and the indefinite(s) following the verb
　　The man *wasn't* saying *nothing*.
　　He *didn't* say *nothing* about *no* people bothering him or *nothing* like that.
2　negative marking of an indefinite before the verb phrase and of the auxiliary verb
　　Nobody didn't like the mess.
　　Nothing can't stop him from failing the course.
3　inversion of the negativized auxiliary verb and the pre-verbal indefinite
　　Didn't nobody like the mess. ("Nobody liked the mess")
　　Can't nothing stop him from failing the course.

4   multiple negative marking across different clauses
    There *wasn't* much that I *couldn't* do (meaning "There wasn't
    much I could do").
    I *wasn't* sure that *nothing wasn't* going to come up (meaning "I
    wasn't sure that anything was going to come up").

Virtually all vernacular varieties of English participate in multiple negation
of type 1; restricted Northern and most Southern vernaculars participate in
2; most Southern vernaculars participate in 3; and restricted Southern and
African American vernacular varieties participate in 4.

ain't
The item *ain't* may be used as a variant for certain standard American
English forms, including the following:

1   forms of *be + not*
    She *ain't* here now.
    I *ain't* gonna do it.
2   forms of *have + not*
    I *ain't* seen her in a long time.
    She *ain't* gone to the movies in a long time.
3   *did + not*
    He *ain't* tell him he was sorry.
    I *ain't* go to school yesterday.

The first two types are found in most vernacular varieties, but the third
type, in which *ain't* corresponds with standard *didn't*, has only been found
in AAE.

Past tense wont
The form *wont*, pronounced much like the negative modal *won't*, may occur
as a generalized form for past tense negative *be* – that is, *wasn't* and *weren't*.
Thus, we may find sentences such as *It wont me* and *My friends wont the
ones who ate the food*. Although the form probably arose through the application of phonological processes to forms of *wasn't* and *weren't*, *wont* now
seems to serve as a past tense analogue of *ain't*, since both *ain't* and *wont*
have a single form for use with all persons and numbers (as opposed to
standard forms of *be + not*, which vary quite a bit by person and number).
Its use is restricted to rural Southern varieties, particularly those found in
the South Atlantic region.

Nouns and pronouns

Constructions involving nouns and pronouns are often subject to socially significant dialect variation. The major types of differences involve the attachment of various suffixes and the use of particular case markings – that is, inflectional forms that indicate the role which nouns and pronouns play in the particular sentences in which they occur.

Plurals

There are several different ways in which plurals may be formed which differentiate them from plurals found in general American English. These include the following:

1 general absence of plural suffix
   Lots of *boy_* go to the school.
   All the *girl_* liked the movie.
2 restricted absence of plural suffix with measurement nouns
   The station is four *mile_* down the road.
   They hauled in a lotta *bushel_* of corn.
3 regularization of various irregular plural noun forms
   They saw the *deers* running across the field.
   The *firemans* liked the convention.

Plural absence of type 1 is found only among varieties where another language was spoken in the recent past and, to a limited degree, in AAE. In category 2, plural suffix absence is limited to nouns of weights (e.g. *four pound*, *three ton*) and measures (e.g. *two foot*, *twenty mile*) that occur with a "quantifying" word such as a number (e.g. *four*) or plural modifier (e.g. *a lot of*, *some*), including some temporal nouns (e.g. *two year*, *five month*); this pattern is found in Southern-based rural vernaculars. Category 3 includes regularization of plurals that are not overtly marked in general American English (e.g. *deers*, *sheeps*), forms marked with irregular suffixes in the standard (e.g. *oxes*), and forms marked by vowel changes (e.g. *firemans*, *snowmans*). In the last case, plurals may be double-marked, as in *mens* or *childrens*. Some kinds of plurals in category 3 are quite widespread among the vernacular varieties of English (e.g. regularizing non-marked plurals such as *deers*), whereas others (e.g. double marking in *mens*) are more limited.

Possessives

There are several patterns involving possessive nouns and pronouns, including the following:

1   the absence of the possessive suffix
     The *man_ hat* is on the chair.
     John_ coat is here.
2   regularization of the possessive pronoun *mines*, by analogy with *yours*,
     his, *hers*, etc.
     Mines is here.
     It's *mines*.
3   the use of possessive forms ending in -*n*, as in *hisn*, *ourn*, or *yourn*.
     Such forms can only be found in phrase- or sentence-final position
     (called ABSOLUTE POSITION), as in *It is hisn* or *It was yourn that I was
     talking about*; -*n* forms do not usually occur in structures such as *It is
     hern book*.
     Is it *yourn*?
     I think it's *hisn*.

The first two types of possessives are typical of vernacular varieties of AAE,
and the third type is found in vernacular Appalachian English and other
rural varieties characterized by the retention of relic forms, although it is
now restricted to older speakers in these varieties.

Pronouns

Pronoun differences typically involve regularization by analogy and rule
extension. The categories of difference include the following:

1   regularization of reflexive forms by analogy with other possessive
     pronouns such as *myself*, *yourself*, *ourselves*, etc.)
     He hit *hisself* on the head.
     They shaved *theirselves* with the new razor.
2   extension of object forms with coordinate subjects
     Me and him will do it.
     John and them will be home soon.
3   adoption of a second-person plural form to "fill out" the person–
     number paradigm (*I*, *you*, *he/she/it*, *we*, *you*, *they*)
     a   *Y'all* won the game.
          I'm going to leave *y'all* now.
     b   *Youse* won the game.
          I'm going to leave *youse* now.
     c   *You'uns* won the game.
          I'm going to leave *you'uns* now.
4   extension of object forms to demonstratives
     Them books are on the shelf.
     She didn't like *them* there boys.

5   a special PERSONAL DATIVE use of the object pronoun form
    I got *me* a new car.
    We had *us* a little old dog.

The first four types of pronominal difference are well represented in most vernacular dialects of English. The particular form used for the second-person plural pronoun (type 3) varies by region: 3a is the Southern form, 3b is the Northern form, and 3c is the form used in an area extending from Southern Appalachia to Pittsburgh. The so-called personal dative illustrated in 5 is a Southern feature that indicates that the subject of the sentence (e.g. *we*) benefited in some way from the object (e.g. *little old dog*).

Other pronoun forms, such as the use of an object form with a non-coordinate subject (e.g. *Her in the house*) and the use of subject or object forms in possessive structures (e.g. *It is she book*; *It is he book*), are quite rare in most current vernaculars, except for those still closely related to a prior creole. The use of possessive *me*, as in *It's me cap*, is occasionally found in historically isolated varieties which have some Scots-Irish influence.

Relative pronouns
Differences affecting relative pronouns (e.g. *who* in *She's the one who gave me the present*) include the use of certain relative pronoun forms in contexts where they would not be used in general American English and the absence of relative pronouns under certain conditions. Differences in relative pronoun forms may range from the relatively socially insignificant use of *that* for human subjects (e.g. *The person that I was telling you about is here*) to the quite stigmatized use of *what*, as in *The person what I was telling you about is here*. One form that is becoming more common, and spreading into informal varieties of general American English, is the use of the relative pronoun *which* as a coordinating conjunction (i.e. *and*), as in *They gave me this cigar, which they know I don't smoke cigars*.

In general American English, relative pronouns may be deleted if they are the object in the relative clause. For example, *That's the dog that I bought* may alternately be produced as *That's the dog I bought*. In most cases where the relative pronoun is the subject, however, the pronoun must be retained, as in *That's the dog that bit me*. However, a number of Southern-based varieties may sometimes delete relative pronouns in subject position, as in *That's the dog bit me* or *The man come in here is my father*. The absence of the relative pronoun is more common in existential constructions such as *There's a dog bit me* than in other constructions.

Existential it/they
As used in sentences such as *There are four people in school* and *There's a picture on TV*, the American English form *there* is called an EXISTENTIAL,

since it indicates the mere existence of something rather than specific location (as in *Put the book over* **there**). Vernacular varieties may use *it* or *they* for *there* in existential constructions, as in *It's a dog in the yard* or *They's a good show on TV*. *They* for *there* seems to be found only in Southern-based vernaculars; *it* is more general in vernacular varieties.

Other grammatical structures

There are a number of additional structures not included in this overview of vernacular grammatical constructions. Some of the excluded forms include those that were once thought to be confined to vernacular varieties but have been shown to be quite common in informal standard varieties. For example, we did not include the structure known as "pronominal apposition," in which a pronoun is used in addition to a noun in subject position, as in *My father, he made my breakfast*, because this feature is found in practically all social groups of American English speakers, even though it is often considered to be a vernacular dialect feature. Furthermore, it is not particularly obtrusive in spoken language. It has also been found that the use of inverted word order in indirect questions, as in *She asked could she go to the movies*, is becoming just as much a part of informal spoken general American English as indirect questions without inverted word order, as in *She asked if she could go to the movies*. Other differences, such as those affecting prepositions, have to be treated on an item-by-item basis and really qualify as lexical rather than grammatical differences. Thus, forms such as *of a evening/of the evening* ("in the evening"), *upside the head* ("on the side of the head"), *leave out of there* ("leave from there"), *the matter of him* ("the matter with him"), *to* for *at* (e.g. *She's to the store right now*), and so forth have to be treated individually. Infinitive constructions such as *for to*, as in *I'd like for you to go* vs. *I'd like you to go*, or even *I'd like for to go* also constitute a case of a restricted lexical difference. Similarly, cases of article use or non-use, such as the use of articles with certain illnesses and diseases (e.g. *She has the colic*, *He had the earache*) affect only certain lexical items in particular dialects. Traditional *Linguistic Atlas* surveys and the *Dictionary of American Regional English* give much more adequate detail about these forms than can be given in this overview.

Glossary

absolute position   The position at the end of a clause or sentence; for example, *his* is in absolute position in *The book is his*, but not in ***His book is here***.

accent   (1) A popular label for dialect, with particular reference to pronunciation. (2) Speech influenced by another language (e.g. "She speaks with a French accent"). (3) See **stress**.

acronym   A word formed by combining the initial sounds or letters of words, for example *NATO* or *UN*.

additive dialect   See **bidialectalism**.

address form   The name used in speaking to or referring to a person; for example, *Ms Jones, Chris, Professor Smith*.

addressee   A person to whom speech is directed.

advocacy research   Research that includes work to benefit one's subjects in some way. See **empowering research**.

affix   A morpheme that attaches to the base or root word; in *retells*, *re-* and *-s* are affixes.

African American English   The variety of American English spoken by some people of African descent in the US. Often abbreviated AAE.

African diaspora   The dispersal of people from Sub-Saharan Africa, usually as a result of the slave trade, into other parts of Africa, the Caribbean, and North America.

age-grading   The association of certain linguistic usages with a particular stage in the life cycle (for example, teenagers make heavy use of slang). See **apparent time hypothesis**.

agreement   A co-occurrence relationship between grammatical forms, such as that between the subject and verb of a sentence; in the following sentence, the third-person singular subject agrees with the verb because it is marked with the morpheme *-s*: *She likes dialectology*.

alveolar   (Of a sound) produced by touching the blade of the tongue to the small ridge just in back of the upper teeth.

analogy   The application of a pattern to forms not previously included in a set, as in the regularization of the plural *ox* to *oxes* or the formation of the past tense of *bring* as *brang* on the basis of *sing* and *sang* and *ring* and *rang*.

> **four-part analogy**; also **proportional analogy**   The changing of irregular forms for words on the basis of regular patterns (e.g. *cow* : *cows* :: *ox* : *oxes*).

> **leveling**   (as a subtype of analogy) The reduction of distinct forms within a grammatical **paradigm**, as in the use of *was* with all subject persons and numbers for past tense *be* (e.g. *I/you/(s)he/ we/you/they was*). See also **dialect leveling**.

> **minority pattern analogy**   The changing of a form on the basis of an irregular pattern; for example, the formation of the past tense of *bring* as *brang* on the basis of *sing/sang* rather than the regular *-ed* past tense pattern.

Anglicist hypothesis   The contention that African American English is derived historically from dialects transplanted to America from the British Isles. The **Neo-Anglicist hypothesis** also holds that African Americans derived their basic language from British dialects, but contends that it has since diverged considerably from European American varieties.

apex   A dialect pocket, or the regionally restricted extension of one dialect area into an adjacent one; for example, the Hoosier apex is an extension of Southern speech in Southern Indiana and Illinois.

apparent time hypothesis   The assumption that one's speech reflects the state of the language at the time one learned one's language as a child. For example, a speaker born in 1950 would reflect the dialect of their community spoken as they were growing up, whereas a speaker born in 1980 would reflect the state of the language thirty years later. Based on the apparent time hypothesis, researchers often infer patterns of language change by looking at the speech of different generations of speakers at a single moment in time.

applied dialectology   The application of sociolinguistic knowledge about the nature of dialect diversity to educational and other social issues.

argot   A deliberately secretive vocabulary or **jargon**; often used with reference to criminal activity.

aspect   A grammatical category pertaining to verbs which indicates type or duration of activity; for example *has written* (perfect aspect) vs. *has been writing* (imperfect aspect). Compare **tense** and **mood**.

aspiration   A puff of air after the production of a stop, as in the pronunciation of *p* in *pie* [pʰaɪ]; usually indicated by a raised [ʰ] after the sound.

assimilation   The modification of sounds so that they become more like neighboring sounds; for example, the negative prefix *in-* assimilates to *il-* when preceding an *l* (e.g. *illogical*).

attention to speech The approach to **style shifting** which maintains that style shifting is conditioned primarily by the amount of attention given to speech: The more attention paid to speech, the more formal the style will become.

audience design The approach to **style shifting** that maintains that speakers adjust their speech based primarily upon the attributes of people in their audience of listeners.

auditor A person in a speech situation who is considered to be a legitimate participant in the conversational interaction but is not directly addressed.

auxiliary A form occurring with a main verb, traditionally referred to as a "helping verb"; for example, *has* in *has made, done* in *done tried*.

avertive A grammatical form that denotes an action or event narrowly avoided, figuratively or literally. The form *liketa* in a sentence such as *It was so cold I liketa froze to death* functions as an avertive.

back formation The creation of a shorter word from a longer word based on the removal of what appears to be an affix but is in reality part of the original word; for example, *burgle* from *burglar, conversate* from *conversation*.

back vowel A vowel produced with the tongue toward the back of the mouth; for example, the [u] of *Luke*, the [o] of *boat*.

backchanneling The linguistic and extralinguistic strategies used by a listener to indicate that the speaker may continue with an extended conversational turn; for example, *uhmm* and *right* may serve as backchanneling devices.

bare root The root form of a verb. With certain verbs, it may be used to indicate past tense in vernacular dialects; for example, *give* may be used as a past tense form in sentences such as *Yesterday they give me a present*.

basilectal stereotype The portrayal of a dialect, whether by linguists or non-experts, in its most vernacular form.

bidialectalism The position in teaching standard English that maintains that the standard should co-exist with a vernacular variety rather than replace it.

bilabial See **labial**.

blending The creation of a new word by combining portions of different words; for example, words such as *smog* (*smoke* + *fog*) or *twirl* (*twist* + *whirl*) were formed through blending.

borrowing A language item that is taken from another language; for example, *arroyo* "gully" from Spanish.

bound morpheme A morpheme that cannot stand alone as a separate word but must be attached to another item; for example, the *-s* in *boys*. Compare **free morpheme**.

breaking See **vowel breaking**.

broad *a* A non-technical label for the vowel found in words such as *bat* and *back*.

broadening See **semantic broadening**.

bundle of isoglosses A set of isoglosses that cluster together and serve to set apart dialect areas on a map.

camouflaged form A form in a vernacular variety that looks like a standard usage but is used in a structurally or functionally different way; for example, constructions such as *They come here talking that nonsense* in AAE appear to be like standard structures such as *They come running* but actually carry a unique meaning of speaker indignation.

Canadian Raising The production of the nucleus of the /ai/ and /au/ diphthongs as a mid central vowel rather than low vowel, as in [rəɪt] for *right* or [əʊt] for *out*.

cascade diffusion The spread of language features from areas of denser population to areas of sparser population. Also called **hierarchical diffusion**. See **gravity model**. Compare **contagious diffusion, contrahierarchical diffusion**.

case A form that indicates the role of a noun or pronoun in a sentence. For example, *I* is the subject of the sentence in *I hate cheaters* and therefore is in **subjective case**; *me* is the object of the verb in *Dogs hate me* and thus is in **objective case**.

chain shifting The shifting of a series of vowels in **phonetic space** in order to preserve phonetic distinctiveness among the vowel sounds. See **vowel rotation**.

change from above A change in a language form of which speakers are consciously aware.

change from below A change in a language form of which speakers are not aware on a conscious level.

change from outside A language change that takes place due to borrowing from other languages or dialects.

change from within A change that is initiated from within the language itself, due to the internal dynamics of the linguistic system.

channel cues Features accompanying speech that may help determine which speech style is being used; for example, laughter or increased tempo may be a channel cue for a more casual speech style. Also called **paralinguistic channel cues**.

clipping The formation of a new word through the removal of syllables, such as *dorm* for *dormitory*.

code switching Switching between two different languages; compare **style shifting**.

coining The creation of a new word not based on any previous form; for example, *meehonkey* for "hide and seek" on the island of Ocracoke, North Carolina.

colloquial Informal. Compare **slang**.

Communication Accommodation Theory An updated version of **Speech Accommodation Theory**. Among the updates is increasing emphasis on ways of achieving psychological convergence with one's addressees other than linguistic convergence – for example, talking *more* rather than less to encourage a speaker who talks very little.

communication network A group of people who are linked together via lines of communication.

community of practice A group of people who come together through some shared social enterprise, for example, an aerobics group, a group of graduate students, etc.

complement A word, phrase, or clause that completes a predicate; structures co-occurring with particular verbs (e.g. *painting* in *The house needed painting*, the clause *the house was dirty* in *I told him that the house was dirty*).

completion task A format used to elicit an item in which the interviewee completes an incomplete sentence (e.g. "The hard inside of a peach is called a_____."). Also known as "fill-in-the-blank."

completive A form signaling that an action has been completed at a previous time, with emphasis upon the completion; for example, "completive" *done* in *He **done** took out the garbage* or *You **done** messed up this time*.

compound A word created by combining two or more words, as in *lighthouse* from *light + house*.

concord See **agreement**.

conflict model A model of social class in which differences are interpreted as the consequences of divisions and conflicts within the society.

consensus model An approach to social class in which it is assumed that all groups in a society agree on the norms of prestige and social ranking.

consonant A sound produced by momentarily blocking airflow in the mouth or throat; for example, [b] and [t] in *bat*.

consonant cluster The sequencing of two or more consecutive consonants without an intervening vowel; for example, [st] in *stop* or [ld] in *wild*.

consonant cluster reduction The elimination of a consonant in a cluster; for example, the [st] in *mist* [mɪst] may become [s], as in *mis'* [mɪs].

constraint (on variability) A linguistic or social factor that increases or decreases the likelihood that a given variant in a fluctuating set of items will occur. For example, the voicing of the following consonant is a constraint on the variability of /ai/ in Southern speech, since /ai/ is more likely to be pronounced as [a] when the following sound is voiced than when it is voiceless.

contagious diffusion The spread of language features from a central point outward in geographic space. See **wave model**.

content validity The extent to which a test measures the content area it claims to measure.

content word A word having referential meaning, such as the noun *dog* or the adjective *blue*. Compare **function word**.

contraction The shortening of words by omitting sounds, often resulting in the attachment of the contracted word to another word; for example, *is* + *not* contracts to *isn't*, *she will* contracts to *she'll*.

contrahierarchical diffusion The spread of language features from sparsely populated areas to those of denser population. Compare **cascade diffusion, contagious diffusion**.

contrastive drill A language-learning drill in which structures from two different languages or dialects are placed side by side to focus on the contrast between forms; for example, a sentence pair such as *The man nice* vs. *The man's nice* focuses on the contrast between copula absence and presence.

contrastive linguistics The study of different languages or dialects by comparing structures in each of the varieties to determine points of similarity and difference between the varieties.

convergence (1) In **Speech Accommodation Theory**, the notion that speakers will adjust their speech to become more like that of their addressees. Compare **divergence**. (2) The adjustment of a language variety over time to become more like another dialect or other dialects. Compare **divergence hypothesis**.

conversion The creation of a new word by using an existing word as a different part of speech; for example, the verb *run* may be used as a noun in *They scored a run*.

copula The form used to "link" a subject with a predicate; in English, a form of *be* when used as a linking verb, as in *She is nice, Tanya is the boss*.

copula deletion The absence of the copula, as in *You ugly* for *You're ugly*; the term usually is extended to auxiliary uses of *be* forms as well, as in *He writing a book* for *He's writing a book*.

covert prestige Positive value ascribed to language forms which is based on the local social value of the forms rather than their value in larger society. See **overt prestige**.

creole language A contact-based language in which the vocabulary of one language is superimposed upon a specially adapted grammatical structure composed primarily of the structures common in language contact situations. See **pidgin language**.

creolist hypothesis The contention that African American English developed historically from an ancestral **creole language**.

critical age hypothesis The hypothesis that true language mastery can only occur during a given age period, namely, during the prepubescent period.

crossing The use of a non-native dialect or dialect features.

cultural difference approach An approach to the study of language and gender that views differences in men's and women's speech as a function of their different sociocultural experiences. Compare **deficit approach, dominance approach**.

dative   The grammatical case in which forms occur when they function as the indirect object of a sentence; for example, *Terry* in *Todd gave the ball to Terry*, *Howard* in *They made a glossary for Howard*. See **personal dative**.

debt incurred   See **principle of debt incurred**.

decoding   The process of breaking down the written word letter by letter and relating the letters to the sound units or phonemes of spoken language.

decreolization   The process whereby a historical creole language loses the distinguishing features of its creole predecessor, usually through contact with a standard variety of the language.

deficit approach   With reference to language and gender studies, the approach that considers women's language traits as deficient versions of men's language. Compare **dominance approach, cultural difference approach**.

deficit–difference controversy   A controversy which took place in the 1960s and 1970s in which linguists argued with educators that vernacular varieties of English should be considered as different dialects of English rather than deficient versions of standard English.

definition by ostentation   The indication of knowledge about a language feature by demonstrating its use.

density   The extent to which members of a social network all interact with one another; if there is a high degree of interaction (i.e. if "everyone knows everyone else"), the network has **high density**; if not, it has **low density**. See **social network**.

derivational morpheme   A prefix or suffix that changes the basic meaning and/or word class of an item; for example, the *-er* in *buyer* changes the form from a verb to a noun.

devoicing   The phonetic change of voiced sounds to their voiceless counterparts, as in [d] to [t] (e.g. *bad* to *bat*) or [z] to [s] (*buzz* to *bus*).

dialect   A variety of a language associated with a particular regional or social group.

dialect awareness programs   Activities conducted by linguists and community members that are intended to promote an understanding of and appreciation for language variation.

dialect discrimination   In testing, penalizing speakers of vernacular varieties on the basis of dialect differences; for example, in language-acquisition testing, treating the use of a dialect form as evidence that the standard form has not been acquired.

dialect endangerment   See **endangered dialect**.

dialect leveling   The reduction of dialectal distinctiveness through mixing with other dialects.

dialect reader   A reading text that incorporates the speech of a vernacular-speaking community.

dialect rights   A position advocating that students should not be asked to give up their dialect, either by replacing it or by adding a standard variety.

dialectally diagnostic   With reference to language features, serving to differentiate social and regional groups from one another.

differentiation   The development of internal dialects in a country whose dominant language originated in another country.

diffusion   The spread of language features; typically used with reference to regional spread but may also be used with reference to spread across social groups. See **cascade diffusion, contagious diffusion, contra-hierarchical diffusion**.

diphthong   A "two-part" vowel consisting of a main vowel, or **nucleus**, followed by a secondary vowel, or **glide**; for example, the [aɪ] of *bite* and the [ɔɪ] of *boy* are diphthongs.

diphthongization   See **vowel breaking**.

direct transfer model   A model accounting for dialect influence in writing on the basis of direct carryover from spoken to written language.

directive   A speech act in which the speaker directs the listener to do something; for example, *Take the garbage out.*

discrimination drill   A drill in which two forms or structures are given side by side and the listener judges the form as either "the same" or "different"; for example, *She run* vs. *She runs.*

dissimilation   Changing similar sounds so that they become more distinctive from one another; for example, the first *l* of *colonel* has been changed to [r] to make it less like the final *l*.

divergence   (1) In **Speech Accommodation Theory**, the notion that speakers may adjust their language to distance themselves from addressees. Compare **convergence**. (2) The development of a language variety or language structure so that it becomes more dissimilar from other varieties or structures.

divergence hypothesis   The contention that contemporary African American Vernacular English is becoming increasingly dissimilar from corresponding vernacular European American varieties.

dominance approach   With respect to language and gender, the interpretation of female–male language differences as the result of power differences between women and men. Compare **deficit approach, cultural difference approach**.

double modal   The co-occurrence of two or even three modal forms within a single verb phrase, as in *They might could do it* or *They might oughta should do it.*

double negation   See **multiple negation**.

dropped *r* See *r*-lessness.

early adopters The first people in tightly knit groups to adopt incoming changes; they typically are central figures in these groups but adventuresome enough to adopt changes.

eavesdropper A person who is not known to be part of a speaker's audience but who may be listening in on a conversational exchange.

Ebonics See **African American English**.

elicitation frame A question designed to lead an interviewee to produce a word or structural item (e.g. *What is the hard inside part of a peach called?*).

empowering research Research that seeks to address the community's desires and goals and is undertaken with the community. See **advocacy research**.

endangered dialect A dialect that is in danger of dying via (1) the recession of distinguishing dialect features in the face of the encroachment of features from other varieties, or (2) the loss of speakers of the dialect.

endonormative stabilization The adoption of local, indigenous norms as opposed to those from the outside. See **exnormative stabilization**.

environment See **linguistic environment**.

eradicationism The position on teaching standard English that maintains that the standard dialect should be taught in place of a vernacular one – that is, used as a **replacive dialect** – thus "eradicating" the vernacular variety.

error analysis An analytical procedure which starts with the set of actual non-normative responses produced by a speaker rather than non-normative responses which are predicted on the basis of a structural comparison of the varieties.

error correction See **principle of error correction**.

ethnolect A variety of language which is strongly associated with a particular ethnic population, for example African American English, Cajun English, or Latino English.

European American An American of British or Continental European (especially Northern European) descent, popularly labeled "White" in American society. Often used as a "catch-all" to refer to anyone who does not consider themselves, or is not considered by others, to have a marked "ethnic" identity, due in large part to the longstanding societal dominance of Northern European American culture in the US.

existential A form used to indicate existence but having no referential meaning of its own; for example, the form *there* in *There are four students taking the course*. Also called **expletive**.

exnormative stabilization The establishment of language or dialect norms based on an external model. See **endonormative stabilization**.

expletive (1) An interjection, often used with reference to profane words (e.g. *Damn!*). (2) See **existential**.

extension See **rule extension**.

eye dialect The use of spelling to suggest dialect difference; the spelling does not reflect an actual dialect difference; for example, *wuz* for *was*.

figurative extension The extension of the meaning of a word to refer to items which are quite different from its original referents but which share a meaning feature with the original set of referents. For example, *submarine* has been figuratively extended to apply to a type of sandwich which is similar in shape to the seafaring vessel.

fine stratification See **gradient stratification**.

first order constraint The factor that has the greatest systematic effect on the variability of an item; the second most important factor is referred to as the **second order constraint**.

flap A sound made by rapidly tapping the tip of the tongue to the **alveolar** ridge, as in the usual American English pronunciation of *t* in *Betty* [bɛDi] or *d* in *ladder* [læDɚ].

floor The right to speak, as in *holding the floor*.

focal area A regional area at the center of dialect innovation and change; changes radiate from this area outward.

focusing The selection of only a few dialect features to mark an entire language variety.

folk dialectology See **perceptual dialectology**.

folk etymology Altering words so that they are transparent in terms of known meanings and forms, as in *cold slaw* for *cole slaw* or *old timer's disease* for *Alzheimer's disease*.

Formal Standard English The variety of English prescribed as the standard by language authorities; found primarily in written language and the most formal spoken language (e.g. spoken language which is based on a written form of the language).

fossilized form A form that occurs during the learning of a second language and persists while other forms continue their development toward the second-language norm.

foundation stage The first stage in the spread of a language into a region where it was not previously spoken; typically characterized by heterogeneous usage patterns by speakers from different dialect areas.

founder effect The enduring effect of language structures brought to an area by the earliest group of speakers of that language settling in the region.

four-part analogy See **analogy**.

free morpheme A morpheme that can occur alone as a word; for example, *boy* in *boys*. Compare **bound morpheme**.

fricative A sound produced with a continuous flow of air through a narrow opening in the mouth so that there is "friction" at the point of articulation (e.g. [f], [s], [θ]).

front vowel A vowel produced toward the front of the mouth, as in the [i] of *beet* or the [æ] of *bat*.

function word A word used to indicate grammatical relations between elements of a sentence rather than referential meaning; for example, articles such as *the/a*, prepositions such as *to/at*. Compare **content word**.

g-**dropping** The production of *ng* in unstressed syllables as *n'* (e.g. *swimmin'* for *swimming*); in spelling, this is usually indicated by *n'*, but the actual phonetic shift involves the change from the back nasal [ŋ] to a front nasal [n].

Geechee See **Gullah**.

gender The complex of social, cultural, and psychological factors that surround sex; contrasted with sex as biological attribute.

general American English A term used to refer to varieties of English that are not characterized by a particular dialect trait under discussion. For example, the use of *a*- prefixing in some rural and Southern dialects may be contrasted with its non-use in "general American English."

general social significance The social evaluation of a form that holds regardless of the geographical area in which it is found.

generic *he* The use of the masculine pronoun *he* for referents which can be either male or female; for example, *If a student wants to pass the course, he should study*. The noun *man* historically has also been used as a generic, as in ***Man** shall not live by bread alone*.

genre A language style associated with a well-defined situation of use; often formulaic and performative. Compare **register**.

glide The secondary vowel of a **diphthong** (e.g. [ɪ] in *bite* [baɪt]). So called because speakers glide from the main vowel or **nucleus** to the secondary vowel in the production of the diphthong.

glottal stop A rapid opening and closing of the vocal cords that creates a kind of "popping" sound. In some dialects, a glottal stop may occur instead of a [d] or [t] in *bottle* [baʔl].

gradient stratification The distribution of socially significant linguistic structures among members of different social groups along a continuous scale rather than on the basis of discrete breaks between adjacent social groups. Also referred to as **fine stratification**.

grammar The formation of words and sentences out of their constituent parts.

grammatical (1) (With reference to sentences and forms) that which conforms to the unconscious rules of a language or dialect; linguistically "well-formed" as opposed to "ill-formed." (2) In popular usage, referring to language forms and constructions that conform to norms of social acceptability; in this usage, "grammatical" constructions may or may not be linguistically well formed; conversely, linguistically well-formed constructions may or may not be socially acceptable. Compare **ungrammatical**.

grammaticalization   The encoding of a unique meaning onto a form; for example, in AAE, the invariant form of *be* has become uniquely associated with habituality in sentences such as *You always be acting weird*.

gravity model   A model of dialect diffusion which holds that linguistic features spread via **cascade** or **hierarchical diffusion**.

group-exclusive   With reference to language forms or patterns, confined to one particular group of speakers.

group-preferential   With reference to language forms or patterns, concentrated in a certain group of speakers but found to an extent among other speakers.

group reference   Identification with a particular group in terms of sociopsychological self-definition.

Gullah   A **creole language** spoken primarily by African Americans in the Sea Islands off the coast of South Carolina and Georgia. Also called **Geechee**.

habitual   (With reference to an ongoing activity or activities) taking place at intermittent intervals over time (e.g. as signaled by the use of *be* in the AAE structure *When I come home, I usually be taking a nap*).

hierarchical diffusion   See **cascade diffusion, gravity model**.

high density   See **density**.

high vowel   A vowel made with the tongue in high position in the mouth, as in the [i] of *beet* or the [u] of *boot*.

historical present   A present tense form used in the recounting of a past time event, as in *Yesterday, I go down there and this guy comes up to me . . .* ; generally used for dramatic vividness.

homophones/homophonous words   Different words that are pronounced the same, as in *dear* and *deer*; in some Southern dialects of English *pin* and *pen* are homophones.

Hoosier apex   See **apex**.

hypercorrection   The extension of a language form beyond its regular linguistic boundaries when a speaker feels a need to use extremely standard or "correct" forms. See **statistical** and **structural hypercorrection**.

independent linguistic constraint   See **linguistic constraint**.

indirect speech act   A speech act used to accomplish another type of speech act; for example, a statement such as *The garbage is overflowing* when used to request a person to empty the garbage.

inflectional morpheme   A suffix that augments a word without changing its basic meaning or its word class; for example, the *-s* in *dogs* or the *-er* in *bigger*).

Informal Standard English The spoken variety of English considered socially acceptable in mainstream contexts; typically characterized by the absence of socially stigmatized linguistic structures.

inherent variability Variability between items within a single dialect system; speakers sometimes produce one variant and sometimes another. For example, sometimes speakers say *drinking* and at other times they say *drinkin'* in the same social context.

initiative style shift A shift in speech style motivated by the speaker's desire to shape situations, relationships, and/or personal identity in some way.

innovators The first people to adopt changes; they typically have loose ties to many social groups but strong ties to none.

interdental A sound produced by placing the tongue tip between the upper and lower teeth; sounds such as the [θ] of *think* and the [ð] of *the* are interdentals.

interruption "Breaking into" the speech of the person holding the floor without waiting for a signal which indicates that the speaker is ready to relinquish the floor.

intervocalic Occurring between vowels; for example, *r* in *Mary*, *t* in *butter*.

intonation The pitch contours that accompany phrases and sentences; for example, question intonation on *Are you going?* vs. statement intonation of *You are going.*

intransitive verb A verb that does not take an object; for example, the verb *jog* in *The students jogged* is intransitive.

intrusive Additional, as in the additional *t* of *acrosst* or the *r* of *marsh.*

intuition In linguistics, the ability of native speakers to judge the well-formedness of particular kinds of sentences. With reference to vernacular dialects, judgment of well-formedness, or **grammaticality**, may be in opposition to judgments of social acceptability. For example, the sentence *Sometimes my ears be itching* is a well-formed, grammatical sentence as judged by native speaker intuitions but is socially unacceptable.

inversion A reversal of the "typical" order of items; for example, *Are you going?* vs. *You are going*, or *Can't nobody do it* vs. *Nobody can't do it.*

irregular form An item that does not conform to the predominant pattern; for example, the *-en* plural of *oxen*, the past tense of *come* (*came*). Compare **regular form**.

isogloss A line on a map indicating a boundary between the use and non-use of a particular linguistic feature. See also **bundle of isoglosses**.

isoglossal layering See **layering**.

jargon A particular vocabulary characteristic of a group of speakers who share a certain interest; for example, computer jargon, sports jargon.

junk language See **mock language**.

labial A sound produced primarily with the lips; the [p] in *pit* is **bilabial**, involving both lips, while the [f] in *four* is **labiodental**, since it involves the lower lip and upper teeth.

labiodental See **labial**.

language acquisition The unconscious learning of language rules which results in implicit knowledge of language.

language ideology Ingrained, unquestioned beliefs about the way the world is, the way it should be, and the way it has to be with respect to language.

language learning The conscious learning of rules of language which results in more explicit knowledge of language.

language register See **register**.

language sample Language data based on conversational interviews, as opposed to the direct elicitation of items.

language transfer See **transfer**.

lax vowel A vowel produced with comparatively little muscular tension; the [ɪ] of *bit* is a lax vowel compared with the [i] of *beet*, which is a **tense vowel**. See **short vowel**.

layer See **layering**.

layering A hierarchical arrangement of dialect features in which successive areas show differing levels of shared dialect forms. See **primary, secondary, tertiary dialect area**.

leveling (1) a type of **analogy**. (2) **dialect leveling**.

lexicographer A person who compiles a dictionary or **lexicon**.

lexicon The vocabulary of a language, including words and morphemes.

lexifier The language that provides the base for the majority of the lexical items in the formation of a **pidgin** or **creole language**; for example, English is the lexifier language for Jamaican Creole or Gullah.

linguistic constraint A linguistic factor, such as a type of linguistic environment or structural composition, which systematically affects the variability of fluctuating forms. Also referred to as **independent linguistic constraint**.

linguistic environment The linguistic context that surrounds a form, such as the sounds that occur next to a given sound.

linguistic geography The study of dialects in terms of their regional distribution.

linguistic gratuity See **principle of linguistic gratuity**.

linguistic inferiority principle The principle which holds that the language of a socially subordinate group is linguistically deficient compared to the more standard variety spoken by the superordinate social group.

linguistic intuitions Inner feelings or unconscious knowledge about the regular patterns that underlie the use of linguistic structures.

linguistic marketplace Those aspects of the socioeconomic realm that most directly relate to linguistic variation; for example, a receptionist may use standard language forms due to considerations of the linguistic marketplace. A **linguistic market index** is a scale which measures the importance of standard English in various jobs.

linguistic profiling Discrimination based on the identification (whether correct or incorrect) of a person's ethnic or other social identity based on their voice.

linguistic rule (1) An unconscious pattern which governs the occurrence of a particular language form. For example, *a-* prefixing is governed by a rule which states that the *a-* prefix may be attached to *-ing* forms which act as verbs but not as nouns or adjectives (as in *The women went a-hunting* vs. *The women like* **hunting**). (2) An explicit statement about the patterning of linguistic forms; a precise statement describing where a form may occur structurally.

linguistic variable A varying linguistic structure (e.g. *-ing/-in'*) which may correlate with social factors such as region or status, or with other linguistic factors, such as linguistic environment.

long vowel In English, a tense vowel, as in words such as *feet, bait, boot*, and *vote*. No longer corresponds with actual temporal length in English. Compare **short vowel**.

low back merger The merger of the vowels in word pairs like *cot* and *caught*.

low density See **density**.

low vowel A vowel produced with the tongue in a lowered position in the mouth; for example, vowels such as the [ɑ] of *father*, the [ɔ] of *caught*, or the [æ] of *bat*.

marker See **social marker**.

meaning shift A change in word meaning so that one of the word's sub-referents, or a referent originally only loosely associated with the word, becomes the new primary meaning of the word; for example, *bead* used to mean "prayer" but now refers to a type of jewelry.

merger The elimination of contrast between sounds; for example, the formerly distinct vowels in *caught* and *cot* now sound the same in many American English dialects. Also called **neutralization**.

metalinguistic task A task that involves talking about language rather than simply using language. Usually performed to give researchers insight into the structure and function of language forms.

metathesis The rearrangement of sounds in a sequence, as in [æks] for *ask*.

mid vowel A vowel produced with the tongue in the middle range of tongue height, as in the [ɛ] of *bet*, the [ʌ] of *but*, or the [o] of *boat*.

minimal word pair A pair of words that are phonetically identical except for one sound; word pairs such as *bit* and *pit* or *bit* and *bet* are minimal word pairs.

minority pattern analogy   See **analogy**.

mock language   The use of language based on linguistic and cultural stereotypes to parody a particular group. Also known as **junk language**. Typical cases are Mock Ebonics and Mock Spanish.

modal   An auxiliary verb which expresses certain "moods" related to permission, obligation, suggestion, or the speaker's attitude toward the truth of her or his assertions; for example, *can*, *may*, *will*, *shall*, *must*. See also **double modal**.

monitoring   The act of paying attention to how one is speaking during the production of speech.

monophthongization   The reduction of a two-part vowel, or diphthong, to a one-part vowel, or monophthong, through the elimination of the glide, as in [ta:m] for *time* or [bɔ:l] for *boil*. A single vowel without gliding is referred to as a **monophthong**.

monosyllabic   Consisting of one syllable, as in *go* or *but*.

mood   A grammatical category which pertains to speakers' attitudes toward the truth of their assertions (e.g. possibility, probability) or to speakers' expressions of obligation, permission, and suggestion. Mood is usually indicated in English through **modal** verbs, such as *must*, *should*, and *may*.

moribund dialect   A dying dialect; see **endangered dialect**.

morpheme   The smallest meaningful component of a word; for example, in *dogs*, *dog* and *-s* are morphemes.

morphology   The level of language which concerns words and their meaningful components, or **morphemes**.

morphosyntactic   Pertaining to the marking of a syntactic relationship through a particular morpheme; for example, third-person *-s* in *Tyler works hard* indicates a relationship between the subject and verb.

multiple negation   The marking of negation at more than one point in a sentence (e.g. *They didn't do **nothing** about **nobody***). Also called **double negation**, **negative concord**.

multiplex network   A social network characterized by the interaction of individuals in a social network in a number of different spheres, such as work, leisure, and neighborhood. See **social network**.

multiplexity   See **multiplex network**.

narrowing   See **semantic narrowing**.

nasal   A segment produced by allowing air to pass through the nasal cavity, as in the *m* of *mom* or the *n* of *no*.

nativization   The differentiation of a transplanted language in a newly independent country from the language variety/varieties of the country from which it was originally transplanted. In nativization, the language variety becomes associated with the new country.

naturalistic speech   Speech that represents how people talk under normal, ordinary circumstances.

negative concord   See **multiple negation**.

neo-Anglicist hypothesis   See **Anglicist hypothesis**.

Network Standard   A variety of English relatively free of marked regional characteristics; the ideal norm aimed for by national radio and television network announcers. See **Standard American English**.

neutralization   See **merger**.

nonstandard   With reference to language forms, socially stigmatized through association with socially disfavored groups.

nonstandard dialect   A dialect that differs from the standard dialects spoken by mainstream or socially favored population groups; usually it is socially disfavored. It is used synonymously with **vernacular dialect** in this book.

Northern Cities Vowel Shift   A vowel shift or **rotation** in which the low back vowels are moving forward and upward and the short front vowels are moving downward and backward; found predominantly in Northern metropolitan areas of the US.

nucleus   The core or base of a vowel sound; in a word like *bike* [baɪk], the [a] is considered the vowel nucleus.

objective case   The form which a noun or pronoun takes when it is the object of a verb (e.g. *me* in *Tanya likes me*). See **case**.

observer's paradox   A widely accepted tenet in sociolinguistics which holds that the best speech for analysis is that which occurs when people are not being observed.

open *o*   The [ɔ] vowel; occurs in words such as *caught* or *song*, as produced in some dialects of English.

oppositional identity   Identity as defined primarily in terms of disassociation from another group; for example, defining Black or Latino behavior as "non-White."

orthography   The spelling system of a language.

overhearer   A member of a speaker's audience whose presence is known to the speaker but who is not considered to be a participant in the conversational exchange.

overt prestige   Positive value ascribed to language forms which is based on the value of the forms in mainstream society. See **covert prestige**.

paradigm   A grammatically restricted class of forms, such as the set of different forms a verb may take when used with different subjects (e.g. the forms *am*, *is*, and *are* of the verb *to be*).

paralinguistic channel cues   See **channel cues**.

participle   A word derived from a verb, having qualities of an adjective or noun as well as a verb; for example, *charming* in *He was charming*, *taken* in *It was taken*.

perceptual dialectology   The study of how non-linguists classify different dialects, as well as their beliefs about and attitudes toward different dialects and their speakers. Also called **folk dialectology**.

personal dative   A pronoun in dative case (i.e. indirect object form) which refers back to the noun in subject position and is used to indicate that the subject benefited in some way from the object of the verb in the sentence. For example, in the sentence, *She ate her some lunch*, the subject, *she*, benefited from the object, *lunch*. Typically found in Southern dialects of American English.

phoneme   A basic unit of contrast, or meaning difference, in phonology. Usually established on the basis of "minimal word pairs." For example, /p/ and /b/ are considered to be different phonemes in English because they can be used to make meaning differences, as in *pit* and *bit*.

phonemic brackets   The slashes / / surrounding sounds which are used to indicate that the enclosed symbols represent phonemes rather than phonetic or orthographic elements.

phonetic brackets   The symbols [ ] which are used around sounds to indicate that they are being presented in their phonetic form, particularly as opposed to their phonemic or orthographic form.

phonetic space   The area in the mouth in which language sounds, particularly vowels, are produced.

phonics   An approach to reading based upon the letter-by-letter processing of written symbols; letters are "sounded out" and combined with each other to decipher words.

phonology   The sound system of a language.

phrase timing   The timing of syllables in which stressed syllables in phrases are held longer and unstressed ones shortened by comparison.

pidgin language   A language used primarily as a trade language among speakers of different languages; it has no native speakers. The vocabulary of a pidgin language is taken primarily from a superordinate language, and the grammar is drastically reduced.

possessive   An item indicating possession, such as the suffix *-s* in *John's hat* or the pronoun *his* in *his hat*.

postconsonantal   Occurring immediately after a consonant, as in the *r* of *brought*.

postvocalic *r*   The sound *r* when it follows a vowel, as in the *r* of *poor*.

pragmatics   The level of language organization pertaining to language use; takes into account such matters as speakers' and hearers' beliefs, attitudes, and intentions.

prefix   An affix attached to the beginning of a word base, such as *re-* in *retell*.

preposing   The shift of an item to the beginning of a sentence; for example, *Yesterday* in *Yesterday Marge ran*, as opposed to *Marge ran yesterday*.

Prescriptive Standard English   The variety deemed standard by grammar books and other recognized language "authorities." See **Formal Standard English**.

prestigious See **socially prestigious**.

primary dialect area That portion of a dialect area which exhibits the greatest concentration of shared dialect features.

principle of debt incurred The sociolinguistic tenet which holds that linguists should use data from their research to benefit the community that provided them with data.

principle of error correction The sociolinguistic tenet which holds that linguists should use knowledge gained from their research to correct errors about language in society and education.

principle of linguistic gratuity The tenet which holds that linguists should proactively seek ways to use data from their research to benefit the community that provided linguistic data.

principle of linguistic subordination The tenet that holds that the speech of socially subordinate groups will be interpreted as linguistically inadequate by comparison with that of socially dominant groups.

pronominal apposition The use of a co-referential pronoun in addition to a noun in subject position; for example, *mother* and *she* in *My mother, she came home early*.

proportional analogy See **analogy**.

prosody The aspects of pitch, intensity, and timing that accompany the segments of spoken language.

raising Pronouncing a vowel with a higher tongue position; for example, the **Northern Cities Vowel Shift** is characterized by the raising of /æ/ to near /ɛ/ position, and Tidewater Virginia speech is characterized by the raising of the nucleus of /ai/ to **schwa** position.

recutting Reanalyzing words into component parts different from the original parts; for example, *a napron* historically was recut into *an apron*, and *an other* is currently being recut into *a + nother*, as in *a whole nother*.

reduplication The repetition of a word or part of a word, as in *teensy-weensy*, *boo-boo*.

referee design The component of the audience design approach to **style shifting** that focuses on referee groups and initiative style shifting.

referee group A non-present group with whom speakers attempt to identify when they engage in an initiative style shift.

regional standard English A variety considered to be standard for a given regional area; for example, the Eastern New England standard or the Southern standard.

register A language variety associated with a particular situation of use – for example, the math register or the "babytalk" register.

regular form An item conforming to the predominant pattern, such as the regular plural form *cats* or the regular past tense form *missed*. Compare **irregular form**.

regularization The process in which irregular forms are changed to conform to the predominant or "regular" pattern; for example, *oxen* becomes *oxes*, or *grew* becomes *growed*.

relative clause A clause that modifies a noun; in *The man who took the course was demented*, *who took the course* is a relative clause.

relative pronoun A pronoun that introduces a relative clause, such as *who* in *The woman who liked the class was a linguist*.

relic area An area where older language features survive after they have disappeared from other varieties of the language.

replacive dialect See **eradicationism**.

retroflex A sound produced with the tip of the tongue curled upward; the consonant sound *r* in *run* and the vowel sound *ir* in *bird* are retroflex language sounds.

r-**lessness** The absence or reduction of the *r* sound in words such as *car* and *beard*.

rotation See **vowel rotation**.

rule See **linguistic rule**.

rule extension The expansion of a rule of limited application to a broader set of items.

saturated With reference to language features, used by the vast majority of speakers within a given speech community. Saturated features contrast with **unsaturated** features, or those used by only a few speakers in the speech community.

schwa A mid central vowel symbolized as [ə]; for example, the first vowel in *appear* [əpir]. Generally occurs in unstressed syllables in English.

second order constraint See **first order constraint**.

secondary dialect area That portion of a dialect area showing the second highest concentration of shared dialect features.

semantic broadening Meaning shift in which a word can be used to refer to a more general class of items than previously. For example, in American English *holiday* has been broadened to refer to all days off from work rather than just "holy days," or days of religious significance.

semantic derogation Meaning shift in which words take on more negative connotations or denotations. For example, the word *mistress* was once the female counterpart of *mister* but has taken on negative meanings not matched by its male counterpart.

semantic narrowing Meaning shift in which words come to refer to a less general class of items than previously. For example, *girl* could once be used to refer to a young child of either sex; *deer* was once used to refer to all animals but now refers only to one specific type of animal.

semantic shift See **meaning shift**.

semantics The level of language organization which pertains to word meaning.

sharp stratification A distributional pattern for socially significant language features, characterized by a clear-cut division between social groups. Compare **gradient stratification**.

short vowel In English, a lax vowel, as in *bit*, *bet*, and *put*. No longer corresponds with actual temporal duration in English.

sibilant A sound produced with a groove in the middle of the tongue through which the air passes, creating a "hissing" sound; sounds such as the [s] of *see* and the [z] of *zoo* are sibilants.

slang Words with special connotations of informality and in-group solidarity that replace words with more neutral connotations (e.g. *rad* for "great"; *wasted* for "drunk").

social dialectology The study of language variation in relation to social status or other social relationships.

social indicator A language feature whose usage correlates with social group but not speech style; speakers do not indicate awareness of such features or their social meaning.

social marker A language feature whose usage correlates with both social group and speech style; speakers are aware of such forms and their group associations but do not comment overtly upon them.

social network The pattern of social relationships that characterizes a group of speakers.

social stereotype A language feature that speakers are aware of and comment upon. May be stigmatized (e.g. *ain't*), prestigious (e.g. [vɑz] instead of [veɪs] for "vase"), or simply "unusual" (e.g. *hoi toid* for "high tide").

social variable A social attribute or characteristic such as status, ethnicity, or gender that may correlate with linguistic variation.

socially diagnostic With respect to language features, serving to distinguish a certain social group of speakers.

socially prestigious Socially favored; with respect to language forms or patterns, (items) associated with high-status groups.

socially stigmatized Socially disfavored, as in a language form or pattern associated with low-status groups (e.g. *He didn't do nothing to nobody*).

socioeconomic status Status determined on the basis of an objective set of scores for factors such as occupation, income, and residency.

sociolect A dialect defined on the basis of a social grouping, such as a social class or ethnic group, as opposed to a dialect defined primarily on the basis of region.

sociolinguistics The study of language in relation to society; the study of language in its social context.

Southern Vowel Shift A vowel shift or rotation in which the short front vowels are moving upward and taking on the gliding character of long vowels, the long front vowels are moving backward and downward, and the back vowels are moving forward.

speaker design An approach to **style shifting** that focuses on style as the proactive projection and performance of identity rather than a reactive response to situational factors such as audience or topic.

speakerly text A text written to project the spoken voice; the text typically uses a form of literary dialect.

Speech Accommodation Theory An approach to **style shifting** which maintains that speakers shift style based on their social-psychological adjustment to the addressee; strategic adjustment toward the addressee is **convergence**; adjustment away from the addressee is **divergence**.

speech act An utterance which accomplishes a social action. For example, *Take out the garbage!* is a directive speech act in which the speaker directs the hearer to perform an activity.

speech community A group of people with shared norms, or common evaluations of linguistic variables. Members of a speech community may use language forms in different ways, but all members orient toward common norms – i.e. believe certain language forms are "good" and others are "bad," or "appropriate" vs. "inappropriate."

spelling pronunciation The pronunciation of an item based on its spelling rather than its conventional spoken form (e.g. *often* pronounced with [t]).

Standard American English A widely socially accepted variety of English that is held to be the linguistic norm and that is relatively unmarked with respect to regional characteristics of English. See **Network Standard**.

standard dialect The dialect associated with those socially favored in society; the dialect considered acceptable for mainstream, institutional purposes. See **Formal Standard English, Informal Standard English, Network Standard, regional standard English**.

statistical hypercorrection The quantitative overuse of a prestigious or standard language form; usually found among those groups attempting to emulate a higher social group, for example, the overuse of postvocalic *r* in New York City by lower middle-class groups in formal speech style.

stigmatized See **socially stigmatized**.

stopping The process of producing fricatives as stop consonants, as in *these* [ðiz] being pronounced as *dese* [diz].

stress Force or intensity which is given to a syllable. Syllables spoken with such force are **stressed syllables**, those without such force are **unstressed syllables** (e.g. in *pity* [pɪ] is a stressed syllable, [ti] is unstressed).

stress timing See **syllable timing**.

stressed syllable See **stress**.

structural hypercorrection   The extension of a linguistic boundary in the attempt to produce more standard or "correct" English; for example, the use of *whom* in ***Whom** is it*, where the objective form is extended to a subject function.

style   One of the speech varieties used by an individual; different speech styles tend to correlate with such factors as audience, occasion, degree of formality, etc. Speakers also often use speech styles to shape situations, relationships, and personal identity.

style shifting   Variation within the speech of a single speaker; often correlates with such factors as audience, degree of formality, etc.

subjective case   The form which a noun or pronoun takes when it is in subject position in a sentence (e.g. *I* in *I like students*). See **case**.

substrate [effect]   The influence of a language or a language contact situation on another language variety after the former language has ceased to be a source for immediate transfer or after the original contact situation has long passed. For example, some varieties of Italian English are influenced by Italian vowels, even among speakers who do not speak Italian itself.

substrate hypothesis   The position that African American English has maintained a persistent substrate effect even though it accommodated to and mixed with regional dialects early in its development.

suffix   An **affix** attached to the end of a base or root word, as in the *-s* of *bats*.

Superstandard English   Forms or styles of speech which are more standard than called for in everyday conversation (*It is I who shall write this*).

superstrate   A language spoken by a dominant group which influences the structure of the language of a subordinate group of speakers. Often used to refer to the dominant language upon which a **creole language** is based.

supra-regional norm   A dialect norm that is generally adopted regardless of the regional location of a group. Often used with reference to contemporary African American English.

suprasegmental   Pertaining to elements of language such as stress and intonation that accompany the sound segments (e.g. consonants and vowels) of language.

swamping   The inundation of a longstanding dialect area with speakers from other dialect areas.

syllable timing   Timing of utterances in which each syllable in a phrase has approximately equal duration. Contrasts with **stress timing**, in which stressed syllables have greater duration. For example, a phrase like *in the house* may be produced with equal duration assigned to each syllable (syllable-timed rhythm) or with longer duration to the stressed item *house* and shorter duration to the other words in the phrase (stressed-timed rhythm). Languages and language varieties may exhibit stress timing vs. syllable timing to a greater or lesser degree.

symbolic capital   Symbolic rather than genuine worth or power. Often accrued through use of language features associated with those with genuine worth/power, whether a standard variety, or a local variety that has economic worth (perhaps to tourists interested in the local culture).

syntax   The formation of words into phrases and sentences.

taboo word   A word having a social prohibition against its ordinary use, such as the "four-letter" words of English (e.g. *shit, damn*).

tag question   A special type of question formed by items attached to, or "tagged," on to the end of the sentence (e.g. *right* in *You're coming to class, **right?*** or *aren't you* in *You're coming to class, **aren't you?***).

task interference   In testing, an impediment to valid testing due to the way language is used to obtain information.

tense   (1) Produced with more muscular tension; for example, the sound [i] in *beet* is a "tense" vowel, whereas the [ɪ] of *bit* is a **lax vowel**. See **long vowel**. (2) The time reference of an activity or event (e.g. "past tense" in *Jason missed the lecture*).

tertiary dialect area   The third-ranked, outer, area in the layered, hierarchical concentration of shared dialect features.

transfer   The adoption of a form from another language, usually a form from a first language carried over into a second language in the process of acquiring the second language.

transitional zone   An intermediate area existing between two established dialect areas.

transitive verb   A verb that takes an object (e.g. *like* in *Students like movies*).

transparency principle   The tendency for languages to mark meaning distinctions as clearly as possible, to avoid obscurity in meaning.

turn-taking   Shifting from one speaker to another in a conversational exchange.

ungliding   The loss or reduction of the glide, or second half of a diphthong; for example, in many Southern varieties, the /ai/ vowel in words such as *time* [taɪm] is unglided to [a], as in [taːm].

ungrammatical   (1) Outside the parameters of a given linguistic rule, usually indicated by placing an asterisk in front of the form or sentence (e.g. **She is tall very*). (2) Socially unacceptable (e.g. *I seen it*); although "ungrammatical" is often used in this sense by non-linguists, linguists do not generally use the term in this way, restricting its use to the technical sense given in (1).

uniplex network   A social network characterized by the interaction of speakers on one sphere only (e.g. speaker A works with B but does not socialize with B; speaker B socializes with C but does not live near C, etc.).

unsaturated See **saturated**.

unstressed syllable See **stress**.

uptalk The use of high-rising final intonation, or question-like intonation, on declarative statements. Also known as **upspeak**.

variants Different ways of saying the same thing, whether different ways of pronouncing the same sound, different ways of forming the same construction, or different words for the same item or concept. For example, *-in* and *-ing* are variants of the *-ing* ending on words like *swimming* or *fishing*.

velar Sounds produced by touching the back of the tongue against the "soft palate" or **velum** at the back of the mouth; the [k] of *cow*, the [g] of *go* and the [ŋ] at the end of *sing* are velar sounds.

vernacular The indigenous language or dialect of a speech community. The term **vernacular dialect** is often used to refer to **nonstandard** or non-mainstream varieties as opposed to the standard variety.

vernacular principle The contention that the speech style that is most regular in its structure and in its relation to community patterns of language change is the vernacular, or style in which least attention is paid to speech.

voiced sound A sound produced by bringing the vocal cords close together, causing them to vibrate when air passes through them in the production of speech sounds (e.g. [z] as in *zoo*, [v] as in *vote*).

voiceless sound A sound produced with the vocal cords open and not vibrating, as in the [s] of *suit* or the [f] of *fight*.

vowel breaking The process by which a one-part vowel, or **monophthong**, is divided, or "broken," into a two-part vowel, or **diphthong**, as in some Southern pronunciations of words like *bed* [bɛɪd] and *bid* [bɪɪd].

vowel nucleus The segment that serves as the core or center of a **diphthong**, or two-part vowel.

vowel reduction The change or neutralization of a vowel to the quality of a **schwa** [ə]; usually takes place in unstressed syllables (e.g. the second *o* of *photograph* [foɔɡræf]).

vowel rotation The systematic shifting of the phonetic values of a set of vowels, as in the **Northern Cities Vowel Shift** or the **Southern Vowel Shift**.

wave model A model for the diffusion of language change which views change as radiating outward in a wavelike pattern from a central point, or **focal area**. See **contagious diffusion**.

weakening Changing the pronunciation of sounds so that they involve less blockage of airflow in the mouth; for example, changing [t] to [θ] between vowels.

word-medial Occurring in the middle of a word, as in the sound *k* of *baker*.

References

Abd-el-Jawad, Hassan (1987) Cross dialectal variation in Arabic: Competing prestigious forms. *Language in Society* 16: 359–68.

Adger, Carolyn T., Donna Christian, and Orlando Taylor (eds.) (1999) *Making the Connection: Language and Academic Achievement among African American Students.* Washington, DC: Center for Applied Linguistics.

Alim, H. Samy (2001) I be the truth: Divergence, recreolization, and the equative copula in Black Nation Language. Paper presented at NWAV 30, Raleigh, October.

Alvarez, Louis, and Andrew Kolker (1987) *American Tongues.* New York: Center for New American Media.

Anderson, Bridget (1999) Source-language transfer and vowel accommodation in the patterning of Cherokee English /ai/ and /oi/. *American Speech* 74: 339–68.

Ann Arbor Decision, The: Memorandum, Opinion, and Order & The Educational Plan (1979) Washington, DC: Center for Applied Linguistics.

Arco's Practice for the Armed Forces Tests (1973) New York: Arco.

Bailey, Guy (2001) The relationship between African American Vernacular English and White vernaculars in the American South: A sociocultural history and some phonological evidence. In Sonja L. Lanehart (ed.), *Sociocultural and Historical Contexts of African American English.* Philadelphia/Amsterdam: John Benjamins, 53–92.

Bailey, Guy, and Marvin Bassett (1986) Invariant *be* in the Lower South. In Michael Montgomery and Guy Bailey (eds.), *Language Variety in the South: Perspectives in Black and White.* Tuscaloosa: University of Alabama Press, 158–79.

Bailey Guy, and Natalie Maynor (1987) Decreolization. *Language in Society* 16: 449–74.

Bailey, Guy, Natalie Maynor, and Patricia Cukor-Avila (eds.) (1991) *The Emergence of Black English: Text and Commentary.* Philadelphia/Amsterdam: John Benjamins.

Bailey, Guy, Tom Wikle, Jan Tillery, and Lori Sand (1993) Some patterns of linguistic diffusion. *Language Variation and Change* 5: 359–90.

Ball, Martin J. (ed.) (2004) *Handbook of Clinical Sociolinguistics.* Oxford: Blackwell.

Baranowski, Makiej (2004) Doing the Charleston. *Language Magazine* 3 (5) (January): 40–4.

Baratz, Joan (1968) Language in the economically disadvantaged child: A perspective. *ASHA* (April): 143–5.

Bauer, Laurie, and Peter Trudgill (eds.) (1998) *Language Myths*. New York: Penguin.

Baugh, John (1983) *Black Street Speech: Its History, Structure, and Survival*. Austin: University of Texas Press.

Baugh, John (1984) Steady: Progressive aspect in Black Vernacular English. *American Speech* 59: 3–12.

Baugh, John (1988) Language and race: Some implications for linguistic science. In Frederick J. Newmeyer (ed.), *Linguistics: The Cambridge Survey*, vol. 4. New York: Cambridge University Press, 64–74.

Baugh, John (1991) The politicization of changing terms of self-reference among American slave descendants. *American Speech* 66: 133–46.

Baugh, John (1996) Perceptions with a variable paradigm: Black and white speech detection and identification based on speech. In Edgar W. Schneider (ed.), *Focus on the USA*. Philadelphia/Amsterdam: John Benjamins, 169–82.

Baugh, John (2003) Linguistic profiling. In Cinfree Makoni, Geneva Smitherman, Arnetha F. Ball, and Arthur K. Spears (eds.), *Black Linguistics: Language, Society, and Politics in Africa and the Americas*. New York: Routledge, 155–68.

Bayley, Robert (1994) Consonant cluster reduction in Tejano English. *Language Variation and Change* 6: 303–26.

Bayley, Robert (1997) Variation in Tejano English: Evidence for variable lexical phonology. In Cynthia Bernstein, Thomas Nunnally, and Robin Sabino (eds.), *Language Variety in the South Revisited*. Tuscaloosa: University of Alabama Press, 197–209.

Bayley, Robert, and Lucinda Pease-Alvarez (1997) Null pronoun variation in Mexican-descent children's narrative structure. *Language Variation and Change* 9: 349–71.

Bayley, Robert, and Dennis R. Preston (eds.) (1996) *Second Language Acquisition and Linguistic Variation*. Philadelphia/Amsterdam: John Benjamins.

Bayley, Robert, and Otto Santa Ana (2004) Chicano English grammar. In Bernd Kortmann, Edgar W. Schneider, Kate Burridge, Rajend Mesthrie, and Clive Upton (eds.), *A Handbook of Varieties of English*, vol. 2: *Morphology and Syntax*. Berlin/New York: Mouton de Gruyter, 167–83.

Beebe, Leslie, and Howard Giles (1984) Speech-accommodation theories: A discussion in terms of second language acquisition. *International Journal of the Sociology of Language* 46: 5–32.

Bell, Allan (1984) Language style as audience design. *Language in Society* 13: 145–204.

Bell, Allan (1999) Styling the other to define the self: A study in New Zealand identity making. *Journal of Sociolinguistics* 4: 523–41.

Bell, Allan (2001) Back in style: Reworking audience design. In Penelope Eckert and John R. Rickford (eds.), *Style and Sociolinguistic Variation*. Cambridge: Cambridge University Press, 139–69.

Bell, Allan, and Gary Johnson (1997) Towards a sociolinguistics of style. *University of Pennsylvania Working Papers in Linguistics* 4 (1): 1–21.

Bernstein, Cynthia (2003) More than just yada yada yada. *Language Magazine* 3 (2) (October): 41–4.

Bing, Janet M., and Victoria L. Bergvall (1996) The question of questions: Beyond binary thinking. In Victoria L. Bergvall, Janet M. Bing, and Alice F. Freed (eds.),

Rethinking Language and Gender Research: Theory and Practice. New York: Longman, 1–30.

Blanton, Phyllis, and Karen Waters (producers) (1995) *The Ocracoke Brogue*. Raleigh: North Carolina Language and Life Project.

Boberg, Charles (forthcoming) The North American Regional Dialect Survey: Renewing the study of lexical variation in North American English. *American Speech*.

Bodine, Ann (1975) Androcentrism in prescriptive grammar: Singular "they," sex-indefinite "he," and "he" or "she." *Language in Society* 4: 129–46.

Bordewich, Frank (1996) *Killing the White Man's Indian: The Reinvesting of Native Americans at the End of the Twentieth Century*. New York: Doubleday.

Brasch, Ila Wales, and Walter Milton Brasch (1974) *A Comprehensive Annotated Bibliography of American Black English*. Baton Rouge: Louisiana State University Press.

Britain, David (2001) Space and spatial diffusion. In J. K. Chambers, Peter Trudgill, and Natalie Schilling-Estes (eds.), *The Handbook of Language Variation and Change*, Oxford: Blackwell, 603–37.

Brown, Claude (1965) *Manchild in the Promised Land*. New York: New American Library.

Brown, Penelope, and Stephen C. Levinson (1987) *Politeness: Some Universals in Language Usage*. New York: Cambridge University Press.

Bucholtz, Mary (1996) Geek the girl: Language, femininity and female nerds. In Natasha Warner, Jocelyn Ahlers, Leela Bilmes, Monica Oliver, Suzanne Wertheim, and Melinda Chen (eds.), *Gender and Belief Systems: Proceedings of the Fourth Berkeley Women and Language Conference*. Berkeley: Berkeley Women and Language Group, 119–31.

Bucholtz, Mary (1999) "Why be normal?" Language and identity practices in a community of nerd girls. *Language in Society* 28: 203–23.

Butters, Ronald R. (1989) *The Death of Black English: Divergence and Convergence in White and Black Vernaculars*. Frankfurt: Lang.

Callary, Robert E. (1975) Phonological change and the development of an urban dialect in Illinois. *Language in Society* 4: 155–69.

Cameron, Deborah (1996) The language–gender interface: Challenging co-optation. In Victoria L. Bergvall, Janet M. Bing, and Alice F. Freed (eds.), *Rethinking Language and Gender Research: Theory and Practice*. New York: Longman.

Cameron, Deborah, Elizabeth Fraser, Penelope Harvey, M. B. H. Rampton, and Kay Richardson (1992) *Researching Language: Issues of Power and Method*. London: Routledge.

Carter, Phillip (2004) *The Emergence of Hispanic English in the Raleigh Community: A Sociophonetic Analysis*. MA thesis, North Carolina State University.

Carver, Craig M. (1987) *American Regional Dialects: A Word Geography*. Ann Arbor: University of Michigan Press.

Cassidy, Frederic G. (editor-in-chief) (1985) *Dictionary of American Regional English*, vol. 1, A–C. Cambridge, MA: Harvard University Press, Belknap.

Cassidy, Frederic G., and Joan H. Hall (eds.) (1991) *Dictionary of American Regional English*, vol. 2, D–H. Cambridge, MA: Harvard University Press, Belknap.

Cassidy, Frederic G., and Joan H. Hall (eds.) (1996) *Dictionary of American Regional English*, vol. 3, I–O. Cambridge, MA: Harvard University Press, Belknap.

Cedergren, Henrietta (1973) The interplay of social and linguistic factors in Panama. PhD dissertation, Cornell University.

Chambers, J. K. (1973) Canadian raising. *Canadian Journal of Linguistics* 18: 113–35.

Chambers, J. K. (2003) *Sociolinguistic Theory*, 2nd edn. Oxford: Blackwell.

Chambers, J. K., Peter Trudgill, and Natalie Schilling-Estes (eds.) (2001) *The Handbook of Language Variation and Change*. Oxford: Blackwell.

Chapman, Robert L. (ed.) (1986) *New Dictionary of American Slang*. New York: Harper and Row.

Chapman, Robert L. (1995) *Dictionary of American Slang*, 3rd edn. New York: HarperCollins.

Childs, Becky, and Christine Mallinson (2004) African American English in Appalachia: Dialect accommodation and substrate influence. *English World-Wide* 25: 27–50.

Committee on College Composition and Communication Language Statement (1974) Students' rights to their own language. *College Composition and Communication* 25 (special issue, separately paginated). Champaign-Urbana: National Council of Teachers of English.

Coupland, Nikolas (1980) Style-shifting in a Cardiff work-setting. *Language in Society* 9: 1–12.

Coupland, Nikolas (1985) "Hark, hark the lark": Social motivations for phonological style-shifting. *Language and Communication* 5 (3): 153–71.

Coupland, Nikolas (1996) Language, situation and the relational self: Theorising dialect-style in sociolinguistics. Paper presented at Stanford University Workshop on Stylistic Variation, Stanford, CA, February.

Coupland, Nikolas (2001a) Dialect stylization in radio talk. *Language in Society* 30: 345–75.

Coupland, Nikolas (2001b) Language, situation and the relational self: Theorizing dialect-style in sociolinguistics. In Penelope Eckert and John R. Rickford (eds.), *Style and Sociolinguistic Variation*. Cambridge/New York: Cambridge University Press, 185–210.

Coupland, Nikolas (guest ed.) (2003) *Sociolinguistics and Globalisation* (theme issue). *Journal of Sociolinguistics* 7 (4).

Crosby, Faye, and Linda Nyquist (1977) The female register: An empirical study of Lakoff's hypothesis. *Language in Society* 6: 313–22.

Cukor-Avila, Patricia (2001) Co-existing grammars: The relationship between the evolution of African American and Southern White Vernacular English in the South. In Sonja L. Lanehart (ed.), *Sociocultural and Historical Contexts of African American English*. Philadelphia/Amsterdam: John Benjamins, 93–128.

Dannenberg, Clare (2002) *Sociolinguistic Constructs of Ethnic Identity: The Syntactic Delineation of a Native American Indian Variety*. Publications of the American Dialect Society 87. Durham, NC: Duke University Press.

Dannenberg, Clare, and Walt Wolfram (1998) Ethnic identity and grammatical restructuring: *Bes* in Lumbee English. *American Speech* 73: 153–69.

Dillard, J. L. (1972) *Black English: Its History and Usage in the United States*. New York: Random House.

Downes, William (1998) *Language and Society*, 2nd edn. London: Fontana.

Dubois, Betty Lou, and Isabel Crouch (1975) The question of tag questions in women's speech: They don't really use more of them, do they? *Language in Society* 4: 289–94.

Dubois, Sylvie, and Barbara Horvath (1998a) From accent to marker in Cajun English: A study of dialect formation in progress. *English World-Wide* 19: 161–88.

Dubois, Sylvie, and Barbara Horvath (1998b) Let's tink about dat: Interdental fricatives in Cajun English. *Language Variation and Change* 10: 245–61.

Dubois, Sylvie, and Barbara Horvath (1999) When the music changes, you change too: Gender and language change in Cajun English. *Language Variation and Change* 11: 287–313.

Dubois, Sylvie, and Barbara Horvath (2003) The English vernacular of the creoles of Louisiana. *Language Variation and Change* 15: 255–88.

Dubois, Sylvie, and Megan Melançon (2000) Creole is, creole ain't: Diachronic and synchronic attitudes toward Creole identity in South Louisiana. *Language in Society* 29: 237–58.

Dumas, Bethany K., and Jonathan Lighter (1976) Is slang a word for linguists? *American Speech* 51: 5–17.

Eakins, Barbara, and Gene Eakins (1978) *Sex Differences in Human Communication*. Boston: Houghton Mifflin.

Eble, Connie (1989) *College Slang 101*. Georgetown: Spectacle Lane Press.

Eble, Connie (1996) *Slang and Sociability: In-Group Language among College Students*. Chapel Hill: University of North Carolina Press.

Eble, Connie (2004) Slang. In Edward Finegan and John R. Rickford (eds.), *Language in the USA*. Cambridge: Cambridge University Press, 375–86.

Eckert, Penelope (1989a) *Jocks and Burnouts: Social Categories and Identity in the High School*. New York: Columbia University Teachers College.

Eckert, Penelope (1989b) The whole woman: Sex and gender differences in variation. *Language Variation and Change* 1: 245–67.

Eckert, Penelope (2000) *Linguistic Variation as Social Practice*. Oxford: Blackwell.

Eckert, Penelope (2001) Style and social meaning. In Penelope Eckert and John R. Rickford (eds.), *Style and Sociolinguistic Variation*. Cambridge: Cambridge University Press, 119–26.

Eckert, Penelope, and Sally McConnell-Ginet (1992) Think practically and look locally: Language and gender as community-based practice. *Annual Review of Anthropology* 21: 461–90.

Eckert, Penelope, and Sally McConnell-Ginet (2003) *Language and Gender*. Cambridge: Cambridge University Press.

Eckert, Penelope, and John R. Rickford (eds.) (2001) *Style and Sociolinguistic Variation*. Cambridge: Cambridge University Press.

Ehrlich, Susan, and Ruth King (1994) Feminist meanings and the (de)politicization of the lexicon. *Language in Society* 23 (1): 59–76.

Ewers, Traute (1996) *The Origin of American Black English: Be-Forms in the Hoodoo Texts*. Berlin/New York: Mouton de Gruyter.

Farr, Marcia, and Harvey Daniels (1986) *Language Diversity and Writing Instruction*. Urbana, IL: National Council of Teachers of English.

Farr-Whiteman, Marcia (1981) Dialect influence in writing. In Marcia Farr-Whiteman (ed.), *Writing: The Nature, Development, and Teaching of Written Communication*, vol. 1. Hillsdale, NJ: Lawrence Erlbaum Associates, 153–66.

Fasold, Ralph W. (1968) A sociolinguistic study of the pronunciation of three vowels in Detroit speech. Unpublished manuscript.

Fasold, Ralph W. (1969) Tense and the form *be* in Black English. *Language* 45: 763–76.

Fasold, Ralph W. (1970) Two models of socially significant linguistic variation. *Language* 46: 551–63.

Fasold, Ralph W. (1972) *Tense Marking in Black English: A Linguistic and Social Analysis*. Arlington: Center for Applied Linguistics.

Fasold, Ralph W. (1976) One hundred years from syntax to phonology. In Sanford Seever, Carol Walker, and Salikoko Mufwene (eds.), *Diachronic Syntax*. Chicago: Chicago Linguistic Society, 79–87.

Fasold, Ralph W. (1981) The relation between black and white speech in the South. *American Speech* 56: 163–89.

Fasold, Ralph W. (1984) *The Sociolinguistics of Society*. Oxford: Blackwell.

Fasold, Ralph W. (1990) *The Sociolinguistics of Language*. Oxford: Blackwell.

Fausto-Sterling, Anne (2000) *Sexing the Body: Gender Politics and the Construction of Sexuality*. New York: Basic Books.

Feagin, Crawford (1979) *Variation and Change in Alabama English: A Sociolinguistic Study of the White Community*. Washington, DC: Georgetown University Press.

Feagin, Crawford (1987) A closer look at the Southern drawl: Variation taken to the extremes. In Keith M. Denning, Sharon Inkelas, Faye C. McNair-Knox, and John R. Rickford (eds.), *Variation in Language: NWAVE-XV at Stanford* (Proceedings of the Fifteenth Annual Conference on New Ways of Analyzing Variation). Stanford, CA: Stanford University, 137–50.

Ferguson, Charles A., and Shirley Brice Heath (eds.) (1981) *Language in the USA*. New York: Cambridge University Press.

Finegan, Edward (1980) *Attitudes toward English Words: The History of a War of Words*. New York: Teachers College Press.

Finegan, Edward, and Douglas Biber (1994) Register and social dialect variation: An integrated approach. In Douglas Biber and Edward Finegan (eds.), *Sociolinguistic Perspectives on Register*. New York: Oxford University Press, 315–47.

Finegan, Edward, and Douglas Biber (2001) Register variation and social dialect variation: The register axiom. In Penelope Eckert and John R. Rickford (eds.), *Style and Sociolinguistic Variation*. Cambridge: Cambridge University Press, 235–67.

Fischer, John N. L. (1958) Social influences on the choice of a linguistic variant. *Word* 14: 47–56.

Fitzgerald, James R. (2001) The Unabomb investigation: A methodological and experiential study from a forensic linguistic perspective. Unpublished manuscript, Georgetown University.

Fordham, Signithia, and John Ogbu (1986) Black students' school success: Coping with the burden of "acting white." *Urban Review* 18: 176–206.

Foreman, Christina (2000) Identification of African-American English from prosodic cues. *Texas Linguistic Forum* 43: 57–66.

Fought, Carmen (2003) *Chicano English in Context*. New York/Basingstoke: Palgrave Macmillan.

Fought, Carmen, and John Fought (2003) Prosodic rhythm patterns in Chicano English. Unpublished manuscript.

Francis, Nelson W. (1983) *Dialectology: An Introduction*. New York: Longman.

Frank, Francine, and Frank Anshen (1983) *Language and the Sexes*. Albany: State University of New York Press.

Frazer, Timothy C. (1983) Sound change and social structure in a rural community. *Language in Society* 12: 313–28.

Freed, Alice F. (2003) Reflections on language and gender research. In Janet Holmes and Miriam Meyerhoff (eds.), *The Handbook of Language and Gender*. Oxford: Blackwell, 699–721.

Fuller, Janet (2004) "Come in Mrs Johnson – or is it Miss?": Female title usage in the South Midlands. Unpublished manuscript.

Galindo, Letticia D. (1987) Linguistic influence and variation on the English of Chicano adolescents in Austin, Texas. PhD dissertation, University of Texas at Austin.

Gates, Henry Louis (1988) *The Signifying Monkey: Towards a Theory of Afro-American Literary Criticism*. Oxford: Oxford University Press.

Gauchat, Louis (1905) L'unité phonétique dans le patois d'une commune. *Festschrift Heinreich Morf: Aus Romanischen Sprachen und Literaturen*. Halle: M. Niemeyer, 175–232.

Giles, Howard (1973) Accent mobility: A model and some data. *Anthropological Linguistics* 15: 87–105.

Giles, Howard (ed.) (1984) *The Dynamics of Speech Accommodation* (special issue of the *International Journal of the Sociology of Language* 46).

Giles, Howard (2001) Couplandia and beyond. In Penelope Eckert and John R. Rickford (eds.), *Style and Sociolinguistic Variation*. Cambridge: Cambridge University Press, 211–19.

Giles, Howard, Justine Coupland, and Nikolas Coupland (eds.) (1991) *Contexts of Accommodation: Developments in Applied Sociolinguistics*. Cambridge: Cambridge University Press.

Giles, Howard, and Peter F. Powesland (1975) *Speech Style and Social Evaluation*. London: Academic Press.

Glowka, Wayne A., and Donald M. Lance (eds.) (1993) *Language Variation in North American English: Research and Teaching*. New York: Modern Language Association.

Gold, David L. (1981) The speech and writing of Jews. In Charles A. Ferguson and Shirley Brice Heath (eds.), *Language in the USA*. New York: Cambridge University Press, 273–92.

Goodwin, Marjorie Harness (1990) *He-Said-She-Said: Talk as Social Organization among Black Children*. Bloomington: Indiana University Press.

Gordon, Matthew J. (2001a) Investigating mergers and chain shifts. In J. K. Chambers, Peter Trudgill, and Natalie Schilling-Estes (eds.), *The Handbook of Language Variation and Change*. Oxford: Blackwell, 244–66.

Gordon, Matthew J. (2001b) *Small-Town Values and Big-City Vowels: A Study of the Northern Cities Shift in Michigan*. Publications of the American Dialect Society, 84. Durham, NC: Duke University Press.

Graff, David, William Labov, and Wendell A. Harris (1986) Testing listeners' reactions to phonological markers of ethnic identity: A new method for sociolinguistic research. In David Sankoff (ed.), *Diversity and Diachrony*. Philadelphia/ Amsterdam: John Benjamins, 45–58.

Grandgent, C. H. (1889) The first year of the American dialect society. *Dialect Notes* 1.

Green, Lisa J. (2002) *African American English: A Linguistic Introduction*. New York: Cambridge University Press.

Grimes, Andrew, and Ryan Rowe (producers) (2004) *Princeville Remembers the Flood*. Raleigh: North Carolina Language and Life Project.

Gumperz, John J. (1982) *Discourse Strategies*. New York: Cambridge University Press.

Guy, Gregory R. (1988) Language and social class. In Frederick J. Newmeyer (ed.), *Linguistics: The Cambridge Survey*, vol. 4. New York: Cambridge University Press, 37–63.

Guy, Gregory R. (1993) The quantitative analysis of linguistic variation. In Dennis R. Preston (ed.), *American Dialect Research*. Philadelphia/Amsterdam: John Benjamins, 223–49.

Guy, Gregory R., B. Horvath, J. Vonwiller, E. Daisley, and I. Rogers (1986) An intonational change in progress in Australian English. *Language in Society* 15: 23–52.

Haeri, Niloofar (1997) *The Sociolinguistic Market of Cairo: Gender, Class and Education*. London/New York: Kegan Paul International.

Hall, Joan C. (editor-in-chief) (2002) *Dictionary of American Regional English*, vol. 4, P–Sk. Cambridge, MA: Harvard University Press, Belknap.

Hannah, Dawn (1998) The copula in Samaná English: Implications for research on the linguistic history of African American Vernacular English. *American Speech* 72: 339–72.

Harrison, Linda (1975) Cro-magnon woman – In eclipse. *The Science Teacher* (April): 8–11.

Hartman, James W. (1985) Guide to pronunciation. In Frederic G. Cassidy (gen. ed.), *Dictionary of American Regional English*, vol. 1. Cambridge, MA: Harvard University Press, Belknap, xli–lxi.

Hazen, Kirk (1997) Past and present "be" in Southern ethnolinguistic boundaries. PhD dissertation, University of North Carolina at Chapel Hill.

Heath, Shirley Brice (1976) A national language academy? Debate in the new nation. *International Journal of the Sociology of Language* 11: 8–43.

Heath, Shirley Brice (1983) *Ways with Words: Language, Life and Work in Communities and Classrooms*. New York: Cambridge University Press.

Henley, Nancy M., and Cheris Kramarae (1994) Gender, power, and mis-communication. In Camille Roman, Suzanne Juhasz, and Cristanne Miller (eds.), *The Women and Language Debate: A Sourcebook*. New Brunswick, NJ: Rutgers University Press, 383–406. (Reprinted from N. Coupland, H. Giles, and J. M. Wiemann (eds.) (1991), *Miscommunication and Problematic Talk*. Newbury Park, CA: Sage Publications, 18–43.)

Hibiya, Junko (1988) A quantitative study of Tokyo Japanese. PhD dissertation, University of Pennsylvania.

Hill, Jane H. (1995) Junk Spanish, covert racism, and the (leaky) boundary between public and private spheres. *Pragmatics* 5: 197–212.

Hill, Jane (1998) Language, race, and White public space. *American Anthropologist* 100 (3): 680–9.

Hindle, Donald M. (1979) The social and situational conditioning of phonetic variation. PhD dissertation, University of Pennsylvania.

Hines, Caitlin (1999) Rebaking the pie: The woman as dessert metaphor. In Mary Bucholtz, A. C. Liang, and Laurel A. Sutton (eds.), *Reinventing Identities: The Gendered Self in Discourse*. Oxford: Oxford University Press, 145–62.

Hock, Hans Henrich, and Brian D. Joseph (1996) *Language History, Language Change, and Language Relationship: An Introduction to Historical and Comparative Linguistics*. Berlin/New York: Mouton de Gruyter.

Holmes, Janet (ed.) (1999) *Communities of Practice in Language and Gender Research* (special issue of *Language in Society* 28 (2)).

Holmes, Janet, and Miriam Meyerhoff (eds.) (2003) *The Handbook of Language and Gender*. Oxford: Blackwell.

Horvath, Barbara M. (1985) *Variation in Australian English: The Sociolects of Sydney*. New York: Cambridge University Press.

Huffines, Marion Lois (1984) The English of the Pennsylvania Germans. *German Quarterly* 57: 173–82.

Huffines, Marion Lois (1986) Intonation in language contact: Pennsylvania German English. In Werner Enninger (ed.), *Studies on the Language and the Verbal Behavior of the Pennsylvania Germans*. Wiesbaden: Franz Steiner Verlag, 26–36.

Huffines, Marion Lois (2002) Fading future for ferhoodled English. *Language Magazine* 2 (2) (October): 26–31.

Hutcheson, Neal (producer) (2000) *Indian by Birth: The Lumbee Dialect*. Raleigh: North Carolina Language and Life Project.

Hyatt, Harry Middleton (1970–8) *Hoodoo-Conjuration-Witchcraft-Rootwork*, vols. 1–5. Hannibal: Western Publishing.

Hymes, Dell (1962) The ethnography of speaking. In T. Gladwin and W. C. Sturtevant (eds.), *Anthropology and Human Behavior*. Washington, DC: Anthropological Society of Washington. (Reprinted in Joshua A. Fishman (1968), *Readings in the Sociology of Language*. The Hague: Mouton.)

Hymes, Dell (1974) Ways of speaking. In Richard Bauman and Joel Sherzer (eds.), *Explorations in the Ethnography of Speaking*. Cambridge: Cambridge University Press, 433–51.

Illinois Test of Psycholinguistic Abilities (1968) Champaign-Urbana: University of Illinois.

Ives, Sumner (1971) A theory of literary dialect. In Juanita V. Williamson and Virginia M. Burke (eds.), *A Various Language: Perspectives on American Dialects*. New York: Holt, Rinehart, and Winston, 145–77.

James, Deborah, and Sandra Clarke (1993) Women, men, and interruptions: A critical review. In Deborah Tannen (ed.), *Gender and Conversational Interaction*. New York/Oxford: Oxford University Press, 231–74.

James, Deborah, and Janice Drakich (1993) Understanding gender differences in amount of talk: A critical review of research. In Deborah Tannen (ed.), *Gender and Conversational Interaction*. New York/Oxford: Oxford University Press, 281–312.

Jespersen, Otto (1922) *Language: Its Nature, Development, and Origin*. London: Allen and Unwin.

Johnson, Ellen (1996) *Lexical Change and Variation in the Southeastern United States*. Tuscaloosa: University of Alabama Press.

Johnson, Sally (2001) Who's misunderstanding whom? Sociolinguistics debate and the media. *Journal of Sociolinguistics* 5: 591–610.

Johnson, Sally, and Ulrike Hanna Meinhof (eds.) (1997) *Language and Masculinity*. Oxford: Blackwell.

Johnstone, Barbara (1999) Uses of Southern-sounding speech by contemporary Texas women. *Journal of Sociolinguistics* 2: 69–99.

Johnstone, Barbara, Neeta Bhasin, and Denise Wittofski (2002) "Dahntahn" Pittsburgh: monophthongal /aw/ and representations of localness in Southwestern Pennsylvania. *American Speech* 77: 148–66.

Johnstone, Barbara, and Scott Kiesling (2001) Steel town speak. *Language Magazine* 2 (2) (December): 26–8.

Keenan, Elinor (1974) Norm-makers, norm-breakers: Uses of speech by men and women in a Malagasy community. In Richard Bauman and Joel Sherzer (eds.), *Explorations in the Ethnography of Speaking*. Cambridge: Cambridge University Press, 125–43.

Kiesling, Scott Fabius (1996) Language, gender, and power in fraternity men's discourse. PhD dissertation, Georgetown University.

Kiesling, Scott Fabius (1998) Men's identities and sociolinguistic variation: The case of fraternity men. *Journal of Sociolinguistics* 2: 69–99.

King, Pamela (1972) An analysis of the Northwestern syntax screening test for lower class black children in Prince George's County. Unpublished MA thesis, Howard University.

Kitzinger, Celia, and Hannah Frith (1999) Just say no? The use of conversation analysis in developing a feminist perspective on sexual refusal. *Discourse and Society* 10: 293–316.

Kochman, Thomas (1981) *Black and White: Styles in Conflict*. Chicago: University of Chicago Press.

Kortmann, Bernd, Edgar W. Schneider, Kate Burridge, Rajend Mesthrie, and Clive Upton (eds.) (2004) *A Handbook of Varieties of English*, vol. 2: *Morphology and Syntax*. Berlin/New York: Mouton de Gruyter.

Krashen, Stephen D. (1982) *Principles and Practice in Second Language Acquisition*. Oxford: Pergamon Press.

Krashen, Stephen D., Robin Scarcella, and Michael Long (eds.) (1982) *Child–Adult Difference in Second Language Acquisition*. Rowley, MA: Newbury House.

Kretzschmar, William A. (1996) Quantitative areal analysis of dialect features. *Language Variation and Change* 8: 13–40.

Kretzschmar, William A., and Edgar W. Schneider (1996) *Introduction to Quantitative Analysis of Linguistic Survey Data*. Thousand Oaks, CA: Sage Publications.

Kroch, Anthony (1978) Towards a theory of social dialect variation. *Language in Society* 7: 17–36.

Kurath, Hans (1939) *Handbook of the Linguistic Geography of New England*. Providence, RI: Brown University.

Kurath, Hans (1949) *A Word Geography of the Eastern United States*. Ann Arbor: University of Michigan Press.

Kurath, Hans (1971) The origins of the dialectal differences in spoken American English. In Juanita V. Williamson and Virginia M. Burke (eds.), *A Various*

Language: Perspectives on American Dialects. New York: Holt, Rinehart, and Winston, 12–21.

Kurath, Hans and Raven I. McDavid, Jr. (1961) *The Pronunciation of English in the Atlantic States.* Ann Arbor: University of Michigan Press.

Labov, William (1963) The social motivation of a sound change. *Word* 19: 273–307.

Labov, William (1966) *The Social Stratification of English in New York City.* Washington, DC: Center for Applied Linguistics.

Labov, William (1969) Contraction, deletion and inherent variability of the English copula. *Language* 45: 715–62.

Labov, William (1972a) *Language in the Inner City: Studies in the Black English Vernacular.* Philadelphia: University of Pennsylvania Press.

Labov, William (1972b) *Sociolinguistic Patterns.* Philadelphia: University of Pennsylvania Press.

Labov, William (1972c) Some principles of linguistic methodology. *Language in Society* 1: 97–120.

Labov, William (1972d) The logic of nonstandard English. Ch. 5 in *Language in the Inner City: Studies in the Black English Vernacular.* Philadelphia: University of Pennsylvania Press, 201–40.

Labov, William (1976) Systematically misleading data from test questions. *Urban Review* 9: 146–69.

Labov, William (1982) Objectivity and commitment in linguistic science. *Language in Society* 11: 165–201.

Labov, William (1984) The intersection of sex and social factors in the course of language change. Paper presented at NWAVE, Philadelphia.

Labov, William (1985) The increasing divergence of black and white vernaculars: Introduction to the research reports. Unpublished manuscript.

Labov, William (1987) Are black and white vernaculars diverging? Papers from the NWAVE-XIV panel discussion. *American Speech* 62: 5–12.

Labov, William (1990) The intersection of sex and social class in the course of linguistic change. *Language Variation and Change* 2: 205–54.

Labov, William (1991) The three dialects of English. In Penelope Eckert (ed.), *New Ways of Analyzing Sound Change.* New York: Academic Press, 1–44.

Labov, William (1994) *Principles of Linguistic Change,* vol. 1: *Internal Factors.* Oxford: Blackwell.

Labov, William (1998) Coexistent systems in African–American vernacular English. In Salikoko S. Mufwene, John R. Rickford, Guy Bailey, and John Baugh (eds.), *African American Vernacular English.* London: Routledge, 110–53.

Labov, William (2001a) The anatomy of style-shifting. In Penelope Eckert and John R. Rickford (eds.), *Style and Sociolinguistic Variation.* Cambridge: Cambridge University Press, 85–108.

Labov, William (2001b) *Principles of Linguistic Change,* vol. 2: *Social Factors.* Oxford: Blackwell.

Labov, William (2001c) Applying our knowledge of African American English to the problem of raising reading levels in inner-city schools. In Sonja L. Lanehart (ed.), *Sociocultural and Historical Contexts of African American English.* Philadelphia/Amsterdam: John Benjamins, 299–318.

Labov, William, Sharon Ash, and Charles Boberg (1997) A national map of the regional dialects of American English. Unpublished manuscript, University of Pennsylvania.

Labov, William, Sharon Ash, and Charles Boberg (2005) *Atlas of North American English*. New York/Berlin: Mouton de Gruyter.

Labov, William, Paul Cohen, Clarence Robins, and John Lewis (1968) *A Study of the Non-Standard English of Negro and Puerto Rican Speakers in New York City*. United States Office of Education Final Report, Research Project 3288.

Labov, William, and Wendell Harris (1986) De facto segregation of black and white vernaculars. In David Sankoff (ed.), *Diversity and Diachrony*. Philadelphia/Amsterdam: John Benjamins, 1–24.

Laferriere, Martha (1979) Ethnicity in phonological variation and change. *Language* 55: 603–17.

Lakoff, Robin (1973) Language and woman's place. *Language in Society* 2: 45–80.

Lakoff, Robin (1975) *Language and Woman's Place*. New York: Harper and Row.

Lanehart, Sonja L. (ed.) (2001) *Sociocultural and Historical Contexts of African American English*. Philadelphia/Amsterdam: John Benjamins.

Leap, William L. (1993) *American Indian English*. Salt Lake City: University of Utah Press.

Leaverton, Lloyd (1973) Dialect readers: Rationale, use, and value. In James L. Laffey and Roger W. Shuy (eds.), *Language Differences: Do They Interfere?* Newark: International Reading Association, 114–26.

LePage, R. B., and Andrée Tabouret-Keller (1985) *Acts of Identity*. Cambridge: Cambridge University Press.

Lighter, Jonathan E. (1994) *Historical Dictionary of American Slang*, vol. 1: A–G. New York: Random House.

Lighter, Jonathan E. (1997) *Historical Dictionary of American Slang*, vol. 2: H–O. New York: Random House.

Lippi-Green, Rosina (1997) *English with an Accent: Language, Ideology, and Discrimination in the United States*. London: Routledge.

Locklear, Hayes Alan, Natalie Schilling-Estes, Walt Wolfram, and Clare Dannenberg (1996) *A Dialect Dictionary of Lumbee English*. Raleigh: North Carolina Language and Life Project.

Lopez-Morales, Humberto (1981) Velarization of -/n/ in Puerto Rican Spanish. In David Sankoff and Henrietta Cedergren (eds.), *Variation Omnibus*. Edmonton: Linguistic Research, 105–13.

Lourie, Margaret A., and Nancy Faires Conklin (eds.) (1978) *A Pluralistic Nation: The Language Issue in the United States*. Rowley, MA: Newbury House.

McClive, Tom (1995) Ethnolinguistic groups and identity markers in the endangered dialect of Ocracoke Island. Unpublished manuscript, University of North Carolina at Chapel Hill.

McConnell-Ginet, Sally (2004) Semantics, pragmatics, and beyond: Family values? Paper presented at Linguistic Society of America Annual Meeting, State of the Art Panel on Language and Gender, Boston, January.

McDavid, Raven I., Jr., and McDavid, Virginia G. (1951) The relationship of the speech of American Negroes to the speech of whites. *American Speech* 26: 3–17.

McElhinny, Bonnie (2003) Theorizing gender in sociolinguistics and linguistic anthropology. In Janet Holmes and Miriam Meyerhoff (eds.), *The Handbook of Language and Gender*. Oxford: Blackwell, 21–42.

MacKay, Donald G. (1983) Prescriptive grammar and the pronoun problem. In Barrie Thorne, Cheris Kramarae, and Nancy Henley (eds.), *Language, Gender, and Society*. Rowley, MA: Newbury House, 38–53.

McMillan, James B. (1978) American lexicology, 1942–1973. *American Speech* 53: 141–63.

McMillan, James B., and Michael Montgomery (1989) *Annotated Bibliography of Southern American English*. Tuscaloosa: University of Alabama Press.

Mahl, G. F. (1972) People talking when they can't hear voices. In A. W. Siegman and B. Pope (eds.), *Studies in Dyadic Communication*. New York: Pergamon, 211–64.

Mallinson, Christine, and Becky Childs (2005) Communities of practice in sociolinguistic description: African American women's language in Appalachia. *Penn Working Papers in Linguistics* 10.2.

Mallinson, Christine, and Walt Wolfram (2002) Dialect accommodation in a bi-ethnic mountain enclave community: More evidence on the development of African American Vernacular English. *Language in Society* 31: 743–75.

Maltz, Daniel, and Ruth Borker (1982) A cultural approach to male–female miscommunication. In John J. Gumperz (ed.), *Language and Social Identity*. Cambridge: Cambridge University Press, 195–216.

Martyna, Wendy (1978) What does "he" mean? *Journal of Communication* 28 (Winter): 131–8.

Martyna, Wendy (1980) The psychology of the generic masculine. In Sally McConnell-Ginet, Ruth Borker, and Nelly Furman (eds.), *Women and Language in Literature and Society*. New York: Praeger, 69–77.

Meier, Deborah (1973) Reading failure and the tests. An Occasional Paper of the Workshop for Open Education, New York.

Melançon, Megan E. (2001) Stirring the linguistic gumbo. *Language Magazine* 2 (1) (September): 29–32.

Mencken, H. L. (1962) *The American Language: An Inquiry into the Development of English in the United States*, Supplement 1. New York: Alfred A. Knopf.

Mendoza-Denton, Norma (1997) Chicana/Mexican identity and linguistic variation: An ethnographic and sociolinguistic study of gang affiliation in an urban high school. PhD dissertation, Stanford University.

Mendoza-Denton, Norma (1999) Fighting words: Latina girls, gangs, and language attitudes. In Letticia Galindo and Maria Dolores Gonzales (eds.), *Speaking Chicana: Voice, Power, and Identity*. Tucson: University of Arizona Press, 39–56.

Miller, Cristanne (1994) Who says what to whom? Empirical studies of language and gender. In Camille Roman, Suzanne Juhasz, and Cristanne Miller (eds.), *The Women and Language Debate: A Sourcebook*. New Brunswick, NJ: Rutgers University Press, 265–79.

Milroy, James (1992) *Linguistic Variation and Change: On the Historical Sociolinguistics of English*. Oxford: Blackwell.

Milroy, James, and Lesley Milroy (1999) *Authority in Language: Investigating Standard English*, 3rd edn. London: Routledge.

Milroy, Lesley (1987) *Language and Social Networks*, 2nd edn. Language in Society 2. Oxford: Blackwell.

Milroy, Lesley, and Matthew Gordon (2003) *Sociolinguistics: Method and Interpretation*. Oxford: Blackwell.

Modan, Gabriella (2001) White, whole wheat, rye: Jews and ethnic categorization in Washington, DC. *Journal of Linguistic Anthropology* (special issue titled *Discourses of Whiteness*, guest ed. by Mary Bucholtz and Sara Trechter) 11 (1): 116–30.

Modaressi, Yahya (1978) A sociolinguistic investigation of modern Persian. PhD dissertation, University of Kansas.

Montgomery, Michael (ed.) (1989) Language. In Charles Reagan Wilson and William Ferris (eds.), *Encyclopedia of Southern Culture*. Chapel Hill: University of North Carolina Press, 757–92.

Montgomery, Michael (2004) Solving Kurath's puzzle: Establishing the antecedents of the American Midland dialect region. In Raymond Hickey (ed.), *The Legacy of Colonial English*. Cambridge: Cambridge University Press, 410–25.

Montgomery, Michael, and Janet Fuller (1996) Verbal -*s* in 19th-century African American English. In Edgar W. Schneider (ed.), *Focus on the USA*. Philadelphia/Amsterdam: John Benjamins, 211–30.

Montgomery, Michael, Janet Fuller, and Sharon DeMarse (1993) The black men has wives and sweet harts [and third person -*s*] jest like the white men: Evidence for verbal -*s* from written documents on nineteenth-century African American speech. *Language Variation and Change* 5: 335–57.

Montgomery, Michael B., and Joseph A. Hall (2004) *Dictionary of Smoky Mountain English*. Knoxville: University of Tennessee Press.

Montgomery, Michael, and Margaret Mishoe (1999) "He bes took up with a Yankee girl and moved to New York": The verb *bes* in the Carolinas and its history. *American Speech* 74: 240–81.

Moon, Seung-Jae (1991) An acoustic and perceptual study of undershoot in clear and citation-form speech. PhD dissertation, University of Texas at Austin.

Morgan, Marcyliena (2001) "Nuttin but a G thang?": Grammar and language ideology in hip hop identity. In Sonja L. Lanehart (ed.), *Sociocultural and Historical Contexts of African American English*. Philadelphia/Amsterdam: John Benjamins, 187–209.

Morgan, Marcyliena (2002) *Language, Discourse, and Power in African American Culture*. Cambridge: Cambridge University Press.

Moriello, Rebecca, and Walt Wolfram (2003) New dialect formation in the rural South: Emerging Hispanic English varieties in the Mid-Atlantic. *Penn Working Papers in Linguistics* 9 (2): 135–47.

Mufwene, Salikoko S. (1996) The development of American Englishes: Some questions from a creole genesis hypothesis. In Edgar W. Schneider (ed.), *Focus on the USA*. Philadelphia/Amsterdam: John Benjamins, 231–64.

Mufwene, Salikoko S. (2001) *The Ecology of Language Evolution*. Cambridge: Cambridge University Press.

Mufwene, Salikoko S., John R. Rickford, Guy Bailey, and John Baugh (eds.) (1998) *African American Vernacular English*. London: Routledge.

Munro, Pam (1989) *Slang U!* New York: Harmony House.

Myers-Scotton, Carol (1998) A theoretical introduction to the markedness model. In Carol Myers-Scotton (ed.), *Codes and Consequences: Choosing Linguistic Varieties*. New York: Oxford University Press, 18–38.

National Council of Social Studies, Task Force on Ethnic Studies (1976) *Curriculum Guidelines for Multiethnic Education*. Arlington: National Council on Social Studies.

Newman, Michael (2003) New Yawk Tawk. *Language Magazine* 3 (1) (September): 40–4.

Nichols, Patricia C. (1976) *Linguistic Change in Gullah: Sex, Age and Mobility*. PhD dissertation, Stanford University.

Nichols, Patricia C. (1983) Linguistic options and choices for black women in the rural South. In Barrie Thorne, Cheris Kramarae, and Nancy Henley (eds.), *Language, Gender, and Society*. Rowley, MA: Newbury House, 54–68.

Nilsen, Alleen Pace (1977) Sexism as shown through the English vocabulary. In Alleen Pace Nilsen, Haig Bosmajian, H. Lee Gershuny, and Julia P. Stanley (eds.), *Sexism and Language*. Urbana, IL: National Council of Teachers of English.

Orr, Eleanor Wilson (1987) *Twice as Less: Black English and the Performance of Black Students in Mathematics and Science*. New York: Norton.

Patrick, Peter L. (2002) The speech community. In J. K. Chambers, Peter Trudgill, and Natalie Schilling-Estes (eds.), *The Handbook of Language Variation and Change*, Oxford: Blackwell, 573–97.

Pauwels, Anne (2003) Linguistic sexism and feminist linguistic activism. In Janet Holmes and Miriam Meyerhoff (eds.), *The Handbook of Language and Gender*. Oxford: Blackwell, 550–70.

Payne, Arvilla C. (1980) Factors controlling the acquisition of the Philadelphia dialect by out-of-state children. In William Labov (ed.), *Locating Language in Time and Space*. New York: Academic Press, 143–78.

Peñalosa, Fernando (1980) *Chicano Sociolinguistics: A Brief Introduction*. Rowley, MA: Newbury House.

Pickering, John (1816) A vocabulary, or collection of words and phrases which have been supposed to be peculiar to the United States of America. In M. M. Mathews (ed.) (1931), *The Beginnings of American English: Essays and Comments*. Chicago: University of Chicago Press.

Podesva, Robert J., Sarah J. Roberts, and Kathryn Campbell-Kibler (2002) Sharing resources and indexing meanings in the production of gay styles. In Kathryn Campbell-Kibler, Robert J. Podesva, Sarah J. Roberts, and Andrew Wong (eds.), *Language and Sexuality: Contesting Meaning in Theory and Practice*. Stanford, CA: Center for the Study of Language and Information, 175–89.

Poplack, Shana (1978) Dialect acquisition among Spanish–English bilinguals. *Language in Society* 7: 89–103.

Poplack, Shana (ed.) (2000) *The English History of African American English*. Oxford: Blackwell.

Poplack, Shana, and David Sankoff (1987) The Philadelphia story in the Spanish Caribbean. *American Speech* 62: 291–314.

Poplack, Shana, and Sali Tagliamonte (1989) There's no tense like the present: Verbal -*s* inflection in Early Black English. *Language Variation and Change* 1: 47–84.

Poplack, Shana, and Sali Tagliamonte (1991) African American English in the diaspora: Evidence from old-line Nova Scotians. *Language Variation and Change* 3: 301–39.

Poplack, Shana, and Sali Tagliamonte (2001) *African American English in the Diaspora*. Oxford: Blackwell.

Preston, Dennis R. (1989) *Perceptual Dialectology: Nonlinguists' Views of Areal Linguistics*. Dordrecht: Foris.

Preston, Dennis R. (1991) Sorting out the variables in sociolinguistic theory. *American Speech* 66: 33–56.

Preston, Dennis R. (1996) Where the worst English is spoken. In Edgar W. Schneider (ed.), *Focus on the USA*. Amsterdam/Philadelphia: John Benjamins, 297–360.

Preston, Dennis R. (1997) The South: The touchstone. In Cynthia Bernstein, Thomas Nunnally, and Robin Sabino (eds.), *Language Variety in the South Revisited*. Tuscaloosa: University of Alabama Press, 311–51.

Preston, Dennis R. (2003) Where are the dialects of American English at anyhow? *American Speech* 78: 235–54.

Pyles, Thomas, and John Algeo (1982) *The Origins and Development of the English Language*. New York: Harcourt Brace Jovanovich.

Rampton, Ben (1995) *Crossing: Language and Ethnicity among Adolescents*. London: Longman.

Rampton, Ben (guest ed.) (1999) *Styling the Other* (theme issue). *Journal of Sociolinguistics* 3 (4).

Rickford, John R. (1991) Grammatical variation and divergence in Vernacular Black English. In Marinel Gerritsen and Dieter Stein (eds.), *Internal and External Factors in Language Change*. Berlin/New York: Mouton de Gruyter, 175–200.

Rickford, John R. (1997a) Unequal partnership: Sociolinguistics and the African American speech community. *Language in Society* 26: 161–98.

Rickford, John R. (1997b) Prior creolization of AAVE? Sociohistorical and textual evidence from the 17th and 18th centuries. *Journal of Sociolinguistics* 1: 315–36.

Rickford, John R. (1999) *African American Vernacular English: Features, Evolution and Educational Implications*. Oxford: Blackwell.

Rickford, John R. (2001) Style and stylizing from the perspective of a non-autonomous sociolinguistics. In Penelope Eckert and John R. Rickford (eds.), *Style and Sociolinguistic Variation*. Cambridge: Cambridge University Press, 220–31.

Rickford, John R., and Renee Blake (1990) Copula contraction and absence in Barbadian English, Samaná English, and Vernacular Black English. *Berkeley Linguistics Society* 16: 257–68.

Rickford, John R., and Faye McNair-Knox (1994) Addressee- and topic-influenced style shift. In Douglas Biber and Edward Finegan (eds.), *Sociolinguistic Perspectives on Register*. New York: Oxford University Press, 235–76.

Rickford, John R., and Angela Rickford (1995) Dialect readers revisited. *Linguistics and Education* 7: 107–28.

Rickford, John R., and Russell John Rickford (2001) *Spoken Soul*. New York: John Wiley and Sons.

Rickford, John R., and Christine Théberge-Rafal (1996) Preterite *had* + V-*ed* in narratives of African-American preadolescents. *American Speech* 71: 227–54.

Rogers, Everett M. (1995) *Diffusion of Innovations*, 5th edn. New York: Free Press.

Ronkin, Maggie, and Helen E. Karn (1999) Mock Ebonics: Linguistic racism in parodies of Ebonics on the Internet. *Journal of Sociolinguistics* 3: 336–59.

Ross, Sarah H., Janna B. Oetting, and Beth Stapleton (2004) Preterite *had* + V-*ed*: A developmental narrative structure of African American English. *American Speech* 79: 146–66.

Rowe, Ryan (2004) "If it's true then the crew gon' sense it": Analyzing Hip Hop Nation Language as an in-group performance register. Paper presented at University of Georgia Linguistics Conference, Athens, GA.

Rulon, Curt (1971) Geographical delimitation of the dialect areas in *The Adventures of Huckleberry Finn*. In Juanita V. Williamson and Virginia M. Burke (eds.), *A Various Language: Perspectives on American Dialects*. New York: Holt, Rinehart, and Winston, 215–21.

Sankoff, David, and Suzanne Laberge (1978) The linguistic market and the statistical explanation of variability. In David Sankoff (ed.), *Linguistic Variation: Models and Methods*. New York: Academic Press, 239–50.

Santa Ana, Otto (1991) Phonetic simplification processes in the English of the barrio: A cross-generational sociolinguistic study of the Chicanos of Los Angelos. PhD dissertation, University of Pennsylvania.

Santa Ana, Otto (1993) Chicano English and the Chicano language setting. *Hispanic Journal of Behavioral Sciences* 15: 1–35.

Santa Ana, Otto, and Robert Bayley (2004) Chicano English phonology. In Edgar W. Schneider, Bernd Kortmann, Kate Burridge, Rajend Mesthrie, and Clive Upton (eds.), *A Handbook of Varieties of English*, vol. 1: *Phonology*. Berlin/New York: Mouton de Gruyter, 407–24.

Schiffrin, Deborah (1987) *Discourse Markers*. Cambridge: Cambridge University Press.

Schilling-Estes, Natalie (1995) Extending our understanding of the /z/ → [d] rule. *American Speech* 70: 291–302.

Schilling-Estes, Natalie (1996) The linguistic and sociolinguistic status of /ay/ in Outer Banks English. PhD dissertation, University of North Carolina at Chapel Hill.

Schilling-Estes, Natalie (1997) Accommodation versus concentration: Dialect death in two post-insular island communities. *American Speech* 72: 12–32.

Schilling-Estes, Natalie (1998) Investigating "self-conscious" speech: The performance register in Ocracoke English. *Language in Society* 27: 53–83.

Schilling-Estes, Natalie (1999) Reshaping economies, reshaping identities: Gender-based patterns of language variation in Ocracoke English. In Suzanne Wertheim, Ashlee C. Bailey, and Monica Corston-Oliver (eds.), *Engendering Communication: Proceedings of the Fifth Berkeley Women and Language Conference*. Berkeley: Berkeley Women and Language Group, 509–20.

Schilling-Estes, Natalie (2000) Investigating intra-ethnic differentiation: /ay/ in Lumbee Native American English. *Language Variation and Change* 12: 141–74.

Schilling-Estes, Natalie (2004) Constructing ethnicity in interaction. *Journal of Sociolinguistics* 8: 163–95.

Schilling-Estes, Natalie, and Walt Wolfram (1994) Convergent explanation and alternative regularization patterns: *were/weren't* leveling in a vernacular English variety. *Language Variation and Change* 6 (3): 273–302.

Schilling-Estes, Natalie, and Walt Wolfram (1999) Alternative models for dialect death: Dissipation vs. concentration. *Language* 75: 486–521.

Schneider, Edgar W. (1983) The origin of the verbal -*s* in Black English. *American Speech* 58: 99–113.

Schneider, Edgar W. (1989) *American Earlier Black English: Morphological and Syntactic Variables.* Tuscaloosa: University of Alabama Press.

Schneider, Edgar W. (ed.) (1996) *Focus on the USA.* Philadelphia/Amsterdam: John Benjamins.

Schneider, Edgar W. (2003) The dynamics of new Englishes: From identity construction to dialect birth. *Language* 79: 233–81.

Schneider, Edgar W., Bernd Kortmann, Kate Burridge, Rajend Mesthrie, and Clive Upton (eds.) (2004) *A Handbook of Varieties of English*, vol. 1: *Phonology.* Berlin/New York: Mouton de Gruyter.

Schulz, Murial R. (1975) The semantic derogation of women. In Barrie Thorne and Nancy Henley (eds.), *Language and Sex: Difference and Dominance.* Rowley, MA: Newbury House, 64–75.

Shuy, Roger W., and Frederick Williams (1973) Stereotyped attitudes of selected English dialect communities. In Roger W. Shuy and Ralph W. Fasold (eds.), *Language Attitudes: Current Trends and Prospects.* Washington, DC: Georgetown University Press, 85–96.

Shuy, Roger W., Walt Wolfram, and William K. Riley (1967) *Linguistic Correlates of Social Stratification in Detroit Speech.* USOE Final Report No. 6-1347.

Shuy, Roger W., Walt Wolfram, and William K. Riley (1968) *Field Techniques in an Urban Language Study.* Washington, DC: Center for Applied Linguistics.

Simpkins, Gary C., and Charlesetta Simpkins (1981) Cross-cultural approach to curriculum development. In Geneva Smitherman (ed.), *Black English and the Education of Black Children and Youth.* Detroit: Wayne State University, 221–40.

Simpkins, Gary C., Charlesetta Simpkins, and Grace Holt (1977) *Bridge: A Cross-cultural Reading Program.* Boston: Houghton Mifflin.

Singler, John V. (1989) Plural marking in Liberian settler English, 1820–1980. *American Speech* 64: 4–64.

Singler, John V. (1991) Liberian settler English and the ex-slave recordings: A comparative study. In Guy Bailey, Natalie Maynor, and Patricia Cukor-Avila (eds.), *The Emergence of Black English: Text and Commentary.* Philadelphia/ Amsterdam: John Benjamins, 249–74.

Singler, John V. (1998a) What's not new in AAVE. *American Speech* 73: 227–56.

Singler, John V. (1998b) The African-American diaspora: Who were the dispersed? Paper presented at New Ways of Analyzing Variation 27, Athens, October.

Sledd, James (1976) Language differences and literary values: Divagations from a theme. *College English* 38: 224–31.

Smith, Lee (1983) *Oral History.* New York: Random House.

Smith, Lee (1988) *Fair and Tender Ladies.* New York: Random House.

Smith, Philip M. (1985) *Language, the Sexes and Society.* New York: Blackwell.

Smitherman, Geneva (1977) *Talkin' and Testifyin': The Language of Black America.* Boston: Houghton Mifflin.

Smitherman, Geneva (1991) What is Africa to me? Language ideology and African American. *American Speech* 66: 115–32.

Smitherman, Geneva (1994) *Black Talk: Words and Phrases from the Hood to the Amen Corner*. Boston: Houghton Mifflin.

Spears, Arthur K. (1982) The Black English semi-auxiliary *come*. *Language* 58: 850–72.

Spender, D. (1980) *Man Made Language*. Boston: Routledge and Kegan Paul.

Stanley, Julia P. (1977) Paradigmatic woman: The prostitute. In David L. Shores and Carole P. Hines (eds.), *Papers in Language Variation*. Tuscaloosa: University of Alabama Press, 303–21.

Steffensen, Margaret, C. C. Joag-dev, and R. C. Anderson (1979) A cross-cultural perspective on reading comprehension. *Reading Research Quarterly* 15: 10–29.

Steinmetz, Sol (1981) Jewish English in the United States. *American Speech* 56: 3–16.

Stewart, William A. (1967) Sociolinguistic factors in the history of American Negro dialects. *The Florida FL Reporter* 5 (2): 11, 22, 24, 26.

Stewart, William A. (1968) Continuity and change in American Negro dialects. *The Florida FL Reporter*, 6 (2): 3–4, 14–16, 18, 30.

Stockman, Ida J. (1986) Language acquisition in culturally diverse populations: The black child as a case study. In Orlando L. Taylor (ed.), *Nature of Communication Disorders in Culturally and Linguistically Diverse Populations*. San Diego: College-Hill Press, 117–55.

Stockman, Ida J., and Fay B. Vaughn-Cooke (1986) Implications of semantic category research for language assessment of nonstandard speakers. *Topics in Language and Language Disorders* 6: 15–25.

Strevens, Peter (1985) Standards and the standard language. *English Today* 2 (April): 5–8.

Tannen, Deborah (1984) *Conversational Style: Analyzing Talk among Friends*. Norwood, NJ: Ablex.

Tannen, Deborah (1987) *That's Not What I Meant! How Conversational Style Makes or Breaks Relationships*. New York: Ballantine.

Tannen, Deborah (1990) *You Just Don't Understand: Women and Men in Conversation*. New York: Ballantine.

Tannen, Deborah (ed.) (1993) *Gender and Conversational Interaction*. New York/ Oxford: Oxford University Press.

Tannen, Deborah (1995) *Talking from 9 to 5: Women and Men at Work*. New York: Quill.

Tarone, Elaine E. (1973) Aspects of intonation in Black English. *American Speech* 48: 29–36.

Taylor, Orlando L. (ed.) (1986) *Nature of Communication Disorders in Culturally and Linguistically Diverse Populations*. San Diego: College-Hill Press.

Terrell, Sandra L. (ed.) (1983) *Nonbiased Assessment of Language Differences: Topics in Language Disorders*, no. 3. Rockville, MD: Aspen.

Thomas, Erik R. (1993) Why we need descriptive studies: Phonological variables in Hispanic English. *Proceedings of the First Annual Symposium about Language and Society–Austin*. Austin: University of Texas Linguistics Department, 42–9.

Thomas, Erik R. (2001) *An Acoustic Analysis of Vowel Variation in New World English*. Publications of the American Dialect Society 85. Durham, NC: Duke University Press.

Thomas, Erik R. (2002) Sociophonetic applications of speech perception experiments. *American Speech* 77: 115–47.

Thomas, Erik R., and Jeffrey Reaser (2004) Delimiting perceptual cues for the ethnic labeling of African American and European American voices. *Journal of Sociolinguistics* 8: 54–87.

Torbert, Benjamin (2004) Southern vowels and the social construction of salience. PhD dissertation, Duke University.

Trudgill, Peter (1972) Sex, covert prestige, and linguistic change in the urban British English of Norwich. *Language in Society* 1: 179–95.

Trudgill, Peter (1974) *The Social Differentiation of English in Norwich*. Cambridge: Cambridge University Press.

Trudgill, Peter (1983) *On Dialect: Social and Geographical Perspectives*. New York: New York University Press.

Trudgill, Peter (1990) *The Dialects of England*. Cambridge, MA: Blackwell.

Vaughn-Cooke, Anna Fay (1983) Improving language assessment in minority children. *Asha* 25 (June): 29–34.

Viereck, Wolfgang (1988) Invariant *be* in an unnoticed source of American English. *American Speech* 63: 291–303.

Ward, Martha Coonfield (1971) *Them Children: A Study in Language Learning*. New York: Holt, Rinehart, and Winston.

Weaver, Constance W. (1970) Analyzing literary representations of recent Northern urban Negro speech: A technique, with application to three books. PhD dissertation, Michigan State University.

Weldon, Tracey (1996) Copula variability in Gullah: Implications for the Creolist Hypothesis. Paper presented at New Ways of Analyzing Variation 25, October.

Whiteman, Marcia F. (1976) Dialect influence and the writing of black and white working class Americans. PhD dissertation, Georgetown University.

Williams, Frederick (1973) Some research notes on dialect attitudes. In Roger W. Shuy and Ralph W. Fasold (eds.), *Language Attitudes: Current Trends and Prospects*. Washington, DC: Georgetown University Press, 113–28.

Williams, Joseph M. (1975) *The Origins of the English Language: A Social and Linguistic History*. New York: Free Press.

Winford, Donald (1997) On the origins of African American Vernacular English – a creolist perspective, Part I: The sociohistorical background. *Diachronica* 14: 304–44.

Winford, Donald (1998) On the origins of African American Vernacular English – a creolist perspective, Part II: The features. *Diachronica* 15: 99–154.

Wolfram, Walt (1969) *A Linguistic Description of Detroit Negro Speech*. Washington, DC: Center for Applied Linguistics.

Wolfram, Walt (1974a) The relationship of Southern White Speech to Vernacular Black English. *Language* 50: 498–527.

Wolfram, Walt (1974b) *Sociolinguistic Aspects of Assimilation: Puerto Rican English in New York City*. Washington, DC: Center for Applied Linguistics.

Wolfram, Walt (1980) *A*- prefixing in Appalachian English. In William Labov (ed.), *Locating Language in Time and Space*. New York: Academic Press, 107–43.

Wolfram, Walt (1981) Varieties of American English. In Charles A. Ferguson and Shirley Brice Heath (eds.), *Language in the USA*. New York: Cambridge University Press, 44–68.

Wolfram, Walt (1982) Language knowledge and other dialects. *American Speech* 57: 3–18.

Wolfram, Walt (1984) Unmarked tense in American Indian English. *American Speech* 59: 31–50.

Wolfram, Walt (1985) Variability in tense marking: A case for the obvious. *Language Learning* 35: 229–53.

Wolfram, Walt (1986) Language variation in the United States. In Orlando L. Taylor (ed.), *Nature of Communication Disorders in Culturally and Linguistically Diverse Populations*. San Diego: College-Hill Press, 73–115.

Wolfram, Walt (1988) Reconsidering the semantics of a- prefixing. *American Speech* 63: 247–53.

Wolfram, Walt (1991) *Dialects and American English*. Englewood Cliffs, NJ: Prentice Hall.

Wolfram, Walt (1993a) Ethical considerations in language awareness programs. *Issues in Applied Linguistics* 4: 225–55.

Wolfram, Walt (1993b) Identifying and interpreting variables. In Dennis R. Preston (ed.), *American Dialect Research*. Philadelphia/Amsterdam: John Benjamins, 193–221.

Wolfram, Walt (1995) On the sociolinguistic significance of obscure dialect structure: NP$_i$ *call* NP$_i$ V-*ing* in African American Vernacular English. *American Speech* 69: 339–60.

Wolfram, Walt (1996) Delineation and description in dialectology: The case of perfective *I'm* in Lumbee English. *American Speech* 71: 5–26.

Wolfram, Walt (2003) Reexamining the development of African American English: Evidence from isolated communities. *Language* 79: 282–316.

Wolfram, Walt (2004) Dialect awareness in community perspective. In Margaret C. Bender (ed.), *Linguistic Diversity in the South: Changing Codes, Practices, and Ideologies*. Athens: University of Georgia Press, 15–36.

Wolfram, Walt, Phillip Carter, and Beckie Moriello (2004) Emerging Hispanic English: New dialect formation in the American South. *Journal of Sociolinguistics* 8: 339–58.

Wolfram, Walt, and Donna Christian (1976) *Appalachian Speech*. Washington, DC: Center for Applied Linguistics.

Wolfram, Walt, Donna Christian, and Carolyn Adger (1999) *Dialects in Schools and Communities*. Mahwah, NJ: Lawrence Erlbaum.

Wolfram, Walt, Clare Dannenberg, Stanley Knick, and Linda Oxendine (2002) *Fine in the World: Lumbee Language in Time and Place*. Raleigh: North Carolina State Humanities Extension/Publications.

Wolfram, Walt, and Ralph Fasold (1974) *The Study of Social Dialects in the United States*. Englewood Cliffs, NJ: Prentice Hall.

Wolfram, Walt, Kirk Hazen, and Natalie Schilling-Estes (1999) *Dialect Maintenance and Change on the Outer Banks*. Publications of the American Dialect Society 81. Tuscaloosa: University of Alabama Press.

Wolfram, Walt, Kirk Hazen, and Jennifer Ruff Tamburro (1997) Isolation within isolation: A solitary century of African American English. *Journal of Sociolinguistics* 1: 7–38.

Wolfram, Walt, and Jeffrey Reaser (2004) *Dialects and the Ocracoke Brogue*. An 8th grade curriculum. Raleigh: North Carolina Language and Life Project.

Wolfram, Walt, and Natalie Schilling-Estes (1995) Moribund dialects and the endangerment canon: The case of the Ocracoke brogue. *Language* 71: 696–721.

Wolfram, Walt, and Natalie Schilling-Estes (1997) *Hoi Toide on the Outer Banks: The Story of the Ocracoke Brogue*. Chapel Hill: University of North Carolina Press.

Wolfram, Walt, Natalie Schilling-Estes, and Kirk Hazen (1997) *Dialects and the Ocracoke Brogue*. An 8th grade curriculum. Raleigh: North Carolina Language and Life Project.

Wolfram, Walt, Natalie Schilling-Estes, Kirk Hazen, and Chris Craig (1997) The sociolinguistic complexity of quasi-isolated southern coastal communities. In Cynthia Bernstein, Tom Nunnally, and Robin Sabino (eds.), *Language Variation in the South Revisited*. Tuscaloosa: University of Alabama Press, 173–87.

Wolfram, Walt, and Erik R. Thomas (2002) *The Development of African American English*. Malden, MA: Blackwell.

Wolfram, Walt, Erik Thomas, and Elaine Green (1997) Reconsidering the development of African American Vernacular English: Lessons from isolated speakers. Paper presented at New Ways of Analyzing Variation 26, Québec, Canada.

Wright, Richard (1961) *Native Son*. New York: New American Library. (Originally published 1941.)

Young, Richard, and Robert Bayley (1996) VARBRUL analysis for second language acquisition research. In Robert Bayley and Dennis R. Preston (eds.), *Second Language Acquisition and Linguistic Variation*. Philadelphia/Amsterdam: John Benjamins, 253–306.

Index